THE MEANING OF LIFE

Russell Hasan

This book is dedicated to Professor Stephen Cox, my editor at Liberty Magazine, without whose support and warm yet critical feedback my career as a writer might never have existed.
I would also like to thank the following people, all of whom were influential to my philosophy: Ayn Rand, Friedrich Nietzsche, Aristotle, Mortimer J. Adler, Ronald E. Merrill, Thomas of Aquinas, and, yes, Plato, and Jesus Christ. Also my professors of philosophy at Vassar College, with emphasis on Jennifer Church and Douglas Winblad, and the law professors of The University of Connecticut School of Law, in particular Patricia McCoy and Lewis Kurlantzick.
And also a special thanks to my readers, too. Thank you!

CONTENTS

THE MEANING OF LIFE: MY ANSWER TO JORDAN B. PETERSON

According to Objectivism, what is the meaning of life? The meaning of life is: You. You are the meaning of your life. The meaning of your life is you. There is nothing else. Your life, and you living it, and the joy, and sadness, and whatever it means to you, that is the meaning of your life, that is the meaning of life for you. Jesus Christ is not the meaning of your life. Helping the poor, and Karl Marx, is not the meaning of your life. No. You, and only you, are the meaning of your own life.

But that means that you have to work, and work hard, to create a meaningful life, to create meaning and intention and purpose and achievement for your life, to make your life meaningful. You have to do it, but it is something only you can do. Now, you could choose to have Jesus Christ be the meaning of your life, and many people have done that, but then that is about you, it isn't really about Jesus Christ. It's about what Jesus Christ means to you; it is not about Jesus Christ himself. And, likewise, you could choose for the meaning of your life to be helping others, but then it isn't really about helping others, it's really about you and the meaning that you create for yourself by choosing that as your purpose in life, as the focus of your life. People think that "What is the meaning of life?" is an impossible question to answer, but if you change it into "What is the meaning of my life?" then it becomes possible for you to answer it. But if you fail, if you do not create meaning and find meaningful people, events, emotions, goals, etc., in your life, then you fall into the void, the abyss, nihilism, then your life would have no meaning.

When we say that we mean something, what we often mean, is that this was our intent, that our meaning is our intention, so, the meaning of your life, and what you mean by the act of living, is often the same thing as your intention for your life, what you intend for your life to be about. Having a family and raising kids, finding true love, having a successful career, having lots of fun, taking vacations and seeing the world, etc., are all valid meanings, much as religion or politics could be, but you have to really mean it. The gay man's desire for sex could become the meaning of his life, or the LGBTQ rights activist or Black Lives Matter activist could find that their political activism and their quest for equality is the meaning of their lives, for other examples. Often, you will have a goal, and there will be obstacles in-between you and your goal, and you will struggle to overcome those obstacles and achieve that goal, and the struggle becomes the meaning of your life, or one of the meanings in your life. But the struggle only matters because you assigned meaning to that goal. If the goal lacked meaning, then the struggle would also be meaningless. The difference between faking it, and having it be real, if the thing itself is merely a meaning, the only difference is whether you really meant it.

And, of course, many people believe that the meaning of your life can't possibly be you, because it has to be something greater than you, something bigger than you, in comparison to which you are small and humble and trivial, so it has to be something huge, like Jesus Christ or helping the poor, but that is never true, it is always you, it always was you and the meaning of your life always will be you, but you can choose to use a cause that is bigger than yourself in order to create a narrative of meaning for your life that extends beyond the immediate physical reach and spatial and temporal scope of your individual life. I would not go so far as to say that such narratives are fictional, but I would say that they are merely extensions of yourself, mere add-ons, not the original thing, which is you yourself.

The big things, the big meanings, they are only the meaning of your life to the extent that they matter for you, because you chose them, they are never bigger or grander than you in any absolute sense, you only use them to make your life feel larger. But the size, the scope, the importance of your life, never has an absolute value that can be measured, it is only whether your life is very important and meaningful to you, or not, or whether your life is important and meaningful to another person, like a husband or partner, or to other people, like friends and family, or to many other people, like a community or a nation, etc., but there is no way to measure this, and every life matters, the only question is the degree to which your own life matters to you. Objectivism, with its focus on ego and rational selfishness, says that, yes, your own life should matter to you a lot, and, if it doesn't, then you should do the work to make it so until it does.

Choose a goal or a set of goals, and then go after it or them, and then build a narrative around your quest, and then that narrative becomes the story of your life, and then you derive meaning from that story. For example, if you are a woman, and the meaning of your life is being a wife and a mom, then the narrative of what is going on with your family right now becomes the story of your life, and that is where the meaning in your life comes from. But all of that meaning originates with you, and what you do for your family, on your quest to be a good wife and mom.

What you choose as the meaning of your life says something about your values--in fact, it says everything about your values--so who you are, as an individual, and what type of person you are, will limit the scope of available options for what you can take meaning from. For example, someone who gets meaning in their life from anime and science fiction novels and comic books and tabletop role-playing games, in sum, from geeky nerdy stuff, has chosen a different set of values than someone who takes their meaning from their collection of fine French wines, a high-paying office job, and making a million dollars a year, and driving an expensive car, and the suffering he derives from the love/hate relationship he has with his second wife. You can't say that one set of values is better or worse than others, you can only say whether a set of values is authentic or inauthentic to a person who chooses them.

Meaning is something you choose, but it is also something that chooses you. Take, for example, a teenager, and all their friends are geeks and nerds, so they try to get meaning in their life from anime and RPGs, in order to fit in with their group of friends, but, for that person, it is inauthentic, that isn't the real them, they are faking it because all their friends are doing it, and then they discover that the set of values represented by sports and football and baseball and hockey is more true to who they are as a person, so they stop pretending to be a geek and instead become more of a jock and sports fan, and then they are happy because they have found the meaning of their life.

Also observe that the thing which has meaning exists objectively, but the fact that you have chosen it for what it means to you was a subjective decision on your part, so, if you get confused and think it would objectively mean the same thing for everyone, that creates trouble, because the next step is for you to try to force it onto other people by force--such as, for example, someone who believes that Jesus Christ has saved their soul, and then fights a Crusade or war of conquest against other people, to force them to convert to Christianity, by the sword, and then leaves a trail of bloody corpses and tears and crying women and children behind them in their path of destruction, doing harm instead of good because they believed that a meaning which was good for them would be good for everyone.

And for some such people, at some point, their meaning itself becomes conquest, and the meaning of their life is their quest to force everyone to convert, so there could be a meaning of someone's life which was wrongful and evil, too. This sin of imposing your meaning onto non-consenting others is a crime of both religious zealots on the Right and political zealots on the Left.

Even some Objectivists get confused by this, and we assume that the philosophy of Objectivism would mean for everyone the same thing that it means to us, but for many other people it doesn't carry the same meaning, and they don't share the same set of values as us, even though the underlying philosophical truths are necessary and universal. So, by mistake, some Objectivists condemn others who disagree with us, with fire and anger and judgment, even though, from those other people's point of view, they have to be, and should be, true to the meaning of their own lives, and what it means to them, which was not the same as ours. Reality exists objectively, and each person exists objectively, but the meaning of your life is something that you subjectively assign to these things, so people can legitimately differ. Meanings, as belonging to a set of individuals, where each person's meaning is unique and special to that person, works best in a climate where you are free to choose your meanings, in other words, in freedom.

Indeed, for the Libertarian or Objectivist, the fight for freedom from government, and for the freedom to freely choose, can become the meaning (or one of the meanings) of their life, much as the political activist's fight for democracy, and against dictatorship and totalitarianism, can be the meaning of their life--that the meaning of his life, is the fight for other people to have the freedom to have meaning in their lives.

The meaning of your life is your answer to the question: Why? Why do I wake up in the morning? Why do I go to work all day? Why do I live my life? Why am I alive? For what purpose? What is my motivation? Why am I here? Why did God create me? What was I put on this earth to do? For what reason? And the interesting thing about the answer to this question is: you do not discover the answer to this question. Instead, you get to decide what the answer is. You choose what the meaning of your life is. You choose to assign meaning to something, and to then live for that purpose. But you make that choice, for a reason, or for a set of reasons, and that has to be organic to who you are, and it has to reflect the values that you really believe in, or else it won't work, and you won't really mean it.

It's like the Objectivist prog rock band Rush once sang: "Why are we here? Because we're here. Why does it happen? Because it happens." You choose why you are here. You choose a reason to be alive, and then you act that reason out.

Ultimately, the answer to the question: Why am I here? Is: To be you. God made you for you to be you. Your purpose in life is to be yourself. To be who you are. No one else could do it, because they are not you, but you are who you are. But that means you have a job to do: to live your life. And, my position is, that the philosophy of Objectivism, more than any other religion or philosophy, offers a set of useful tips and tricks, for how best to do your job.

Much has been made of the work of Jordan B. Peterson among the public, especially on the Right, within the last decade. Having looked at his work, I see it as Right-wing Christianity, no different from most other Right-wing Christianity. His only unique contribution was his concept of "meaning," that Christ becomes the meaning of your life, and you build a narrative of the meaning of your life that is built around Jesus Christ. Apparently, this struck a nerve and there was a huge demand for the meaning of life from people looking for the meaning of life, which explains his popularity. So, I took this opportunity, here, to tell you what the meaning of life really is. And, no, it isn't what he says it is.

However, he is completely correct when he says that a person should seek meaning instead of happiness, although, contrary to what he said, the reason for this is not that meaning is superior to happiness, instead the reason is that seeking meaning is actually a faster path to happiness than is the path of directly seeking happiness itself, because finding the meaning of your life, and having it, will make you happy. Meaning fills the great empty void of human existence, causing happiness, far more effectively than any of the outwards trappings of happiness as pleasure, such as drugs, sex, partying, vacations, fun, friends, a big fancy wedding with an expensive honeymoon, or a diamond wedding ring, a large family with a husband and many children, owning a mansion house or a yacht, money, status, prestige, a fancy university degree, an antique car or rare work of art, etc., any symbol of pride, greed, or lust, having true meaning in your life will make you happier than any of those things, unless one of those things actually holds a special meaning for you that you have assigned to it, so it becomes a vessel that carries your life's meaning, in terms of the meaning and purpose of your life. As means to the end of happiness, mere objects are initially empty, but they become full of joy by holding the meaning of your life for you.

Unlike "JP," I find that the best source for the discovery of meaning is not religion, instead it is philosophy, the civil, rational, ethical, logical contemplation of human existence and our place in reality, which can help you think through your goals and intentions and find what you really want out of life.

LUDWIG WITTGENSTEIN'S "PHILOSOPHICAL INVESTIGATIONS"

First, let me express my view of what position Ludwig Wittgenstein is asserting. Then, having defined his views, I will attack his views.

Wittgenstein's positions can be summarized as:

(1) Language is an arbitrary set of rules.

(2) Words have no meanings, only uses, and words have no precise uses, only imprecise vague uses.

(3) The "Big Questions" in philosophy are illusions and deceitful traps, to which there can be given no precise answers, and there is no use to be had in trying to answer them.

(4) People have access to language, but no access to any underlying reality underneath language.

(5) Everything is relative to a language. There is no absolute truth.

(6) He calls every language a "language-game," that language is a game people play by making a series of moves in the language-game to achieve practical results through usage of language. One could broadly call it the language-game theory of language. I believe Wittgenstein chose to call his theory of language as a "language-game," because a game is, fundamentally, an arbitrary set of rules, which you can follow, and you can achieve either a better practical outcome or a worse practical outcome by obeying that set of arbitrary rules.

(7) This isn't explicit in the book, but his followers went in this direction, which is suggested by the book: logic is an arbitrary set of rules, but it has no meaning, only uses, so you can prove or disprove that someone followed the set of rules called logic (syntax), but you can never prove that something is true or false (semantics), logic has no meaning, indeed, "true" and "false" have no precise definitions, and there is not much use for those words absent a hard commitment to the semantics of logic. So being logical merely means that you obeyed an arbitrary set of rules, it is no indication of the truth or falsehood of your arguments.

I would categorize Wittgenstein's theory of philosophy using the following four categories:

(1) Language Subjectivism: There is no objective reality, there is only language, we have access to language, not to objective reality.

(2) Language Relativism: Everything is relative to a language, there is no absolute meanings.

(3) Language Pragmatism: The only thing that matters about language is that it works, there is no need for precise definitions provided that it works in a useful way for a practical purpose. Language has pragmatic syntactical uses, but no semantic meanings.

(4) Language Behaviorism: You can observe people using language, and evaluate whether their usage achieved their objectives, but you have no access to their mental states relating to their use of language, and language implies only behavior, not a set of mental states (such as, for example, the mental state of knowing what you mean when you talk, or the mental state of understanding what someone else said).

So here are my objections to Wittgenstein:

(1) Time and again, Wittgenstein switches between different definitions of the same word, in order to argue that words have no precise meanings. This does not prove that conclusion, it merely proves his skill with verbal trickery and sleight-of-hand. Take, for example, when he speaks of knowledge, and compares knowing something all the time, that someone would say "I knew that all along," with saying "I know it!" right when you manifest and use your knowledge. He points out the obvious paradox, that you don't know when you knew it.

Obviously, if we used the linguistic precision that he lacks, this is not one word "knowledge", but two different definitions, one of "knowledge" as potential, and the other of "knowledge" as actual, as actualized knowing manifested in action, and if we wanted to be perfectly precise, we would use two words, one for each different meaning, but most people for convenience would use one word. But he lumps them together into one word, then uses the one word with two different meanings, then argues that this one word cannot have any precise meaning, and then he argues that we have no idea what we mean by "knowledge," we merely have uses for that word without a rigid understanding of why it works.

(2) The big question, in philosophy, is always: Why? Why are things the way they are? Why is this thing what it is? Why does existence exist? The questions that Wittgenstein hides from, are all variations of: why? If words have no meanings, then why do we use words? What usage does a word have other than to convey a meaning, and why would it have any other uses? Why can't a word have a precise meaning, if someone gives a precise definition for it? How, precisely, does language work? What is a language? What is the precise definition of the word "language"?

Because Wittgenstein, being a clever man and a crafty philosopher, knows that he cannot provide answers to those questions, he instead attacks the questions, by saying that asking the big questions in philosophy is forbidden, taboo, off-limits, a superstition. His theory is false, so he says there is no such thing as truth. He has no explanation for why language works, so he says that "why" is not a practical useful question. He can't define what a language is, so he says that there are no precise definitions. His is an entirely self-serving, crafty move in his language-game, trying to hide his lack of answers to basic philosophical questions that everyone is entitled to ask, by shutting down the questions, saying that those questions are not legitimate.

(3) Assume a high school Spanish teacher who tried to teach Spanish, but without giving precise definitions for any of the words, without giving any explanation for why the grammar rules are what they are, and letting the students just try to copy the behavior of a Spanish speaker and then be observed by the results of the words they speak when they say them to a Spanish-speaking audience, without regard for what those words mean, and without regard for the students' mental states as to whether their minds understand what the words mean, or not. Such a Spanish teacher would fail, miserably, and should be fired. If the students were tested, and got any questions on the test right, which is unlikely, those right answers would be due to random chance, not because the students spoke Spanish. That is not, in reality, how language is taught. That isn't how language works.

If you speak Spanish, then you know a set of words, you know each thing in reality that each one of those words refers to, and you understand, mentally, that each one of those things in reality is the meaning of each Spanish word that you know. You don't just memorize the grammar rules for using "las" or "los," you understand why those rules exist. "Amarillo" means yellow, and "roja" means red. Those are words, in the Spanish language, they have precise meanings, and the meaning of the word is the thing it refers to or corresponds to in reality. It's just that simple.

And you might say, if students observe the behavior of someone speaking Spanish, and they copy that behavior, they might end up speaking Spanish, and if someone observes the students copying the behavior of a Spanish speaker, they might think that the students are really speaking Spanish. But I would say, the students do not truly speak Spanish unless, on the basis of observing that behavior, they have figured out what the words mean. For example, they observe a person saying "comida" and then eating, so they figure out that "comida" means "food," and only then do they know that word. But you might ask, how do they know, just from observing behavior, that "comida" means food, when it might mean "I'm hungry," or it might have some other meaning, or it might have been purely random behavior. And the answer is, they would have to observe the Spanish speaker's behavior at a point where the difference between the possible meanings makes a difference in his behavior, and then they would see which was his meaning. They might even have to observe his behavior where it makes a difference whether he had a meaning at all or whether his behavior was random.

An arbitrary rule is a command, to be obeyed, without understanding why. A non-arbitrary rule, a rule that exists for a reason, is a principle to be understood. Wittgenstein seeks to replace a philosophy based on the discovery of principles, with philosophy as a doctrine of obedience to a set of commands.

(4) Wittgenstein is very popular among Analytic philosophy professors, because he provided, not an accurate theory of language, but a methodology for how to do philosophy, an effective program for philosophy professors to have something to do, so that they can keep their jobs. They do nothing but debate the syntax of logic, endlessly, over and over again, never opining on its semantics, never needing any theory of how to prove truth or falsehood using logic, never needing to draw a connection between logic and an objective physical reality underneath language, with no concern for any objective reality underneath their language at all, and all they spend their day doing is talking about words, and using arcane esoteric terminology in this way or that way, but they are fully protected from ever having to make sense to ordinary people, because no one is entitled to demand that they give precise definitions for the words they are using, and no one has the right to demand what is the real meaning of their words, as opposed to their usage in the game they play, and whether that meaning corresponds and refers to things in objective reality, and is true, or does not, and so is false.

When there is no meaning, meaning is lost. When people don't believe in truth, truth dies. So the philosophy professors talk, and talk, and talk, but never say anything, but they are all playing their clever little "language-game," and they are all in on it, and they craftily, cleverly make moves in their language-game, as if the philosophy professors were playing one big game of chess against each other, and they only care about their game, and scoring points against each other, they do not care about reality or truth anymore. Their goal is not to study reality and explain why things exist or why human experience is such as it is, their job is merely to score points against each other in their massive intricate language-game of philosophy.

Someone might object: But really, logic has no meaning, it really is just an arbitrary set of rules, after all, right? And, no, that is not correct. To say that something is logical, means that it is at one with itself, and logic is always true, because reality is at one with all real things, so each thing must be at one with every other thing in reality. The solution to a logic puzzle is the proposition of which all statements in the puzzle can be predicated as true as one thing, with each statement at one with all other statements, without contradiction, and a contradiction is two (or more) things that cannot be at one with each other, because they contradict and are opposed. That is what logic means: oneness, wholeness, unity, or, as it is called in Objectivism, integrity, that all premises integrate into one conclusion without contradiction, and thereby have (moral, rational) integrity.

What is missing from Wittgenstein's theory of language, is meaning. That your words have meanings. Those meanings can be true or false. And your meaning is what you intend for your words to show to your listener or audience of readers, your meaning is your intention, your purpose, your will, your willfulness. Under his views, there could be no truth, because there would exist no meaning. The meaning of something is frequently the answer to the question: why? For example, if you ask someone: why did you say that? Their answer is probably: because my meaning was such-and-such, and I wanted to convey that meaning.

THE PROBLEMS OF PHILOSOPHY

I had been thinking of applying to and obtaining a PhD in philosophy, recently, but, having studied it extensively, I have decided not to, and here, I want to explain why. The way that I do philosophy--and the way that Ayn Rand did it--is completely different than how the academic philosophy professors in today's universities do it, although I maintain that both ours, and theirs, are, in fact, things that you can legitimately call "philosophy," we are two schools within one area, or two methods for trying to achieve the same result. The philosophy professors, are, overwhelmingly, obsessed with answering this question, in one form or another: "How many angels can dance on the head of a pin?" Not literally angels, of course, but it's all that type of question. Virtually any question they ask, in any research paper, could be translated into the above: some sort of theoretical question with no answer, where you could make any argument, and it becomes like a test of oratory and rhetoric to see how sophisticated you can sound, the answer doesn't matter, the answer could be anything. And I don't care how many angels can dance on the head of a pin. I just don't care. If you could tell me, I wouldn't want to know. That type of question does not interest me.

When I philosophize, and this was also true of Ayn Rand, I do so by writing books. My readers pay me a small sum of money, for a book, when they buy a book, and in return, my book needs to help the reader, somehow, in some way--otherwise, I failed, my book failed to earn the money I was paid in return for that book. So my philosophy, of necessity, is a practical philosophy, useful for real people. Ayn Rand's novels are the same, and early in her career she was poor and she relied on book sales to make money, and, yes, people paid her to be entertained by her novels (and they take months to read, so it was a lot of entertainment), but the unique thing about Rand's novels was always her philosophy, so she, like I, had to do philosophy in a practical way, that normal readers could read and understand, and which would benefit ordinary people.

Compare and contrast the typical research philosophy paper written by a philosophy professor today. The purpose of the paper is not to be read by ordinary readers--normal people could neither read nor understand it, without the background context of a philosophy PhD. What is the purpose of a philosophy professor's philosophy paper? To help other philosophy professors. To help them do what? To help them write other philosophy papers. It becomes circular. It has no purpose. It is a means without ends. They aren't helping anyone, other than themselves. I think part of this is that, for a normal person, money holds you accountable, a normal person's need for money forces them to get a job, and be nice and polite to their boss and coworkers, and not show up to work drunk or stoned in the morning, etc. But the philosophy professors, the ones with tenure, at least, live in their Ivory Towers, and their salary is paid, and they don't need to make money, they are insulated from all financial need and want, so reality has no way of holding them accountable. Their money comes from endowments, from donors, who can't read or understand philosophy papers, so they just assume that a professor at Yale or Harvard is legit, and they would be incapable of forming an opinion that it is a scam or a con.

For example, if someone advances the position that consciousness does not exist, which is obvious bullshit and any person with self-awareness can prove this isn't true just by being self-aware, such a paper, if it had enough bells and whistles and ornaments of fancy words and arguments written in the style popular in academic philosophy right now, might get published in a peer-reviewed philosophy journal, and then it actually serves the professor's career, instead of hurting them as it would a normal person--if a normal person showed up at work, and said consciousness is an illusion, and he really meant it, his coworkers would call 911 and say he was crazy or on drugs. There isn't a way to measure the truth or falsehood of what philosophers say, so the universities are using the number of peer-reviewed papers that get published, as a measure of the philosophy professors' quality, and donors fund grants on that basis, and the number of papers published only correlates to conformity, orthodoxy, obedience to the most popular methodology, to doing things the same way that everyone else does them, it does not correlate to truth, or to logic, or to reason, or to rationality.

Of course, you might say that in many areas of academia, like physics or math, the professors write papers whose only purpose is to help other professors write papers, and the end is the goal of advancing human knowledge. But, in physics, math, etc., that body of knowledge ultimately has a practical usefulness for real human beings, as technology, etc. With philosophy papers, it doesn't help real people in any practical way, nor is it ever intended to. This, too, is why Objectivism is so unpopular among professors, and why they refuse to take us seriously--we do things differently from them, but we are the only ones who do, so, if we did not exist, people would have nothing to compare them to--and the comparison is unfavorable to them. It isn't clear, to me, that there is something that lots of philosophy professors could do, that would actually make enough money to earn a salary--and here, as elsewhere, I define "to make money" as meaning "to create value for self or others to consume."

How does one do philosophy? Take consciousness, as a philosophical problem, for example. You could adopt one of several positions with respect to it. It exists. It doesn't exist. It's an illusion. It's the spiritual soul. It's the physical brain. We can have knowledge of it. We cannot have knowledge about it. And then the arguments for and against, and pros and cons, of each position. It's all very obvious, really, and every smart person already understands this debate. You make your arguments, the person listens to the debate, they choose what they believe, and that's it, and then they move on. There's nothing more for a philosopher to do. Yes, if the person chooses the wrong position, then they live for the rest of their lives with the consequences of believing something that is false. But that's on them. You can prove, using logic and deductive proof, that a position is true, but the audience still has to choose to see your proof and think it through and understand it, or else they are not persuaded, even by logic. So there isn't that much work for a philosopher to do.

One might say, but in a philosophy class, a professor asks the students "Does consciousness exist?", and maybe one of the students had never thought about it before, but now she thinks about it, and it makes her see the world with a fresh set of eyes, so this opens her mind up to the wonder of thinking about philosophy or thinking about life in a philosophical way, and that makes her a better thinker. Yes, a philosophy teacher can do that, and that is worth money to the student, if it makes her a better thinker. But a high school philosophy teacher could do that. Any person can do that. That isn't the goal of a PhD-holding philosophy professor at Yale philosophy or Harvard philosophy. That wasn't the goal of what their graduate philosophy studies were teaching them how to do.

Now, in the debates, in philosophy and politics, the Objectivism position and the Libertarian position are often left out, so I have a lot of work to do, because not every side is represented in the debate yet, so a person can't yet make a fully informed decision, because they haven't heard our side yet. But for the philosophy professors? There is not that much work for them to do. So they waste their time with busy-work, trying to look sophisticated so that people will think that they are smart, with arguments bordering on mere mysticism, arguing in paper after paper about how many angels can dance on the head of a pin. I don't have much to gain from them, and they don't really have much to gain from me. They are not my intended audience. But they are their own only intended audience.

You might ask me for specific examples. Take modal logic, and counterfactuals. Those are the hot trending topics philosophy professors love nowadays. Modal logic is based on the logic of all possible worlds. But there's a problem. In reality, there aren't any worlds other than the reality that you and I live in. It's bullshit. It's a crock of dog shit, dumped on the street, for everyone to smell. Papers on that topic literally make me want to vomit.

Counterfactuals are not nearly as repulsive, but they are one of the hot topics in academic philosophy, and, as far as I am concerned, they are completely unimportant. A counterfactual is an If P then Q statement where P is false. Every element of them that has true importance in logic could be summed up in a single paragraph, maybe even a single run-on sentence. There is nothing special about them. And yet there are dozens of papers on this topic every year. It's insane. Again, they view it as having to do with other possible worlds, that If P Then Q is true even if P is false because there is some other world where P actually is true in reality. And they don't mean hypothetically; they mean that there really is an actual reality where P is true, an alternate universe that exists. I know, it's weird, right?

The problem is that the logicians never came up with a principle of inductive logic, from which you could relate P and Q to reality on the basis of true or false, so they return, again, to modal logic, and, again, they make me want to vomit.

In my books I have explained inductive reasoning and the points of connection between logic and physical scientific empirical reality, but, alas, they are ignorant of my work, and I blame them for not having thought of it themselves. I can only assume these topics are really popular because it is easy for the philosophy professors to write about them, and it is impossible to ever know whether what they say about them is really true.

Maybe, at some point, originally, some of them, in their examination of counterfactuals, were looking for the analysis I presented and proved in my essay "If P Then Q," about the logic of science and how to use logic for observations, but they were not smart enough to arrive at my end result, so they got lost along the way. They don't know how someone could know that If P Then Q is true if P itself is false. It's sad. It's like they've never done an actual philosophical analysis of something in physical reality, from which anyone would see how you can know such things. "If the cow had been born without a mouth, it would have died." The farmer knows that, because he knows cows, and he understands how they work. It has nothing to do with other possible worlds, it has only to do with this world. But the philosophers don't know how to connect logic to perception, such that you can see what is or is not truth. So they think it all comes from intuition, and inner knowledge of other possible worlds, which is sheer mysticism. There are no other possible worlds. There is only one reality.

There is nary an original thought in all their heads. They just eat, and then regurgitate, and then re-eat, the vomit that other philosophy professors vomited, after those other professors had eaten the vomit--I mean, the work--of David Lewis, which itself was not a contribution to human progress in any meaningful way. It is a syndrome Ayn Rand described: the death of originality, the rise of mediocrity, the end of new ideas, the conformity to conformity itself.

WHAT IS PHILOSOPHY?

Philosophy studies these topics. Any answer to any question on these topics, to the extent plausible and based on argument and analysis, is philosophy. Who decides what is plausible? That too is for philosophy to study. To answer a question pertaining to these topics, or to take a position with respect to any aspect of one of these topics, to say what one of these things is, why it is such, how it works, that it is one or two opposed to each other or many, or to assert that it does not exist, and to then explain why it does not exist and how we humans are to go without it--is philosophy. Any method or tool by means of which these topics are studied constitutes the tools and methods of philosophy.

Call this, if you will, the Hasanian Taxonomy of Philosophy.

The topics:
1. Metaphysics and Ontology
I. Being
II. Reality
III. Objectivity
IV. Reason and Reasoning
V. Induction and Deduction
VI. Things and their Relations
VII. Substance and Form

2. Epistemology
I. Knowledge
II. Language and Truth
III. Logic and Proof
IV. Universals
V. Essences
VI. Definitions
VII. Abstractions and Ideas

3. Ethics and Morality
I. Free Will

II. Right and Wrong, Good and Evil
III. Moral Absolutes and Moral Relativity
IV. Consequences, and their Moral Significance
V. Means, Usage of Things for Purposes, and Its Moral Significance
VI. Human Action and Motives and Ends
VII. Ideals

4. Philosophy of Mind
I. Minds
II. Persons, and Personal Identity
III. Emotions, specifically What Are They
IV. Mental States, and Thought
V. Self-Knowledge
VI. Self-Reference
VII. Consciousness

5. Philosophy of Science
I. Science, specifically What It is, and What is Its Nature
II. Cause and Effect
III. Necessity and Coincidence
IV. Math and Numbers, specifically What They Are, and What Is Their Nature
V. Sensations and Phenomena and Empirical Data
VI. Perception
VII. Physical Substance, the Physical World, Space and Time

6. Religion and Theology
I. God
II. Souls
III. Virtues
IV. Sins
V. Intuition and Revelation
VI. Faith
VII. Meaning and Purpose

7. Social and Political Philosophy
I. Politics, Its role and purpose, and Its causes and effects
II. Economics, Its role and purpose, and Its causes and effects
III. Freedom, Its role and purpose, Its causes and effects, and Its creation and destruction
IV. Government, Its role and purpose, Its causes and effects, and Its creation and

destruction, as Well as Its Means and Ends

V. Individual Rights (if any exist), Their role and purpose, their causes and effects, and their creation and destruction, and Collective Responsibilities (if any exist), Their role and purpose, their causes and effects, and their creation and destruction

VI. Utopias and Ideal Political-Economic Conditions, How They are Defined, If They Can Exist, How or Why Then Can Exist, or, If They Cannot Exist, Why They Cannot Exist, and What Conditions of Society are Acceptable Without Them, and What Role the Ideals of Utopias Play in Non-Utopian Conditions

VII. Practical Philosophy (for example, Philosophy of Law): The application of any answer to a question pertaining to a theoretical topic of philosophy where such application is to a practical or methodological area of human life and human action, such as, for example, the practical implementation of an abstract philosophical position.

You might object: But what about aesthetics? I left out an entire branch of philosophy! But aesthetics, as commentary about works of art, or a theory of art, would come in under other categories, for example, art that was about, or art criticism that used works of art to comment upon, for example, being, or moral and ethical ideals, or spiritual meaning and purpose (for example, either to say or imply what it is, or to say or imply that it does not exist), would be aesthetics, as philosophy, relating to one of those above topics. Theories of works of art, as they relate to beauty, or to love, would come in under human action, or under emotions, or under ideals, or under being. There is no one right answer to how or why aesthetics is philosophy (maybe? About that, too, we can debate), but I would argue that my system covers everything there is in philosophy, pretty much.

One might also ask: Then every religion is a philosophy? Yes. Every theology is a philosophy. Theology is a type of philosophy. It is one type among many types.

The unifying theme that unites all these topics, is that they are the deepest, most abstract, most theoretical topics available to us humans. Or maybe something else. Or perhaps there is nothing that all of these topics share in common. That too is for philosophy to decide.

Then the next question: who is a philosopher? A philosopher is any person who studies these topics and forms a belief therefrom or who formulates a position on a topic combined with an argument or analysis to justify that position.

FROM THE OBJECTIVIST POINT OF VIEW, CAN PEOPLE RIGHTFULLY BELIEVE IMMANUEL KANT?

From the point of view of Objectivism, do people have the right to believe the philosophy of Immanuel Kant? Rand said he was evil and blamed much of the moral decline of contemporary philosophy on his influence. She attempted to de-legitimize him and say that he was an idiot, and not a real philosopher. But, I say, people have the right to be Kantians. Kantianism, German Transcendental Idealism, is a legitimate philosophy. It is not the objectively correct philosophy. It is not an accurate description or explanation of reality. It is possible to prove that it is objectively incorrect. But Kant had a set of answers to the problems of philosophy, and he had an analysis, and arguments, to support those answers, and some people believe his arguments. His arguments are wrong, and people are wrong to believe them. But other people have the right to be wrong. People have the right to believe whatever they want, and Kant was a philosopher, and people can believe him. And the philosophy professors who are Kantians have every right to believe Kant and to make arguments in his favor which seek to persuade their students. This is not brainwashing; it is merely debate.

If we don't want people to believe Kant, we must simply do a better job of persuasion than the Kantians to express our philosophical positions as alternatives to him. The fire-and-brimstone Orthodox Objectivist will accuse me of defending Kant. I am not defending Kant. I am defending freedom of speech. Freedom of belief. Intellectual freedom. Nothing more or less. I am not a Kantian and I have no vested interest in defending his beliefs. Then other Objectivists might say, but his philosophy promotes irrationality, which leads to political oppression or violence, which violates my rights. Well, but other people have the right to believe what they want, so long as they do no violence to you. And, at the point at which they do violence to you, then you have the moral right to use force for self-defense against them, and against any violence directed at you which was inspired by Kant or any other irrational philosopher, such as Marx. And if your self-defense wins, then you remain free. Such is life.

People have the right to believe Kant, Marx, or anyone. And Kant, and Marx, and most famous philosophers, are legitimate philosophers, who made arguments, and gave answers, according to the tools and methods which define philosophy, and which answers problems and questions which are within the realm of philosophy. Other people can believe whatever they want, and it's none of your business, but that doesn't make their beliefs right. Many other people believe Kant, but, as Sartre said, "Hell is other people."

ON IMMANUEL KANT

I took it upon myself to read the Critique of Pure Reason. That lasted a few days, before I couldn't pick it up anymore. But I will say this: say what you want about Immanuel Kant, he was a great enemy of Objectivism, but he was also a great writer. He takes the fact that his theory is so absurdly crazy that there literally are no real-world examples of his ideas, and turns that to his advantage: "I sacrificed examples in the interests of clarity," is basically what he says, but he says it so much more elegantly. He says "this is the last work there needs to be in philosophy, ever, this answers every question, and you have no choice but to agree with me, you must agree with everything I say," then, in the next sentence, obviates any anger the reader might feel at being talked to with such arrogance, by saying that any previous philosopher, who put forward any theory of the soul or reason, was actually being far more arrogant than Kant--which is obviously not true, but the quality of Kant's prose form was so good that he makes the reader feel as if it was true. I think Kant's staying power in philosophy, at 200+ years and counting, owes more to how good of a writer he was, and far less to the quality of his philosophy.

By the way, I had previously read "Prologue to Any Future Metaphysics Seeking to Present Itself as Science" and "Groundwork of the Metaphysics of Morals," cover to cover, while in college, so, yes, I have read Kant in his own words. After all, I did earn my college degree with a major in philosophy!

PHILOSOPHICAL WISDOM

(1) The Logical Positivists held that everything which cannot be verified by science has no meaning. My position is precisely the reverse: that everything which has a meaning can be verified by science.

(2) Nietzsche once said: "Every philosopher must be forgiven for his first followers." I have a similar motto: every writer must be forgiven for their first book.

(3) Nietzsche said, or meant, in gist, something similar to this: "We hold the greatness of geniuses a safe distance above ourselves for the purpose of considering ourselves unable to reach it." Similarly, people who choose to be stupid look up to smart people in order to relieve themselves from the burden of having to think.

(4) What is a Libertarian?
A Libertarian is someone who doesn't obey the rules.
But then how do they know what to do, if they don't follow rules?
You would have to think for yourself.
Precisely.

(5) The history of philosophy, summarized in one paragraph: Pre-Kant, there were the empiricists, who had sensations but not reason, and the rationalists, who had reason and the analysis of concepts, but not sensations. The empiricists were like Pavlov's dogs, merely animals reacting to sensations like a smell or a noise, or to a mental image, without thought; the rationalists were like blind men, having a mind that could think but lacking eyes that can see. Kant "combined" the two, by saying that reason and the analysis of concepts imposes truth onto sensations, and he called this scientific. And the popular narrative of the history of philosophy calls Kant a hero, for having done that. I might be viewed as having said the opposite: that reason acts upon sensations, but it is the sensations which impose truth upon reason, and it is the sensations which impose truth upon the analysis of concepts, and that this is what science is.
　　But that is a shallow, two-dimensional view of my work. My philosophy runs deeper. There is no sharp distinction between sensations, on the one hand, and reason

and the analysis of concepts, on the other hand, the former is object, the latter, subject, you could not have a sentence without the form of "Subject verb object." The subject does something to the object, or else nothing would happen, but the subject is subject, and the object is object. What the subject actually does to the object is summed up by this pithy quote: "Nature, to be commanded, must be obeyed."

(6) If someone from another country, a long distance away, in a land where they grow mangos but not apples, and he has never seen an apple before, if he asked you, "what does an apple look like?" How would you answer? The only true answer is that an apple looks like an apple. A thing is what it is. And a thing's appearance is what it looks like. If you have seen an apple, then an apple, itself, is something that you have seen. The apple's appearance, what the apple looks like, is equal to the visual properties of the apple itself, of the apple in itself, the thing as such, the thing in itself. So, if something looks like an apple, then it has an apple's appearance.

If something looks good, then you know that it is good-looking, because these are one and the same thing, and if something looks ugly, then you know it is ugly looking, because that is what it looks like, and good-looking and ugly are properties of visual aspects of things, and so those can be directly perceived. If you see something, then you know what it looks like, but that doesn't necessarily mean that you know what it is, in the sense that you don't necessarily know what is underneath its appearance, you don't know what structure is there, what physics of body and mass, what chemical composition, or what actions the thing can do, what its purpose is, and so on. Any one of those things could surprise you, if you assume, absent proof, that the thing is exactly what it looks like it is.

But to see a thing, and to then have knowledge of what it looks like, is incorrigible, and the only way to truly know what a thing looks like, is to see it. Sensations are simple, what Ayn Rand called "the irreducible primary," they do not break down as visual appearances into smaller components, although the visual things can be described using abstractions, like "blue" or "cloudy" to describe how the sky looks, etc.

But things themselves as such are not simple or irreducible, it is only the directly perceivable properties of things, which is what an appearance is, that are of this sort. And, of course, you could draw a picture of an apple, to try to show the foreigner what an apple looks like, but that is merely an abstraction, and sensations are always fully concrete, so it is not the same, seeing a drawing of an apple is not the same experience as seeing a real apple (although it is the same as seeing a drawing of an apple), because of what sensations are. This is why to experience something is to have an experience, which is a unique, simple, irreducible thing. There are some philosophers who say, "you cannot say what experience is." But you can. Experience is experience. That says everything that there is to be said. And, no, that isn't a tautology, because there are plenty of philosophers of logic who would disagree with me. You can say what it is, in a statement that is true, but that isn't the same as experiencing it.

However, experiences can be analyzed, using logic and reason, because they are things, like, for example, asking why an apple looks the way that it does, for what purpose, and how this shape helps the apple seeds become trees, and such. The experience of seeing a hammer, for example, is the perceivable and sensory aspect and attributes of the hammer itself: the hammer is the sensation, plus the substance, such as, in this example, the logic of why this shape and this material can hammer nails, and so on, which reason and logic can analyze. The hammer as a perceived thing is-plus the set of sensations; you see the sensations, but it is also true that you see the hammer, that you see the thing itself, because the thing itself is the sensations plus other properties. A thing is a set of properties, and an experience is a set of sensations which are properties of a set of perceived things. The things, as such, exist in objective reality, so the things that you perceive do in fact exist objectively, outside of your own subjective mind; experience is not in itself subjective, although your own mind and point of view and angle from which you see experience is.

Sensations can give us a path to knowledge of the depth behind the surface appearance. Such things can be real, or illusions, but reason and logic can tell the difference, much as a scientist might look to empirical data to see if his research is on the right track or has hit a dead end. In general, as I have written elsewhere, if the sensations were what a theory would expect, they serve to confirm it, to the extent that those sensations are a statistically significant sample set of the entire thing, but if the sensations were not what a theory would expect them to be, they refute the hypothesis.

A caveman in ancient times could see the stars at night, and he knew what stars look like just the same as we do, but we know that they are stars, which the ancient cavemen did not know, because we have science and reason built upon generations of research and scholarship, and he had only the knowledge that came from immediate experience of the sensations of stars. The difference between what he knew and what we know is the difference between empirical knowledge and rational knowledge.

(7) Some philosophers would say "a dollar bill on Mars isn't a dollar bill, it is just a piece of paper." But, no, it is still a dollar bill--because the dollar bill always was just the piece of paper. There are some who have said that a hammer isn't really a hammer objectively, it is only a hammer for human beings, because that identity, being a hammer, exists only relative to our human purpose. No. It is a hammer--that is a fact in objective reality--it is useful precisely because, in reality, it has a handle of wood, and a head of metal, with this hardness, in thus-and-such a shape, that makes it useful for hammering--the fact that humans can use it to hammer nails into wood is a fact in reality, which is true because of what the hammer is--because it is a hammer---it is not

a merely a subjective wish or feeling. What humans find useful, is a fact in objective reality--whether we succeed or fail, whether we live or die, exists objectively. Also, if a human actually used a hammer to hammer nails, the fact that they did so would be objectively true, and would be fully objective.

(8) Mark Twain once said "Be yourself. Everyone else is already taken." He also said "Do the right thing. This will please some people and astonish the rest." I would combine the two: "Do the right thing. Everything else is already being done."

(9) If people are not allowed to be proud of their virtues, then they will be proud of their sins.

(10) What is Heaven for one man is Hell for another.

MY METHODOLOGY,
AS A PHILOSOPHER,
FOR PHILOSOPHY

I was reading the entry entitled "Contemporary Philosophy" on Wikipedia and reading the subsection on "The Professionalization of Philosophy" and it said something like, and I paraphrase: "Now only philosophy professors can be philosophers, and philosophy is something that is done by publishing academic papers in highly technical trade journals, which non-philosophers cannot understand and which are not designed to be read by non-philosophers, and the age of the amateur philosopher with no technical training and no PhD who writes genius philosophy books intended for a mass audience, the age of philosophers like Descartes or Spinoza or David Hume, is over," and I remember thinking, "That's me! They're talking about me! I'm a precocious amateur genius who writes philosophy books! They are saying the age of me is over!" And I don't think my age is over. Here I am.

So, to decide whether to pursue philosophy at a graduate level in academia, I took it upon myself to look at all the philosophy departments' websites, to see whether there are philosophy professors under whom I would want to study or do a doctoral dissertation. There aren't. And it isn't because I think I'm smarter than them, as many of them seem smart and highly educated and scholarly. The reason is that none of them--0%--focus on the areas in philosophy that I focus on. The reason is that none of them study Objectivism or Libertarianism, in any extent.

There are a handful of sort-of-fake professors whose chairs are endowed by the Ayn Rand Institute and their donors and related grants, and there is a cluster of Libertarians at George Mason University (which does not offer a PhD in philosophy, by the way), but, in academia, mostly, there are no prestigious, seriously regarded professors who are studying Objectivism, and there are maybe a handful of Libertarian professors, but most of them aren't even real Libertarians, they are Far Left Libertarians who are more like anarcho-socialists pretending to be libertarian and are not real Libertarians (Zwolinski, the so-called bleeding-heart libertarian, who truly is a bleeding-heart liberal, and whose vision of a supposedly libertarian utopia would actually have higher taxes than socialism, for example), and then there are some Elitist professors who say they are Libertarian but are more like Republican conservatives who strongly support the free market (Epstein of NYU Law, for example, who says libertarian things but functions like an establishment elitist in methodology. Volokh of Reason Magazine is the same way.). There is one, and only one, Libertarian professor, at the University of Colorado, who is legit and well-regarded and seems smart, but, ironically, that is the one university I would not consider going to, because it sits atop the Rocky Mountains, and I have a fear of heights.

I Googled it, and, yes, the official position of academic philosophy is that Objectivism (and, for different reasons, Libertarianism) is not a real philosophy, is not to be taken seriously, and is not to be studied, and is not to be given any image of legitimacy. So, of course, I work exclusively, as a philosopher, in the Objectivist and Libertarian tradition, so there is no place for me there, in academia, and there never was.

Why are things like this? I could blame the problem by saying that the university culture attracts elitists and snobs, because the highly educated view themselves as smarter and better educated than the great unwashed masses, and socialism appeals to the elites because it lets them condescend over the poor and use the poor as an excuse to wield economic political power, while Objectivism and Libertarianism are useful for real people in real ordinary life, so they have more of a populist appeal, and would never win among an academy of elitism.

I could say that. But I won't. It's probably really more of a network effect. If there were Objectivist professors, then there would be more Objectivist students, who would become a higher number of Objectivist professors themselves in the next generation. But the cycle can never begin, because the number of professors who study Objectivism is zero, so there is never a professor, so no students are taught, so no students go on to become professors. It's a vicious cycle. It could not be broken, either, unless Objectivism becomes so popular that large numbers of people pursue PhDs in philosophy despite a culture and environment hostile to them, which they would know, going in, was going to be highly hostile and toxic towards them. Who knows? It could happen, in 50 years, or 100 years, or 200 years. But it may never happen.

WHAT IS A PHILOSOPHER?

What is a Philosopher? A philosopher is someone who explores religion by means of reason instead of by means of faith. A philosopher is someone who knows God by means of reason, not by means of faith and intuition or divine revelation. To say, of the world, that God made it in this way, and why, that the metaphysical nature of things is this or that, or not, or to say what God is, or even to say whether God exists, are philosophical claims, but, at the same time, they are religion, and religious claims. Objectivism, as a philosophy with a set of virtues and sins, of right and wrong, good and evil, that necessarily arise from its cosmology of ontology and metaphysics, is, perhaps, the most truly, an atheistic religion. It is not a cult, it is not the cult of Ayn Rand, but, as a philosophy, it does function like a religion, but with the innovation, the evolution, of knowing God by means of reason, and rejecting faith, which, perhaps, was the methodology of Thomas of Aquinas, and Aristotle, before Rand.

So, if you know God by means of reason, then you could have reasoned debates about what you choose to believe, instead of obeying Ayn Rand as a prophet who had unique divine access to God. Rand said that God did not exist, but if, as Spinoza did, one was to say that God is the physical world of space and time, or that these things arise from God's nature, that God is everywhere and God is everything, then philosophy merely uses reason to study reality, and this is the same as using reason to study God, it just depends on how you define the words, and that the world is the expression of science, science is the outline of math, and math is the shadow of logic, and logic is God, then Ayn Rand would have had a theory of God.

And, by the way, John 1:1 from The Bible can be translated as "In the beginning was logic (literally, the 'logos,' in the original Ancient Greek text of The Bible, which, translated, means 'the rational understanding of things as expressed in language'), and logic is God." This is often mistranslated as "In the beginning was The Word, and The Word was God."

Logic is at one with all things, because logic is the principle that each thing must be at one with itself and be at one with all other things because reality is at one with all things and reality is at one with itself, and, for you to be at one with who you are, and for you to treat reality as what it is, for your actions and behavior to be at one with reality, is for you to live an ethical life.

The religious, the faithful, say that God can only be known by means of faith, and that God cannot be understood through reason, so they hate us, because we challenge their assumptions, which, when challenged, have no rational defense, and they are not smart enough to use reason, so they resort to faith, because they have nothing else.

Religion is the study of God by means of faith, whereas philosophy is the study of God, and the world God made, and why God made the world the way that it is, by means of reason.

ARISTOTLE AND THE SEVEN DEADLY SINS

Let us see if we can combine Aristotle's theory of the Golden Mean, which holds that the good is a ratio, virtue lies in the middle ground between two extremes, and that the ethical behavior is in between one extreme of excess and one extreme of deficiency, with the Christian doctrine of the Seven Deadly Sins, defining each sin as an extreme of excess:

My statements will always take the following form: First, the sin of excess, then, a naming of the virtuous middle virtue, then the sin of deficiency. I will then state the topic to which the degrees of too much or too little pertain.

Take this example: Too Much, Just Right, Too Little. Virtue.

(1) Lust, Healthy Sexuality, Involuntary Celibacy. Sex.

(2) Gluttony, Healthy Eating, Anorexia. Eating.

(3) Envy, Inspiration from Others' Achievements, Apathy towards Goals. Comparison and Competitiveness.

(4) Pride, Self-Esteem (but also being Humble and Grateful), Low Self-Esteem or Self-Criticism. Self-opinion.

(5) Wrath, Righteous Anger against Injustice, Complicity or Weakness. Anger.

(6) Sloth, Relaxation and Enjoyment, Stress and Anxiety. Idleness or Laziness.

(7) Greed, Rational Self-Interest and a Healthy Desire for Money and Ethical Selfishness, Poverty. Money.

If this is true, then the Christians completely misunderstood their own doctrine, because they believe that, for example, any desire for money is greed and is evil, or any desire for sex is lustful and is therefore evil, so a truly virtuous person holds zero desire for money and zero desire for sex, so they are led down the wrong path by their misunderstanding of their own Bible. In reality, for ethics and virtue and morality, you can do the wrong thing, but you can also have too much of a good thing, which itself becomes another wrong thing, and, because a good person desires goodness, doing too much of the right thing might be an even greater temptation than doing the wrong thing.

Take, for example, this question: if eating lots of cake and junk food tastes good, then how can it be true that perception is truthful, which is the position held by the philosophy of Objectivism, because the cake tastes good, but eating it is bad for you? But I hold that the cake tasting good is truthful, because the cake is good, it is only bad to eat it because eating it is too much of a good thing, for example, too much fat and too much sugar, so the fact that fat and sugar taste good is not evidence that the senses are deceptive or that perception lacks accurate knowledge of objective reality, fat and sugar taste like exactly what they really are in reality.

Similarly, for sex, it looks hot and beautiful because it is hot and beautiful, but the naked human body is also gross and disgusting and dirty, as an animal body, so sex looks exactly like what it really is. One should want some food, but not too much and be fat, or too little and starve; one should desire some sex, but not too much and be dirty and disgusting, or too little and be mired in sexual frustration and a lack of pleasure in life.

There are countervailing arguments against me: for example, that greed is the love of money in itself, which is an unhealthy attitude towards money, whereas a healthy attitude towards money is to use money as a means to an end but never as an end in itself, and so on for sex, food, etc., so it is a question of attitude, not a question of degrees. There is also the argument that I get Christianity wrong (and, I admit, most theologians would not agree with my analysis), that food, money, sex, self-esteem, etc., are the tools by means of which a person stays alive in the physical world, and any behavior that clings to life in the physical world is wrong, and true virtue lies in renouncing the physical world, which purifies the soul for its journey to Heaven upon death. That is one extreme Christian view, although, if that is the official Christian position, then, obviously, my theory is not Christian, it is merely a synthesis of certain elements of the Bible with certain elements of Aristotle.

One may, of course, point to sex, food, money, and self-opinion, as things that tempt one into betraying one's moral integrity, such as, for example, if money is a temptation to commit a crime, or if sex tempts you to betray a friend for a woman (or for a man), or if pride leads you to an act of arrogance or grandiosity or to steal credit for someone else's achievement. Envy, or wrath, could also be an emotional influence that tempts you to evil. To betray law-abiding society (by crime, for money), to betray someone else (for sex), or to do the worst thing you could do, to betray yourself, is the ultimate evil. Betrayal, symbolized by Judas in the story of Jesus Christ, is the one true evil, but, expressed on our lives, it is our own betrayal of our ethics and our moral integrity. So defined, one could say that the seven deadly sins are merely a list of temptations to betrayal, to evil. If so, then, used in a good or ethical way, food and sex and pride etc. would not be sins, they would only be sins when expressed as the temptation to bait you into betraying your own soul.

The next two books in this volume deal with forgiveness, as seen from the point of view of logic and Objectivism. The later books in this volume deal with moral integrity and ethics in general, and also the application of ethics and moral integrity to laws and politics, as well as the integrity of logic applied to epistemology philosophy.

ON FORGIVENESS

INTRODUCTION

This is an essay on forgiveness, not in the religious sense, but in a purely secular meaning, as in, when one person forgives another person for something they did wrong. The primary focus is on self-forgiveness, where a person forgives themselves, a concept which this essay explains as "moral bankruptcy," using debts and credits and bankruptcy and economics and finance as a metaphor for the moral debts and moral credits that you owe to yourself and to others, that you owe it to yourself to be a good person, and you owe it to other people to be good to them, and, where you fail, you owe them a debt. The human brain evolved in such a way that humans tend to subconsciously seek to repay moral debts through the infliction of emotional pain, either inflicting emotional pain upon the self for debts owed to self (guilt), inflicting pain upon the self for debts owed to others (shame), or inflicting pain upon others for debts they owe to you (anger). This essay, despite being atheistic and secular in nature, does explore forgiveness in the context of areas that are commonly thought of as religious sins: lust, greed, pride, envy, and evil, as well as shame and guilt. The key central idea is that self-forgiveness, "moral bankruptcy," can help set you free from any guilt, shame, and anger that is holding you back in your life, and forgiveness will enable you to live a happier life, by giving you the confidence to act, and to achieve, with a greater resistance to fear of feeling guilt or shame if you fail, thereby tranquilizing fear of rejection or fear of failure or fear of disappointment. This theory of emotions will define honor, emotional maturity, self-esteem, and confidence, as well as explaining all of the seven major emotions: happiness, sadness, love, fear, guilt, shame, and anger. This book is cold, logical, no-nonsense wisdom about forgiveness, and is not mere wishy-washy empty generalities like most self-help books.

MORAL BANKRUPTCY

In The Genealogy of Morals, Friedrich Nietzsche put forward a theory of emotions which I refer to as emotional capitalism. If one of your friends or loved ones owes you a moral debt, and does not repay in kind, you may exact payment by being mean and nasty to them. If you owe them a moral debt, you can repay by being nice to them, or by letting them be mean to you. If someone owes you, you may seek their feelings and expressions of gratitude to pay the debt, or inflict emotional pain to recover your debt. Emotional capital is the debts and credits you owe, or are perceived to owe, to the people in your life.

Emotions can be explained in this way: you feel guilt if you owe a moral debt to someone else to give them your pain in order to pay off your debt. You feel shame if you owe a moral debt for failing social norms or if you owe a debt to society, again, to give your suffering to your creditor as payment. And you feel anger toward someone if they owe you a moral debt which they are not repaying, to extract what you owe from them by getting pain from them when you cause pain to them.

For example, say that you feel you have been a good employee for several years and you deserve a promotion, and your boss passed you over for a promotion and promotes someone else instead. You might get angry at your boss, because, either consciously or subconsciously, you desire to cause your boss pain equal to the moral debt that your boss owed you when he wronged you. Obviously to get angry in this way would be a great way to get fired from your job and lose your salary and ruin your life. Later it will be shown how forgiveness, implemented as moral bankruptcy and emotional maturity, would enable you to forgive your boss, and be a happy productive employee at work.

This theory takes its most interesting turn with the idea that, when you owe something to yourself and fail to obtain it, you owe to yourself a debt you cannot repay, which you must then pay to yourself by inflicting pain and punishment upon yourself: this is the theory of emotional guilt. Moving forward this essay will frequently refer to guilt as the self-inflicted pain of a debt owed to self, and refer to shame as a debt owed to others, although there are some nuances and wrinkles in these definitions. Later it will become clear that shame usually causes guilt to go with it, because you let yourself down by not being good enough for the others whom you sought to impress, and, for this reason, guilt and shame can function as one entity in reality.

From here we finally see the groundwork laid for a theory of moral bankruptcy.

In legal bankruptcy, the law forces creditors to absolve the debts of the debtor, in order to give the debtor a fresh start and freedom. Absent bankruptcy it would probably be inevitable to bring back debtors prison and indentured servitude, which is a road to slavery. Moral bankruptcy operates along similar principles. Michel Foucault once hypothesized that there is an Internalized Other in each person's head whereby society conditions a person to cast society's judgment upon himself internally. To the extent that a person has a sense of social judgment, and an accounting of one's emotional capital, one acts in this capacity as bankruptcy court judge, and one then looks in the mirror and sees oneself as debtor to oneself as creditor, to the extent one failed in what one was morally obligated to give to oneself.

You were stupid in how you applied for a job, you did not try hard enough to obtain a goal, you did not put up enough of a fight to save a romance, etc. You look at yourself and declare that you are filing for moral bankruptcy. The judge then absolves all emotional debts, you are forgiven, you have absolved yourself for the sin against yourself that you had committed, and you move on with your life.

The definition of emotional maturity is explained by the theory of emotional capitalism. It is the constant forgiveness of small debts to other people in your life who have been good to you in the past. Someone annoys you with some small wrongdoing against you and you forgive them instead of seeking to recover what they now owe to you, and you forgive them in your emotions, and hold no urge nor feeling to get pain from them.

This is a sound way to do business in a capitalist economy. This is like a car dealer who pays off your loan as the cost of making the sale happen. Between two merchants who frequently do business with each other, forgiving small debts is a matter of convenience and practical necessity. Such is the definition of being emotionally mature.

In contrast, an emotional toddler is someone whose recovery of tiny debts owed to them is swift and extreme. Such people will throw a temper tantrum to make you feel bad if they feel bad and blame you in any small extent, either consciously or unconsciously. If they resent you, such as by categorizing you as the type of person from whom they blame their miserable lives, or if they feel that the type of person you are, or you specifically, have treated them unfairly, they will seek to recover what they feel owed in the most juvenile way possible.

Honor is defined as the quality of repaying and taking debts owed by you or to you according to your own internal moral ledger without needing any external pressure to be forced to do so. Honor and emotional maturity do not contradict, because an honorable man strives to repay outgoing debt (debts owed to others) whereas a mature man strives to forgive incoming debts (debts owed to him). Because you own debts owed to you, you may do as you please with them, and forgive them, and this is not theft. This is true if you owe a debt to yourself. In contrast you cannot force someone else to forgive a debt because that would be theft.

Debts can have orders of magnitude, also known as scale. A higher order debt can offset a lower order debt, for example, I owe you $50 and you owe me $5, we can cancel $5 by one debt paying off the other and now I owe you $45.

A kid may recover a lower order debt by being mean to them if the parent did something wrong, but the kid's higher order debt to the parent (being given life and love, etc.) outweighs it. The kid will not know it offset but the parent will, so the parent may think the kid wronged them and be mean to the kid to recover that lower order debt, which the kid may see as a new debt owed to them that the parent wronged them again. In this way, two people must calibrate their ledgers to each other or the result can be chaos if each feels owed debts which the other does not recognize or is unaware of.

Just as the absence of bankruptcy leads to slavery, the absence of moral bankruptcy leads to emotional slavery, whereby one person takes control of another person on account of real or perceived emotional debts so high they cannot be repaid. Such is evil and the antithesis of freedom, although one's honor may naturally seek to repay debts to the fullest extent one can.

An emotional thief is someone who seizes emotional capital without paying for it, either by intentionally failing to repay emotional debts earned in the normal course of business of social relationships, or by causing pain with no remorse, not giving what is owed on their side of the ledger. Such people are evil and have dishonor.

In addition to a ledger of what is owed to a person, we humans seem to keep a mental ledger of good and bad done to us today, what life owes us. If one person after the next after the next is mean to us, we reach and break our limit, and then throw a temper tantrum to be mean to random passersby to try to recover some of what life owes us. If life is very kind to us we feel blessed and elated to have a moral surplus, and may then be in a kind and generous mood towards strangers, repaying life for what it gave to us.

Interestingly, like men, nations and races maintain an emotional ledger, and may seek repayment of debts for wrongs or rights done 700 years ago or even older. This explains much about why war or peace exists.

Parenting is also informed. The unconditional love of a (good) parent for a child will forgive any sin in return for the joy of having a child. Also, maybe we try to protect children, not from a parental instinct, but because we feel they are too young to have done anything to deserve bad things happening to them. An emotional debt arises between two people from their actions and exists irrespective of whether one has "passed moral judgment" upon the other. Debts exist objectively, not subjectively, much as if someone loans you $20, your debt to them exists objectively because the $20 is a real physical object in your pocket. But it must be conceded that emotions and psychology are mental attributes, although what a person does is something which physically exists in objective reality, if only as what their voice says or what their body enacts (although in other books I have argued the mind and brain are identical, I don't intend to rely upon that premise in this book). What is owed and what one believes is owed may be identical, because only honor motivates most of the emotional economy, so only what people believe is owed will ever be paid, and a debt is not fully real unless we expect to collect on it somehow.

What is owed is based on the context of what you know. For example, if you know X, and because of X Jane owes you a debt, so Jane goes out of her way to be nice to you, and then you learn that X was never really true, then you now owe Jane a debt equal to what she paid you, or potentially greater if the ignorance was your own fault.

This has applications to Objectivism and Libertarianism. Objectivism is a cruel, strict master, which calls upon a person to be rational 24 hours a day, 7 days a week, with any intentional act of unreason deemed as black, putrid evil. Objectivism as ethics is to some extent a form of Perfectionism, and you are expected to be a smart person and achieve the very best that your ability could have made possible. That is a tough standard to maintain. Moral bankruptcy, if viewed as rational, can play an important role in an Objectivist's moral life.

In libertarian political philosophy, moral bankruptcy forms a basis for "real" bankruptcy, legal bankruptcy, absent which some might view it as a debtor immorally stealing what is owed to, and owned by, a creditor. Some libertarians view bankruptcy as theft. But it is a natural part of human existence. It also justifies the libertarian darling called jury nullification: if a jury knows there is guilt under the facts and the law, but feels the accused should rightfully be forgiven, then they may vote to acquit. The theory of emotional capitalism and moral bankruptcy can play an important role in the emotional health of Objectivists and libertarians, and everyone else, too.

GREED AND LUST:
SINS, OR VIRTUES?

Let us begin with definitions and axioms, and then see where logical deduction leads.

Assume that a human being is an animal which speaks and thinks. The human as animal is body. The human as thinking entity is mind. The human as one who speaks is soul (personality, identity).

Let us assume that one human can be sexually attracted to another human because of one or more of three traits: body, mind and soul.

Define love of the body as animal love.

Define love of the soul as Platonic love.

Define love of the mind as Randian love.

We can immediately deduce that each of these three types of love possess fatal flaws. Animal love lowers oneself to a capacity one shares in common with animals and is not distinctly human. As such it lacks our highest capacity as humans. It is our basest and most disgusting nature. While the pleasure of the body is actualized, the mind and soul, our distinctly human nature and higher capacity, are ignored.

But Platonic love denies the existence of lust and the physical world. As such, it may engender mutual esteem, but not true love, since it creates regard but not sexual desire. Lust without love should not exist, but love without lust cannot exist. Platonic love shares all the faults of Plato: seek to deny the physical world, and you will repress and deny reality, and then reality itself will undermine you and condemn you to frustration.

Then there is Randian love. Ayn Rand lived this is her relationship with Nathanial Branden: she believed that one person's love of another person's mind, with no regard for liking the other person's personality and with no lust for them physically, that mere shared intellectual values and having in common a philosophy, could form the basis for love. Randian love leads to the repression of both body and soul: you love the mind, but do not like the personality and are not attracted to the body. Then your repressed desires will eventually explode, as when the Rand-Branden affair ended with fireworks.

A form of love exists which shares none of the above flaws, which we may term

Aristotelian love. Aristotelian love calls upon each person to find a ratio of body to mind to soul which is the correct expression of what they want in a lover, and to then seek that. This can be expressed as a percentage. For example, a person may care 20% about body, 10% about mind, and 70% about soul. Or a person may care 60% about body, 15% about mind, and 25% about soul.

The aspect from Aristotle is the Golden Mean: you do not want to choose too much or too little, you want just the right amount, and your correct ratio is unique to you as an individual. Too much body and you are a mere animal. Too much soul and you are a mere ghost. Too much mind and you become a mere brain without genitals.

There may be feelings of guilt if one hews to an extreme and away from the Golden Mean, as, if, for example, one cares 96% about body, 2% about mind, and 2% soul. But this is a personal choice and it would be difficult to prove that you were objectively incorrect (or to prove that you are correct). What you desire is an expression of who you are, and the only wise guidelines are "know thyself" and "to thine own self be true."

Also, for love, what each person wants must match with what the other person has. If you care about soul and someone has a great personality and sense of humor and is friendly and loving, they might be perfect for you, but if what they love is mind and, let us say, you lack a college education and are coarse and unrefined, they will not want you. What someone is and what they want have no correlation: a person may have a great body yet desire a boyfriend with a great soul, or they may have a great body and crave only another great body for pleasure, or they may have a great body and care 33% about each if the three attributes.

In true love, if and when such a thing exists, you, what qualities you possess, will satisfy all or most of what your partner seeks and vice versa. And, in reality, there is an added even deeper level of complexity, because people often feel guilty about their desires or are confused by them and so will be dishonest and lie about what they really want, making it even harder to win a good match and find real love, since you will know if you love them but might find it hard to tell if you are what they truly desire. Something similar may be said of greed. Greed is the love of money, but it may be subcategorized into three types for analysis.

Getting money is the love of acquiring money, and is really the joy of spending money, of consuming value. We may call this selfish greed.

Making money is the joy one takes in the act of creating value, the pride that a maker has in the act of making something good, or the pride one takes in a job well done. We may call this proud greed.

Then, albeit more rarely, there is what may be termed economist's greed, which is the desire to plug into the economy and do one's job and perform one's role for the good of the economy, on account of the various economic theories which prove that it is a net benefit to society when the individual makes money. Economist's greed is honorable greed, the desire to do the work to pay all the other people in the economy who make the stuff you use, by making stuff for them to buy.

Selfish greed taken to an extreme will inspire one to theft or fraud or unethical behavior to maximize the amount of money one has. The rich people who engage exclusively in selfish greed may rightly be termed the evil rich, and there is no shortage of scams or government-enabled graft and corruption by the evil rich.

But proud greed to too great an extreme ignores the whole point of money, which is the joy of spending it and experiencing the pleasure it buys. Someone with too much proud greed might be a workaholic and work excessively, spending too much time making things instead of spending time with his family or enjoying a hobby, for example.

Economist's greed taken to an extreme can devolve into a belief, even among capitalists, that society is more important than the individual. A lot of actual economics professors are capitalists who believe this, but it undermines the moral foundation of capitalism, which is individualism. People may want to do their duty to society by working their job, but ignore their own legitimate needs for joy and pleasure. As with lust, in greed one should discover a ratio between selfish greed, proud greed, and economist's greed, by which one avoids being evil while still selfishly enjoying life. For example, one may be motivated 75% by selfish greed, 20% by proud greed, and 5% by economic greed. Or, if one really loves one's job, and does not enjoy shopping much, one may be motivated 50% by proud greed, 30% by selfish greed, and 20% by economic greed.

One final point on the topic of lust: if lust is not a sin, then being gay/lesbian/LGBT is not a sin, and every legitimate non-criminal sexual desire/fetish is not a sin, for the same reason. However things like pedophilia and bestiality are evil, because they defy human nature and the role and purpose of sexuality, which is sex and love with consenting adults. Children and animals lack human sexual capacity physically, so human nature could not have intended them subjects of sex.

This concludes my account of lust and greed as analyzed by analytical logic with special reference to Aristotle's ethical theory of the Golden Mean.

ENVY: KEEPING SCORE

Men can compare themselves to others and fall short in many ways. One can measure and compare:

Health,

Beauty,

Wealth,

Charisma,

Intelligence,

Luck,

Strength.

One can also compare accomplishments:

Family,

Friends,

Lovers,

Children,

Career,

Skills,

Education,

Amount of joy consumed,

Amount of money made,

Amount of joy your actions enabled other people to have the freedom to consume (social libertarian political activism), and

Amount of money your actions helped other people be free to make (economic libertarian political activism).

Because technically speaking a human should be good in every area, but in reality no one has the resources to pay the cost to achieve at a high level in literally every area, you will probably always envy at least one or more other people, if only because they chose to spend their time on an area where you spent far fewer resources and so in that area you achieved far less than they.

One might think then that wisdom lies in achieving the goals best suited to your personality and desires, for example, is your highest value becoming a doctor, or finding true love, or going on lots of vacations — because you have finite discreet limited "life resources" to spend (time and money being the big two) so you can't have everything. But in practice this wisdom can be difficult — you want to be a doctor with a love life who takes long vacations, and if you choose one you will envy everyone who chose the other two, intimately knowing the flaws of your choice but seeing only the virtues of theirs. A Buddhist might tell you to renounce the goal of achievement. A conservative, or a strict parent, might say you had better fucking achieve or else. Neither path will make the pain of failing to achieve hurt any less.

Wisdom dictates a different path: try your best to achieve but forgive yourself if you fail. Prioritize your goals and spend resources accordingly, mindful that, as Rand said, subjugating a lesser value to a greater one is not a sacrifice, but vice versa is (and see her essay on this topic, in The Virtue of Selfishness).

To paraphrase Nietzsche: esteeming the greatness of the achievements of other men enables us to hold the achievement of our own dreams a safe distance away from ourselves. He also might have said, or should have said: we are all of us human, all too human, and therefore must either move above our humanity or else forgive ourselves for being human. It is also instructive to study self-esteem, in light of Rand's The Fountainhead. Take sex, for example, with a focus on what is known as "body image problems." There are those who feel that if you are hot then you deserve to have sex and are worthy (really, that you deserve to be loved) and, if you are not hot, you don't. But being hot does not correlate with deserving to have sex, only, in a practical sense, for some people it has some small impact on the game of chance of getting lucky, and no more. Self-esteem is what correlates with deserving to have sex.

We can distinguish two things: a source of self-esteem, which can be attacked but can never truly be destroyed, and the pretense of self-esteem, which can be taken away. These two things can exist for any given purpose, for example, hotness is a pretense of self-esteem for the purpose of having sex, and can be taken away (if a man says "you look fat" to a woman or to a gay man, for example). But if, for example, the source of your self-esteem for dating is confidence, that cannot be destroyed, and a woman's rejecting you may test it but will not crumble it.

A body image problem arises if your pretense at self-esteem really is based on looks and you are plausibly critical of your own hotness. As Rand artistically rendered in The Fountainhead, pull out the foundation of self-esteem and the soul collapses: this is what Toohey does to Peter Keating, and what Dominique tries and fails to do to Roark.

One can have a source or pretense of self-esteem for any purpose: career, job skills, a hobby, a friendship, your religion, your favorite author or favorite music, any facet of your identity, and it can always be attacked or challenged by other people or events or even by new facts, but self-forgiveness is a very useful tool for repairing it or fortifying it. For example, forgive and accept your body and then fret no more over it.

The basic premise of being fat-shamed is that you owe it to other people to be perfect for them so if you're not then you don't deserve to be loved. In reality there is no objective rational reason why you would owe perfection to others or need it to achieve the relatively mundane social status of love and acceptance. You deserve to be loved, you deserve to have the boyfriend or girlfriend or wife or husband of your dreams, and you deserve to have sex at will. Every good human being does.

The only obstacle is that men can use low self-esteem to exploit and control women, which is also an LGBT problem as one gay man can do this to another, much as Toohey manipulates Keating because Keating's pretense of self-esteem as an architect arises from social approval (Toohey's art criticism as the voice of society), and so there are systemic structural elements in our social existence which enable attacks against our self-esteem at any time. Adults and "normal" people are less vulnerable — unless it is their sense of normalcy itself which gets attacked. While one is forgiving oneself for being less than perfect in a romantic context, it is also wise to forgive one's boyfriend or girlfriend or wife or husband for being less than perfect, although it is a personal decision how much is too much to forgive and when to walk away. Generally, flaws and faults should be forgiven, and such forgiveness and emotional maturity is necessary to have a healthy relationship, but pure evil should not be forgiven.

If confidence is a source of self-esteem whereas body image is not, and is a mere pretense, it may be asked how one achieves confidence. Roark in The Fountainhead is illustrative. He is a good architect, and he knows that he is a good architect. This is true even while at times in the novel everyone else is saying he is a bad architect.

You are a good person, and therefore you deserve to be loved, and your knowledge should always match the truth about objective reality, so you should know that you are a good person, and then you should know that you deserve to be loved, because these facts are true. You really are a good person, and you really do deserve to be loved. This in a sense is pride, and, in that sense, pride is a virtue, not a sin, and pride is the antidote to low self-esteem.

FORGIVENESS OF EVIL

We must ask: what if you commit a truly evil act? Is your own forgiveness enough? Or do you need God's? Or your victim's?

We must begin by asking: why did you do it? Did bad luck, circumstance, or a villain, drive you and pressure you to do it? Was it a necessary evil brought about by desperate times or an emergency? Where there is no freely chosen decision to act, there is no volitional free will so there can be no blameworthy nor culpable status.

But what if you commit the most evil sin? What if you fundamentally betray a friend, a family member, or, as I believe the most evil sin to be, what if you betray yourself and violate your integrity as an ethical human being?

What if you sell your soul, metaphorically, trading your moral righteousness and integrity to evil in return for what you want: money, power, sex, an easy way to gain success without doing hard work, or a sense of self esteem arising from how society sees you when you conform and betray who you really are by pretending to be someone else, or other vices like these? What if you looked the other way while your friend or your boss committed a crime? What if you fall into a life of crime yourself? What if you betray a friend and have an affair with his wife and lie to him repeatedly about it? Even worse crimes than these can also exist, especially in times of war or with political corruption. Even good men can be tempted to evil.

The great appeal of The Fountainhead (which nobody realizes) is that Ayn Rand addresses this. Peter Keating and Wynand both sin against Roark, but Wynand is forgiven. In the novel, climaxing at the end, Peter Keating sells his soul to Toohey for power and the pretense of self-esteem. Peter Keating gets his sense of self-esteem from how society views him, making him into the slave of social critic Ellsworth Toohey, who represents (and controls) the voice of society. Here I explore Keating's actual black sin of evil, betraying his friend and the voice of any trace of integrity left in his life, Roark, to Toohey, not even for any tangible profit but because Toohey has become his master and he has no self-respect left with which to resist the command of society for obedience.

Rand was cognizant of this betrayal as sin, and as Keating destroying his own soul, a long, drawn-out process which begins with his letting his mother pressure him to become an architect when he really wants to be an artist, grows when he abandoned the woman he loves to marry his boss's daughter to gain social status at work and in the eyes of the architecture professional, and culminates in handing evidence that

Roark bombed Cortland Homes to Toohey, which Toohey wants to use to send Roark to jail, to break his spirit by force because no amount of social pressure or stigma has succeeded in getting Roark to contradict himself and renounce or sacrifice his soul to gain Toohey's (society's) favor. There is a point in the famous Toohey speech at the end of The Fountainhead where Toohey explicitly says that Keating sold his soul to him.

Rand even acknowledged this tongue in cheek where Toohey says to Peter Keating "ever read Faust?" (a German play where the main character Faust makes a deal with the devil Mephistopheles) when Keating hands him the contract that Keating and Roark signed for Roark to build Cortland Homes while Keating takes all the credit and praise for it, which Toohey needs as evidence in the courtroom trial against Roark, whereby Keating sells Roark to Toohey.

The scene much earlier in The Fountainhead where Toohey comments upon the Biblical verse "what should it profit a man, if he gaineth the world, but loseth his own soul?" (Mark 8:36), with Toohey replying "then to be truly rich one should collect souls?" is Rand's sense of humor about this issue of Keating selling his soul to the devil. In Ayn Rand's lectures on writing fiction she once said "nothing in my novels is accidental," so it is open season for us to read these religious interpretations into little details in The Fountainhead.

Wynand, too, betrays his own inner integrity, succumbs to pressure, and sells Roark to the masses to save his newspaper, at the end of the novel, again, for money, power, and the pretense of self-esteem that having built a newspaper empire makes his life meaningful. Toohey finds what Wynand built his self-esteem upon, the newspaper, takes control of it, and thereby breaks Wynand, much as he breaks Keating through his self-esteem depending on what other people think of his career and social status as an architect. This act, to betray your integrity in return for trivial sham rewards, is what I regard as the blackest sin.

But Roark forgives Wynand. Wynand in the end cannot forgive himself but as one final gesture lets Roark build the Wynand Building. He says to Roark, in the most poignant scene at the very end of the novel, "build it as a monument to that spirit which is yours . . . and could have been mine," which sums up the quest for integrity and speaks to his overwhelming sense of guilt for having betrayed Roark and for having betrayed and defiled the good in him (his friendship with Roark) in service to evil (his newspaper, the stupid masses who read it, and Toohey who controls them). But Roark forgives him and builds the building.

I think there are two lessons. If you commit the blackest sin, betraying your integrity, selling your soul to the devil, there is no external elements to this crime, it is merely your choice, so if you repent, and if you are a good person, you can forgive yourself. You control what is in you. Your moral status, whether you are good or evil, is within your control. Second, Keating simply is evil, and Wynand just is good, it is what they are, you are what you are and your choices and actions can't ever truly change your soul. If you are a good person, that will be with you always, and any crime to which you are driven, hands stained red with blood by ill fate, cannot change what you are. If there is still goodness in your soul, if you still see the light, if you know the difference between right and wrong, this is a sufficient basis to forgive yourself, spell out your sentence of penance for you to punish yourself, repent, pick yourself up and then move on. Were you truly evil you would know only the darkness, so if you can still see light, this is proof that you have a rational basis to deserve to forgive yourself.

This is if the person you betrayed is yourself. If instead you stabbed someone else in the back, if someone died for you to live, then, in moral capitalism, you owe it to the world to save someone, or to save as many people as whose lives you ruined. This explains why religions based on guilt are so often missionary religions. Even in this case, one can earn the repayment of debts owed. And wrapped around this entire analysis stands moral bankruptcy if you have the balls to absolve punishment for a sin as black as night. Even if you hurt others, the moral injury is a wound to your own soul, which you own, and thereby you own the debt and have the legal right to forgive it.

At no point in this exposition has it become apparent that you have any need for God or religion. Yours can be a Do It Yourself forgiveness of sins. You do not need God's forgiveness because your own forgiveness is what matters, and is the moral reflection of your soul, or your moral self-worth.

What if your crime has an external victim whom your actions have wronged? When you hurt someone, you sin against three beings: your own soul as your capacity to be good and the corresponding debt you owe to yourself to be the best you that you can be, your victim equal to the emotional capital (money and/or joy) which hurting them has robbed them of, and also you sin against society, the brotherhood of all men, our great human undertaking to build a world where we help each other to be as happy as possible.

The law exacts the payment of moral debts owed to society (by fines or jail, the quintessential Nietzsche paradigm of causing pain to repay a debt from pain wrongfully caused), and this essay does not examine the laws as such, so I will not explore that area. You repay the debt to yourself and the debt to your victim with guilt, unless you forgive yourself, and unless you beg for and are granted forgiveness by your victim, in which you will no longer regard yourself as owing him your guilt. In a worst case scenario, if you are being crushed by guilt and depression, you can file for double moral bankruptcy: forgive yourself for your sin against your own soul, and forgive yourself for failure to obtain your victim's formal declaration of his forgiving you.

Ultimately if you repent with sincerity then there must still be good in you, which is a sufficient basis to "save your soul," pick up the pieces and try to put your life back together and be a good person from now on, and forgive yourself for having done evil. People's emotions tend to believe what other people say they owe, children especially so because they don't know any better and lack a frame of reference from

THE MEANING OF LIFE

which to doubt. Social capitalism relies upon external validation, and children and teens do so a lot, although adults do also, to a degree inverse to their emotional maturity.

Social capitalism is emotional capitalism as it relates to, and impacts, social interaction with your peers. Your moral ledger (your mental sense of debts and credits owed) guides how you behave towards others. How others treat you, and what they say to you, is external validation or contradiction, feedback which your emotions use to calibrate the accuracy of your ledger.

For someone who was abused or bullied, as a child or teen or as an adult, the bully is essentially telling you that you don't deserve to be happy, that you don't deserve to live, and your emotions will read that as external feedback. Your emotions can be tricked into thinking you have sinned and exact payment as guilt or self-inflicted punishment. Here the act of self-forgiveness will clear the emotional fraud off the ledger. You are not, and are never, to blame for being bullied or abused, because bullying and abuse are evil by nature and so will always reflect an unjust account of debts or credits owed.

Taken to an extreme, honor combined with guilt may lead to an act of suicide, because the person seeks to repay whatever debt they feel they owe by literally giving their life to their moral creditor, but this is irrationality, and filing for moral bankruptcy is always what such a person should do instead. At the point of death, one can no longer be good nor do good, so suicide arising from a moral basis of extreme guilt is a contradiction: one tries to do the right thing by destroying one's own moral capacity. Moreover no good creditor would ask that as repayment, so you should not ask that of yourself, and if others do then they are evil and their evilness toward you must offset whatever you think you owe them, and they can hold no moral claim upon you. Guilt can be crippling but here the wisdom of Rand and Nietzsche is that you must have the stoic discipline for your reason to control your emotions and reach into your soul and turn off the feelings that are not objectively warranted by what you really owe to yourself or to others in the long-term.

When someone dies, we pray that they will forgive us for what we did to them in life, and we also forgive them for whatever they owed us, because the relationship is over so it is time to close the ledger and reconcile all debts and credits. Usually we feel that we treated them unfairly and were too miserly and stingy and immature, which we know only when it is too late to correct, because we were greedy and were not forced to undertake an audit until now. If, after we reconcile the ledger, we find that we owe the dead a debt which we will now never be able to repay, then we hold and cherish our memory of them for the rest of our lives, to try to repay our debt. We feel sadness to pay to the dead what we owe them, by giving them our pain (our grief), and also as a signal to our friends and loved ones to request support and comfort in any amount that our friends owe to us or are willing to lend us.

HUMAN MOTIVATIONS

Some men give to charity to seek penance for the sin of greed, to atone for being rich. That is charity from shame. Others give to charity out of an overflowing abundance of joy, that they are so happy and prosperous that they want everyone else to share their joy too. While the result is identical from the point of view of the recipient, shame is evil, and joy is good.

Our reaction to perfection is similar. Some of us, if we see someone with a perfect body or a perfect personality, immediately feel that they deserve to be loved, which reminds us that we ourselves are less than perfect, and then we feel we don't deserve love, and are sad. In times like these we must instantly forgive ourselves for being less than perfect and move on.

Other types of people, seeing someone who seems perfect, will simply feel glad for them, and share in their happiness, because they have self-esteem and confidence, and the perfection of others does not challenge and call into question their own worth. That is the type of person who can give to charity because they are so happy and proud that their joy overflows and spills over to give to others.

The perfection of others as a challenge to our own sense of self-worth relates to a similar syndrome in all social interaction: the fear of rejection. If we "bare our soul" to someone else, if we assert not merely a minor detail about ourselves but something essential to our identity, of if we seek to share something personal and deep and meaningful with someone, we expose ourselves to rejection and make ourselves vulnerable. If you are to do so, you must be prepared to instantly forgive yourself for not having been good enough for the other person in the event that they criticize or attack your self-esteem.

Two types of people can face opportunities for rejection with other people without fear: those who are so confident that they don't expect to be rejected, and those who know that if they were rejected they would forgive themselves immediately and completely for it, and know how to do so.

Obviously it goes without saying that you owe it to yourself to act for the sake of the best within you and to thereby actualize your highest potential for joy and happiness. To actualize your highest potential is to act for the sake of the best within you. In Objectivism (from a certain point of view) your soul, your highest potential, and the best within you, are the same thing. To be good, and to be happy, you must live life to the fullest with no regrets — or with regrets that you can find it within yourself to forgive yourself for. Failure to do so is the ultimate sin, for which you will need your own forgiveness, if at the end of the day you want to be able to look in the mirror.

POLITICAL MOTIVATIONS

The inflicting of pain in order to obtain payment for an owed debt may be referred to as retribution, justice, or revenge. Such is the motive of many voters and political activists. For example, someone sees a forest get destroyed, then becomes an environmental activist to get revenge against polluters on behalf of the trees. Or someone is denied an employee benefit by her boss and then votes for a pro-labor leftist politician to get revenge against big business. Or a man sees a picture of an aborted fetus and becomes a pro-life activist to get revenge equal to the loss suffered by the fetus which he feels is now a debt owed by the pro-choice movement that created the freedom for it to happen.

But in politics, as in social reality, there can be an equivalent of emotional maturity, which in this context we might name policy maturity. A higher order debt cancels out a lower order debt by offsetting the amount owed. Just having a job at all may be so important to long-term survival that the employee owes more to the employer for creating the job than the amount lost on a denial of requested benefits. Big business, by making the money that enables a society to be prosperous, might pay for conservation efforts which otherwise the human race could not afford — after all, dirty energy is cheap and clean energy is expensive, so if we couldn't afford to pay for it we would burn more coal and oil. The debt a fetus owes to its mother for existing probably exceeds any debt the mother would owe to the fetus as an obligation to be pregnant with it and give birth to it, or, at the very least, the debt of fetus to mother equals what mother owes fetus so the two debts would offset and leave a net zero.

Generally, emotional irrational thinking among voters is the equivalent of being an emotional toddler in social reality while logical rational thinking and seeing the big picture enables policy maturity. One final point is that misattribution and misdirection may be present as well: you feel that one individual injured you and owes you an unpaid debt so you seek retribution by voting for a politician who will punish the group or category of people to whom your debtor belongs — a race, by voting for a racist politician, for example. This is obviously irrational and insane, because other people are not morally responsible for what one person has done so you should not punish a race for a debt owed by an individual. But in politics many voters behave irrationally and lack maturity.

Men give their votes to social justice crusade politicians to pay wronged groups of people for what you feel you as a member of society owe to them, so that the government will pay off your moral debt for you. You may also vote for a particular politician if you feel that he personally helped you, either individually or by aiding a group or class you belong to, because you owe a moral debt to them. And then there are voters who feel blessed to live in a good society and feel it is a repayment of what one owes for being given this blessing to vote for a politician who will fight for goodness and virtue and truth and justice. Libertarian policy is generally superior to socialism, but such a basis for votes in emotional capitalism are usually based on how you feel about the politician, not how you feel emotionally about his policy. There are many ways in which forgiveness and sin play out in politics. People see a group or class of citizens whom they feel have been wronged, and then vote for a government to right that wrong, to give those people what they are owed, which is called fairness and justice and is really the repayment of debts owed so that both sides of the ledger even out. But the libertarian point of view is that, if you feel a wrong has been done, it is your job, not the government's job, to help fix it, spending your own money, not other people's money, because you have the right to spend money you own but lack the right to take money from others even for a good cause.

But what if by yourself you don't have enough money to fix it, so collectively pooling money is necessary for justice? Then persuade large numbers of others to freely and voluntarily donate to your charity, don't force them to give money against their will by government tax and spend. The money you would owe to the taxpayers you robbed would equal any justice of debt repaid to an oppressed class.

It is not the job of government to forgive us for being human and for making mistakes, by removing our freedom to make mistakes and replacing it with a dictator's control. Instead, forgive yourself by doing the work necessary to get what you want, and then you will obtain it, and the only thing that could stop you then is bad luck, for which you should feel no blame. I am not a Christian but believe strongly in this: "Ask and ye shall be given, Seek and ye shall find, Knock and the door shall open." (Matthew 7:7). If you want money, go get it. If you want a job, find one. If you don't choose to get what you want, that is a sin, but government can't fix that, that is something only you can do. If you hit rock bottom, are poor or homeless, file for moral bankruptcy, stop feeling sorry for yourself and start over.

There are also those who feel they are not worthy to be happy and lack self-esteem and feel they don't deserve to live, so embrace any dictatorship that will punish them to give them what they feel they are morally owed: suffering, a total lack of responsibility for making the decisions which control your own fate, and, eventually, death. These people need to forgive themselves and seek a sense of self-worth, but, absent that, we the living must not allow ourselves to be dragged into Hell by those who are half dead already.

When the government has total control, regardless of whether politicians are good or evil, the citizens have no free will, hence cannot make mistakes, hence can do nothing for which they need to be forgiven. But it is also true that, lacking free will, they can commit no blessings nor virtues and do nothing that is right and good, having no ability to make any decision or ethical choice of right or wrong at all. Such a scenario is manifestly repugnant to the moral lives of human beings.

With respect to politics, it is also wise to remember this Bible verse: "All those who sin are a slave of sin." (John 8:34). If you sacrifice your moral integrity, you will very quickly find yourself under the control of evil men, and, ultimately, of evil politicians or dictators. The evil in you will seek out the evil in them, and, having turned to the darkness, you will not have the light within you to shine at them to drive them away. If someone else controls your self-esteem then they can destroy you, so your soul becomes their slave. Although I am a Libertarian, I want to point out that any type of politician may seek to exploit you: the socialists, liberals, conservatives, and, if there were any, libertarians. Remember with warning what Toohey says: "It's the soul, Peter, the soul, not whips or swords or fire or guns. ... The soul, Peter, is that which can't be ruled. It must be broken. ... You won't need a whip — he'll bring it to you and ask to be whipped."

MORAL ECONOMICS

Let me point out that, in Atlas Shrugged, in the scene where James Taggart accuses Cherryl of having a shopkeeper's morality and she accuses him of seeking the unearned in spirit, Rand gets at her closest to articulating an idea that pervades Atlas Shrugged, the idea that moral value and economic value is equivalent, that morality and finance are comparable. Esteem is to be paid for by being a good person, success is to be paid for by doing the right thing ethically. Moral value as a human is to be earned by doing the hard work of living an ethical life. And you earn your social and romantic relationships by doing the work to make the relationship work and to give the other person what they enjoy in return for you getting what makes you happy.

Emotions are like money, in this way: money is a loan, in that the owner of a $1 bill is owed $1 worth of value; the dollar bill is a promissory note that the economy is to give back $1 worth of value if the owner hands over the dollar bill to the economy. An emotion is a record of money on your moral ledger; for example, if you love someone, then you owe them your devotion because they have already paid you for it by being the person you are in love with or by loving you. Your emotions tell you what you owe and are owed, just as a $10 bill tells the economy that it owes you $10 worth of value, $10 worth of goods and services to consume, because you lent the economy an hour of labor at your job that paid you a salary of $10/hour.

Values — moral values — can be earned, stolen, bought, sold, traded, and, yes, loaned or borrowed or repaid. The thesis of this paper is to take this concept seriously, and then understand how bankruptcy works in a moral economic system. Much as the finance system and capitalism in the USA could not function absent bankruptcy law to govern debtors and creditors in the event of insolvency, so too moral capitalism cannot exist absent a formalized system of forgiveness. It is then a logical analysis of human nature to say that our emotions evolved as our ledger in moral capitalism, telling our conscious minds to take what we are owed and give back where we owe debts.

Feelings and emotions, in this way, are vital to ethics, and it is also worth noting that emotions are not inherently irrational and illogical as such, and play an important role in a rational life. However your subconscious mind may have a different belief about your debts than your conscious mind, which is where reason and emotions might conflict, and you must reconcile how you feel with what you believe. Do not assume that your reason is correct and your emotions incorrect, nor vice versa, but undertake a substantial detailed analysis to discover the truth.

It might be asked why the human brain tends to subconsciously dish out pain (or pleasure, as discussed in the next chapter) to repay moral debts and credits. My position is that this is simply a feature of human evolution, although one might see it as a moral fact, that your brain tries to give you what you deserve. Humans seem to have evolved from primates who survived as pack or tribe animals. They formed tribes, and families within those tribes, which would have required a precise calibration of how to assign help to each other, as for sharing food, or hunting, etc., and who owed what to whom. Our biological ancestors were "social animals," to take a phrase from Aristotle which is probably better translated as "social by nature." As such, not only our reason and mind, but also our social reactions, are highly evolved. I see moral economics as an aspect of the human brain arising from our evolution as social animals.

Here I will share a happy thought. So you sinned. You let yourself down. You failed. Your wife and kids are mad at you. You're not the greatest person at your job. You wanted to do something very much but lacked the courage or the will to do it. You reasoned that you should pursue a path but let irrational fears talk you out of it. Or something similar. You sinned against your own soul by failing to act for the sake of the best within you. Or you sinned against someone else. You didn't buy the best gift for your girlfriend because you didn't want to spend the money. You were not supportive of a friend in a time of need because it was too difficult and stressful. You were a doctor and made the wrong decision and a patient died, or you were a soldier in a war and one of the other soldiers died in combat to rescue you and you survived but they died.

You feel guilt, to make yourself suffer in order to repay the debt that you cannot otherwise repay: a debt you owe to yourself, or to someone else. For the doctor who owes life to the dead or the soldier with survivor's guilt, in their emotional capitalism ledger they may feel the need to hurt themselves with guilt in an amount equal to the value of life itself, because they feel they owe a life to the person who died.

But that's humanity. That's being human. You sinned. So what else is new? We all fail. Everyone does. Forgive yourself. Use moral bankruptcy. You are a good, special, wonderful person. You still deserve to be happy. Repeat that: you deserve to be happy.

You're a good person and you deserve to be happy. And you deserve to love, and you deserve to be loved. Never forget that. They say "forgive and forget." Yes, forgive. But never forget that you deserve to be happy.

CONCLUSION

This essay has succeeded in explaining a theory of emotions, motivations, and ethics, which explained everything that it set out to explain. Guilt and shame and anger have been explained by reference to the infliction of emotional pain to repay, or retake, pain as payment for moral debts that are owed. Honor was explained as the willingness to repay the moral debts that you owe to others without being forced to do so, while emotional maturity was explained as a tendency towards forgiveness of small debts on a daily basis. Moral bankruptcy was presented as the paradigm for self-forgiveness, using finance and economics as a metaphor for moral economics.

However, happiness, love, sadness and fear have not yet been discussed. Just as the human brain inflicts pain upon someone in order to be repaid for a moral debt that they owe, so, too, the human brain evolved to feel pleasure as payment for moral credits that are owed to it. So your brain rewards you for being a good person, to self or others, with happiness, literally, with emotional pleasure, because you earned it. Happiness is the pleasure that you give to yourself when you owe yourself a moral credit, while love is the pleasure that you give to others when you owe them a moral credit for them having been a good person or having been good to you (precisely, for them having been or done something worthy of your love). If this is true, then living an ethical, moral life is the key to living a happy life.

In this way, happiness, which is pleasure given to yourself for a moral credit, is the opposite of guilt, which is pain inflicted upon yourself for a moral debt, and love, which is pleasure given to others for a credit, is the opposite of anger, which is pain inflicted upon others because of an unpaid debt. Happiness and love can be termed the positive emotions, while guilt, shame and anger are the negative emotions.

I am tempted to define another emotion, pride, and say that pride is the opposite of shame, in the sense that pride is the pleasure you feel from people seeing what a good person you are, that you reward yourself with for having impressed others with your virtue, while shame is the pain you feel when others watch you fail. However, I am resisting this temptation, because the word "pride" has many meanings, some positive and some negative: pride can mean joy in being good, or one's own knowledge and conviction that one is a good person, or joy in other people seeing oneself as good, or pleasure as reward for having done a good job, but it can also mean hubris and arrogance, or an unjustified inflated ego.

It is even true that, from the Objectivist point of view, self-knowledge of one's own virtue is the key to self-esteem, whereas virtue in the eyes and opinions of other people is a mere pretense of self-esteem (usually), so it is very ambiguous whether pride is actually virtuous or unethical, and the definition of the word is too muddy to admit of clear and precise usage. Pride, as an emotion, would merely be a type of happiness, happiness arising for a specific reason, anyway.

With respect to the seven major emotions: happiness, sadness, love, fear, guilt, shame, and anger, this leaves only fear and sadness in need of an accounting. I briefly touched upon sadness before, when discussing grief and mourning, but I will elaborate more broadly here. Sadness seems to be a biological reaction to the experience of things going wrong in your life, such as when you start crying or feel tired and apathetic, and it seems to have evolved to trigger a person to act to remove the cause of the sadness, or, at least, to notify one's friends and family so that they will try to help you.

On this analysis, sadness is similar to guilt, except that guilt is a specific reflection of you having done moral wrong, whereas sadness is precisely a reaction to things in your life going wrong, regardless of moral blameworthiness. To the extent that your guilt makes you sad, this is the emotional expression of the moral fact that having done the morally wrong thing will cause things to go wrong in your life.

The author views fear as largely a biological mechanism that evolved to make an animal flee from and run away from a threat. The only extent to which fear now matters for humans from a psychological or ethical point of view, as opposed to a biological point of view, is when the threats are social or emotional or moral, rather than a danger to survival, in which case the brain feels fear or anxiety to motivate escape.

Fear can be perfectly moral and rational if you are in a situation where running away would really be the right thing to do, such as if you have to flee from a fight you know you would lose in order to save your life, but fear can become irrational or unethical if the situation is such that you feel a need, or a desire, to escape, but the right thing to do in this situation is to face your fear, which really means, to stand up and put up a fight against whatever is threatening you.

For example, being in a new social situation where you have no friends can be scary, and might trigger social anxiety, and then you must choose whether to stay and try to talk to people and make new friends, or whether to leave because you can't stand your anxiety. The fear is your desire to flee, but what you really fear is the shame you will feel if people reject you. As such, fear itself can pose a moral test, as to whether you face your fear, or flee from it in cowardice, and this is the most common scenario where fear will possess any moral significance, as seperate and distinct from a mere biological urge to run away from physical life-threatening danger. A similar case is the person who fears starting a new job or a new career, or an athlete who fears a clutch moment in a sports game, because they fear failure, and what they truly fear is the guilt they will suffer if they fail, or the shame they will feel if other people watch them fail.

This is why, if you are practiced at the art of filing for moral bankruptcy, and you can use self-forgiveness to eliminate guilt, shame, and anger, this will also eliminate your fear of failure or your fear of rejection, because what you really fear is the guilt or shame that you will inflict upon yourself if you fail, and, with moral bankruptcy, you will no longer have to live in fear of those other negative emotions, and so you can have the ability to act, and to go after your life goals, be they friends, family, career, money, love, or whatever, without fear of feeling the pain of guilt or shame if you fail, and without fear of anger. In this way, the theory of moral bankruptcy can help you to succeed and achieve in life.

TO BE LOVED, LOVE; TO BE LIKED, BE NICE TO PEOPLE; TO BE AN ADULT, FORGIVE PEOPLE: EMOTIONS AND SOCIAL INTERACTIONS, EXPLAINED

INTRO

This book explains a system for improving social skills and psychological health and emotional well-being. This system is based on a set of principles, based on math and logic and reason. Each principle is stated in a clear, simple way. Each principle is then given an analysis. Math and logic are used for this analysis, but only at a level that every person can understand.

The math and logic describes basic aspects of human existence that you will relate to. You will see what I mean when you read the book. This book is, basically, the math and logic of depth psychology, and how it can help you master your emotions, make people like you, and live a happy life.

The book assigns a separate chapter to each principle. As a result, this book has a lot of chapters, but each chapter is short and easy to read.

This is a self-help book. But it is not typical. It is unique. It uses math and logic to explain the depth psychology behind a variety of social dynamics in human behavior. If you understand how these dynamics work, you can use that understanding to your advantage, to further your goals.

This is not a book of words of affirmation. There are other books that say "You are a good person, you deserve to be loved, you deserve to be happy, you are special, you can achieve any goal you set your mind to." I have written other books that say exactly that. Such statements are all true. But this book doesn't say that. Instead, this book will tell you, in detail, **how** to get people to love you, **how** to be happy, and **how** to achieve your goals. With precise, specific details. With tactics, and strategies, that you can understand.

This book's unique purpose is not give you warm, fuzzy feelings in broad, general terms. Many other self-help books, my own included, already do that. Instead, this book tells you strategy and tactics for maximizing your social skills and social interactions, and explains the psychological and social dynamics of the groups of people you interact with, at work, at school, in business, in friendship, socially, or romantically. With tips for how to handle each social dynamic, described using math and logic.

A lot of this book is focused on common mistakes and pitfalls that people fall into often, and intelligent, clever ways to avoid those pitfalls, or ways to climb out after you have accidentally fallen in. Ways to escape from anger, addiction, depression, and fear are described. Tools for motivation are offered. But this isn't just about problems and bad stuff. It is also about being happy, friendly, cheerful, trusting, faithful, positive, and optimistic. How to be more polite. How to get people to like you. And ways to become more emotionally mature and insightful and perceptive about other people's feelings.

If, after reading this book, you go out into the world, and you feel like you now understand more of the different types of behaviors you are seeing people do, than what you knew before reading this book, then, for this book, it is mission: accomplished.

I hope you enjoy reading this book as much as I enjoyed writing it for you!

THE BASICS

The basic element of the analysis is a mathematical logical equation, of the form, for example:

Y +N to O as Emotion for O +N to Y as Speech.

So let's go through each item of syntax (symbols) one by one and explain the semantics (what it means).

Y: You. The Self. A representation of the person from whose point of view the analysis is conducted.

+: Positive, giving, giving something from the person on the left side of the equation (Y) to the person on the right side (O). + indicates giving a benefit, or something positive. The contrasting symbol would be –, which indicates a detriment, or something negative. + is plus. – is minus.

N: A number. Indicates a quantifiable, measured amount. It can represent any amount, until you plug an actual number or unit into the variable N.

To: indicates that the +N was given "to" O (from Y).

O: The Other. A representation of another person, who is not Y, but whom Y interacts with.

As: This indicates that the next term will qualify the form in which the +N manifested.

Emotion: Indicates that the +N was a positive emotion.

For: For the benefit of. The expression "A for B" means that A was done because of B, A exists because of B, B pays for A, A repays B, or A is for the benefit of B. The expression on the left was payment "for," or given in return "for," the expression on the right.

Speech: A qualifier of the +N that O gave to Y, that it was spoken verbal speech or written words, in some form of language.

So, here, Y gave +N as emotion to O in return for O giving +N to Y as speech. So this statement could mean, if we plug those variables in, if N is a small amount, it be translated to mean that O was polite towards Y, so now Y likes O.

But, if N is a large amount, it could mean that O asked Y to marry them, so Y is happy and loves O.

The statement can mean different things based on what values we enter into the variables in the expression. That is why this system is flexible and can describe most any social situation, as we shall see.

MORAL DEBTS

Let's consider three typical Hollywood movie scenes.

In an action movie, the villain kills the hero's friend, and then the hero tells the villain: "You will pay for what you did to my friend!" (This is a version of a quote from the movie Hellboy 2, where the hero kills the villain's accomplice, and the villain says to the hero "You will pay for what you did to my friend," to which the hero sarcastically replies: "You take checks?")

In a drama, a man is released from prison after serving a twenty year sentence, and an onlooker observes: "He paid his debt to society. He earned his freedom." (Many movies have scenes like this.)

In a police thriller, the older veteran cop saves the rookie cop's life from a shooter, and then the veteran says to the rookie: "You owe me, kid. You owe me one, big time." (A ton of cop drama TV shows and action movies have scenes like this.)

Please carefully consider the above quotes. They speak of debt. But they do not mean a literal money financial debt. The villain isn't going to pay the hero with dollar bills. The debt to society was repaid with jail time, not by the criminal defendant giving a sum of money back to society as compensation for his committing a crime. The rookie cop does not owe a precise dollar sum to the veteran, as repayment, and the veteran does not expect money from the rookie cop. That is not what they mean when they say these things.

What these quotes mean is a moral debt. To be repaid by pain.

The hero will make the villain repay the moral debt he owes, by inflicting emotional pain upon him, equal to the pain caused by his friend's death.

The criminal paid the moral debt that he owed to society, by means of the pain he suffered from two decades in jail, with the understanding that the pain of twenty years in prison is pain equal to whatever wrongfulness or pain his crime caused to his victims for which he was convicted and sent to prison.

The rookie cop owes a moral credit to the veteran cop, who now owns a moral credit against him, to be repaid by the rookie doing or saying something of benefit to the veteran, equal in amount to the good that the veteran did to the rookie.

This book takes the position that moral debt and moral credits, to be repaid by the infliction of emotional pain or the causation of emotional pleasure, permeates human existence, and affects every aspect and facet of human life, but it does so mostly subconsciously, by means of emotions, so most people are still not consciously aware of how it works. So everyone gets what those movie quotes mean, but no one realizes that financial debt is a metaphor for moral debt, that this is central to human existence, and that most human morality is a system of repayment of what is owed and earned. This book will explain how it works, and what it means, to repay a moral debt through emotional pain, or to be owed a moral credit that has earned emotional pleasure. This book will analyze emotions, using that insight.

Of course, the first objection that will enter everyone's thoughts, is that this idea would mean that most human emotions are a mere this-for-that buy-sell trade, a trade of pain for debt, or pleasure for credit, which would suck all the joy and meaning out of the depth and beauty of real human emotions, and which would be limited in usefulness as a tool for analysis. Other sections of this book address, and refute, that objection. I will fully explain my theory first, and then refute objections and challenges to it, later.

O –N to Y as O wrongs Y, O does wrong to Y.

This statement implies that O now owes a moral debt to Y in an amount equal to N.

Then there exists a set of possible solutions:

Y –N to O as to right a wrong: this can be called Justice, Retribution, or Revenge.

If done by laws and government, often by imposing jail time onto O as –N, it is called justice. If done by one private individual against another individual, it is often called revenge, or vigilante justice.

Or: O +N to Y for O –N to Y, O pays penance or pays compensation to Y or apologizes to Y for O's wrongdoing.

Or: O –N to O for O –N to Y: O feels guilt to atone for doing wrong.

Or, as discussed elsewhere in this book: Y F(–N) = Zero, Y gives spontaneous, complete forgiveness to O. Then O does not owe a moral debt to Y after having been completely forgiven. Such forgiveness is a gift, instead of a trade of –N for –N (revenge) or +N for –N (compensation).

Definitions:
Time T: The time when a statement happens.
= Now: A qualifier of T, that means today, the present.
= Future: An alternative qualifier of T, which means some time in the future.
= Past: Another T, which means at some point in the past.

The statement
O +N to Y at Time T = Now
implies that Y owes a moral debt to O at Time T = Future where the amount of the

moral debt is equal to N, which can be repaid to O by Y as

Y +N to O

Or (maybe) as

Y –N to Y for O.

So we can state this as:

(Y +N to O or Y –N to Y for O) for (O +N to Y)

Take this statement:

Y +N to Y as Action for Y +N to Y as Emotion.

We can also write this statement as:

SD MD(N) owed to SC for SC MC(N) owed to SD.

Let's define the terms:

SD: Self as Debtor. When you loan emotional capital to yourself, you owe yourself a debt. One person, but in relation to themselves as debtor (to themselves as creditor, on the other side of the expression). SD receives a moral credit as a loan and thereby owes a moral debt.

MD: Moral Debt

N: A number. Any quantifiable measured amount.

Owed to: Indicates that SD owes MD(N) to SC. SD owes a moral debt to SC in an amount equal to N.

SC: Self as Creditor. Gives loans of moral credit in return for moral debt, and receives repayment for moral debt.

Loaned to: Indicates SC loaned N to SD. SC's credit to SD equals SD's debt to SC.

This statement can also be stated as:

SD +N to SC at Time T=Future for SC +N to SD at Time T=Now.

At: Means the expression on the left happened or took place at the time value on the right.

What does this mean? The expression is broad and could describe many things. Its precise meaning depends upon the values that fill the variables. It could be that you loaned an amount of courage to yourself necessary for you to ask your boss at work for a salary raise or a promotion, which moral credit you repaid to yourself by actually asking your boss for a raise or promotion. It could be that you loaned yourself the self-confidence and trust to ask someone out on a date, which you repay to yourself by doing so, the happiness and satisfaction that comes from it.

Why does this matter?

This book has a theory of the emotions: guilt, shame, anger. That they arise because the human brain naturally seeks to inflict emotional pain to repay moral debts. For anger, if a person owes you +N, and they don't repay with +N to Y, you exact payment by causing them pain equal to –N to O. For shame and guilt, a person naturally repays +N to Y with +N to O, but, where Y is unable to, the human brain evolved such that, naturally, Y will try to repay unpaid +N to O with –N to Y. Shame is pain repaid for a moral debt to others or to society. Guilt is pain inflicted upon the self to repay an unpaid debt that self owes to self.

Anger: Y –N to O as Anger (to cause pain) for O –N to Y as perceived moral wrong O did to Y.
Shame: Y –N to Y as Shame (pain) for Y –N to O as social mistake or awkwardness or social failure for Y owed +N to O (behavior that you owe to society, or benefit that you owed to someone else).
Guilt: Y –N to Y as Guilt (pain) for Y –N to Y as unpaid moral debt for Y +N to Y.

This book will show that anger, guilt, and shame, are factors in a lot of social scenarios and social dynamics. The book shows how to use forgiveness to master your emotions and take control of these situations. This takes the form:
Y F(–N) = Zero (to Y and/or to O).
This book describes forgiveness, by metaphor and analogy, as "moral bankruptcy," that you wipe the moral debt off the emotional ledger, you forgive the debt, and absolve the debtor. If you do that, then the self, or the other, doesn't owe you anything. And if no one is owed pain, then the human brain has no natural urge to inflict such pain. Then you can eliminate the guilt, shame, or anger, not by repressing it or hiding it, but by forgiving the underlying emotional unpaid debt that was causing it when the brain tried to inflict pain to repay or take repayment for unpaid moral and emotional debts.

Moral debts: what you owe
Moral credits: what you are owed
In general, moral debts are repaid with the infliction of emotional pain, while moral credits are paid off with the providing of emotional pleasure.

O +N to Y as Love (pleasure) for Y +N to O as Love and Emotional Support (a moral credit that Y was owed by O)

Y +N to O for O +N to Y. For example, as Speech, Y is polite to O because O was polite to Y.

Y –N to Y for O, for O +N to Y. Y owes a moral debt to O but cannot repay, so Y feels Guilt (Y causes emotional pain to Y on behalf of O, to repay O by giving Y's pain to O).

Y –N to O as Anger for O –N to Y as Action (as Moral Wrongdoing that Wrongs Y). O owes a moral debt to Y for having morally wronged Y, so Y takes payment as Anger, by getting angry at O, and thereby causing emotional pain to O to repay the moral debt that O owes to Y.

They're moral debts and moral credits, not literal financial debt of loans and amounts of money owed. I have to say this over and over again, and repeat it, so that people understand. I'm not talking about money debts. I'm talking about moral debts. That you owe it to people to be good to them. And that when someone morally wrongs you, they thereby owe you a moral debt. Or that when you do good and do the right thing, you are owed a moral credit by the people you did good for (self, or others). It's moral debt. It's moral bankruptcy. It's not money debts. It's not actual bankruptcy.

I am talking about morality. Please wake up and pay attention. Please understand.

DEFINITIONS: +N, –N

To: at, directed at, towards.

For: Because of the morality and moral debts or moral credits of, for the benefit
of.

+: Plus.

–: Minus.

N: An amount, a quantity.

As: Manifested as, embodied as, taking the form of.

$: Physical.

+N: Positive energy
Being there, showing up, staying, not leaving
Emotional support
Love
Happiness
Pleasure
Kindness
Hope
Trust
Compassion
Politeness
Respect
Friendliness/Being Friendly
Cheerfulness/Good Cheer
Optimism
Commitment

Honesty/Openness
Emotional availability
Doing work to make a relationship work
Appreciation
Being supportive in the face of negativity
Staying positive
Giving them a loan of social or emotional capital

–N: Negative energy
Not showing up/Leaving early
Rejecting someone
Keeping someone waiting/Sending someone away
Pain
Anger
Sorrow
Misery
Distrust
Pessimism
Gloom
Hopelessness
Depression
Sadness
Guilt
Shame
Rudeness
Disrespect
Theft of emotional capital
Negativity
Being annoying
Being manipulative
Being insecure (to lack trust)
Being emotionally dysfunctional
Being abusive

+$N:
Logistical support
Money
Tangible achievement
Tangible favors
Being relied upon

Doing work
Making stuff
Physical love

–$N:
Theft of money
Dishonesty
Being unreliable
Being manipulative
Using someone as a means to an end
Taking stuff
Physical violence

Y: The Self, You.

O: The Other, another person.

P: To perceive, to believe, to know. X P(Y) means that person X perceives Y to be true or believes that Y is true or holds Y as knowledge.

Hide: To repress, submerge, or misdirect one's emotions. X Hide(Y) means that X is hiding Y.

F: Forgiveness, to Forgive, moral bankruptcy.

G: A Goal, any goal, any end state that is the object of desire.

Day: Today's good luck or bad luck, and anyone who happens to be near you today.

Life: The sum total of everything that has happened to you, either –N or +N.

EMOTION AS MORAL DEBT AS A FORM OF MEMORY OF PRESENT EXPENSE TO BE REPAID BY FUTURE ACTION

An explanation of the eight most important human emotions:

Memory as moral debt or moral credit in emotional accounting ledger.

For example:
Y –N to O as Anger for O –N to Y as Action at Time T = Now
Y –N to O as Action for Y –N to O as Anger at Time T = Future

This theory explains eight of the most important emotions in human existence:

The negative emotions: (pain for moral debts)

(1) Anger: Y –N to O as Pain (for O –N to Y as Action, usually)

Solution: Forgive. F(–N) to O = Zero Anger.

(2) Guilt: Y –N to Y as Pain (for Y –N to Y as Action, usually)

Solution: Forgive. F(–N) to Y = Zero Guilt.

(3) Shame: Y –N to Y as Pain (for Y –N to O, usually)

Solution: Forgive. F(–N) to Y for O = Zero Shame.

(4) Sadness: Y –N to Y as Pain for Life –N to Y as Action (usually, but can also be Life –N to Y as Pain)

Solution: O +N to Y as Family and Friends' Support and Comfort. That is the best solution.

(5) Fear: Y Avoids Risk N = Risk of –N to Y (and, sometimes, Y –N to Y as Pain/ Sadness for Y avoided Goal G for Fear of Risk N = Attempt G –N to Y and thereby Y caused Y to miss opportunity G out of Fear)

Solution: Confidence that you will forgive all –N against yourself if you fail. That eliminates, for example, fear of rejection, fear of guilt or shame as fear of failure, and fear of disappointment. Then give yourself a loan of courage and self-confidence that you give to yourself as Y +N to Y where +N = Risk(–N).

The positive emotions: (pleasure for moral credits)

(6) Love: Y +N to O as Pleasure (for O +N to Y, usually)

(7) Happiness: Y +N to Y as Pleasure (for Y +N to Y as Action, usually)

(8) Pride: Y +N to Y as Pleasure for Y +N to O as Action or as Accomplishment of Goal G (usually)

Emotions as pain inflicted to repay a moral debt owed by a moral debtor or pleasure given to pay off a moral credit owed to a moral creditor. Emotions are not irrational. Emotions are logical and mathematical and exist for a reason.

Conceding the theory of negative emotions as the infliction of emotional pain to repay moral debt, we can then see the extreme usefulness of a theory of forgiveness as moral bankruptcy, where Y F (–N) = Zero N owed to Y. This serves to prevent emotional accounting from becoming excessively mean and cruel or potentially unjust and too harsh to survive. Moral bankruptcy sets the debtor free, and gives them a fresh start in moral reality, set free from pain imposed upon them.

An emotional decision is one based on seeking to obtain positive N for oneself (or others), or to inflict negative N upon others (or upon self), in contrast to a rational decision, which seeks the best means to achieve a Goal regardless of the emotional pain or pleasure that those means causes to others or to self. However, often, emotions, and managing emotions, is itself a part of the most rational means to achieve a Goal, at least where human action is involved.

F: FORGIVENESS

The mathematical logical formula for forgiveness:

F(–N) = Zero: When you forgive negativity equal to N, the result is zero, a moral blank slate, no emotional negativity.

Y F(–N) = Zero to O: Where Y had felt an emotion equal to –N towards O, Y has forgiven O for an amount equal to N, such that –N becomes Zero.

WORDS

Saying these words to someone is Y +N to O as Speech where N = Amount of politeness and amount of being pleasant and nice. Obviously you can't say these in a mechanical or formulaic or robotic way, or as though you were reading a script. They have to flow naturally. And you have to really mean them. But these are some examples of +N as Speech:

The seven ways to say something nice to someone and to make someone feel good about themselves because they talked to you:

I. Salutations and Farewells (Y +N to O as Politeness)

Hello
Goodbye

II. Words of Polite Request (Y +N to O as Politeness for Y –N to O as Asking O to Do Something for Y)

Please
Please (do this)
Yes, please.
Thank you
You're welcome

III. Words of Sympathy (Y +N to O for Life –N to O)

How are you?
I'm good. How are you?
How's it going?
Hey, what's up?
I'm glad that you are feeling well/I'm glad that (something good).
I'm sorry that you are feeling bad/I'm sorry that (something bad happened).
I'm sorry that you feel that way/I'm sorry for you that (something bad).
Best wishes.

My condolences.
Get well.
Feel better.
I hope (person) gets better/feels better.
Have a good day!
Have a nice day!

IV. Words of Affirmation (Y +N to O for O +N to O)

I'm happy to see you!
You look nice today/Those are really nice (clothes they are wearing, your hair looks really nice/you have a really nice haircut today, your makeup looks nice, that's a really nice sweater, etc.).
(Any compliment.)

V. Words of Thankfulness or Words of Apology (Y Offers Y –N to Y for O)

Thanks, I appreciate that/I appreciate your help/I appreciate you saying that.
I'm sorry. I apologize.
I'm happy to help (you).
It was no problem.
I hope you enjoy (thing)/I hope you have a good time doing (event)/at (place)!
I understand. That's okay.

VI. Words of Joy or Words of Love

I like you!
I love you.
Hey, do you have any plans for/are you doing anything on (this weekend/tonight/lunch/dinner)? Would you like to hang out with me? Maybe doing (event/hobby/activity) with me?
(Smile at someone.)
(Listen to a person who is talking to you. Listen actively. Listen intently.)
(Laugh at someone's joke.)

VII. Words of Respect

I value your opinion
I appreciate you telling me that/I appreciate your honesty
Thanks for telling me that. I learned something from you today.
I agree.

I'm glad you said that, I found that helpful, I learned a lot from what you just said.

(Address someone by name. Their first name if in a casual setting. A formal Mr./Ms./Mx. And their last name if in a formal setting.)

GIVE THEM A LOAN

Emotional capital/An emotional loan: Giving someone a loan of emotional capital means giving them love, hope, trust, and treating them like they are a great friend or treating them like they are the love of your life, now, today, early in the relationship, before you know whether they are a good person or a bad person and whether they will treat you well or badly. They then repay the loan by being a good person and loving you and having a good relationship with you over the lifetime of the relationship. First you love them, then they earn your love.

In its most extreme form, this is love at first sight. In a more moderate form, it is becoming best friends with a person you just met. In its most minor form, this is, for example, going to a party, and giving a stranger a small loan by saying hello to them and talking to them warmly and opening up a conversation with them, which loan they repay by having a polite friendly conversation with you for a few minutes. You take a risk, you invest, you give a loan, then the other person is nice or friendly or loving to you for a period of time, and that is your profit on the loan.

People are rational moral actors trying to maximize their self-interest. To get people to be nice to you, you have to give them something in return. So if you are nice to them, they will be nice back to you in return, because you were nice to them. That is what "giving a loan" means. You are nice to them, before you know for sure whether they will be nice or nasty back to you in return.

In contrast, you take a loss if the other person does not repay the loan: if they leave, if they are mean, if they mistreat you and are rude and disrespectful to you and treat you badly. You can take an emotional loss on the loan if what you get is less than what you gave, or you can try to recover the value of the unpaid debt from the other person by causing them pain equal to your moral loss as what they owed you, by breaking up with them, un-friending them, coldly walking away from them at the party and not talking to them anymore, etc.

You have to give people loans of emotional and social capital, to take risks, in order to "make a profit" socially and emotionally, you have to take the risk of investing in your friends and your romantic relationships, to make them grow, or else you won't have any. A loan is a risk. And, to be emotionally mature, you must forgive small loans that go bad in your life, with the people in your life and with the people whom you love, and to forgive, constantly, daily, instantly and completely.

Things to which you can give a loan:

A person

Self (for example, loaning yourself self-confidence)

Others

A lover (for example, loaning them your trust)

A friend (loaning them the time and energy to hang out and have fun with them)

A romantic partner (loaning to them the belief that they are destined to be the love of your life, and treating them as such, before you even know everything about them, loving them before you know whether they deserve your love)

A situation (for example, a loan of courage and conviction to take a risk to move to an apartment in a new city or move to another country)

A new job or career (for example, loaning it hope, loaning to it the grit to overcome early anxiety and fear about it, and loaning it the time it takes for it to develop to see whether you like it and/or are good at it)

A new belief or theory or idea (loaning it the resources of an experiment to test it and see if it works for you, and then loaning it the resources to put it to work for you in real life)

A religion or philosophy

An activity or hobby or interest (for example, loaning it your time and energy, and expecting some enjoyment as repayment from it after the work is done)

An undertaking or venture or goal-seeking endeavor or quest (for example, loaning it the belief that achieving that goal will make you happy, to give a sense of meaning and purpose to your quest)

ON FAITH

O seeks to achieve Goal G

O requires positive energy (self-confidence) = N in order to achieve Goal G

Y +N to O as faith, trust, hope, believing in O that O can do this

O +N to Y as achieving Goal G in order to repay Y for Y's trust and confidence in O.

That is the psychology of why, if Y expects O to succeed, O is more likely to succeed (or, if Y expects O to fail, O will more likely fail). Your faith in them is what morally motivates them to succeed.

When you are a member of a team, if every team member needs to excel in order for the team to win, then it is imperative that each team member trust the other members of their team and believe in them and have confidence in them and have faith in them, because the team will lose if they don't. The best way to unlock each team member's maximum +N is by the other team members' +N to them.

It doesn't matter whether your faith in them is justified at the outset. They will earn it, over time, by performing. You don't have to know that someone will succeed in order to have faith in them. You don't know. You don't know in advance whether they will succeed, or fail, but you choose to have faith in them that they will succeed, anyway. That is why it is called faith, or trust, or hope, that you give to them, or loan to them, as opposed to merely a prediction that they will win.

In contrast:

Y −N to O as distrust or doubt

Then O's +N + Y's −N = Less +N for O, less self-confidence and courage and conviction with which to achieve G, which makes O less likely and less able to achieve Goal G.

The principle is similar if it is Y who believes in Y as self-confidence and believing in yourself.

Y +N to Y for G at Time T = Now as a loan

Y achieves Goal G by means of self-confidence = N at Time T = Future

Y repays loan of Y +N to Y at Time T = Past with Y +N to Y as joy and happiness for success of Goal G at Time T = Far Future.

This is why, if a person has hope, then they still have the chance to succeed, but if they lose their hope, then they have no chance to succeed: it is because, if they still have hope, they can rationally justify giving themselves a loan to pay the emotional and moral costs of continuing the fight, as Y +N to Y for Goal G, and then they continue to give themselves loan after loan of hope and self-confidence and courage until they win (or lose), thereby still being able to win, but, if they lose hope, then they can no longer (rationally) give themselves a loan, because it would be a guaranteed loss, with no return on investment and no interest or principal repaid, so they lose all "emotional financing," the emotional and moral capital with which to continue the struggle.

I think that when the Christians say that they have faith in God and that they believe in God, what they really mean is precisely the opposite: that they want God to have faith in them and they want God to believe in them. God would have no use for their faith, and God would not need their faith. In contrast, they would very much need God to have faith in them. And the so-called "Protestant work ethic" simply means that, if God shows faith in you, and you are given the opportunity to succeed, then you should earn God's faith in you by succeeding, by doing the hard work and labor and time and effort to succeed, thereby proving that you were worthy of God's faith in you.

This theology contrasts sharply with Kierkegaard's "Stairway to Heaven" critique, that some Christians believe, which says that humans are always so weak and sinful that we could never earn God's faith, and so we must always ask for it as an undeserved gift, arbitrarily given for no reason.

MAKING OTHER PEOPLE LIKE YOU BY BEING NICE TO THEM

Other people liking you: O +N to Y.

The key to getting other people to like you is:

Y +N to O (as Speech, Action, Emotion, Loan of Emotional Capital, Loan of Social Capital (trust, hope, love)).

O +N to Y for Y +N to O.

And resist the temptation to:

Y –N to O (being mean to them, if you want them to like you or if you like them),

or Y –N to Y for O (being mean to yourself, self-deprecating, self-insulting to yourself, on behalf of someone else, to get them to like you. Being negative towards yourself is a type of being negative, which no one likes and no one enjoys).

O +N to Y for Y +N to O

It isn't a direct this-for-that buy-sell trade. It's a bit more complicated than that.

Y +N to O at Time T = A long period of time

Eventually, O likes Y (If O can like Y, if O ever will like Y, if O + Y is a combo of types of people that will get along and like each other)

Then O +N to Y Because O likes Y.

If Y's strategy is "O +N to Y for Y +N to O," then "it's not about you," instead "it's about them." The focus of Y should be on +N to O, which is what Y controls, Y should not be focusing on O's +N to Y. Y should not be selfish or have an ego about it, in the bad sense of those words, instead Y should focus on sincerely liking O and projecting positive energy +N to O. Y's +N must be real and sincere and Y should mean it, it can't be fake and phony. If it's fake, it's like trying to buy something with counterfeit money, which is fraud, whereas the right way to earn value is by paying for it with real legitimate hard-earned cash. Money is a metaphor for this, but it is literal truth that Y is trying to earn O's esteem by +N to O. To be loved by someone, you must love someone. To be loved, love.

HOW NOT TO BE MANIPULATED, AND HOW TO HANDLE CONFRONTATION

Adult/Mature: Y +N to O for O +N to Y.

Childish/Abusive: O –N to Y as Threat of Higher O –N to Y If Not Y +N to O.

O uses –N if O lacks the social skills to use +N or if O is simply too mean, not nice, or too evil to use +N.

Can be O Threatens O –N to O for Y If Not Y +N to O.

O threatens –N to O because of Y unless Y agrees to give +N to O.

For examples:

–N: "Go on a date with me or I'll cut myself."

+N: "I really like you a lot. Please go on a date with me."

–N is the abusive, dysfunctional, passive-aggressive, personality disorder way to interact with people.

+N is the healthy, mature, sane, good behavior, normal way to interact with people.

For another example, of a married couple with kids who are having a fight:

–N: "I will take the kids away from you and take them with me to another country and you will never see your children again if you divorce me."

+N: "Please, let's see a marriage counselor. I want to stay in this marriage, I love you. But, if we can't work things out, let's at least stay civil and polite, and stay friends, for the sake of the kids."

Definitions:

Exceed: Is Greater Than. That, if N Exceeds N(2), the amount equal to N was higher, greater, a bigger number, than the amount equal to N(2).

N(2): A second N in a formula, not the same number as N. N, by implication, means N(1).

So what does Y do after O Threatens Y? Y has to confront O, and have a confrontation with O.

How does Y do that?

There are two paths. By means of +N, or by means of –N.

Healthy, adult, mature confrontation:

Y +N to Y for Y Confront O where Y +N to Y Exceeds O –N to Y. And then Y +N to O when Y faces O in confrontation.

For example: Y gives Y a loan of emotional capital as hope and trust and self-faith and self-confidence in Y that Y can handle this (and/or Y seeks emotional support for this from Y's supportive friends and family), then Y confronts O, Y engages O and talks to O, Y tries to get help for O and to be nice and friendly to O and to talk O out of it; if that fails, Y takes legal steps to protect Y, O (and kids) from O.

Y says No to O (assuming, in these examples, that Y doesn't want the date, or that Y wants the divorce), but Y says it in a polite way, and it is spoken in a nice, respectful way, evidencing respect for O, so that Y's No = Y No to O as Y +N to O. This way, O does not perceive Y's No as equal to Y –N to O, for which O would then counter in anger with O –N to Y. If Y's No is perceived as +N to O by O, then that is Y +N to O, which negates O's feeling of O –N to Y for Y –N to O, which would leave O feeling Zero towards Y, and that ends the confrontation.

Abusive, juvenile, immature confrontation:

Y –N to O for O –N to Y, where Y's Goal is for Y's –N to O to Exceed O's –N to Y.

Example: Y gets nasty and abusive back to O and Y Threatens O, with Y's goal being to be more mean to O than O was to Y, and for Y's threats to be worse and more scary, to threaten and bully O into backing down from O's threats.

Later this book will discuss the difference between positive confrontation and negative confrontation:

In positive confrontation, the strategy is Y +N to Y as Emotion and as Action, and Y +N to O as Action, and the goal is for your +N to Exceed your opponent's –N. That your positive energy, your maturity, your responsibility, and your good cheer and love, overcame their negativity.

In negative confrontation, the strategy is Y –N to O as Emotion, Speech, and Action, and the goal is to use your –N to Exceed the enemy's –N. This very quicky becomes a race to the bottom where the worst person wins. That is not a good way to win. It is neither nice nor smart.

It becomes a war of bullying.

If O wins, then Y changes Y's No to Yes out of fear and intimidation. Y says Yes, when Y doesn't want to, and Y really means No, because Y fears O's Threats. This, then, only lead Y to repress Y's true feelings, which was a No, until Y explodes in anger. And then O will create a bullying dynamic against Y, to force Y to stay. This leads to a dysfunctional, abusive relationship.

But this tends to only happen if Y tried to use –N to counter O's –N. If Y instead chooses the strategy of +N, Y can gain the confidence and self-trust to leave the relationship, to exit, to leave O, by means of Y giving a loan of emotional capital equal to +N to Y, where N equals the emotions of self-confidence and self-trust and self-faith that are necessary for Y to confront O and/or to leave O.

Or, if Y wins, it is because Y was so mean and nasty and scary to O that Y pressured and scared O into abandoning O's initial threats. But then O's Threats made Y become a mean, nasty, scary, angry person. That is not a good, healthy way to win the confrontation. And the relationship between O and Y would continue to be defined by the dynamic of –N. Hence be abusive and dysfunctional. Even if Y doesn't date O or if Y divorces O, and Y scared O into not acting on O's threats if Y does so.

"Give yourself a loan" of self-confidence and self-trust and self-faith (having faith in yourself) that you are able to succeed. To enable you to face confrontation.

How do you give yourself a loan?

It's easy.

You spend it (use it) today.

You pay for it (earn it) in the future.

It's not complicated.

And, using the term "loan" for this type of thing is a metaphor. I use finance and capital as a metaphor for emotional capital and social capital. Emotional capital is love, trust, faith, hope, optimism, positive energy, good vibes, everything you have to loan someone (or to yourself) at the start of a relationship or to undertake a goal, in order to have the confidence and the trust and faith to do it. Social capital is what you spend (really, what you do) to make people like you and to become part of a group or be in a relationship.

Loans are a metaphor. An analogy. I'm not talking about literally giving people actual loans with real money. Wake up. Pay attention. This is a metaphor only.

But then that leads to another useful metaphor. Moral bankruptcy. As the forgiveness of loans of emotional/social capital. As the forgiveness of debt. It's a useful way to understand how to forgive self and others. For the guilt/shame/anger that you may feel you owe to them.

The reason why people who have hope will put up a fight, is that they can rationally justify giving themselves a loan. If you have no hope, then you can't give yourself a loan, at which point the fight ends.

Manipulation:

O Threatens –N to Y unless Y gives Goal G to O

O's –N to Y Exceeds Y's –N to O

What can Y do?

Y more –N to O until Y –N to O Exceeds O –N to Y: Confrontation, fight, make it be more trouble than it is worth.

Or:

Y seeks help from X: The law and police, friends, a third party, a person in a position of authority, and X –N to O where X –N to O Exceeds (O –N to Y and O –N to X)

Of, if Y is stick in that situation and cannot fight back:

Y Ignore (–N) = Zero, until Y exits, Y leaves or escapes from O and from that situation.

Y should never give G to O unless Y is forced to. If Y gives G to O, usually O –N to Y anyway, and Y has signaled weakness to a bully, and then O asks Y to give a second goal G2 with threat of –N, and then O asks for G3, and then G4, and then GN where N equals the number of iterations of this cycle. If Y allows O to bully Y, it won't end, unless and until Y causes it to end.

HOW TO SAY NO
TO SOMEONE

O asks Y for a Yes

Y wants to say No to O

Y No to O = Y –N to O

Y is afraid that O will get angry at Y if Y says No

If Y says it politely and/or with apology, it becomes

(Y +N to O as Y –N to Y) for (Y –N to O as Y saying No to O)

Then Y +N to O = Y –N to O

Then O does not owe any –N to Y as Anger, Y has offset the moral wrong (of hurt feelings) to O so Y owes no moral debt to O

O might still get angry, but this anger is unjustified because of Y's politeness and/or apology, and so Y can safely ignore it without guilt.

COPING WITH REJECTION

If Y asks O to be their friend, or to be their work-friend, or to date them, or to be their lover, if O rejects Y, or Y thinks that O doesn't like Y, if Y takes it personally:

Y P(O –N to Y) where N = Value of Y.

That Y feels a wrong or a negative directed at Y where the amount is equal to the very value of Y themselves, that N equals the value of Y as a person, the value of Y's life, because Y as a person is what was rejected by O, that O didn't like Y as a person enough to accept Y. Or, if O's acceptance would have been joy = +N, then O's rejection equals the same amount of negative where sorrow and sadness = –N and N sadness = N joy that would have been.

The solution is:

Either:

Don't take it personally, don't perceive rejection as O –N to Y.

P(rejection = Zero).

Or:

If you take it personally, and it hurts: Forgive yourself for having failed and for having been rejected.

Y F(O –N to Y) = Zero.

Give yourself a fresh start and an emotional blank slate. Use moral bankruptcy. Then try again, without owing any fear or guilt to yourself for your next attempt because you failed the last time.

HOW TO HEAL

"Time heals all wounds." "Forgive and forget."

Definitions:
P: Perceive (to perceive, to think, to remember, to be aware).
For example: Y P(O +N to Y) means Y perceives O +N to Y, or Y thinks that O +N to Y is true.

Forgetting about someone who has hurt you is the most insulting thing you can do them. It is worse than anger. Worse than hatred. Worse than making a plan to murder someone. It is the worst insult. That they, and what they did to you, doesn't matter to you enough for you to think about it or remember it.

But

If Y Forget O

Then

Y P(O −N to Y) = Zero and (Y −N to O for O −N to Y) = Zero, Because Y Not P(O Anything). Y P(O = Zero).

Then Y P(−N to Y from O = Zero).

So, if Y forgets about the hurt that O gave them, then Y is unaware of any pain, Y feels no anger towards O, but also Y knows no self-disadvantage from having been hurt, because Y has forgotten about it.

To forget, or to forgive, is not the same thing as to repress, or to hide. Each of these four things is exactly what it is.

To forget means to forget.

To forgive means to forgive.

To repress means to repress.

To hide means to hide.

This discussion involves only to forget.

TO FORGIVE ANGER

Y –N to O as Emotion for O –N to Y as Action.
Then Y –N to O as Action for Y –N to O as Emotion.
So Emotion –N = Debt of –N that Y owed –N to O as Action.

This is the paradigm of petty, vindictive anger directed as people around you to recover what you are owed for perceived wrongs against you.

Debt = Future based on Now, or Now based on Past.
Emotions hold memories of what is owed. Emotion is memory of morality, and of moral debts (and credits), to be later repaid as inflicted emotional pain for debts, as anger to others or guilt and shame to self, (or given as emotional pleasure for credits, as love to others or happiness to self).

The solution to solve petty, vindictive anger: Is forgiveness.

Y F(–N) = Zero owed to O.

Moral bankruptcy. Y forgives the debt owed to O. Y absolves debtor O of debt –N owed to O instead of giving the –N debt owed to O as anger. Then the emotion of anger ends, because the anger was just the memory that stored the debt on your emotional ledger, and the debt no longer exists, it was wiped away by moral bankruptcy.

The paradigm of forgiveness, as emotional maturity. To forgive, instead of anger.

Anger, as a biological responsive, is hardwired into the human brain. If something, or someone, annoys us or anger us, we get angry. It is natural.

Forgiveness is not easy. But it is virtue. And it can be used as the foundation of a system for emotional health and psychological well-being.

ON MORAL BANKRUPTCY

How to use moral bankruptcy to fight guilt, shame, anger, fear of rejection, fear of failure, fear of shame (social anxiety).

Y in Social Situation with O

Y –N to O by accident as goof/awkwardness/mistake

Y –N to Y for O as Guilt, Shame

Maybe also: Y –N to O as Anger for Y –N to Y as O –N to Y (Anger because of Guilt)

Y –N to Y as Fear of Guilt, Shame, Anger, as Denying Y a Loan for Future Social Attempts (Fear of Failure, Fear of Rejection)

Solution:

Y F(–N) = Zero. Y forgives Y. Y forgives O for judging Y in Y's perception of O and for Y's anger at O for causing Y's guilt.

Then Y gets a fresh start.

Then O +N to Y for Y +N to O as social success,

Or:

If failure again, then forgive again, and repeat until success.

EMOTIONAL MATURITY

What is the difference between an emotional toddler and an emotional adult?

If Y is an emotional toddler, and O –N to Y, then immediately Y –N back to O, as Action, frequently as being rude or getting angry at O or throwing a temper tantrum.

But, if Y is an emotional adult:

Y (as an emotional adult) is the master of Y's emotions, so, whenever someone is rude to Y or annoys Y or if Y thinks that they don't like Y, when O –N to Y, as Emotion, Speech, or Action, Y stops, and thinks, and decides how Y wants to react to that –N directed at Y:

Do I retaliate with anger? In emotion? In speech? In action?

Do I forgive?

Do I forget and ignore?

Do I hide and repress, until some time in the future?

Y may still choose to do Y –N to O for O –N to Y. But the emotional adult thinks about it first. The child doesn't think first. For the child, –N to others is an instinctive, automatic, instant reaction to any –N directed to them. So they have no self-control.

That's the difference between maturity and childishness.

PASSIVE-AGGRESSIVE BEHAVIOR AND REPRESSION

Definitions:

Hide: A Hide from X (B), means A hides or is hiding the action, emotion, or whatever, that is equal to B, from person X. A might be aware of A's Hiding either consciously or subconsciously, and A might be aware of B either consciously or else only subconsciously.

Passive-aggressive behavior: Y Hide from O (Y –N to O)

For example, talking trash about someone else behind their back, to vent your anger at them. For example, you are angry at someone for a long time but lack the ability or desire to express your anger directly to their face.

There are three possible solutions:

(1) Honesty: Get angry to O to their face, say mean things to them, vent, and let that cleanse the –N out of your system,

(2) Forgive, Y F(–N) = Zero, or

(3) Continue passive-aggressive behavior indefinitely. But then it will cycle until N builds up to the point where Y no longer has the ability or will to hide an N of that size, then Y explodes in anger to O's face as –N.

Repression: Y Hide from Y (Y –N to Y as Guilt or Y –N to O as Anger or some other emotion or feeling or belief, such as Fear of desire for Goal G = –N, or Fear of attempt to achieve Goal G = –N). For example, Y secretly desires to make the attempt to achieve Goal G, but Y's fear holds Y back, so Y has chosen not to make the attempt for G, and now Y is repressing his/her/their desire for G, in order to make the decision not to seek G more tolerable.

There are three possible solutions:

(1) Honesty: Recognize how you really feel and come to terms with it and accept it and express it openly. Get angry at Y or O to their face, vent, express your honest emotions and feelings, and let that cleanse the –N out of your system, or, in the desire example, realize that what you really want to do is to go after Goal G, and you cannot eliminate your desire for it, so go for it, choose to go after Goal G despite your fears, and with courage and bravery to yourself as a loan of self-confidence = Y +N to Y for Goal G.

(2) Forgive, Y F(–N) = Zero, for example choose not to seek Goal G and then forgive all guilt, shame, and regret for that choice, and totally commit to it, and eliminate all –N that you had been repressing, or

(3) Continue self-repression behavior indefinitely. But then it will cycle until N builds up to the point where Y no longer has the ability or will to hide an N of that size, then Y explodes in anger (or guilt, or whatever) to Y's face as a total nervous breakdown or to O's face as –N as a fight and anger or confrontation or argument.

You can't hide from your feelings forever. The truth always comes out in the end. This can have either embarrassing and humiliating results, or even life-threatening and self-destructive results, sometimes.

Forgiveness is the best solution, but honesty is second best. To intentionally continue passive-aggressive or self-repressive behavior is wrong.

Misdirection is another type of passive-aggressive behavior, where O –N to Y, but either Y is too cowardly to –N to O or Y is too weak and O too powerful for Y –N to O, so Y assigns blame for O to a scapegoat, and then Y –N to scapegoat for O –N to Y. The choice to assign blame in this case is entirely subjective and irrational, but it is deemed Y +N to Y for Y –N to scapegoat, and Y Hides it from Y. Y can also scapegoat someone else for Y –N to Y and then Y –N to O to offload Y's guilt onto their scapegoat, or Y can scapegoat the Self for the benefit of an Other. The question, then, is always, if someone is angry at you, are they really angry at you, or are they angry for some other reason and they are misdirecting their anger towards you, and, if so, what do you do about it? It is irrational so there is not much you can do.

HOW TO ALWAYS
BE CHEERFUL

How to be a happy, cheerful, positive person:

Forgive F(–N to Y) = Zero

O/Day/Life –N to Y
Y F(–N) = Zero
Y +N to O/Day/Life

For example:

Life –N to Y: Some terrible tragic accident. Someone in your family is diagnosed with a severe illness. You trip and break your leg. And then your health insurance declines the bill for medical treatment for your broken leg.

Day –N to Y: You're having a bad day today, you get bad luck, you miss the bus, there is a hair in your morning coffee, your favorite chair has gone missing and you have to sit on a very uncomfy chair. So you're in a bad mood, which means you have a tendency to get angry at anyone around you, to punish them for the bad luck that today gave to you.

O –N to Y: Person O was rude to you. Person O dumped some of their anxiety and fear onto you as –N. Person O said or did something that hurt your feelings. Person O vented their own annoyance by means of them saying or doing something negative towards you.

Then:

F (–N) = Zero: You forgive. You file for moral bankruptcy, on behalf of yourself and what anyone else owes to you. The moral debt that Life, or the Day, or person O, is forgiven, the debt absolved, taken off the books, wiped out from your moral ledger. You are owed no +N and you owe no one any –N.

Day –N to Y, Y F (–N) = Zero owed to Day, is the very definition of "emotional maturity," that a true adult is someone who forgives all of the minor annoyances of the day, instead of getting angry about those annoyances, and so is calm and rational and happy. Contrast the "emotional toddler," who is grumpy and resentful and tends to get angry at everyone nearby, which they do in order to try to reclaim revenge for all the wrongs done to them, in a juvenile, immature, hurtful way.

Then:

Y +N to O: Y is nice to O. Not forced being nice or faking being nice. Y is nice to O, and really means it. No anger, resentment, or malice. Just love, kindness, and respect.

Y +N to Day: Y is nice to everyone who happens to be near them.

Y +N to Life: Y projects positive energy and good cheer and optimism and happiness about life in general. Friendly, cheerful, positive. Everyone likes this type of person. You will be happy to be this type of person.

And, of course, the person who hurt you might be yourself. Then:

Y –N to Y

Y F(–N) = Zero

Y +N to Y as Self-Love.

REMEDIAL ACTION

If you make a mistake socially or do a social faux pas, as Y –N to O, these are some things you can do:

Make a self-deprecating joke about what you did as Y –N to Y for Y –N to O. It doesn't have to be all that funny. It's the thought (the moral intention) that counts.

Apologize, as Y –N to Y offered to O for Y –N to O. Don't make it dramatic. Just say enough so they know you are sorry.

Affirm the other person, be very nice to them or say something nice about them and flatter them, as Y +N to O for Y –N to O. Make sure they understand you are making the effort to be nice to make up for it. +N as an implied apology for –N.

These are constructive behavior solutions.

In contrast, shame, or guilt, or anger because of shame, are destructive coping behaviors.

THE DOWNWARD SPIRAL PATTERN: INTRO TO THE DOWNWARD SPIRAL

Pattern:

Y –N to Y as Action for Y –N to Y as Emotion for Y –N to Y as Action for Y –N to Y as Emotion, to infinity until Sum(–N)=Point of Explosion.

For example, the drugs and/or alcohol downward spiral to drug addiction or alcoholism. You feel sad, so you drink or do drugs. Then you feel sad because you drank or did drugs. So you use more drugs and/or alcohol because you feel bad and trashy because you used drugs and/or alcohol. That would, in theory, just spiral, until you were doing so much drugs and/or alcohol that your life was in danger.

Solution: F(–N) = Zero breaks the cycle. So you would forgive yourself for the last time you used, and then not use the next time (at least, not because of your prior usage).

SELF-ESTEEM

Here I introduce another set of definitions:

SE: Self-Esteem

+SE: Positive self-esteem, or an amount by which your self-esteem goes up.

–SE: Negative self-esteem, or the amount by which your self-esteem goes lower.

SE = What +N or –N Y feels that Y deserves, in sum.

+SE = Deserves +N to Y.

–SE = Deserves/are owed –N to Y.

SELF-ESTEEM AND
DEATH SPIRALS

Definitions:
SE: Self-Esteem
+SE: High Self-Esteem, or an amount by which SE increases
−SE: Low Self-Esteem, or an amount by which SE declines

SE = the +N or −N that you expect to receive and that you feel you deserve.

Y +SE for +N to Y.
+N to Y affirms Y's +SE.

Y −SE for −N to Y.
−N to Y affirms Y's −SE.

Y −SE for O −N to Y as Abuse or for Y −N to Y as Self-Abuse.

Y +SE for O +N to Y as Being Nice and/or Loving or for Y +N to Y as Self-Love.

Because SE = Expected +N/−N, if Y has +SE, Y will seek out, demand, and expect, +N from O, and will surround themselves with Others who will give +N to Y.

So O +N to Y will cause +SE, but +SE will cause Y to seek out O who will give +N to Y. So +SE becomes a self-fulfilling prophesy upward spiral.

If Y has −SE, Y expects O −N to Y. So Y will gravitate towards Others who will Abuse Y. Then it becomes a self-fulfilling prophesy downward spiral: Y −SE because O −N to Y, and O −N to Y because Y chooses those O because Y −SE.

This can be described in math as:
Y −SE.
Y Seek Out (O −N to Y) Because Y −SE.
O −N to Y.

Y –SE for O –N to Y.

Solution to the death spiral formula: Y +N to Y, be nice to yourself and treat yourself with respect, until you recover enough self-esteem to put people in your life who will love and respect you and affirm a higher self-esteem. Also Y F(O –N to Y) = Zero for Y, Forgive yourself for the pain and shame and low-self-esteem inflicted upon you by the abuse of others.

The spiral pattern can exist in several forms:

The Fight:
X –N to A as Anger for A –N to X, plus
A –N to X as Anger for X –N to A
Then cycle repeatedly, and with each cycle, N increases, until:
Fight, confrontation, explosion, or
Forgiveness of –N by X for A and/or A for X = Zero, or F(–N) equals a de-escalation in the amount of –N as perceived moral wrongdoing against the Self that was forgiven. For one person to forgive the other person, is for the forgiver to "be the bigger adult," to be the grown-up in the relationship, in comparison to an emotionally immature person, who doubles down on their anger, to get what they perceive is the revenge and justice they are owed, by getting angry at the other person for wrongs committed against them, in order to cause pain to the other person equal to the pain that the other person caused to them.

The Downward Spiral of alcoholism and drug addiction:
Y –N to Y as drugs and alcohol for Y –N to Y as Guilt and Low Self-Esteem
Y –N as Guilt and Low Self-Esteem for Y –N to Y as drugs and alcohol (and drugs-and-alcohol-induced behavior)
Cycle, and N increases with each cycle, until:
Death or a total nervous breakdown, or
F(–N) = Zero, as forgiveness of the guilt that comes from being an alcoholic or a drug addict and the moral failure that is perceived to be, and
Y +N to Y, where +N offsets –N, as Recovery and Quitting and Cleaning yourself up, or
O +N to Y, where +N offsets –N, as Support, as, for example, an intervention by loved ones, or a support group such as Alcoholics Anonymous, or treatment by a therapist.

The Low Self-Esteem Spiral:
Y –N to Y as Self-destructive Action (treating yourself like a piece of trash) for –SE as Low Self-Esteem (feeling like your self-worth equals a piece of trash),

Y −SE to Y as Low Self-Esteem for Y −N to Y as Action

Cycle, and N increases with each cycle, until:

Death or a total nervous breakdown, or

Y +N to Y, where +N offsets −N, as taking steps to boost self-esteem and recover your pride in being yourself, such as some achievement or hobby, or

O +N to Y, where +N offsets −N, as Support, as, for example, support by loved ones, or a support group, or treatment by a therapist.

SE is the +N or −N that you expect, so:

Early success causes +SE

+SE leads to +N to Y

+N to Y leads to +SE

It becomes like a plane taking off from a runway.

Early failure causes −SE,

−SE causes a loss of self-confidence as inability to trust yourself or give yourself a loan,

−SE causes failure = −N to Y

−N to Y causes −SE to Y

So early failure can cause a downward spiral, like a plane where one engine fails and then the plane crashes.

This is why early success is so important to long-term success. If you have early failure and spiral down, the solution is to catch yourself before you crash, forgive all −N = Zero, then try again to have a small success as a source of +SE, and then build on whatever small successes you have to rebuild +SE to the point where your self-confidence would enable bigger successes = +N to Y, and then get back on the track of the "upward spiral" of +N for +SE, +SE for +N.

THE URGENTLY FELT MOST PRESSING EMOTIONAL NEED

Every human being's most urgent emotional need:

+N to Y for –N to Y

Support, comforting, justice, help, validation, vindication.

O is nice to Y after Y's hardship, O helps Y clean up the mess and heal the pain, Y loves O for it. O makes Y feel better. After a cry, a hug. After a bloody fight, bandages. After a breakup, a new love. After stress and anxiety, comfort.

Every politician and advertiser wants to sell this. People just want sympathy, justice, or to feel better.

EXAMPLE: THE OFFICE

Some people are being mean to you at work. O –N to Y.

You resent them as a result. Y –N to O as Emotion for O –N to Y as Action.

So you get angry and are mean back at them. Y –N to O as Action for Y –N to O as Emotion.

Your being mean and angry at work makes the people at work hate you even more. O –N to Y for Y –N to O.

Repeat the cycle of O –N to Y for Y –N to O for O –N to Y until Sum(N) = Everyone at work hates you, you hate everyone, and you feel miserable at the office, or where N exceeds Point A where A = the amount of –N that triggers an explosive fight or violent confrontation.

The solution: Y F(–N) = Zero, then Y +N to O, until O +N to Y for Y +N to O.

Step 1: Forgive them. Forgiveness is key. Forgive, and really mean it. (The difference between forgiving negativity, on the one hand, and repressing or hiding from negative feelings and pretending you don't feel them, will be explained later. The TLDR is that with forgiveness, you forgive the moral debt they owe you, so you don't feel they owe you, so your negative emotion towards them ceasing to exist.)

Step 2: Be cheerful and friendly towards them. Even to the mean ones. Having forgiven them, you won't feel anger towards them, so you don't just pretend to be nice, and go through the motions. You have to really mean it.

Step 3: Eventually, this "remedial" being nice will change the perception of you at the office. People will like you. And then they will be friendly to you, because they like you. Maybe some of the really mean, rude ones will still hate you. But you will just forgive them, every time, and so it won't affect or impact your office cheerfulness and friendliness, which will make any normal person or group of people like you.

THE STORE CLERK: AN ETIQUETTE STORY

X walks into Store A. There he meets Store Clerk A.

Clerk A tells X about Rule A. For example, no T-shirts or sandals allowed in the store. And X is wearing a T-shirt and sandals. But that is only one possible example; for another example, maybe X had an appointment to pick something up at the store, and X is five minutes late, so A has to tell X that X is too late and X has to return tomorrow to pick up his package. Or maybe customers aren't allowed to bring food into the store, and X brought some food, and A has to tell X to throw it out or else leave. Any example of –N to X as a customer in a store works.

A seeks to enforce Rule A against X. A asks X to comply or else to leave the store.

This is: A –N to X.

What happens next:

Either:

X complies. X +N to A as compliance, X +N to X as enjoying the store.

Or:

X gets angry. X –N back to A.

Then A gets angry in response to X's anger. A –N to X.

Next:

Either:

X –N to A and A –N to X until N escalates to the level where they have a fight,

Or:

A tells X to leave immediately.

Then:

Either:

X leaves. X cuts losses where loss to X = A –N to X. –N to X is capped at whatever level it was at the point at which X left.

Or:

A kicks X out. A –N to X and A cuts losses where loss to A = X –N to A. Then all future –N to A from X is capped at past levels.

Or:

They argue, but A tries to be nice and respectful to X as A +N to X, X feels appreciated and respected and reciprocates with respect = X +N to A, then their argument takes the form of a peaceful debate about Rule A, and then X agrees to peacefully:

Either:

Comply: X +N to X as stay and enjoy, X +N to A as comply and end making a scene in the store.

Leave: X +N to A as respect, X +N to X as get whatever relief comes of getting out of that situation.

In this situation, it is a cost-benefit analysis for A and X of how they can maximize +N to them. X wants to wear a T-shirt and sandals, but X also wants to enjoy shopping in the store. A wants to enforce the rules that it is part of A's job to enforce, but A also doesn't want to make a scene in the store and make other shoppers uncomfortable. Social Skills and social IQ, in this situation, is reading the other person's motives, and using +N to the other person as Speech (as politeness, respect, de-escalation) to try to get the other person to make a decision that you can win under.

If X chooses to leave, there is often:

The Parting Shot:

X rude to A on the way out: X –N to A where A cannot be rude as –N back to X (because X has left).

Then A –N to X as Emotion (futile frustration or anger), which A might then misdirect and vent at other customers, or A F(–N) = Zero to X and just forget the whole thing and move onto the next customer with a cheerful emotional state.

Or:

A rude to X as X exits: A –N to X that X can't repay/retaliate, because X just left.

Then X –N to A as Emotion (frustration, anger), which X might redirect and vent at any random person who is nearby or by being angry at life in general, or X F(–N) = Zero to A, and just move on with a clear mind and a clean soul.

Instead of The Parting Shot, sometimes, there is The Parting Forgiveness:

A F(–N) to X, and A is polite and friendly to X as X leaves, as A +N to X to repay A –N to X.

And/or:

X F(–N) to A, X is polite to A while X exits, as X +N to A to offset X –N to A as refusal or unwillingness to comply and inconvenience to A as store employee.

But, if X stays, this might happen:

A F(–N) to X and A gives good customer service as A +N to A for X + $N to A as X spends money and shops and buys stuff from A,

Or:

A Hide(–N) to X as resentment, for example, the waitress giving the "sneeze muffin" to the customer she doesn't like, that she sneezed on it behind the counter out of sight, and then serves it to him.

And:

X F(–N) to A, for example X leaves a tip + $N to A as a symbol of X +N to A to show appreciation and support,

Or:

X Hide(–N) to A, for example leaves a negative online review of A's store, or calls A's manager the next day to complain about A's service.

If X complies and chooses to remain, and if A intends to be nice to X, A will read X's body language to determine whether X wants A to hover over X and say nice things and make small talk, or whether this makes X feel self-conscious and awkward and X would rather be left alone to shop while being ignored by A. Thus, the behavior that X wants is how A can express +N to X, but there is no "one size fits all" of what is +N, instead A has to read X, and then what X happens to want is what gives +N to X. Or, of course, if A resentfully wants to give some pain to X, giving X whatever X doesn't want is –N to X, if X doesn't want hovering and constant friendly small talk or if X doesn't want to be left alone and ignored.

To begin this story at the end, with a "prequel," A is aware that all of this might happen, so, in order for A to approach X and ask X to comply and inform X of Rule A, knowing that a confrontation and fallout might occur,

A Loans +N to A as Courage such that +N Exceeds –N where –N = A's Fear of X –N to A.

But in this case, in this story, it has a happy ending, because A is perfectly polite to X and A displays respect for X when A approaches X and asks X to comply with Rule A, A is so nice and friendly that X wants to reciprocate by complying to make life easier for X (and so that X can enjoy this store, which seems nice and good-looking), it turns out that this is a clothing store, and X buys a long-sleeved shirt and shoes and immediately puts them on, thereby complying with the no T-shirts and no sandals rule, A is friendly and warm and nice to X while X shops in the store, and X leaves a $5 tip for A as a sign of emotional appreciation and joy.

Add this detail to the middle of the story:

X chooses to stay in the store, and X is shopping.

A is helping other customers. X signals to A that X needs A's help.

A keeps X waiting. A is helping someone else and this other customer is very needy and is taking a lot of time for A to help them.

X doesn't like to wait. X is kept waiting for a long time. X feels that this behavior is A –N to X as Action.

X gets angry. X –N to A as Emotion.

So what happens next?

Either:

X screams at A "Hey, hello over there! I'm waiting! I've been waiting a really long time!" as rudeness = X –N to A as Action.

Or X F(–N) A, and X politely waits, to be nice.

What does A do if X is rude to A?

This is the key to great customer service.

This is what A should not do: A can –N to X as Action as A being rude back to X, saying "I'm sorry, sir, you are just going to have to wait your turn, these other customers need help also, please wait," in a nasty tone.

Then X –N to A as rudeness back, A –N to X as rudeness back for that, and the interaction collapses. It becomes a contest to see if one person's –N to the other person exceeds the –N the other person directs back at them. The "winner" is the person who delivers the biggest –N as rudeness, anger, aggression, and that person feels they established dominance over the other person, because their –N was bigger.

This is what A should do:

A F(–N) = Zero to X. A should just forgive X, instantly and completely. And then be pleasant, nice, and friendly back to X. A shouldn't just fake being nice. A can really mean it. Because A has forgiven X, A feels no emotion of anger towards X.

Then A helps the other customers, but A runs over and tries to help X also at the same time, and A does A's best to help X as soon as possible, or apologizes in a nice, friendly, polite tone. X may appreciate it. Or X may still feel that A hasn't helped X enough. But A +N to X as being friendly and polite and nice and cheerful is the best way to get X to spend +$N in A's store. That is what A earns a salary equal to +$N in return for doing: forgiving X, being nice to X, and giving great customer service (meaning: polite, friendly) to X.

But this requires A to have the maturity to forgive, instead of getting angry, and then getting sucked into the power struggle for dominance of who can assert more rudeness and anger as –N against the other person and get away with it. If A forgives X, then it doesn't matter how much anger, rudeness, aggression, or dominance X asserts to A as –N, the size of X's –N to A doesn't matter, because A F(–N) = Zero, A forgives X's anger, rendering it a nullity.

MASON JONES: A STORY ABOUT RECOVERY

Let M = Mason Jones (he/they)

M is a soldier in a war.

M and M's friend are soldiers on the battlefield.

M's friend dies in combat, M tries to save him but cannot. M survives.

M –N to M as Emotion: Guilt where N = Value of Friend's Life (Survivor's Guilt). M subconsciously/emotionally blames self for friend's death, and M's life is a symbol of blame = Guilt where –N = the value of a human life. So M feels that M deserves to die, where M –N to M for M –N to M's friend.

M uses drugs and alcohol as +N to M as Emotion (pleasure of drugs and alcohol) where –N Guilt = +N drugs.

M drugs and alcohol Hide(–N Guilt = Survivor's Guilt) as numbness/painkilling +N.

M –N to M as Emotion: Guilt as feeling guilty about using drugs and alcohol.

M drugs and alcohol Hide(–N Guilt = guilt from addiction).

Repeat: M uses drugs and alcohol to Hide(–N as Guilt from using drugs and alcohol).

Cycle as Sum(–N as Guilt) grows itself.

M –SE = Sum(–N).

M tries to get sober.

M sober for Time T = +N.

M –SE = M expects to not deserve M +N to M, so +N to M causes M –N to M as Guilt for M +N to M.

Net result of being sober is –N to M as Guilt ("I'm not a good person, sober me is not the real me, I'm only human and imperfect.")

M uses drugs and alcohol to Hide this M –N to M.

Repeat/Cycle for each attempt to sober up.

Then M –N to M as Guilt for each failure to sober up or stay sober.

Repeat/Cycle.

Then one of two things happen:

Repeat/Cycle until Sum(–N) = M –N to M where N is an amount equal to death or total collapse and self-annihilation of any attempt to live a normal healthy happy life. Punishment for being alive as drugs and alcohol, punishment for being an addict and alcoholic as drugs and alcohol, punishment for being sober and trying to be a better person than you feel you really are as drugs and alcohol.

Or:

M files for Moral Bankruptcy.

M F(–N) to M = Zero for: drugs and alcohol, failure to be perfect and failed sobriety, having not been able to save his friend and still being alive.

M owes MD(Zero) to M: M does not owe drugs and alcohol use to himself as punishment.

M owes Zero to M as Emotion: End of emotional pain and guilt. A fresh start.

M sobers up.

M enters Rehab and AA, where group therapy and moral support equals +N to counter and offset –N to M that can manifest as addiction.

M F(–N as Emotion: Shame stigma embarrassment of being an addict) to enable M to have the courage to face Rehab/AA and to keep going without embarrassment or shame.

M builds back M's life, by M +N to M, where Sum(+N) = Rebuilding life.

M achieves Goal G = Sobriety.

M achieves Goals G = Get a job, get married, have kids, climb Mount Everest.

M +N to M as Emotion: Happiness for M +N to M as Achieved Goal G = Rebuilt Life, Live Life.

M, with a friend from AA, visits the cemetery where his friend from the war is buried. M leaves a wreath of flowers at the friend's grave. M cries. M leans on his AA friend's shoulder, and sobs in tears. M cries until all the tears are gone.

M leaves the cemetery.

M lives his life. Without guilt. Without pain. Without drug addiction and alcoholism.

Without the downward spiral of cycle/repeat –N as Action, for –N as Emotion, for –N as Action, for –N as Emotion, to infinity, until death.

MOISHE GOLDSTEIN: A STORY ABOUT SELF-ESTEEM

Let M = Moishe Goldstein (he, him, his)

M is a math and science genius in high school. M is proud of being so smart. M uses his high IQ as the basis of his self-esteem, as a young man. M has high self-esteem because of his very high IQ.

M gets into an Ivy League college named X.

M is from a poor family. $N limits scope of N. M's family cannot afford tuition for X.

M is rejected for a scholarship due to bad luck. The school runs out of grants before they reach his application.

M has to go to a low-ranked state college instead. The state school gives an in-state tuition discount and a grant.

M –N to M as Guilt where N = value of Ivy League status to M's self-esteem SE.

X as a symbol of IQ as a basis of SE. Absence of X as a basis of low self-esteem = M –SE to M.

M uses alcohol as –N to M as punishment for Blame = –N for X.

M –N to M as alcoholism for P(M –N to M as Action as not being good enough or smart enough to go to X).

M alcoholic behavior –N to O (to everyone around him, including at work) as M –N to M for M –N to M.

M's drunken anger as M –N to O for M –N to M.

M alcoholic crazy stupid behavior as M –$N to M as M ruining M's career.

M –$N to M as symbol of M –N to M to punish M for M –N to M as failure to get into X.

M gets a civil engineer license and gets a job as a civil engineer, because his genius is evident, even though everyone knows he is an alcoholic.

M is an alcoholic and gets drunk daily and gets angry and engages in self-destructive behavior daily.

M goes to parties. He gets drunk. He gets angry at everyone (himself and everyone else). He pukes all over. He drunkenly passes out. He wakes up on the street, or in some random motel room naked, or at home while still wearing his vomit-stained clothes.

M is drunk and angry. M meets some random stranger at a bar one night. M is complaining to everyone near enough to hear him about how unfair life is. The stranger hears M complain about M's life story. The stranger immediately understands M. The stranger explains to M that M needs to forgive M for his failure to go to an Ivy League college as a symbol of his low self-esteem, and that self-forgiveness will set M free from anger, shame and guilt. This stranger explains the math and logic behind this. The stranger finishes his beer, and leaves. M never sees him or meets him ever again. M ever doesn't learn the stranger's name.

M wakes up, hung over and with beer-stained clothes, the next morning. But he remembers what the stranger told him. He wakes up that morning sober, and he understands. He chooses not to drink that day.

M F(–N = X) for M, M F(Blame M), M F(–N = career failure).

M F(–N = Indicia of Low or Average IQ).

M recovers +SE = High science and math IQ as basis of SE as "I am a smart, intelligent, good person."

M recovers High IQ = High SE Basis = M +N to M as career achievement.

M sobers up. M stops drinking. Permanently.

M, in order to get back in the habit of doing high-level civil engineering work, takes up a hobby of reviewing the blueprints and engineering plans of local buildings, to look for ways to improve them and sell himself as an applicant by mentioning his ideas for this to local architecture firms.

M reviews the local building blueprints on record in the public records file at M's local Town Hall.

M notices something. Something bad. Something scary.

The much-hyped new development the Super Skyscraper Skyrise has an engineering flaw.

It was based on a 100-story building that was built in California.

It is going to be built in New York.

When winter comes, in a blizzard, with snow and high winds, its roof will collapse.

In California, this design never had blizzards.

No one noticed. Everyone just assumed that, because the California architect was famous and a genius, that it would be fine. No one carefully double-checked every detail of the design against pressure from intense heavy snow plus high wind gusts. No one understood the weight of snow plus the pressure of intense wind at precisely the right place in in the blueprint to crush the roof.

The building is being built by a famous New York architecture firm. Their engineers examined the blueprints. They just didn't notice. They assumed. They didn't understand how wind and snow could combine. M's science and civil engineering brain immediately understood after he looked at the blueprints. Then he did the math. He has proof.

A billion dollars is invested in this office building. M's local town is counting on it to revitalize their downtown economy. So much was riding on this building.

Construction is 75% complete. $750 million has been spent.

What has been built is worthless. Unsafe. It has to be torn down. And rebuilt.

M says this to the Town's civil engineering safety commission.

The building developer begins a smear campaign against M. Calls him an alcoholic. A loser. A liar. He wants to finish the building.

The developer petitions the civil engineering board to have M's license revoked.

The board holds a joint hearing, on M's license and the building's permit.

The developer's lawyers ask M about M's education. M answers calmly. Without anger. Any trade of anger will confirm the rumors. M would lose at trial. M stays calm. He feels no anger. "But you didn't get into X, did you? "No." "You're not an Ivy League graduate, are you?" "No." "You went to that crappy local state school, didn't you?" "Yes." "And you don't work for a high-prestige firm, do you?" "No." "You have caused minor disturbances, while drunk, haven't you?" "Yes." "You have a reputation as the town drunk, don't you?"

"Objection." "Sustained. M seems reasonable. M, what is your proof?"

M calmly, clearly explains the math and science of the building's design flaw. He is happy to get to share his knowledge with people who want to learn. He explains. He is passionate. He is smiling. He proves his argument.

The developers' lawyers look at each other. The board are engineers themselves. They understand.

The lawyers know they've lost.

The building is scrapped and rebuilt. Hundreds of lives are saved as a result.

The case attracts national attention. M gets a reputation as a smart person.

A local, high-prestige engineering firm offers M a job.

M takes it.

M stays sober, has his self-esteem, is confident that he is smart, feels no blame and no guilt and no shame, is happy, works as a civil engineer doing big-money high-stakes work, continues to review local blueprints for flaws as a hobby, and lives a long and happy life.

ABNER AND XANDER: A FISH OUT OF WATER – A LOVE STORY

Let A = Abner Lewis (he, him, his)

Let X = Xander Willems (he/she/they)

At Time T = Past, someone A trusted, named person P (a parent, teacher, friend, coworker, lover, partner, spouse) was in A's life. P betrayed A = P –N to A. P told or implied to A that A was worthless. A –SE = –N at Time T ≈ Now for P –N to A at Time T = Past.

A has low self-esteem. A feels stung and void because of P's betrayal. A hides the pain, frequently in beer. But the scar never healed, it was submerged in alcohol instead, like an iceberg beneath water.

A dates partner B.

A tried to derive self-esteem +SE = Value of B.

B's flaws = –N to A's SE.

B is not good enough for A.

A dumps and breaks up with B.

Repeat with person B2, person B3, person B4.

Cycle for person BN where N is the number of boyfriends A has previously broken up with for not being good enough for him.

A goes to a singles bar. The name of the bar is "A Fish Out of Water."

A sees X. X seems like the perfect person for A. X seems perfect.

A's stare meets X's gaze from across the bar. A stares into X's beautiful eyes. A instantly falls in love. A gazes longingly at X's beauty.

A P(X's value = High +N).

A doubts that A can seduce X. A isn't good enough. X is worth too high a price for A to pay. X is out of A's league.

A is at the bar that night with A's wingman, A's friend, D.

A points out X to D. D says go for it. A says he can't. He is too afraid. A isn't good enough for X.

D gives A this advice: Give him a loan. Give yourself a loan.

A says: What?

D explains: Give him a loan. Loan him the belief that he is the love of your life. That you and he will fall in love, marry, and live happily ever after. I know that you don't believe in love at first sight, Abner, but, for this guy, act like you believe in love at first sight, and that he is it. Talk to him and behave like you have fallen in love with him, from day one, from your first conversation with him. Love him that much. Be nice to him that much. Begin by believing that he is your soul mate, and love him, before you have gotten to know him. Then let that love happen during the relationship, naturally, as you get to know each other, after you have already believed it would come true. A loan of hope and trust and faith. A loan of love, repaid by being loved.

Give yourself a loan. Believe you can do this. Trust yourself, and have the self-confidence to do this. Know that you can do it. Know that you've got this. Then you'll actually find out whether you really can do it, later, after you have already done it. Loan yourself self-confidence today. Loan to yourself the knowledge that you will succeed. Then prove that the loan was justified, pay for it, repay it, tomorrow. With your successful relationship as the interest repaid to you on the loan capital.

A: Okay.

And then A downs a few beers, A does one shot of vodka to chase the beer down, and A goes over to X, and A initiates a conversation with X. A says hello, and starts talking, and makes a joke, and asks X what X's hobbies and interests are, and gets X talking to A. X is smart, funny, interesting, and shares a lot of the same interests as A. A and X get along very well together, and X thinks that A's jokes are funny. A flirts with X, A and X talk and laugh and make jokes, they have some drinks, A hits on X and A asks X to come home with him, X comes home with A, they hook up, and the next morning they eat breakfast together of coffee, toast, and scrambled eggs, at A's apartment, and they decide to date. They watch TV and cuddle together that night, and are inseparable thereafter. They are partners, lovers, and best friends, and they make each other incredibly happy.

X dates A.

A is happy. A +N to A as Emotion for A +N to A as Action as having won X for X +N to A as Action and Emotion as X's love and what a great guy X is and how much A likes X.

But then, as they get to know each other, A learns that X has a dark secret. A learns X's dark secret. X is imperfect. X has flaws. In this example, X is physically attractive, and X put himself through college and law school and paid for it by having a career as an adult film star and adult content creator. A is horrified when A learns this, and A now views X as dirty and trashy and horrible. X has been with hundreds of lovers. By contrast, A has only had less than a dozen lovers and partners in A's entire life.

A P(X's Flaws = N and X –N to A as –N to A's SE).

A confronts X, gets angry, and screams at X, in tears, while crying. A dumps X and breaks up with X, even though A loves X and X is the love of A's life.

A is sad. A –N to A as Emotion: depression for A –N to A as Emotion: Guilt for A –N to X as Action: Breaking up with X.

A is depressed. A gets drunk every day and is drunk 24/7 to kill the pain. A screams at D. A wakes up hung over, drenched in vomit and tears. A cries.

A goes to counseling. A's therapist explains the principles of moral psychology to A.

A F(X –N to A where N = X's imperfection).

A +SE = A F(A –N to A for the betrayal at Time T = Past) = Zero.

A now is not using X's value as a basis of A +SE. A isn't trying to use X +N to A as Value of X to compensate or repay for P –N to A at Time T = Past.

A loans +N to A for A apologize to X.

A meets X at the bar where they first met. They see each other from across the bar. They walk towards each other.

X cries, X hugs and kisses A, X and A reunite and get back together. X loves A. A loves X.

X has already forgiven A for breaking up with X, because X is emotionally mature and knows how to choose to forgive someone, like a true adult.

A +N to X as Love. X +N to A as Love. A as Debtor +N to A as Creditor as Happy Life for Loan = Courage to face X again after their fight.

A and X live a happy life together and having a loving romance and get married and have kids and grandkids and grow old together and live happily ever after.

DANIEL DOMINIC: A STORY ABOUT FORGIVENESS

Let D = Daniel Dominic (he, him, his)

D is a child.

D stands to inherit estate = $N from D's father.

D's father dies.

D's father leaves the estate to D's sister.

D Blames D's mother, who he thinks talked his father into it.

D –N to mother as anger, as Emotion.

D grows up and becomes a young adult.

D cuts D's mother out of D's life as D –N to mother as Action. D is originally from the South. D moves to the Northeast, away from all his Southern family and relatives.

D –N to Life as anger, Blaming Life in general for Life –N to D as Life (Life = bad luck, fate, the world, everyone) –$N to D.

D drinks an amount of alcohol = D –N as anger towards Life.

D has money trouble. He gets drunk a lot. He can't hold a job for long. He works as a carpenter and electrician and plumber.

D Blames problems on mother –$N to D.

D offloads Blame = –N from D onto D's parents.

D –N to mother for D +N to D as Not D –N to D as Blame.

D asks the bank for a loan. At first the bank says no. D is angry. D drinks his anger away.

A few months pass. Then the bank calls D. The bank is willing to offer a loan to D.

D gets a loan of $N(2). The bank says they gave D the loan because the loan was guaranteed by a pledge of collateral from a mysterious person, who does not choose to disclose their identity to D. D wonders if it is D's girlfriend, somehow, because she has a rich uncle, although D has never met him. But D doesn't mention it to his girlfriend.

D uses $N(2) to start a small business. Remodeling houses.

D succeeds in business. Small business Goal G is achieved by D.

G +$N to D. G +N to D as happiness. D forgives Life for some –N to D.

Time passes. D is now an adult.

D's money problems go away. D becomes happy. D marries his longtime girlfriend. They have three little kids together.

D decides it is time to travel home. To forgive D's mother.

D drives a long drive down to the South, in a pickup truck, with the windows down. It is summer.

D meets D's sister, at a restaurant as a neutral site, to confront her, and also to forgive her.

When she sees him, she expects him to scream at her. But he is perfectly polite and friendly to her. He seems relaxed. Not angry. He seems happy now.

D's sister explains that, because D was a child when D's father died, and a legal minor, had the estate been left to him in his father's will, the state could have seized it under state law. D's mother talked D's father into leaving it to D's sister, who was of the age of majority at that time, for D's benefit. D, as a little child, was too young to understand, and by the time had he grown up, he was too angry at them for them to talk to him about it. D's sister was the mystery loan guarantor to the bank, but she only helped D get the loan because D's mother told her to. D's mother was always just trying to save D financially. (D's sister doesn't personally like D all that much. But his mother loves him.)

D meets his mother, face to face, at their old estate mansion. They see each other for the first time in decades. She has grown old, ancient. Her skin is wrinkled. Her hair is gray.

What do you want from me? She asks him.

To forgive… his voice trails off.

I forgive you, she says.

Thanks, he manages to say, in a soft voice, struggling to speak through his emotions.

They hug. They have afternoon tea together on the patio. They cry. They hug again. He leaves. He returns home, to his business, and to his wife and kids, in the Northeast.

D F(–N = anger) = Zero. D forgives his mother, his father, his sister, and Life in general.

D stops drinking alcohol. D sobers up. D no longer needs the alcohol. D is no longer angry at Life.

D lives happily ever after.

HOW TO BE TAKEN SERIOUSLY

There are two human languages, in every language: LNS (Literal, Not Serious) Language, and SNL (Serious, Not Literal) Language. Whether you take what someone says literally, but not seriously, or whether you take them seriously, but not literally.

To tell whether someone likes you, it depends upon whether they communicate using LNS or SNL.

In LNS, you just ask "Hey, do you like me?" And they answer yes or no.

But, if they speak SNL, then asking "Hey, do you like me?" comes across as awkward and socially unskilled. It's too direct and abrupt.

In SNL, you read social cues, like body language, whether they laugh at your jokes or not, whether their eyes light up when they see you or they roll their eyes when they see you, whether they go out of their way to meet you or go out of their way to make excuses to avoid being at events you are at.

Do they look happy when they see you?

Do they make eye contact with you?

Do they avoid you?

You can also make a "symbolic gesture" to ask them whether they like you, and then interpret their answer. For example, ask them to dinner one on one, or ask them to see a movie with you. Make sure you are alone with them when you ask, so there is no social pressure on them, from your group of friends or such. They should give you an honest answer of yes or not, which can represent their answer to the question: Do you like me?

SNL is Huff, snort, moan, sigh Language:

Huff/snort: O –N to Y

Moan: O –N to O for Y

Sigh: O P(Y –N to O or Life –N to O)

Often, LNS is socially inappropriate and looks awkward and comes across as harsh. Saying the same thing in SNL looks normal and appropriate.

LNS states literal meaning. SNL states by implication of an indirect statement or inference from tone and body language. SNL sugar-coats the message with +N to O, because you don't have to hear the harshness and cruelty of the literal meaning, you just see it implied softly.

Consider these statements, which sound rude in LNS, but are frequently stated in SNL:

"I want to have sex with you tonight."

"Do you like me?"

"I don't like you."

"I think that I am superior to you." "I think that I am smarter than you."

"I don't want to see you or spend time with you." "I don't want you to be around me."

These are implied, and you take the hint or get the message in SNL, which you translate into LNS in your own mind to understand the literal meaning of what was implied. You should never say any of these out loud, because they are huge –N to Others. But, if you think them, you can imply them, and you should always listen for them. You can't say such things because it looks bad, but if you state them in SNL then there is nothing there to see so nothing looks bad.

Some people, for example, feel that sexuality is gross, so they don't want to directly address any statement that involves sex (or dating and romance, to the extent those involve sex), so you can't say anything about sex to them directly, but if you imply it and discuss it in SNL then they can talk about it without having to directly or consciously face it and feel grossed out by it. They want sex, but they don't want to have to think about it or talk about it.

This is true for any ugly truth, such as one person hating or disliking another person, especially for an unpleasant reason such as arrogance/sense of superiority. A person can believe that they are better than other people, but that is a cruel truth to face, so people want to imply it without ever directly saying it, if they want to say it at all.

If X says that X is better than A in LNS, that is seen as X –N to A as arrogance (or as racism or as sexism, etc.), for which any listener or audience out of a sense of justice will impose –N to X as Judgment and Shame on behalf of A.

But if X says the same thing in SNL, listeners are not confronted with the thing that X has meant, so they don't feel (or feel to a lesser extent) a need to punish X with –N to X for A as condemnation.

Taken to an extreme, one could say everything in SNL, which is what politicians do, using nothing but double-speak and never saying anything literally because any literal meaning that they assert would offend one or more groups of voters with a sense of judgment against the politician. But then, if you only use SNL and never assert literal plain honest truth in LNS, people might judge you for that overuse of SNL, too, much as some people view politicians as tactful but dishonest.

HOW TO CLOSE A DEAL

There are five types of businesspeople in this world, when it comes to making deals:

(1) The ones who want Y +N to O. So you take them to the right restaurant, buy them the right bottle of wine, buy the right gift for their spouse, meet them at a meet-and-greet at the right business conference at the right resort hotel, get a personal reference from the right friend of theirs, say the right things, and look good, attractive, normal, and be perfectly polite and well-spoken and sophisticated, and have the right picture-perfect spouse and kids that you have pictures of on your desk, and hang the right impressive high-pedigree diploma on the wall, and work in the right nice-looking office filled with beautiful people when they visit your office for a meeting to discuss the deal, and all that. What they want is +N to them from you, as sensations of pleasure from doing business with you, and the more +N you give to them, the more likely they are to close the deal. This is what it means to say that you want them to form the right impression of you as someone they want to do business with.

(2) The ones who want Y +$N to O. They are looking to make money. They don't care about politeness or rudeness. They don't want attractiveness or beauty or pleasant sensations. They care only about money. You could be polite or rude, or look professional or amateur. They don't care. What matters is your proof, in numbers and data, about how much cash the deal will bring in for them. That proof, and only that proof, is what persuades them.

(3) The ones who want O –N to Y. They want to be mean to you and be rude to you and make you jump through hoops and accept inconveniences which they impose upon you, in order to establish their dominance over you, as a symbol of O –N to Y. They want you to let them display –N as their aggression towards you. If you submit, and they feel that they own you, that is when they will do the deal. They want to be the "alpha wolf," and the more you enable that, the more you are likely to close the deal. Your +N to them, your actually being nice or trying to look professional or good-looking to them, won't be noticed, other than that they read it as a sign of weakness. The story comes to mind (and this is a true story) of the Silicon Valley software tycoon mogul who would demand of people that they discuss business deals while naked together in his giant jacuzzi bathtub with him at his Silicon Valley mansion, and he would walk away from the deal if they said no, as the classic example. The other person

THE MEANING OF LIFE

wants to feel a sense of power over you, so you let them, to get the deal. So you essentially pay for O +$N to Y with O –N to Y, if you feel that is what you want to do, possibly with Y F(Y –N to Y for O –N to Y) = Zero, that you forgive yourself for feeling dirty that you let them do that do you in order to close the deal, which is the adult mature choice, if you had to do it financially. They want to dominate, and they want you to submit. But doing this for the deal, doesn't mean you have done it for your soul. Their dominance ends when you leave work and go home for the day. You don't take it home with you. If you feel angry or resentful at home, after work, because of how this person treated you, then you should forgive yourself. You did what you had to do, or, if you wanted the deal to close, then you did what you wanted to do. If it reaches that point, you have to decide whether it is really worth it, and when to walk away. Some people have situations where they need the deal to close, and the other person is that type of person. Then what is very useful to you is: F(O –N to Y) = Y owes Zero (forgive yourself = no shame, no guilt) to Y and Y owes Zero to O (forgive them = no anger, no resentment). It should be just about the money, in business. You shouldn't take it personally. Then your emotions won't hurt you. Submitting in this context is not Y +N to O. Submitting in this context is Y –N to Y for O +$N to Y. What they want is a detriment to you, not a benefit for them. It is inherently negative and self-destructive, not positive and life-affirming. But some people, in business, ask for, expect, and demand this. As will be discussed in this book, some people use –N, instead of +N, to get what they want out of people, as a social skills strategy, and such people will enjoy O –N to Y, with their leverage of Y wanting or needing to close a deal. But you are free to choose to seek to close a deal with such a person. Then, to get what you want in business, the math is Y –N to Y for O +$N to Y for Y +N to Y. The happiness you give yourself from success in business, by means of submitting on a selective basis, exceeds the emotional pain, or hit that your self-esteem takes, or damage to your pride, from demeaning or belittling yourself for someone else, to close the deal and make the sale.

(4) The next type in business are the ones who will test you with O –N to Y as rudeness and aggression, because they are looking to see if you will fight back with Y –N to O by being angry and assertive back at them, or whether you will respond with Y F(–N) = Zero or Y Hide(–N to Y) and then Y +N to O as being polite and nice and friendly back at them and ignoring their rudeness and mistreatment of you, because they want to see how you will react in a fight, to see how tough you are, to see whether they want to do a deal with you. If you handle their –N well, with grace, depending on whether they had wanted to see –N to O (fight back) or +N to O (forgive, shrug it off, and be nice and friendly and polite) as your reply, that will make them see you as someone, as the type of person, that they want to close a deal with. So the math looks like: O +N to Y as Respect for Y –N to O as Pushback and Assertiveness for O –N to Y as Rudeness or Aggression or Domination. Or: O +N to Y as Appreciation and Being Impressed for Y +N to O as Being Cheerful and Polite and Calm and Nice for O –N to Y as Rudeness

or Aggression or Domination. Of course, obviously, O has been rude to Y, and that's not nice of O, even if O did it just to test Y and see how Y reacts. It would be normal for Y to get angry at O, or, if Y is not allowed to express anger at O because then Y loses the deal, it is normal for Y to repress and for Y to get angry at Y because of O. If Y represses anger, then Y's politeness seems forced and unnatural, or the anger builds up and then Y explodes and Y is openly rude to O, and then all prospects of a deal are gone, because O takes offense and walks away. But Y can forgive O, instead of getting angry and repressing anger or exploding in anger. Because Y is a mature adult. So Y is the master of Y's emotions, and Y doesn't care. If Y truly forgives, then Y isn't angry. Y does, in fact, wish positive energy and good vibes to O, regardless of O's behavior. Then Y's +N can be sincere and honest, and will come across as such. That is what impresses and earns respect. If you are a nice person, people will like you. And that helps Y get the deal closed. In this scenario.

(5) The last type of person in business is the one who will mix the first four types. One common combo is type one plus type two, so they want you to be polite and attractive and good-looking and classy and business-savvy and have great business professional etiquette, but they also want to be persuaded that the deal will bring them a huge amount of money and profit. Or someone could combine types three and four, that they will try to dominate you, and want to, but if you put up a fight and resist and fight back, that impresses them and causes them to respect you. Or, as is common in business, the decision to close a deal will be made, not by one person, but by a committee or group or board of directors, and each member might have one of these five styles, so that a combination of styles will evaluate you to decide to close the deal.

It's really important, to close a deal, that, as soon as possible, you identify which of these five types of styles you are dealing with, so that way you know what to focus on in order to close the deal, but giving the decision-maker what they want to have to persuade them to decide to choose your deal, and not all the other potential suitors offering deals to them. And if you are wrong about what the other person wants, you might give them the wrong thing, and so lose the deal. So you have to read the other person continuously to see what it is that they want, to make sure you have not misread them and given them the wrong thing and that you are giving them what they want to close the deal. You should also try to seek out favorable matchups, such as, for example, that the math and science geek who knows hard numbers does better proving a profit equal to +$N, and the really handsome or beautiful nice person who is well-schooled in fancy restaurants and expensive wines and resort hotels and who is fun to be around and who can be the life of the party does better at giving +N.

In dealmaking there is often a scenario where the other person gives –N to you as them trying to force you to accept deal terms favorable to them and unfavorable to your side. The question is, do you push back, with your –N towards them, because if you don't they will take every advantage they can get and take the shirt off your back, but, if you do push back, if your –N offends them they may walk away from the deal completely. How much –N to give back is a judgment call, for you to make as a negotiator and dealmaker, that for the most part depends on what deal terms your business requires from the other person in order to make a profit. You demand the terms you need, and walk away if you don't get them. You concede the terms you don't need or want, to be nice and polite. And then it's a judgment call how big of a fight to put up for deal terms in the gray area of what you want but don't absolutely need. Deals fall through because one side pushed too much, all the time. But deals also happen where one side gets less than they could have gotten or should have gotten. Again, it is a judgment call for you as negotiator and businessperson. And then there is the classic technique of trading –N in one area of the deal terms in return for +N in another area of the deal terms, which you can do.

If the deal falls though, and you get blamed for that, it will look like you –N to your own business where N = the value of that deal to the business. If you boss won't forgive you, and you can't plausibly blame it on someone else, then the thing to do is to accept it with honor and apologize to your company as you +N to them for the –N to them that you caused. So, for your own point of view, you have to compare the other deal party's –N to you in dealmaking, against the –N your boss and your business will give you if you fail to make the deal and fail to close the deal.

MEN AND WOMEN

Definitions:

G: Any Goal, any end result or goal or objective that a person seeks or desires to obtain. Any goal that Y or O pursue.

Anger, aggression, force:

Y seeks Goal G from O by Y –N to O Exceeds O –N to Y.

The primary quality for causing –N is strength, to cause –N to O, and toughness to withstand pain, to accept –N from O without yielding to O. These are often thought of as a man's virtues. As such, the path of aggression and force is often associated with masculinity.

Attractiveness, pleasantness, trade:

Y seeks Goal G from O by O +N to Y as G for Y +N to O.

The primary qualities for causing +N are attractiveness, beauty, social skills, and emotional IQ. These are often thought of as a woman's virtues. As such, the path of attractiveness and beauty is often associated with femininity.

Trade, in economics, is often considered masculine, but peacefulness is seen as feminine, and trade is the inherently peaceful way to seek G, in contrast to force, which is the inherently warlike or argumentative way to seek G.

The paradigmatic relationship of man to woman is Woman +N to Man for Man –N to Enemies where Man's –N to Enemies Exceeds Enemies –N to Woman. The man uses aggression and strength to protect the woman from their enemies, and the woman is nice to the man in return and gives beauty and pleasantness to the man in return.

This is the model of gender that existed for cavemen in the last Ice Age, and during the Dark Ages and ancient times. The prototypical, paradigmatic caveman model is that:

the man hunts for food, by hunting animals, (aggression)

and he fights other men, if they threaten or approach the woman, (toughness)

and he fends off predators, by fighting off wild animals, (strength)

while, in return,

the woman gives the man sex, (beauty, attractiveness)

and she raises the children, (social skills and emotional IQ)

and the woman gives emotional support to the man (social skills and emotional IQ)

and she keeps the man happy. (pleasantness)

So the man needs strength and aggression and toughness, and the woman needs beauty, social skills, and being emotionally adept.

The mathematical formula: Woman +N to Man for Man –N to Enemies.

Woman loves man, and her love forms their family, and, in return, man protects woman from their shared common enemies, man protects woman from danger, and man fights battles for woman.

Women would express their emotions, as +N to Man or as Woman's Need for +N from Man, but a man would not express his emotions, because this would be perceived as a sign of weakness, as Man –N to Man as Getting Emotional and being Vulnerable for Man +N to Man as being Emotionally sensitive and Managing his Emotions. Any sign of –N to Man would be interpreted as a sign of weakness, that would lessen the degree to which Man –N to Enemies Exceeds Enemies –N to Man. So women are thought of as emotional, while men are thought of as tough. Women always tell men to ask for help, but a man never wants to be helped in order to do something, because needing help is a sign of weakness, and a man always wants to be strong.

However, in modern times, anyone: man, woman, or any person, of any gender, can choose to use +N as a tool to achieve Goal G, or could choose to wield –N as a tool for seeking Goal G. They are not inherently limited to either gender, at least not in today's world. +N is the path of peaceful trade of value for value, of getting what you want by being good-looking and attractive and being nice and polite to people. –N is the path of getting into a fight in order to win and to conquer.

In traditional times, men used muscle to defeat their enemies. In modern times, a new type of man has emerged: the masculine nerd geek, who uses his brainy intelligence and his high IQ, instead of his muscles, to cause –N to his enemies, such as, for example, by devising schemes and plans to cause pain to his enemies, or by using his intelligence to figure out a way to defeat his enemies. A businessperson or lawyer, for example, wins in business, or in court, not by punching his enemy in the face and beating them up, but by outsmarting them, by making sales and crafting advertising campaigns, or by filing the correct motions and persuading a judge. The businessperson's success comes at the expense of his direct competitors, just as the lawyer's victory comes at the expense of his trial adversary, so those are fights, but fought with IQ, not with muscle.

In today's world, the attribute of causing –N to others has also served men well in business, and in sports, both of which can be viewed as competitions where you win by inflicting more –N onto your opponents than the amount of –N they inflicted onto you, such that If Y –N to O Exceeds O –N to Y, Then Y wins. It is a contest where the size of –N matters, and the biggest –N wins.

This may explain why business, and sports, are often male-dominated. A woman could succeed, in business, or in sports, but, to enjoy great success, she would have to win by inflicting –N onto her enemies, not by exceeding others' +N with her +N. Because that is how you win in a fight. And professional sports, and competition in free market capitalist business, are, ultimately, types of fights. You fight the other team to score more points. Or you fight the other competing businesses in your market for market share.

This book explains ways to defuse fights by means of projecting +N and Forgiveness of –N, but that doesn't "win the fight," it instead causes the two people to not have a fight. The focus of this book is on social skills, and using +N to achieve Goals, so the strategy and tactics to win by means of –N are not discussed in this book. But a person has to understand the +N and –N psychological dynamics, in order to read how people are behaving in a social situation, whether someone is trying to use +N, or whether someone is looking to have a fight and wield –N. There are situations where +N can defeat –N if the size of the +N Exceeds the size of the –N directed against it. The light of your positive energy outshines the darkness of their evil. However, if you face someone using negativity to achieve their goals, and if your +N does not Exceed their –N, if they are more negative than you are positive about whatever is involved, and if you are not willing to actually have a fight and have your –N Exceed their –N by being more mean and rude and angry and cruel and nasty and abusive and insulting than they are, then the other option is to walk away from that situation. Those are the three choices you have, most of the time: use +N, use –N, or walk away. Your approach should be that you should read the situation, and then choose the best option from among those three choices to achieve your Goals.

Insecurity about being a man or being a woman, and how this can be exploited psychologically for manipulation, is discussed elsewhere in this book.

Definitions:

Aggression: The willingness to seek out and engage in risks and dangers without fear, under the belief that you can cause an –N that exceeds the –N that can be done to you.

Strength: The ability to cause –N to Enemies. For example, being able to craft mean, hurtful insults and formulate verbal abuse.

Toughness: The ability to withstand –N that Enemies cause to You, without crumbling or giving in or being defeated. For example, the ability to be verbally insulted in a brutal, hurtful way, without really caring about it and without feeling pain or suffering from it.

Assertiveness: the quality of trying to take control of any situation you are in, and to assert yourself and assert your beliefs and goals and desires onto any situation.

Attractiveness: The ability to give +N to the Other. For example, beauty as a set of sensations that cause pleasure.

Social IQ: The ability to manage a trade of +N for +N, or of +N to O for O –N to Enemies. The ability to manage emotions and expectations in a long-term relationship, for example.

Positivity: The ability to cause +N in general, to both Self and Others. Being nice, for example.

"The men fight while the women flirt." Or, to quote the rock band Garbage, "The boys wanna fight while the girls just want to dance all night." Given the textbook caveman gender roles of Woman +N to Man for Man –N to Enemies (man fights other men, fights predators, hunts food, for woman), we can see that, in the traditional gender roles social and social psychological dynamic, Assertiveness and Aggression and Toughness and Strength are Masculine virtues, for Men, because they are used to win a fight, while attractiveness, social IQ, and positivity, are Feminine virtues, for Women, because these are what Women need to survive and trade in return by getting the Men to protect them and fight their battles for them.

Obviously, in Third Millennium Earth, with our modern contemporary progressive views on gender, this traditional caveman view of gender is laughable and absurd. But, still, the role of Man and the role of Woman in this social dynamic does still explain a great deal about the actual behavior of men and women in real life. Whenever the size of –N to challenged, whenever a man's –N is challenged, he will fight back, and resist, against any perceived force that seeks to demean his manhood. Women tend to become insecure in, and can be goaded into compensating for, their ability to give +N, for example insecurity about their beauty, or fear of a failure in social skills, such as not being popular.

But "man" and "woman," in this sense, are gender roles that any human person can perform, such as, for example, women in women's sports causing –N to the other team in a fight to win a game, or women in business using their high IQ to cause –N to win economic wars against competing businesses in their marketplaces, are women winning in a man's fight, or men in fashion and beauty industries being good at causing +N, or men as actors in the theater or movies known for their good looks, are men succeeding in a woman's industry. But you would tend to see men who perform the male gender role to gravitate towards and be more interested in areas where –N causes success, like sports (strength to cause –N) or business and technology (where high IQ is used to cause –N to opponents), and women who perform the female gender role as more interested in areas where attractiveness leads to success, like getting married and raising a family or child education (where teaching social IQ to children causes success) or customer service or fashion or music or internet/social media (where producing +N for an audience causes success).

In politics, the Right tends to be the more Manly, Masculine side. The Right value strength, and assertiveness, and domination against enemies (in foreign policy and wars, for example), and they view government control and regulations as a challenge to their manhood as the king of their household and independent ruler of their own life, and they value the toughness to be resilient against pain and to take a beating without getting knocked down.

In contrast, the Left tends to be more on the Womanly, Female side. The Left wants everyone to be taken care of and that no one should ever have to take risks or face danger, and everyone must always be protected by someone else (by the government), and they want everyone to always be treated in a nice respectful way, with people not being allowed to ever be mean or rude or disrespectful.

Socialism is, in essence, the forced feminization of the populace, placing the populace into a role of female weakness and helplessness to then be protected by the government in the role of male. As such, the men of the Right bristle at, and reject, all socialism, while socialism is cheered by the women and LGBTQs of the Left, and by the men of the Left who feel destined to assume the role of government with its power and authority to protect those women and LGBTQs on their behalf. Any group whose identity and sense of self-esteem comes from being a victim and from projecting self-pity and needing to be protected by someone else, would also naturally fall into the female position of weakness in relation to a male government as protector, and they would naturally support socialism. (The math for self-pity is Y –N to O for Y as Self-Pity, where Y perceives that O owes +N to Y as sympathy but O isn't giving +N to Y to Y's satisfaction. It is similar to other such psychological dynamics, such as loneliness and/or depression as Y –N to O for O owes +N to Y as comfort, or Y –N to O as grouchy moodiness for O owes +N to Y as cheering up.)

Socialism imposes womanhood onto the public, and the socialist government claims the man's role as protector, and so the men of the Right inherently feel that socialism challenges their manhood as individuals and seeks to deny and take away their status as men, which would make them feel weak in relation to their own women and feel unable to fight their battles as men. So the Right will always oppose any position that the Left takes, for government and regulations and policy, and they will oppose them for the sake of opposing them, for the sake of preserving their masculinity, and not because they have a substantive rational objection to why this or that policy will not work, even if, by random chance, the government's position is objectively correct, and opposition is crazy, for that particular political issue. This explains why the Right sometimes takes positions that are crazy: they do so in order to oppose the Left, not because they really care about the issue itself. The Right would favor personal responsibility and, for example, gun ownership or the freedom to run a business, because the men of the Right feel competent to fight their battles themselves, and to win, instead of needing the government to fight their battles for them.

While the Left claims to be progressive on gender, the Left's political gender dynamic is, ultimately, merely a variation of the traditional caveman psychological dynamic, where the caveman government protects the cavewoman public and fights all battles on her behalf.

The Fascism of the Right, is, in essence, the forced masculinization of a society, where an entire nation is put into a state of masculine anger and aggression, and the goal is to dominate all enemies and triumph by conquest. The fascists' goal is to win all fights by means of their –N exceeding the enemy's –N, so they want to be as negative as possible, and their strategy is to engage in any and every fight possible, for this purpose: to strengthen their powers of –N to be as high as possible, because every fight that they win tests, hones, and improves their powers of causing –N. Fascists tend to persecute political dissidents and to punish dissent as Y –N to O, and they also tend to seek out wars of conquest as Y –N to O, as fighting for the sake of fighting, conflict solely for the purpose of making a display of manly, muscular strength. They have no mercy and no sympathy, and they walk the path which, in history, belonged to, for example, the Roman soldier or the Viking warrior, as bloodthirsty conqueror.

In contrast to socialism and fascism, in a libertarian, liberal, free democracy, such as today's United States of America, each individual has the liberty to choose his, her, or their, gender role for themselves, and there is no national gender imposed upon society.

The Right tends to want men in male gender roles and women in female gender roles, because their men and women still rely upon "men being men" in the caveman model, their men need to be men, and their women rely on their men to be men for them, so they become insecure about their gender roles when they face gender-fluidity and their gender is challenged. That explains their love of tradition, it dates back to the caveman dynamic, which, to be fair to the Right, is how humans evolved 10,000 years ago and how we survived until the past century.

The Left is more gender-fluid and LGBTQ, which defines them as more progressive and modern, because they are more willing to have anyone in any gender role, and they can use women in male roles or men in female roles with success, and so they are less dependent upon men acting out the male gender role in order for their men and women to survive.

Despite the fact that strength and power are Right virtues and softness and sensitivity are Left virtues, Right and Left do not necessarily correlate to Right control/ dictatorship and Left freedom/democracy, it is not true that the Right is always dictatorial and the Left is always pro-freedom. Each could be either. The freedom Right are, for example, the libertarians. The dictatorial/control Right are the fascists, who desire total control by a dictator. The dictatorial/control Left are the socialists, the communists, and the progressives, who desire total control by the government. The democracy/freedom Left would be, for example, moderate center-left tax-and-spend liberals. Tyranny is the condition of total control, regardless of whether it is by a Right dictator or by a Left government. In contrast, true freedom requires democracy and civil liberties and a free press, regardless of whether the Left or the Right is the political party that happened to most recently obtain the most votes.

Economic freedom tends to be male freedom, the freedom for the strong: free market capitalism, gun rights, no government control. Social freedom tends to be female freedom, the freedom to be beautiful, or freedom for the weak: things being being nice and polite and being free from rudeness and from offensive behavior, abortion rights, LGBTQ rights, gay marriage, or, as a type of freedom to be weak, protection from racism, the right to use recreational hard drugs, immigration freedoms.

The social Right tends to be, not freedom, but men attacking female freedom, and men oppressing women: preventing women from having abortions, attacking the legal rights of transgender female youth, attacking the freedom to engage in LGBTQ sex or LGBTQ identity, etc. Similarly, the economic Left tends to be, not freedom, but men attacking male freedom on behalf of women, and men oppressing other men, such as men telling other men what they have to do, how they have to behave, forcing people to conform to safety instead of taking risks, and forcing them to obey the government, instead of just letting them do whatever they want.

The Right is masculine, the Left is feminine, and Libertarian is the political non-binary, Libertarians are on the Right on economics and on the Left on social issues.

Envision a grid, where the Right side is male, the Left side is female, the bottom is Collective, and the top is Individual.

Right: Masculine: Collectivist - Fascists, Social Conservatives: Men rule men and women on behalf of men, domination, 100% controlled by men, women are oppressed, (often) a dictator, but economic freedom because that gives men the freedom to use their strength and intelligence, and freedom such as gun rights because that gives men the freedom to engage in physical violence, and freedom to be rude or offensive.

Left: Feminine: Collectivist - Socialism, the Economic Left: Men rule men and women on behalf of women in order to protect women, 100% controlled by men for women, no economic freedom, but (often) social freedom for women's rights, such as freedom from the rude and offensive, freedom for abortion, LGBTQ freedom, etc. There is an emphasis on safety, that the government will protect everyone (weak women) so that no one has to be strong enough to win a fight (as a man), and also the government will force everyone to be nice, polite, and respectful, so that there will be only female beauty, and no male ugliness, that is visible in discourse. They also champion the ideal of equality on the belief that men ruling for women will bring the women up to equal status as men, that the weak and oppressed will be lifted up to the level of the ruling class, by a ruling class that fights for the rights of the weak.

Right: Masculine: Individualist - Far Right Libertarians (Market Anarchists, Anarcho-Capitalists): There is no government, only market anarchy, so there is 100% freedom for men, because there is no government to nag them and whine at them and boss them around and rely on their tax dollars and treat them like an annoying housewife treats her husband. With market anarchy, there is no government to tell a man what to do, so the man has 100% total domination within the sphere of his own individual life, although he loses the fascist domination of men against women, because, absent government, no politics exists at all.

Left: Feminine: Individualist - Moderates and Independents, Liberals on the Center-Left: They want some freedom and so oppose total socialism, and they want some economic freedom, but they are deeply committed in principle to women's freedoms, abortion rights, LGBTQ rights, feminism, equality, and justice, and, in general, they want people to be nice and polite and respectful, and they take offense at the rude and offensive.

A "Non-Binary" is the name for someone who does not accept the gender binary or who does not fit within the gender binary or who adopts both masculine and feminine traits at the same time, or who is transgender and changes back and forth between being a man and being a woman. It is a term used often in the LGBTQ community, although I am the first author to assert that Non-Binary is the gender identity which is expressed in "political gender" as libertarian.

The Libertarian Non-Binary: economic freedom, which is freedom for men to be strong men, plus social freedom, which is freedom for women to be free women, free from oppression. Economic Right + Social Left.

The reason why Libertarianism always fails: Men on the Far Right, who embrace freedom and fall in love with the ideal of libertarian freedom, then realize that the principle of freedom would require freedom not only for men but also for women, as a matter of principle, and then they retreat, in fear of women, afraid of female freedom, and they return to fascism and social conservatism. And the men and women of the Center-Left, who become excited about freedom, that women can be truly free, later realize that the principle of freedom would also require freedom for men to be men, the freedom to be rude and offensive, the freedom to be strong, and so they become afraid of male freedom, and they retreat back to the Left, and have no place to go other than back to socialism. People are too afraid of true freedom because of their gender insecurity, because men can't stand seeing women be free, and women can't stand seeing men be free, so they retreat back into the gender safety of fascism for men and socialism for women.

The Libertarian hypothesis:

The condition of perfect male freedom is free market anarchy with zero government: a set of conditions where there is no government of men on behalf of women to boss around men and tell men what to do.

The condition of perfect female freedom is no oppression, which means, no laws that oppress women.

If there is no government, then there exists no government that can pass any laws, and, if there are no laws, then there are no laws that oppress women or violate women's rights. Under free market anarchy, men are free from government interference, and women are free from government oppression.

Therefore, the condition of perfect masculine freedom, and the condition of perfect feminine freedom, is the same set of conditions, which is equal to perfect freedom.

The anarcho-capitalist Far Right libertarians (known within the movement as the "An-Caps") have a principle, namely, Austrian economics. But the Non-Binary "Economic Right plus Social Left" libertarians, too, have a principle, although it is a different principle. The Non-Binary libertarian principle could be summed up as: "less government, more freedom." Let people do whatever they want.

132

In general, when the government stops telling people what to do, in economics, the result is behavior that the Right favors. People will trade in free markets, and be capitalists, unless the government forces them to pay taxes and obey regulations. But also, in general, when the government stops telling people what to do, in social policy, the result is behavior that is on the Left: absent government laws enforced by the police that ban the public from doing so, people will do drugs, people will use prostitutes, people will come in across borders from other countries, people will have gay weddings, people will have abortions, etc.

So, if you begin from the principle of "less government, more freedom," then you arrive at a place where your policy positions are economic Right plus social Left.

In general, social conservatives and the social Right are the ones who attack freedom in the social arena, while the economic Left are people who attack freedom in the economic sphere. Therefore, to be a "social Left plus fiscal Right" Non-Binary libertarian (whom we could call by the abbreviation "NBL"), is to be opposed to both the social conservatives and fascists, and to oppose the economic Leftists and socialists, which means, to be opposed to government control and power as such, and to be a defender of liberty.

The economic Right is men being free. The social Right is men dominating women and preventing women from being free.

The social Left is women being free. The economic Left is men, on behalf of and for women, dominating men and preventing men from being free.

So a position that is economic Right plus social Left combines men being free and women being free.

This explains why the Non-Binary libertarian, the NBL, is on both the social Left and the economic Right.

In contrast, the true tyrant dictator would combine the social Right with the economic Left, much as the Nazis did, because the true tyrant desires to oppress and dominate both men and women, and allow neither one to have any degree of freedom.

In theory, along the lines of the gender of politics and the Libertarian as Non-Binary, there could also be a type of Libertarian, on the Left, who is a Libertarian only because they want freedom for women, and freedom for the weak and the oppressed, and they believe anarcho-capitalism is the best system suited to achieve this, and they do not care about men or freedom for men at all, men are not their area of concern. Such people do exist, although they seem to be rare and uncommon.

According to this theory of the gender of politics, a person who was neither on the Left nor on the Right, but who is unique, and is not on the political Left-Right binary at all, would also be a type of Non-Binary Libertarian, because they are not Left and not Right, they are not masc and they are not fem. However, we would expect each such type of person to have their own unique politics, so there would not be one name or word to describe their political identity.

Obviously, a state is the most common form of government, but, even in the condition of anarchy, even in a fully stateless society, I would define the initiation of violent force in order to achieve social, moral, or political goals, as a type of government, and as governing, even if the violence was used only by private individuals against other private individuals. This is why the Libertarian Party asks for a "loyalty oath," that a member will never initiate violence against a non-violent other to achieve social or political goals: because that oath really means you will not govern others. To the libertarian, violent force may be used only for individual self-defense, never to govern other people.

Libertarians often use a visual picture called The Nolan Chart, which is a diamond, with the Right on the right, the Left on the left, Freedom on the top, and Tyranny on the bottom. It is intended to show that Freedom would combine the economic side of the Right with the social side of the Left. It can be updated, using my analysis presented in this essay, merely be adding Masculine to the Right, Feminine to the Left, Collectivist to the bottom, and making the top Individualist.

Some concluding thoughts on these topics:

To be LGBTQ gay: to appreciate the beauty of strength.

To be a feminist: to appreciate the strength of beauty.

As with politics, where a side of Left or Right can have a gender, so, too, a race, as a political class, can also have a gender. We often see a vulnerable or oppressed race move to the Left when it is weak and chooses to be submissive in order to rely on the strength of the government to protect it, and then, once the race has its footing and is stable, the men of that race then move to the Right in order to assert their masculinity.

We saw this in America with the Jews, who used to be on the Left when they were weak but moved to the Right as they became strong, and, more recently, the Latinos have made the same move, the same dance step, they were politically weak and they had been on the Left, but the Latino men are moving to the Right today in order to assert their manhood and masculinity, against what they perceive as a weak, girly, womanly Left.

Interestingly, the men of the Black race seem not to do this; the Black people seem locked in a position of weakness and submitting to the state and relying upon the government for power on the Left side of politics. Black young men (and this is probably merely a false racial stereotype, or it may be true of some Black men but not be true of other Black men) tend to assert their manhood through violence, aggression, sex with women, drug use, gangs and gang-inspired music, daring feats of strength against the police and against authority, etc., instead of through Right-wing politics. There is also a certain type of white young man who copies the Black young man's criminal behaviors in order to assert his own white-young-man's masculinity, by doing drugs and having sex and breaking the law and such, although, being white, he is arrested for it far less frequently than the Black man.

The above is not intended to be racist towards the Black race. This is not intended to describe all Black men, but, instead, it describes a certain type of Black young man who is insecure in his masculinity, because these behaviors are done to assert one's manhood, and to overcome one's masculine insecurity. The math and logic of it is that, when a person breaks the law or defies authority, he is asserting that his negative N against the police and against the government is bigger than their negative N was against him, which is why he won his fight against them. And, when he has sex with a woman, he feels that his negative N was large enough to overcome her negative N against him, that he conquered her by having sex with her.

These behaviors are common in young men of every race, at the age where they are insecure in their masculinity, but, for whatever reason, media and culture tend to focus on this lifestyle among Black young men (and Latino young men, too). Possibly, because historically the Black race and the Latino race were oppressed and conquered by the white race for such a long time, and so they feel that they were dominated in the way that a man dominates a woman, some Black and Latino young men enter the world feeling that their masculinity has already been called into question, so they overcompensate by asserting their manhood in such cheap and easy ways as drugs and crime and gangs. It is all about the size of one's power to inflict negative N, the size of one's masculinity. Obviously there are entire classes of normal middle-class law-abiding Blacks and Latinos who are fully secure in their masculinity (or femininity) and to whom such would not apply, and these people tend to blend in with the moderates and independents of the white race, within the space between Right and Left.

It is also worth speculating that a certain type of political activist or politician feels masculine insecurity due to a history of racial or gender or class oppression against them, and then attacks people with their Leftism and attacks people with their socialism, against what they perceive as the complacent capitalist middle class or their foes on the political Right, in order to assert their negative energy against others to reclaim their lost manhood, by means of politics.

But we see in those rare cases when a Black man does achieve wealth and power, and when he no longer benefits from reliance upon the government for help, he too will move to the political Right in order to assert his masculinity, as, for example, with a very famous and notorious Black man United States Supreme Court Justice on the Right, Clarence Thomas, or else he will assume the white male position of privilege and power in the Left, as for example with America's recent Black President, Barack Obama, who had far more in common with rich white men on the Left than he did with the poor Black man on the streets.

In the United States of America, historically, the white race, in general, seems to be gender-male, and historically the white man had expected white women to submit to men. This explains the Right's fascination with the white race: it is because both of them are gender-masculine in their gender-performance. But people can be racist whether they are on the Right or on the Left. The white men on the Left tend to come to power on the Left, and to rise to the top of the Left, and they are the men who fight for women, they are the men who fight on behalf of those whom they deem weak, they are not themselves gendered as women, they wield negative N for women, not positive N as women. To hold power, and use helping those who are weak as your pretext and propaganda to rule, is certainly not the same thing as actually really being weak yourself. A rich man who donates millions of dollars to charity is not himself a beggar, and he has power and will never suffer as the beggar does; nor is a white man on the Left someone who truly is gender-feminine. He says he fights for them, but he is not them, he has no way to relate to them, it is a pretext to wield power over men on the justification of helping women.

Note here that I define "man" as someone who uses negative N as their survival strategy, and I define "woman" as someone who uses positive N as their survival strategy. I do not intend to refer to men and women by their bodies; here I speak of men and women as gender roles. In practice, sometimes, however, the body, the gender role, and the race, and the politics, will all blur together.

Also note that, while the caveman gender dynamic calls for a man to attack his woman's enemies with his causing –N to them, the man, to be as strong as possible, will fight everyone around him, in order to build toughness and strength, and, so, often the man will attack his woman herself with his –N also, just because she is nearby, even though protecting her in return for her +N to him was the basic premise of their social contract. Thus, man will attack woman's enemies, and man will attack woman at the same time, and this makes sense, from the man's point of view, as agent of –N.

This is why the Black woman leads the most challenging life: she is a woman, and so caveman gender roles define her as weak and submissive and for a man to dominate, and then she is also Black, so racial expressions of gender roles again treat her like the cavewoman gender role.

However, the solution for caveman gender is not for the Left to defeat the Right, as both Left and Right assume this caveman-cavewoman dynamic; the author feels that the Non-Binary Libertarian will emerge as the superior method of achieving gender freedom. The men in power on the Left do not truly desire gender equality, although the Leftist activists and radicals on the streets believe that they do; instead, the men want power, and they think they get more power if they wield it in the name of women and against men, by ruling the economy. But the Right is no better, because they only want freedom for men, and they desire to rule women, and so, despite their rhetoric of freedom, they are no friends of liberty. Only the Non-Binary Libertarians can achieve perfect freedom.

I will conclude this section with this thought, which is that, in perfect socialism, the people have only positive N, however, all their capacity for inflicting negative N is taken by the socialist government, and the government itself then inflicts negative N, on behalf of the people, against all critics and dissidents and rebels. This is why, much as the fascist men in power on the Right will censor or jail or shoot and murder their critics, political dissidents, and rebels, so, too, the socialist men in power on the Left would do the same thing, and cause incredible extreme negative N, despite the fact that their premise is everything being nice and pretty and beautiful and one big happy family of +N for everyone.

+N and –N are inherent in human existence, positive energy and negative energy is inherent in the very fabric of reality itself, in physics and chemistry, so +N and –N will never go away, the only question is which social and political institutions we choose to channel them into a form that we prefer, be they Left, Right, and/or Libertarian.

Insecurity in being a man: Fear that –N isn't big enough for Y –N to O. "I'm not strong enough."

Insecurity in being a woman: Fear that +N isn't big enough for Y +N to O. "I'm not good-looking enough."

Challenge to masculinity: Test of Y –N to O by means of O –N to Y.

Challenge to femininity: Test of Y +N to O by means of competitor or rival's +N to O.

Why adults tend to be more confident than young people: They have survived to adulthood, which proves, mathematically and logically, that the size of their N is big enough for them to survive.

Advertiser and politician manipulation: Subconsciously challenge masculinity or femininity (see above for how this is done), then sell a symbol of boost of Power = –N to men, or sell a symbol of boost of Beauty = +N to women. It doesn't have to be the real thing, what they sell is just a symbol of the thing.

STRATEGIES FOR HOW TO MAKE FRIENDS OR GET A ROMANTIC PARTNER

The ten strategies for obtaining a relationship with someone you like:

Definitions:

Y: You

O: the Other person

+N: Positive energy (as social or emotional value/benefit/capital)

−N: Negative energy (as social or emotional forcefulness/willfulness/dominance)

As: the form that N takes in a particular trade.

For: for the benefit of, for a trade of that in return for this.

(1) Y +N to O as Beauty/Attractiveness (beauty for women, muscles for men, a pretty face, a nice body, a handsome face, beautiful eyes, wearing fancy beautiful clothes, or being good at dancing and partying, or cooking tasty flavorful food for them, or being good at sex. It is the providing of sensations of pleasure to the other person.)

(2) Y +N to O as Speech attractiveness: being funny, clever, witty, enjoyable to talk to, fun to hang out with, being fun to do things with

(3) Y +N to O as Being Nice, polite, friendly, cheerful

(4) Y +N to O as Love (or as a loan of love, such as "falling in love at first sight")

(5) Y −N for O as Assertiveness, Aggressiveness, Confidence

(6) Y +$N to O as Money, buying them gifts, paying for stuff for them, or just giving them money

(7) Y +$N to O as logistical Support, such as letting them crash on your sofa, renting a hotel room for them to hook up with you, running errands for them, letting them share your alcohol cabinet and/or your 420 drawer, etc.

(8) Y −N for O and Y +$N to O as Y Protecting O from danger/risk = N, from either physical danger, emotional danger, bullying, from other people, or from financial

danger.

(9) Y –N to Y for O +N to Y, or O +N to Y as Unpaid-for Gift: Present yourself as a victim of unfairness, and ask for O's love out of sympathy and mercy, for them to make you feel better, or ask for love and friendship as an unpaid-for gift, where you give nothing in return. If O takes pride in helping others and in being a nice person, then O +N to O for O +N to Y, so you pay O for O's love by giving O the opportunity to "be a good person" by helping you and being nice to you.

(10) Y –N to Y for O as Presenting yourself as someone who is weak and in need of protection, as someone who needs to be protected and is looking for a protector, and then O –N for Y to Enemies as O +N to Y as Protection completes the relationship. But, normally, what O gets in return for protecting Y is for O to know Y's beauty, so it helps if Y has beauty to "sell" in return for a strong, forceful, dominant, muscular protector to take care of them.

#1 and #10 are the traditional "female" methods of "getting a man to fall in love with you" in caveman gender roles, while #5 and #8 are the traditional "male" methods. #8 is what a man offers to a woman to get her to become his wife, traditionally. #9, in sex, is called "sympathy fucking," and in dating and friendship #9 is called "charity," or "feeling sorry for someone."

The plan is, you do one or more of these, for O +N to Y back to you in return, as a relationship, friendship, love, or fun.

To be loved, love. To get something, give something.

DATING PROFILES

This advice is for dating profiles, but also works for going on dates, and while being in relationships, in general.

Do this:

Y +N to O as friendly, attractive, polite, positive (positive about Y, and positive about O).

Do not do this:

Y –N to O as complain, as you have to deal with my baggage, as negativity.

Y –N to Y for O as self-deprecation, as I apologize for what a bad person I am, as self-criticism, as self-doubt, as negativity.

Always remember: You are trying to make the sale. Your goal is not to lose the sale by being honest about flaws. Trust me, if the flaws are there, they will get noticed. There is no need for you to draw attention to them. Being positive gets results. Negativity drives people away. Also, your hurting yourself and your image for the other person's benefit will not, in fact, make them like you. It just presents yourself more badly than you had to.

WHAT MAKES SOMETHING ENJOYABLE (+N)

The nine affirmations that express +N in such a way as to create an enjoyable experience:

(1) Pleasurable sensations: pleasure, beauty, awe, grandeur, joy, a sense of meaning, stimulation, amusement and entertainment, relaxation, excitement, jokes, humor, music, drama, something that so fully engages the mind that the person ceases to be aware of their problems.

(2) People being nice to them.

(3) A symbol of their self-esteem which affirms their self-esteem as SE+.

(4) A sense of belonging or community.

(5) Feelings that they have done moral good, are appreciated by others, have done right, have been judged worthy.

(6) Seeing O +N to Y through the point of view of someone they can relate to.

(7) Something that matches their unique subjective preferences of what they like (and the absence of what they don't like).

(8) Removal of stress and anxiety, or a symbol of defeating some symbolic challenge to their self-esteem.

(9) A feeling that they are loved or that they have a friend. This, more than anything, motivates someone to get married and/or start a family.

If you want to motivate self or others to seek to achieve a Goal G, offering them +N of one or more of these forms as a reward is the surest technique for motivation.

CONFIDENCE, OR ARROGANCE

Confidence: Believing in yourself and in your ability to succeed. Giving yourself a loan of self-confidence and trust in yourself.

Y +SE, Y +N to Y as Loan of +N for +SE.

Arrogance: To put someone else down in order to lift yourself up over them, by measuring your self-esteem as your value minus their value, so the less value they have, the higher your (pretense of) self-esteem becomes.

Y −N to O for Y +SE = (Y − O).

Mathematically and logically, confidence and arrogance are two completely different things, although they look the same, and people often confuse the two. The only thing they have in common is that they are both tactics based on increasing one's self-esteem, one's opinion of one's own worth and value.

EARNING VS. ENTITLEMENT

Definition:
For (Y=Y): For who Y is, what Y is, Y's status or title or identity.

Deserving/earning: O +N to Y for Y +N to O as Action.
A sense of entitlement: O +N to Y for Y=Y (because of who Y is or because of what Y is).

Then disdain/condescension is Y –N to O for O –N to Y as O Not +N to Y for (Y = Y). If Y expects to be given +N because Y=Y, then Y feels that O owes +N to Y. So, then, if O doesn't given +N to Y, Y interprets that as O –N to Y. And then Y will give –N back to O for O's perceived –N to Y. And "giving someone attitude" means giving them –N when they expected you to give them +N because of who they are.

IS LOVE A TRADE?

Y +N to O for nothing in return (for Zero) = Y Gifts +N to O.

There is a belief that true love, true friendship, truly being nice to someone, is a gift.

But if someone gives you a gift of this sort, if you are a nice person or a good person, you always want to repay by being nice back, even if the gift was freely given with no expectation that they would get anything back from you.

So, socially:
One way to get everyone to like you,
Is to be nice to everyone,
But expect nothing in return and ask for nothing in return.
Everyone likes kindness and generosity and being friendly to strangers and good cheer and good vibes. If you display those traits, people will tend to like you.

The Charitable Person:
From an overflowing abundance of Y and/or O +N to Y,
Y Gifts +N to O.
If O is a nice, good person, if O is able,
O might, or will, try to repay Gift +N to O with O +N to Y (as Speech, Emotion, or Action).
If O is a mean or petty or insensitive person,
O won't care,
O won't try to repay,
Or O will be negative back.
O Zero to Y or O –N to Y for Y Gift +N to O.

So you make a huge profit by giving lots of gifts away. But this only works if you really mean it. You really intend it as a gift, not in order to get something back in return, not for a purpose of selfish profit. Any socially skilled person can detect your intentions. They will see giving gifts for the purpose of getting people to like you as fake and shallow and evil and manipulative. You have to really intend Y +N to O as a gift.

If you don't really mean lots of Gifts of +N, then fall back on the trade model: Y +N to O as a Loan of Emotional Capital or Social Capital for O +N to Y as ROI (Return on Investment) Profit.

OBJECTIONS TO MY THEORY, AND MY REPLIES

Objection:

Y +N to O for Because it's the right thing to do

O +N to Y as Appreciation for O Likes Y, O esteems Y to be a good person because Y +N to O

But that is not O +N to Y for Y +N to O

If Y +N to O is right, and if Y is a good person, then Y +N to O even if O –N to Y

Reply:

O +N to Y for Y is a good person because Y +N to O.

If Y is a good person, Y +N to O as a Gift, or else Y +N to O is not the right thing to do unless Y owed +N to O or for some other moral reason.

Then, if Y +N to O as a Gift, O +N to Y as Appreciation, that is described accurately by my theory, and if Y +N to O for moral debt from O +N to Y, my theory also describes that.

Objection:

O +N to Y for Because O likes Y, not for Y +N to O

If O dislikes Y, O –N to Y even if Y +N to O

People +/– N to Y Because they like or dislike you, and their liking or disliking you is an irreducible primary that cannot be analyzed or changed, regardless of Y +/– N to O.

Reply:

Yes, I concede that O +N to Y because O likes Y is often the most accurate description of reality, but someone liking you can be analyzed, and, yes, it is difficult to predict who will like you or why they like you, but liking can be adjusted for:

Y +N to O at Time T = Now is the situation, and the condition, that makes it most possible and most likely for O to like Y.

Y +N to O maximizes the potential that O likes Y.

Y +N to O as Y being nice, polite, friendly, respectful, caring, loving towards O, is (usually) a necessary condition, but not a sufficient condition, for O to like Y.

And so: O +N to Y for O likes Y for Y +N to O.

Objection:

True love and true friendship is not a trade of O +N to Y for Y +N to O. It cannot be quantified. Love transcends analysis. Love defies math and logic.

Reply:

No, love absolutely can be analyzed, and it can be quantified. However, love and friendship are not a direct buy-sell trade. I never asserted that. It is a gift, for which you might receive appreciation, or it can be given as a loan, which can be repaid by having a relationship. You can use math and logic to better predict how to maximize the love and friendship in your life. Love and friendship are rational. People, even nice people, to the extent that they are rational, act according to rational self-interest. So if you love someone and you are someone's true friend, it is more likely that they will love you or be your friend, in return. That doesn't mean it was "selfish" in that sense that you were only using them to get a selfish benefit out of them for yourself. If you truly loved them or you were their true friend, you had to have sincere care and concern for them and their well being, for their sake in addition to your own. You should not fake caring about other people, you should mean it. But, yes, all social relationships can be described rationally.

Objection:

Real social reality isn't cut-and-dried enough to quantify with math and logic. It is messy, unpredictable, and emotional.

Reply:

My theory does not purport to be complete. But my theory is an accurate description. It correctly describes a lot of why humans do what they do. Also, emotions, too, can be analyzed using math and logic.

Objection:

In a real relationship, often, you love X, hate X, Y +N to X, Y –N to X, X –N to Y, X +N to Y, all at the same time, and it does not evaluate to a net sum. So math and logic do not describe it.

Reply:

My theory describes this. It's just that my theory has nothing to say about what you should do in a relationship like that, other than to just live it and do what you want with it. I never asserted that all the +N and –N would sum to a net sum, or, if it did, that the net sum would have any special meaning.

Objection:

Forgiveness, moral bankruptcy, as (Y or O) –N to Y, then Y F(–N) = Zero, then Y +N to (Y or O), describes what to do, but actually doing it in reality is very, very difficult. My system says you should forgive a lot. And then be cheerful, after you got hurt, because you have forgiven the pain. That is hard to do. Very, very tough thing to do. No one could always forgive everything. So nobody can ever always be cheerful and never get angry, 100% of the time.

Reply:

Philosophy doesn't change people's lives. People change people's lives, but philosophy can tell them how to change their lives. Forgiveness is the tactic that could enable you to be cheerful instead of angry, but, yes, you have to actually do it, or else it doesn't work. And it only works for the period of time when you do it, so, if you don't always forgive, then my theory doesn't expect you to always be cheerful and never get angry. You're only human, but that, too, can be forgiven.

Forgiving someone who really hurt you is a lot of hard work. Feeling pain hurts. Forgiving all anger and all annoyances, all the time, is a ton of hard work. For some people, for many people, it might be impossible, especially if their gut reaction, their instinct, is to get angry at people. So being cheerful 100% of the time would be a ton of hard work.

But, in theory, F(–N) = Zero is a way that it could be done. Doing it is the hard part. But forgiveness is the key to being emotionally mature.

I never said my system was easy. It would be difficult to do it perfectly all the time. In reality, I would expect people to use it as much as possible, and get whatever help it provides, but not to use it all the time, not to be 100% perfect and consistent with it. If you aren't cheerful, or you get angry, that is –N, but, later, tomorrow, you can forgive yourself for that –N, too, and ask others to forgive you for any –N you directed at them as anger or sadness or not being cheerful and friendly. Forgiveness is sad, in a way. It means that something bad happened, which is so bad that it needs to be forgiven. But life is tough. My system is a system for living life, as a real human being. If you didn't forgive, you might be angry or resentful all the time, and never be able to be happy.

The theory will make your life better, probably, in certain ways, if you apply it to solve the various problems that it describes. If you do it, it works. Lots of things in life are difficult. Making money is difficult. Diet and exercise for being healthy is difficult. Forgiveness, too, is difficult. But it is the right thing to do. It rewards you with happiness, just as doing the hard work of making money rewards with wealth, or doing the hard work of diet and fitness rewards with health. But this is a realist, practical theory, for using psychology and math and logic to improve your life. It is not an imaginary magical fantasy that you will always be perfectly happy without having to do lots of hard work to use the theory.

EVERYTHING IS SOMETHING: A PHILOSOPHICAL DIALOGUE ABOUT LOGIC, LANGUAGE, WORDS, MEANINGS, TRUTH, AND THE THEORY OF THINGS

I. INTRODUCTION: WHY DO WE NEED PHILOSOPHY?

Hello, Friend.

Hi! Nice to see you today. Hey, what is that? What's that thing you're holding?

This? I bought this at the pet store. Today.

Um... What is it?

The pet store told me it's a dog.

(You believe the pet store without question or doubt. You don't feel an urgent need to question other people's assertions or to think critically about what an authority tells you. You feel no desire to do critical thinking or to think for yourself. You do not need philosophy. You can put this book down now.)

Or...

But what I want to know is: Did the pet store tell you the truth? Is it really a dog? It looks sort of like a dog. It also looks sort of like something else, that isn't a dog.

What is a dog? How do I know if it's a dog?

What is a dog? (Metaphysics, Ontology).

How do I know if it's a dog? (Epistemology, Logic).

What does the word "dog" mean? How do we know what "truth" is, to know whether the pet store told you the truth? (Philosophy of Language).

If it looks like a dog, can I just believe that it's a dog? Is there anything more to it being a dog, than just looking like a dog? (Philosophy of Empirical Perception and Sensory Experience).

If I believe that it's a dog, does that mean it really is a dog? (Philosophy of Realism and Objectivism or Subjectivism).

Well, friend, let's consider some possible answers.

It doesn't matter whether it's a dog. Because the answer to that question makes no real practical difference to you or me. (Pragmatism).

We can't know whether it's a dog. No one ever really knows anything. There is no way to know. (Skepticism).

We can't know whether this is a dog, because it's in the physical world, but there is another realm, a spiritual world, where knowledge is possible (Platonism, German Idealism, Kantian Transcendentalism).

It isn't a dog. It isn't anything. Nothing is anything. Everything is nothing. (Continental philosophy, Existentialism, Nihilism).

If it looks like a dog, it's a dog. To be, is to be perceived, and sensations are the only things which exist. There is no knowledge or logic or analysis, only raw, naked sensations. Only perceptions are real. (British Empiricism.)

We can't define what a dog is, but if we remove all analysis, and just let whatever this thing is present itself to us, then we would see, by our naked intuition, what it is. (Continental philosophy, Phenomenology.)

Or...

We can define what a dog is. We can know what a dog is. We can know whether this thing is or is not a dog, on the basis of whether it meets the criteria, the necessary and sufficient conditions, of the definition of a dog. We can analyze whether this thing is a dog, using logic, and analysis. A thing is something. Everything is something. A dog is something. This thing I bought from the pet store is something. And we can analyze whether this thing I bought from the pet store is a dog.

Ah, that sounds like Analytic philosophy! I like it! Let's you and I continue down this path of Analytic philosophy, and see where it leads.

"Dog" refers to something in the set of all dogs. A dog is a member of the set of all dogs.

But how do I know if this thing belongs to that set?

Let's think through some more possible answers.

Someone arbitrarily creates the name "dog" and defines the set of necessary and sufficient conditions in the definition of that word. Our language arbitrarily, subjectively chooses whether this belongs to the set of all things named "dog."

That doesn't seem right....

The word "dog" refers to a Platonic Idea, or Kant's Pure Reason, some strange thing in the spiritual world, from which things in the physical world get their identity. We would have to refer to the being of "dogness" in the spiritual world or in the world of intuition, to see if whatever this thing is, participates in the idea of dogness or not.

Hmmm. I would sort of like to know whether this is a dog or not, just from this thing alone. I don't feel comfortable communicating with the spiritual realm to answer this question. I do not feel any feeling such that I possess intuition that would automatically tell me the answer to this question. That is why I want to use philosophical analysis to answer this question.

So then let's try this approach. The set of all dogs is defined as the set of things that have an essential property, the property of being a dog, and that essential property does exist, physically and objectively.

What is it? What is the essential property of being a dog?

I'll float a definition for the sake of argument. A dog is a four-legged canine animal with a tail, which barks. Having that set of properties is the property of being a dog.

But what about a three-legged dog? My family owned one when I was a child growing up! It was a dog too! (The attack from borderline cases.)

Okay, then. A normal dog is a four-legged canine animal with a tail, which barks.

What is "normal"? What the heck does normal mean? Is anything ever really normal?

I guess probably nothing is ever perfectly normal. And I don't want to define "normal" here. Okay. Your dog had three legs. But it barked, and it was canine, and it had a tail. So it was a dog.

What is barking?

It's the sound that a dog makes.

Well, you can't define barking as the sound a dog makes, and define being a dog as being something that barks. That would be a circular definition. It would be useless. Does your pet bark, by the way? It seems very quiet.

I don't want to define dog by means of a circular definition! Let's try something else instead. I could say, a dog is a canine, and a canine is a mammal, and a mammal is an animal, and an animal is a living thing, and a living thing is a thing. That gets at a lot of what a dog is. That defines several properties that every dog has.

You could say that. Except that, for a dog to be any or all of those other things, it must first be a member of the set of all dogs. And we have not yet established how to determine whether it is a dog. From which to determine if it belongs in that set of all dogs.

II. ESSENCE: WHAT IS SOMETHING?

Let us assume that a dog is a thing, and that a thing is one thing. What action, or act of being something, does that set of cells or molecules or atoms, do as a whole, to be a dog? What unifies them and makes them be one thing? What properties cause a dog to be a dog? What properties cause a thing to be a dog?

A dog is:

(1) A dog shape, which math and three-dimensional spatial geometry can describe.

(2) A dog's behavior, which science and observation can describe.

(3) A dog's DNA, which science and chemistry and biology can describe.

Let's call the name of dog "f(dog)," (pronounced "f of dog" or "the naming function of dog"), the naming function that names dogs. This function is satisfied only by the set of all dogs, and by nothing else. If you call this function, it returns the set of all dogs. The condition of being a dog returns the set of Objects defined by this function. If any Object X is data that is a solution to f(dog), then it is a dog. If f(dog) describes X then X = dog.

But what is a dog? You have given it a name, and a very fancy name at that, but you have not said what it is. What is its being? How did we define the name f(dog)?

A thing is a set of properties. Having the essential property or properties X is what makes a thing be an X or be an X type of thing. A consequential property is a property that having an essential property causes or requires a thing to have. Having an essential property causes a thing to have all its consequential properties, such that, where the essence equals X, and the consequence equals Y, we can say that All X Are Y. Because X is defined by reference to the essence of X, so all X have it, and the essence of X causes (or requires) Y, therefore all X must have Y.

So what is the essence of being a dog? What is doghood?

The essence causes the consequences, so we should define the essential properties of being a dog as what will cause a thing to be a dog, what will cause all its necessary and sufficient properties to count as a dog. Having dog DNA causes a thing to have a dog shape, and causes a thing to do dog behavior. So that must be the essence. That must be the essential property or essential set of properties. Then a three-legged dog with dog DNA is a dog.

But what if dog DNA changes and then dogs had six legs?

(1) Then what a dog is, would have changed. Then what is a dog has evolved. So that is still a dog.

(2) Then there would be two things, an old dog, which has dog DNA, and a new dog, which has this new six-legged dog DNA, and we would want two words, for two different things, and have a word for each thing, for purposes of logical analysis and semantic clarity. Linguistic precision dictates that, where there is the X property, the Y property, and the Z property, and, in reality, there are two things, an XY and an XZ, that, instead of just calling them both by the name for X, precision requires a distinct name for XY and a distinct name for XZ. Then it would still be true that a dog is a dog, as we defined it. An old dog is an old dog, and a new dog is a new dog.

Logic is the study of what things are, according to the axiom that a thing is itself, a thing is what it is, and everything is something. Essential logic then posits that a thing is a set of properties, a thing refers to the set of properties as one thing, while "what a thing is" refers to the thing as the set of various different properties. An essential property or an essential set of properties, also called an "essence of a thing," is used to define a thing. And the consequential properties are whatever set of properties would be caused by having the essence, that having the essence will cause (or require) a thing to have the consequence. Then let the essence equal X and the consequence equal Y, and we achieve the holy grail of logic, proof that All X Are Y. Add the axiom that things, as sets of properties, are directly perceived, by empirical experience and sense perception, that things can be directly perceived as sensations, and you then arrive at Empirical Essential Logic: That if you see X, then you can know that All X Are Y, an analytical a priori-type claim, from experience that would be commonly thought of as contingent a posteriori knowledge. Note that, if the consequence of X is Y, but another consequence of X is Z, then All X Are Y and All X Are Z, even though Y and Z might be completely dissimilar to one another. Logic is both pure reason and practical reason. It is true, but it is also useful.

How do you define a word? How do you choose f(X)?

To define an Object, you just point to it. To define an idea? Well, for example, to define f(apple), we begin with the assumption that someone already knows what the essence is, that this person will teach it to others. Then you could take an apple, point to it, take another apple, point to that, say "I mean this," then point to a banana and a pear and an orange and say "but not those." That way, a person, the Audience for the Speaker of word f(apple), would be able to see what properties those two apples have in common, but which the other non-apple things do not share in common with the apples. That gives a starting point for forming a definition. Although more analysis may be necessary to formalize and finalize that definition. The two apples are examples of being an apple, where, based on this, we can define "example" as any specific thing presented for the purpose of inferring an essence from that specific. Those two apples are examples of an apple, and, to that extent, those two apples are also an example of an example.

What do you mean by an Object?

An Object is a concrete, a real thing T, at place R(S) and time R(S), where T means Thing, R means Real, and S means Specific or Specifics (as in "specific properties," which are those properties of a thing that are non-essential). The three types of Things are properties, Objects, and Essential Things. A thing is merely a set of at least two, or more than two, properties, unified together by one thing being both, by one thing having both properties. One property by itself is a property, not a thing, although you can also analyze a property as a thing.

Wow. This is complicated. But I am trying to follow along. I can see how, if everything is things and their properties, then everything is something, and you would want to use logic to understand everything. What is an Essential Thing?

An Essential Thing is a thing, as an object of thought and contemplation and analysis, which has the essential properties of X, but lacks all specific properties of any real X. Because it has only X and nothing else, whatever we reason must be true of the Essential X, must be the consequence of X, and will therefore be true of all real X. But Essential Things do not exist, in themselves. They exist only as real things. The great mistake of Plato is that he thought Essential Things are real, in themselves, and he called them Platonic Ideas, otherwise known as Platonic Forms.

How can an Essential Thing exist as a Real thing?

To explain that, I must define is-plus, vs. is-equals. For there is a horrific lack of clarity in the English language, that there is one word, "is, to be," and it has three different meanings. And that word is used a lot, so that creates a ton of confusion.

So you're saying it depends on what the definition of the word "is" is? Okay. What is it? What is "is"?

Say that X is a property and Y is a property. Let us say that XY is the thing that has both the X property and the Y property. XY equals X multiplied by Y, XY equals X times Y. So XY is an X, and XY is a Y. But we would also say that XY is XY. I assert that these are two different meanings. If we say that XY is an X, what we really mean is that XY is-plus an X, that XY has the property of being X, but also has other properties. If we say that XY is an XY, we mean that XY is identical to XY, that XY has the complete set of properties that defines XY.

A philosopher once said "A white horse is a horse, but a horse is not a white horse," to prove a contradiction, but that is mere sophistry. With proper words, we can now say that a white horse is-plus a horse, but a white horse is-not-equal-to a horse (assuming that being a horse is a property, and being white is a property, and a white horse is the thing that has both properties). A white horse is-equals a white horse, and a horse is-equals a horse.

So when I say that every real dog is the Essential dog, I mean that every real dog is-plus the Essential dog, because it has the property of being a dog, but real dogs will also have many other properties, each specific to that actual real dog. We can never say that the Essential dog is-equal to any real dog, because the Essential dog lives only in our minds and thoughts, but real dogs are in Reality, in the external world, in objective existence. The property of being a dog is not in our minds, it exists out in the external world, but that property, as such, is-plus every real dog. The logical notation for "X is-plus Y" is "X =+ Y," and the symbol for "X is-equals Y" is "X == Y". These are the two senses in which you can assert that X is Y, that an X is a Y.

Going back to what we said before, a dog is-plus a canine, a canine is-plus a mammal, a mammal is-plus an animal, an animal is-plus a living thing, and a living thing is-plus a thing. But a dog isn't-equals a living thing, as such. If being an animal is one thing, and being a plant is one thing, and animals and plants are living things, then there is one property, the property of being a living thing, that both animals and plants have, but an animal also has another set of properties, as an animal, that plants do not have, and having those animal properties make a living thing be an animal and not be a plant. If we define animal as X, define plant as Y, and define living thing as Z, then an animal is XZ and a plant is YZ, and XZ is-not-equals YZ, but XZ is-plus Z and YZ is-plus Z, so both XZ and YZ are-plus Z, and it is also true that Z is-equals Z. Animals and plants are the same thing as a living thing, but are different types of living things as the types of living things they are.

You mentioned three meanings of "is, to be." You only defined two meanings. What is the third?

That to be, is to exist. To exist means to be something in objective reality, which means, to have the property of existing objectively. To exist objectively is to have specific properties of being at a place and time in Reality, in our spacetime, and also to have the property of being objective. To be objective is to not be subjective, which means, to exist outside of consciousness, to be independent of, and completely separate from, the insides of our minds, and to be independent and separate from perception and awareness.

If objective reality is separate from perception, then we never see it?

No. That is not a position that follows logically. You could see, and directly perceive, objective reality. If something is not created by your mind or by your act of perceiving it, and what you are looking at is outside your mind, is literally outside of your physical brain, then it could be objective. There is no reason to assume that what you see, only exists subjectively, in your mind, or that sight and thought bias the objects that are seen or thought about. That is an assumption, axiom, or position, that you can choose to believe, but, in logic, it is not the only possible position. You could take the position that the world that you experience in sense-perception does exist objectively.

III. PROPERTIES AND NAMES

You said that XY is X times Y. What did you mean by that?

There is an analogy, that for a thing to have two properties, for it to be one thing but to be two things at the same time, is like a number, which is the product of multiplying two other numbers together, such that being each number becomes a property of the product, so the product is-equals itself but is-plus also each of the original numbers in relation to the other number.

For example, 3 times 2 is 6. 6 is two sets of three things. To be number, is to be a set of things, where set is that number of things. So, 6 is 2, six things is two things, because six things is two things where each of those two things it itself a set of three things. And, likewise, 6 is 3, because six things is three things where each of those three things is itself a set of two things. Six is equal to XXX + XXX, which is two sets of XXX, which is two things, which is the number two. Six is also equal to XX + XX + XX, which is three sets of XX, which is three things, which is the number three. So 6 is-plus 2, and 6 is-plus 3. And 3 times 2 is-equal to 6. So I would say, for the sake of convenience, in my language of essential logic, that XY is X times Y.

Take this example. A red chair is both red, and a chair, it has the property of being red, and it has the property of being a chair, so, conceptually, a red chair, as a thing, is red times chair. 2 x 3 = 6. Red x Chair = Red Chair. A red chair is red in relation to being a chair, but it is a chair, in relation to being red. It is both red and a chair, so a red chair is-plus red, and it is-plus a chair, although it is-equals a red chair. And so on.

Being red is an attribute, a property, of the chair, but I would also assert that, for the red chair, being a chair is an attribute of its redness, being chair-shaped and chair-structured is a property of that red color. This is why I prefer to speak of things and properties, and not to speak of a substance and its attributes. In Ancient Greece, their logic, which is sort of similar to mine, said that they assert attributes of a substance. But, for a thing, all of its properties are primary, there is no primary and secondary properties, so you could never say that one property is a substance, and others are the attributes of that substance, you can say only that one property is essential relative to other properties as specifics, and that, for this thing, this set of properties is all one thing, as a thing.

So that is XY. It's like logic is analogous to math. But then, given your theory of multiplication and products, what about X squared?

Well, 3 squared, would be three sets of three, which is why 3 times 3 equals 9.

For an example of non-arithmetic things, say, for example, that economics squared is economic economics, but compare it to, for example, philosophical economics. Philosophical economics would seek to study economics and its subject matter using the methods and rules of philosophy. But economic economics, in other words, economics squared, would seek to study economics and its subject matter using the methods and rules of economics. This is an imperfect example, but surely you get my point.

Wow. I have never heard of philosophical economics. What is it?

Ha ha, I think that is a long subject, outside the scope of us figuring out whether Fluffy here is a dog. I have named her Fluffy, by the way. But that does introduce one other point, which I would like to clarify. A thing, and what it is, and what it is as a certain type of thing. Like with is-plus and is-equal, there has been a remarkable lack of clarity and precision in the English language, which most philosophers did nothing to solve. A thing is a set of properties, as a thing, which means, as one thing. What a thing is, is the thing, but with a focus on the individual set of properties, with each property in that set being considered individually, even though the analysis understands that, ultimately, it is one thing. And, when you speak of a thing as something, the word "as," indicates that you are talking about what the thing is, but with special emphasis or focus, for your inquiry, on only that property, within what it is, that is the essence of the thing that you are thinking of it as. That is the meaning of the word "as."

For example, Fluffy here has the property of being in this basket that I am carrying her in, and she has the property of being alive today, but she also has the property of maybe being a dog or some other type of animal, she has a property of being a type of animal, although we don't know what that property is, yet. She is a thing, and her properties are all one thing as a thing, but what she is, as a type of animal, is precisely what we are trying to figure out. Which means we are looking at her (a thing), then we are looking at all her properties (what the thing is), and then we are isolating her property as a dog or as a type of an animal (the thing as a dog), and then we are trying to analyze that one property, but in relation to Fluffy in her entirety.

We can look at Fluffy and examine her, obviously, but we are attempting to figure out, using logic, what conditions she would have to meet, to be a dog. For which we need to know what it means for any thing to be something and meet the conditions necessary to count as a thing of such-and-such a type. And that is where we are in this analysis. In this sense, every real dog is the essential dog as dog, but real dogs are not the essential dog as a real dog. Also, to speak of "a thing as such," which also means, "a thing in itself," is to refer to a thing as that thing whose essence is the entirety of its properties of being that thing. The logical notation for "as" is: X = e(XS as X), which, translated to English, says "The property of being X is the essence of an X as X where X also has other specifics S," where "e(X)" means "the essence of X," X is a thing, and "S" means "Specifics, a set of specific properties that are non-essential relative to the essence under consideration."

Do we need to get Fluffy's DNA tested, then? Since that is the essence of being a dog?

Well, we could, and we would have to, to be 100% certain. But I intend to take her home, and observe her behavior, today. If she behaves like a dog, and behaves like no other animal besides a dog, then I would feel confident in saying that I was 99% certain that she is a dog, because only being a dog, only having dog DNA, would cause her to be dog-shaped, and to behave like a dog, and I know of no other property which would cause that, so I can infer the essence, because the consequence requires it. And, for all practical purposes, there is no difference between knowing something that is 99% certain knowledge, or being 100% certain knowledge, although there could always be borderline cases that act as challenges where there is a real difference between 99% knowing vs. 100% knowing. 99% of the time there is no difference between being 99% certain or being 100% certain. And when we say 99% certain, we mean that the thing will be true 99% of the time, in other words, most of the time, but, if I am 100% certain, then it will always be true, necessarily and universally, hence 100% of the time.

I am looking at Fluffy, and she does look sort of dog-shaped, now, doesn't she? So I'll take her home, see if she behaves like a dog, eats dog food, drinks from the toilet, plays fetch, and barks, and marks her territory when I walk her. That is my hypothesis, which experience can confirm, on the basis of logic. On the other hand, if she behaves exactly like a cat, or like a large hamster or gerbil, and if she does not behave like a dog at all, then empirical observations and experience will refute my theory, and I will go back to the idea that she might not be a dog. For the logic of science, first, logic will define the set of expectations that you would expect to see if a theory is true, and then, you actually look at reality, and see if it exists, to prove your theory true, or false, if what you had expected to see does not exist, using the logic of science.

So now we can tell whether your pet is a dog. But did we ever decide what the word "dog" means? I guess it just refers to the essence of being a dog? To that set of properties that constitutes dogness? Or does it refer to the essential dog? Or does it refer to the set of all real dogs, as dog?

Well, yes, the word "dog" is a symbol or set of symbols, in a language, the English language, and that symbol, according to the rules of that language, has been mapped to a thing, what it refers to, and the thing that it refers to or corresponds to in the language-map, the map that maps symbols to things where each symbol corresponds to and refers to something, that corresponding thing is the meaning of the word. But, yes, then, the issue is, for a proper name, like Fluffy, we know that it refers to this Object in my basket, but with a word like "dog," what does it really refer to, and how does it do so?

There are many position a person could take, as you alluded to. That the word "dog" is a naming function which refers to the set of things that satisfy its conditions.

That the word "dog" names a form or class, such as a Platonic Idea, which class or form then gets instantiated in reality, in every real dog which participates in that idea, and so identity comes from ideas in our minds, and things are just merely in our minds. You could take the position, as the great Objectivist philosopher Ayn Rand held, that the word "dog" refers to an abstract idea, and that abstract ideas are merely a way to organize and sort and group concretes together, so there isn't an actual thing, as such, that the word refers to, it means only a certain way of organizing concretes.

Then there is my position: that the word "dog," used in reference to an abstract or theoretical dog and not to any specific real dog in its sentence or statement where used, refers to the essential dog, but, because the essential dog has only the property of being a dog and no other property, logically it really refers to the essential properties of a dog, and, because every real dog has that essence as a dog, the word "dog" by implication can refer to the set of all real dogs. Because every real dog is-plus the essential dog. So, if you say "A dog is man's best friend," you are talking about all real dogs, but you are talking about them as dogs, because they are dogs, which means that you are referring to them by means of referring to that essential property they all possess that makes them be a dog, and you are not referring to them by reference to some other property.

Because the essential dog is a dog, although it is not a real dog, the essential dog would be included in that set of all dogs you are talking about, because the essential dog has the property of being a dog (but no other specific properties). When thinkers do what is called a "thought experiment," what this really is, (at least when done correctly,) is asserting the Essential Thing, in their imagination, and then deducing the consequences of that Essential Thing. It is based on logic, not on "teasing out intuitions," which is a misinterpretation of thought experiments. What is true of the Essential X must be true of all real Xs, as Xs. The focus of logic is objective reality and the external world, not imagination or intuition.

For another example, say that you have four people in a room, four people named Bob, George, Jessica, and Vanessa. Bob is black-haired, Vanessa is red-haired, and George and Jessica are blonde-haired. The phrase "the blonde-haired people in the room" is a naming function that is solved, and is only solved, by George and Jessica. That statement refers to those two people, but it picks them out only by their hair, the condition that they meet, to be what the statement, the naming function, refers to. George and Jessica are-plus blonde hair. But, if someone instead enters the room and asks to speak to Bob, then he picks out the object named Bob, by proper name, and Bob is-equals Bob, a person. So, if, to extend the example, these four people are actors, looking for roles, and the casting director needs to cast two blonde people, they should ask for "the blonde-haired people in the room," and they get George and Jessica because George and Jessica are blonde, but if they specifically want to see Bob audition for a role, that he might be perfect for, they should ask for Bob by name, and they will get Bob. The proper name and the phrase are both naming functions that are solved by things which have the defined condition, it is just that the proper name is solved by one real Object, but the phrase is solved by an essential property. If the casting director asked for "the black-haired people in the room," she would get the same object as if she asked for Bob, but for a different reason, because she picked him out by his property of being black-haired, not by his property of being Bob, even though being Bob does include being black-haired plus lots of other stuff.

Great, so it sounds, to me, like you are defining the set as everything that satisfies the conditions of having the essential properties for that set (to be included in that set), and then you define the word as a name that names everything such that the name is a naming function that is solved by the set of all things that have that property, and the naming function simply refers to its solution. Am I right? Do I understand you correctly?

IV. MATH AND LOGIC

Yes. And here we can now discuss Bertrand Russell's Paradox, and the reason why, to me, it is mere sophistry, and shows a lack of understanding of logic, on his part. His paradox is simply this: consider a set that is defined as a set that has a property of not being a member of itself. If it is not a member of itself, then it is what it is, but then it would have the property of not being a member of itself, under which condition it would be included in that set, in which case it would then be a member of itself. But if it is a member of itself, then it is not what it is, which was the set of all members which are not a member of that set. You see? But, actually, with essential logic defined correctly, there could never be a set that was not a member of itself, because, to define a set, you name, define, describe, an essence, a property or set of properties, and then anything which has those properties would be in that set.

For example, the set of all dogs is always a member of itself, because the set of all dogs is the set of all dogs, and the set has the property of being itself, and therefore it is within that set, because it is-equals that set of things which are within that set, and therefore it is included in itself. In other words, the set is-equal to the set of all of its members, and all of its members are within the set, therefore the set as a whole is within the set, therefore the set is always a member of itself, because the set is-equal to all the members of itself. So a set, which was not a member of itself, would be a thing, that would lack its own essence as that type of thing, and then it would not be that thing. I think the only way Bertrand Russell's Paradox would cause concern for someone is if they didn't fully understand what a set is, and what it means to be a member of a set. A set is the set of all things that have the essential property or properties that define the set. So a set will always be-equal-to all of its members, and, if the members are members of the set, then the set is a member of itself.

So, in my opinion, Bertrand Russell named and stated a contradiction, but, by its own very nature, that contradiction could never exist, it could never be something, it could never be. So he named and pointed out a contradiction, but it poses not threat to logic, because its actual existence, in reality, ever, is impossible. And yet, at the time when he articulated it, all the great and famous logicians ran around like chickens with their heads cut off when the sky is falling, because they thought he had discovered something that posed a threat to logic, or which disproved logic. Logic can never be disproved, if a thing is a thing. If everything is something and every thing is a thing, then logic will always be true. No one will ever be able to refute or disprove logic, as such.

But what about a thing which is not a thing? It would be a thing, but, as what it is, it would not be a thing.

What you are referring to is zero, which is zero things, which is not anything, which is a thing for which the negation of every property is asserted. To be a thing is to be something, to have some property, so a thing which is not a thing would be a thing with all properties negated, and that thing, is-equal-to zero, because zero is that thing which has the negation of every property. For example, if X is red, then Not X is a thing that has the property of red negated, that literally is not red, that does not have the property of being red. If X is 5, then Not 5 = Not X, Not X is the negation of 5, and Not X describes every thing that lacks the property of being 5 things. But, if X is a thing that has literally every property negated, it would have no properties, it would not be a thing. And I define zero as that thing which has every property negated. Zero is the negation of every property, and therefore is the negation, as such, of being a thing.

Zero is zero things, zero is nothing, the void, absence. It has the numeric property of being zero, but it also has exactly zero properties of being any actual number. But it is zero things, therefore it is zero real things, and therefore it is zero things in physical reality, so it has no existence, as such, as zero, as void, in our reality. It is merely a conceptual place where we end up, if we assert that a thing is not X, and is not Y, and is not Z, and so on, but then we assert that it is not every property, from the set of all properties, such that it is not any thing, and we are then left with nothing, zero, void, not-everything, nothingness, non-existence. But, again, it does not exist, because it is not a thing which exists. You and I, my friend, on the other hand, we do exist. So it need not trouble and concern us. Zero is, in the sense you describe, is a contradiction, it is X as a thing and is Not X as zero things, but it is a contradiction that does not and cannot exist. Because it does not exist, and cannot exist, it poses no problem for us. If logic is true, we would expect every logical contradiction to not exist, and to be unable to exist. Logic is true.

Why is logic always true? Can you prove it?

Yes. To be true is to be a word or statement that refers to something that exists. In contrast, to be false, is to be a word, or statement, that refers to something that does not exist. That is the definition of true and false. True or false are properties that belong only to words and statements in a language. A language is a map that maps things or sets of things to symbols or sets of symbols, where the symbols are arranged according to the rules of the language to form statements, where the symbol or set of symbols is a word, or a statement (a sentence), and the thing or set of things, that the symbol refers to or corresponds to according to the language-map, is the meaning of the word or statement.

So, for example, the statement "I just named this dog Fluffy," is true, if, in reality, the thing shown by the words, the thing to which the statement refers, exists, but, if the statement says a thing which does not exist, then it is false, and, if I say something false, that means I lied.

Logic is always true, because logic will necessarily only state true things, because to be logical is to not be in a contradiction, so that which is illogical is a contradiction. It then remains only for us to prove that a contradiction cannot exist. Zero is not a thing, yet zero is a thing. Zero is a contradiction. Every contradiction always resolves to zero, or else it resolves to two things, one of which is X, and the other of which is Not X, but that resolves to X minus X, which, again, equals zero. Take, for example, "X or Y, and Not X." In logic, the solution, then, is Y. X, as a solution, is a contradiction. Why? Because if X is the solution, then X is true, but the second statement said Not X, which means that X is false, so, if X is true, then X is both true (as the solution) and false (per the second statement). Then X is not at one with itself, X is not one thing, it is two things, and is therefore not a thing, and is therefore zero. And, X minus X, which is equivalent to X and Not X, would equal zero. You can always say, that being X, will cause the thing that is both X and Not X, to be X, which will cause it to not not be X, so the thing that is both X and Not X could never exist. A contradiction will always reduce to zero, and zero is always zero real things in existence.

Why, then, given the above, do you know that Y is true?

Because of the first statement, which said that Y could be true (and also said that, other than given other statements, X could be true). Y can be true, X or Y can be true, but X cannot be true, which leaves behind Y as the only option that could be true. Therefore, Y is necessarily true. When logic proves that only one solution can be true, then that solution must be true and is necessarily true. To say that X is "proven" true, means that a logical deduction showed that X as true is the only solution. And to say that X is "known," or is "knowledge," simply means that we believe that X is the only true solution that is possible, to say that X is knowledge means that we believe X is necessarily true and cannot be false, according to our belief (and that belief, itself, is the actual knowledge). In any deduction, you begin with axioms, definitions, and propositions, all of which are asserted as conditions of the solution, a true thing which exists, and the solution is that one thing (or set of any things) of which every statement in the proof can be asserted without contradicting itself or any other statement that is true (for the solution). A proof asserts every statement, which includes every definition, axiom, and asserted proposition, of one thing, and the one thing that solves and satisfies all statements without contradiction is the solution, which is the conclusion of the proof.

Logic must always be true, and can never be false, because any contradiction will resolve to zero, so the illogical cannot exist, and to say that something is logical, is to say that it is proven, and known, to resolve to one, to resolve to being at one with itself, and not to be equal to a zero, not to be a contradiction. On the other hand, that which is logical, always resolves to One, that X is X, that X is one thing equal to X, that X as X is one, that X is one thing, that X is at one with itself, being without a contradiction that would make it two opposed to each other, an X that is X and an X that is not X. This is what the axiom "A is A," the axiom of identity, in logic, really means.

Therefore, my logic is complete and consistent, in the sense that every proposition, which is logical, could be proven, given a sufficient set of data from which to deduce the truth. Being an empirical essentialist, I hold that things, as sets of properties, are directly perceived, so, yes, analytical truths, which are necessarily true, are a posteriori, are synthetic, and arise from the world of experience and the physical world. We are not born having read Kant's Critique of Pure Reason, instead, we learn it (if we learn it), as do we learn all things. Try asking a three-year-old child what they know analytically a priori. Nothing, and yet that is the extent of Kantian or Platonic intuition, as knowledge that does not arise from experience and inference and having been learned in the physical world of sensations.

Wittgenstein once objected to my theory of language, by saying that, when we know the meaning of a word, we do not look it up in a set of language-maps, corresponding each symbol to some thing, to then arrive at a meaning. But we did. In school, as children, learning our language, we did. It takes us years, as children, in school, to learn language. We do not look up every word on our map, now, only because we memorized the map, that comprises the English language, and so now we can do so, from memory, at an instant.

To say that "X means Y" is to say that what thing the symbol "X" refers to, according to the language-map of this language, either is-plus or is-equals whatever thing is referred to by the symbol "Y" according to this language map. A translation from one language to another, merely takes one language-map, such as a map that maps symbols to numbers such that {X:1, Y:2}, takes another language-map, such as {A:1, B:2}, and then infers the meaning from one set of symbols and then infers the second set of symbols from the meaning, to arrive at the second set of symbols, the translation in the second language. So the translation is {A:X, B:Y}.

I use brackets and colons to indicate a map of symbols to meanings in a language-map. If, in language L, the language-map is {A:1, B:2, C:3}, then, when speaking L, you could say "A plus B equals C," and you would mean that $1 + 2 = 3$. A sample of a small subset of the English language-map is {apple: "apple," dog: "dog"}, where the word refers to the thing so named, and the word in quotation marks refers to the word that names the thing.

Although, often, when one says "X means Y," one is asserting that X is-plus Y but also implying that X is the thing and Y is what it is. A normal fluent speaker will have his language-map of symbols-to-meanings memorized, to be recalled from memory at a moment's notice. And if we can't, then, still, we look up the meaning of a word in a dictionary, or look up the meaning of a statement in an encyclopedia. Language, like logic, is entirely learned from experience, none of it really comes from a priori intuition or instinct, although when we say "I know X by intuition," what we really mean is, we know X, but we do not understand how we arrived at that knowledge, nor do we understand X well enough to assert a conscious definition of X.

But, being an empirical essentialist, and an Essentialist Objectivist, I have a principle of empirical induction, for the a posteriori synthetic analytic necessary and universal truth, which other Empiricists lack, and which renders Immanuel Kant entirely unnecessary, within the realm of philosophy. It is simply this: you see things, and you see a thing's properties, so the essential property, too, is directly perceived. If you perceive a real X, you perceive the property that is the essence of X, you see X being an X, but you see that property also being many other properties, like being at a real specific place and time, and other specifics, that all real things have. Having then been known, and learned, you can quite easily use essential logic, as I explained it to you, to deduce the consequence of the essence, and then say "All X Are Y," where X is the essence, and Y is the consequence.

Perception, induction, deduction, and proof, all existing in perfect harmony. For example, some philosophers would say that "2 + 2 = 4" is the textbook analytical a priori claim. I can prove it empirically, a posteriori, in a way that is necessary and universal, using symbols themselves as symbols of all things. Say that X is X and Y is Y. Say that X is-plus Z and Y is-plus Z. Picture two Xs and two Ys. I can diagram:

XX + YY.

Now consider them as Zs.

XXYY becomes

ZZZZ.

Given the postulates:

XXYY = ZZZZ.

XXYY is 2 + 2 as 2 Xs and 2 Ys.

ZZZZ is 4 as 4 Zs.

Therefore 2 + 2 = 4.

And, because these symbols could mean anything, because they have no specifics other than the essence of being something that can be counted, this must be true of anything.

If you count the number of Xs, Ys, and Zs, you can reason that 2 + 2 = 4, just by looking at XXYY and ZZZZ. But these symbols, as things, could represent anything. So the claim is proven universal, and necessary for any thing. This is similar to how deduction and proof in geometry work, where what you prove of a drawing, which represents all shapes of a type, must be true of all shapes of that type, because you proved it is true because the drawing possesses the essential properties of that shape, and no non-essential properties interfered, and so the drawing actually represents the Essential Thing, and you deductively proved the consequence of the essence by asserting a conclusion of this drawing of an Essential Thing, but using the physical, sensation-perceived drawing itself as an example.

Math, proven by these symbols, these Xs and Ys and Zs, that you are looking at, and seeing, as sense-perceived sensations, by your own eyes. The a posteriori synthetic contingent physical matter, manifesting itself as a priori analytic necessary logical truth. Because basic numbers of things, like 2 things or 4 things, a group of 2 things or a set of 4 items, are a directly perceivable property, you can see a group of four things, you could look out your window and see four dogs playing with each other, for example, so you are seeing four dogs as four things, and four things is-equal to the number four, you can infer that essence from sensations, and then quite easily deduce a universal necessary consequence from the essence, and reason that 2 + 2 = 4, from a combination of induction from sensations and then deduction from logic.

V. ON LANGUAGE, TRUTH, AND PROOF

You have said some complicated stuff, friend. Hold on, there. Please slow down. Can we please unpack it? If we perceive essential properties, if we see the number four when we see four dogs, then why can't we just look at poor little Fluffy and know immediately whether she is a dog?

What does it mean, "to assert something"? And, for example, what does it mean, to say "X is Y"? I seem to remember, from logic class in college, that really means "There exists an X such that for all X, X equals Y," or something like that, right?

If you say "The present king of France is bald," what does that statement refer to, because no such thing exists? Is that statement true or false?

If you say "Apollo visited me in a dream last night," what does the name Apollo refer to (assuming you believe Greek mythology is fiction)?

What about the statement "I wonder whether William Shakespeare was really Francis Bacon"? Are you referring to Shakespeare or Bacon or both or neither? And is that statement true, or false?

You also mentioned that zero is a thing, in a sense, but it is not really a thing. What does it mean to refer to something "in a sense"? When you use language, do you refer to a reference, but you mean it in a certain sense, such that reference and sense are different, and the meaning of the statement combines them both? Sense is not logical and can't be analyzed, it is an amorphous emotional feeling, the way the word feels, really, so that might throw a monkey wrench into your logic.

Ha ha, thank you, for challenging me, my friend! Yes, I can unpack all of that. One by one. I can see a dog behaving, and see a dog's shape, and then infer the essence. Some properties are directly perceived, and, for things for which those are the essence, those essences are directly perceived. But some properties of things are not directly perceived, they are inferred from knowledge that comes from sensory experience, but are not known directly by being directly seen themselves. I can taste fried eggs, and I perceive their essence as fried eggs, and I know that my wife cooked them for me this morning, but I infer that, from a set of sensations plus logical deduction and inference, I do not see that directly. So the essence of the eggs as what my wife cooked is inferred, not perceived, although I know it through physical sensation plus logical inferences.

Fluffy's doghood and dogness, sadly, is not one we can see, instead we must figure it out, from what we can see, on the basis of what we see.

You could very easily translate "X is Y" into "There exists an X such that for all X, X equals Y," although the two statements are not identical, and each one means exactly what it says. Typically, when someone says "X is Y," because of the confusion about the different meanings of "is, to be" all lumped together in English, what they really mean is this: "I assert that X exists, and I assert that X is-plus Y." If someone says "The present king of France is bald," that statement, by implication, reduces to two statements: "France presently has a king," and "that person from the first clause so described, the present king of France, is-plus bald." France does not presently have a king, so the first clause's meaning is false, and France does not presently have a king, so the king of France can be neither bald nor full-haired, so the meaning of the second clause is neither true nor false.

If someone says "Apollo visited me in a dream last night," they assert "Apollo visited me in a dream last night," and also, it is implied that they assert that "Apollo exists" and "Apollo is the Greek God of Light, who did such-and-such in this-or-that Greek myth," which anyone who knows who Apollo was, would understand. It is true that Apollo is that Greek God so described by Greek myths, so that clause is true, but Apollo does not exist, so the clause that asserts he visited you, is false.

With respect to "I wonder whether William Shakespeare was really Francis Bacon"? The "I wonder" part is true if you really wonder it (if the "you" that is wondering it exists, in other words, if you exist and you are wondering it). The "Whether William Shakespeare was really Francis Bacon" second asserts that Shakespeare was the Shakespeare known to have written such-and-such plays, asserts that Bacon was the historical figure Bacon, but then asserts that Shakespeare is-equals Bacon. That assertion is a factual claim, which only historians could answer, or perhaps, no one will ever answer. Questions can be neither true or false, because they do not assert that a thing exists, instead, a question asks whether a thing exist, so a question calls for an answer, and the answer can be true or false.

But how can you refer to something that doesn't exist? For a false statement.

The statement itself exists, but the object to which it refers, does not exist. The statement is false. The set of symbols exist, which, according to the language-map and the rules of this language, would assert that X exists, or that X is Y, but X does not exist, or X is not Y. If X does not exist, it is false. If X is not Y, it is false, but only because X is not Y (because the X that is Y does not exist), not because the Object named by X does not exist. Usually, when you say X is Y, you can always isolate the clause as asserting that X exists, from the clause that asserts that X is-plus Y.

For example, if I say "Water is H2O," I mean that water exists, and water is H2O, although, by implication, I also mean that the consequence of the essence of being water is being H2O, which means that all water is H2O. One statement may assert each of these things, and you must analyze the statement, to see what it really means, to see which things it asserts. Water is one thing, but the word "water" identifies it by being a clear, tasteless liquid in oceans and rivers and that humans drink, while H_2O identifies it by its chemical composition. "Water is H_2O" asserts that water is-plus H_2O, which really means (probably) that water is water because water is H_2O, that water is a clear, tasteless liquid in oceans and rivers and that humans drink, because it has the chemical composition H_2O.

Thus, it is yet another example of an empirical analytical claim, disproving the old wives' tale that an assertion is either factual/empirical/synthetic or a priori/analytic/necessary, or that it can't be true that "Water is H_2O, yet water is water, and H_2O is H_2O," because water isn't-equals H_2O. The properties that the word "water" picks out, are not-equal-to the properties that H_2O picks out, but "Water is H_2O," again, really means that the essence of water has the consequence of being H_2O, in which case "All water is H_2O." It is not correct to categorize assertions based on whether they are analytic/necessary or synthetic/contingent. Water is necessarily H_2O relative to the consequence of the thing as that essence. But this is a claim that arose from empirical observations and science, not from abstract "Pure Reason," not from mind turned in upon itself and never looking at the outside world.

What the analytic/synthetic distinction is getting at, is that "water is-equals water" is analytic, but "water is-plus H_2O" is synthetic, yet they know that water, by its definition, will always be H_2O, the word f(water) will always return the set of all H_2O, hence it also seems necessary, and this confuses the Kantians. Using essential logic could solve all their problems.

Water is-equals H_2O only in the sense that water is one thing and that one thing will always be picked out by the naming function "water" or by the separate and semantically distinct naming function "H_2O," despite the fact that the essence of water as water is-not-equals the essence of H_2O as H_2O, one is a directly observable property and the other is a property discovered only by chemistry and inference. But with the right words, this is not a problem.

The same issue would arise any time Y is a consequence of the essence of X but where the X property is-not-equal-to the Y property. X is not Y, in a necessary sense, because the X property is not identical to the Y property, yet all X are Y, in a necessary sense, because, for all X, X is Y, because Y is the consequence of the essence of X, so being X will cause being Y, so every thing that is X is Y necessarily. The essence-consequence "All X are Y" essential logic, as distinct from saying that "the X property is-equals the Y property," is the correct way that linguistic precision solves this problem. We should retire the analytic/synthetic, necessary/contingent lens, and just use logic and language correctly. You could have two different naming functions, each of which returns the same set of Objects, but for different reasons. So you could say the two functions are contingently identical but analytically distinct.

Yet, what if the reason why they are the same set, is because one function names the essence, and the other function names the consequence? Then, they are identical analytically as the analysis of the essence and consequence, but not analytically as the definitions of the naming function, from prior to the essential deductive logic. So a set of Objects can be contingently identical, analytically identical, and analytically not identical, at the same time, but in different sense.

Here let me briefly mention, Aristotle's first principle of logic, "A thing cannot both be and not be, at the same time, and in the same respect," where "respect," here, means "as measured in relation to the same thing," and I often say "sense" when I mean "respect." Twelve inches long is one foot long, and twelve is not one, so one thing cannot be both twelve long and be one long at the same time, but one thing can be twelve long in relation to one thing (inches) and be one long in relation to a different thing (feet), at the same time, and that is not a contradiction, because they both are and are not, at the same time, but in different respects.

Good gravy, I learned a lot, already, just from passing you by on the street and meeting you by chance and stopping to chat with you today! And I feel like I may learn more, too. You say that logic is complete and consistent. I seem to recall... from Philosophy 101 in college, or, wait, was it Logic 101? Someone, someone famous, proved that no system of arithmetic logic can ever be complete and consistent. I remember it... It was kind of a big deal.

Yes. You refer to Kurt Gödel's Incompleteness Theorems. Much was made of them. Much ado about nothing. They are mere sophistry, based upon a complete and utter misunderstanding of the concepts involved, namely, the concept of logic and the concept of language.

Can you please explain your refutation of Gödel to me?

Certainly. Gödel translated his native language, German, into a language where words and statements were expressed as numbers. He then invented a way to deduce the logical results of statements, through arithmetic and logic operations on these numbers, in his language. For my refutation, we must first assume, as an axiom, that any language can be translated into any other language, and, in every language L, if we apply logic to statement X, we will get logical result Y, where Y is the result of logic applied to X, in language L. Here, L can be any language. We must assume that the Gödel language is not special, and the only special thing about it, was a certain genius in using math for expressing semantic content. Gödel then used the statement "This statement is unprovable," then he used math to cause the statement to refer to itself within his proof function math, and he showed that, in his Gödel language, that statement was, in fact, numerically such that it could be neither proved true nor proved false, or, if it was proved by his math to be true, then it was false, and then it was a contradiction, and therefore could never be proven. He took this as proof that there is at least one statement that logic can never prove true or false, and therefore every system of logic is necessarily never perfectly complete.

And he was wrong, why exactly?

Because, to be a statement, in a language L, the statement must refer to a thing, other than itself, according to the rules and symbols-to-meanings language-map for L. To be proven, is to be proven true, and a statement can only be true or false, if it asserts something, that can exist or not exist. And a statement is proven true, if and only if logic proves that the thing existing is the only condition that can exist and that the thing not existing cannot exist, in other words, that it is necessary that this thing exists, because if the thing does not exist, if the statement was false, then a logical contradiction results.

A statement cannot refer to itself. A statement that refers to itself is not a statement. "This statement is unprovable," is true, if it is false, and is false, if it is true, to infinity. But "This statement" does not refer to anything, because self-reference is impossible, there is no thing with meaningful semantic content to which "This statement is unprovable," refers, self-reference contradicts the essence of language. So the Gödel sentence never begins with any truth or false value, and so is never true, then false, then true, then false, into infinity. It cannot be proven, but it is not a statement, so it does not prove that logic is incomplete for all statements. Logic is complete for all things, therefore logic is complete for all statements which assert things.

The Gödel statement is not a statement. It cannot be proven true or false because it fails to make an assertion that something exists, which would be true if it did exist or false if it did not, and which would be proven true if its logic resolves to the condition that its existence is necessary or proven false if logic resolves to the condition that its existence is a contradiction. And this would be the result of logic applied to the Gödel sentence, if the Gödel sentence is translated into any language: Gödel's number language, English, German, Spanish, Japanese, or any language L, where L is a language. That the Gödel sentence is unprovable, fails to prove that logic is incomplete, because it fails to prove the existence of a statement that can't be proven true or untrue by logic, because the Gödel sentence is not a statement.

Mere sophistry. And yet he is regarded as one of the greatest logicians and philosophers of all time, within Analytic philosophy. Little more than a scam artist or con artist. His math muddies the waters to make them appear deep. And, while he asserted that his conclusions applied only to set theory and arithmetic logic, most people assumed it would apply to all logic. The semantics clearly would have. And that was the end of any serious attempt by philosophers to create a complete, consistent system of logic. Other than me, and a handful of others, all of whom were ostracized and excluded from the university academia environment.

The Gödel argument is similar to the so-called Liar's Paradox, that puzzled philosophers for a long time, that someone says "This statement is false," and, if it is false, it is true, but then it is false, but then it is true, etc. That statement is also not a statement. There is nothing to which "This statement" refers, and, because it fails to assert a thing, it can be neither true nor false, because there is not a thing that would exist, to cause it to be true, or not exist, to cause it to be false, which it is referring to, as a statement, when it says "This statement." The statement itself exists, as a statement, but not as a thing asserted by a statement, and a statement cannot refer to itself and assert its own existence in a directly self-referential way, language simply cannot do that, it defies the nature of language. The Liar's Paradox sentence is neither true nor false, and it has no meaning. It is formed by words, which each have meanings, but when you put those words together, in this way, such that the meanings would combine and would be one meaning, it means nothing.

You can form sentences that have no meaning and which are not statements. If you take a collection of random words and toss them in the air, you could form a sentence, but it is just random words, it would not be a Speaker asserting a thing to an Audience. "Hat car retrospect August inviolate orchid Grizzly negligent Michael it's could Basketball terminated lazy exceptionally," is a sentence, and each word has a meaning, and you could add the meanings of each word together in sum to try to form a meaning for the sentence, but, really, it has no meaning, it's just random words, it does not assert something, so it can't be true or false, and can't be proved or disproved. Only things can exist or not and be proven to exist or not, so logic only deals with statements that assert things, with statements that have meanings. Sentences which have no meaning are properly outside the scope of logic, but they have no meaning, hence they do not matter, and they do not limit the scope of logic in any meaningful way. The Gödel sentence, and the Liar's Paradox sentence, likewise, contain words with meanings, and you can sum those words to attempt to find a meaning for the statement, but there is no thing that is being asserted, because the statements attempt to be self-referential. As statements, they have no meanings.

On a related note, relating to the nature of language, too, if you take all the words in the English language, and arrange them, randomly, into every possible combination of words, and fill an infinite library with infinite books so created, you would not, in fact, have every possible statement and every possible book. Why? Of course, an actual infinity is impossible in physical reality, unless you define infinity to include non-actualized potential in the future, because infinity is a never-ending series, so you could never have an actual library with an infinite number of books. But we can solve that problem, by defining a finite length for the books, say, for example, two thousand pages long. Because the books are finite, and the number of characters and symbols in the English language is finite, you could, in theory, have a library with every possible book, defined as such, and the library could be actual because the set of books is finite. That isn't the reason why it won't work. But it won't work.

Then why?

Because none of the sentences in any of the books are statements, and none of the books in this library are books. The library contains no books, where "books" are defined correctly, as symbols used to assert something, because no meaning was intentionally asserted, by a Speaker, to an Audience. They are just random words, sets of random symbols. If "The cow jumped over the Moon" was created by rolling dice randomly to choose words at random, it would not have a meaning. It has a meaning because you, I, and everyone, knows that those words were arranged, for a purpose, by a Speaker, to show a thing, to an Audience, and they are not a random chaos.

We infer the meaning of a statement from the Speaker's act of meaning something, the meaning is the thing that the Speaker asserts, which we infer from the set of symbols that we see, because we know the language rules for how those symbols are arranged to sum into a thing asserted by a sentence.

The meaning of a statement is the thing the Speaker seeks to show, it is the Speaker's meaning, their intention, their message. If there is no Speaker then there is no assertion, and, similarly, if there was no Audience whatsoever, there could also be no language, you could still have those markings on a page, but they would not be symbols as symbols anymore.

There is a thing, that the Speaker has in mind, and then there are symbols, and the Audience infers what was in the Speaker's mind, the thing they asserted, from the symbols, and then that thing is in the Audience's mind. Absent Speaker, and meaning, and intention, there is no meaning, just random symbols on a page, which just happened to match what could have been a statement if someone had stated it.

In theory, you could have a private language, if you were both the Speaker and the Audience, provided that you had defined a language-map that maps a set of symbols to a set of things, and you used these symbols to represent things by asserting them as a Speaker, to show things to yourself as Audence in your thoughts. But a private language, for your own thoughts, would not function precisely the same way as a public language, because there would be no need for a formal precise public set of definitions to enable another person to understand you, and you could redefine your words at will without hesitation, so a private language would be nothing more than a person's own thoughts and their own mind and consciousness, really.

It is worth speculating that, maybe, the brain itself is a language-map, that maps neurons and neural impulses as symbols, to the sensations that are received by the body's sense-perception cells as things, such that the neurons in the brain become symbols of sensations out in external reality, and the brain and its reason then computes these symbols, to arrive at a set of neural synapses in the brain, that map to essences and essential things, what is abstracted, as theory, from the set of sensations, as specifics. Such that those maps in the brain, are concepts, and, when you experience something in reality, those sensations enter the brain, they are solved by the naming functions, that is, the concepts, that describe them, and that is how your brain knows what the sensations are, and that knowledge then enables your brain to choose a response or reaction to what those sensations are, which your brain then sends to your muscles. If that is true, we could say that pure reason is practical reason, because reason is the tool by means of which a human engages with the realm of sensory experience. But that is mere speculation. Only biologists and scientists could prove that. I cannot prove that.

Also note that I am not saying that reason is merely a set of responses mapped to a set of sensory stimuli, like a behaviorist might say. I am saying that thought, reason, logic, philosophy, consciousness, self-awareness, would enable you to make conscious decisions, that were not mere fate, but your brain is a tool that could enable this, and the realm of experience is where there would be the things with respect to which you could be making these decisions, such that thought and mind could physically exist. You would not even be conscious of your brain as language-map, you would only be conscious of the objects that your brain was aware of by means of that brain-language.

Ludwig Wittgenstein once said that language and words do not have meanings, only uses, only usage. If words had no meanings, we would have no use for them. The usage of a word, is to show a thing, for a Speaker to assert a thing to an Audience. The usage is based on the meaning. A Speaker uses a statement to show a meaning to an Audience. When I ask you, "how do you use this word?", it is only because I intend to infer its meaning from how you use it. Absent this act of intention, of meaning something, that a Speaker asserts something to an Audience, you do not have language or words, in their full and properly defined necessary and sufficient conditions.

Wittgenstein, having asserted that words have no meanings, then says that language is merely a series of moves in a language-game. And the Analytic philosophers of language embraced that position, and exploited it, seeking to solve every problem and answer every question in the history of philosophy, not by solving the problems, but by redefining words so that the problems could not be stated, so that the questions cannot be asked. But that so-called solution, the philosophy of language, does nothing to solve problems or answer questions, it is merely a tool that philosophers lean on when they have no answers and can't solve the problems, but they must pretend that they do have a solution, to maintain their appearance of wisdom and knowledge.

There is a type of person for whom language is merely a language-game. The dishonest person. For whom it is a game which they play to see how much dishonesty they can get away with, by means of language, before they are caught in a lie. Or, for another example, politicians, and government, view language as merely a series of moves in a language-game, because they seek to change the meanings of words, thereby making it impossible to make statements that criticize them by referring to the objects that are the evidence of political misconduct and political corruption. Again, they play the game to see how much dishonesty they can get away with, not merely by telling lies, but by changing what words mean.

Hence, censorship will always attack language itself, much as it does in the novel "1984." For dishonest people, and for politicians, language is merely a series of moves in a language-game to play. For an honest person, language is never a game, because an honest person takes honesty seriously, and, therefore, they must always know what their words means, in order to know what they assert, so that they can verify that their statements are true.

Okay. But if self-reference is impossible, for any word in a language L, then what does the word "I" refer to?

And you mentioned "sense." Again, does a word have a sense, as isolated from its reference?

And, while you discuss what "I" refers to, if I refer to my thoughts, feelings, or sensations, to what thing do I refer? If I talk about the pain I feel, what thing am I referring to? And if it isn't a thing, is that not something, very real and important, outside the scope of logic?

When people speak of sense and reference, what they really mean, is that, when they state a statement, they assert two things, one of which is the reference (the thing referred to by explicit, conscious intention), and they also assert a second thing, the sense (the thing they refer to by implicit, unconscious emotion), but the sense and the reference are both things, as such. Take, for example, the statement "Webster Woods is selfish." This statement, as intended by the Speaker and as understood by the Audience according to the rules of the English language, may really mean: "Webster Woods exists, Webster Woods is-plus a person, Webster Woods is-plus selfish, and to be selfish is-plus evil and bad." Evil and bad, for most people, are a thing which, when they think it, they feel a corresponding emotion, a sense, or feeling, of badness, wrongness, and evil. That is all a "sense" is: a thing, asserted by implication, which, in most Audiences, will trigger some sort of feeling or emotion.

"Selfish" here is reference, as a property of Woods, and "selfish" is sense, as a thing that people feel is wrong and sinful. But a sense, in that sense, is a thing. (Note that to say "in that sense" really means "as that thing.") And any thing can be studied by logic. For example, an Objectivist might say "Webster Woods is selfish," but Objectivist morality holds that being selfish is rational, because it is based on the logic that you are yourself and therefore you should take care of yourself and put yourself first, such that selfishness, rational self-interest, has moral integrity, and is coherent to the logical statement that you are yourself, that "you = you" and "I = me," and therefore being selfish is good and ethical and moral and a virtue, so the sense, for an Objectivist, might be the opposite, that Webster Woods is selfish, so you should feel good about him. And, when you assert good, the Audience gets a warm fuzzy feeling. That is what sense is. You know the object it refers to, but you have a sense, a feeling, of what it means, but that sense is merely another thing that is asserted, which manifests more as an emotion, and less as an Object.

Emotions and feelings, too, are things. We feel them, even though we might not know what they are. They are entirely within the realm of logic and the correspondence-reference theory of language. For example, if I draw a smiley face on your birthday card, I am asserting a warm, happy feeling at you. The smiley face is true, if the feeling exists, and it is false, if I am faking it and I don't really mean it and there is no such warm happy feeling. Some would say that the smiley face communicates by sense, not by reference. I say that it does refer to something. Everything is something.

The word "I" refers to the Speaker, "I" refers to whomever said it. It is self-reference, but it is not self-reference as a word. "I" refers to the person who said it, it does not refer to the word "I" itself. I would say, for example, "I wear glasses. I am a human being." I would not say "I am the word that is the first word in this sentence." That does not make any sense. In a children's story, perhaps, you could assign personhood and self-awareness to the letter I, and have I tell a story about itself, but the letter I, the word "I," cannot actually talk about itself, in the first person, in objective reality. But people, humans, can talk about themselves using "I."

"I" is self-reference as a person, not as a word, not as the word "I." So linguistic self-reference, in the sense of the Gödel sentence, remains an utter impossibility. "I", as a naming function, is objective-relative, it is relative to who says it, but its meaning is, nonetheless, objective, not subjective. Much as the naming function f(X) = "X + 5" defines X relative to 5, but the set of things that it names, is defined in an objective way, with an objective meaning that can be true or false. If X is 4, it is true that f(X) is 9, and it would be false that f(X) is 10, and that is objective, but relative, its truth is measured in relation to 5. The word "I" is always in relation to who says it, it always points back at the Speaker, only the one who says it, solves it.

If you refer to pain, the thing you refer to is pain. That isn't the real question. The real question is, what is pain? What are sensations? People know what the word "pain" refers to, but they don't know what pain is, which is the real question to which they refer when they say they do not know what the word means. I won't prove an answer to that question, here. I think that sensations are things in objective external reality that are perceived, such that what pain is, is really the object that is causing harm to your body, but we'll leave that discussion alone, for now. But you know what you mean. Even if you don't know it well enough to formally define it. And others, by analogy to their own pain, they know what that word means. So, too, when you refer to your thoughts, or your mind. Other people cannot see your thoughts or your mind. But they can infer what you mean. Much as you can infer what mental states other human beings are talking about. I am not an Empiricist. To be is not to be perceived. There can be depth, behind appearance, which exists, in the physical world, but you don't see it, instead, you reason that it exists, on the basis and justification of what you did see.

For another example of this, what is temperature? Temperature is the speed at which atoms, as atoms, move at an atomic level. Heat is fast atomic movement, cold

THE MEANING OF LIFE

is slow atomic movement. You can feel hot and cold, as sensations, you can directly perceive hot and cold, but you cannot directly perceive what hot and cold are. Science was necessary in order to infer what hot and cold are. So you can refer to them as sensations, or you can refer to them by their scientific descriptions. Temperature is one thing, but you could name it two ways, by means of referring to it by means of two different properties that it has. It will always be both, because a thing is what it is. You directly perceive pain as a sensation, so you can refer to it in that way, even if you do not know what pain is.

Can you prove that a thing is always what it is?

Yes, sure. Thing Theory, The Theory of Things, that I have been explaining to you, is, ultimately, merely a consideration of a thing as such, of the essential thing Thing. What you can prove is true about a thing, as such, must then be true of all things, because every thing is-plus a thing. So, when I say that a thing is one thing as a thing, this must be true, of all things. And a thing is what it is, because what it is, is the thing's set of properties, and a thing is-equal to its set of properties.

You had mentioned things that are implied, or stated by implication. How does that work?

If you assert X, and, for X to exist, X will require Y, then, when you assert X, you are also asserting Y, by implication. You did not actually assert Y, but it is implied that you are asserting Y, because the existence of X requires the existence of Y, and you have actually asserted X. Y is a logical implication of X, if logic can prove that Y must be true if X is true.

Let me conclude thusly, before you and I part ways, and you go and walk away from me, and you return to your daily routine. Although I hope that you and I will meet again, tomorrow. And I hope that you spend tonight thinking about what we just discussed, and thinking up all the criticisms and critiques and questions and doubts and refutations, that you could think up, to attack all of my positions. Critical thinking demands nothing less. I think my Theory of Things can withstand all attacks.

I have an objection. Already. Can logic fully describe all the depth and wonder and wisdom and mystery of human existence? Can logic describe the depth and meaning of the human experience? Are not these things outside the scope of logic, yet very much within range of philosophy, and incredibly important?

The depth and meaning of human existence. Is that a thing? Is it something?

Yes. I think so.

Well, if it is something, then logic can analyze it, precisely because it is a thing. And, if it isn't something? If it is not a thing? Then it is of no concern. Every thing can be analyzed by logic, as a consequence of what being a thing is. I am aware of the depth and meaning of human existence. I am aware of wonder, and mystery, and wisdom. But these are things. Each one of them is something. Therefore they are absolutely within the scope of logic. Either something is something, or else it is nothing. If it is something, then logic can analyze it. If it is not a thing, then it is illogical, and such things are of no importance in my philosophy.

But let me turn your own philosophy back against you, my friend. I assert that the wonder and depth and mystery of the human experience exists. But I do not assert that it is-plus a thing. The question is whether everything that exists, is-plus a thing as a thing.

Everything is something. To exist, is to be a thing in objective reality. Therefore, one of the properties of existing, is being something. Therefore, yes, everything that exists is-plus a thing.

It looks like the bus is nearly here. I see it coming down the street. Here you and I part ways, my friend. You and I will not meet again, until tomorrow. I will leave you with this: A description is a named set of properties that identifies something, or a set of things, which have those properties. A definition is a description of essential properties, for a thing or type of thing. People often say "by definition" when what they really mean is "as a consequence of the essence." A bachelor is an unmarried man, by definition. Yes? No. A bachelor is an unmarried man as a consequence of the essence of being a bachelor, which are the set of properties, of being unmarried, and of being a man. Being XY requires a thing to contain the set of properties of X and Y, so, at least, XY is always the essence of XY as XY, and then being XY is also the consequence of being XY as XY. If an essence contains some property, then that something is always a consequence of that essence, because to contain it will require it.

I can also define what is meant by "the necessary and sufficient conditions" such that an X is an X, for the definition of X. Let us define a thing named A as equal to the property of being X plus the property of being Y. When we say A is XY, we mean a thing that has the property of being X and the property of being Y.

Then we can make these statements:

X is necessary for A but is not sufficient.

XY is necessary and sufficient for A.

XYZ is sufficient but not necessary for A.

So, when philosophers talk about the necessary and sufficient conditions of something, what they mean is the properties that define its essence, but they don't know what they mean. They know what thing they mean, but they don't know what it is. By which I mean, they know enough of its properties to be able to refer to it on the basis of those properties, but they do not know all of its essential and consequential properties.

Fluffy looks hungry. I think she just growled at me. I think you should go feed her.

I hope she eats dog food. The pet store talked me into buying some dog food for her. If she turns out to not be a dog, it will be a disaster. What will I feed her?

Let me know how Fluffy and the dog food turns out. I would love to know if she really was a dog. Let's meet at this bus stop again, this time tomorrow. You can let me know all the details. I will try to think about what we discussed today. I'll think about it tonight, and give you my opinions, when we meet again tomorrow. See you tomorrow, Gloria!

Goodbye, Cindy! Talk to you tomorrow! Bye!

VI. BONUS CONTENT: POEMS OF LOVE AND LOGIC

Integrity:

To be at one with yourself, as one thing, as an ethical being, as a person, as a human, is to have moral integrity.

A Leftist can be at one with Leftism. Or not.

Leftism cannot be at one with itself, because it cannot pay for the cost of what it wants to spend to help the poor.

A Conservative can be at one with Conservatism. Or not.

But Conservatism cannot be at one with itself, because its core virtue is freedom, yet it opposes freedom across a broad range of "social" issues, like abortion and gay marriage and recreational drug use.

An Objectivist can be at one with Objectivism. Or not.

Objectivism can be at one with itself. It has no internal contradictions.

Therefore only an Objectivist at one with Objectivism is perfectly at one, perfectly logical, without contradictions, coherent, with integrity.

Self-Esteem:

Having low self-esteem is bad.

Having a small ego is good.

But self-esteem = ego.

Is having a big ego good?

Ayn Rand:

Objectivism is the philosophy of Ayn Rand.

Ayn Rand was human and therefore fallible.

But Objectivism = The Truth.

Truth can't be false, therefore, The Truth is infallible.

Can Objectivism be added to, by someone not named Ayn Rand, if she were wrong about something?

Angels:

How many different names for the elements of logical syntax can the philosophy professors define?

How many angels can dance on the head of a pin?

How many licks does it take to get to the center of a Tootsie Pop?

Academics:

The philosophy professors don't take Ayn Rand seriously.

Ayn Rand is a plausible interpretation of Aristotle.

Aristotle and Plato are the foundation of (Western) philosophy, and that is a historical fact.

Therefore the philosophy professors don't take philosophy seriously.

Objectivism:

The Leftist Marxists seek to seize control of the means of production, and redistribute it to the poor. Objectivism holds that intelligence, and human minds, are the means of production. Therefore, in logic, this reduces to: The Leftist Marxists seek to seize control of the mind. And Ayn Rand's "Atlas Shrugged" argument is, simply, that minds do not enjoy being ruled and controlled, minds enjoy freedom, so it won't work. But it will collapse into an ugly dictatorship. This would be true, in logic, whether it was socialist Marxist-Leninist dictators, or "democratic socialists," who say that they want socialism with democracy and freedom, not dictatorship and tyranny. They will fail, and they will fail because of logic, it will become a dictatorship because socialism is what it is. This is why the Left hates logic. Logic refutes them. They will all seek to seize control of the mind, which is the means of production, and controlling minds requires armies, censorship, a police state, the loss of all civil liberties, the loss of all freedom, and, eventually, to be fully realized, it requires a dictatorship.

Economics and Politics:

There are two rooms, Room A, and Room B. A closed door separates them. The door can open, but right now the door is closed.

In Room A, there is a person named X, and a person named A.

X makes a product called Y, and A makes a product called B.

X trades Y to A in return for B.

X then consumes B. A then consumes Y.

In Room B, there is a person named Z. Z is armed with a gun.

(1) If X and A had a conflict, if Z knew about it, Z would provide courts and a legal system to resolve the dispute, in a fair and just way, and would provide police to enforce the court's rulings.

(2) If Z knew about X and A, Z would force X to give Y to A, or force A to give B to X, until the possessions and property of X and A were perfectly equal.

(3) Z had left the room, Z is not in Room B. Room B is empty.

Now assume that:

In Room A, there are three people, X, A, and C. X makes product Y, A makes product B, and C makes product D.

X trades Y to A in return for money, A trades B to C in return for money, and C trades D to X in return for money. In each trade, the money is a symbol of value, such that it represents receiving an equal value at a future point in time, like a note of debt. X then consumes D. A consumes Y. And C consumes B.

In Room B:

(1) Z is in Room B. If X and A, A and C, or C and X, had a contract dispute, regarding their sales and trades, if Z knew about it, Z would provide courts and a legal system to resolve the dispute, in a fair and just way, and would provide police to enforce the court's rulings.

(2) Z is in Room B. If Z knew about X, A, and C, Z would take all the money in Room A away by force, burn the money, and Z would then take all the Y, B, and D, put it into one pool on the floor, and force X, A, and C, to share it equally.

(3) Room B is empty. There is nobody in Room B. Z had gone away.

Now further posit:

(1) X, A and C are unarmed.

Or:

(2) X, A and C are each of them armed and carry a gun.

Then assume:

(1) X, A and C are happy, and each feels better off for having made the trades and sales that they did in fact choose to make. They can achieve happiness independently and self-autonomously.

(2) X, A and C are unhappy, and each feels that they were victims of, and exploited by, and taken advantage of by, one or all of the other two. They would love it if someone would protect them and guide them, from an external source.

And:

(1) If Z knew that X, A and/or C are unhappy, Z would use Z's gun, by force, to try to rectify and fix the conditions in Room A.

(2) If Z knew that X, A and/or C are unhappy, Z would do nothing.

(3) If Z knew that X, A and/or C are unhappy, Z would use Z's gun, by force, to try to rectify and fix the conditions in Room A, but only if, and to the extent, that Z obtained a tangible benefit by doing so.

To finalize and make our points, let us name Room A as "The Economy," and let us name Room B as "The Political System."

This thought experiment proves, analytically, by means of the analysis of concepts, that economics is distinct from politics, and proves that capitalism, socialism, and anarcho-capitalism, are all possible. This proves that you could have economics and capitalism without any state or government, and, if that is true, then you can also have economics and capitalism with as small and as limited a government as possible.

A SYSTEM OF LEGAL LOGIC: USING ARISTOTLE, AYN RAND, AND ANALYTICAL PHILOSOPHY TO UNDERSTAND THE LAW, INTERPRET CASES, AND WIN IN LITIGATION (A SCHOLARLY MONOGRAPH)

METAPHYSICAL LOGIC

This paper begins with a glossary of philosophical terms and then applies them to construct a system of legal logic. The system of legal logic presented herein will go a good way towards introducing much-needed clarity and precision in how lawyers and judges think about the law. To the extent that everyone is governed by a legal system, it is also good reading for everyone (although a high intelligence and knowledge of the law, and a background in philosophy, may be required to grasp the academic legal details).

T: a Thing, a set of properties, can also stand for one isolated property.

X: an X, a T as the object of analysis.

p(T): a perceived T. The object.

P(T): a perception of T. The means of perception.

W(T): a witness of T. The subject.

e(X): the essence of X, the property from which X derives ontological being as X, what makes X be an X.

S: specific properties nonessential relative to an essence.

>: the arrow of inference, which indicates that the content on the left side evaluates to the content on the right side by a direct inference of reasoning.

X minus S > e(X).

R(X): a real X. An X which exists in Reality.

p(X) > X.

X = S plus e(X).

Therefore p(X) > e(X).

p(R(X)) > R(X).

E(X): the essential thing X. A T which lacks S and lacks R and has only e(X).

C(e(X)): the consequence of the essence of X. Those properties which e(X) will cause T to have.

XY: a T which has the property of being X and the property of being Y (i.e. X times Y). For example 2 x 3 is the number two having the property of being in a set of three: XX + XX + XX = 6.

The Essential Syllogism: e(X) > E(X) > C(E(X)) > C(e(X)).

The Essential Argument: if a Thing must have the essence of X in order to be an X, and having the essence of X causes a Thing to have the property Y, as a consequence of the essence of X, then all X are Y, because being X causes T to be Y, therefore each X is Y, therefore all X are Y. It is necessary and universal that all X are Y if you can establish a "because" relationship between e(X) and Y. If a critic asserts that some X is not Y then if it had the essence of X this would cause it to be a Y because it was an X, therefore it is not an X after all, because it lacks e(X), or else it would have been Y if it had e(X).

The Empiricist Argument: if a thinking entity can gain knowledge of X from p(X) and gain knowledge of e(X) from X and gain knowledge of C(e(X)) from e(X) then there exists the possibility of a posteriori knowledge of necessary and universal truth, arising from the empirical perceived immanent ontology of things, not from the mind imposing categorical conditions onto subjective experience.

The Objectivist Argument: that the means of perception do not create or bias the act of perception, that p(T) = T and p(T) causes P(T). Therefore we see and experience objective reality, and the phenomena are the noumena. The argument holds that p(T) cause, are prior to, and exist separately from and independently of P(T), that we see p(T) by means of P(T) but the T we actually see is p(T) and R(p(T)), whereas P(T) exists in our minds (actually as nerve signals in our optic nerves and brains).

The Closed Eye Argument: that from perceiving something, then not perceiving it, then perceiving it again, one can infer that it existed while one was not perceiving it, therefore it exists objectively, and from this one can infer R(R), that Reality is real.

The Painted Box Argument: assume a box with each side painted a different color. Four people on four different sides look at the box. Each sees a different color, but each side is the color that is seen, so all four are objectively correct, and their perceptions are not subjective. For each side R(p(T)) therefore R(Sum(p(T))).

The Color Blind Argument: that color blind people see less of Reality, not a different Reality. For example purple equals red times blue so if you see both blue and purple as the same color you see blue but only the blue part of purple.

The ABC Principle: C(e(ABC)) = C(e(A) and e(AB) and e(ABC) and e(B) and e(BC) and e(C) and e(AC))

b/c: because.

Non(X): Not X, a Thing is not X, or lacks the property of being X. If Q is X was asserted as an assertion this means that statement is False, it is not True.

N: the number in a series of a potentially infinite set.

The CD Principle: e(ABC) > D, e(ABNon(C)) > Non(D), either C > D or AB x C > D.

r: Reason, especially Essential Reasoning. The substantive analysis of why e(X) causes Y. Always reduces to a b/c relationship, that X causes Y physically, Y is a part of X in other words X contains Y e.g. X = ABCY, or X requires Y as X's means or the cause of X where Y is the only possible cause of X. Must be done at the level of specificity of the subject matter, e.g. philosophy for e(T), chemistry for e(water) > becomes ice when freezes, that case's specific evidence for a trial.

K(T): to know T. Semantically identical with: to believe R(T).

Conceptual Identification(ConID): $p(X1) > (X = e(X) + S(X1)) > e(X) > E(X) > C(E(X)) > (C(e(X)) = Y) > (p(X2)$ and $Non(p(Y))) > K(X2 = Y)$. To reason that all X are Y, see an X but not see Y but know that Y is present despite no empirical direct evidence. The basis of analytical philosophy as logic.

The Blue Green Fallacy: inferring that all X are Y from repeatedly seeing XY without r(b/c), i.e. without establishing a because relationship between essence and consequence.

The Lab Rat Fallacy: X is an M, Y is an M, scientist establishes all X are Z and asserts all Y will be Z because of M, and then a Non(Z)Y is discovered and it looks like r is not necessary and universal, but in Reality X was Z because of S(X)M so not all Y are Z.

The Black Swan Fallacy: the definition of the word W is commonly known, all W are Q, but then a Non(Q)W is found and it seems logic teeters, but it turns out that W had two meanings(M): T1 and T2 which are found together 99% of the time but only all T1 is Q and this was a Non(Q)T2. Which definition is correct? Actually it is best to coin one W for T1 and a second word W2 for T2. S is always relative to e(T) so this will produce the correct C(e(T)).

The three consequential mechanisms:

Cause: the essence directly causes a thing having it to have the consequence because of what it is.

Contain: e.g. being B is a consequence of being AB.

Means/Effect: the essence requires the consequence as its means of being or the consequence is the only cause of that essence as its effect.

The 99% Rule: 99% of the time there is no practical difference between being 99% certain or 100% certain. For example the extent to which you Know that the Roman Empire existed because a big lie about it is too implausible.

C%: degree of certainty.

TR%: degree of trust.

C% = TR% + K(C(e(X)) + p(X).

How to prove a negative: prove all X are Y, Y is not Q, therefore all X are not Q, not Q is proven.

The Space Time Statement: $R(T) = R(T(S(location))) + R(T(S(time)))$.

R: Reality. (Intentionally uses the same letter as R the property of being Real.)

Metaphysical Possibility (Meta Po): that T is possible in theory, that the nature of R allows it, that no essence to consequence relationship contradicts it.

Mechanical Possibility (Mech Po): that R(T) is possible, that the physical means of R(T) does in fact exist, that T is possible in practice.

Ignorant Possibility (Ig Po): that we do not know (1) if T exists or (2) if T is metaphysically or mechanically possible so (3) we say T might exist.

PW: the Physical World.

Descartes' Demon and Hume's Darkness (DDHD): Skepticism, the belief that

Non(R(PW)) is possible, that the physical world might all be an illusion and we cannot prove that the Sun will rise tomorrow morning.

R(R): that Reality is Real.

R(PW) that the Physical World is real, which may imply R = PW.

Valid and Invalid Possibility Inferences:

Valid:

Meta Po from Mech Po,

Mech Po(T) from R(T),

Non(Ig Po(Not(T))) from R(T).

Invalid:

Meta Po from Ig Po,

Mech Po from Ig Po.

The Anti-Hume Postulate: that it is invalid to infer that T is possible from imagining or conceiving of T.

The Anti-DDHD Argument: if in the first instance you can affirmatively infer empirically from p(T) that R(T) therefore R(Sum(T)) therefore R(PW) and from this infer Non(Ig Po(Non(R(PW)))) therefore Non(DDHD). Also if C(e(PW)) > R(PW) then Non Meta Po Non(R(PW)) therefore Non Ig Po Non(R(PW)) > Non(DDHD).

The Objective Relative: the theory that a measurement of X in relation to Y is objectively true, not Subjectivist or relativist, if R(X) and R(Y) and R(X/Y).

SOM: Standard of Measure. The T in relation to which X is measured.

The Aristotle Caveat: A cannot be Non(A) at the same time and in the same respect, but can be in a different respect, meaning in relation to a different SOM or as a different essential property.

Paradigm: a very broad doctrinal or mindset-level SOM.

If (A + B = C) and (R(A) and R(B)) then R(C).

If p(T1) > T2 > T3 > TN then R(TN) b/c p(R(T1)) and R(T1) > R(T2) > R(T3) > R(TN).

If (p(A) + B = C) then R(C) only if (p(B) or p(T1) > R(TN) > R(B)).

I(X): X is irrational, meaning K(X) but Not r(X). X is irrationally believed.

If (A + B + C = D) and (p(A) and r(B) but I(C)) then Ig Po(D). D may or may not be R. If in the next step r(R(C)) then r(K(R(D))).

Pure reason (Pure(r(X))): Reason only from perceived things or conclusions validly drawn from them, with no irrational premises.

The Purity Postulate: that perfectly pure reason admits of 100%C because R causes P which causes K(R(T)). Impure logic should not be trusted until all premises are empirically verified.

Scientific Experiments: ((IV + Cf) = DV) = (X – S(X) = e(X) > C(e(X)))).

IV: independent variable.

DV: dependent variable.

Cf: confounds.

PA: patterns in data.

SIG: statistically significant patterns in data. To the extent that a SIG DV is found and all Cf are not causing it, because they were controlled for and their effects were subtracted out, it must be caused by IV because there is nothing else there to cause it and it was SIG hence not just random, therefore DV=C(E(IV)).

Statistically significant conclusions based on random samples admit of the degree of certainty of its probability but only up to 99%.

The Essential Argument of cause and effect of essence justifies the necessity of the If Then statement in formal logic.

X = ABC, p(AB), is it X? Is AB enough for X? Only up to 99%C from circumstantial evidence. The more important thought in that scenario is C(e(AB)). If that cannot answer the question then Ig Po(X).

The Essential Thing Method: if you can assert Y of E(X) then it must be C(e(X)) because there is no S there to cause it, there is only e(X) there present to cause it.

The Aristotle Method: the essence of X is that thing which when removed does not leave behind that thing of which it was the essence, so to find the essence conceptually remove properties from a Thing until you would no longer regard it as an X.

LEGAL LOGIC

The Philosophy and Law Postulate: the Law is applied philosophy.

The Legal Logic Postulate: the Law defines an act Y that the government will take if a judge finds that Facts F are equal to X, therefore L is the statement Y because X, therefore the Law defines the legal consequence of the essential properties of a set of Facts.

F: Fact or Facts.

L: the Law or laws.

RA: the Rationale of the holding of a judge in case law, which states why he held as he did, i.e. X b/c Y.

Elemental Logic: breaking F into T and matching them up to the elements of a claim in L. A process of Legal ConID of identifying a set of F(T), breaking L into a set of e(T) where C(e(T)) = the desired legal outcome, and matching the properties in T to e(X). To match all elements is to state a claim, to prove all F(e(L)) is to prove your case.

EL: an element of a claim of L. An EL is an e(T) where L = (O = C(e(EL))).

O: outcome, what the government will do if a set of R(F) satisfies L(EL). The goal of a lawyer is the client's optimal or desired O.

Statute: legal text defines L = e(X) explicitly, or you infer using canons of statutory construction and definitions.

Common Law: opinion says L = T b/c RA, you must infer e(T) from RA.

Max C%: the maximum potential r(L)C%. Unless the Law and its definitions are perfectly explicit and clearly define L, the Max C of L is 99% or less depending on how clear L is. For a multifactor balancing test with high judicial discretion, Max C %(L) might be 1%. Max C%(F) = the degree to which the consequence of the essence is proven from p(T) of every EL, which can be 100% or the lesser degree of TR% of circumstantial evidence.

The burden of proof: a definition of Min C%(minimum degree of certainty) to prove that all facts necessary to prove all elements of a claim are proven.

Max C%(Case) = Max C%(L) + Max C%(F). The opposite of it is DDHD(Case).

The Prediction Postulate: All X are Y is the basis of the belief that K(L) enables predictions of future O where future F = X2 given future F because L = e(X) where FN = (X + FN(S)).

Making the Pro Argument:

Step 1: p(F1) or p(T) > r(T) > r(TN) > F1 (prove the facts).
Step 2: EL1 = e(X) (interpret the Law).
Step 3: F1 = EL1 (the facts satisfy the elements of the Law).
Step 4: repeat for FN = ELN (the facts satisfy all elements needed to win).
Step 5: O = C(ELN) (win the case and be awarded the desired outcome).
Answering the Con Arguments:
Assume case law is one case such that:
Holding = L1
Facts = F1 + F2 + F3
Rationale = RA1
Your client's Facts are F4 and F5.
You want L1 to apply to your F.
You argue:
(L1 = e(F1) b/c RA1) and X = e(F1 as L1) therefore X = EL1, and F4 is a type of X (is of the category of X) because F4 = e(X) + S(F4).

This is your Analogy: F4 is like F1 in the way significant to the Law as shown by RA1.

Opposing counsel's arguments are Distinction:
F1 is not e(L1), instead F2 is EL1, and F4 plus F5 is Not e(F2).
EL1 = F1 + F2 and F4 = F1 but F5 Not = F2.
S(F4 + F5) adds something that blocks C(e(X)) because of RA1.
Non(F4 or F5).
F4(SOM) Not = X(SOM).
DDHD. C% or TR% is too low.
In plain English: EL requires F not present here to be met, you are wrong about which facts in the opinion are legally significant, you are wrong about what was the essence of the legally significant fact, you misread the Rationale hence the previous two counterarguments, the specifics of the facts in your case change the legal significance of your facts matching the essence of the case law's facts in a way indicated by the case law rationale, the essence are not the same because you use a different paradigm to interpret and analyze your facts than the case law used, you failed to prove your facts even if your elemental logic was correct. You did not prove knowledge of the facts sufficient to meet the burden of proof against skepticism of your facts.

You then reply to each counterargument by making the Pro argument directed at it.

Analogy: these facts have the same essence but different specifics as the legally significant essence defined by the facts of case law or the definitions in statutes.

Distinction: the essence is different.

Horizontal counterargument: you say X, I say Not X.

Vertical counterargument: you say X, I say Y (and If Y Then Not X).

The Philosophical Rule of Evidence: the goal of evidence at trial is 100% Certainty. This explains the demand for firsthand testimony and authenticated evidence sufficient from which to infer each element of a claim, and other things, such as the rule against hearsay. It is an Empiricist philosophy that all knowledge must originate in direct perception and then be logically inferred from that.

Authenticating Evidence: establishing the Purity of the line of reasoning from perceived things (firsthand evidence) to the conclusions. The chain of custody of evidence shows the decision-maker a basis to trust the line from $p(T)$ to $K(F)$. Hearsay and the other rules of evidence are based in the principle of Pure reason that all conclusions must ultimately be based upon and grounded in $p(T)$. If $p(TN)$ can be introduced into evidence and proves F as a consequence of the essence then C% can equal 100%, otherwise C% is limited to TR% of circumstantial evidence from which to infer F. Tangible physical evidence that judge or jury can see for themselves can be 100%C, otherwise where a Witness W testifies that she saw T this can be like $p(T)$ for the line of r but is limited to TR%(W).

The Closed Eye Method: prove objective $R(T)$ by corroboration or that T existed between periods of being perceived as T is asserted to be.

The Painted Box Method: explain away differing accounts as different POV but all consistent with the underlying $R(F)$.

The Color Blind Method: explain away differing accounts by deficiency in POV, means of perception, $P(T)$, compared to the ideal perfect POV that saw your asserted F.

POLITICAL LOGIC

To extend the analysis of law by philosophy and logic, let us ask this question: Can we derive the Law conceptually and analytically from the analysis of concepts?

H: the property of being Human.

R(H): a real person, a realistic person as analyzed by logic.

X: a person. (X = E(Human)).

A: a second person. (A = E(H)N/X).

X/A: the relationship between X and A.

What is C(E(X/A))? What political relationship emerges between X and A from nothing other than their essence? What conditions must be met within X/A for a specific politics to arise?

POLI = C(e(X/A)).

How does POLI define the Law or limit the scope of possible Laws? What conceptually understood contingencies cause a Law potential in a POLI to collapse into an actuality?

A thought experiment is relevant here in order to answer the preceding questions. As a theoretical challenge, let us ask, and answer, this question: can Libertarianism be justified pragmatically using a priori logic? If so, how and under what conditions?

A priori: from before, from the analysis of concepts without reference to empirical research.

Pragmatic: practical, justified by its usefulness and benefit to real human beings.

Assume a thought experiment:

X is a person.

A is another person.

Y is X's belief, what X believes is good. A believes Y is evil.

B is A's belief, what A believes is good. X believes B is evil.

Assume X and A are members of one political system.

Assume these possibilities:

1. X can let A be free to do B.

2. A can let X be free to do Y.

3. X can impose Y onto A by force.

4. A can impose B onto X by force.

5. X can fight in self defense against #4 but cannot stop A from trying if A wants to.

6. A can fight in self defense against #3 but cannot stop X from trying if X wants to.

Game Theory Question One: given this hypothetical, can we infer all possible scenarios and rank them from the a priori point of view, in other words, before we know what Y and B are and which is good and which is wrong? Do we have sufficient information to do so?

Scenario One: #1 and #2. Freedom and peace between X and A. X happily does Y and A happily does B, marred only by each's knowledge that somewhere the other exists, to the extent each has a legitimate interest in controlling the other.

Scenario Two: #3 and #4, the war of all against all, the struggle for power, might makes right, the fight to seize control and impose your values onto the dissenting other.

Scenario Three: #1 and #4 which leads to either: 7. A defeats X and rules X or kills X or else it leads back to 5: X succeeds in self defense, which reverts to #5 but X can either maintain #1 or switch to #3 which becomes Scenario Two.

Scenario Four: assume #2 and #3, then either 8. X rules and conquers A or to #6 where A can continue #2 or switch to #4 which leads to Scenario Two.

Game Theory Conclusion One: Scenario One is the optimal outcome because X is able to do Y and A is able to do B and every other outcome entails greater risk of one or both of these conditions failing but the game theory shows that X and A cannot force each other to resolve to Scenario One. X can try to give #1 to A in return for #2, and A can give #2 to X as payment for #1, a reciprocity of freedom, and this would be practical from a pragmatic a priori point of view of before we know who X and A are, what position on which issue Y and B are, or even whether X likes or hates A personally or vice versa.

Game Theory Conclusion Two: any #3 or #4 leads to scenarios where a Scenario Two outcome is more likely: the slippery slope.

Now with the basics under our belt let's explore more variations of this game.

Assume this argument: X says he should force Y onto A because he would let A force Y onto him in return or as payment or for fairness.

Posit this counterargument: the equivalent of X's Y for A is B, not Y, so if X tries to force Y onto A the reciprocal or fair and equal outcome is for A to force B onto X.

Assume the following argument: X is a crusader for justice who believes Y is good and B is evil so wants to escalate to Scenario Two and win the war.

Posit these counterarguments: from the a priori point of view X does not know who will win the war so in this "from before" perspective it maximizes the chances of the maximum existence of Y and minimizes risk of loss of Y to choose Scenario One, and this is true even if X firmly believes B is gruesome horrific evil because this is a pragmatic argument to maximize Y. The only objection is the extent to which B's very existence injures X but we can isolate these into moral revulsion, which is merely an emotion that can be ignored as the price one pays to coexist in civilized society, or a physical intrusion of B into X's moral space, which would theoretically revert to X's right of self defense in #5 and the path back to #1 and Scenario One.

Now it's time to assess decision-making authority and its allocation.

Assume these possibilities:

9. X decides between Y and B for X.

10. A decides between Y and B for A.

11. X decides for A between Y and B.

12. A decides for X between Y and B.

Note that any attempt to escape this question by removing an option or choice from its scope reduces to #11 or #12. For example to say "we will give X only B and remove the possibility of Y so there exists no choice nor decision to be made" is logically equivalent to "A chooses B for X."

Game Theory Question Two: can we infer the logical result of all possible scenarios and see what this fact pattern evaluates to given the postulate that we do not know a priori the intelligence, IQ, knowledge, expertise, education level, ignorance or lack of knowledge or lack of wisdom of X and A? What possibilities does this set resolve to?

Scenario One-a. #9 and #10. This is the epistemic corollary of Scenario One.

Scenario Two-a. X seeks, or achieves, #9 and #11, which, if X chooses Y for A, as X probably will, leads to #3, then Scenario Two.

Scenario Two-b. A seeks or achieves #10 and #12, leading again to Scenario Two.

We can deduce that as a practical matter #9 and #10 maximize Y because they avoid Scenario Two and thereby protect and guarantee at least X's Y while leaving open the possibility that X may persuade A as decision-maker for A to freely choose Y over B as a result of reasoned dialogue and persuasion.

Assume that:

13. The decision of Y vs B for X impacts only X.

14. The decision of Y vs B for X impacts X but also affects A.

15. The decision of Y or B for A only has a result or effect for A.

16. The decision of Y or B for A had results and effects for both A and X.

If #13 and #15 are true then we may say that Scenarios One and One-a meet the condition of being fair and just: X bears the result of X's choice, A takes responsibility for the decision for which A is responsible. However it is also logically true that #14 and #16 are not incompatible with Scenario One and One-a if, and only to the extent that, X if #16 asserts #5 and uses force for self-defense to the extent necessary to protect himself from intrusive impacts of A and #12, and the same for A that if #14 and #11 then #6.

The Libertarian Assumptions:

The First Libertarian Assumption: assume that there is no difference between social conduct or economic conduct, beliefs, religions, morality, behavior, what to say, think, or do, or plans for how to manage the economy or distribute resources or assign productive efficiency, in terms of what substantive content can be plugged into the variables Y and B.

The Second Libertarian Assumption: in the state of nature X and A can (a) delegate their right of self-defense to the government or (b) delegate their war to impose Y or B onto each other to the political process so that the war of bloodshed becomes a war for votes to elect politicians who will impose either Y or B onto the public.

From this we can assess a certain set of policy questions:

Let the individual or the government decide what an individual can do with his property and money?

Let individuals or the government decide the banking interest rate? Let the individual or the government decide how much of his money to spend on social causes or charity for the poor (taxes)?

Let the individual or the government decide which medical treatments or medications he can or can't use (FDA)?

Let the individual or the government decide to what extent a person may harm his own body (recreational drug use, obesity-causing food, the legality of suicide for the terminally ill, etc.)?

Let the individual or the government decide whether he (and by extension his religious sect) should recognize gay marriage as legitimate?

Let the individual or the government decide whether she should have an abortion?

Let the individual or the government choose what he is allowed to say (free speech vs libel laws)?

Let the individual or the government decide whether to recognize immigrants as members of his social and political community?

Let the individual or the government decide the terms of the individual's economic interactions with foreigners and trade across borders? Let the individual or the government decide what religion he is?

Let the individual or the government decide with whom he does business, whom he sells to, buys from, hires or fires?

Let the individual or the government decide with whom a person can interact socially, whom they can date or marry and on what terms (the terms of a marital relationship, the legality of prostitution, Jim Crow-era racial segregation where the government forced whites and blacks to be kept apart, etc.)?

Let the individual or the government choose his or her healthcare?

Let the individual or the government choose their children's education?

Game Theory Conclusion Three: In the classic game of game theory, the prisoners' dilemma, two prisoners are separated and may confess or lie. Their benefit is maximized if they both lie but because each can't force the other to lie they are both motivated to individually confess. This is deemed a collective action problem where the efficient solution is to force both prisoners to lie, which by analogy justifies the government to force citizens into behaviors to solve real large-scale collective action problems. With the XYAB game the problem is similar yet different: X and A cannot force each other into the optimal Scenario One given that the freely chosen non-violence and peace-selecting behavior of the other is necessary to achieve it. But because Scenario One entails freedom from government interference and political domination, it would also be difficult to solve this collective action problem by having the government impose it by force or by law. In an ideal outcome, the voters would freely choose Libertarianism, having been persuaded in their capacity as decision-makers. The next best thing is for the law to assign decision-making authority for each individual to that individual, to enable each person to have a right of self-defense physically and/or legally, and to use constitutional law to safeguard the rights of the individual against the tyranny of the majority. However no system can render Scenario One fully necessary as a result of a political system because it will always rely on the contingent free choices of X to choose #1 and of A to choose #2.

This system is self-validating: a libertarian wants to be free to make his own decisions but will not impose his values onto others by force, so he would let someone else be free to oppose libertarianism and be an adherent of tyranny and an enemy of freedom, but the libertarian would not let his enemy impose his tyranny onto the libertarian by force.

The XYAB Thought Experiment neatly translated into the common law:

(1) X decides for and has decision-making authority and freedom individually for his life, liberty, body and property.

Let LLBP be defined as Life, Liberty, Body and Property.

(2) Constitutional law: protect X from A imposing B onto X by means of votes and politicians, in other words, protect the individual from the government by creating a system of laws which the government is forced to obey. Protect X's LLBP from public intrusions.

(3) Criminal law: disallow A to violate X's LLBP by violent intentional force.

(4) Torts law: disallow A to violate X's LLBP by violent accidental force.

(5) Property law: protect X's LLBP from private intrusions, especially into X's decision-making authority, and establish rules to determine what is or is not within the scope of X's LLBP.

(6) Contract law: establish rules for how X may trade parts of his LLBP in return for compensation, which, if based on X's freedom to make decisions, entails

interpreting the intent of X in choosing the deal and what terms of the deal X intended to consent to, as well as whether X received the compensation which justifies assigning his LLBP to the other party.

(7) Due process: giving X the right of self-defense for his LLBP by giving him a hearing where he can legally put up a fight to defend his rights, and notice so that he can attend the hearing.

(8) Environmental law: prevention and/or compensation to the extent that A's pollution injured X's legitimate interest in his LLBP (and note that, if X's LLBP is legitimate, no huge amount of profit by A could justify violating it at a theoretical level, because it is a moral right prior to economics).

(9) Intellectual property: balancing the extent to which X gains LLBP by inventing or artistically creating inventions or works of art with the extent to which these do not physically exist and/or are preexisting things which are discovered, not created, and hence would fall outside the scope of X's LLBP as inventor or author.

MORAL LOGIC

We begin this section with a reference model mapping the scope of LLBP: 1. Self/mind/soul/consciousness, 2. Free will, 3. Choice, 4. Body executing choice, 5. Do work/make money/perform social behavior, 6. Actions go out into the World, 7. The economy, society, and other people interact, 8. The World sends the result of your chosen actions back to your body, 9. Your body receives the result and 10. The result is experienced by the self. LLBP covers the scope of the body as it expresses choices in such a way as to create property or relations which have a physical moral component of a result that impacts, rewards or punishes the self as decision-maker by the property and/or body receiving a benefit or detriment, liberty as the freedom for this moral lifecycle, and life as a self living in a body whose choices and actions create the sustenance (physical rewards) to keep the body alive.

This mode of thinking is useful for lawyers and helps make legal arguments. Consider the following questions:

Who is your client? Or, if you are doing policy advocacy, who is your stakeholder?

What was the scope of his LLBP? Where in the LLBP Lifecycle was it? From what source did it originate?

What choice did your client make? What was the result? What should have been the result?

How did the other party wrong your client? How was his LLBP violated? What choices gave rise to the conduct at issue? Who was responsible? How can they get what they deserve?

How did the other party disrupt your client's LLBP Lifecycle? How could the healthy circuit be restored? What damages would accomplish this?

Can the Law impose the result that would have resulted had your client been free to defend himself or been properly defended by the government as the agent to which he delegated his right of self-defense?

To what extent would it be wrongful or unfair had someone else done to the other party what they did to your client? This can establish wrongful conduct or doing the reciprocal back to the other party might be a measure of the fairness of damages.

Was your client's freedom impaired under the justification of protecting others? Can you make the pragmatic a priori argument that those third parties would benefit more from freedom for everyone than from this instance of protectionism?

We can analyze what might be called Scenario Two Law: a L designed to impose control or to collapse a law-abiding democracy into a dictatorship. X uses the government to impose control or grab decision-making power. By regime:

In torts, an excess of liability and litigation, to the point where ordinary people live in fear of the Law.

In contracts, the tyranny of fine print that nobody ever actually consents to.

In property, the replacement of inalienable rights grounded in human nature with a set of arbitrary entitlements arbitrarily assigned by society.

In environmental law, a takeover by regulators of all natural resources.

In intellectual property, a regime where our employers own our minds and owners censor and control our ideas.

In due process, the belief that the government can trample over us and crush us after notice and a hearing.

In constitutional law, the removal of all meaningful limits on government power.

$d(X = X)$: do the action based on X being X, treat an X like it is an X, behave in reaction to $R(T = X)$.

$d(X = Y)$: do the action based on X being Y, treat an X as a T of type Y, treat this X as a member of category Y, behave in reaction to $R(T = XY)$.

If (If X then do(Y)) then $Y = d(X)$. Belief X is the Premise of Action Y.

$d(R(X))$: behave as if X is Real.

$R(d(R(X)))$: the objectively correct way to behave as if X is Real.

$X(do(Y))$: X does the Y action.

$X(do(Y)while(Z))$: X does the Y action while Z is true or while the Z condition is met.

O+: a good outcome.

O-: a negative outcome.

Assume X is a hammer and Y is a pillow. If you try to build a house, and you use a hammer to hammer nails into wood, you can succeed. If you try to hit nails with a pillow, you will fail. You succeed by treating a hammer like a hammer in Reality. Conversely, if you try to sleep, and you treat a hammer like a pillow, and rest your head on it, you fail. If you treat a pillow like a pillow, you fall asleep by resting your head on the pillow. Treating a hammer like a pillow seems insane but the principle is real and widely applicable: do you treat yourself like the person you really are? Do you do the right things at work? Do you treat each person as who they really are? Do you treat politics and economics and laws as what they really are?

The R in $d(R(T))$ causes O+. If you do the right thing then you will do an action well and treating Reality like what it is enabled you to conquer Reality. In Law, treating the R(F) like what they really are will enable the truth to emerge before the jury, and treating each L as what it is will enable accurate legal reasoning.

OBJECTIVIST LOGIC

J: the Japanese Distinction, which holds that Non(R(X)) is not equal to X = Non(T). To not exist is not the same as to not be something. T is to be something whereas R is to exist. (In English there is one word "is/to be" whereas the Japanese language has two distinct words.)

Objectivist Logic: the logic that follows from Non(J).

Objectivist Logic in sum: If(Not(1 < T)) then T = zero. If a thing is not something then it is nothing. If it is something then it is one with everything, lacking contradictions. This is true of TN so each T can never contradict a second T.

Objectivist Logic rejects J: to be something is to exist in Reality because 1=R, PW=1 and T=1, to be something is to exist is to be one thing is to be part of the one world that exists, to be a contradiction is to be two things at odds with each other or in conflict or where one severs itself into two so half can hide from the other half of the truth, therefore every T will integrate into R because they are already part of 1 thing and 1 is at one with itself so part of 1 cannot contradict 1 and R is 1 and all T are part of R therefore a contradiction cannot exist and the real will always integrate into Reality. Contra the reification of the zero, to think that something could be nothing, that a 1 could not exist, to be a walking contradiction or an irrational human.

<: the symbolic logical notation for the Objectivist Inference, that what is on the right side of the operand integrates into what is on the left side without contradiction.

K(PW) < p(T): the key Objectivist method of analysis.

Essential Logic: T > C(e(T)).

Objectivist Logic: 1 < T.

If (1 < T) and (R=1) then T/R: if a T is really something at one with itself then it exists in its proper relationship and ratio to Reality. Reason as a ratio of T to R.

If (Not(X < Y)) then Not X or Not Y.

Reason as the art of non-contradictory identification: integrate your sensory experience into your knowledge of reality. If it integrates without contradiction, then know it. If it resolves into a contradiction, a contradiction cannot exist therefore either K(PW) or p(T) is wrong. Think and look to the evidence you know is true to determine what the truth is and which one is true. Reality is one thing, it cannot be two at odds with itself, therefore a contradiction is impossible.

CONT: a contradiction.

To use some empirical examples from the Objectivist novel Atlas Shrugged:
In summary:
Rearden: ethics < sexual desire = CONT.
Dagny: Looter PW < p(Galt) = CONT.
Galt: Capitalist PW < p(20th Century Motor Co. socialism) = CONT.
The K(PW) or the P may be false but something must be true.
More detailed Objectivist examples from the Randian novels:
Howard Roark = Architect as 1. He has integrity to one principle: he will be true to the fact that he is (and wants to be) an architect, he is one thing with no contradictions.

Rearden: sexual morality as acceptance or toleration of evil < sexual desire for Dagny = CONT, resolved by reforming morality.

Galt: knowledge of morality and reason, that goodness must succeed because it is good < the sight of the Communists winning at the 20th Century Motor Factory = CONT, resolved by depriving evil of the permission of the victim.

Dagny: her worldview that the achievers and people of ability can save the world < Galt and the uncontrollable collapse of the world = CONT, resolved by accepting Galt's morality and the ideas in his speech.

These examples show that K(PW) or P(X) can be wrong when K(PW) < p(T). If it resolves to 1 then true, if it resolves to CONT then find your mistake and check your premises (question each of your assumptions and beliefs and the empirical evidence that gave rise to them).

The best method for executing Objectivist Logic: (K(PW) < p(T)) > If K(PW) then X > T=X or T=Not X.

< as Integrate: if X < Y then Y integrates into X without CONT. Then we can say INT(X < Y).

Integrity: INT(You < You(do(X))). The one principle that a T must be consistent and coherent with to have organic consistency. For example, for Howard Roark, d(You=Architect).

Politics: INT(H < POLI and Law).

The Objectivist Logical Argument of Politics: Assume you could choose either Y or B. If Y or B is True you need the freedom to reason which one and choose that one in order to survive, b/c d(R) = O+, and ultimately doing right or wrong leads to life or death. The moral and only the moral is inherently practical because d(R)=O+ and r is the means of K(R(T)), and since alive or dead are the only two contingent conditions for H and morality implies choice and free will it must be true that moral status is defined by which of life or death it achieves.

Objectivist Logic for Lawyers: view the case as 1 story where everything must fit in without CONT to make sense and CONT is a clue to a lie. View the statute or case as 1 and the legal interpretation that assimilates into it without contradiction and has integrity to the Law is true. So:

Case law < your reading of the law.

Statutory text < your legal interpretation.

Body of law or legal regime < your legal reasoning and paradigm.

Your case and its story < every fact.

Objectivist Logic values Integrity as the intellectual and philosophical foundation of reason. A lawyer whose reason and story of the facts of the case and legal analysis has Integrity is more trustworthy and credible.

Rational: resolves to 1, does not resolve to CONT.

If (X < Y) then XY is rational as a T or X + Y is rational as a whole or group of T or (if X then Y) or (if X then Po. Y) is rational.

Three key Objectivist concepts: integrity, consciousness, and the choice to think.

Integrity: to be one thing, to = 1(T), to be T as 1. To be true to one unifying principle of who you are("to thine own self be true".) R(H) as 1. Then, in epistemological terms, to integrate sensory experience into your previous knowledge without contradiction: epistemic integrity, that R = 1 and H(K(R as 1)).

Consciousness: the H as knower of R as 1. The mind as the thing that sees and reasons and integrates and chooses. Consciousness is the act of non-contradictory identification: the signature Objectivist epistemology.

The choice to think: because Reality exists objectively and is one thing, if you open your eyes then you will see it, and it defines you, and you plus Reality defines what you should do, and what you should do defines your choices, so your only really free choice is to open your eyes or choose to close your eyes. If you choose to think, your consciousness can and will reason from sensory experience to knowledge of Reality.

To blank out: to choose not to think. This involves splitting the one consciousness into two halves: the mind that knows the truth (inevitably), and the mind which hides from what it knows. What happens to James Taggart at the end of Atlas Shrugged is the horror of knowing you lied to yourself.

To apply this to lawyers: make your arguments as if the Judge is really very smart. If he is, opposing counsel will fail. If he isn't, you still look smart and may (and should) win. And the higher up the appellate court chain you climb on appeal, the smarter the judges tend to be. Really open your eyes and see the case, reason from the facts, know the law, and a winning argument (or the argument that should win even if it does not, which you can't help) will naturally emerge by applying the law to the facts with logic. The same with jurors, as at the end of The Fountainhead: treat the jury with intellectual respect, don't talk down to them, reason with their minds, and engage them cognitively. You cannot predict how a herd of sheep will stampede, so you may lose anyway if the jury is stupid, and therefore you have nothing to lose by making smart rational arguments to a jury based on reason and reality.

This paper offers a brief account of foundational bias. Foundational bias happens when a party at trial asserts that the other side is biased. If the other side makes a substantive argument or argues that they are not biased, both arguments can be dismissed as biased and therefore not credible. If your argument that you are not biased is itself asserted to be biased, it can become impossible to win the argument absent the tools of legal logic with which to defend yourself. To counter the assertion that X is biased when X asserts Y, X must do three things: assert Y, assert that he knows Y, and assert that it is possible for him to know Y. Further, if Y is factual and the asserted bias is some sort of subjectivity, X must not only assert Y but must also assert that Y exists objectively, that X knows this, and that X can know this. If Y is a legal interpretation, a lawyer must be ready to assert the degree to which it is knowledge and not mere opinion, and why and how he knows it. The lines of reasoning and methods of inference explained in this paper, and the relatively simple system of shorthand notation to organize legal logic, which can be used to diagram and explain proofs, can empower you to make each of the arguments that you need to make in order to overcome accusations of foundational bias, skepticism at its most fundamental, and to prove your case.

THE LOGICAL PROOF THAT EXISTENCE EXISTS

The Anti-Cogito Ergo Sum Argument:

Version 1: R(R)? = R( ) + R?, R( ) = R, if R then R(R).

Version 2: R(R?) = R(R or Not (R)) > R(R) and R(Not(R)) > R(R) = R and R(Not(R)) = CONT = 0.

Version 3: R? = R or Not R. If Not R then R(Not R) = CONT = 0.

In other words, to ask if reality is real, there must be a reality and real beings there to ask that question. If the question of whether reality is real is asked, the question is real, so something is real, so the real exists, so reality exists. If nothing is real then the question of whether reality exists is unimportant and the question itself is not real so there would be no doubting of reality absent that question so the question would not be asked.

The main application of this is to summary judgment (where a litigant can win without going to trial if there is no genuine issue of material fact for a jury to decide). If a real question exists, summary judgment should not be granted. If the only issue is whether to grant summary judgment then it should be granted. The Reality of the issue is what the inquiry should focus on: can R(F)? be asserted in logic without contradiction?

TRIAL LOGIC

This section begins with an account of de novo vs. clear error review and judge's discretion vs. mandatory outcomes and questions of first impression vs. stare decisis and binding precedent. Reasoning is a lot of work and the legal system only wants to pay for it once. If $F > r > L$ at the trial level, the appellate judge can review the facts to determine the correct outcome, or review the trial judge's reasoning, which takes the validity of his cognitive choices for granted, at which point he is just checking the structural soundness of the logic, whether it is logical, which reflects the clear error standard of review. The same is true of state decisis: the legal system only wants to do the work of spending money and costly doctrinal heavy lifting once. In questions of first impression or where a judge has been granted discretion by the laws he is technically unbound. But this account of freedom vs. mandate is deceptive. A judge has free will and can always do whatever he wants. In the case of A v. X a judge can rule for A or X at trial and an appellate judge on a clear error standard can hold for A or X and can say any plausible analysis as his opinion.

But Reality always defines one clear outcome, because the Facts exist objectively and the party who should win is defined by applying the Law to the Facts. Truth, justice, and $L = C(e(R))$ vs. Anything goes, the arbitrary relativist subjectivist stance that every position has pros and cons and you should just arbitrarily pick a position with pros you like and cons you can live with, is a dichotomy, essentially of free will vs. determinism and Objectivism vs. Relativism, that is true for every judge in every case realistically, regardless of binding precedent or standard of review. A judge should always pursue the Truth and hold according to Justice, and a lawyer can argue for truth and justice, instead of adopting the relativist stance that his job is merely to make arguments and the Judge can plausibly choose among positions from whichever pros take his fancy or cons don't dissuade him. R as $1 > L = 1$. If X then do Y, R(X), therefore L(do(Y)). (X v. A(apply L to F)) > (X or A) = rightful winner.

BONUS CONTENT: LEGAL APHORISMS

As some bonus content at the end of this paper, please enjoy this legal wisdom:

The law is opinion ossified into knowledge. So there are two types of arguments: the argument from subjective opinion, and the argument that old subjective opinions are knowledge that can't be questioned.

Lawyers are the guns of modern duels.

A lawyer is a warrior of words.

The law is common sense justified by obscure technicalities. So there are two types of arguments: the argument from common sense, and the argument from the obscure technicalities. A lawsuit tells a story about right and wrong. There is only one winning argument: my client was a good person and the other party wronged him.

On any legal question there is always room for debate, but about this statement, too, there is room for debate.

A lawyer who cannot argue both sides of any issue will very quickly find himself with only half a clientele.

God, country, Jesus, and the US News & World Report law school rankings, but not necessarily in that order.

There are two types of lawyers: the arrogant elitist snobs, and the ones who were too stupid to become arrogant elitist snobs.

Textualism: what the law says. Originalism: Thomas Jefferson's subjective feelings.

(A) A criminal law judge protects goodness from evil.

(B) A criminal law judge protects clean people from trash.

(C) A criminal law judge is a rich white man who has been given the authority to ruin poor Black young men's lives by sending them to jail.

Have I not just said the same thing three times from different points of view?

Rigid rules, unfettered discretion, or the unfathomable compromise somewhere in between?

The law is what a lawyer says it is until someone proves him wrong.

The first thing we do is we kill all the people who tell lawyer jokes that aren't really funny.

Legal writing should be written to be as strong as possible.

Make your legal writing strong.

MAKE your legal writing STRONG!

Be aggressively reasonable.

Go in, make your point, and get out. Don't narrate.*

Be entertaining but informative, for a jury.

Persuasive public speaking, legal research, or technology: win in at least two of these three areas to win at trial.

Never make opposing counsel's argument for them.*

Never say never. Never say always.*

Be aggressively honest and assert the truth even to your own detriment. Juries tend not to believe lawyers whom they view as dishonest.

A case opinion which does not enable a lawyer to predict future holdings on similar yet different facts, and which does not enable law-abiding citizens to predict whether they break or obey the law, is as ephemeral as a puff of smoke, and as dangerous to the health!

The Legal Realists say that a Judge rules based on what he ate for breakfast. This is true only if he ate for breakfast poison that shut down the language and cognitive function centers in his brain.

A multi-factor fact-specific balancing test? Oh, you mean just let the Judge do whatever he wants and do whatever his feelings tell him to do, right? Why not just say so?

A Partner has to succeed. An Associate has to avoid failure.

If the Associates are the exploited slaves of the Partners, they are the most well-compensated slaves in human history.

A great trial lawyer plans out in advance the inferences the jury will draw and when they will draw them.

The benefit to society of the legal profession should be measured by what happens to people who hire bad attorneys. (Hint: what happens is they get a trove of horrors when their lawyer messes up their case!)

Lawyers dance across the hot coals of legal uncertainty every day.

A client is paying his lawyer to be superhuman.

A trial is like an election. It's a popularity contest, high IQ is not always what wins, and sometimes people cheat.

The judge can do whatever he wants. Whether he is right or wrong to do it is another matter entirely.

The art of legal writing is the art of making arguments to a judge who is too busy to consider your arguments. As such, what you say does not matter, but what you seem to have said is all-important.

What does it mean in legal doctrines to say that something must be "reasonable", such as the reasonable expectation of privacy for the Fourth Amendment, reasonable expectations in contract law, or reasonable precautions in torts? "Reasonable" either means nothing or else it means everything. It means not too much and not too little and whatever standard of measurement is asserted as the truth for measuring too much and too little—ah, but how to measure is nothing or everything!

*The ones marked with an asterisk I must attribute to various friends and/or my past law professors.

RAND'S AXIOM PROBLEM: ON OBJECTIVITY, ONTOLOGY, ESSENCE, EPISTEMOLOGY, DEDUCTION, INDUCTION, AND THE FOUNDATIONS OF KNOWLEDGE

INTRODUCTION TO RAND'S AXIOM PROBLEM

The purpose of this paper is to analyze and solve problems in Ayn Rand's epistemology, particularly Rand's theory of axioms. Her main problem is that she fails to offer proof of the axiomatic propositions, which I believe can be debated and denied and are therefore in need of proof, so that Rand's epistemological foundation has a hole in it where a proof of the axioms should be. I will challenge Rand's intrinsic-objective-subjective analysis and posit that a theory of essences intrinsic in reality is necessary to prove identity and existence and to support a theory of reality as objective and concepts as non-arbitrary. I will also seek to offer a new understanding of proof and demonstration as capable of being grounded in empirical observations rather than logical or mathematical deductions. Such an understanding benefits a philosophy of empirical reasoning such as Rand's.

My approach in this paper will employ two different tactics. I will argue that Rand's epistemology, particularly her theory of axioms, is guilty of an internal contradiction. The internal contradiction will be explored in depth below, but can be summarized by saying that the axioms assert that they cannot be proved by reason, yet they form the foundation for all reasoning, hence all reasoning depends upon things that cannot be known by reason, and if a thing cannot be known by reason then it must be accepted on faith, therefore all reason is ultimately founded on unproven beliefs that must be accepted on faith, therefore Rand's epistemology reduces to the statement that reason is based on faith.

But I will also argue that Rand's epistemology contains what I call an "external contradiction". By "external contradiction" I mean that reality exists objectively and Rand's philosophy is not a complete and truthful account of reality as it really exists, hence one may say that Rand's philosophy is contradicted by reality. An internal contradiction happens when someone says that a thing is and also says that it is not, while an external contradiction happens when reality says that a thing is and someone says that it is not. To show Rand's external contradiction, I will offer my own unique, original theory of epistemology, based on the theory of essence. My theory describes reality as it really exists, and Rand's philosophy fails to match it. Note that my argument is not that Rand is wrong because she disagreed with my view, which is of no importance. Rather my argument is that Rand is wrong because her theory does not match reality, which can be known because my theory is a better description of reality than hers. Also, here at the beginning of my argument, I will concede that this paper is merely an introduction to my theory, and many details to my ideas exist that would require a longer discussion to be explained, such that the account given here is incomplete. I fully explain my theory elsewhere, but this paper contains enough of the gist of my ideas for the reader to undertake an evaluation of my claims regarding Rand's epistemology.

In this paper I am going to criticize Rand's position regarding axioms, by which I mean her claim that the propositions "existence exists" and "A is A," which she also referred to as "existence" and "identity," are axiomatic (Rand 1990, 55). She also considered "I exist," in other words consciousness, to be axiomatic, and although I won't deal specifically with that axiom, my argument applies to it also. Once I have established that her position on axioms is contradictory I am going to offer a different theory to replace hers. My purpose is not to show that axioms are false and therefore Objectivism falls apart. On the contrary, my purpose is to show that there are holes in Objectivist epistemology where a proof of the axioms should be, but the axioms can be proved, so that Rand's philosophy can be made much stronger and put on a more stable foundation if the holes are filled.

I do not dispute the truth of existence and identity. I merely dispute whether they are axioms. My main argument is that Rand, by claiming that existence and identity are axioms, claims that these propositions cannot be proven, but that they must be believed, and the only logical result of this is that they must be taken on faith. Nothing should be taken on faith, and I believe that those two propositions should be proved and can be proved. The problem I will seek to solve is how to prove the truth of "existence exists" and "A is A." I also believe that Rand's mistake regarding axioms trickles down and causes problems with her account of objectivity, necessity and universality.

I will begin by offering Rand's view of axioms in her own words. I will proceed to explore what Rand's axioms mean and discuss the problems with axioms and axiomatic concepts. I will look at Rand's arguments about the impossibility of rejecting the axioms without also accepting them, the non-existence of non-existence, and the stolen concept. I will then examine the difference between premises and implications. I will explain my approach to proving existence and identity by using perceptions as premises combined with essential reasoning. I will conclude by critiquing Rand's intrinsic-objective-subjective analysis and her theories of objectivity, necessity and universality.

RAND'S AXIOMS IN
HER OWN WORDS

Rand's position regarding axioms is evident from a passage in John Galt's speech:

"'You cannot *prove* that you exist or that you're conscious,' they chatter, blanking out the fact that *proof* presupposes existence, consciousness and a complex chain of knowledge: the existence of something to know, of a consciousness able to know it, and of a knowledge that has learned to distinguish between such concepts as the proved and the unproved.

'When a savage who has not learned to speak declares that existence must be proved, he is asking you to prove it by means of non-existence—when he declares that your consciousness must be proved, he is asking you to prove it by means of unconsciousness—he is asking you to step into a void outside of existence and consciousness to give him proof of both—he is asking you to become a zero gaining knowledge about a zero.

'When he declares that an axiom is a matter of arbitrary choice and he doesn't choose to accept the axiom that he exists, he blanks out the fact that he has accepted it by uttering that sentence, that the only way to reject it is to shut one's mouth, expound no theories and die.

'An axiom is a statement that identifies the base of knowledge and of any further statement pertaining to that knowledge, a statement necessarily contained in all others, whether any particular speaker chooses to identify it or not. An axiom is a proposition that defeats its opponents by the fact that they have to accept it and use it in the process of any attempt to deny it'" (Rand 1957, 956).

Rand says much the same thing in her "Introduction to Objectivist Epistemology":

"Since axiomatic concepts refer to facts of reality and are not a matter of 'faith' or of man's arbitrary choice, there is a way to ascertain whether a given concept is axiomatic or not: one ascertains it by observing the fact that an axiomatic concept cannot be escaped, that it is implicit in all knowledge, that it has to be accepted and used even in the process of any attempt to deny it" (Rand 1990, 59).

We can summarize Rand's argument regarding axioms. First, she claims that the axioms cannot be proved, because proof presupposes or assumes knowledge already contained in the axioms or in an attempt at proof. Second, she attacks anyone who asks her to prove the axioms by claiming that they seek knowledge of existence from non-existence. Third, she argues that the only way to reject the axioms is to shut up and die, and fourth, she argues that one must believe the axioms even though they cannot be proved, because it is impossible to reject them without also accepting them at the same time. We can reduce this to three basic ideas: first, the impossibility of denying the axioms, second, the non-existence of non-existence, and third, the stolen concept. I will address each of these ideas later, but first I would like to look at the theory of axioms more generally.

WHAT DO RAND'S AXIOMATIC PROPOSITIONS MEAN?

Rand believed that "existence exists" and "A is A" are axioms, but to see whether this belief is problematic we must inquire into what Rand's axiomatic propositions mean, and what it means to be an axiom (Rand 1957, 933-34). One dictionary defines "axiom" as "established or accepted principle" or "self-evident truth," and defines "self-evident" as "obvious; without the need of proof or further explanation" (Thompson 1998, 52, 826). Rand refers to Aristotle (not by name, but as "the greatest of your philosophers") when first explaining her belief in axioms, so it may be useful to examine Aristotle's understanding of axioms (Rand 1957, 934). Aristotle, in describing his theory of logic as demonstration from premises in "Posterior Analytics" Book I Chapter 2, defines an axiom as a "basic truth," i.e. a proposition in a syllogistic demonstration that has no proposition prior to it, which a pupil must know in order to learn anything even though it cannot be proved by the teacher (Aristotle 1947, 12-13). In Book I Chapter 10 he says of basic truths that they cannot be proved, and that axioms express necessary self-grounded fact and must necessarily be believed (28-29).

I would define axioms as propositions that are self-evident and form the basis of all reasoning. Rand says that "axioms are usually considered to be… fundamental, self-evident truth," and axioms are made of axiomatic concepts (Rand 1990, 55). Rand's axiomatic concepts are "primary," meaning that they are irreducible (55). She doesn't say that axioms are the beginning of all cognitive activity, but her description indicates that the purpose of the axioms is to act as "guidelines" for and to "underscore" and "delimit" all conceptual thought (59). The function of the axioms is "delimiting (knowledge) from non-existence, imagination, falsehood, etc." (261). She claims that axioms are the "base" of knowledge (Rand 1957, 956). From this it seems that Rand's axioms are the foundation for all conceptual thought in the stage of adulthood, and that Rand's axioms really are axioms in the Aristotelian sense.

What did Rand mean by the phrases "existence exists" and "A is A"? The closest Rand comes to explaining what "existence exists" means is her explanation of existence as an "axiomatic concept" as found in "Introduction to Objectivist Epistemology" (Rand 1990, 55-61). Rand claims that existence is a quality that applies to everything (56). If existence were a concept that applied to everything, then it would have no real meaning, at least no more so than the concept "everything." The phrase "existence exists" should mean more than simply "everything is everything," which is an empty statement. "Everything is everything" is an empty statement with no real meaning because the proposition "everything is everything" does not reveal new information about the term "everything."

What, then, is Rand's definition of "everything," or of "existence"? Rand doesn't believe that "existence" needs to be defined at all: "Since axiomatic concepts are identifications of irreducible primaries, the only way to define one is by means of an ostensive definition—e.g., to define 'existence,' one would have to sweep one's arm around and say: 'I mean this'" (41). The only problem is that "this" has no meaning, or if it has a meaning it is so vague and imprecise as to be useless for rational thought. Rand offers a way to refer to existence, not a definition of existence, not a description of what existence is. If it is impossible to give an intelligible definition for some idea, a definition capable of explanation, then that idea's usefulness for rational thought is highly dubious. Concretes are perceived, and so they can be defined by pointing to them; for example, I could point to an apple on my desk and say "I mean this apple." But existence and identity are abstractions, not concretes, and as such they are not directly perceived and should not be defined that way.

Of course, Rand believed that existence and identity are concepts that are perceived directly (55). My objection to this is the observation that I can see a chair, or a table, or a book, or an apple, but I do not see the concept of "existence" as such, and Rand fails to explain how one arrives at the universal abstraction "existence" via induction from perceptions of specific concretes.

"Existence exists" has a meaning. One dictionary defines "exist" as "have a place in objective reality," and defines "existence" as "all that exists" (Thompson 1998, 303). I argue that "existence" means not just being, but also having a physical, objective existence at a specific place and time, and "physical" and "objective" are not axiomatic concepts and can be debated. "Existence exists" means "reality is real," which means "everything in this world is physical and objective," and that is a statement which has content. I would argue based upon my understanding of the English language that the definition of the concept of "exist" reduces to three distinguishing characteristics: that the existing thing has the quality of being at a specific place and time, that it is made of physical substance, and that it is objective.

Rand rejected this view, arguing that "existence exists" does not reduce to "there is a physical world" (Rand 1990, 245-51). But Rand fails to adequately address two problems: first, that if "existence exists" does not mean that, then it has no meaning other than "everything is everything," which has no content, and secondly, that based on the definitions of words in the English language, the best interpretation of "existence exists" is "reality is physical and objective." Rand claims that even a primitive savage who believes in supernatural spirits has grasped that "existence exists" (248). But if that is true then we must ask: what does the savage really know? And why doesn't this knowledge prevent him from believing in spirits? If "existence" is so general, then it really is no different from saying "everything is everything," which has very little meaning.

It seems that Rand really intended "existence exists" to mean "everything is everything." She says "…what's the difference between saying 'existence exists' and 'the physical world exists'? 'Existence exists' does not specify what exists" (247). She also says "the concept 'existence' does not indicate what existents it subsumes: it merely underscores the primary fact that they exist" (59). If it is really true that "existence exists" does not specify what kinds of things exist, and is not the same as "existence is physical and objective," then Rand's axiom would not contradict the proposition "existence is made of Platonic Forms." If Rand is right then "existence exists" has virtually no content whatsoever.

Perhaps looking at the purpose of the axioms will shed light on their meaning. Rand says that axiomatic concepts enable one to know that what is true at one point in time is true at every point in time (56-57, 260-61). But how do axiomatic concepts accomplish that purpose? Her answer to that question is vague and imprecise (261). She says that the axioms' purpose is to distinguish object from subject (57, 261). But she is unclear about precisely how they do so. And she says that axioms underscore primary facts and confine knowledge to reality (261). But if "existence exists" does not say anything specific about what reality is, then how does it limit knowledge about reality? I found no intelligible explanation of how axioms accomplish these purposes in "Introduction to Objectivist Epistemology". I don't consider it a defense on Rand's part that she believed that axiomatic concepts could not be analyzed, such that the answers to my questions should be self-evident (55). If she had consistently applied the belief that axioms are incapable of analysis then she would not have been able to fill a whole section of her book on epistemology with an analysis of axiomatic concepts.

I will concede that Rand attempted to add content to her axioms in Galt's speech. She says: "existence exists—and the act of grasping that statement implies two corollary axioms: that something exists which one perceives and that one exists possessing consciousness…. To exist is to be something, as distinguished from the nothing of non-existence, it is to be an entity of a specific nature made of specific attributes. … Reality is that which exists; the unreal does not exist…" (Rand 1957, 933-34).

She says that existence exists and that to exist is to be something, in which case "existence exists" reduces to "everything is something." I argue that there are three problems with that reduction. First, "everything is something" might reduce to "A is A," making the first axiom redundant. Second, Rand does not give a significant analysis of what it means to be something or to have a specific nature, such that "everything is something" has little content.

My third and central problem is I believe that non-existing things are things with identities, so that "existence exists" cannot reduce to "everything is something." Regarding this analysis, I argue that "to exist" and "to be something" are different concepts. I call this analysis the Japanese Distinction, because in the Japanese language there are two completely different words for "to be" and "to exist". Japanese uses the word "desu" for "to be something" and the word "arimasu" for "to exist." (Japanese also has a third word, "imasu" which means "to be alive, to exist as a living thing".) For Rand's understanding of "existence exists" to be correct there must be no difference between the terms "to be something" and "to exist". In the English language the word "to be" has both meanings, but I argue that this is a coincidence and not a philosophical insight. This ties into Rand's idea of the "reification of the zero," which is that, according to her, only existing things are things, and nonexistent things are not really things at all, nothingness as such does not exist and is not a thing, and every truthful description of a non-existent actually reduces to a description of existents because non-existents can be known only in relation to existents (Rand 1990, 58, 60-61, 149-50).

My critique of Rand's reification of the zero argument has several parts. First, the terms "exist" and "be something" are conceptually distinguishable. One can say "a nonexistent thing" and "a non-identity" and mean two different things. One can also say of a gigantic bronze statue of Ayn Rand inside the main concourse of Grand Central Terminal in New York City that it does not exist, however it is something, and it has an identity. It has attributes of substance, appearance, and location, so one cannot say that it is not a thing. Second, it seems to me that it should be impossible to know anything about something that has no identity, so that if non-existents are not things, they would be unknowable. But one can possess some degree of knowledge about Platonic Forms, pink elephants, fictional statues of Ayn Rand, what one experiences in one's dreams, or for that matter Howard Roark, the hero of Rand's novel, who is fictional and therefore does not exist but who has a knowable personality. Rand's idea, if followed to its logical conclusion, prevents us from describing the things that don't exist. I concede that nonexistent things cannot be known except in relation to that which exists, but that doesn't mean that they have no identity.

Third, it seems to me that when something is destroyed and ceases to exist, what happens is not that it ceases to have an identity, but that it ceases to have an identity with attributes of being at that place and time in physical reality. And fourth, if Rand were right then the number "zero" would not be a thing, yet it seems to me that zero is a number and has a mathematical identity. I agree that zero does not exist, but I do not agree that it has no identity. Regarding this point Rand might have argued that zero is a concept of method, a claim that she made regarding imaginary numbers (35-36, 304-6). My dispute with numbers as concepts of method is that while the numbers may be used as a means of discovery, the numbers in themselves, e.g. the square root of negative one, must either be something or not be something, because anything else would be a contradiction. Rand's concepts of method are ambiguous as to whether they refer to things or not.

I must clarify that I believe that everything that exists is a thing, but not that everything which is a thing exists. It is difficult to make a distinction between "to exist" and "to be" because every existing thing is something. However the distinction can be done on the basis of things that don't exist, e.g. zero, and it is equally difficult, or impossible, to distinguish "to exist" from "to be objectively physical at a specific place and time," because every existing thing also has that attribute. If Platonic Forms and pink elephants are non-existing things, as I argue, then there must be something more to "exists" than merely "is something." And I posit that the something more is being physical and objective at a specific place and time.

CAN RAND'S AXIOMS BE DEBATED OR DENIED?

If it is truly impossible to debate or deny existence and identity then they are not in need of proof and Rand's axioms do not have a problem. I believe that Rand's axioms can be denied, even if they mean exactly what Rand intended them to mean and do not mean what I claimed they should mean in the previous section. In order to argue that Rand's axioms can be debated, first I will argue that linguistically it is possible to frame propositions that contradict the axioms in a manner capable of being understood and discussed, second I will argue that if the axioms cannot be proved then logic is circular reasoning, and third I will briefly discuss two famous philosophers, Plato and Derrida, whom I think would not have agreed with Rand's axioms as Rand meant them.

To argue that one can state contradictions in a way capable of being understood and debated it may be useful to analyze the term "coherent." That term has two meanings, a common English meaning and a technical philosophical meaning, and it helps clarify the use of the word to distinguish the two meanings. The technical meaning of "coherent" is "not entailing any contradictions," or in other words, non-contradictory and logical (personal correspondence, 3 May 2009). The common meaning of "coherent," found in a dictionary, is "intelligible and articulate," and this dictionary defines "intelligible" as "able to be understood" (Thompson 1998, 158, 460). If one were to fail to carefully distinguish the two meanings one might think that incoherent propositions cannot be understood because they are contradictory, but I argue that it is possible to understand ideas that are contradictory and illogical. For example, the statement "hgteagleajrg bjergaoejighl gikhalighi" is unintelligible, whereas the statement "if you achieve knowledge of spiritual reality then it will be revealed to you that the physical world is really not the physical world" contains a contradiction, but has a meaning that is capable of being understood and debated.

If you can state contradictory propositions in a way that is intelligible then you can debate whether they are true or not, and it becomes necessary to prove that A is A in order to refute the truth of illogical propositions. Contradictory propositions that are intelligible and debatable can be formulated. It might be hard to imagine someone believing "a cat is not a cat" or "a triangle is a square circle." However, a more easily imaginable example is that a person can say "humans do not need to think in order to survive, but only need to believe in God," which Rand might have thought violated the principle "Man is Man," which violates the axiom "A is A," so Rand might have considered such a statement to be contradictory (Rand 1957, 934). Similarly one can imagine a person believing the economic theory that "inflation creates jobs," which someone else might believe to be a contradiction.

One might believe that existence and identity cannot be denied except by an insane person. It is difficult to imagine a sane person believing that A is non-A, and it is difficult to find a philosopher who openly claims that logic is useless. But a quote from Rand's Toohey speech sheds light on this: "Men have a weapon against you. Reason. So you must be very sure to take it away from them. Cut the props from under it. But be careful. Don't deny outright.... Don't say reason is evil—though some have gone that far and with astonishing success. Just say that reason is limited. That there's something above it. What? You don't have to be too clear about it either. The field's inexhaustible. 'Instinct'—'Feeling'—'Revelation'—'Divine Intuition'—'Dialectic Materialism.'... Suspend reason and you play it deuces wild. Anything goes in any manner you wish whenever you need it" (Rand 1943, 637). Rand seems to be saying that illogical thinking is widespread, and that a person can deny logic not by denying identity openly, but by believing in something besides logic. Based on this quote Rand seems to agree that logic can be denied, in fact she seems to be saying that religion and Marxism both reject reason, and if reason can be denied then it can be debated, and if it can be debated then it is in need of proof.

If "A is A" is not demonstrated then all logic is mere circular reasoning: if logic is valid because "A is A," and "A is A" is true because it is logical, then logic is a circle. It might be illogical to disbelieve that "A is A," but if logical belief in a proposition requires proof by demonstration, and "A is A" cannot be proved by demonstration, and all logic is based on belief in the proposition "A is A," then logic is not based on logic, which means, logic is not logical. To say that logic needs special rules for axioms is to concede that axioms are not logical. Either obedience to logic has an intellectual origin, in which case we have the problem of showing what that origin is, or else there is no reason to believe that one should be logical, and logic is merely arbitrary and without a foundation. My problem is more than the mere question of why one should believe in logic, although it includes that question. My inquiry is the question of where logic comes from, because if logic's foundation comes from intuition and is incapable of rational proof then it is no better than any other intellectual strategy that comes from intuition, particularly faith in God. If you cannot demonstrate that "A is A" then faith is the only basis for claiming "A is A," and if you choose to believe in unproven, undemonstrated axioms then it is mere preference whether you prefer the axiom "A is A" or the axiom "God exists," since both would be equally unproven.

I accept that it is impossible to dispute identity, the principle of non-contradiction, without being illogical, but if a person does not begin with the belief that thinking should obey the rules of logic then one has no way of knowing that it is wrong to think illogically. Rand's argument that you can only put the negation of the axioms into practice by abandoning language and committing suicide would be true only if one had to put the negations into practice in a way that was strictly consistent. But if you negate identity you no longer bind yourself to be strictly consistent, and the axioms can be denied in a way that is irrational and contradictory, but not impossible, e.g. you can believe in the physical world and in a spiritual world at the same time.

I must also note that I can think of two philosophers who might dispute Rand's axioms; I cannot be sure about what either of them would have said about Rand's axioms but I can make educated guesses. I would guess that Plato would not agree that "existence exists." He would say that existence, the perceivable world, is a mere shadow of the world of Forms, as for example in his famous cave metaphor in "Republic", or his discussion of Forms in "Phaedo" (Plato 1997, 57-73, 1132-35). And based upon what I have read about Derrida I would guess that instead of agreeing with "A is A" he would try to deconstruct that statement. Insofar as "A is A" claims to be a perfectly rational statement that perfectly represents the real world, Derrida might critique it as logocentric presence, and would dispute that any language can capture objective universal truth (Appignanesi 2007, 77-81). Because the axioms can be debated and denied we need a demonstration of them to show to doubters in order to prove to them that the axioms are true.

THE NON-EXISTENCE OF NON-EXISTENCE AND THE STOLEN CONCEPT

Before I show how it is possible to prove that existence exists and that A is A by means of essential reasoning from sensory experience, let us consider two of Rand's ideas that she offers in support of her axioms: the non-existence of non-existence and the stolen concept. Rand's non-existence of non-existence idea contains two parts: first, that the negation of existence, i.e. non-existence, doesn't exist, and therefore you have to accept existence; and second, to obtain proof of existence one would need to go outside of existence, into the realm of non-existence (Rand 1957, 956). This argument can be seen as a form of proof. But this argument is a negative proof, not a positive proof: she proves that non-existence does not exist, not that existence exists. To justify Objectivism we need positive proof. If a negative is not a positive, as Rand claims (for example, "light is not 'the absence of darkness,'.... Existence is not a negation of negatives,") then disproving the negative of "existence exists" is not the same as proving the positive "existence exists" (941-42). Rand's argument defines reality by what it is not rather than by what it is, yet her sharpest criticism of the concept of God is that it is defined only by what it is not (951-52).

Rand argues that the person who wants proof of existence wants it to come from outside of existence (956). Her general idea is that existence is all around us, so the people who doubt it want knowledge from outside of existence. This may be true for her anti-reason critic, but it is not true for the honest inquirer. Do we need to not have bodies in order to prove the truths of biology? Do we need to not contain chemicals in our bodies in order to prove the truths of chemistry? Do we need to live in a world with no geometric shapes in order to prove the truths of geometry? Does proving something within existence require you to have a point of view from outside of existence? I do not believe that it does. Why would we need non-existence in order to prove that existence exists? Critics of objectivity might claim that you would need a point of view outside of experience to claim objective knowledge, but that view is not consistent with a belief that objectivity is possible.

The stolen concept argument is that when you reject the axioms you also accept the axioms, or when you deny the axioms you use the axioms in the process, and therefore they must be accepted and can't be rejected (956). But to make this argument two things are necessary. First, you have to prove that the concepts are stolen. When this is done you establish a contradiction: you both accept and reject the axioms. Proving the theft in a persuasive manner is a big problem. It is hard to argue that the proposition "existence does not exist" contains or relies upon the proposition "existence exists," or that "A is not A" borrows the idea "A is A." The Socratic claim "I know that I know nothing" does not seem like a claim to knowledge. It seems like a claim to ignorance, with a meaning that is identical to "I know nothing" or "I do not know anything." This refutes the Randian argument that the statement "I know that I know nothing" both claims and denies knowledge, such that it entails a contradiction and accepts that knowledge is possible. I will flesh out my objection to this aspect of Rand's argument further when I discuss premises and implications in the next section.

Second, having established that a theory or idea contains a contradiction, you have to also prove that contradictions don't exist for the contradiction to be a problem. Even if you could prove that the axioms are "stolen," which would be difficult, you would still need to prove that the laws of logic should be obeyed in order for the theft to be problematic, assuming that you don't begin with an unproven law of non-contradiction. The argument that "contradictions exist" is contradictory is a circular argument: if you don't already have a proof that contradictions don't exist, then proving that "contradictions exist" is contradictory does not invalidate it, because something could exist despite being contradictory. The negative proof results in circular reasoning, and the only solution is a positive proof of "A is A."

PREMISES AND IMPLICATIONS

Nietzsche in "Twilight of the Idols" claimed that philosophers confuse the last with the first, the most abstract with the most basic, and the ultimate goal of thought with the intellectual point of origin (Nietzsche 1990, 47). This is precisely Rand's mistake. "Existence exists" and "A is A" are perhaps the most abstract propositions possible, so it makes little sense to say that thought begins with those, or that they form the base of all reasoning. It would be better to say that thought begins with induction based on the observation of the objects of perception, the most specific or "concrete," and ends with axiomatic propositions, the most general or "abstract."

I argue that Rand's theory of axioms is itself a contradiction. But I believe that her mistake is probably not random. I would conjecture that Rand made her mistake for two reasons: first, she herself did not fully understand how she had arrived at her knowledge of existence and identity, and because she did not know how to reason them, she claimed that they could not be proven. When you are sure about something but you don't know the reasons behind your knowledge, the temptation is to say that it is self-evident, which translates into the statement "I know it but I don't know why." Second, she saw that it seems as though you would have to know existence and identity in order to do any reasoning, including any reasoning that would prove them: after all, doesn't existence have to exist in order for you to be able to reason that existence exists, so wouldn't any proof be circular? (Rand 1957, 956). Regarding the first problem, I have something that Rand lacked, a proof that existence exists. But regarding the second problem we must ask: does all reasoning use those two axioms as premises?

How can you possibly reason that A is A without already knowing it? How can you engage in any reasoning or any thought without the premise that A is A and the premise that existence exists? If that were true then these ideas would have to be in the mind at birth, and they would be intuitions accepted on faith, which is precisely the problem with Rand's belief in axioms. The problem here was that Rand was confused about the difference between implications and premises. Something that is implied by an act of reason is different than something that is a premise in an act of reason. I would define an "implication" of reasoning as something that makes the reasoning true and has to be true in order for the reasoning to take place, and a "premise" of reasoning as that belief, proposition, or source of knowledge that is actually what the conclusion of the logical argument is deduced from. Identity and existence are implied by all reason, in that obviously there would be no reasoning taking place if existence did not exist in order to our brains to exist and think, and there would be no logical thought possible if things were not themselves.

But the principles of existence and identity are not what knowledge, in its origin, is actually deduced from. They are implied in all reason, but they are not the premises of all reason. Sensory experience is what all rational conclusions are ultimately reasoned from. Sense-perceived objects are the premises of all reason, since all reason begins with specific sense-perceived objects and proceeds via induction to general abstractions. Rational knowledge begins with the objects of sensory perception, and then proceeds by deriving general principles from specific perceived objects. In other words, reason integrates concepts from sense-perceived concretes. The foundation of all thought is not axioms. The foundation of thought is the specific sensory perceptions from which our concepts are formed. Rand's belief about axioms is chronologically backwards. She has us beginning with what comes only at the end. Identity and existence are not our most fundamental premises. In fact, they are the two most abstract and general concepts of all our conceptual abstract generalizations, which means they are the pinnacle of thought, not the start of thought. They are implied by all reason, but they are not the first premises of all reason.

Rand did put forward a theory of "implicit" concepts (Rand 1990, 159-62). But she seems to suggest that an implicit concept is one that is implicitly present because the material from which to integrate it is present and the mind is in the stage or process of integrating it (162). Thus, Rand's "implicit" is something in the process of being integrated, rather than something that must be true in order for reasoning to take place, and so her analysis is not precise enough to mesh with my argument. For example, I would disagree with Rand and say that the laws of physics are implicit in all reasoning (162). I would also say that an infant or young child has no awareness that existence exists or A is A, because sophisticated cognition is necessary to grasp those concepts (162). Because she was imprecise about whether an infant is actually aware of an implicit concept or not, simply saying that it is "not yet conceptualized, but it is available," it is difficult to know to what degree Rand would have disagreed with me about that (161).

I have a problem with Rand's belief that axioms are the foundation of all thought. You do not begin with the laws of logic inherent in the mind and then apply logic to the perceivable world. That is a Kantian approach to epistemology (Kant 1977, 38-49, 63-64). I believe that in the human mind as it develops for real human beings, in babies and young children, you begin with an empty mind, you experience sense-perceived objects, and then you reason from the specific perceived objects to general abstractions. You begin with sense-experience and then derive the laws of logic from that experience, using inductive reasoning. You do not begin with the laws of logic and then use them as the foundation for all cognition. Rand might have agreed with me about intellectual development because she believed that children integrate abstractions from concretes (Rand 1990, 11-13, 19-21). But if she did agree she would be contradicting herself, because beginning with the laws of logic and applying them to the world is no different from beginning with unjustified axioms and applying them to the world. Both approaches lead inexorably towards Kantian epistemology in which the laws of logic come from pure reason prior to empirical experience. The origin of reason can be either self-evident axioms or inductive reasoning from sensory experience, but not both. If axioms could be derived by inductive reason from experience then they would not be self-evident, because the observations from which they were reasoned would prove them and be the evidence supporting them.

PROOF, DEMONSTRATION, AND PERCEPTIONS AS PREMISES

To solve Rand's axiom problem we must discover a way to prove existence and identity. Before I offer my solution to Rand's problem, I must address the question of what "proof" is and what it means to be "demonstrated," and also what "self-evident" means. It is possible for someone to believe that nothing is logically demonstrated or proved unless the demonstration begins with premises and demonstrates that the premises prove the conclusion by means of demonstrated mathematical computations or the rules of symbolic formal logic. Such a person might believe that logic enables deductions, but that sensory experiences only enable mere inferences, but never deductions. Aristotle may have believed this: in "Posterior Analytics" Book I Chapter 31 he claims that perceptions do not provide the scientific knowledge of demonstration, because perceptions are of particulars and demonstrations are of universals (Aristotle 1947, 66-68). But in Book II Chapter 19, where Aristotle grappled with the problem of the origins of axiomatic knowledge, he states that knowledge of basic truths comes from induction from sense-perception, but he then contradicts himself by saying that it comes from intuition (106-9).

The belief that demonstration comes from logic and mathematics but not from perception is a flawed, one-sided account of reason: it accepts deductive reason as proof, but rejects inductive reason, which takes sensory experience and derives generalized abstractions and premises from that experience. If inductive reason is incapable of proof, then how can you prove the premises that logic begins with? The argument "If P then Q, P, therefore Q", or "If P then Q and R, not Q, therefore not P", and all other similar syllogisms, are mere abstract theory detached from any basis in practical reality if we lack a principle of induction capable of telling us whether P is true or false. Similarly, the logical argument "all money is made by doing work, it is good to make money, therefore it is good to let people be free to do more work," depends upon proof that making money is caused by doing work, which can only be proved via induction from sensory observations, and cannot be derived entirely from deductive logic and axioms. Unlike Rand and Aristotle, I have solved the problem of induction, by means of my theory of essence, and through empirical essential reasoning I can achieve proof and demonstrations of universals by reference to specific concrete observations.

In order to understand the theory of essential reasoning as inductive proof, we must be precise in what we mean by proof and demonstration. Something has been demonstrated, and you have proof of something, if you can point to a source of knowledge and show how you can reason a conclusion from it that is true if the source of knowledge is real. In other words, something is proven if you have evidence that proves the conclusion. The claim "a cat is in the room" can be proven if you see a cat in the room: if your perception of the cat is accurate, in other words if the cat that you see is real, then the cat itself, which you perceive, is the proof of the truth of the proposition, and you can prove it to someone else by pointing out the cat to them. The problem of induction is how we can point to one cat in the room and infer "all cats are mammals" from this one cat which we perceive, and essence is the tool that enables inductive reasoning to infer from specific to general.

It seems to me that an induction-deduction dichotomy, which could also be called a perception-logic split, is appropriate for philosophers like Kant and Descartes who want all proof to come from the analysis of concepts and who believe that logic and mathematics are pure but that the temporal physical world is muddled and illusory. But for a philosophy that believes that reason should properly be focused on the physical world and which thinks that truth can be known from empirical observations, we need to accept that induction is necessary for logic and that perceptions can be premises in deductions. I do not believe that we should draw a sharp distinction between inductive and deductive reasoning, because the two terms merely describe different phases of the same process. It is beyond the scope of this essay to prove that sense-perception provides accurate knowledge of reality which admits of absolute certainty (although I will discuss objectivity below), but it seems as though Rand accepted that it does (Rand 1957, 934).

Regarding the term "self-evident," I would argue that perceptions are the only premises that can be self-evident. I believe that a "self-evident" premise is not one that needs no proof, because something that cannot be proved would require faith in order to be known. A self-evident premise is one that contains the proof of itself within itself, in other words it proves itself just by being perceived. When I see a red apple, the apple itself is the proof that it is red, and that it exists. It contains the proof of itself within itself, therefore it is self-evident. If someone argues that the apple is not red, you simply show him the apple: the apple is the proof of its redness. One might say along these lines that "the proof is in the pudding," or as the English say, "the proof in the pudding is to be found in the eating." The proof of the thing's existence is in the thing itself, as perceived by the senses. Self-evidence is therefore a property that belongs only to specific sense-perceived objects, and not to ideas. To rephrase this in Randian terms, concretes can be self-evident, but abstractions, such as existence and identity, cannot be self-evident.

THE SOLUTION OF
ESSENTIAL REASONING

My solution to Rand's axiom problem is to claim that perceived things, the objects of sensory perception, are self-evident, and universal laws such as existence and non-contradiction can be reasoned from sense experience by means of inductive reasoning. If you can reason from the experience of an apple that the apple cannot be ripe and rotten at the same time, then you can deduce a universal idea of non-contradiction from a specific instance of non-contradiction. Once derived from specific cases, universal principles can then be applied by deductive reasoning to all future instances. The propositions "existence exists" and "A is A" are best defended, not by any of Rand's arguments, but by arguing that the knowledge of existence and identity can be grasped by inductive reasoning applied to sensory experience, and that this constitutes proof.

But there is a big problem here: how do we go from specific experiences to universal principles? How does inductive reasoning work? We can go from a specific instance to a universal law by a process that I call "the necessary consequence of the ontological essence." Some Objectivist readers might react with horror to my use of the concept of "essence," but this issue will be addressed in the following section. My solution to Rand's axiom problem depends on the idea of "essence," so I will proceed to argue that reason is best understood as relying on essences. In order to argue this I must explain my view of how essential reasoning works. It took me 120,000 words in a philosophical treatise (An Essay on Reason and Perception, by Russell Hasan) to fully explain my theory of essences, essential reasoning and essential things, but let me try to do so now in five paragraphs. First I will define "ontological essence" as whatever quality or attribute a thing has that makes it be a particular kind of thing, and then define "the consequence of an essence" as whatever being or attributes a thing has that is caused by it having an essential attribute. In other words, a thing's essence is what makes it be that thing, and the consequence of the essence is whatever results from having that essence.

There are three ways in which an essence of a thing may result in the consequence of the essence in that thing: first, by causation; second, by requirement; and third, by containment. For example, the essence of iron will cause it to sink in a pool of water, because being iron causes a thing to be heavier than water, so that it will sink in water is a consequence of the essence of iron. Wood will require something that cuts it to be harder than wood as a means of cutting it, so the essence of being a thing that can cut wood will require the thing to be harder than wood, so that if iron cuts wood then a consequence of the essence of iron is being harder than wood. And being a metal is part of the act of being iron, because to be iron is to be a metal, so the act of being iron contains the act of being metal as a part of it, hence being metal is a consequence of the essence of being iron. From this essential reasoning we can conclude that iron is a metal, that it sinks in water, and that it is harder than wood. This will be true of all iron everywhere, such that if a thing is iron then it will do those things, and if something does not do those things then it cannot be iron.

The best example of essential reasoning comes from geometry. Reason begins with inductive reasoning: for example, you see the cover of a box, which is a red cardboard square. Your eye sends information to your brain, and this information in your brain is the perception of the red cardboard square. You analyze this information and separate the different aspects of the object. In its aspect as a red object, it is red. In its aspect as a shape with four equal sides, it is a square. By thinking this through you create the concept of a square in your brain: the processed perception becomes a concept. This is inductive reasoning. Reason can then take the essences known from perception and abstract more essential qualities from them to build knowledge of more abstract essences, such as going from the concept "square" to the concept "shape."

What makes a thing a square, in this case having four equal sides, is the essence of the square, and the consequence of that essence is whatever qualities a thing has that are caused by having that essence. You can reason the consequence of the essence of a square by thinking about the essential square, an object that has four equal sides and has no other qualities. The essential square has four right angles, because the consequence of the essence of having four equal sides is having four right angles. Having four equal sides causes a thing to have four right angles. This is deductive essential reasoning.

What is true of the essential square must be true of it because of the essence of square. Therefore what is true of the essential square must be true of all squares in the real world, because to be a square all those objects must have the square essence. If a thing did not have the essence of a square, then it would not be a square, so for a thing to be a square requires it to have the square essence, and the essence causes the consequence, so we can infer that everything that is a square has four right angles, because being a square will cause it to have four right angles. Therefore it is impossible for something to be a square and to not have four right angles. It is necessary for every square to have the consequence of the square essence, because everything that is a square must have the square essence in order to be a square, and having the square essence causes a thing to have the square consequence. By isolating the essence of a thing from a specific perceived thing and then employing essential reasoning, a person can achieve inductive reasoning and can infer general propositions from specific instances. This also shows that universal laws are obeyed because of things in themselves, not because of the structure of the mind, contrary to Kant.

Every essence is an attribute (and every attribute is an essence relative to the other non-essential attributes of that thing), and the attribute of having four equal sides is the square essence. The square essence is an aspect of squares in the real world, but the essential square does not exist: it has no specific place or time, and existing things always exist at a specific place and time. You can take essential reasoning from the essential square and apply it to new squares that you encounter. You see something square which is new to you and which you have never encountered before and yet you know instantly that it has four right angles because it is square. This is essential identification. You can take one thing as the representative of all of its kind, for example geometric reasoning from one square applied to all squares, only if you reason from the square essence of your representative square, which everything of that kind must have in order to be that kind of thing. This is why a geometric demonstration using one specific square as an example to show that every square in the universe has four right angles is effective, even though the example is just one square and there are other different squares with different measurements of the lengths of its sides. A demonstration is universal because the demonstrator deduces his proof from the square essence of the example square.

The three central mistakes that people make in their thinking are all mistakes in essential reasoning. First, some people think that what happened repeatedly in the past will always happen again in the future, confusing coincidence with necessity because they don't look for the consequence of the essence. For example, if someone sees one hundred wooden square boxes they may infer incorrectly that all squares are made of wood. This is why correlation is not causation. This is also the origin of belief in magic, e.g. someone does a dance and it rains so they conclude that doing a dance causes the sky to rain. Second, some people believe that something necessary is merely a coincidence, again because they don't grasp the consequence of the essence. This is the origin of skepticism. And third, some people believe that essential things are real, leading to a belief in a non-physical world of spiritual ideas. I posit this last mistake as the origin of Platonic Forms. This is a concise summary of my theory of essences.

If we can reason that an apple cannot be both ripe and rotten because it is an apple, then we can say that if a thing is both ripe and rotten, it is not an apple. In this way we can go from one apple to every apple, and the ontology of the thing itself, in itself, requires reality to universally obey what we believe. If the essence requires the consequence then everything of that kind must have that consequence because to be a thing of that kind requires having that essence. It follows that if a thing did not have the consequence of the essence it could not be that kind of thing because having that essence causes that consequence and the absence of the consequence would show the absence of the essence, and so being what it is requires a thing to obey the demonstrated conclusions of essential reasoning.

The line of essential reasoning that proves "A is A" is: a contradiction is both A and not-A, there are some pairs of essences for which being one kind of thing causes a thing to not be the other kind of thing (this would be reasoned by induction from specific instances, e.g. being a dog causes a dog to not be a cat because a dog must have different organs and DNA than a cat in order to be a dog, being ripe requires an apple to have a different appearance and chemical molecular substance than a rotten apple), A and not-A are such a pair because a thing is not-A by not having the essence of A and a thing is A by having the essence of A, therefore the consequence of the essence of being A is not being non-A, therefore the essence of being A will cause the thing that is both A and non-A to cease to be non-A if it continues to be A as a consequence of being A, therefore a contradiction cannot exist.

The line of reasoning proving that "existence exists," if it means "everything (that exists) is something," is: to exist is an attribute, to have an attribute is to be a something (which is deduced from the essence of "thing," which is abstracted from perceived things,) therefore everything that exists is something.

If "existence exists" means "reality is physical and objective," it is reasoned as follows: one forms a concept of the perceivable world as physical and objective by observing perceived objects, e.g. by touching a book you learn that it is physical, by seeing a book both before and after closing your eyes you learn that it exists separately from your perception of it (because it continued to exist while not seen and therefore your vision did not create it), which means that it is objective. Because the essence of existing is being physical and objective, it follows that everything that exists, in other words existence, must be physical and objective. Another line of reasoning proves this: a thing to be perceived must be at a specific place and time, to be at a place it must exist in space, to exist in space it must be physical, to be physical it must be made of physical substance, and to be made of physical substance it must exist outside of consciousness and perception, which proves that the perceivable world exists physically and objectively.

When you reason something from some source, you can point to your source and your reasoning and say that this constitutes proof, that you have not asserted your conclusion, instead you have demonstrated your conclusion. You need only point out an apple to someone and show how you can reason that it cannot be contradictory and that it is physical and objective, and then show how to go from one apple to everything, and you have proved identity and existence to that person.

THE FLAW IN RAND'S INTRINSIC-OBJECTIVE-SUBJECTIVE ANALYSIS

Any reader of mine who is well-versed in Rand's epistemology will now exclaim about my theory: "But that's intrinsic, not objective!" That objection is the fundamental source of Objectivism's rejection of essences (Rand 1990, 52-54). So let's deal with that objection, and see how my theory can improve Rand's account of the objective.

When Rand rejects the theory that essences are in objects rather than in the mind, she is thinking of Plato as the representative of the "intrinsic" position; her problem with Aristotle is that he is too much like Plato (141). The differences between my theory of essences and Plato's Forms come in two parts. The first difference is that Plato's Forms can never be known by sense perception, and my essences can only be known by sense-perceiving objects that have those essences, or by conceptually combining or analyzing the different essences that you have reasoned from perceived objects. The second is that Plato's Forms are in a world apart from the physical world, they are spiritual, and my essences are in the physical world, they are in physical objects. Really the essences are the physical objects, or, to phrase it more precisely, they are physical objects when they are thought about in a certain way, by focusing thought on the essential aspect of the objects. For example, the essence of a dog is every real dog thought of as dog, focusing only on what makes it a dog and not on any of its other characteristics. Also, as I mentioned, it is useful for essential reasoning to think about essential things, but an essential thing does not exist, it is merely a conceptual took for isolating and analyzing the essences of real physical things.

Thus, my essentialism does not reduce to Platonic Forms, and is fully compatible with Objectivism. Rand's objection to intrinsic essences centers on her claim that they can only be known by revelation, and that they exclude consciousness from reality (53, 141). She doesn't consider the possibility that essences could be known by perception, or that they might be in things in themselves but be known though an intellectual process such as essential reasoning which abstracts essences from perceived objects, perhaps because this might damage her intrinsic-objective-subjective idea, which is itself a contradiction. She claimed that a theory such as mine reduces thought to perception (53). But that is not true: the essence is perceived, for example you can see that a dog is a dog, but the act of abstracting the essence from a specific perceived object is an act of thought, for example it is an act of thought to go from a perceived real dog to the essential dog. In fact, her criticism here could more accurately be directed back upon herself, in the sense that she reduces thought about "existence exists" and "A is A" to perception, as if the abstract axioms were seen directly instead of being integrated from inductive reason.

Being, what makes a thing be what it is, what can be called essence, is either in things in themselves, outside of the mind, which Rand rejected as "intrinsic," or else it is in the mind, in which case it is subjective. There is nothing in between. For being to be both in things and in the mind is a contradiction. And if being is in the mind, but is based on reality, then what precisely is it in reality that it is based on? Rand writes that "A concept is a mental integration of two or more units possessing the same distinguishing characteristic(s), with their particular measurements omitted" (13). Either the "distinguishing characteristic" is in the thing, which Rand rejects as "intrinsic," or it is in the mind, in which case Rand's epistemology reduces to subjectivism. Rand also says that the definition of a concept must be by its most essential characteristic, the one that causes and explains all or most other defining characteristics (45, 71, 230-31, 238-39, 304). If this quality of being essential is merely in our minds and not in reality, if it is epistemological rather than metaphysical, then how is our concept not subjective?

Rand's "objective" is a contradictory compromise between "intrinsic" and "subjective," an attempt to claim that being is somehow in between reality and the mind. The truth is that being is in reality but is known by the mind, but Rand's "objective" does not accomplish this.

She says that essence is "epistemological," not "metaphysical," but essence is another word for being or what makes a thing be what it is, therefore Rand's statement reduces to the claim that being is in the mind, not in reality (52). If we are going to be rational then we must conclude that the "intrinsic" position is what makes objectivity possible. This also reflects what is visible, for example, what makes a square be a square is its four equal sides, and this is in the square, not in our minds: it is metaphysical, but it is known by epistemology. Rand's intrinsic-objective-subjective account contradicts what she says elsewhere, namely that the attributes of entities are metaphysical, not epistemological (277-79). A square's essence, as square, is its attribute of having four equal sides, and every being's essence is merely whichever attribute it has that is essential as that type of thing.

When Rand claims that the objective is between the intrinsic and the subjective, the implication is that the objective is in the mind rather than intrinsic to external objects, but yet it is still somehow related to something outside the mind. That is a contradiction. If essence is in the mind but is related to reality, then what in reality is it related to? If definitions refer to essential characteristics, what are these characteristics if not essences? Either the defining characteristic of a thing is in the thing itself, which Rand rejected as "intrinsic," or it is in the mind, in which case it is subjective. Rand asks "to what precisely do concepts refer in reality? Do they refer to something real, something that exists—or are they merely inventions of man's mind, arbitrary constructs or loose approximations that cannot claim to represent knowledge?" (1). Yet this, the question of what concepts refer to in reality, is what Rand fails to answer, and what she cannot answer because she rejects the idea of essences. An essence is a thing's identity as a specific kind of thing which is in the thing itself, so if there are no essences then concepts have nothing to refer to.

If we reject Rand's intrinsic-objective-subjective analysis, then what becomes of objectivity? A good theory of objectivity was put forward by Aristotelian philosopher Mortimer J. Adler in his "Ten Philosophical Mistakes" (Adler 1996, 5-82). Adler argued that the problem of objectivity is an interrelated conceptual and linguistic mistake. The word that is missing from the discussion is "of," which denotes the object of a subject. When I see an apple, the apple is not a perception. The apple is the object of a perception. The perception is in my mind, whereas the apple that I see is out in the external world. When I think about a dog, the concept of "dog" is in my head, but the dog itself is out in the world, if it exists, or if the dog doesn't exist, then it isn't anywhere, and I am thinking about something that doesn't exist.

Perceived things and thought-about essences are the objects of consciousness, whereas the perceptions and concepts are the means by which I perceive or think about things. Perceptions and concepts are in my mind, whereas what I see and think about is in reality. If I am thinking about a square, the concept of "square" is in my mind, but the essential square, the object of thought, does not exist, and I am really thinking about all the squares that exist as such, as squares. Adler argued that since perceptions and concepts are in the mind, if we see perceptions and we think about concepts, we become trapped in subjectivism and we can only see and know what is within the mind. I extend that argument by claiming that what we perceive is objective reality precisely because what we perceive is that which we perceive, not the means by which we perceive it, and this fact is itself perceptually verifiable, e.g. when you look at a book you see the book, not your eyes.

If we use "of," if we are aware that what is in the mind is only the means by which we perceive and think, rather than the objects of perception and the contents of thought, we can escape from this problem. Rand, who advocated a belief in an objective reality, should have said that we perceive an objective reality, a world outside of our mind, a world separate from the mind and independent of the mind. But she didn't understand how to put this belief on a solid logical footing. Because Rand claimed that the things that we see are perceptions made of sensations, and that things such as existence and identity and everything else abstract are concepts, her epistemology reduces to subjectivism (Rand 1990, 5, 10). But the problem is easily fixed: simply know that existence is not a concept, it is a thing to which a certain concept refers, and the things that you see are not your perceptions, they are the things in objective reality which the perceptions in your mind are your means of perceiving. Being itself is in things in themselves, but our concepts of beings are in our minds.

This enables us to say things that Rand rejected, but should have said: that concepts and perceptions physically exist in our brains, but refer to objects outside of our brains, that the mind reduces to the brain, that the self reduces to the body, and that the mind-body relationship is a question whose answer lies in philosophy, not science (154, 290). This also clears up Rand's confusion and imprecision over whether concepts physically exist as concretes or not (154-58). I would argue, contrary to Rand, that a mind cannot understand itself or the world around it in any meaningful way until it grasps its relationship to its body, the relationship of consciousness to self. And once you deduce that perceptions come from the impact of external objects on your body's sense organs, you can reason that everything that you perceive exists objectively.

OTHER PROBLEMS WITH RAND'S EPISTEMOLOGY

Rand might have challenged me to show in what way the essence is not arbitrarily defined, but I don't consider that to be a problem. The essences are in things in themselves, but which essence you are thinking about is a matter of your choice. A thing is a set of attributes, and essential reasoning chooses one attribute and then reasons the consequence of the essence which then applies to everything which has that attribute. For example, if you have a red cardboard square, thinking about it as a square rather than as a red thing is a choice, but the four sides producing four right angles is not a choice. Rand's disciple Peikoff might have objected that if non-essential qualities are contingent rather than necessary then we enter the problem of the "analytic-synthetic dichotomy," but I disagree with that as well (115). A thing's non-essential qualities are contingent relative to the essential quality, but are absolute when the thing is considered as a whole. Rand seems to think that an Aristotelian essence is a physical object within a thing that gives it identity, as if there were an organ inside of humans that made them human, and each organ is identical (139). I dispute this. An essence is an attribute of an object, such that the details of what I do and what you do may differ, but our act of being human, as such, is identical, in that we are both beings which think and have human DNA and generally human-shaped bodies. If there was nothing identical between us then we would not both be humans.

Where are the universal laws of logic, such as identity? Where are metaphysical facts? If they exist in this world, where are they so that we can point to them and look at them and touch them, or if they exist in a different world, how is that not a non-physical world of spirit, which contradicts Rand's metaphysics? Why are the laws of logic necessary, and why are they true everywhere and at every time? Rand says that things act a certain way because a thing "must act in accordance with its nature," but where precisely is a thing's "nature"? (287-88). Is it in the thing itself, or in some other plane of existence? What exactly is a thing's "nature"? And if one goes from concretes to universals by means of measurement-omission, precisely how does the mind go from a concrete measurement to a universal measurement-omission? (11-12). Specifically, how does the mind know that any measurement may be substituted for the omitted measurements? (18). What are the "characteristics" that determines whether a concrete is included in a concept or not, which Rand seems to admit are the basis of conceptual categorization, if not an essence in the things in themselves? (17).

Rand's theory has no answers for these questions, but my theory does. Metaphysical facts and the laws of logic do not exist separately from the physical world. They are the essences in physical objects. The essence of "thing," the essence of a thing as a thing, in other words a thing as such, requires it to be itself and to not be not itself. A thing must have the essence of a thing in order to be a thing, so the essence requires obedience to the laws of logic, and the metaphysical fact of identity is the essence of a thing. This is why propositions stated as metaphysical facts are necessary for all things of that kind. For example, a consequence of the essence of water is that it is a liquid when it is at room temperature, so all water, not just some water, is a liquid at room temperature. A thing's essence as that thing is its "nature," that is why it behaves in a certain way, because it has that being. The essence of water is being H2O, so if a scientist reasons that water is liquid at room temperature because of its chemical composition, then this is proved as a universal truth for all water. For a thing to be water it must be H2O, and being H2O causes a thing to be a liquid at room temperature, so the essence of water will require all water to be liquid at room temperature.

The essences are in the things in this world. Essences are the things of this world thought about using essential reasoning, so they exist physically in our world, and not in a separate Platonic world of spirit. But it is the essence, not the mind's essential reasoning, which requires that things in reality obey the metaphysical facts and act according to their nature. Necessity comes from the essence itself. The essence requires the consequence of the essence, and having that essence is being that thing, so being the thing will cause the consequence. Essential reasoning enables the mind to go from specific things to universals, because induction derives a concept of the essence of a type of thing from one, a few, or a group of some real things with that essence, and deduction then reveals the consequence of that essence which must be true for all things with that essence.

Rand admits that concepts must match "essential" characteristics, and that "essential" characteristics exist, but claims that this is the case because cognitive efficiency and practicality dictate it (52, 65, 70-72). It would make more sense and be less arbitrary if the justification was that the essential characteristics actually exist, in other words if essences exist. Rand acknowledges that definitions should be based on "fundamental" characteristics which cause or explain most other characteristics (42, 44-45). If this is the case, how is the fundamental characteristic not an intrinsic essence if it is in things in themselves, and if it is not in things in themselves, then how are definitions based on objective reality? Rand posited rules for the formation of concepts, but the same critique applies to her rules as well: if a black swan is a swan because of attributes of the black swan itself, then those attributes are an essence of "swan," and if it is a swan merely because it is mentally useful for humans to classify it as one, then the concept of "swan" is hopelessly subjective (70-73).

RETHINKING RANDIAN NECESSITY AND UNIVERSALITY

My theory also corrects a problem in Rand's account of necessity, which is based on her theory of the metaphysical vs. the man-made (299). For her the metaphysical could not be different than it is because God did not create the Universe, but the man-made, because man has free will, could have been different. My problem with her analysis is, first, that she says that metaphysical facts were not created by God, but she does not explain where they come from, and second, that while she explains why metaphysical facts are necessary, she does not explain why it is necessary for the objects in reality to obey those metaphysical facts, she offers no detailed mechanism for explaining how necessity functions. My theory explains where metaphysical facts come from, e.g. "squares have four right angles" comes from the essence of squares. My theory of essences provides a clear, understandable mechanism for how necessity is created: because a thing must have the essence in order to be that kind of thing, and the essence causes the consequence as a result of having that essence, everything of that kind must have the consequence because it is what it is, e.g. every square must necessarily have four right angles because it is a square, and if it did not have four right angles then it could not have the square essence and it would not be a square.

My analysis extends to solve another contradiction in Rand's epistemology, her belief that all knowledge is contextual (42-43). Rand's thoughts on necessity as it relates to her metaphysical vs. man-made distinction and universality as it relates to contextual knowledge are captured in a bit of dialogue about water in "Introduction to Objectivist Epistemology" (295-301). A "professor" asks her how we know that water boils at a certain temperature, and why we know that all water boils at this temperature rather than merely all the water that we have known in previous experience. She begins by saying: "By whether you can or cannot establish a causal connection between what you have determined to be the essential characteristic of water and the fact that it boils at a certain temperature" (295). I fully agree with this statement, and this quote supports my theory of essences rather than Rand's own intrinsic-objective-subjective idea. But when asked how to establish the connection,

Rand ducks the question by saying that the answer lies in science, not philosophy, because it involves molecular chemistry. When pressed on why molecular knowledge matters, she says that it is simply because we have gained more knowledge. This I disagree with: it is not merely more knowledge, rather it is knowledge of cause and effect, of the consequence of the essence of water, and this is where necessity and universality come from.

Rand, without this idea, then posits that water boiling at that temperature is necessary because it is metaphysical and not man-made, and says that this knowledge about water applies only to specific cases, and could be proven wrong if we were to learn more knowledge, because all knowledge is contextual (296, 298). It is true that there are certain specifics to the case of water boiling at a certain temperature, but these all must be considered in essential reasoning, to arrive at the essence whose consequence you want to reason. In other words, water is an essence, water at a high altitude is another more specific essence, water at a high altitude with salt in it is an even more specific essence, and each essence has its own consequence. Thus, when you have reasoned the consequence of an essence, you can say that your knowledge is necessary and universal, without any possible exceptions, regardless of any new "context." But when Rand claims that not just some, but all knowledge is contextual, she paves the road to skepticism or relativism. For her position to be applied logically, all knowledge is merely relative to one's context, and everything that one knows, literally everything, could be disproved by a new context. This is a form of skepticism since it makes absolute knowledge impossible, and it is relativism because it makes all knowledge relative to one's context.

Rand claims that a new context will never contradict previous knowledge, but she never proves why this will be the case (43-45). If your context changes and forces you to give up on knowledge or definitions that you had previously held to be true, it would seem that your previous knowledge has been disproved. She claims that mathematical knowledge is not contextual, but this leads to an analytic-synthetic split: math would be analytical, empirical science would be synthetic (202-3).

Rand's contextual knowledge is a contradictory concession to those who claim that empirical reason cannot provide absolute certainty. If all knowledge is contextual then no knowledge can claim to be truly universal. The solution is to see the difference between more knowledge and consequence of the essence knowledge: the former can be overturned by still more knowledge, whereas the latter is necessary and universal, in all cases. Essential knowledge is not just more knowledge. It is a special kind of knowledge.

Our theory of necessity and universality is of the utmost importance. In my opinion the great appeal of Kant is that he offers a comprehensive theory of necessity and universality. Kant claimed that necessity is created because the mind applies the laws of science to everything that it experiences with no exceptions (Kant 1977,

63-64). Thus Kantian subjectivism creates universality. If we are to challenge Kant's supremacy we will need an account of necessity and universality that comes from things in themselves, which is impossible if we accept Rand's intrinsic-objective-subjective analysis.

CONCLUSION TO RAND'S AXIOM PROBLEM

For Rand, because concepts are "merely... our way of organizing concretes," without reference to essence in things in themselves, it is impossible for Rand to justify universal knowledge, or to claim knowledge of things in the future (Rand 1990, 307). Nowhere in "Introduction to Objectivist Epistemology" does Rand explain how, if concepts are not based on essences, they are not arbitrary, nor how, if they are merely groupings of concretes from previous experience, do they offer knowledge of the concretes that one is going to experience in the future. If concepts are merely a way to mentally organize concretes, then how is conceptual reason capable of proof? Rand's concepts, just because they are "open-ended," do not enable her to prove truths about the future, because her concepts do not refer to essences in concretes and so she has no basis for knowing that concretes in the future will resemble concretes from the past (17, 27, 66). She claims to have solved the "problem of universals," but her answers are problematic (1-3).

Because things in themselves are required to have the essence in order to be that kind of thing, since they would not be that kind of thing if they did not have the essence, and the essence causes the consequence, my essences offer universal knowledge. Only essential reasoning enables your knowledge of the present and the past to produce conclusive, demonstrated knowledge, in other words proof, about the future and the things that you have not yet experienced. My theory also enables reasoning that is purely empirical, in other words, which is purely the result of deductions from sense perceptions. Essential reasoning solves the problem of induction. Rand's axioms are assumptions dressed up in a fancy name, and as soon as you base your reasoning on unreasoned assumptions instead of perceptions, you can no longer claim to base your knowledge on empirical observation of the perceivable world. Indeed, reliance on the axioms is based on faith in the axioms, and Rand's theory of axioms contradicts her commitment to reason.

My theory will give an epistemological foundation to Rand's metaphysical, ethical and political ideas that is stronger and more logical than the theory of axioms. My theory will also introduce a more logical conception of objectivity, necessity and universality than is found in Rand's writings. I agree with Rand's vision of reality as objective and as something that can be understood and mastered by the reasoning human mind, but the details of her epistemology betray and contradict that vision. Fortunately we have a solution to Rand's axiom problem.

Let me add a concluding postscript to this paper. When I first submitted it to "The Journal of Ayn Rand Studies," it was rejected for two reasons: first, because the reviewer asserted that I was accusing Rand not of an internal contradiction, but merely of disagreeing with my personal epistemology, and second, because I did not fully explicate my epistemic theory of essences alluded to in the paper. The conception of this paper as incomplete is a straw man. The rest of this book explains the details of my philosophical beliefs, but the above presentation gives enough of the gist of my ideas for my critique of Rand to be thoroughly understood. Secondly, my argument is undeniably one based on Rand's own internal self-contradiction, as well as her external contradictions.

Rand believed in reason and rejected faith, but she accepted the axioms without reasoned proof that the axioms are true. If the reader of this paper considers the natural, reasonable proposition that something which cannot be proven by reason must be accepted on faith, since the origin of any idea is either reason or faith, then it follows that Rand's premises collapse into a contradiction, in that reason is based on axioms and axioms must be accepted on faith, hence reason is based on faith. Merely disagreeing with my argument, in the absence of a well-reasoned critique, does not refute my argument. Disagreement does make clear whether the reader of this paper possesses blind faith in the ideas of Ayn Rand, or whether he or she is willing to check Rand's premises and question the Randian philosophy using a serious philosophical methodology.

REFERENCES:
Correspondence
Chris Matthew Sciabarra, 3 May 2009
Publications
Adler, Mortimer J. 1996. Ten Philosophical Mistakes. New York: Touchstone.
Appignanesi, Richard and Chris Garratt. 2007. Introducing Postmodernism. Cambridge: Icon.
Aristotle. 1947. Introduction to Aristotle. Edited by Richard McKeon. New York: Random House.
Kant, Immanuel. 1977. Prolegomena to Any Future Metaphysics That Will Be Able to Come Forward as Science. Translated by Paul Carus, revised by James W. Ellington. Indianapolis: Hackett.
Nietzsche, Friedrich. 1990. Twilight of the Idols/The Anti-Christ. Translated by R.J. Hollingdale. New York: Penguin.
Plato. 1997. Complete Works. Edited by John M. Cooper. Indianapolis: Hackett.
Rand, Ayn. 1957. Atlas Shrugged. New York: Signet. ___. 1990. Introduction to

Objectivist Epistemology. 2nd ed. Edited by Harry Binswanger and Leonard Peikoff. New York: Meridian. ___. 1943. The Fountainhead. New York: Signet. Thompson, Della, ed. 1998.

The Oxford Dictionary of Current English. New York: Oxford University Press.

MORAL LOGIC AND ECONOMIC LOGIC: ON KNOWLEDGE, CHOICE, WILL, DESIRE, THE MORAL IDEAL, ECONOMICS, AND ECONOMIC VALUE, WITH A SYSTEM OF SYMBOLIC LOGICAL NOTATION

INTRODUCTION

As a philosopher, I am dedicated to the position that logic can, and should, be applied to literally every area of human existence, as a guide and tool for how to think and how to make decisions. Much work has been done historically, in the history of philosophy, on the logic of mathematics. In the academic tradition, the scope of logic is largely limited to math, and, even there, within academic math, the most influential works in the philosophy of logic are those which purport to limit logic, and to prove that logic can never completely describe math.

My position is radically different. The scope of logic is universal and infinite. Logic has no limits. Either something is logical, in which case logic can analyze and describe it, or else that something is illogical, and, if and to the extent that it is illogical, it is of no concern and need be given no heed by rational intelligent people. Emotions, and appeals to emotion as a form of persuasion, can be analyzed by logic, quite easily, actually. See, for example, my essay "On Forgiveness," which explains all human emotions, using logic.

In my most popular essay, "A System of Legal Logic," I explained a new system of logic, using the Aristotelian theory of "essence," which describes legal logic, and which proves that the common law, the legal system of the United States of America, and the decision-making process of a trial by jury, can be perfectly derived from, and completely described by, logic.

After having dealt with legal logic, I then turned my attention to scientific logic, in another popular essay of mine, "If P Then Q." That work proved that science, and scientific experiments, and theories in science, can be justified and explained, in whole, by logic. That essay proved that logic is the foundation of science, and showed how to use science as an analytical logic of sensory experience and of the physical world.

In this essay, which you are now reading, I apply logic to two other areas: first, ethics and morality; and second, economics and capitalism. My goal is to prove that it is possible for logic to fully define and describe an ethics, and an economics, which is capable of being functionally implemented in human existence, and that logic can be a necessary and sufficient condition for ethics to exist, and for economics to be understood. Despite a very broad scope, this is a very short paper: I say only what needs to be said, and nothing more, with minimal narration and exposition on the core principles expounded herein.

Is moral logic possible? Is economic logic possible? If so, how, and under what conditions? The goal of this paper is to answer those questions.

Please note that this paper stands alone. You do not need to have read "A System of Legal Logic" or "If P Then Q" or "On Moral Psychology and Moral Philosophy" first. However, if you finish this, and enjoy it, those are your recommended next reads. I must also note that, as a philosopher, I work largely in the "Objectivist and Libertarian" tradition, so other recommended reads to supplement the context of this essay include Ayn Rand's famous novel "Atlas Shrugged," and the various popular books about Libertarian politics, such as Murray Rothbard's "For a New Liberty," F.A. Hayek's "The Road to Serfdom," and Milton Friedman's "Free to Choose."

With that, I conclude this introduction.

PART ONE: MORAL LOGIC

This paper attempts to derive a system of ethics and morality conceptually from analytic logic. The attempt begins with premises, and definitions, and then applies deductions, to reach a conclusion. The basic proof sketch of the argument is this:

Knowledge, Desire, Choice, and Will, are what they are;

Ethics and morality arises because Humans have a choice between Good and Evil;

and Life or Death are the only two things that human choice can make any real difference with respect to;

therefore Life is Good and Death is Evil;

A logical ethics will define Good by reference to logic, and assess the necessary and sufficient conditions of Good Choices;

For Humans, the moral ideal will be the condition of harmony, or alignment, in which you feel a Desire, you Know what you Desire, you Know that it is possible for you to achieve your Desire, you Choose to achieve your Desire, and you Will that which you Desire, and thereby you have and hold and possess the object of your Desire;

In the condition of the moral ideal, a person will have The Will to Live, and will thereby live a long and happy life.

If one concedes, or begins with, Desire, Knowledge, Choice, and Will, as defined and explained in this paper, then it follows as an inevitable, logical, proven conclusion, that moral alignment and harmony and The Will to Live are the moral ideal.

A set of attributes, arising from deductive logic, comprised of Knowledge, Knowing what you Know, and Strength of Willfulness, Willing your IQ, Willing What You Can Take, Overcoming all Obstacles, and Choosing to achieve your Desires, form a description of "The Objectivist Hero," the personified ideal of moral logic.

The argument can be summarized in English as: "The moral ideal is to Ask for what you want and to Will what you want, but this requires that you Know what you want, for which, either you already have a Desire, in which case you use Self-Awareness to Know what you Want and to then Know that you Know what you Want, or, if you do not already have a Desire, you Choose what you Want, and then you Mean your Choice of what you Want. The moral ideal also requires harmony, in that you Want something, and you also Want to Want what you Want. If you Ask for what you Want, and you Will what you Want, then you maximize the Actualization of your Potential to be Happy, and thereby achive to the fullest extent possible your Will to Live."

In Logic, this can be stated as:
Moral Ideal = Ask(D) and W(D),
which Requires K(D).
D or Not(D).
If D then K(D) and then $K^2(D)$.
If Not(D) then C(D) and M(C(D)).
AND Moral Ideal = $(D = D^2)$.
Then (W(Life) = 100% and Act.(Po.) = 100%) = Achievement of Moral Ideal.

A second and correlated set of propositions may be articulated in English: "In order to Will something to be, you must first Know that it is possible and that you have the ability to Will it, and you must Know that you Know this, because your Knowledge of what you can do defines the Limits of your Will. In contrast, if you Know that something is impossible then you cannot Will it, and then, because you do not Will it, it will not be.

You must also be looking at what you are doing and be thinking about what you are doing, in order to Will success, because perception and thought define the Scope of your Will. You can only Will something if you can see what you are doing and if you are thinking about what you are doing. That collectively defines the Scope and Limits of Will. Knowledge that you can do it and Perception of what you are doing are necessary conditions, but not sufficient conditions, for Will; they are preconditions, which, if met, put you in a place to be able to Will what you Desire. Once all preconditions are met, if you do actually Will something, and if you do Will that which you Desire to be, then that thing necessarily will be, and your Will will actualize Potential into Actuality, and actualize Desire into the Will to Live. If something is Potential, and if you Will it, then it will be Actualized. If something is possible and if someone Wills it then it is logically necessary that it will exist, because that is what Will is, Will is the Actualization of Potential by means of Choice, Desire, and Knowledge."

These propositions can also be stated in Logic:
If K(N(Po.)) then N(W(Po.(Act.))).
If (N(P(W)) or N(Con(W))) then N(W).
If (Po.(X) and W(X)) then Act.(X).

DEFINITIONS

X: A Universal-scope variable. X is a variable with infinite scope: X can be virtue, career, friends, family, money, sex, hobby, politics, going to out to a restaurant for dinner tonight, putting cream and sugar in your morning coffee, writing a book, travelling to Paris and Rome on vacation, anything. X can also stand for any K (Knowledge), D (Desire), C (Choice), or W (Will).

X^2: X squared.

X(Y): Usually pronounced "X of Y," although this varies based on context.

K: Knowledge. This can stand for Knowledge, or for a thing that is Known.

D: Desire, to want. This can mean either your feelings of Desire, the act of feeling Desire, the act of wanting something, or the object of the Desire, the something that you want.

C: Choice. This can mean choosing, or a choice. W: Will. This can mean the act of Willing, or the thing Willed.

K(X): "To know X" or "the knowledge of X."

D(X): "To desire X" or "the desire for X."

C(X): "To choose X," or "the choice to do X."

W(X): "The Will to do X," or "Willing X to be," "Willing X to exist."

K(D): Knowing what is your Desire. To know what you want.

C(D): Choosing the object of your Desire.

W(D): Willing the object of your Desire.

K = D: Your Knowledge aligns with your Desires, such that what you Know is in harmony with what you Desire. For example, you desire to buy a new house, and you know that you have the money and job with which to do so. In contrast, if K was Not equal to D, for example, you would desire to buy a house, but you would know you can't afford to.

K(D) = D: Your Desire is equal to what you know you Desire. For example, you desire to buy a house, and you know that what you want is to buy a house.

W = D: What you Will is equal to (the action implied by) what you Desire. For example, you desire to buy a house, and you Will yourself to buy a house.

R: Reality/Real

N(X): Not X

Non-X: Not X

Po.: Potential (The state of Becoming, of being Possible)

Act.: Actual, Actuality (The state of Being, of Existing)

Po.(X): X is Possible.

Act.(Po.): Actualize Potential

Po.(Act.): The Potential to become Actualized.

K(Po.): To Know that something is possible.

W(Act.): To Will something to become actual, to Will the actualization of potential.

M: Meaning

M(X): to Mean X.

W(Live): The Will to Live.

CONT: Contradiction.

V: Virtue (Goodness)

A: Assign, Assignment

P: Perception

Con: Consciousness

SA: Self-Awareness

#: Any number

W#: The Strength of Will, where the number is a measure of Strength.

A(W#) > X(W#): A's Will is stronger than X's Will. Literally, that the number on the left is greater than the number on the right. Likewise, < would be mean less than.

Means(W), W(Means): The Means of the Will, the means and methods and tools by which the Will is done.

Thwart: to frustrate or block a Will.

Obstacle: A thing which thwarts.

W(Life): The Will to Live

D(Life): The Desire to Live

+: Goodness, positivity, positive numbers in math

-: Evil, negativity, negative numbers in math

1: Integrity, unity, wholeness, one thing, the number one in math

Logical: Resolves to 1, resolves to integrity, coherence, unity.

Illogical: Resolves to zero or -1, resolves to a contradiction, is not at one with itself, cannot be at one with itself.

Do(X): To do the X action, or to do that behavior which is implied by X being true.

KNOWLEDGE, DESIRE, CHOICE, WILL

The Rumsfeld Principle of Knowledge: "There are known knowns, and then there are known unknowns. There are the things we know we know. And then there are the things we know we don't know."

You could also not know what you know, or not know what you don't know.

K(X): To know X.

$K^2(X)$: To know that you know X.

The ideal condition of knowledge: $K = K^2$, to know that you know what you know.

K(D): To know what you want. As in, for example, "I want a man who knows what he wants."

N(K(D)): To not know what you want.

D^2: To want to want what you want. To desire to hold the desire that you hold. Same as D(D). $D^2(X)$: To desire to desire X, to want to want X, to desire for yourself that you would hold a desire for X and want X.

$K(D^2)$: To know what you want to want (to know what you think you should want).

$N(K(D^2))$: To not know what you want to want.

W(D): Will what you want. Take the object of your desire, and will it to be. This can also be stated as: If D(X) Then W(X). If you desire X then you will X.

K, C, W, D, AND POTENTIAL VERSUS ACTUALITY

Potential becomes Actual when all Potential collapses into one Actuality, when all possible outcomes resolve to one and only one outcome.

K(X): Knowledge has two necessary and sufficient conditions: first, that you believe X is true; second, you believe that X only is true against all Non-X alternatives (and nothing that makes X be false is or can be true). Knowledge is the belief that only this belief can be true. When K(X), all Non-X alternatives collapse into one possibility, X.

C(X): To choose X has two necessary and sufficient conditions: first, you will do X; second, you will do only X and will not do any alternative to the exclusion of X. Choice is the action of doing one chosen action and not doing anything else. When C(X), all Non-X alternatives collapse into one possibility, X.

$W = C^2$

W(X) (the same thing as $C^2(X)$): To will X has two necessary and sufficient conditions: first, that you will choose the choice to do X from among all competing alternative choices; second, that you will choose only the choice to do X, and will make, consider, mean, and think, no alternative choices to the choice to do X. To Will X is to Choose the Choice to X, it is to Choose only that Choice and to Choose no other Choices. When W(X), all Non-C(X) alternatives collapse into one possibility, C(X). You mean X – You *really* mean X.

K^2: To know that you know X has two necessary and sufficient conditions: first, that you know that you possess the knowledge that X is true; second, that you know that only your knowledge of X is true, and that no other knowledge that knows or implies that you do not know X can be known. When you Know that you Know something, you belief that only this Knowledge is Known, and no other Knowledge can be known. When $K^2(X)$, all Non-K(X) alternative knowledge collapses into one possibility, K(X).

The opposite of K^2 is Doubt(K).

K and D and C are directed at the object. They are attributes of the object, or of the subject in relation to the object. In contrast, K^2, D^2, and W are attributes of the subject, or of the subject in relation to the subject's relation to the object.

D: Desire is the feeling or belief that there is a condition or scenario, which can exist, and that, from your point of view, this condition or scenario should exist. The degree to which you Desire X is the degree to which only this condition or scenario should exist and no other conditions or scenarios are acceptable to you or should exist from your point of view. Note that "point of view" is inherent in the definition, therefore all Desire is subjective.

D^2: The Desire to Desire means that there is a feeling or belief that there is a Desire, which can exist, and that, from your point of view, this Desire should exist (in other words, that you should feel this Desire). The degree to which you Desire a Desire is the degree to which you feel that only this Desired Desire should exist or is acceptable, and that no other Desires, or no other competing alternative Desires, should be felt, and all competing Desires should not exist.

For examples:

I prefer: {A, B, and C}.

I eliminate A and B.

I Desire C.

Say, for example, that, out of {A, B, and C}, I would prefer C over A or B by five to one.

Then my Desire for C = 80%.

My Opinion is: Maybe {A, B, and C} are True.

I eliminate A and B.

I Know C.

Only C can be true, and that is my belief. That is what Knowledge is.

I plan on possibly doing: {A, B, and C}.

I eliminate A and B.

I am doing C.

Then I have Chosen C. That is what a choice is. Action to the exclusion of any alternative.

I am considering my choice to do C and my choice not to do C.

I eliminate my choice not to do C.

Then I Will C. My Will to do C = 100%. That is what Will is.

Say, for another example, that I am 90% committed to Choice C, but there is a 10% chance I would waffle and say "maybe" and choose Choice A or Choice B instead.

Then my Will to do C = 90%.

I consider my Knowledge that I Know C and my Knowledge which contradicts C.

I eliminate all Knowledge that contradicts C.

I Know that I Know C.

I consider my set of Desires: {A, B, and C}.

I prefer Desire C over Desires A or B such that I prefer C five times more than A or B.

Then I have an 80% Desire to Desire C.

But if: I only desire to hold Desire C, and I eliminate Desires A and B, then I have a 100% Desire to Desire C. (This does not mean that I desire C. It only means that I want to desire C, that I desire to desire C.)

Knowledge is a belief which is believed to be impossible to be false. As such, perhaps, only logic can achieve knowledge, because only a logical proof can prove that all alternativs to a true position resolve to a false condition or resolve to a contradiction, leaving behind one and only one possible true belief.

As Knowledge is to Truth, Choice is to Action, and Desire is to Scenarios, and Will is to Choice. It is the property, of a subject in relation to an object, of removing all possible alternatives and contradictions, leaving behind only one.

WHAT IS WILL?

$W = C^2$

Will is the choice to choose one's choice. Not only the choice to do X to the exclusion of all alternatives to X, but the choice to choose to do X to the exclusion of all other possible choices. To "go all in" on the choice to X. If you choose to choose, that means you really mean it. Hence $W = M$ (usually).

Examples of what I mean by "Will":

"You have to *mean* it, Harry!" – Harry Potter, Book Five.

"*Insist* on it." – Ayn Rand, The Fountainhead.

"Do, or do not. There is no try." – Master Yoda, Star Wars, The Empire Strikes Back.

"Much must be risked in war." – The Return of the King, Lord of the Rings.

"The World as Will and Representation." – Arthur Schopenhauer.

"Intentionality." – John Searle's The Construction of Social Reality.

"Manifestation." – Husserl's Phenomenology.

"Don't tell me what I can't do, tell me how to do what I want to do." – J.P. Morgan.

"Don't pull your thing out, unless you plan to bang. Don't even bang unless you plan to hit something." – OutKast, Bombs Over Baghdad. $W(W)$, W^2: The will to will something. To have Willed something, and then to really mean that one has Willed it. To Will Will. To Will what you Will.

POTENTIAL AND ACTUALITY, AND SELF-FULFILLING PROPHESY

If W(X) and Po.(X) then X. There are no exceptions to this rule. If you will it, and it is possible, it will be, it will be done.

"Where there's a will, there's a way."

If Po.(W(X)) and W(X) then X. (And, this context, X = R(X).)

If X is possible, and if you Will X, then X will happen. There is no "might," "maybe," "probably," "should," or "likely." X *will* happen. That is what Will is.

If K(N(Po.(W(X)))) despite Po.(W(X)) then N(Po.(W(X))).

If X is possible, but if you Know that X is not possible, then you cannot Will X. Your mind won't let you do so. Your belief that X is impossible will prevent you.

If K(N(Po.(W(X)))) then N(Po.(W(X))) because won't C(W(X)) therefore can't W(X). Won't W(X) = Can't W(X). N(W(W(X))) = N(W(X)).

The Principle of the Self-Fulfilling Prophesy:

If K(N(Po.(X))) then N(Po.(W(X))). If you know, or believe, that X is impossible, you will never choose X and really mean it. You won't allow yourself to believe it, you won't allow yourself to do it, you won't allow yourself to mean it.

But if you know that it is possible, and if it really is possible, then you can Will X.

W(Po.) = Act.

Po. – Act. = Moral Failure

Therefore, Po. – W(Po.) = Moral Failure

(Act.(Po.) = 100%) = (Moral Failure = 0%)

(W = 100%) = The Condition of Moral Perfection, The Ideal

Your highest or best potential, your potential to be the best you, your moral potential, minus the actualization of that potential, equals your moral failure, which is equal to your sin, or guilt. To be moral is to will the actualization of moral potential. Therefore moral achievement arises from willing one hundred percent of your potential to become actual.

This condition of moral perfection is not impossible, by definition, because we have defined your potential to include only that which is possible, not the impossible, and, if something is possible, you have the ability to actualize that potential, by means of willing it to be, because, if something is possible, and you will it to be, it is.

Guilt is a Moral Contradiction. A Contradiction embodies the statement (1 N(=) 1). Guilt is a Contradiction embodied in Morality. Guilt can take these forms:

C(N(C(X))) + C(X) or

C(X) + do(N(X)) or

Do(X) + D(N(X) or

D(X) + D2(N(X)).

Guilt is the opposite of Moral Integrity, which matches the Ideal Conditions (1 = 1, and 1 = 12) defined above.

W(Po.) = Act.

Po.(You) – W = Guilt, Regret, Moral Failure (in the sense that Morality calls upon you to Actualize your full or highest Potential, what Ayn Rand said meant living "for the sake of the best within you.) This is pronounced as "Your Potential minus Willing the Actualization of that Potential equals your Guilt, Regret, or Moral Failure."

If you have Potential, and you can Actualize it by Willing it to be, why would you not do so? You would have a reason to. And no reason not to. And the ability to do so. Not doing so would be illogical.

(W = 100%) = (Po. = Act.) = Moral Success, To fully live your life, a fully willed self-actualization.

W#(W = 100%): A fully strong Will to the extent necessary to actualize one's full or highest potential.

(Ethics, Will, Moral Significance, Subject,) and (The World, Representation, Math, Object.)

Life = Subject Willing Object.

Do(W): Do what you Will. To do as you Will. 100%W(W): To fully Will that which you have Willed. To really mean it, fully. If this condition is met, Guilt necessarily equals zero.

W(Po.(+))100%: To be the best person you can be. To Will and thereby Actualize yourself as a Good person, to the fullest extent of your Potential for Goodness.

N(W(X)): To not have the Will to do X.

W(N(X)): To Will X to not be.

W(IQ): To Will your intelligence.

W(IQ#): To Will your level of intelligence, to Will how smart you are.

STRENGTH OF WILL

The Means of the Will, Means(W): If W(X), this is how X becomes, this is how W(X) makes or causes X to be.

Objectivist Means(W): Reason, Logic, Math, Science, Truth, Honestly, Virtue, Goodness, Perception, Consciousness, Self-Awareness, Strength of Will.

Obs: Obstacle

Thw: Thwart

Thw(W): To Thwart Will

Obs(Thw(You(W))) if Obs(W#) > You(W#) or if Obs(Thw(You(W(Means))))

An Obstacle can thwart your will:

If they "want it more than you," if their Strength of Will for thwarting you exceeds the Strength of your Will for doing it; or

If the Obstacle thwarts the means of your will, if they sabotage or block the tools and methods necessary for your Will to Actualize the Potential at issue, the Means by which your Will Actualizes your intention.

Defy: If your Will exceeds the Obstacle's will, you Defy the Obstacle, preventing it from Thwarting your Will.

Ally: An Ally helps you succeed by contributing their Will to your Will, so that the Strength of Will to overcome the Obstacle equals the sum of yours plus your Ally's Wills.

To Overcome by Force of Will or Strength of Will:

"Who wins depends on who wants it more." If A(W#) > X(W#) then A's Will will overcome X's Will, and what A wills will become actual, and what X wills will remain potential. Newton's Third Law of Motion: "For every action, there is an equal but opposite reaction."

Newton's Third Law of Motion applied to Morality: "For every action, there is an equal but opposite reaction."

Resistance Overcome = Amount of Reward Achieved.

Pain = Gain.

"No pain, no gain."

Work(X) = Will(Do/Make X)

WYCT: What You Can Take. The amount of resistance you can withstand before physically or psychologically breaking down or giving up, in order to achieve a goal. This is the limit of Work that you are capable of doing to achieve X, above which you "can't take the pain," or will lack the Will to withstand the Resistance needed to be Overcome in order to achieve X.

The more X is very difficult to achieve, the higher is WYCT(X).

Greatness/Genius: W((WYCT) = WYCT(X)). Will yourself to be able to withstand whatever pain and hardship and "blood, sweat and tears" is necessary to achieve X.

W(W#): "Don't be lazy." "Don't tell me what I can't do, tell me how to do what I want to do."

The more "comfy" you are about doing X, the easier to W(X).

The more "awkward" with doing X you are, the more difficult it is to W(X).

A main purpose to training, education and gaining real-world experience, is just to make your more comfy, only because X only if W(X). In contrast, true awkwardness, hesitation, reticence, indecisiveness, means you are trying to do X with only half a Will to do X. Which would have only a 50% chance to succeed.

To be comfy is to be confident is to W = 100%.

To be awkward is to be insecure is to be W = 50%.

To "Choke" is to become awkward only when pressure is high or the stakes are high.

To be "Clutch" is to feel comfy and thereby have a full Will to succeed when pressure and stakes are high.

A "natural" is someone who feels comfy in a situation instantly, with no training or wading into the waters first.

Comfy = "Don't worry. Don't panic. Relax." Confidence and Optimism.

ON MEANING

M: Meaning M(X):

To Mean X

W(Act.) = Speak(M)

Your Meaning, your true intent, is what you Will, finalized and fully Willed by having been Actualized.

"The Word is the Will made Flesh."

Language: To Infer M from words is to infer the speaker's W from his visible Act. You see Act. and infer W. Like a lawyer trying to infer the M of the Legislature, the W of the People, from the text of a passed law. The Legislature's vote is W, and the legal text speaks M.

To Ask for what you want: Ask(D) = W(D) = M(D) = (if Po.(D) Act.(D))

Matthew 7:7: "Ask and ye shall receive; Seek and ye shall find; Knock and the door will open."

To Ask for what you desire is the embodiment of Willing that which you desire.

Ask(X) = W(X): Going to the gym and lifting weights regularly is how you say you want big muscles, it is how you ask for big muscles, for example.

WHAT IS THE MIND?

P: Perception

Con: Consciousness

SA: Self-Awareness

Con = P^2. Consciousness is the perception of one's own perception. It is the act of perceiving one's act of perception.

SA = Con^2. Self-Awareness is being conscious of one's own consciousness. It is the awareness of awareness as such.

$P(K^2)$: To see details and really notice them and pay attention to what they mean and know what they mean. To grab hold of objects in the periphery of your vision or awareness and drag them into the sight o your full attention.

Thought plus Sight = Scope of Range of W. You can't Will something if you can't see what you're doing or if you don't know what you're doing.

You consider your choices.

You choose a choice.

Having chosen that choice, you do it – you will that choice to be.

It goes from being potential to being actual.

THE WILL AND SELF-RELIANCE, AND POLITICS

You can only have the freedom to C(X) if you can W(X) yourself without reliance on someone else. If Means(W(X)) involves reliance on one or more others, the other person's free will is the limit of the scope of your will.

W(X) as of Right: X will happen if W(X).

W(X) Discretionary: X will happen if Other People allow X to happen and W(X).

The difference is whether you have the Potential to Actualize X by yourself, or whether the Actualization of X in some way depends upon one or more Other People also as well as you.

Politics: The Will of the People vs. The Will of the Dictators.

Free Will is free. A choice is not a choice unless it is freely chosen. Therefore political tyranny and the thwarting of freedom are the enemies of C and W and W(D).

FREEDOM!!!

THE HERO OF THE WILL
AS MORAL IDEAL

The Randian Hero of Ayn Rand's novels as the Hero of the Will.

Happy people Will the objects of their Desire. Sad people don't. The Randian Hero is a happy hero who Wills what he/she/they wants. They Overcome any Obstacle by Strength of Will, and by Willing their IQ to be equal to the level so that their Knowledge can be the Means of their Will to succeed.

Because the Objectivist Hero is happy, they have The Will to Live. So they end up happy. And live happy lives.

The Atlas Shrugged heroes W(Make Stuff) and W(Solve Problems) and thereby run their business = W(Make Money).

The Randian Hero Wills the actualization of their highest potential. They fully live their life. They live life to the fullest, as moral humans.

The Objectivist Hero: W(Life)100%. The Objectivist Hero has the Will to Live and Wills himself/herself/them to be alive with a 100% Strength of Will.

The Objectivist Villain: W(Life) – 100% = Envy/Resent(Hero). The Will to Live minus 100% equals the Villain's Moral Failure, which equals the degree to which he envies or resents the Hero's full and complete Will to Live. If W(Live) = 100% then Envy/Resent = Zero.

THE WILL TO LIVE

If W(Live) and Po.(Life) then Act.(Live)

If N(W(Live)) then Act.(Die)

If D(Live) then W(Live)

If N(D(Live)) then N(W(Live))

Objectivism = (Life = V) (Life, in the mortal flesh-and-blood physical world, is goodness, life is the standard and measure of all virtue. It's good to be alive, therefore it's virtuous to will your life to continue.)

Therefore: if Objectivist then C(D(Life)), which causes or motivates W(Life).

Objectivism is "The Morality of Life."

MORAL HARMONY AND ALIGNMENT OF DESIRE

"The Heart wants what it wants." D = D. It is very difficult to C(D). Nor would there be any reason to want to do so, unless your Desire is evil, in which case you would simply choose not to Will it, in order to be ethical. If you Choose to be a good person, your Desires will naturally tend towards Goodness.

Heart (Desire) > Head (How to) > Hand (Do)

NOT Head (which Desire) > Heart (that Desire) > Head/Hand (How to/Do)

The ideal state: $D = D^2$. Moral harmony of desire.

A moral contradiction between what you desire and what you believe you should desire (what you want to desire): $D\ N(=)\ D^2$.

You desire desire. You do not choose, or will, desire.

$K(D)$ is passive. You can't change $K^2(D)$. However you can will to choose to desire something $(W(C(D)))$, with unpredictable results. The results depend upon whether $M(W(C(D)))$, whether you really mean it, which, if you do, then you do desire it.

$W(K)$: To act upon what you know. To Will your knowledge, which means, to Will based upon what you Know.

$W(K(N))$: To do what you know you should not do. To act contrary to what you know.

Objectivism: $A(V(W(K)))$

Moral Integrity: $W(K) = D$

But if $(D = W(K(N)))$ (You desires contradict the actions based upon your knowledge) and $D^2 = W(K)$ (you desire a desire that is in harmony with acting upon your knowledge) then $CONT(D\ N(=)\ D^2)$ (Your desire is not equal to what you want your desire to be): Somewhere in your thinking there is a contradiction. Either you must Will your Desire to match your Knowledge, or else figure out where your Knowledge is wrong and make your Knowledge align with that which you Desire.

Happiness: $W(D)$. And $W(You(W\#) > Obs(W\#))$. "If you want something, go after it," and "Put up a fight!"

Principles of Happiness:

$K(D)$ and $C(W(D))$ and $K^2(K(R))$ and $Ask(D)$ and If $A(V(X))$ then $W(X)$.

$K(X)$ and $C(X)$ is "Feel the Force," $K^2(X)$ and $W(X)$ is "Control the Force." On your path to becoming a Jedi Knight.

One Life Objectivism: You only have one bullet with which to hit the target. Shoot wisely. If you have the shot, take it immediately. But if you don't have the shot, back out without hesitation and without remorse, and wait for the shot to come up. The one wrong thing to do is to hesitate and get caught in between: then you miss the shot even if you have it.

The condition of Alignment, the Moral Ideal:

$C = W = K(D) = K^2(D) = D = D^2 = C(W(K(D))) = 1.$

You know what you want, you choose to will what you know you desire, you know that you know your knowledge, and you also desire to desire what you desire. So you can fully mean it, with all your heart, mind and soul.

THE PERFECT STATE,
THE IDEAL CONDITION,
ALIGNMENT, HARMONY

$K^2(D(X) = D2(X))$ and

$K^2(Po.(W(X)))$ and

$W^2(X)$,

Therefore W(D) and

Therefore Act.(X). Therefore Act.(D). Therefore D(Live). Therefore W(Live). Therefore Act.(Live).

The Ideal State: $(K = K^2)$ and $(D = D^2)$ and $(C = W)$ is based on the ideal state of $(1 = 1^2)$. According to Objectivist logic, 1 is good, oneness is moral integrity (to be at one with self) and to be at one with Reality (to live without contradiction).

W(D) or N(W(D)) is the only real choice. All else flows from that. C(W(Live) or N(C(W(Live) flows from that. If you have what you want you are happy. If you are happy then you want to live. If you want to live then you will yourself to stay alive. If you will yourself to stay alive, then you live your life.

Assign Virtue to X: A(V(X))

If A(V(X)) then do(X) = Moral/Ethical/Right/Good.

If A(V(X)) then N(do(X)) = Immoral/Unethical/Wrong/Evil.

Moral Integrity vs. Compromised Moral Integrity/Hypocrisy

Should you A(V(X))? Ask:

Is (V(X)) objectively true?

Is A(V(X)) rational?

Is it justified? Do you have a reason to do so?

Is the reason sincere?

Is the reason plausible?

Do you choose A(V(X))?

Do you will A(V(X))?

If the answer to all these question is yes, then yes, you should A(V(X)).

Examples:

A(V(electronic dance music or classical symphony orchestra music))?

A(V(sex or chastity))?

Objectivism = A(V(Life)).

WILLING SHARED ENDEAVORS, JOINT UNDERTAKINGS

To "initiate": To Will. For example, "to initiate confrontation." "To initiate sex." Sex can only be Willed with the consent of the other person. Lacking consent, it is not Possible to have sex. Without consent, it would be rape, not sex. Rape is a type of violence. Rape is not a type of sex. This is true by definition. To rape, or to initiate violence against another human being other than for purposes of self-defense, is evil. For a more full explanation of the ethics of self-defense and violence, see the Applied Ethics section of this essay. However, with sex, even if both people consent, someone has to Will it, for it to be. Otherwise the Potential would be there but not Actual. So too it is with any shared human undertaking. There must be shared consent, which is C, then someone must initiate the thing, which is W, then it gets done.

MATHEMATICS AND ETHICS

W(+): Will Goodness. Will positive energy. Will addition, creation, production.

W(–): Will Evil. Will negative energy. Will subtraction, negation, destruction.

Objectivist Logic: R = 1. Reality is one thing. It is the set of all Real things, as one. Therefore:

$R = 1$ and $1 = 1^2$

Reality is really Real.

$1 = (-1)^2$

$R = (N(R))^2$

The Realness of Reality is the Unreality of Unreality in relation to itself.

i = the square root of -1 = (1 or -1) = Choice, the choice to do good(+1) or to do evil(-1). Because $(1 \times -1 = -1)$, only (1 or -1) could be its square root, since the square root would have to be 1 once and be -1 once.

Evil, -1, arises from choice, i. If there was no choice between good and evil, there would be no evil, but there would also be no choice, hence no morality at all.

Math arises from the properties of the number One, in relation to itself.

Geometry = $Math^2$

Physics = $Geometry^2$

Chemistry = $Physics^2$

Biology = $Chemistry^2$

Morality (Philosophy and Religion) = $Biology^2$.

One = Goodness, therefore Reality is Good, and Life is Good. Therefore Objectivism is the correct Morality.

Life is a perpetual motion machine. Life is any action that acts to cause itself to continue to do its own action for an indefinite or infinite progression of time. Life = $Action^2$. A living species, which sexually reproduces at each generation, and which always spreads out to find new food to eat and new places to live, will live forever. Given a sufficient IQ for a sufficient science and technology to defeat all environmental obstacles.

EXPERIENCE AS A SERIES OF SENSATIONS OR A SET OF THINGS

Sex altered my view of the evidence of the senses. Prior to that, for much of my entire life, I had believed that what you perceive are "perceived things" – e.g. a table, an apple, a chair – and each perceived thing is a set of properties as one thing, an object, wherein the set of properties, as one thing, was directly perceived, such that the thing was directly perceived, and a thing is a set of properties, so the set of properties is directly perceived. I gained the concept of sensations directly perceived – the look of wood, the redness of an apple, the feel of a chair – as such, only from my first sexual experience, which I had relatively late in life. That having been conceded, I am now of the position that sensory experience is composed of perceived things, a series of directly perceived objects, each of which is a set of properties directly perceived to be a thing, directly perceived to be what it is, but the mind can, and will, break a perceived thing down into sensations and sense-perceptions when it has the desire or occasion to do so. I had previously considered Objectivism to be a type of Realist Empiricism. However, now knowing that "Empiricism" means the position that to be is to be perceived *as a sensation or sense-perception*, such that they define experience as merely an unending series of sensations, and not as the world of perceived objects, I no longer categorize Objectivism as a type of Empiricism.

Mere animals respond to a series of sensations. In contrast, humans engage with a set of objects. In other words, experience is *things*.

"There is no such thing as the sensations of sweetness or sour. There is only atoms and void." No, that is not the truth. The truth is that the sensations of sweetness and sour are what atoms and void taste like – among other flavors, depending upon which foods the atoms have been arranged into the molecules of.

"The brain of a brain-damaged man may mistake his wife for a hat. Therefore knowledge is impossible." For him, you, and your idiot readers and followers. Not for me and mine.

ON KNOWLEDGE

Tradition held: To be knowledge, there are three necessary and sufficient conditions: first, that it is a belief; second, that the belief is true; third, that the belief is justified.

The problem is the second condition.

My question is, how do you know that something is knowledge, you would have to know that the belief is true, but then it is circular.

Let B(X) mean "Believes that X is true," or the Belief that X is true.

Assume R(X), that X exists in objective Reality, corresponds to the statement "X is true."

For the sake of argument, assume the Traditional view: K = B(X) + R(X) + Justification(X).

Assume B(X) = B(R(X)).

Assume that Y asserts K(X) (regardless of whether Y is asserting that Y knows X, or Y is asserting that a third person knows X).

Then Y asserts B(X), Y asserts R(X), and Y asserts Justification(X).

But how does Y know R(X) in order to assert R(X) as part of K(X)?

Y asserts R(X) because Y(B(X)). Then the second element factors out. So the assertion of K reduces to the assertion of B, with some bells and whistles tacked on.

Or Y might say that he asserts R(X) because Y(K(X)). But then Y(K(X)) because R(X) (it is the second element), and Y asserts R(X) because Y(K(X)). That is a circular loop.

Does "That it is true" mean that it really is objectively true? How does Y prove that X is objectively true independent of Y's own subjective knowledge of X, in other words, Y's belief in X? How does Y prove R(X) outside of Y's own point of view, which is the scope of Y(B)? K would require objective knowledge of R(X) separate from Y's B(X).

Objectivist epistemology can do this, can prove objective true, can prove R(X) for Y independent of Y's subjective point of view. But academic tradition is most definitely not Objectivist. So that won't save them.

Does it mean that the person who holds the knowledge subjectively believes that it is true? If the latter, there is no difference between knowledge and belief. But if the former: Who knows what the truth is? For Person A to say "Person Y knows X," Person A has to prove that X is objectively true. Because if it isn't "The Truth" then it cannot be "Knowledge." Then you open up the Pandora's Box of proof, knowledge, and how you prove that X is objectively true – given that, in academic philosophy, many philosophers are skeptics or subjectivists anyway, in which case they think no one has knowledge.

But, even if you were a Realist, and you B(K), this classic definition of K falls apart: For Y to know that X is true, X must be true, but "X is true" presupposes the person who knows that statement – if that person is Y, then "Y knows X" reduces the statement "Y believes X." If you really believe X is true, and you really mean it, you will assert that you believe X, and you will assert that X is true. So by "knowledge" they seem to really mean "belief," but they want to pretend that their belief, their "knowledge," is somehow a level above the mere "belief" of everyone else, of the layperson non-philosopher.

If we are merely to say that "X is true," the question then is, when you assert that someone knows something, how do you know that X is true, as separate from Y's believe that X is true? Is it the third-person omniscient narrator who knows X is true, or God knows X is true, or someone else knows X is true, or you sweep this question under the rug and seek to forget about it?

This issue only arises if you have a concept of K2. The problem with their definition of Knowledge is that you could never Know that it was Knowledge, although you could Know an X.

You might say that Y knows X is true because of Y's justification, therefore B(X) is justified, so we are all justified to believe that "X is true." But the classic model places the justification as a third element, distinct from the second element.

K, B, X, and "X is true" all presume a subject who knows, believes, asserts, or says that X is true. Tradition ignores this, and mixes the objective "X is true" as an element of Knowledge of people, from the person's own point of view, when asserting that an individual person holds Knowledge, that Y(K(X)), for example.

My theory of K does away with all these errors. K does not resemble the traditional definition at all. The traditional definition does not correspond to any entity in Reality.

Having a subjective point of view does not prevent Knowledge of objective Reality. According to Objectivism. The key is proving that the act of perception and means of perception do not bias nor constitute nor mediate the perceived thing as seen by the mind's eye. In which case what you see, the world of experience, exists objectively, it is not subjective. Why this is true is beyond the scope of this essay; I have written other books about that.

APPLIED ETHICS

Scenario One: Honesty

The Year is 1935. You are a Jewish father with two young children. You live in Germany. Sensing the danger in Nazi Germany, you make your escape. At the border, almost there, one final Nazi guard catches you. The Nazi asks you whether you are German, or Jewish. You know that if you lie, he will let you go, and your path to America is clear. If you tell the truth, he will send you back to Germany. You believe that dishonesty is unethical.

What should you do? You should tell the lie – but doing so is not "unethical" in the moral sense. Why? Because to "tell the truth," in that situation, would be dishonest, because it would be *faking Reality*, it would be to pretend that Reality is not what it is, to pretend that you could live in Nazi Germany. By lying, you are trying to live an ethical human life. By telling the truth, you would be ceasing to intend and will an ethical, moral life, a life as a human being. To quote myself, "Humans live as humans, or else we do not live, because we are human." "The value of Life is paramount over all other virtues." You should lie, and live, but doing so is not an "exception" to the universal principle that dishonesty is evil. To tell the truth, in that context, is the more dishonest act.

Scenario Two: Self-Defense, Gun Freedom and Gun Rights vs. Gun Control, and Vaccine Mandates vs. Health Freedom

The Year is 2112. A plague strikes the human race. There is a vaccine, which early studies suggest is highly safe and highly effective. But some people are skeptical of the vaccine. Does the government have the right to force the public to take it?

To paraphrase Robert A. Heinlein in "The Moon is a Harsh Mistress," "What is the difference between the government and any individual? The government cannot morally do anything to us other than what one individual could morally do to another individual." The question is: Could you force me to take it? Should you force me to take it?

The answer depends on the plague. If the plague is so deadly and contagious that me sneezing on your face is the moral equivalent of me shooting at you in the face with a gun, if the odds that you would die from a sneeze is the same as the odds that you will die if shot in the face, then you could defend yourself, as self-defense, by force, from everyone sneezing at you, to precisely the same extent as defending yourself from someone shooting at you. If that means you force me to take the vaccine, then you do. Anything less than (sneeze = firearms) would not justify it.

But then that brings in the question of gun control. If you can force the vaccine to avoid the risk of being shot in the face, why not take everyone's guns away to avoid the risk of being shot in the face?

I might sneeze at you, but until I do, I have not. If I own a gun, I might shoot at you, but I have not yet done so. Does that justify you taking my gun away from me, by force, because of a fear of risk? If so, not only vaccine mandates, but total gun control, is justified.

The answer is, with the plague, everyone has to travel in human public areas on a regular basis, or else cannot live, so people would be sneezing at you all the time, and any reasonable person would expect them to do so. Much as if people were to shoot at you with guns every morning when you walk to work, you could shoot back, and that would be self-defense. So you could force the public to take the vaccine.

If people are responsible adults, a reasonable person would expect them, if they choose to own a gun, to be a responsible gun owner. Much as the plague would have to be super-deadly and super-contagious to justify a vaccine mandate on the grounds of unreasonable risk, so, too, humanity would have to be super-crazy to justify gun control on the grounds of the unreasonable risk of crazy mentally-ill shooters going on a rampage. And humans are generally sane, and smart. If we humans were not, we would have gone extinct by now.

You have the right to use force for self-defense. Self-defense is the only moral use of violent force. Any other use of violent force violated the free will of individuals, thereby robbing them of their moral and ethical capacity as humans, the freedom to make choices as human, which takes away the ability to live *as human*. They could live as robots or puppets under the state's control, but that is not the same thing as a human life.

To use force on the grounds of mitigating unreasonable risk, the risk must be so severe and deadly as to be the moral identical equivalent of violent force. Only then could you use force to prevent risk. So only for those risks would any government action be moral. Government action is, by definition, the use of violence, of force – the moral right to use force by the consent of the governed and by the social contract for a shared system of self-defense, is the definition of "government" and "public," as opposed to "citizen" and "private." The public (politics) is the realm of violent force, the private (economics) is the realm of freedom and choice. If government action was not backed by threat of police and army, no one would obey it, it would be mere suggestions, not laws.

The citizen delegates the right of self-defense to the government. However, while delegating their right of self-defense against wars and foreign armies and foreign invaders, the citizen keeps the right to self-defense against local criminals (or against their own government if it descends into dictatorship, much as the patriots of the American Revolution did, when they founded the USA). Thus the citizen has the moral right to bear arms, and no exceptions to this right can exist.

PART TWO: ECONOMIC LOGIC

This section seeks to assess what principles and conditions of economics can be deduced purely from the analysis of economic concepts. A thought experiment, in which the essential features of an economy are present, but all specifics and details have been omitted, (other than fanciful fictitious details to make the reading more enjoyable), such that we can see that which must be logically true for this economy, and, hence, for any economy.

"Capitalism is good, Socialism is evil" is true, but it is an assertion, not a deduction. The attempt to prove it by empirical research is dubious, because all such empirical research is accused of bias, and most voters lack the cognitive tools to assess the empirical research, so they would need to rely on experts to assess the research, and can't arrive at the truth for themselves, in which case the empirical research is merely an assertion by the experts. What is missing is the logical proof, presented in such a way that everyone can see its truth. Here it is.

THE DESERT ISLAND
THOUGHT EXPERIMENT
FOR ECONOMIC ANALYSIS

Sailor Bill is on a ship. The Year is 1651. He sails in the Atlantic Ocean. The ship gets shipwrecked. Sailor Bill washes up on a tiny unknown island along the shore of what will one day become the great State of Connecticut, USA. The island is large, and rife with apple trees.

Sailor Bill wants to survive. Sailor Bill becomes Farmer Bill, on his desert island.

Farmer Bill climbs apple trees and reaps a harvest of apples. During the farming, during harvest season, he eats 10 apples a day for 150 days (and nothing else). He consumes 1,500 apples. From his crop, he harvests 1,500 apples.

The next year, in 1652, he consumes 1,500 apples. But it rains a lot, which the orchard likes. He harvests 3,000 apples that year.

He consumed 1,500 apples.

He produced 3,000 apples.

He made a profit of 1,500 apples.

What does this prove? Profit (and economics) would exist on a desert island. It is not created by capitalism. It does not represent the exploitation of the working class by the capitalist class. Profit is revenue in excess of cost. The cost is whatever is consumed in the act of producing the revenue. The revenue is the consumable value created by the productive process which consumes the cost.

In Year Three (1653), the weather is dry. Many apple trees die. Farmer Bill eats 1,500 apples. But he only harvests 1,000 apples.

He took a loss of 500 apples. Again, economics exists, as a fact of nature, on a desert island. It is not a human invention. And humans cannot alter the laws of economics by their choice or desire. Economics simply is.

Farmer Bill eats those 1,000 apples in 1654. The weather is the same, and the orchard recovers to the same level as, 1651. Farmer Bill would have made 1,500 apples. However, in 1654 Farmer Bill works harder, makes more of an effort, reaches more trees and picks more apples, and works longer hours, and sleeps less. He did not like having so few apples last year, and it puts the fear of God into him. By working harder, despite having fewer Resources to spend (only 1,000 apples consumed, instead of 1,500 consumed), Farmer Bill harvests 3,500 apples, so 3,500 apples produced. This year, by working harder, which really means, spending more time and energy, Farmer Bill made a profit of 2,500 apples.

The next year, in 1655, Farmer Bill builds a boat, sails to the mainland to explore, makes contact with the British Colony of Connecticut, and learns of other humans in the New World.

In 1655, Farmer Bill trades 1,000 apples to a Colony Merchant in return for a horse and buggy.

In 1656, Farmer Bill has made a profit of 1,000 apples. He again wants to trade them to the Colony Marchant for a horse and buggy. But the Merchant does not desire apples. He desires a set of new clothes for his family. The tailor has clothes the Merchant wants. But the tailor does not desire a horse and buggy. The tailor loves apple pies. The tailor desires Bill's 1,000 apples.

Farmer Bill does something smart. He decides to invent money. He trades 1,000 apples to the tailor in return for a promissory note or letter of debt entitling the holder of the letter to claim a new set of clothes from the tailor. Bill then trades the letter to the Merchant in return for a new horse and buggy. The Merchant then shows the letter to the tailor. The tailor gives the Merchant a set of new clothes for the family, in return for the letter of debt for 1,000 apples.

And so money is created. The money is made, by making the set of new clothes, by doing the work to have a horse and buggy to give, by harvesting the 1,000 apples of profit to trade. And the money is spent, to consume the apples, to wear the clothes, to travel in the horse and buggy. Again, the economic principle of money arises from the nature of human existence, from economics, it is not an artificial nor unnatural occurrence. Farmer Bill does not create the money by magic. He does not get given the horse and buggy by magic. He does so by means of being a farmer at a good enough level to make a 1,000 apple profit. And to then choose to sell, to trade, those apples, for something else he wants, that he wants to consume but cannot produce himself.

In 1657, the same scenario unfolds, except that now a British Merchant has arrived. The Colony Merchant will give Bill one new horse and buggy for Bill's note of debt for the tailor. But the British Merchant thinks the tailor's American clothes would be a big hit in London. To get them, he offers to trade to Bill two new horses and buggies in return for the letter of debt (the paper money).

Here we see a full picture of economics come into view. Bill, as consumer, gets to choose who to buy from, which seller to spend his money on, which defines who gets the value of 1,000 apples represented by the money, even though those applies ultimately go to the tailor. We can also begin to see the "Money Supply Ratio," the ratio of value to dollars, and the question of whether one American horse and buggy is worth two British horses and buggies, or what is the ratio of value between them, in relation to 1,000 apples. If Bill chooses to buy the two British horse and buggies, then each horse and buggy is worth a half-note (say, for the sake of argument, it is a $1 note, so each horse and buggy costs 50 cents), and 50 cents is worth 500 apples, so each British horse and buggy is worth 500 apples. The money changes hands, the trades happen, Bill consumes 2,500 apples, harvests 3,500 apples, gives 1,000 apples to the tailor, the tailor gives the new set of clothes to the British Merchant, the British Merchant gives the two British horse and buggies to Farmer Bill, and the British Merchant turns around and sails back to London and sells the American clothes to a British noble family. All involves a circuit of trades of goods for $1. We can also see that Bill's choice of which thing to buy would actually set the ratio of apples-per-horse and buggy, at 1,000 per one or 1,000 per two, which would also define the value of the money in relation to the goods it can buy.

In 1658, Farmer Bill wants to expand his farm by investing in new technology: a ladder made of hand-wrought iron. The British Merchant gives him a new iron ladder. Farmer Bill, as a result of the ladder, climbs higher up, reaches the high branches of more trees, harvests 6,000 apples, and consumes 2,500 apples, so his profit is 3,500 apples. But without the ladder he knows he would have only harvested 3,500, and consumed 2,500, so his profit would have been 1,000 without the ladder. So he made a 2,500 profit (equal to 3,500 minus 1,000) on the ladder. He gives the ladder back to the British Merchant, plus 2,000 apples as a thank-you for letting him borrow his ladder.

Bill keeps 500 apples of the 2,500 he produced because he had the iron ladder.

In 1659, The British Merchant doesn't have a new iron ladder. The Colony Merchant does. Yet he no longer wishes to do business with Farmer Bill. But the British Merchant has 2 $1 notes. So he loans the $2 to Bill. Bill buys a one-year rental of a new iron ladder from the Colony Merchant for $2, which $2 was given to Bill by the British Merchant. Bill makes 2,500 additional apples to consume because of the new iron ladder. He then gives 2,000 apples to the tailor in return for a $2 letter of debt, and Bill gives the $2 back to the British Merchant, as a thank-you for a loan of $2. Bill keeps 500 apples that he grew because of the loan.

The next year the same thing happens, except the British Merchant tells Bill that if he loans him $2, he wants to get back $3. Bill gets the newest iron ladder, works harder, and repays the $2 loan with $3. Bill is better off by his marginal apple profit on the new ladder, the British Merchant makes interest on his loan, and the tailor gets to eat a lot of apple pies. Then, eventually, not only the tailor, but the butcher, baker, smith, and hunters, begin accepting Farmer Bill's $1 notes. Then they all buy and sell for $1 notes to each other, trading $1 for something (buying something for $1, what a shopper does in a store) or trading something for $1 (selling something for $1, what an employee does by selling work for a salary).

And so debts, credits, loans, capital, investment, banking and capitalism are invented. Farmer Bill has a friend, Jolly Joseph. In 1660, Bill consumes 1,500 apples and harvests 3,000 apples.

Farmer Bill gives the 1,500 extra apples to Jolly Joseph. In return, Jolly Joseph builds a wooden shed for Farmer Bill to store surplus apples in. That shed never would have existed absent Farmer Bill's profit. Jolly Joseph's job never would have existed absent Farmer Bill's profit to pay Jolly Joseph's salary. Absent that profit, Jolly Joseph would have no job. But they are both the better off. Bill gets his shed. Joseph gets food to eat.

In 1661, the same, except Bill pays Joseph for the shed with a $1 note of debt, and Joseph later trades the $1 note to Bill in return for 1,500 apples.

In 1662, an evil British Lord visits the Connecticut Colony. He brings a gang of British soldiers with him on his ship. Farmer Bill harvests 3,000 apples, on a cost of consuming 1,500 apples to gain the time and energy to harvest those 3,000 apples. The 1,500 apples pay for 3,000 apples. So Bill gets a 1,500 apples profit. The British Lord decides to tax Farmer Bill's profit. The British Lord likes apples. But he doesn't want to trade or give anything in return for them. He just wants to take them, by force. Backed by the King of England, he declares a tax. He takes 1,500 apples from Farmer Bill, as a tax. With British soldiers aiming guns at Bill's head and Bill's family, Farmer Bill has no choice but to let the evil British Lord do so.

In 1663, Bill consumes 1,500 apples and produces 3,000 apples. The British Lord takes a tax. But this time, the British Lord collects $1 from Farmer Bill as his tax. The British Lord gives that $1 note of debt to the tailor, in return for a new set of clothes. The tailor then gives the $1 note to Bill. Bill, in honor, has no choice but to give 1,500 apples to the tailor in return for $1 (given that a Connecticut Colony $1 note of debt is worth roughly one set of clothes, or 1,500 apples).

In 1664, the evil British Lord decides to mint some new money. He and his British soldiers forge a new $1 bill, that looks exactly like the Connecticut Colony's money. The British Lord hands this newly printed $1 to the tailor. The tailor gives the British Lord a new set of clothes. The tailor then gives the $1 note to Bill. Bill, in honor, has no choice but to give the tailor 1,500 apples in return for the $1 note. But now there is an extra $1 note in circulation. Bill spends it. With more dollars chasing the same amount of goods, that exist in the Connecticut Colony, prices go up. Everything becomes that much more expensive. The precise amount that prices go up equals the pro rata per everything else value of the $1 note that was newly printed. Because the total amount of wealth, the total of quantity and quality of value, in Connecticut, is represented by the total number of Connecticut dollars, the money supply, in circulation in the Connecticut Colony economy. So the value of $1, what I owe to you if you give me a $1 note of debt, is equal to total wealth per total dollars, pro rata for each dollar.

That is how capitalism works. There is no exploitation. There is no theft. There is no crime. Other than by the government. It is just cold, hard economic logic. And freedom. And productivity to create value, and then happiness when you consume value.

Farmer Bill is free to choose who to spend his money on, and his only limit is his farm, the weather, his harvest, how hard he works, and how big of a loan he can talk the Merchants into giving him. And how much the British Monarchy steals. It is perfectly fair. But it is scary as fuck. Yes, if he were to operate at a loss for a few years, if he consumes all his apples, and then harvests 500 apples, but needs to consume at least 1,000 next year to have the time and energy to work a harvest at all, then he goes "below the line" of viability. He does not merely "go bankrupt," he goes hungry. And, if he starves to death, he dies.

But that is how life in the Colony of America is. The New World is tough. His death is fair. It is not unfair. There is no one to blame it on. This predates the Industrial Revolution. There is no super-rich capitalist class, to say, they should have given him charity, to save his life.

He might ask in the town for charity, for crumbs to eat, and get it, or not. But that is each person's individual free choice to give Bill charity or not. If Bill works hard, he is likely to survive. And if he fights, and puts up a fight, and works, and works, and works, and wills himself to survive, he does survive. There is no way that a system, such as socialism, could make life less scary. Socialism cannot change economics. Capitalism would exist on a desert island. It is not a social construct. So human choices cannot change it. It is metaphysical. It is not human-made. Capitalism did not create economics. Economics created capitalism.

The risks are inherent in life. People need to eat. Farms make food. They don't always make enough, or it's never certain that they will make enough – for you to eat, or for the farmers themselves to eat. In this world that could not be taken for granted. Yet stealing from some to feed others does not create new value. If not enough value is there, you consume what you already have, to survive. If you run out, you die. So you will yourself not to run out. Farmer Bill, facing starvation, could steal an apple pie from the tailor. Then the tailor goes hungry and the tailor's family starves. It's a zero-sum game.

Or, centuries later, a socialist government could steal trillions from some, and give trillions to others. And jail the political dissidents who complain. Which is unfair, yet done in the name of fairness. It's still a zero-sum game. Unless, somewhere, someone makes a new apple pie, and chooses to give it to Farmer Bill as charity of their own free will. And that just buys Bill an apple pie's worth of time, maybe a few days, in which to work harder and try to jumpstart his farm and get back "above the line."

Have courage in the face of life. We need the courage to be capitalists. Socialism isn't magic. It pretends to make things safer, for cowards, to soothe their anxiety, by means of mere tricks and sleight-of-hand. By sacrificing freedom for the sake of an illusion of safety. Which thereby leaves an impoverished masses dependent upon

THE MEANING OF LIFE

government to survive, and a government in total control, with life-or-death power over every person, with a military to enforce its theft-as-charity. And there was no capitalist exploitation or theft happening in Farmer Bill's capitalism, to justify any socialism whatsoever. "Those who would sacrifice freedom for safety, deserve neither freedom, nor safety."

Farmer Bill's life was tough, but he was free. It is mere emotional toddlers and those with the maturity (or intelligence) of tiny little children who would prefer a parent-as-government to run their lives for them and "keep them safe" forever, instead of growing up and becoming free adults and making their own decisions and taking full responsibility for those decisions. Farmer Bill was free back then. He had rugged individualism. Today, we need that freedom again.

It is theoretically possible – and whether this is really true is an empirical question, not a question for logic – that there could be an entire class of people below the line of a middle class lifestyle, people who simply are not smart and hard-working enough to make the money (to create enough value) to pay the cost of the material objects of a happy middle class life, given the objective per-person costs of creating that set of physical objects which constitute a middle class lifestyle.

Logic can say that, if there was such, there would be no reason to tax the rich, or the middle class, to pay for this class of people to live a middle class life which they themselves do not pay for. You could not say that "they did not deserve it." You could not say that it was "unfair." Such elements simply do not exist. People can choose to work harder, or to work less hard. People choose to be smart, or stupid. People will their lives. People have free will, hence personal responsibility for themselves. There would be no reason to assign any virtue to such socialist redistribution of wealth. There would be no reason nor justification to do so.

I will conclude this section thusly: I might be accused of cruelty, to say that such people's lives are worth less than middle-class or rich people's lives, that they deserve a lesser, cheaper lifestyle. I have not said that their lives are worth less. The moral value of a life cannot be measured in dollars. History is full of great people, and loving people, and happy people, who were happy but not rich. I assume that many people are. The value of their lives, and basic human dignity, is not at issue. The economic value of objects can, and must, be measured in dollars. If a middle class life requires a refrigerator, washer and dryer, television, phone, internet, and microwave oven, then those must be created, and the cost must be paid to create them, and the value must be created that gets consumed as the cost by the productive processes which created them – much as Farmer Bill must eat apples, to have the time and energy, to harvest apples. His apples have a cost. If he didn't pay the cost, he would not have more apples. He could not have more apples. Not by anyone's choice, but because of economics. It is simply not possible for something to exist, in economics, unless someone pays for it. The next section explains why.

GOVERNMENT SPENDING

Government spending either gets paid for by the taxpayer, as higher taxes, or gets passed onto the consumer, by means of higher prices caused by inflation. Something, in order to exist, must be paid for. To make money is to create value. To spend money is to consume value, so the value that gets consumed, has to be made by someone, it has to be taken from somewhere.

For a clear and simple example, Farmer Bill eats six months' worth of apples, 2000 apples for example, and spends six months, and builds a house, for example. Then the 2000 apples were the cost of the house. And the money value of 2000 apples, what dollars could be trades to buy them, was the money cost of the house. You can't just magically declare, by fiat, that the house is free, and give the house away, to the poor, or to the friends of the government. If the cost wasn't paid, the house would not exist. The house could not exist. Someone had to eat the apples, or else they would not have been alive for the six months they spent to build the house, and they had to have those apples to eat, with whatever those apples cost, paid for, to spend six months building a house, instead of spending those six months harvesting food. If the owner of the house pays for the 2000 apples, that is capitalism. If, for example, Bill builds a house to be able to house some farm workers, and their productivity will result in 2000 or more new apples harvested, that is capitalism. If the government declares that the house of free, and is to be built by Bill and given away to the poor for free, and then forces Bill to eat 2000 of his own apples at his own expense, to be forced to spend six months to build a house for the poor, instead of spending six months farming, that is socialism. That is taxation. Taxation is theft.

Government spending does not happen by magic. The stupid, and the uneducated, and the ignorant, and the Left, believe that it happens by magic. They say it's "free" because the government gave it away. But somebody makes whatever the government gives away. If nobody made it, it would not be there. And whoever made it, has costs, what it cost to make. Those costs were paid for when the thing was made. Something, in order to exist, must be paid for. Nothing is "free."

They say it is paid for by the rich. But which rich people do they mean? What they say cannot logically be true, because they also say that the rich are thieves who get rich by stealing money, yet, to pay for government spending would require creating the value that gets consumed by the beneficiaries of government entitlements, so only the rich people who make money, who create vast new amounts of value, would pay for it, the rich people who are thieves and do not create value, could create no value for the government to give away. So it taxes people according to their productiveness, and punishes people for their virtue, for creating value, for willing life to exist.

Of course, taxes literally steal money from the taxpayer at the point of a gun with the threat of being thrown in jail, so that is easy to understand. The sheep and idiots believe that this theft is justified, so they desire it, blinding themselves that they have condoned theft, which is an inherent and intrinsic evil, to take what is earned away from the person who earned it by willing it to be.

Inflation is the only wrinkle complex enough to stump people a few grades higher of IQ. The government prints money. Someone has to create the value that gets consumed when that money is spent. Otherwise it's just Monopoly Money, just pieces of inked rectangular paper, which you can't consume, can't eat, can't spend. The government steals value for this new money with sleight-of-hand. The government buys things with its phony Monopoly Money, and forces the sellers to sell actual real value in return for that paper-with-ink-on-it, more buying raises prices (that's simple supply-and-demand), the consumer has the same amount of money-per-value, yet now there's more money in the economy, so he/she/they has to create more value to buy the same things they used to, "create more value" means work harder, make more money, create more value that's backing the money supply, so the consumer has to pay the higher prices, and that redistributes value from the consumer, through the government, to whomever was the recipient of the government's money.

Remember, "the consumer" is not just a consumer who sits there and makes demands and gets given stuff. The consumer is the worker, the employee, the producer, but with a focus on them as one spending the money they made, while "the producer" is them with a focus on them as one at work. There is one person, the citizen of the economy. The citizen makes money, spends the money they made, and thereby lives. The only other true economics actors are the government, who robs the citizen, and the deadbeat, whom the government gives "free" value to, in return for votes and showing up at protests and rallies waving angry signs. Economic value is moral value. And you have to earn it. The only other way to get it is to steal it. Or else it isn't there.

ECONOMIC SYMBOLIC FORMAL LOGIC

All economic conduct in Capitalism is either producing value, or trading value for value, or trading value for money (a purchase or sale).

The syllogism for creating a value is:

Output = Process of Input

O = P(I)

The symbolic notation: #Y = P(#X)

For example,

3,000 apples = Farming(1,500 apples)

This means the Farming consumed 1,500 apples and produced 3,000 apples.

Or:

A digital ad campaign = Placing a set of digital ads($5,000)

Placing the set of digital ads consumed $5,000 and produced a digital ad campaign.

You could nest statements. You can also add inputs.

For example:

Having read a book = read(10 hours + book = buy a book($10))

Reading a book consumes 10 hours of reading plus the book, which costs $10 to buy. The process results in output of having read the book.

Any productive process can be so described.

Any consumption of value could be likewise described. For example:

Vacation = Taking a vacation($2,500)

Taking a vacation cost $2,500 but produced the enjoyment of a vacation.

That is the symbolic logic of creating a value.

The below deals only with the symbolic logic of trade, and assumes the value is already created:

Symbolic Notation: <- -> -> / <- <- -> &&

This describes a trade or sale, as described in the Farmer Bill story. The format is:

Person First Trader Sells Second Product to<-First Trader->Product One Traded->#· of Units of Product One Traded/# of Units of Product Two Traded<-Product Two Traded<-Second Trader->Person Second Trader Sells First Product To

Bill->apples->1,000/2<-Horse and Buggy<-Merchant

Bill trades 1,000 apples to the Merchant in return for two Horses and Buggies

Tailor<-Bill->apples->1,000/1<-$<-Merchant->Tailor

Bill trades 1,000 apples to the Merchant in return for a $1 note, and the Merchant will then sell the $1 note to the Tailor in return for value equal to $1 which Bill will then give to the Tailor.

The paradigm of a shopper at a store who buys a new TV:

Economy at Large<-Consumer->$->1,000/1<-A new television<-TV manufacturer->Economy at Large

The consumer purchased a new television for $1,000. The Paradigm of an Employee earning a salary: Economy at large<-Employer->$->30/1<-Hours of Labor<-Employee->Economy at Large

The employee sells one hour of labor to the employer for $30. The employee will then turn around and trade this $30 to someone else (represented by "The Economy at Large") in return for $30 worth of values to consume, while the employer will package that hour of labor, with the hours of labor of every other employee, to make stuff, which it will then sell to consumers in return for money, and then trade that money to employees in return for more labor-hours.

&&: "And," for connecting multiple economic logical statements into one full statement.

(X->Y->1/5<-B<-A)&&(X->Y->1/2<-D<-C):

X trades one Y to B in return for 5 A, and X also trades one Y to C in return for 2 D.

In logic, the above statement proves that, according to the choices of all economic actors in sum, in this hypothetical scenario, five B is worth two D. Had money prices been assigned, and Y is worth $1, then B would be worth $0.20 and D would be worth $0.50. This is true given that B and D are to be measured (and priced) in relation to Y.

The Syllogism of Capitalist Economic Logic: Your Work = You(Food, shelter, healthcare, time, energy, love from friends and family, enjoyment and de-stress of leisure and entertainment, news and info, etc.) Economy->$->#/#<-Products<-Your Employer (Your employer as firm)

&&

Your Employer->$->#/#<-Hours of Labor to Make Products<-You (You as employee/producer)

&&

You->$->#/#<-Products<-The Economy (You as consumer)

&&

Your Employer->$->#/#<-Factors and Resources to Make Products<-The Economy

&&

Your Employer->Note of Debt or Shares of Stock->#/#<-$<-The Investor or Bank

Lender Plus details and numbers into the variables in the above template. This can describe any subset of a Capitalist economy.

BONUS CONTENT

My prediction:

Flat Earth:Round Earth::Universe:Fractal.

As Flat Earth was to Round Earth, so Universe will be to Fractal.

We humans saw a Flat Earth, but we reasoned that the Earth is Round.

We see the Universe. We will reason that we live inside of a giant multi-dimensional Fractal.

You don't yet see it because your point of view is too small to see enough of it to see it. Much as, from one person's point of view, the Earth around you looks flat.

But math can give you a broad enough point of view to "see" that the Earth is round.

A Fractal is a cyclical mathematical geometric pattern that is always self-similar yet never perfectly repeats. Thus, every Fractal contains smaller Fractals similar to it yet different from it, and at the same time every Fractal is within a larger Fractal that is similar to it yet different from it. The pattern always repeats, but never the same way twice.

I believe this was Nietzsche's "Eternal Recurrence" – and is also the reason why Nietzsche would have thought of it at all.

My thought for the future:

A robot with morals is not a robot.

A computer with a soul is not a computer. A robot or computer with morals and ethics would be a person, much as any human is a person. But the reverse is also true: A human who had no morals and no ethics is not a person and does not have a soul. Having a soul comes from ethics and morality. Ethics and morality arise from the need for them because you face a choice. Facing choices comes from having free will. As such, C and W, guided by D and K, and contingent upon P, Con and SA, are the hallmarks of personhood. This holds true for humans, robots, computers, cyborgs, genetically enhanced animals, genetically enhanced humans, aliens, and any new technology not yet developed. These principles will always hold true, because they arise from the nature of Reality, and so are true in any and all Universes, for any and all beings.

IF P THEN Q: WHY PHILOSOPHY CAN TEACH YOU HOW TO THINK AND HELP YOU LIVE A HAPPY LIFE BY THE METHODS OF APPLYING LOGIC TO SOLVE THE PROBLEMS IN YOUR LIFE AND ACHIEVE SUCCESS (A SCHOLARLY MONOGRAPH)

ON LOGIC

This book will explain a system of logic that uses science, philosophy, and the scientific method in order to solve problems. Any problem can be solved by means of the system of logic explained herein: problems in the hard sciences, problems in the law, and problems in ordinary everyday human life, will all be used as examples of showing the power of this system of logic.

The basics of logic are assumed: logic begins with definitions and assumptions and then applies deduction and inferences to prove conclusions that must necessarily be true if the definitions and assumptions were true; logic deals with statements, such as P and Q, and these statements can be either True or False; and logic can analyze relationships between statements, such as "If (A and B) then (Not C or Not D)". Common logic operators include AND, OR, and NOT, but the main focus of this paper is on IF ... THEN ... .

DEFINITIONS

P: The idea, hypothesis, theory.

Q: The expectation.

Q is defined by what difference it makes whether P is True or False.

Q is precisely what we would expect to see (to experience in empirical phenomenal perceptions and sensations) if P were True.

The Philosophical Scientific Method (The PSM): The use of "If P Then Q" to connect logic to sensation, where Q is sensations and P is a theory and If P Then Q is the logic that connects them, enabling logical analysis of sensation and experience and data, in order to prove that a scientific theory is true by means of logic.

b/c: Because.

The fundamental model of how a scientific experiment works:

(1) Posit or assert or formulate or guess idea/hypothesis/theory P.

(2) Define expectation Q such that "If P Then Q."

(3) Run an empirical scientific experiment to test and/or measure whether Q or Not Q. This does not need to be a formal experiment with measurement instruments, it can be as simple as opening your eyes and looking at something and seeing whether your own subjective observations conform to Q or not.

(4) Refute P (or, possibly, confirm P, as we will later discuss) based on the scientific findings or experiential observations of Q or Not Q.

Some philosophers refer to "If P then Q" as a conditional statement, that P is a condition that must be met for Q to continue to be true. I prefer to think of it as cause and effect: P's truth, the truth of P, will cause, or make it necessary, that Q is also true. In the scientific use of logic, P will always be the theory or abstract framework, and Q will always be a set of sensations or experiences, or data collected from those sensations and experience, such that Q are caused by P.

THE FALSIFICATION OBJECTION

The Philosophical Scientific Method works like this:

How to refute a theory which is false, by means of an experiment:

    (1) If P then Q. (From analytical logic.)

    (2) Not Q. (Seen from experiments and data.)

    (3) Therefore Not P. (Refutation.)

    And:

    How to prove that a theory is true, by means of an experiment:

    (1) If P then Q. (From analytical logic.)

    (2) Q. (Seen from experiments and data.)

    (3) Therefore P. (Proof.)

But an objection to my "proof" logic can be levelled against me:

(1) If P then Q.

    (2) Not Q.

    (3) Therefore Not P.

    But:

    (1) If P then Q.

    (2) Q.

    (3) Therefore (P or Not P).

Something other than P could have caused Q even if Q is True, therefore Q can't prove P, but, if P were True, P would have caused Q, so Not Q proves Not P. Science can refute (falsify) a theory, but it can never prove that a theory is true, hence science is the great skeptic art, but can never achieve something that we can properly call knowledge. This is the logic underlying the so-called "falsification" theory of science, attributed to philosopher Karl Popper.

In early versions of this paper, I was accused of asserting a logical fallacy: that logical fallacy of "If P then Q, Q, Therefore P," a well-documented type of logical fallacy. No, I am not asserting that this logical fallacy is valid. Yes, I am aware that it is a logical fallacy. But that is precisely the problem: if you define P as a theory, and Q as sensations and experiences caused by P, then science, as knowledge, rests upon this logical fallacy.

The central thesis of this paper is how to prove P from Q without running aground into the dangerous waters of the logical fallacy. Only in this way can science prove that a theory P is true. Otherwise, science can refute a P, can prove that P is false, but can never prove a P is true, can never know P. But the achievement of scientific knowledge can be done, by means of various methods, such as probability math, and building a logical model, or by establishing "Q if and only if P" independently of "If P then Q." In this way, this paper is quite revolutionary, and very important, to both logic, science, and philosophy. This paper elaborates below.

COUNTERS TO THE FALSIFICATION OBJECTION, WHY SCIENCE ACHIEVES KNOWLEDGE

There are a variety of arguments against Falsification, proving that the Philosophical Scientific Method can, in fact, achieve knowledge, because there are logical methods by means of which evidence Q or experience Q can prove that idea P or theory P is True. These various methods of logic are explained in the next sections of this paper.

THE IF AND ONLY IF METHOD (SHERLOCK HOLMES REASONING)

(1) Q If and Only If P. (This is achieved based on the degree of precision that Q is precisely what we would expect if, and only if, P were true. The more precision between P and Q, the greater the degree to which this is true.)

(2) Q.

(3) Therefore P.

Consider this logic, which is similar to Q If and Only If P:

(1) If P then Q. (Given. Established by analytic logic.)

(2) If Not P then Not Q. (Given. Established by analytic logic.)

(3) Q. (Established by sensation and observation or data collection.)

(4) If P then Q, Q, Therefore P or Not P.

(5) Q or Not Q, Q, Therefore Not Not Q.

(6) If Not P then Not Q, Therefore If Not Not Q then Not Not P,

(7) Q, Q or Not Q, Therefore Not Not Q, Therefore Not Not P.

(8) P or Not P, Not Not P, Therefore P.

In a way, this is like the reasoning Sherlock Holmes does in the great short story classics: he sees the crime scene and sees the clues, then he makes a mental analysis of every possible cause of the set of clues he has discovered, he refutes each one of those causes one by one, and, when left with only one possible explanation, he considers that truth, and acts upon it.

This method of Sherlock Holmes is essentially a process of elimination:

A or B or C.

Not A and not B.

Therefore C.

But, when logic is paired with sensation, and we define If P Then Q where P is a theory or hypothesis and Q is a sensation or experience, we might find:

A or B or C.

If A then X.

If B then Y.

If C then Z.
Not X and not Y.
Therefore C.

THE MODEL METHOD

Step 1: Build a Model (a conceptual, theoretical framework of what you think something is, why it is, and, therefore, how it will behave, that will enable you to predict Expectation Q from Model P, in other words, build a mental representation of whatever you are studying that will predict how this subject matter will behave in the future).

Step 2: Take a sample data set, apply the Model to it (a Test). The Process for this is: Take a sample data set, predict what Q you would have expected if Model P were true, assess the data set to see if Q is true, if Q is false then Refine and correct the Model so that your new Model would have predicted the Test data, and, if Q is true, leave your Model alone and increase your confidence score.
Step 3: Refine the Model based on the Test.

Step 4: Retest and Refine until you reach a point of confidence acceptable for real-world usage.

Step 5: Apply the Model to the Real World. This involves making a prediction and relying on that prediction in a real-world situation without first testing the Model on the real-world situation, such that, if your prediction is correct, your get a successful outcome, but if your Model fails, then you fail. (Real-world examples of this scenario are given later in this paper.)

Step 6: Succeed or fail and, if fail, look at the failure data, use that data to Refine the Model again, then repeat Steps Two through Five.

THE PROBABILITY METHOD

(1) Probability = Odds of P based on # Actual Q out of # Possible Q.

(2) If (Probability)P then Q.

(3) (Number of) Q.

(4) Therefore (Probability)P.

If the probability math and statistics were perfect, this would perfectly refute the Falsification Theory, because Q could perfectly prove (Probability)P.

THE X-BECAUSE-Y METHOD

(1) Perceive X. Therefore Know X.

(2) Perceive Y. Therefore Know Y.

(3) Know (X + Y), Therefore Know (X/Y) (because X/Y = f(X + Y)). In other words, the relationship between X and Y is a function of what is X and what is Y, so, if you know what X is, and you know what Y is, you can deduce from X plus Y what is the relationship between X and Y.

(4) If X/Y = X b/c Y, then Known (X Because Y). In other words, if the relationship between X and Y is "X Because Y," that Y causes X, and you know X plus Y, then you can reason from (X plus Y) to (X Because Y), and then you can know that Y will cause X.

(5) If X Because Y, then you can predict that X will be true if Y is true, in the future and at all places and at all times, without any further need for empirical experimentation to confirm or refute this.

(6) If Know (X/Y) then can prove (If Y Then X) and (Y If and Only If X) statements, if those statements are substantively true given whatever X and Y really are.

THE BUSINESS MAKING
MONEY EXAMPLE

A business sells at-home ice-cream-making kits. The kits have three data points: flavor (chocolate or vanilla), profile (brand publicity, how well-known they are, i.e.,publicized or not), and price (cheap, medium, expensive). Those are Q. The R to be predicted is sales, and, by extension, profits.

The ice-cream kits sell well. But the business wants to find the price point that will maximize profits, using the basic formula that sales times price equals revenues. For example, selling 100 kits for $10 yields $1,000.

So, if it raises price, that must more than offset a decline in sales, of, if it lowers price, the increase in sales must more than offset the lower price, for the net revenue to increase.

The business lowers the price. Sales do not improve. The business then adds to its model that lower price does not impact sales, when lowered. So a cheaper price won't help sales, and therefore won't raise profits.

It raises the price, in an experiment. Sales do, in fact, go way down. Then the business knows raising prices lowers sales a lot. And the business sees that the expensive price hurts sales so much that the higher price does not make up for it.

So, the logic for this business to discover the correct price point for maximizing revenue per sales is:

(1) cheap OR medium OR expensive (from logical analysis),

(2) NOT cheap, AND NOT expensive, (from observations and experience)

(3) therefore medium (the conclusion proven by logic).

It tries chocolate and vanilla sales. Then it introduces strawberry flavor. Sales skyrocket, sales go through the roof. But then the business learns that, on the day of its new strawberry product launch, a local major media news outlet wrote a story about them. Was the price surge attributed to profile, or to flavor?

Logic and experience can answer the question. The business runs two experiments. It pays a PR firm to get more publicity. Each time a story runs, sales go way up.

It then temporary stops selling strawberry, and sells only chocolate and vanilla. There is some impact on sales, sales drop, but it is small, it does not drop by enough to impact profits.

So the business infers, using logic and experience, that profile can cause sales to go way up, but the customers don't care that much about flavor options. The business builds a model that customers want this ice-cream kit solution, and they like it, but they don't know it exists yet, so publicity is going to be the key to success, at least for now.

Does the business know this for sure? No. But it has a model, which is validated, by logic. Further experiments could refine the model, but the business will reach a point where the cost of more experiments outweighs the benefits. What matters is that the business builds a model of how to maximize profits, and please customers, and then does so.

You can take any set of data points, for anything: personal, professional, academic, career, business, romance, and plug them into logic, using IF THEN, AND, OR, and NOT, but you must always establish True or False from experience and sensations. Truth comes from sensations, and then "trickles up" through your logical analysis, eventually rising up to the top, where it forms a theory or conceptual framework, a Model, which is proven True by the sensations and the logic.

In this way, the system of logic described in this book uses "If P Then Q" as the point of connection between logic and sensation, enabling an analytical logic of experience, which is called science.

THE CRIMINAL TRIAL EXAMPLES

The Criminal Trial Case: Defendant X is on trial for murder. The murder happened in Boston on the evening of July 15. On July 15, there is entered into evidence that X was seen at a party in Miami that evening, that X's credit card was charged for dinner at a restaurant in Miami on July 15, and that X's cell phone location was logged as being in Miami on the evening of July 15 (although phone geo-location is missing at the precise time of the murder, because there happened to be a signal outage at that time).

But there were no witnesses to the murder, there were no witnesses who saw X at the precise moment when the murder happened, and, simply because the victim had some sort of previous relationship to X and the two were angry at each other, X is a suspect and has been accused, because the prosecutor could not find anyone else who might have done it. The prosecution asserts X did it in person; records show he was too poor to afford to hire a hit man.

Can you convict X? Is this enough to know that X can't be guilty? Why or why not? How does "If P then Q, Q, Therefore P" shed light on the logic involved? Is this an "If and Only If" case, or is this a "Model" case, or could you use either one?

This is the Circumstantial Evidence Problem. Most people will probably say "He obviously couldn't have done it, he's innocent," but some might say "no one saw the murder, so we can't ever really know who did it, it might have been him," and then the jury has to reach a verdict given the condition of imperfect knowledge, with only logic to guide them.

The Criminal Trial Case Part Two: Defendant X is on trial for assault, for getting into a heated argument after someone cut him in line at the cafeteria counter and punching an unarmed woman in the face, in anger. There were no witnesses other than X and the woman; it was late in the evening and most of the workers had gone home for the day. The woman asserts it. X denies it. There is no corroborating physical evidence (doctors could not determine whether there was face trauma).

There is testimony entered into evidence that X gives lots of money to charity and volunteers at charities to help the needy. X's friends and partner and coworkers testify that X is a nice, loving, sweet person. X's published articles and essays advocating pacifism are entered into evidence. A psychological evaluation showing that X's personality type is calm, relaxed, even, and non-violent, is entered into evidence. X's personal history is entered into evidence showing that he has never been in a fight nor been violent before in his entire life. X's medical records show he was not drunk or on drugs at the time.

Can you convict X? Is this enough to know that X can't be guilty? Why or why not? How does "If P then Q, Q, Therefore P" shed light on the logic involved? Is this an "If and Only If" case, or is this a "Model" case, or could you use either one?

This is the Character Evidence Problem. Most people would say "Obviously he isn't the type of person to punch someone over this," but someone might say, "he has free will, so he could be the nicest type of person in the world, and yet he could still have chosen to punch this woman, we don't know," and then the jury must reach a verdict given the human condition of imperfect knowledge, with real people's fates at stake, the man to get a criminal conviction on his record, or a woman's rights to be violated without recourse nor restitution. Logic is the only tool to use for this.

The logic involved in both of these criminal jury trials may actually be best annotated in this way:

(1) If P then Q. (From logical analysis.)

(2) Q If and Only If P. (From logical analysis, independent of If P Then Q.)

If in Miami then will leave a trail of evidence that he was in Miami.

If a nice person, will leave a trail of evidence that is a nice person.

(3) Q. (From sensation, experience, observation or data.)

Evidence of having been in Miami.

Specific evidence that would have been caused by having a nice-person personality type.

(4) Therefore P. The theory is supported.

Being in Miami is inferred from the evidence of a paper trail in Miami.

Being a nice person is inferred from behavior showing that he is a nice person.

(5) If P then R.

If in Miami then not in Boston, and if not in Boston then can't have been the culprit.

If a nice person then wouldn't hit a woman over a pointless annoyance.

(6) Therefore, If Q then R.

(7) Q, therefore R. The evidence proves that the defendant is innocent.

The substantive presentation of the trial evidence, and legal arguments, by the defendants to prove their innocence.

Ultimately, the planes have to fly, and the verdicts must be reached, and the right outcome needs to be achieved or else people's lives are ruined (a plane crashes in a fireball, an innocent man goes to jail for forty years), so someone has to figure out the truth, and know for sure that they are right, and they really have to be right, or, at least, they have to know what are the odds that their probability model is correct, and then act according to those odds.

The great thing about Objectivism is, it says: You are the one who must make that decision, so you have to know, and logic is the method by means of which it is possible for you to know.

Of course, realistically, juries rely on circumstantial evidence and character evidence all the time, without really thinking about it or worrying about the philosophy that justifies it, and airlines fly planes that are not perfectly safe all the time, without going through the philosophical analysis described herein.

But it is also probably true that the innocent go to jail sometimes, and that people sometimes die in plane crashes, and it would be logically true that, had the correct methods of logic been used, and successful outcomes achieved instead, those people's lives could have been saved by means of reason and logic and Objectivism. So this is not mere disembodied abstract theoretical philosophy, these ideas can make a real difference.

THE PERSONALITY EXAMPLE

The philosophy of Objectivism holds that logic is not mere abstract disembodied theory meant for ghosts or armchair philosophers; no, instead it has real meaning and practical usefulness for real people. Consider these example of how a real person might use Logical Modeling. The first example involves sex, the second example involves money.

Assume a young person in college, exploring their sexuality and engaging in self-discovery. Yes, this is an example which some people, myself included, might find strange, but it is a perfect example of how practical and useful logic is for ordinary human beings. Also, by the way, no, not everyone finds themselves sexually in high school, there are college kids, and adults, who find themselves, so this is realistic.

To begin, they have a model, which many young people still assume as their starting point, that they are "straight," in other words, for-opposite-gender. They then have a random casual sexual encounter with someone of the opposite gender, but who is older, and do not enjoy it. Assume that their lover was physically attractive, so beauty/handsomeness would not have been a factor.

Logically, there are four possibilities: they did not enjoy it because their lover was of the opposite gender, they did not enjoy it because their lover was older, or they did not enjoy it because it was casual and not in a serious romantic relationship, or some combination of the first three.

So they Refine their Model to think that they are for-own-gender, and then they try a random casual sexual encounter with a person of the same gender, who is their age, and they enjoy it a lot.

But then their Model poses a question: either they are for-own-gender, or else they are "bi"/"pan"/for-all-genders but they enjoy only people their own age but not older people.

To answer this question, they identify, logically, the experiences Q from which the difference between P or Not P would emerge.

They try a random casual sexual hookup with a person their own age of the opposite gender, and they enjoy it a lot. Next, they try casual sex with an older person who is same-gender, and they do not enjoy it much.

Logically, then, they enjoy sex with any gender, but only with people their own age and not with older persons, and they can enjoy casual sex without a serious romance. So they further Refine their Model to include this. They can now predict the types of persons they would enjoy having sex with, with a good deal of accuracy.

But, in logic, they realize that this does not prove that they would not enjoy sex in the context of serious romance, and that the presence of a serious romantic relationship might, or might not, change what they like sexually, in terms of age and/or genders, they don't know.

So they date and have a serious long-term relationship romantically with a person for a year, and enjoy it a lot, but they find that sex with the other person doesn't matter that much to them when in the context of romance, and, where the sex doesn't matter, age and gender does not matter either.

So, on the basis of using experience to identify Q or Not Q in order to prove P or Not P, and by defining their Q based on what difference it makes whether P is true or false, they used logic and science (by which I mean, logic and logical analysis applied to empirical experience and perceptions and sensations) to learn:

Am I for-opposite-gender, for-own-gender, or for-any-gender?

Am I for-casual-sex, for-romance, for-both, or for-neither?

Am I for-own-age, or for-any-age?

These valuable life lessons then guide this person as they grow up and explore the magical journey of being human and finding love and romance as an adult.

THE JET FUEL EXAMPLE

You are developing chemical formula X for jet engine fuel, to be put into engines of engine type Y. The only variables which will define whether a plane will fly, or get engine failure and crash, are your chemical formula X, and whether it is suitable and correct for usage in a jet engine of type Y which works according the principles of how Y-type motors work. At some point, after your science-and-logic process is done, you need to really make the fuel, and you fuel up lots of planes and lots of engines with this fuel without having tested literally all, or even most, of the planes with this new jet fuel, and the fleet of planes will fly on day one (if you were right), or, if you were wrong, they crash and burn.

You can test as much as you want on one hundred prototype jet engines, but your fuel will go into thousands of planes on the day when the airline business CEO signs off and green lights takeoff, and these will be real planes flying hundreds of routes each day with real people, with thousands of real human beings who might die if any engine fails because of your fuel.

How do you proceed? By means of experiments and trial and error, and trial and failure until trial and success? By means of the Model method? If the Model method, what degree of certainty is acceptable before putting thousands of human lives at risk? Would you just make a random list of chemicals, and pour each one, one after the next after the next, into a prototype engine, to see at random which works the best, using a blind guess-and-check methodology, or would some analysis have to go into the choice of chemical formula, the prediction and hypothesis about what fuel will work, which requires thinking about why the fuel will work?

Or do you not use the Model method? Then do you seek to go by means of the Because/If and Only If method, for which you would have to conceptually understand how the X molecules will function in a Y mechanism, such that every X will work the same way in every Y, because of the metaphysical nature of X and Y? If Know(X Because Y) then you can use that to predict Y from X, for example, if the nature of an Y-type motor is that petroleum-based gasoline-type jet fuel will make it overheat but hydrogen jet fuel will not make it overheat, just because you know the melting point of the material the engine is made from and you know how much heat the different types of fuel combustion will generate, then you can infer with 100% certainty-knowledge that hydrogen fuel will work (or, at least, that hydrogen fuel won't cause the engine to overheat and melt), but that gasoline won't work.

If your science then looks at the amount of energy created by hydrogen combustion, and that amount of energy meets or exceeds the energy requirements of the jet engine for the plane to fly, based on your knowledge of the weight of the plane and the physics of how planes fly, then you just achieved a Model which says that chemical X should be hydrogen, for engine-type Y. This is a Model that you achieved using the X-Because-Y Method. If that is your Model, you then fuel the airplane fleet with your hydrogen jet fuel, watch it take off, and, if you are correct, the airplanes fly, and the passengers are safe and happy. But, if an airplane were to fail, your Model would be refuted, and you would then be forced to Refine your Model, and try a different chemical formula for jet fuel, instead of hydrogen, probably after applying analysis to try to understand why that plane engine had failed, and then applying those lessons learned from that failure in order to Refine your Model.

On the other hand, if you are using just a probability model approach, and you test 100 engines with Fuel X, and 99 of the engines work, then all you learned is that you can infer a 99% chance that X will work. And, if you test X on 100 engines, and 100 of them all work, all you can infer is a 99.999+% chance that X will work, but never 100%, because, even if you only test 100 engines, it might be true that the first 999 engines you could have tested with fuel X would have worked, and then the 1,000th engine that you would have tested would have failed, if you had tested 1,000 motors, instead of only the sample set test of 100 motors that you in fact really did test. But what you can be certain of is that the odds are that the number of them worked out of the total number that you compare it to, if you really conduct a 100% complete test of each unit in your sample set (such that your knowledge of the sample set is 100%, therefore your knowledge of the odds of the basis of testing the sample set is 100%).

For example, if you test 100 motors, and they all work, and you are only going to be flying 200 planes, you can know that at worst you are 50% sure they will all work, because you tested and can know that at least half the planes will have engines proven to have worked. But then, if, statistically, each test of one engine is representative of testing thousands of other motors, because of the similarity between them is so extreme that they are largely identical and there isn't supposed to be any deviation between them, then testing 100 engines might give you odds of having tested a million engines, if the science says that this is true. But what matters isn't having comfy odds, or having a correct Model. You could have a team of highly educated, highly trained research scientists, with the most fancy Model in the world, and then a plane still crashes. What matters is that the fuel actually works. What matters is that the planes need to really fly.

This is the Problem of Human Action: we, as humans, need to act upon our knowledge, and we survive by thinking about the future and trying to predict the future, and we live or die based on whether we are right or wrong (even our ancient ancestors had to predict where in the ground to plant the seed, when to harvest the wheat, in what type of oven to bake the bread, and, if they were wrong, they died), so how do we know, and who decides what to do?

Some common answers are: Refine the model until you are 95% to 99% sure that 95% to 99% of the planes will fly, and then fly the planes. Another common answer is: Don't worry too much about it, keep testing and refining your Model until your research and development laboratory budget runs out of money, which means you did the best you could, and then fly the planes and hope they work. And an economist might say, quantify the risk, and then quantify the value of the airline to the economy as a whole, and spend as much money on safety as is cost-justified by the cost of the planes flying that is paid by the passengers when they buy the airline tickets.

The Objectivist answer probably is: Put a really, really smart scientist in charge of making sure that the jet engine fuel works, and maybe give him some shares of the airline stock so that he gets rich if his chemical formula works, and then fly the planes.

You can even add another wrinkle to this scenario, and say that the chief scientist says it works, but a lab technician thinks it won't work and wants to play whistleblower, and the question then becomes, with human lives at stake, and knowledge holds the key, whose knowledge do you trust, and how do you know, and who makes the decision to fly the fleet or whether to ground the fleet and not trust the jet fuel?

CONCLUSION

A methodology based on Models and statistical sampling might be deemed more "empirical," while a method focused on discovering a universal "X-Because-Y Relationship" might be called more "analytical." Of course, as I have written elsewhere, that which is analytical really is also empirical, because analysis is based on concepts, and all concepts are either first concepts or secondary concepts, and "secondary concepts," like the concept of the red square sofa in your living room or the concept of the Sun, are always created by the brain from "first concepts," such as the concept of the color redness or the color yellow, and the concept of a square shape or of a circle, which form a red square (your sofa) or a yellow circle (The Sun), and these "first concepts" are always formed from sensations, by the human brain, such as by abstracting the concepts of "red" and "square" from the perception and sensation of a red square.

Therefore all concepts, both secondary concepts and first concepts, ultimately arise from sensations, as their root cause, and all concepts are therefore empirical, therefore all analysis is empirical, logical analysis is the achievement of the "analytical a posteriori", to use a Kantian taxonomy.

The empirical really is also always analytical, however, because mere sensations devoid of any intellectual analysis at all would be rendered meaningless and stupid. Sensations only become intelligible when organized and understood by means of concepts and analysis.

But the empirical vs. analytical distinction is, nonetheless, useful for philosophy in this sense: the danger with analytic thought is that, at each leap of inference, if you make a mistake, without knowing it, you might travel deeper down a road of error without any empirical validation to correct you by refuting you, because the empirical data and observations and experiments is not acting as a system of checks and balances upon your abstract thought; while the danger in empirical thought is that you might be holding your eyes down too closely to the data, and fail to see the larger picture and fail to infer universal principles of necessity and/or causation which might actually be fully valid given the data set available to you and your toolkit of logical inference. On the one hand, the analytical cost is a mistake that goes uncorrected, which could later wreak havoc; on the other hand, the empirical cost is a failure to achieve thoughts and conclusions that were possible and might have been highly useful.

There should be a balance between analytical thought and empirical observation in any thought-process, and the precise ratio between the two must be thoughtfully and wisely chosen based on the needs of the task at hand and how much money and intellectual resources are worth investing into either path.

As a concluding note, let me outline how my theory of the PSM replaces the "Paradigm" theory of the scientific method, which was made famous by Kuhn's book "The Structure of Scientific Revolutions". Paradigm theory says that science never achieves knowledge, instead, science creates a theory, the theory works for a period of time, then, over time, the theory collapses under the weight of its own internal contradictions, and every theory is then always replaced with a new theory, in a never-ending series, such that no theory is ever "the Truth," because they will all one day be refuted. Einstein refuting and replacing Newton in physics is the most common example.

Instead, my theory of science is that you have a Model, and you are always seeking to Refine your Model, but, to the extent that the Model is based on logical inference applies to perceptions and empirical sensory experience, to the extent that it is proven by logic, your Model is knowledge, it is The Truth, and, if a Model is correct, it will be capable of making accurate predictions, which is the true test of science, and which is, ultimately, what science is useful for to humans, the purpose of science.

The Truth is not some abstract theory, it means only knowledge, which reflects what really exists in Reality, to help us live happy lives. If we know the Truth, then, in theory, by applying that knowledge, we are better able to deal with, and cope with, Reality, because we can make predictions, and then rely on those predictions, and, when they turn out to be true, we profit, much like, for example, if we predict that a stock on Wall Street will make money, we become able to make a profit off of it. If our Model of the stock was correct, and the Model was based on logic, then our Model was not subjective, instead, it was objectively true, as proven by reason and logic, and it helped us make money precisely because it was The Truth.

Einstein did not destroy Newton, instead, there was one Model, called Physics (really called Science as a whole), and Newton Refined it, and then, later, Einstein further Refined it, such that Newton enabled one set of predictions, which were True, but Einstein later enabled another broader set of predictions, which also proved to be True.

"(1) If P Then Q, (established by analysis)

(2) Q If and Only If P (established by analysis),

(3) Q (from sensation, experience, or data collected),

(4) Therefore P,

(5) If P Then R (established by analysis),

(6) Therefore if Q then R,

(7) Q, Therefore R,"

is a very simple form of logic, but it is powerful. Using this logic, you can take sensations, apply logic, build a model, and then use the model to predict future experience.

Hopefully this essay has helped you to see how you can use logic to solve the problems in your life. Every problem you face in your life can be translated into a "logic puzzle" for you to solve using logic and Models. Logic is not a mere abstract theory, not just an esoteric oddity that Hermione uses to solve Snape's potions logic puzzle. Logic is something that we should all be using in our lives, all the time, because it makes us as humans become more powerful.

THE POWER OF OBJECTIVISM

PREFACE

This is a philosophy essay about the philosophy of Objectivism, the set of ideas presented by Ayn Rand in her book Atlas Shrugged.

This essay, which evolved out of a series of blog posts, is many things:

(A) A high-level summary or synopsis or outline of the philosophy of Objectivism for people too busy to read Ayn Rand's thousand-pages-long books (Atlas Shrugged is over 1000 pages long. In contrast, this essay is around 50 pages long).

(B) A reference to quickly look up the key principles of Objectivism.

(C) A tool for the Author to organize his own thoughts, which hopefully the Reader will also enjoy.

(D) A restatement of the philosophy of Objectivism, with a specific focus on ethics/morality (the study of right and wrong), and epistemology (the study of knowledge, and how knowledge is possible).

(E) This book includes a high-level outline or synopsis or summary of the entire history of Western philosophy, in order to compare other philosophers to Ayn Rand and see how Objectivism fits into the history of Western philosophy.

In the interests of honesty and accuracy the Author must say, up front, that his vision of Objectivism is not limited only to the work of Ayn Rand, and that he incorporates his own philosophical positions and his own unique point of view into the philosophy of Objectivism.

WHAT IS OBJECTIVISM?
WHO WAS AYN RAND?

What is the philosophy of Objectivism? Let's learn about it together! I bet you'll learn something new!

Objectivism is the name of a philosophy--a set of ideas--developed by novelist Ayn Rand in the 20th Century. Objectivists are people who practice Objectivism. What do Objectivists believe? They think that a person should be happy, and that your happiness is the moral and ethical purpose of your life. They claim that rationality and reasoning are your main tools to succeed in the world, and that success causes happiness. They promote capitalism and individualism, feeling that the individual is more important than society.

Did you know? The 1980s were called The Decade of Greed because many people were influenced by Objectivism at that time, including high-ranking officials of the Reagan Administration. Federal Reserve Chairman Alan Greenspan was also a known Objectivist.

Who was Ayn Rand? She was born in 1905 in Russia to Jewish parents. She lived through the 1917 Communist Revolution in Russia, which gave her a lifelong hatred of Communism and socialism. Eventually she escaped the USSR and fled to the USA, where she gained citizenship by marrying an American man. She achieved wealth and fame with her bestselling novel The Fountainhead (1943), and followed it up with her novel Atlas Shrugged (1957). Atlas Shrugged is the foundation of Objectivism, and it is over 1000 pages long!

Did you know? There was a surge of interest in Objectivism in the 1960s, and a large Objectivist movement, centered around New York City. But Ayn Rand had an affair with another one of the leaders of the movement, a man named Nathaniel Branden (who was 25 years younger than her), and when they broke up in 1969, an explosive conflict developed between them, where Rand cast Branden out of her inner circle, and the fallout destroyed the Objectivist movement of the 1960s.

Many people hate Ayn Rand and her philosophy, but she is a hero to her millions of adoring and devoted fans, and her novel Atlas Shrugged routinely ranks as one of the most influential books of all time. Her work has been credited by historians with helping save capitalism from the rise of Marxism in the 20th Century, and she has inspired many people to live happy lives, and changed many people's opinions about philosophy, morality, religion, politics and economics. Love her or hate her, no one can deny her ideas are unique – no one had ever said what she said before, in the entire history of philosophy. Her stunning and groundbreaking defense of capitalism, not on the basis of economics, not because it works or it makes money or it is efficient, but on the grounds of morality, because it is right and good and virtuous, lives on into today's world and continues to change the world for the better.

I hope you enjoyed learning this lesson about Objectivism as much as I did! Thanks for reading!

THE TOP TEN PRINCIPLES OF OBJECTIVISM

This is a summary of the Ten Core Principles of the Philosophy of Objectivism, that I have refined and distilled from my extensive study of Objectivism:

1. Life is Good, Death is Evil. (Your Own Life is Good, Behavior that Causes You to Die is Evil.) Life or Death is Our Only Real Choice, Since Everything Else Continues Regardless, and Choice Creates the Need for Morality (Because Morality is What Tells Us Which Choices to Make), therefore Life is the Basis of Human Morality.

2. Intelligence is Good, Stupidity is Evil. The Human Mind is the Human Means of Survival.

3. You Need to Spend Money in Order to Live, and You Need to Make Money in Order to Spend Money, so... Greed is Good, and High IQ is What Makes Money.

4. Freedom is Good, The Mind Needs Freedom in Order to Function.

5. Capitalism is Good, Socialism is Evil. Capitalism Gives the Mind the Freedom to Make Money.

6. Selfishness is Good, Altruism is Evil. Doing What You Want (Being Selfish) Makes You Happy, which Prolongs Your Life and Makes Your Life Worth Living.

7. Rationality is Good, Religion is Evil (Irrationality is Evil). Rationality Maximizes Survival. Reason is How Humans Gain Knowledge of Reality, and Knowledge of Reality grants Power Over Reality.

8. Integrity is Good, Compromise is Evil. Something is either Good, or else it is Evil, so if it is Good, there is no Need to Make Compromises to Any Competing Positions, since doing so would only Dilute Goodness with Evil.

9. Individuality is Good, Conformity is Evil. Your Own Life is Goodness for You, So, to Be Good, You Must be True to Who You Are, and Be Yourself. Which Means You Must be an Individual, and Not Conform to Society.

10. Desire, and the Fulfillment of Your Desires, is Good, Self-Abnegation and Self-

Denial is Evil. Do What You Want, Do Whatever Will Make You Happy, and Use Reason to Achieve your Goals. This is Rational Selfishness. (And Don't Support Any Government That Won't Let You, and Other People, Do What You Want and Live Happy Lives.)

TEN OTHER PRINCIPLES OF OBJECTIVISM

1. You are personally responsible for yourself.

2. You are not personally responsible for other people.

3. Other people are not personally responsible for you.

4. Other people are personally responsible for themselves.

5. Reality is an absolute. Existence exists objectively.

6. You have to spend money (consume value) in order to live, and you have to make money (create value) in order to spend money. Yes, you can make money without creating value, but only if someone else creates the value that pays for your money, and, again, yes, you can spend money without consuming value, but then someone else gets the benefit of the value that your spent money paid for... and the problem with that is, as British Prime Minister Margaret Thatcher once said, eventually you run out of other people's money. Really, eventually you run out of other people's values. Then the collapse depicted in Atlas Shrugged happens, socialism collapses.

7. Philosophy is not merely a matter of opinion. It is a matter of absolute truth and objective facts.

8. "Nature, to be commanded, must be obeyed." The mind cannot impose its will onto reality subjectively, by wishing for something or believing that something is true. The mind must learn from reality what is true and learn what one should do, and then doing that which one learned from reality will bend reality to one's will.

9. There are two types of people: Prime Movers, and Second Handers. Prime Movers live. Second Handers live for the sake of what other people think about them. The Second Handers are the parasites of consciousness.

10. The Sanction of the Victim: A person who seeks to destroy you will want your blessing in order to do so. If you deprive them of that, it is very difficult for them to destroy you. Evil triumphs only when Good does nothing. A vampire can't get in without an invitation. The whole of altruistic/Marxist/Christian morality has been

created to make people feel guilty for being happy (for being selfish), in order to guilt-trip the smart, productive, selfish people, the Creators, into being the victims (the economic slaves) of the Looters, the evil ones. Objectivist morality teaches Creators to deny the Looters the Sanction of the Victims.

THE TOP TEN VIRTUES FROM THE JOHN GALT SPEECH IN ATLAS SHRUGGED

I have not seen a simple list of the virtues enumerated in Atlas Shrugged, so I made this list:

1. Reason
2. Purpose
3. Self-Esteem
4. Rationality
5. Independence
6. Integrity
7. Honesty
8. Justice
9. Productiveness
10. Pride

For Ayn Rand's explication of these virtues, see pages 932-33, Atlas Shrugged, Signet Paperback Edition.

One can further subdivide this list:

Reason, Purpose and Self-Esteem are "the Big Three Virtues,"

Rationality, Independence and Integrity are "The Intellectual Virtues,"

and Honesty, Justice, Productiveness and Pride are "The Social Virtues."

These three sets of values comprise the bedrock foundation of Objectivist morality.

THE TOP TEN VIRTUES THAT SHOULD BE ADDED TO OBJECTIVISM

1. Courage
2. Confidence
3. Conviction/Commitment
4. Optimism/Hope
5. Self-Reliance
6. Determination
7. Cleverness
8. Forgiveness
9. Love
10. Loyalty (But Never Blind Obedience)

WHAT IS SELFISHNESS? THE TOP TEN ANSWERS (FOR AN OBJECTIVIST)

The top ten answers to the question "What is selfishness?" First, five from a Subjectivist, then, in reply, five for an Objectivist:

Subjectivist

(These first five are the counter-position, that I will refute below in the other five):

1. Selfishness is being a greedy, disgusting pig.

2. Selfishness is prioritizing one's short-term needs over one's long-term needs.

3. Selfishness is prioritizing (in other words, going after, spending your life resources (time, money) in order to achieve) immediate carnal goals, like food, shelter, money, comfort, instead of what one really wants, like, for example, pursuing a life as a writer, which will deprive one of money and "selfish" pleasure even though one really wants to be a writer. (Note that "writer" really is just an example, it is not based on me personally--this actually comes from an essay by philosophy professor Derek Parfit, who used the example of wanting to become a philosophy professor.)

4. Selfishness is prioritizing one's personal goals over the social needs and well-being of one's loved ones and society, for example, by pursuing a career as a writer, because that is what one really wants to do, instead of getting a good steady job as a banker or a doctor to provide money and support for one's wife and kids and to pay more taxes and charity to help the poor.

5. Selfishness is the attribute of taking as much for oneself as one can at the expense of the other people who would have had what you took but for the fact that you have taken it for yourself.

Objectivist:

6. Selfishness is the attribute of asserting and nurturing the self, in other words, your

personality, individuality, who you are. Selfishness means being true to yourself -- literally, to your "self."

7. Selfishness is the system whereby one ranks one's values into an ordinal hierarchy, and then assigns one's life resources to the achievement of one's values, prioritizes a higher value over a lesser value. Thus, pursuing a higher value over a lower value is not a "sacrifice," but sacrificing a higher value to a lower value, is a "sacrifice." Selfishness is the opposite of sacrifice.

8. Selfishness is rational self-interest, such that, if prioritizing one's short-term goals over one's long-term goals was what would rationally be designed to maximize one's own happiness over the span of one's life, one would do so, but, if prioritizing long-term goals over short-term goals was the more rational choice in the context of one's life situation, going after the long-term over the short term would be selfish, in that situation.

9. Selfishness is doing what you want, given your hierarchy of values (that you choose, or discover from self-reflection), so, if being a writer is a higher value for you than is making money to buy nice things for your wife and kids or to have a financially secure comfortable life, then pursuing a career as a writer is selfish, because you are going after what will make you really happy, instead of doing what other people want you to do, but if your wife and kids or comfort are the higher value to you, then abandoning a career as a writer is not selfless, it is selfish, because the more selfish thing would be to be supportive of your family or your finances, since that is what you really want to do, that is what is really important to you. Selfishness tells you to do so without guilt. Note that what matters is not which value society deems the more important, it is which value you want more strongly, it is whichever value is higher to you.

10. Selfishness is the attribute of taking as much for yourself as you can in the context of the fact that, as Ayn Rand said, there is no conflict of interests among human beings as economic actors, so, you take as much as possible for you, but you concede to every other human being the freedom for them to do what they want, and the freedom for them to make as much money as they want, as they are able. So, theft or being a criminal and actually taking money from other people is not "selfish," it is stupid, whereas making money is selfish and smart, it is rational self-interest, as opposed to irrational self-motivated behavior.

With respect to the concept of "Selfishness" in Objectivism, there are three positions one can take. The first position is that Ayn Rand took the classic, old definition of "selfishness," and asserted that it is good, whereas people had thought it was evil before. This means that this position thinks that Ayn Rand said it was a good thing to be a greedy selfish pig and to hurt other people to benefit yourself and to hoard as much money as possible and to use or exploit other people for your own self-interest. I call this the Old Position. The Old Position says, or implies, that capitalism is a system where the rich use and exploit the poor and the working class to get rich, and the rich run scams to get rich, but this capitalism is good, not evil.

There is a position, which I take, that Ayn Rand invented a brand new concept, rational self-interested Objectivist morality, and, because there was no word for it, she chose the most similar word, "selfishness," in essence taking an old word and giving it a new definition. I call this the New Position. The ideal of the New Position is not the pig, it does not take the pig and change our evaluation of old selfishness from evil to good. Instead, it invents a brand-new morality, one which is quite complicated and which you have to read Rand's books carefully to fully understand, but which can be summarized as "rational self-interest." The New Position holds that the old fight of altruism vs. selfishness was "poison as food, and poison as antidote," as Rand once wrote, and that we should not be for or against the selfish pig as the paragon of selfishness; instead, we must reject the selfish pig as the emblem and poster child for selfishness, and instead assert the virtuous human being, like John Galt and Dagny Taggart and Hank Rearden of Atlas Shrugged, people who are very much concerned with doing the right thing regardless of whether doing so hurts them personally and who do not hurt other people in order to advance their own ends, as the symbol of our new definition of "selfishness."

The New Position says that capitalism creates wealth, which helps everyone and lifts everyone up, because when you make more money, then there is more money for you to spend, to pay other people to do their jobs, and then they have more money, and so on, so that, when one person is selfish, and makes money, that actually helps everyone else--there is no economic (or social) conflict of interests among humans. This, in a way, is very similar to the argument that Socrates makes in Plato's "Apology," where Socrates says that he would not corrupt the youth of Athens, because doing so would not help them, and when you help other people you make the world a better place, and when you make the world a better place then the world is a nicer place for you to live in, and your living in a nicer world is a selfish benefit to you, so Socrates would not have chosen to corrupt the Athens youth because that would not be selfish and personally beneficial to him.

In Objectivism, because there is no conflict of interests among men, you do what is best for you, but that does no harm to others--not merely because you did not actively choose to harm them, but because, fundamentally, essentially, logically, when one person behaves rationally selfishly, that does not do harm to the people around that person.

The third position is what I refer to as the Bait-and-Switch Position, which holds that Rand intended the New Position, but the Bait-and-Switch hooks people on the New

Position, and then, because people don't consciously understand the definitions of words or what is at stake, they get switched into the Old Position, which is little more than praising and glorifying people for being greedy selfish gluttonous disgusting pigs. The Bait-and-Switch Position is the position that confuses the New Position and the Old Position, either intentionally or unintentionally, or which holds that the New Position and the Old Position are identical and there exists only one definition of "selfishness," the result of which is that people want to believe in the virtuous, noble New Position, but they get led down into the dead end of the Old Position, where all the old classical altruist criticisms of selfishness (and capitalism) ring true, at which point Objectivists struggle to defend the virtue of selfishness. So the Old Position ideal is a pig, whereas the New Position ideal is the rational self-interest of the smart, productive, ethical, good person.

I want to conclude this list by emphasizing this point: people today are taught to use the words "greedy" and "selfish" when the word they are really looking for is "stupid." Take this example: A person has saved up $50. Their friend is starting a small business, and the friend asks the person to invest their $50 in it, and if the person invests $50 in this business, in six months he will make a return on investment of $500. But, instead, the person spends the $50 to buy a really big, fancy cake, and eats the entire cake in one day, and gets sugar-poisoning from eating too much and vomits. If he had invested, he would have had $500 and could have bought ten chocolate cakes and eaten them over several weeks. The Old Position would say that this person was selfish and greedy. The New Position would say, no, that was stupid. By eating the cake, did the person maximize the benefit to himself or maximize his own pleasure? No. So he was not selfish. Did he maximize the amount of money he had? No, he lost $500. So he was not greedy. But he did do something stupid.

Let us extend this example, and see where it leads, with another example: a man gets an MBA from a top-ranked business school, and he could get a job making $80,000/year as a CFO, he gets that job offer fresh out of B-school. But instead, he goes to Wall Street, starts a Ponzi scheme, and gets investment banks to invest $500 million in his Ponzi scheme (say, for this example, he says he has a startup which has invented a new way to genetically engineer Dutch Tulip bulbs, and it is made up, he tells a lie.) So he now owns $500 million, and he buys mansions, and yachts, and goes on business trips to Hollywood and Paris and London. But then, after six months, he runs out of victims, his Ponzi scheme collapses, the Wall Street analysts look at his numbers and figure out his lie, and he goes to jail, and his wife divorces him. Was he greedy?

He did not maximize the amount of money he owns: he owns zero dollars in prison, but he could have owned $80,000/year. So he was not greedy, because he did not maximize the amount of money that he had, and no rational person would have expected his behavior to do so. Was he selfish? He is unhappy and miserable in jail but would have been happy in the $80,000/year job with a wife and kids and a normal life. So, he did not maximize the benefit to his self, nor did he maximize his own personal happiness. He was not selfish.

But what he did was very, very stupid. There is a certain type of crook or criminal who thinks he is very smart because he thinks he has invented a way to get money without doing work, namely, by being a crook, and stealing money from the hard-working regular folk, whom he regards as suckers and naive fools. But the belief that you can make money without doing work is stupid. That's not how economics works, and it is an idiotic, irrational belief. Interestingly, that is what the socialists think about economics: they think you get rich by being a crook, and that therefore all rich people are crooks, because none of the socialists are "men of ability" and none of them have ever seen a John Galt-like genius invent a new motor that makes billions of dollars, like a real life Steve Jobs of Apple or Bill Gates of Microsoft, they just read the stories in the (liberal media) newspapers about how some Wall Street banker was found guilty of a white collar crime that stole millions of dollars and got off with a slap on the wrist and a million dollar fine, and they think capitalism is corrupt and you get rich through evil. One of the key principles of Objectivism says no, you get rich by being good, and you become happy by being good, not by evil. That is the "Protestant work ethic" that shaped early 1700s/1800s America during the Industrial Revolution, although, really, it is the Objectivist work ethic, that goodness earns prosperity and virtue buys success. Atlas Shrugged described how people really get rich, by doing work. So crime is "stupid," it is not "greedy" or "selfish" in the Objectivist sense of those words.

THE TOP TEN SUMMARIES
OF GOOD AND EVIL

1. Good: Who are able to get a job, get a job.
Evil: Who are able, are too lazy to get a job.

2. Good: Read books or play games or get a hobby. Sober fun.
Evil: Drinks too much, does drugs too much, listens to loud music, strives to numb and kill their own mind in any way possible.

3. Good: Judge people as individuals.
Evil: Collectivist, Tribalist, racist, sexist, homophobic, transphobic.

4. Good: Forgive, and earn love.
Evil: Exact petty revenge, but seek unearned love.

5. Good: Cares about right and wrong.
Evil: Honestly does not care if they are evil.

6. Good: Are loyal and supportive.
Evil: Just use people for their own ends manipulatively.

7. Good: Are tolerant of different types of people.
Evil: Condemns the Other as evil.

8. Good: Is a nice, clean, respectful person.
Evil: Acts like a slob or a piece of trash.

9. Good: Has gratitude. Always compares what they have to the condition of not having it, instead of comparing what they have to other people who have more.
Evil: Ungrateful, envious.

10. Good: To the extent they are able, strives to think and use their IQ.
Evil: Chooses to be stupid; is proud to be stupid.

RAND'S NIETZSCHE VS. HEIDEGGER'S NIETZSCHE

Two versions or interpretations of the famous German philosopher Friedrich Nietzsche exist: The Objectivist Nietzsche or the Atheist Existentialist Nietzsche, what can also be called Rand's Nietzsche vs. Heidegger's Nietzsche. The Existentialist interpretation of Nietzsche is widely known, while the Objectivist Nietzsche is virtually unknown, thanks in part to Ayn Rand explicitly rejecting him and denying his obvious and extensive influence upon her. The purpose of this article is to present a summary of the Objectivist Nietzsche.

Ayn Rand was in Nietzsche denial, saying throughout her adult life that Nietzsche did not influence her and that she owed him no debt – an outright lie, both historically and ideologically. Historically it is known that Ayn Rand read Nietzsche as a teen and went through a phase of explicit fandom (see for example the biography The Passion of Ayn Rand by Barbara Branden). Ideologically, the heroes of Rand's novels are the Overman and Objectivism is the new code of values called for by Nietzsche in his plea to replace Christian morality with something new. What is Objectivism? It is Ayn Rand doing what Nietzsche had said needed to be done, a half century earlier. Rand's criticism of altruism is based on Nietzsche's critique of what he called the Slave Morality, but before we explore how he influenced her, let us look at what Heidegger said and how it misled Nietzsche scholars.

Heidegger's Nietzsche says there is no absolute truth, there are no ideals, there is no such thing as knowledge or eternal principles, reason does not discover the truth, the Rationalism of Descartes and Kant is a fraud, there is only the ever-changing physical world in which we know nothing, we are all mere beings in time with no access to timeless truths or immortal ideals. Christian ideals are empty and meaningless, and God is dead, leaving behind a void, literally a nothingness, for us to believe in. It is in this sense that Existentialism is really Nihilism: Nietzsche removed God as what to believe in, so Existentialist Atheism believes in nothing.

Contrast this with Rand's Nietzsche, who says that Kant, Descartes, and Christianity are wrong, but, instead of a void left by their absence, we need something new to replace them, a new idealism of the physical world to believe in: we need "new values on new tablets," to quote him, in other words we need a new morality, not no morality at all, to replace Judeo-Christian ethics. There is eternal truth, knowledge, and ideals, it is just that the Christian school of thought got them wrong. Nietzsche called for a new morality and Ayn Rand answered his call with the philosophy of Objectivism. Nietzsche predicted a Zarathustra-like sage to find new truth, and Rand's "Atlas Shrugged" created a brand-new morality which did everything Nietzsche had said a new morality must accomplish. Ayn Rand is not a Nihilist, despite rejecting God: she gives us something to believe in, namely, the human ego, our ability to succeed and triumph and our potential for greatness. Her Nietzsche contrasts Roark's temple in "The Fountainhead," a celebration of how high we can go, with Toohey's Stoddard Temple as religion, something whose greatness and grandeur makes us feel small and weak in comparison to it. That Randian attitude towards religion is deeply rooted in Nietzsche's books.

Nietzsche did not specifically predict Rand's ego as ideal or reason as means of knowledge. But he did anticipate her moral vision. Consider this statement, which summarizes one of his ideas: Slave Morality is used to manipulate the strong into being the slaves of the weak by making them feel guilty for being healthy. Now consider this as a sum takeaway of "Atlas Shrugged": Altruism is used by the poor to manipulate the rich into being the slaves of the government by making them feel guilty for making money and being productive. Do you see how obvious and undeniable is the influence of Nietzsche upon Objectivism?

Nietzsche called for the replacement of Slave Morality with a Master Morality, in which people were proud of being strong and healthy and felt no guilt, in which being strong and healthy is virtuous. Rand's Objectivism is a Master Morality. Nietzsche was a signature pioneer in philosophy for being one of the first philosophers to critique and attack altruism, and the rejection of altruism is central to Ayn Rand. Indeed, some of Rand's arguments against altruism in Atlas Shrugged are remarkably similar to things Nietzsche wrote. Nietzsche argued that it is illogical that a value should be unethical if you take it selfishly for yourself but ethical if you give it selflessly to someone else, because the other person is selfish if, and when, they take it for themselves. Ayn Rand copied that precise analysis in the John Galt Speech in Atlas Shrugged. Nietzsche also had his theory of the Overman, the super-human man who would rise and be so strong and tough that he would overcome the weakness inherent in humanity and achieve a new phase of human evolution. Howard Roark and John Galt read like a literary attempt to realistically depict what the Overman is like. They do not behave like real human beings, with emotional depth and inner conflicts and self-doubt such as everyone feels, but they certainly do behave like real Overmen, like supermen heroes.

It is true that Friedrich Nietzsche opposed reason and knowledge, but it was reason and knowledge as defined by Descartes and Kant, reason as a non-physical disembodied thought gaining spiritual knowledge arising from an eternal deity, like reason transcending the world of empirical perception. Given the Kantian definition of the words "reason" and "knowledge", Ayn Rand also opposed reason and knowledge, just like Nietzsche did. Whereas Heidegger's Nietzsche says reason and knowledge are empty illusions, Rand's Nietzsche clears a path to a new reason and knowledge based on empirical experience and the physical world. Rand thought of Descartes and Kant as champions of religion whereas Nietzsche thought of them as champions of reason, but the answer to the question of what enemy is Objectivism opposed to is the same if one defines both Rand and Nietzsche as philosophers of Objectivism.

On the topic of Nietzsche and Rand, it is worth observing that Objectivism is a philosophy and, as a philosophy, Objectivism is an ethics, a system of thought that tells you what is good and evil so that you can make choices and choose goodness instead of evil. Historically, people view Marxism and socialism as the great enemy of Objectivism. But socialism is a politics, not an ethics. The dominant ethics in the Western world, which is opposed to Objectivism, is Christianity, which was the nemesis that plagued Nietzsche throughout his writings. For Objectivism to flourish, it must replace Christianity in the hearts and minds of the Western world. So, really, Christianity (and especially the idea of altruism) is the great enemy of Objectivism. But this is not a position that every Objectivist will adhere to, because we have found, in politics, a great alliance with Christian libertarians and with the Christian Right, who also are enemies of socialism and Marxism. This is a very Nietzschean interpretation of Objectivism.

Indeed, there is a lot to like about Christians, because they at least care about virtue and goodness and right and wrong, whereas the Marxists and socialists tend to be amoral and to reject ethics as such, and they seek to enshrine and worship evil and trash, and, to paraphrase Ayn Rand, the socialists seek to turn the human soul into a sewer or cesspool. The Christians have the wrong ethics, but the Left has no ethics at all. This gets at the heart of Rand's Nietzsche vs. Heidegger's Nietzsche: some see Nietzsche as a champion of amorality and an enemy of ethics, but Rand saw him as an enemy of Christianity and a champion of a new morality. This only works if there exists some morality other than Christianity, which the Existentialists don't know about, because they are largely ignorant of the ethics of Objectivism.

If Christianity and ethics are identical, then Nietzsche opposed ethics and was amoral because he opposed Christianity. But, if there are two ethics, one of which is Christianity, and the other of which is Objectivism, then, logically, it becomes possible to champion ethics but oppose Christianity, by supporting Objectivism. Looking beyond Christianity, at other religions, one could observe something similar, more broadly: if you believe that religion and morality are identical, then you cannot be an Objectivist, because Objectivism asserts that morality is not identical with religion, and Objectivism is an atheistic morality, it is a new code of values based on reason and rationality, not based on faith and theology.

This concludes a brief account of why Friedrich Nietzsche should be considered an Objectivist philosopher, given a plausible alternative to Heidegger's interpretation.

THOUGHTS ON MORALITY

There are two sides of Objectivist morality: (A) Nietzsche's influence: Go to a party, dance, have a few drinks, kiss a stranger, have fun, enjoy life; and (B) the Christian influence: work hard, be good, avoid sin, be a piously virtuous person, be a member of your community, don't drink, and be productive at work, get married and have kids, but with Atlas Shrugged instead of The Bible, and Reason/Rationality instead of Jesus Christ. This is not a contradiction, provided that the value of Life is paramount over all: choose whichever one maximizes your happiness and survival, or choose some ratio between them that is right for you (the Aristotle influence in Objectivist ethics, A / B = C, choose the middle between two extremes, Aristotle's theory of the Golden Mean of Ethics).

There is a question for Objectivists posed by ethicists and philosophy professors, for example, should I be a good employee because I'll impress my boss and get more work or get promoted and make more money, such that if someone paid me more money to be a bad employee I should, or is it because it's the "right" thing to do, always? Then there is the argument that it is right because 99% of the time it will pragmatically maximize wealth so you should do it 100% of the time because you can't predict the 1% of the time when it would be "selfish" to be lazy.

No. It is the right thing--the virtuous behavior--100% of the time. Why? Because to live, as a human, is to work a job--to the best of your ability. If someone pays you money to be evil, you would sacrifice your integrity, and gain nothing. You cannot, and will not, be happy, nor "live" in the human sense of that word, having lost your integrity. Thus, here, the value of Life is a higher value than the value of Greed: you should choose integrity over a large sum of cash. Remember, in the Top Ten Principles of Objectivism, the Atlas Shrugged Deduction, the first axiom is: Life is Good, Death is Evil. All other virtues are deduced from those, so the higher value takes priority over the lesser value that serves it. You get money to be happy, and you are happy in order to live a long life, so if money did not make you happy, it would not be a value.

In the History of Western Philosophy, in this issue in philosophy, honesty is often used as the example--should I always tell the truth, if so, why, and what if it benefits me more to lie? But it does not benefit you to lie. What if you have to lie to save your best friend's life? Why--because your best friend is being held at gunpoint by a gunman, whom you must lie to for tricking him into not shooting your friend? Then, in such dire straits, your friend is probably already doomed, as a practical matter. Saving your friend by lying is not a choice, because saving your friend is not an option, and the insane gunman is likely to kill him, regardless of what you say. And if not--you should tell the truth, because honesty is a human value, and good comes from being good, and being evil will only wreak harm. Humans exist in a reality where honesty is rational, and there is no excuse nor lie that can fake reality. The lie will not benefit you, nor your friend.

Much as it does not benefit a soldier fighting in a just war to run away to save his own life. What life is left--if you betray yourself? And then the army of evil wins anyways, and probably finds and kills the hiding defector/deserter, because they probably kill everyone who was on the side that lost the war. In that scenario, the choice is to fight, and maybe live, or maybe die... or betray yourself. The soldier cannot choose guaranteed survival--that is not an option open to him. Humans live as humans, or else we do not live, because we are humans.

For another example from popular ethics, should I sacrifice one person's life to save five other people's lives? But that is not how ethics works. (That is how socialist propaganda works.) In the unlikely case where you really faced that choice, both options are evil, but you should at least save someone. But the choice to be good or evil is the choice to do right or wrong, assuming the context of your options as a given for your moral logic. You do not get to choose from everything imaginable, only from the slate of options that are real in your context, so the right, ethically, is only the best choice from among your available options. Lying to save your friend is not an option. Escaping the war and living a happy life is not an option. But to choose the most rational option--meta-ethically--that is always doable. And that is Objectivism.

RATIONAL ETHICS

Note that Objectivism is not hedonism. Happiness is not identical with pleasure. Happiness is that pleasure which comes from living a distinctly human life – an ethical life – your life in which you "be yourself."

Mere animal pleasure is not moral in itself but becomes moral arising in the context of the human animal body in a human moral life. A human thing is an animal (body) with a mind (brain) and a soul (free will). To be ethical, according to Objectivism, is to treat a thing as what it really is in objective reality. Therefore, to live the good life, as a human, is to be good at being human. To be good at being a body is to be healthy, which includes sexual health; similarly, to be good at being a mind, requires thinking, and to be good at being a soul, requires the cultivation of an ethical, moral capacity, and ethical choices and behaviors.

Because a human is a body, mind, and soul, ethics must satisfy all three of the human attributes. Food, and sex, and exercise, and medicine, are the good for the body, much as books and news and information and contemplation and thinking are the good for the mind, and culture and meditation and spirituality and ethics are the good for the soul. The virtues of mind are particularly and uniquely suited for making money and being good in business; the virtue of body is good for being a good sexual lover or a strong physical day laborer; whereas the virtues of the soul make for a good friend or a loving family member. But the best virtue, which equips a person to do most anything, is to cultivate all three virtues, in a proper ratio between and amongst them.

One can call this the "Athenian" Model of ethics, because history indicates that the ideal in Ancient Athens was healthy minds in healthy bodies (and, presumably, healthy souls to go with them). I sometimes think of this as the "Head, Hand, and Heart" Model: The Heart (soul) wants something, the Head (mind) designs a plan for how to get it, and the Hand (body) enacts and executes the plan. Thus, the task of ethics is to maximize the health of the Head, the Hand, and the Heart, so that each, working together, at maximum effectiveness, can lead to success as a human being, in the task of being human. And, for Objectivism, getting what you want (rational selfishness), by means of reason (and courage, and virtue) in order to achieve your heart's desire (happiness) is the ethical lifecycle for human existence.

The word "reason" derives from the Latin root "ratio," (hence "rational,") and, in truth, a rational Objectivist morality is the art of finding the correct ratio between body, mind, and soul, for the health of the human being.

This issue of ratio as rationality for "rational selfishness" goes to a point far broader than merely finding the correct ethical ratio between body, mind, and soul. Consider this question: suppose that you have chosen your "hierarchy of values," and one of your values is learning how to play a musical instrument, while another one of your values is becoming better at playing a sport. Which do you choose? Ethics should tell you how to make a decision. But what if they are both high values to you, and you truly desire to do both? Must you sacrifice one love and let it die that another love may live?

But this choice does not need to be an either/or. Instead of a hierarchy of values, you can have a ratio of values. For example, spending three hours learning the musical instrument is worth spending seven hours playing the sport. So, you do not need to sacrifice being musical in order to pay for being athletic. Instead, you do both, but in a ratio that is rational and authentic to your personal desires, as you discover through a process of introspection, reflection, and thought, where you assess and discover or decide what your hierarchy of values, or ratio of values, is.

What if you only have five free hours per week, and you would truly need to commit all five hours to either music or sports to excel and master either, so it truly is an either/or? In that limited scenario, 3/7 could be scaled down to 1.5 hours music per 3.5 sports, but, if that is actually sacrificing mastery in either to do badly at both, then the ratio collapses down into an either/or ordinal hierarchy, but the ratio already implied that playing the sport matters more to you than learning the instrument (because you wanted to spend more hours doing that), therefore rational ethics would tell you to spend 5 hours a week playing the sport, and abandoning music is the cost that pays for the benefit of learning the sport.

In Objectivism, and Objectivist ethics, you are a trader, who trades value for value, and pays for what you have by earning it. The concept of opportunity cost is useful here. A concept from economics, which means that, where you face an either/or of costs and benefits, not choosing one thing is the cost that pays the price of having the other thing, so that if you could have been a great ballet dancer, or made money in business, not being a dancer was the price that paid for you to succeed in business.

This concept is meant to show that not being a dancer was a real cost that really pays, because, absent having gone into business, you becoming the dancer would have been real. This is not to say that it is sad that you could have been a great ballet dancer and instead sacrificed that to get rich, because, in Objectivism, you should pursue your highest value, so, if being a dancer would have made you happy, that is what you should have done, and paid for it by being poor.

If the opportunity cost of playing sports is not playing music, then, if your desire is sports, it follows logically, that your desire is not to play music, because your desire to play music was a lesser value, and sports was a higher value, so your desire to play sports logically evaluated to a desire not to play music (and to play sports instead). However, here is why is it less cruel to think of ethics as a ratio than as a hierarchy, because you could make money by day and do ballet dance by night, as a hobby, in an 8 hours to two hours ratio, so you could get rich and do what you love at the same time, if you were smart about it.

Or you could play sports, and play music, but sleep less, and figure out all the "factors of production," the life costs such as time, and money, and energy, that go into doing something, and figure out the correct payment of costs to buy what you desire, and spend time and money on sports or music in the ratio to achieve what you want to achieve with your life.

Ethics will define the correct ratio of what you pay (time, energy, money) in relation to the values which you choose to pay for, the virtues which you choose to buy (for example, the fun of playing sports). Indeed, here the "ratio" of ethics dovetails nicely with capitalist supply and demand economics, because an ethics ratio of 8 to 2 for sports to music, is similar in concept to a free market where tables cost $80 and chairs cost $20, the ratio of 80/20, which tells the industrial producers to invest 80 units of wood into tables for every 20 units of lumber made into chairs (assuming the wood to make chairs costs the same as wood for tables), which satisfies market demand at a supply defined by the prices consumers have chosen, because tables are four times more valuable than chairs. People choose to pay $80 for a table, and $20 for a chair, because that is what they want, that is the cost the things are worth to them.

In a broader sense, you won't always be choosing whether to play sports or play music; instead, you will be choosing whether to aggressively pursue a career (money, mind), or whether to go after love and romance and getting married and having kids (love, soul), or whether to be scholarly and academic and smart and spend all your time reading books and watching the news on TV and thinking deep thoughts (knowledge, mind), or whether you would be content to just be normal and work a simple job and focus on the enjoyment of comfort like good food and having fun and hanging out with your friends and going on vacations or having an active sex life or going to bars and dance clubs and cannabis parlors (pleasure, body).

Again, the "rational ethics" approach says this is not an either/or, instead, you draw up and choose your hierarchy and then assign each value to a ratio, so that your action plan for how to live life, that ethics teaches you, is an ideal ratio, which could be as simple as how many hours each week to spend, or how much money each month to spend, on the pursuit of each value, in ratio to each other value. This is truly a practical ethics for how to live life on earth.

Note, in conclusion, that it is not my position that there is one objectively correct ratio for you, which you must discover, such that you can be right or wrong about whether you should quest for money, or for love, or for pleasure. That is your choice. You decide that. You assign the moral significance of love or money or pleasure as what it means to you. You choose your hierarchy of values, and you choose your ratio of values. For example, if your desire is to just have lots of hot sex, if that is your truth, then you morally should, and sex would be virtue for you, but if that is not your truth, then you should not, and then an obsession with sex would be unethical for you, because sex would exceed its proper place in the ethical ratio of mind to body to soul for your life. Sex exists objectively, just as every physical object, each and every thing, exists objectively, but what it is, does not inherently define its place in your ratio of values; instead, you get to choose and define your ratio for yourself, by assigning moral significance to objects.

Similarly, the choice to buy a chair, or a table, is a subjective desire, but the chair itself, what you bought, exists, and it is what it is. The subjective becomes the objective in the act of having been chosen by free will. After you have subjectively assigned your moral significance to the objects in your life, if that assignment is authentic and truthful and it is what you truly desire, then those objects become objectively the values in the ratio that you have chosen. This coincides with Objectivist economics, where the choice of what to buy is subjective desire, but it becomes objective and quantifiable when you assign money prices to those choices.

For example, you could choose that you value money three times more than love, and no one can prove that right or wrong. But, if you do choose that ratio, but you then in your behaviors actually spend your time chasing love and throw money away and end up poor, then you betrayed your ideals, and compromised your moral integrity, which is the one objective true evil according to this ethical system.

Once you have a ratio of ethics, which you chose, you have to mean it, and commit to it. If you can't, then maybe you never really meant it to begin with, and you should reconsider your ethical ratio, and "re-evaluate all your values," to paraphrase Nietzsche.

Indeed, going back to the idea of Nietzschean ethics vs. Christian ethics, the Nietzschean ideal of being healthy and proud and strong and having fun or the Christian ideal of being spiritual and humble and sober and hardworking, there, too, there is a ratio between the two, that you must choose what works for you to live a full human life. It is not an either/or, much as mind or body is not an either/or, the Objectivist ideal is a healthy mind in a healthy body (with a healthy soul), with ethics helping you choose a ratio to achieve that end goal. The fact that Objectivism incorporates aspects of both Nietzsche and Christian ethics is not a contradiction, because it asserts them as a ratio, not as an either/or.

Rational ethics can be turned into a form of "applied ethics" very easily. First, choose your top-level ratio of mind to body to soul, in terms of your desires. Do you love money, or love and friendship, or knowledge, or pleasure and fun, and what concrete specific manifestations of those things do you desire? Those become your goals. Some people love pleasure when they are young, love money when they are middle-aged and working on their career, and love family when they are older, but a person could just as easily have a ratio of all three attributes at any age. It is your personal choice. However, you want the idea from Aristotle of the "golden mean," that you should not have too much body, or you would be merely an animal, nor too much soul, and be a ghost, nor too much mind, and be a disembodied brain. Just as Aristotle said that virtue is the average between too much and too little of any quality, like courage is the average between cowardice and recklessness, so too the correct ratio of mind/body/soul is one that has just the right amount of each for you, specific to you and what you need.

Then, evaluate the values that you have to pay the cost of achieving your goals. You have time, energy, and money, in whatever detail is specific to you. Then create a budget and a plan for how to obtain a goal by paying for it with a cost. The model is: You have Y, you want X, so you trade Y in return for X, and end up with X. Say, for example, that your ethics ratio values body most, and values physical strength and ability as a manifestation of that value. You want to learn karate, you have two free hours after work every evening, so you spend two hours each night getting karate lessons, and then you know karate. A budget can be as simple as a defined unit of either time (a day) or money (your monthly income), and then a list of priorities for how to spend it, in proportion to your ratio of values.

Also make note of how values can pay for values. For example, your goal is to get back together with your girlfriend after you have a fight. You can pay for that with the virtue of honesty, by having a frank honest conversation with her about what you both want and why you should be together. Or you want to ask for a raise at work, but if your boss takes offense you could get fired. You can pay for that with the virtue of courage: own your desire and just do it. Of course, the use of virtue can never guarantee that you will succeed. But in capitalism, there is no safety, only freedom.

AYN RAND AND THE
BANKRUPTCY OF ALTRUISM

Ayn Rand was fond of saying that altruism, and the whole of Judeo-Christian morality, had become bankrupt. In this essay I want to unpack that idea, and then extend it with my own gloss, that altruism is appropriate for children but not as a major important idea for adults.

What does it imply that something has gone bankrupt? There was a loan given to someone, that person promised to repay it by giving something back, and then the person defaulted, they did not, or could not, repay what they had promised.

What did Western civilization loan to altruism, in the era since the Enlightenment? The overarching belief that it was a moral edict to be adhered to by all men, that it was to be a common commandment accepted by all and disputed by no man, as the bedrock foundation of ethics.

What did it promise us in return? As individuals, that it would tell us right from wrong, and that in doing the right thing it would make us happy, as in that warm fuzzy feeling when you rescue a stray kitten or donate to a homeless military veteran.

As a society, it promised that it would make everyone better off by ensuring that those in need got taken care of.

Ayn Rand, at heart, made a very practical argument: altruism made promises and simply and utterly failed to deliver. Atlas Shrugged is some 1,100 pages long, approximately, and I won't waste 50 pages quoting every paragraph where she criticized selflessness. In sum, for society, when you say that you should give from those who have, to those in need, that leads to socialism (back when she wrote, they still called it Communism), which destroys the economy, kills freedom, and erodes civilization and human society. Altruism fails to repay its debt to society after we gave it our trust that it would make society better.

For the individual, you want the warm fuzzy feeling of doing good by helping others. But altruism, taken to its logical conclusion, says your own feeling of happiness is not legitimate. You must want nothing for yourself, not even the happiness that comes from doing right and being good, and care only about helping others, even if you suffer and are made sad by it. Your charity becomes a duty, not a joy. Ayn Rand argued that this is necessarily true if your ethics is based on the other, instead of the self.

The Western world paid altruism a trust, which altruism failed to repay. Instead, it ushered in Communism, and the Liberal wing of the Democratic Party: two villains that Ayn Rand hated. Choosing a morality, from her point of view, is a financial transaction, where you pay with the coin of your loyalty, and get something to consume in return. Altruism is a fraud, with no meat on the bone, nothing for us to consume that pays us back for the loyalty we gave to it.

The true altruist will say we should choose altruism even if it gives back to us nothing, makes no repayment, offers absolutely zero warm fuzzy feeling. Our own desire for a return on investment is selfish, and only the needs of others matter. Ayn Rand critiqued that as irrational, then wrote the 100 pages long John Galt speech to prove that morality should be derived from reason.

One idea of hers from Atlas Shrugged to prove the irrationality of altruism is simply this: why is something good when you give it to others, but bad if you take it for yourself, when, if someone else gave it to you, then it would be good, but you would have it just the same either way? The difference is that with altruism, you wouldn't have earned it. Much as altruism fails to earn its status as a moral underpinning.

The same argument, stated differently: Why is a value selfish if you take it for yourself, but selfless if you give it to someone else, when, if they take it from you, for them, and they enjoy it for their own pleasure, then they are being selfish, from their point of view, by taking a value away from you for their own benefit? For example, if you give $10 of charity to a beggar, everyone would regard that as selfless. Everyone except Ayn Rand, that is. She would ask, when the beggar takes $10 from you, he is taking $10 away from you and spending that $10 on himself, for his own happiness. Why is that not selfish for him, from his point of view? Since altruism, on its face, says that you must deny yourself and only serve others. It might be selfless for you to give, but it is selfish for the beggar to take, so your altruism is only helping the beggar to be selfish, hence unethical according to altruism, therefore altruism is illogical, and collapses into a contradiction.

It is completely illogical, unless "selfless" does not really mean "given to someone else," it means "given to someone because they needed it, not because they earned it." Altruism, then, isn't about being selfless, it isn't about helping others (after all, plenty of money is donated to private charity in capitalist economies), instead it is about destroying the concept of earning and deserving rewards by good behavior, and, ever so far from being a perfect ethics, it destroys morality and virtue, and seeks to corrupt any ethical system where you earn moral status by being good and behaving virtuously.

Of course, the true altruist will say that, when you give something to someone else, it is selfless for you to give it, but not selfish for them to take it, because they need it, and you don't. In the example, you don't need that $10, but the homeless beggar does. But that altruist position, taken to its logical conclusion, leads to the Marxist principle: "From each according to his ability, to each according to his need." This explains why altruism is the moral underpinnings of socialism and Communism. That also explains why capitalism necessarily needs, and must rely upon, Objectivist ethics, the ethics of rational selfishness, in order to survive, and why capitalism cannot survive in a world dominated by Judeo-Christian altruist ethics.

But Objectivism does provide a plausible, superior alternative to altruism, and one which, if understood properly, satisfies the moral desires which are being mistakenly usurped and fulfilled by altruist ethics. Take our examples of helping a stray kitten or donating to a homeless veteran's charity. Say, for example, as many people with compassion feel, that, in that situation, you would choose to help the kitten or the beggar, and you want to choose an ethics that will tell you this is the choice you can, and should, make. But as Ayn Rand said, "check your premises." The Randian method of analysis is always to use logic, where, if the conclusion has integrity, it is true, but if there is a contradiction, then you must climb up the chain of inference, and check your premises, until you find the faulty premise that is introducing a contradiction. Here, the false premise is that your feeling that you want to rescue the kitten or donate to the charity case is inconsistent with Objectivism. You would do it because you feel it is the right thing to do, you have more than enough and they are in need, and it gives you that warm fuzzy feeling. But that virtue, and that warm feeling, make you happy. That is a benefit to you. So Objectivism would define that as "selfish." (Yes, this is a new definition of the word.)

It would only be "selfless" if you really didn't want to do it, and you were doing it, not to bring you that warm fuzzy happy feeling from helping others because you can, but with no selfish benefit to you at all, only to benefit others at a cost to yourself. Selfishness is not just about getting money; it is an ethics where you try to make yourself happy, which includes acting to get happy feelings. If that warm fuzzy feeling from helping others is a higher value to you than $10 that you own, then giving $10 to the homeless, and getting that warm fuzzy feeling of helping the needy in return, is an emotional profit, the benefit to you emotionally exceeded the cost to you financially, so it is selfish, not selflessness.

Selfishness is that which benefits the self, whereby your revenue exceeds your costs, and you make a profit, in your emotions and your happiness and your life, just as much as your wallet and bank account. The selfish person acts to make a profit. It does not mean you hurt others, and it does not forbid helping others. It says only that you must do what you want, for the benefit of your self, according to your hierarchy of values.

If you are rich, then getting a warm fuzzy feeling from a smile on the face of some needy poor person you hand $10 to could very easily be more selfish than keeping $10 for yourself, instead of donating it to charity. Similarly, if you did not believe it was the right thing to do, and you don't feel the rich should ever give money to the poor, then it would not make you happy, and then it would not be selfish, and then you should not do it. That is the personal decision of what is your hierarchy of values, and where the poor homeless veteran or your $10 stand on it. Ethics is the branch of philosophy that tells you how to make choices, and Objectivism is an ethics. In answer to the question: "Should I give $10 to a poor beggar?", Objectivism's answer is: "Yes if you want to, but if you do not want to, then no."

The idea presented here contrasts sharply with the traditional view, an outdated, unsophisticated position which says that giving the $10 to the beggar is "selfless" whereas keeping the $10 for yourself is "selfish." The superior position is a more sophisticated, nuanced, subtle approach, which says that doing what you want, according to your hierarchy of values, is "selfish," but doing something for the sake of others and against your own selfish desires is "selfless." So, logically, being selfish will tend to make you happy, thereby enriching and furthering your life. If rescuing stray kittens makes you happy, then rational selfishness might tell you to pursue a life spent rescuing stray kittens, in the service of helping animals, because that will make you happy, and your own happiness is your highest moral ideal.

But altruism says you must act at a loss, to the detriment of your self, and that you are not allowed to ask why altruism is correct if it makes you unhappy, indeed, if it demands that you regard your own unhappiness as your highest virtue. Altruism will always naturally lead to dictatorship (usually socialist or Communist in nature), because most people will never freely live their lives by a morality which says they should always be unhappy, they would just choose to be happy while feeling guilty about it instead, so a government will rise up to force them to obey altruism and be miserable and to do what they do not desire to do, by means of violent force from police and army.

So, similar to how the AIDS virus protects itself from the white blood cells by attacking the autoimmune capacity, altruism saves itself from bankruptcy by saying that morality is outside the world of returns on investment from ethics.

I differ from Ayn Rand and feel that a little bit of altruism, in moderation, is good, but mainly to teach to young children when they behave like spoiled brats and won't share their toys with their brothers or sisters or friends. A child needs to learn that sometimes, we all have to share, to enable an undertaking that can only be done successfully by a group. Little kids see things only from their own point of view, and can be taught empathy and sympathy and compassion as little kids.

But to take a lesson for a little kid, and say that every adult in the world should obey, and worship, this idea as a core moral principle? As the highest, most important moral edict?

That would be irrational. And, with respect to that precise point, I think Ayn Rand would agree with me.

WHAT IS THE SOUL? THE TOP TEN ANSWERS (FOR AN OBJECTIVIST)

Everyone knows what the soul is according to religious philosophy, such as Platonism or Christianity: a non-physical spirit that occupies and animates a body, a ghost in a machine. But Aristotle and Ayn Rand both wrote much about "the soul," and I suspect they meant something different.

This is a list of my top ten thoughts about how Aristotle and Ayn Rand would define "the soul." Aristotle had some (strange) beliefs about God, but Ayn Rand never conceded the existence of any non-physical aspect of reality, so her conception of the soul is not that it is something that does not physically exist; instead, the soul is an aspect of the moral existence of a human being, which, for Rand, begins with the mind and reason as the fountainhead of morality.

The Soul of a Person is Their:

1. Mind

2. Self

3. Self-Esteem (In The Fountainhead there are scenes where to destroy someone's self-esteem is stated as their soul being destroyed)

4. Their self-aware Brain

5. Their Mind that Sees

6. Their Mind that Thinks

7. Their Mind that Thinks with Integrity and Acts in a Moral Way (so for a person to compromise their integrity is for them to lose their soul)

8. A Human Body Living a Moral Life - in other words, The Person as a "Person," in the Moral Sense

9. Consciousness

10. Purpose in Living Their Life and the Meaning for Them of Their Life - this particularly would mean Aristotle's theory of the "Final Cause," that the end state that something seeks to achieve is literally a cause of its physical existence.

THE TOP TEN METAS
OF PHILOSOPHY

1. Freedom is the freedom to do what you want. Meta-freedom is the freedom to engage in political activism in, and vote for politicians who advocate and enact, the limitation or destruction of freedom, on the ostensible theory that some limits may be necessary for the benefit of the individual or for the good of society. Meta-freedom is the freedom to choose freedom, which implies that you also have the freedom to not choose freedom.

2. Most people on the Left support meta-freedom but oppose freedom.

3. Ethics is the choice of right or wrong, and a code of values to tell right from wrong. Meta-ethics is the condition of being able to choose from among varying codes of ethics, and the system of right ethics and wrong ethics according to which to choose an ethics.

4. Libertarian politics is a meta-ethics, but is not an ethics. It does not tell you what is right or wrong. It only tells you that you should have absolute freedom to choose from among any competing systems of ethics.

5. The Christian Right politics is a meta-ethics, which tells you that you may only choose Christianity as your code of ethics, and seeks to restrict the meta-ethical freedom to choose any competing code of ethics. The Right opposes meta-freedom, but, after you have chosen Christian ethics, the Right supports freedom.

6. Philosophy is the study of the deepest truths about the nature of reality and human existence, which encompasses metaphysics (the study of the nature of things), ontology (the study of being), epistemology (the study of knowledge), philosophy of mind, philosophy of science, logic, ethics, politics, and aesthetics. Meta-philosophy is any attempt to define and refine a system according to which to choose or prefer one philosophy over other competing philosophies.

7. Philosophy professors think they are philosophers. I contend this is not so, because what they are specialists in is meta-philosophy, not philosophy as such. Every philosophy professor is a meta-philosopher--they have to be, it is what they are trained to do and how they keep their job. The philosophy professor who is a true philosopher, someone who creates a new and useful philosophical argument that is not a functional duplicate of work others have already done, in other words a "system-builder," is exceedingly rare. Philosophy professors are not like Kant or Plato or Aristotle or Rand, who were "real" philosophers, they are the hundreds of teeming intellectuals who sit at their desk all day analyzing philosophies and finding little details that make one position slightly better than some other positions. In a sense, the philosophy professors, as a whole, as a profession, comprise their own meta-philosophy, as compared, for example, to Objectivism: if you ask this question: "who should decide which philosophy I believe in?" The Objectivist answers: "you should," the philosophy professors answer: "we should."

8. Objectivism is both a philosophy and a meta-philosophy, and an ethics coupled together with its own meta-ethics. It presents a philosophy, and then tells you that reason and rationality are the system you should use according to which to choose your philosophy, and then deduces logically that Objectivism is the only reasonable, rational choice, according to the nature of reality and humanity. As such, Objectivism as a meta-philosophy is restrictive in the meta-ethical sense: it does not promote the freedom to choose any philosophy, instead it says that only this philosophy is an acceptable choice. Note this careful distinction in Objectivist meta-philosophical freedom: there is the question of who should decide what philosophy you believe (you), vs. which are the acceptable philosophies from which to choose (Objectivism), so there is only one good choice, but the person who has to make the decision is still you. This Objectivist meta-ethics is coterminous with Objectivist ethics as such, which holds that, in every choice, there is only one right choice and many wrong choices, but the person who should make the choice is still that person themselves, organically and independently, someone else should never make that choice for them. Compare and contrast the philosophy professors, who say, with respect to choosing a philosophy, that there are many right choices, but they should get to be the ones who choose.

9. A meta-meta is a system that analyses meta-systems.

10. This list is a meta-meta-list! And this book is meta-Objectivism!

THE TOP TEN PRINCIPLES OF CONSCIOUSNESS OBJECTIVISM

Consciousness Objectivism is a theory that answers the hard question: what is consciousness? These are the top ten principles of the theory.

1. A conscious experience is a thing in reality that you are experiencing.

2. If you experience an apple, the round, red, apple-shaped, apple-tasting sensation that you experience, that looks like an apple and tastes like an apple, is the apple in objective reality, it is not an apple in your head.

3. Color is objective. Color, like all perceived entities, exists objectively. If it did not exist, you would not perceive it.

4. The "phenomenological theater," the sensations and perceptions that you continuously see, hear, smell, etc., in your conscious perception, is objective reality.

5. A conscious experience of a thing that you see is a seen thing, whereas "the sight of something", as designated by the word "of", is the light that brings the seen thing from the thing to your brain where the brain processes the light signals so that your mind sees the object in external reality. The light brings the object to your mind. You do not see light. You see objects, by means of the light they reflect.

6. The meaning of a word is that thing which it brings to your mind when processed by your system of language.

7. The meaning of a work of art is the image or emotion or meaning that it shows to your mind by means of itself. If you see a painting of a woman, you see a woman because the paint in the painting showed a woman to your mind's eye. The experience of a work of art is what the work of art brings to your mind's eye.

8. The content of a computer data file is the object that the computer data shows to the recipient when the recipient translates the data according to the logic of the computer language in which the data was stored, it is the meaning "of" the data.

9. A language is a set of translation rules whereby one thing can carry something from one place to another place, wherein the original thing, the meaning, is encoded into a form for transmittal, carried to its goal, and then translated back into its original form. The message is the means by which the goal accesses the original. The sign "of" a thing shows that thing to the mind's eye. But what you see, or think, or learn, is the original, not the encoded message. For example, the Sun is a star in the sky, the Sun is not the word "Sun."

10. If you exist objectively, then when you look at something, you see reality, not the inside of your own mind.
Credit to Mortimer Adler for this theory, although my interpretation of his thesis is unique.

THE TOP TEN PRINCIPLES OF EPISTEMOLOGY

1. Something is knowledge if you can prove that it is true.

2. You know that what you see/hear/touch/taste/smell is what you see/hear/touch/taste/smell. What you see proves that it looks like what you see. It is literally self-evident.

3. Math can be knowledge, if the deduction is proved.

4. Science can be knowledge, if the probability math that the results of an experiment are not random is proved.

5. Logic can be knowledge, if the deduction is proved.

6. Philosophy, politics, and economics, (and history, and literature, and all of the social sciences and the humanities, all academic knowledge) can be knowledge to the extent it can be proven by empirical perception and observation, math, science, and/or logic.

7. Empiricists believe that knowledge comes from perception.

8. Analytics believe that knowledge comes from the analysis of concepts.

9. An Empirical Essentialist (like me) believes that knowledge comes from the analysis of concepts, but knowledge of those concepts comes (originally, in the first instance) from perception. If you did not begin with empirical perception, you would not have any concepts in your mind at all. All concepts are either first concepts, which are made of perceptions, or are secondary concepts, which arise from putting concepts (either first concepts, or a mixture of first and secondary concepts) together. Concepts come from reality, not from intuition.

10. A Philosophical Scientist (like me) believes that, because the origin of concepts

is perception, after you have analyzed concepts to reach a conclusion, you should be able to test that conclusion against independent perceptions (an experiment) in order to validate the conclusion and prove that it is true. This is why Empirical Analytic philosophy achieves knowledge.

THE TOP TEN PRINCIPLES
OF THE ABORTION ISSUE
FOR OBJECTIVISM

1. Just because you think something is wrong/evil, doesn't mean it should be illegal.

2. Just because you think abortion is wrong, doesn't mean it should be criminalized.

3. But if you think abortion is murder, murder should be illegal.

4. But whether abortion is murder is a gray area debate with pros and cons just like any other debate.

5. You shouldn't force other people to obey your position in any political debate; if you did, you would not be a champion of freedom.

6. You shouldn't force other people to obey your position that abortion is murder.

7. If you become pregnant, you can choose childbirth for yourself.

8. If a woman becomes pregnant, you may use reason and persuasion to talk her into choosing childbirth of her own free will.

9. If you could use force whenever you define something as murder, then everyone could use force all the time--the socialists believe that capitalism is murder, the vegans believe that meat is murder, the environmentalists believe that pollution is murder, etc.

10. Therefore, "pro-choice" is logical and "pro-life" collapses into contradiction.

WHAT IS PHILOSOPHY?
THE TOP TEN ANSWERS

1. Philosophy is the search for truth.
2. Philosophy is the study of that which is true but not obvious.
3. Philosophy is the study of reality.
4. Philosophy is the study of reality, humanity, and the relationship of humanity to reality.
5. Philosophy is the study of humans, what humans know, what humans can or cannot know, and what humans should do about what they know.
6. Philosophy is the study of depth that is achieved by moving beyond appearance.
7. Philosophy is the study of the metaphysical aspects of the physical world.
8. Philosophy is the study of the history of philosophy and what the great philosophers have said to us.
9. Philosophy is the love of wisdom (this is the literal translation of the Ancient Greek "philo (love)-sophia (wisdom)").
10. Philosophy is the study of abstract theories and conceptual ideas that makes a very real life or death difference to your immediate survival and long-term happiness, and, specifically, is the study of how to tell the good ideas, which will help you live, from the bad ideas, which will hurt your happiness.

WHAT IS POLITICS? THE TOP TEN ANSWERS

1. Politics is the system that enables many people to share one space without everyone murdering everyone else.

2. Politics is the articulation and enforcement of human rights.

3. Politics is the arena where the forces of freedom fight the forces of tyranny.

4. Politics is the system that seeks to use wisdom to restrain man's baser instincts and guide man's behavior with wisdom and justice.

5. Politics is the system that enacts and enforces laws, which are arbitrarily and subjectively chosen by humans when they decide how they want to govern themselves.

6. Politics is the system that enacts and enforces laws, by identifying the objective facts about human nature which define the set of laws that humans need in order to live happy lives.

7. Politics is the system whereby the rulers rule over the masses by means of oppression and propaganda, within which rebellions may rise, some of which will topple the old rulers and replace them with new rulers.

8. Politics is the civic lifeblood of the polis.

9. Politics is where the people go who are too rich to be common criminals and too evil to be businessmen.

10. Politics is the area where lives any and every requirement, that the human species has in order to flourish, which can only be, and necessarily is, imposed by force against some or all people without their consent. In other words, economics is the voluntary realm, while politics is the involuntary realm.

WHAT IS ECONOMICS? THE TOP TEN ANSWERS

What is Economics? These are the top ten answers to that question:

1. Economics is the study of how to prioritize society's scarce resources, typically by assigning a money price to each resource and then comparing price values in order to prioritize the usage of resources.

2. Economics is the study of costs and benefits, typically on the understanding of profit as the condition where the sum of all benefits exceeds the sum of all costs for economic actors to the maximum extent possible.

3. Economics is the study of supply and demand, such that the efficient economy is one where supply clears demand at the equilibrium point between supply and demand.

4. Economics is the study of human action, which presumes a subjective desire, a purpose, and at least one or more competing means to achieve that purpose, and the prioritization of some means over other means.

5. Economics is the study of trade in a division of labor economy and how trade works, and, more specifically, the use of money as a common medium of exchange for trade.

6. Economics is the study of rational self-interest and how economic actors act to maximize their self-interest within the context of a broader society of humans.

7. Economics is the study of how politics shapes the material existence of the human species.

8. Economics is the study of the conditions of freedom that enable human beings to survive, thrive, and prosper.

9. Economics is the study of historical economic data from which to infer trends that may be prescriptively applicable to future events.

10. Economics is the study of how people pay for the things that they have.

THE TOP TEN PHILOSOPHY SCHOOLS OF THOUGHT IN WESTERN PHILOSOPHY (WITH PHILOSOPHERS)

A. Ancient

1. Platonic (Plato)

2. Aristotelian (Aristotle)

3. Christian Theology (Augustine, Aquinas)

B. Modern

4. Rationalist (Descartes, Spinoza)

5. Empiricist (Locke, Berkeley, Hume)

6. Idealist (Kant, Hegel)

C. Contemporary

7. Analytic Philosophy (Bertrand Russell, Wittgenstein, Searle, Too Many to Name Them All)

8. Existentialist Philosophy (Nietzsche, Kierkegaard, Sartre)

9. Phenomenology (Heidegger)

10. Objectivism (Aristotle, Nietzsche, Ayn Rand)

THE TOP TEN MOST INFLUENTIAL IDEAS IN WESTERN PHILOSOPHY

1. Plato's Cave Allegory - that the physical world is an illusion, like shadows in a cave, we are looking into a cave (the physical world) with the light (the Ideas, the spiritual world) behind us and we see only the shadows of real things cast onto the wall of the cave, the physical world is just shadows, if one turns away from the shadows one sees the light – Plato's theory of Platonic Ideas (and please make a note of my personal position, which is that the correct English translation of Plato is "Ideas," not "Forms", although these are commonly referred to as Platonic Forms), that only ideas are real, and physical objects get their identity by participating in the ideas.

2. Aristotle's Theory of Logic - that the form of an argument can be correct or incorrect, regardless of its content.

3. Hume's Skepticism - that he can't know whether God exists, he can't even know if the Sun will rise tomorrow. Hume intended this as a critique of Christian faith, but it became an assault against all knowledge as such.

4. Kant's Copernican Revolution - that reality revolves around the mind, instead of the mind revolving around reality, analogous to Copernicus saying the Earth revolves around the Sun, not the Sun around the Earth. What this really means is Subjectivism: the mind imposes its categories onto reality, the laws of science are created by the mind. Kant used philosophy to protect religion from science, and, as Nietzsche said, "Kant muddied the waters to make then appear deep" – Kant's books read like mystical nonsense, but the clear takeaway is religious thinking ("Transcendentalism"). The key Kantian idea is that the physical scientific world is in your own mind, but if you transcend yourself then you access the mystical religious reality outside your mind – he called the subjective/physical "phenomena" and he called the real/religious "noumena". For my answer to Kantian epistemology, see Consciousness Objectivism.

(In a way, Kant is Neo-Platonism: the phenomena are shadows in a cave, the noumena are the light outside, except that Plato did not have to contend with science, science did not exist back when Plato wrote, so Kant had to tweak Plato for a world in which science was achieving incredible wonders in the physical world. Plato and Kant are

THE MEANING OF LIFE

very confused, they think ideas and reason are outside the mind, while the physical world is a mental construct, and ideas (Plato) or reason (Kant) imposes rationality onto the world we experience. The truth is the opposite: the physical world exists outside our minds, we experience reality, and we create ideas and reasoning within our mind in order to gain mastery over the objective physical world.)

5. John Locke's politics - kings are only human, there is no divine right to rule, and all people have rights. Locke led to the global trend to replace kings with democracy, in the Enlightenment, which gave way to a contemporary trend to replace democracy with dictatorship.

6. Karl Marx - Communism (today called Socialism!). The rich capitalists exploit the poor workers, so the working class should rise in revolution, and create a dictatorship in which they are the rulers. The trend among Marxists today is to call it "democratic socialism" so that they can pretend that the end result will be democracy, not dictatorship.

7. Descartes' "I think, therefore I am" - knowledge from the mind turning in upon itself and thinking deductively, instead of by looking outside, at the external world. He claimed the fact that he has a mind proves that he exists and that God (who created him) exists, so knowledge comes from the mind, but no knowledge of the physical world can come from the mind. He called the mind "res cogitans" (things in mind/things of thought) and called the physical world "res extensa" (things in space/ extended things), analogous to Plato's Ideas/things and Kant's noumena/phenomena.

8. Ayn Rand's Rational Selfishness - a meaningful rejection of altruism as the dominant ethical axiom, to be replaced with one's own happiness as one's highest virtue. Rand's key innovation was to present a morality that is rational in the physical world – prior to her, people had either said that morality is spiritual, not rational (Plato, Christianity, Kant) or said that rationality and the physical world are amoral (Nietzsche, Bertrand Russell). Note that by "morality" I mean Virtue Ethics, as opposed to ethics that is not based on right, goodness, and virtue; for example Pragmatism, Utilitarianism or Stoicism, each of which is a rational physical-world ethics.

9. John Searle's The Construction of Social Reality - Everything is a social construct, nothing is objective.

10. Judith Butler's Bodies that Matter - Gender is a social construct, to be overcome, gender is an (political) identity that is arbitrarily assigned to bodies to give them meaning, but you could assign any gender to any body.

I like Aristotle, John Locke, Rand, and Butler... I am not a fan of the others!

It seems clear that Subjectivism is one of the major historical trends in philosophy, which the new philosophy of Objectivism is rebelling against. Plato, Descartes, Kant, and Searle all believe that when we look at reality, we see the insides of our own subjective minds, whereas objective reality is to be found in the ideas (Plato) or reason (Descartes, Kant) or analysis (Searle) outside of the subjective world that we perceive.

They all have it backwards: when we open our eyes, we see objective reality, we see the external world, whereas ideas and reason and analysis are inside our own minds, those are the tools and means by which our mind learns to understand the external world that we see.

THE TEN CIVILIZATIONS CRUCIAL TO THE HISTORICAL DEVELOPMENT OF WESTERN PHILOSOPHY

1. Ancient Athens (Socrates, Plato, Aristotle)
2. The Roman Republic and Roman Empire (Cicero, Marcus Aurelius)
3. Medieval Early Christianity (Augustine, Aquinas)
4. The Aristotelian Arabs during the Dark Ages (Avicenna, Averroes)
5. Continental Europe of the Renaissance (Descartes, Spinoza)
6. Enlightenment England (Locke, Hume)
7. Continental Europe of the Enlightenment (Kant, Hegel)
8. Late 19th/Early 20th Century America (William James, Ayn Rand)
9. Late 19th/Early 20th Century England (Bertrand Russell, Wittgenstein)
10. Late 19th/Early 20th Century Continental Europe (Karl Marx, Nietzsche, Heidegger, Karl Popper)

MY TOP TEN PET PEEVES
OF PHILOSOPHY

1. Only philosophy professors with PhDs in philosophy can be philosophers.

2. It is impossible to prove that you know what you know.

3. All science is defined as that which can be refuted or falsified.

4. The theory of axioms.

5. The conviction that it is impossible to plausibly or correctly explain what consciousness is.

6. The conviction, which no one has ever actually proven, that color is subjective.

7. The belief that only "the great philosophers" deserve to be taught.

8. The academy's absolute and stunning refusal to consider Ayn Rand as a serious and worthy philosopher.

9. The belief that that the success of a philosopher is to be defined by the pedigree and ranking of the school he teaches at and the school he got his PhD from, not by the truth or rationality of his ideas.

10. The overwhelming sense in academic philosophy that the goal of philosophy is to brainwash students into believing your positions (almost always some version of Marxism or altruism or Subjectivism), not to teach students critical thinking skills to view reality with an open mind, equipped with reason and logic as tools, and choose their own beliefs for themselves. In contrast, the true Objectivist prefers reasoned disagreement over blind obedience.

THE TOP TEN POLITICAL PHILOSOPHERS IN THE HISTORY OF WESTERN THOUGHT (WITH MAIN IDEA)

1. Plato (the Philosopher King)
2. Thomas Hobbes (Conservatism: Life will be nasty, brutish and short, and a war of all against all, unless we concede power to an all-powerful, authoritarian, dictatorial big conservative Christian right-wing government, which will block change and maintain tradition)
3. John Locke (kings do not have a divine right to rule; the consent of the governed, men in the state of nature delegate their legal rights to the government by the social contract)
4. Jean-Jacques Rousseau (civilization is corrupt, savages are noble, equality is the ideal)
5. Karl Marx (Socialism: the rich exploit the poor)
6. Ayn Rand (Objectivism: the stupid exploit the smart)
7. John Rawls (liberalism: eliminate privilege in order to equalize the different good luck and bad luck people are born into)
8. John Maynard Keynes (government spending fights unemployment but causes inflation)
9. Murray Rothbard (Libertarianism: the free market economy does not need government, government interference causes both unemployment and inflation)
10. Jacques Derrida (capitalism is oriented towards logic – which he intended as a criticism!)

THE PHILOSOPHER'S REVENGE, WHY EVERY GREAT PHILOSOPHER'S MOTIVE IS VENGEANCE

1. Plato was motivated by his desire for revenge for the death of Socrates, by articulating and extending the Socratic philosophy into its most radical and extremist form, saying that the physical world was an illusion and a prison-like cave, even to the point of the idea that death would set you free, which Socrates implied when he chose to obey the Athenian death sentence against him that Athens had sentenced him to death for the crime of teaching his philosophy to young people, even though his followers offered to help him escape.

2. Aristotle was motivated by his desire to avenge the rejection of the physical world and of physical biology that Plato had taught everyone in that era in Athens, which he believed was wrongfully taught. ("Plato is dear to me, but the truth is dearer still.")

3. Augustine, the great Christian theologian philosopher who defined early Christian thought, wanted revenge against sin for his weakness in giving in to the temptation to what he had deemed was a life of sin before he repented and found Christ.

4. Thomas Aquinas wanted revenge against his parents, who tried to stop him from becoming a Catholic priest, by being the most saintly, scholarly, theoretical, abstract philosopher he could be, giving rise to the complicated intellectual gyrations of Scholasticism.

5. Descartes wanted revenge against Scholasticism, which he deemed corrupt and blamed for having given him a bad education in university, and so he set out to build a philosophy which he believed would replace it and destroy it.

6. Hume wanted revenge for being denied a professor's chair in England because he was an atheist, by attacking Christianity with his Skepticism.

7. Kant wanted revenge against Hume's assault on Christianity, which embodied the Enlightenment turning away from Christianity and towards reason, by creating a religious, mystical philosophy that Hume and reason could not refute. ("David Hume awoke me from my dogmatic slumber.")

8. Nietzsche's life was ruined by sickness, so his revenge was a philosophy where robust physical health, and its intellectual underpinnings, are the central virtue of a new morality.

9. Rand's life was ruined by the Russian Communist Revolution, so her revenge was a philosophy where free market capitalism, and its intellectual underpinnings, are the central virtue of a new morality.

10. Rothbard's early career was ruined by liberal leftist professors, so his revenge was an academically rigorous libertarian economics that the Left could not refute.

THE TOP TEN PRINCIPLES OF WHY AYN RAND BELIEVED PHILOSOPHY WAS IMPORTANT

1. Politics defines freedom, and people need freedom.
2. Politics arises from human behavior.
3. Human behavior arises from human choices.
4. Human choices arise from morality and ethics.
5. Morality and ethics arise from epistemology and metaphysics.
6. Philosophy defines epistemology, metaphysics, morality and ethics.
7. For example, Plato led to The Gospel of John, Christianity, and the Dark Ages.
8. For example, Thomas Aquinas revived Aristotle, which led to the Renaissance and the Enlightenment.
9. For example, John Locke led to the American Revolution.
10. For other examples, Rousseau led to the French Revolution, Karl Marx led to the Communist Russian Revolution, and Kant led to the Contemporary era of philosophy and the return of religion after the Enlightenment.

All of these philosophers defined philosophies that shaped the course of human history which had a very real impact on many real human beings. Philosophy matters.

WHY CAPITALISM IS VIRTUOUS: THE TOP TEN REASONS

1. Selfishness: You own what you produce, so you own the results of your hard work, and you get to enjoy it, for example when you work really hard and work long hours at a demanding job, then you earn money to spend on your own selfish enjoyment. If you work 60 hours a week, doing really hard labor, why shouldn't you get to spend the money you made and eat some strawberry ice cream, without guilt? You traded the money you made to the ice cream shop in return for the ice cream--you earned it. Your selfishness motivates you to make as much money as you possibly can, to maximize your selfish benefit. But making more money benefits society, too--for example, when a businessperson selfishly grows and expands their business, to make more money for themselves, the bigger a business gets, the more jobs it creates. In comparison, in altruism and socialism, in theory, you would force the ice cream shop to give free ice cream to everyone who walked along, with no money changing hands, so the ice cream shop owner can't pay his employees, can't pay rent for his store space, and has no money to buy cream and sugar and strawberries--it very quickly dissolves as a coherent theory if you try to figure out how it works in practice.

2. Intelligence: Capitalism gives people the freedom to achieve greatness and genius and be rewarded by the profits of their work. For example, John Galt, the genius inventor in Atlas Shrugged, invents a great invention, worth trillions of dollars, but... well, I don't want to spoil the plot for you if you haven't read it yet.

3. Greed: Capitalism creates an abundance of prosperity, and everyone is happier and lives better lives with more money to spend. More money buys better healthcare, better cars, more food. Money is not magic--to say that there is more money, really means that people were self-motivated to create and trade more value, which pays for those things--a greedy doctor is profit-motivated to invent a better medicine, an engineer to design a better car, farm workers to work extra-hard to harvest more food. In socialism, people are paid based on need, not greed, which motivates people to have as much need as possible, and to be lazy and stupid. But in altruism, they won't try to maximize need, because they selflessly want to help the people with real needs? Ayn

Rand argued that people are human, so, yes, the corrupt will try to milk altruism and socialism, by competing for who can have the most need, not who can make the most money. And everyone who supports socialism is secretly greedy and thinks they will get to have more money for themselves if money is taken from the rich and given to them. They don't care about the poor, they care about themselves.

4. Rationality: It is a system where every benefit has to be paid for, by the people who make the money that gets spent as the costs of creating the benefits, so it is a sane, rational system, where everything adds up correctly in the accountants' ledgers, in comparison to Utopian socialism that wants to spend far more money than actually exists in the entire world, which is an impossibility that will simply bankrupt everyone if the attempt is put into practice. For example, as stated above, the cost of ice cream is the cream, sugar, the machine to make the ice cream, employees to serve it, a building in which to have the ice cream shop, plumbing and electricity for that building. Those all cost money. If the people who eat the ice cream don't pay for it, by buying the ice cream with money that then pays the cost of it, it doesn't really work, in logic. This is why Ayn Rand said that Marxism was akin to religion and mysticism, it gets really murky and muddy when Leftists try to explain how they think it will work.

5. Freedom: In a system of laws, rights, and private property, you have the freedom to act and to create a sphere of personal autonomy in which you are free to make decisions, and bear the consequences, good or bad, of your freely made choices. But the poor don't have freedom to do anything, you say? The common reply is: the poor have freedom, what they lack is power. If they had the power to do something, no one would stop them, so they are just as free as the rich. And if capitalism is allowed to work, it makes more wealth, which lifts people up and empowers people to rise and gives power to the poor.

6. Individuality: Sometimes, being quirky and different and abnormal and unique makes lots of money, think Apple Computers and their "Think Different" ad campaign that launched the iMac. Capitalism culture is keyed to the concept of "be yourself" and how to sell people tools and props to act out and perform their chosen identity.

7. Integrity: Being intransigent and stubborn and staying true to your own vision is what realizes your highest potential to make money, whereas selling out and conforming to what you think everyone else wants and caving into group-think is not a good way to make money, according to Objectivism.

8. Desire: In capitalism, businesses make money by catering to desire, by selling people what they want, so it maximizes the fulfillment of everyone's desires. In comparison, in socialism, the economic planners have their big fancy plans, but they have no way to know what people want, absent money and prices to send demand signals, and the choice to buy that is the ultimate proof that you wanted something.

9. Life: In capitalism, people run businesses, which succeed, which creates jobs, which pays salaries, so people make money, so people spend money, so people survive. As

such, the businesses are the engine of the survival of the human race, and because life is the standard of virtue, businesspeople are the most ethical and virtuous of us all-- even if motivated only by selfishness and greed (but not stupidity).

10. Capitalism: Capitalism embodies the entire Objectivist morality and Objectivism's code of virtues, whether people realize it or not. Ayn Rand was remarkable for making the argument that capitalism needs a moral defense, that it is virtuous and socialism is evil, not an efficiency defense, that it is more efficient or more practical or builds bigger bathtubs than socialism. But Rand's moral defense of capitalism is really very simple and easy to understand. In capitalism, you make money, and you spend money, so you pay for what you consume with what you produced, and trade value for value, instead of seeking the unearned. If people consume what they did not make, against the will of the producer, then society operates at a loss, and goes bankrupt, as Atlas Shrugged showed, but Atlas Shrugged also showed that socialism collapses into sin and evil, where need, and stupidity, are rewarded, and intelligence, and greed, are punished, thereby destroying the moral fiber of the human soul. When things work right, like in the USA for much of its history, capitalism deserves the credit. The productive become rich, and the crooks go to jail, and you get what you earn, by your choices and your work, reward for virtue and punishment for sin, and you get what you deserve--which is how greed is supposed to work in a rational economic system.

THE APPEAL OF OBJECTIVISM AND LIBERTARIANISM FOR LGBTS (LESBIANS, GAYS, BISEXUALS, TRANSGENDERS)

Noted Objectivist scholar Chris Matthew Sciabarra wrote a famous monograph on this topic. I have not read it, but accounts and reviews indicate its focus is historical, not doctrinal. This essay will seek to show that Objectivism and Libertarianism, as philosophy, hold appeal precisely because of their ideas.

In Atlas Shrugged, John Galt is at one point described as "the man without pain or fear or guilt." This is every LGBT's dream and goal with respect to how we feel about our sexuality. Atlas Shrugged, in the theory of "white blackmail," says that the establishment takes our virtues and tricks us into regarding them as sins, then uses our ensuing guilt to manipulate and rule us. While Rand focused on the sin of greed, logically this is equally true for the sin of lust.

In The Fountainhead, Roark is so committed to being an architect that he will let no one and nothing stop him. The stigma and scorn of society, which criticized and disdained his buildings throughout much of the novel, does not bother him. He tells Toohey, the villain who embodies society's disapproval, "but I don't think of you," when asked how much he hates him. Rand at one point says Roark could walk down a street naked and really not notice if anyone cared.

This disregard for social disapproval is central to the gay agenda. Homophobia does exist, equally among conservatives, moderates, liberals, and, yes, libertarians. LGBTs face scorn and hatred and shame and stigma and the pressure to be closeted. The attitude of not giving a damn what other people think of you embodied in The Fountainhead is a useful tool for gay pride, not politically but rather psychologically.

Rand was herself interesting from an LGBT point of view. Her own sexual repression, and the repression of her 1960s followers, is well documented. She seems to have repressed her sexual desires her entire life and then misdirected them at Nathaniel

THE MEANING OF LIFE

Branden, the much-younger guy she had an affair with as an older woman. She is also known to have had special praise for Mises when he called her "one of the most courageous men in America." Barbara Branden in her biography of Ayn Rand said that Rand was happy that Mises had called her a man. We can wonder what that meant.

Libertarianism is also a good political philosophy for LGBTs, although many gays favor leftism.

"Live and let live," the sum of our philosophy, means every LGBT gets the freedom to do what they want, even if some members of society regard it as evil. In contrast, gay socialists want to force everyone to like gays by outlawing homophobia. This goal of everyone loving gays is impractical and unachievable. We libertarians would agree to outlaw homophobic violence, but we let each person have the freedom to believe what they want. Freedom treats people with respect, and you have the freedom to associate with those who accept you, and avoid the ones that don't. As an extension of this, I have advocated that each church, temple and synagogue be free to choose to recognize or reject gay marriage as they decide according to their own moral compass, with government marriage licenses abolished.

"Stay out of my bedroom" and "mind your own business," along with "live and let live," are key mottoes and mantras for both LGBTs and libertarians. These phrases show that gay political activism and libertarian ideas can share a point of view.

Here I have made a compelling argument that LGBT (and Queer, Non-Binary, Pansexual, etc.) can find a use for Libertarian and Objectivist ideas. If you don't know the definitions of Queer, Non-Binary, or Pansexual, Queer is an umbrella term for every non-straight identity, a Non-Binary is someone who performs male and female at the same time or who switches back and forth between male identity and female identity, and Pansexual is a sexual orientation that is attracted to all people, of every gender and every identity, without exception. Gender fluid, and other similar terms, fall into and out of usage in contemporary vocabulary for LGBTQs. The names change as times and eras change, but it all has one basic meaning: Sexuality. Ultimately, LGBTQ is regarded as evil because of the Christian view that sex is a sin. Objectivism considers sex to be a virtue, not a sin, so it follows logically that, for Objectivism, LGBTQ is virtuous and ethical and good.

The Objectivist virtues of Desire and Individuality and Integrity are all implicated by gay/LGBTQ pride:

Desire: You should act rationally and selfishly to fulfill your sexual desires, in order to make yourself happy (provided that your desires meet a baseline level of Rationality, in other words, only involves sexual conduct between consenting adults);

Individuality: You should "be yourself" and express your individual sexual identity without regard to society or conformity;

Integrity: You should be true to who you are and have integrity to the principle of what you are, with all of your behavior staying true to your unifying principles without contradiction, including who you are in terms of sexual and gender identity.

I also hold the position that the virtue of Rationality is implicated, because homophobia and transphobia are irrational: the idea that "marriage and sex is between a man and a woman" assumes the premise that the only purpose of sex is to procreate, to make babies. Absent that premise, the logic does not resolve to a rational conclusion. In today's world, the survival of the human species no longer depends on maximizing the number of babies, as it did 2000 years ago. So sex for the purpose of pleasure, and sexual identity for the purpose of self-expression, are perfectly Rational. But if that is true, then there can be nothing wrong with being LGBTQ.

Note that the virtue of Individuality means that one person can regard something as beautiful, even if other people regard it as ugly (for example, a gay man regarding a male human body as beautiful, which straight/hetero men would consider to be ugly or unattractive). Please see my book "What They Won't Tell You About Objectivism: Thoughts on the Objectivist Philosophy in the Post-Randian Era" for my essay on The Subjectivity of Personal Taste in Objectivism, which explains why it is legitimate for personal tastes and preferences and desires and aesthetics to be subjective, even though the objects of desire are things which exist in objective existence.

THE POWER OF OBJECTIVISM
- THE TOP TEN REASONS
OBJECTIVISM CAN GIVE
POWER TO YOU, THE READER

1. It enables you to feel desire, and to seek to selfishly achieve your personal desires, such as a desire for money, or a desire for sex, or a desire to be happy, or a desire to do something of which others or society disapprove, without guilt, without shame, without a sense that you have done something wrong, unlike most of the world's philosophies and religions, for example: Christianity (think sexual desires), Buddhism (think your desire to affirm your self and your mind, which Buddhism says you should strive to destroy), altruism (think your desire to put yourself and your own happiness first, selfishly, instead of taking care of other people out of a sense of guilt or shame, when most other people can, or should, take care of themselves), socialism (think your desire for money, or your desire for freedom).

2. It teaches you how to think, by means of reason and logic.

3. It provides a coherent worldview to use as a tool for analysis to understand the world.

4. It empowers you by telling you that your reasoning mind works, and that your five senses have the power to see reality, and that the world of sensory experience is not some mere delusion or fantasy (think Plato, Descartes, Kant).

5. It orients you towards the goal of living a happy life, instead of making yourself the slave of your or other people's misery and guilt.

6. It helps win the fight for capitalism, which makes the world a more prosperous place in which to live.

7. It helps fight basic irrationality, like superstition, mental illness, a belief in witchcraft, etc., which is still very real and prevalent in many parts of the world.

8. It gives you a morality that can be applied to decisions to help you make choices when faced with moral or ethical dilemmas.

9. It's a fun conversation starter at cocktail parties, since everyone either likes The Fountainhead or hates Atlas Shrugged.

10. It is an interesting stepping stone on your path of your own personal intellectual journey to enlightenment and self-discovery, giving you a new and unique point of view to consider and chew over as your arrive at your own conclusions about life and morality.

ON SELF-RELIANCE, SELF-ESTEEM, AND INTELLECTUAL HONESTY

SELF-RELIANCE

SR: Self-reliance.

There is me.

There is me relying on myself. Instead of relying on other people. That is self-reliance.

Then there is me relying on my self-reliance. Instead of relying on my reliance on other people. $(SR)^2$. Self-reliance squared. Self-reliance multiplied by self-reliance. That is self-reliance squared. This can be me relying on my self-reliance emotionally, as a source of courage and confidence. Or me relying on my self-reliance by making it a habit for me to just rely on myself, instead of expecting that other people will help me or do my work for me.

View it as a triangle, where you are at the top, self-reliance is in the lower left corner, and self-reliance squared is in the lower right corner. Your self-reliance squared relies on self-reliance, your self-reliance relies on you, and you rely on your self-reliance squared.

I have to rely on my self-reliance instead of relying on other people.

Nobody is going to help you. If you want things to improve, you have to improve them yourself. It's up to you. It's your responsibility. You are responsible for yourself, for what happens, and you are the one who will experience the outcome. If you want something, you have to make it happen, and you alone are the one who will make it happen. Otherwise it will never happen.

INTELLECTUAL HONESTY:
THAT A THING IS WHAT IT IS

An Objectivist believes that the hallmark of intellectual honesty is the belief that a thing is what it is.

An Anti-Objectivist believes that the hallmark of intellectual maturity and intellectual sophistication and being an intellectual adult is the belief that a thing is not what it is, and that a thing is what it is not.

So the true Objectivist always thinks that Anti-Objectivists are intellectually dishonest, and the true Anti-Objectivists always think that the Objectivist is intellectually unsophisticated and immature and childish, and that will never change, neither side will ever persuade the other, they are incompatible points of view.

For an Objectivist, it is always all or nothing, and absolute, because either a thing is what it is, or else it isn't what it is. Either a thing is something, or else it isn't something. And, if you don't see that a thing is what it is, that's dishonest of you. But that all-or-nothing absolute attitude, which is very off-putting and unpleasant and arrogant to many people, is justified, because, after all, in reality, a thing is what it is, regardless of how people feel about it. For an Anti-Objectivist, there are shades of gray, and areas to compromise, because, if a thing isn't what it is, it could be partially what it is, and be partially what it isn't, a thing could sort of be something, and sort of not be something, so there is a basis for degrees and shades of gray and ambiguity. So, with respect to this debate, about absolutes or compromise, too, there is a fundamental disagreement, at a philosophical level, and the two sides will never persuade each other, neither side will ever budge.

The Atlas Shrugged postulate holds that, for a person, if they act as though a thing is what it is not or is not what it is, someone else must pay for them to do so, or else they don't get away with it. And then Ayn Rand said the Objectivists should decline to pay, and let the Anti-Objectivists die (unless they choose to be moral and repent and convert).

To "cut corners": to treat a thing like it is not what it is or is what it is not, out of laziness or intellectual dishonesty or temptation. To close your eyes to reality, even for a moment, to enable you to pretend that something you wish was true, is true, and to behave as though it is true, even though you know it isn't true in reality.

To cut corners: Metaphorically, when you drive a car, on a winding road, instead of carefully hugging each corner, you go more in a straight line, because that is easier or faster or less difficult for you, treating the road as what it is not, and not treating the road as what it is. Because carefully going along each corner, and making each turn in the road, and treating the road like exactly what it is, would be slower, or require more work, or be more difficult, or need more physical labor, or require more thought, and would require you to pay careful attention to each curve, and require you to pay attention to what you are doing and pay attention to your driving while you carefully maneuver each curve, which is the work of the conscious mind, of the consciousness, which is intellectual labor.

So it might be a lot of work to perfectly drive each corner and treat the street like exactly the thing that it is, but cutting corners is, obviously, more dangerous, and simply will not work on a long enough time line, at some point you would leave the road and crash. So someone else has to do the work of driving the corners for you, or you die.

Literally, to choose not to carefully do every step for accomplishing a task, because you are too lazy to do the work or too intellectually lazy to think through and understand how to do each step and pay attention. So someone else must do that step for you, or else the task won't get done. Someone else must do your work for you, must live your life for you, or else you die, if you choose to cut corners.

The goal of Anti-Objectivist philosophy is to soothe the guilty conscience of those who cut corners by giving them fancy sophisticated arguments to make it seem like it is okay or correct. To say that things aren't what they are, and that things are what they are not, is a badge of sophistication and maturity and being a grown-up. Or that ethics and morality aren't based on reality and that ethical behavior isn't based on what things are. That values aren't based on facts. That no one can derive values from facts. So altruism and socialism and mysticism can't ever be refuted by logic.

The person who relies on their self-reliance can't cut corners because there is no one else to pay for it. Hence they would need Objectivist morality: that intellectual honesty is a sacred virtue to be always adhered to.

People who cut corners favor mutual reliance upon others, their idea being, you help me fake reality and let me rely on you to help me cut corners today, and then I will do the same for you tomorrow. Which can only lead to mutual dependency and collectivism. They don't just want you to rely upon society. They want you to rely upon your reliance upon society. To count on it. To take it for granted. For it to be your source of emotional support, comfort, and safety. That society will take care of you. That not only do you rely on society, but you are relying upon being able to rely on society.

They want everyone to rely upon reliance upon society. That is the condition under which no one can be independent. If everyone is relying upon relying on society, then everyone is dependent upon society. No one would be independent. They would forget how to do so, and have no experience doing so. No one would have freedom. No one could be free, because, if they declare freedom, they are cut off from the society they depend upon, and then they die. They would not know how to rely upon themselves, or how to rely upon their self-reliance to live. And, if society can, it will demand that you help them cut corners, and force you to, when they want to cut corners. It is the perfect opposite of self-reliance-squared.

They may even want you to rely upon society to control other people and force other people to do the right thing, instead of relying upon each other person to be self-responsible and to do the right thing and to control themselves. That is either you relying on someone else's self-reliance or relying on society's control of other people to protect you from them.

There is the issue of whether you rely upon yourself, or you rely upon others. There is the issue of whether you have intellectual honesty or you cut corners. Then there is the deeper, final issue, of whether you are relying upon your self-reliance, or you rely upon relying upon other people. If you are intellectually honest, then you have the ability to rely upon yourself, and you don't need to cut corners. But that doesn't define whether you actually do so. That is a choice you must make.

THE CORE FOUR
OBJECTIVIST PRINCIPLES

(1) You are personally responsible for yourself.

(2) You are not personally responsible for other people.

(3) Other people are not personally responsible for you.

(4) Other people are personally responsible for themselves.

It's pretty obvious how this would be a moral defense of capitalism and ban socialism. It's your job to take care of yourself. If you don't, no one else will. And you should not be counting on someone else doing so, or be expecting them to. So it's okay to put yourself first. To be rationally selfish. You should get as far ahead in life as you possibly can. It's not your job to take care of other people. It isn't other people's job to take care of you, either. That's your job. You should not be a burden on others. Nor should they be a burden upon you.

But it is key to focus on the role of the person relying upon self-reliance instead of relying upon community-reliance, for survival and courage and confidence as well as the logistical tools for success, as a key mechanism for how this works.

Say that a normal person makes $100 a day and consumes $80 a day. Then each person can pay for their own life. But, if one person had to pay for two people, they would both die: they would have $100 income and $160 costs ($80 times two). Now, the socialist would say, each person only needs $80 a day, so take $20 each day as taxes, and use it to fund payment for those unable to pay. That harms no one because each person who makes at least $80 can keep $80 and pay every cost which they otherwise would have anyway.

The Objectivist reply is threefold:

First, nobody can tell the difference between those unable to pay through no fault of their own, and those unwilling to pay due to sheer laziness and not being motivated to desire to be alive, and;

Second, two wrongs don't make a right. One wrong is someone being unable to pay the costs of being alive through no fault of their own. A second wrong is stealing money away from the person who made it and who thereby rightfully owns it. Bad luck is the first wrong. Taxation is the second wrong. They are both evil. Using one evil to justify more evil is itself evil, and;

Third, it's morally right for each person to rely upon his/her/their own self-reliance for survival and to live a happy life. Because of human nature. An ethical life is such that it is built on self-reliance. You can't count on other people. If you want something, you are morally obligated to take control and cause it to happen for yourself.

$(Self Reliance)^2$ = Independence = Reliance upon self-reliance.

But you might say: in a family, you are responsible for other people, and other people are responsible for you. In a friendship, you are responsible for other people, and they are responsible for you.

No. You can help them. You should help them. And they can help you. They should help you. But you should not be relying on them in a dependent way. Nor should they be relying on you in a dependent way. You are, ultimately, in a primary way, personally responsible for yourself, completely, to a 100% degree. And, too, they, for themselves. You may want to help them, need to help them, and be morally obligated to help them, and they to help you. But you must be able to be personally responsible for yourself, and to rely on yourself, and to rely upon your own self-reliance. And you must be prepared to let them rely upon themselves. That is the right thing to do, in family and friendship. If you love someone, let them live as a human being should live, which is living your own life for yourself, as a thing in itself and for itself.

Let me be perfectly clear. If you are in a family or in a friendship, you should help your family and friends. And they should help you. But helping someone, and them relying, for some specific task or some short period of time, upon your help, is not the same thing as them being fully dependent upon you, and relying on you for their very existence, that they could not survive on their own. Helping someone is good. Relying on someone in a fully dependent way is not good. You can be independent, as such, even if you help others and they help you, in their turn, among your family and/or friends. Also, this assumes the people involved are not sick. Sickness can deprive people of their ability of independence. Then they need to rely on other people. And should do so. And their friends and family should take care of them. But here, in what I said above, I spoke of healthy, normal humans.

Half of humanity is honest, nice, decent, respectful, responsible, competent, kind, and good. I really believe that. Half of all humans are abusive, dishonest, petty, immature, manipulative, lazy, stupid, incompetent, and evil. I believe that, too. You never know what someone is, until you rely on them. And it's a roll of the dice, which they will turn out to be. For the important things in life, you should not put all your trust in a roll of the dice. You cannot rely on other people. You should never count on other people, if something has to happen. If you need something to happen, *you* have to make it happen, and *you* are the one who must make it happen.

The Anti-Objectivist will:

(1) Ask the Objectivist to help them cut corners;

(2) Ask the Objectivist to accept Anti-Objectivist morality, altruism where the good is to help the needy, but which really means where the good people help other people to cut corners and get away with not living their own lives, in other words, the good is to help evil people and enable evil people to be evil;

(3) Ask the Objectivist, even if he/she/they don't accept Anti-Objectivist morality, to just go along with it, just pretend they accept it and go along with the charade and pretend that it's okay, because that is normal and mature and adult and what everyone does.

The Objectivist must:

(1) Not help someone cut corners; not pay for someone else to cut corners;

(2) Reject Anti-Objectivist morality;

(3) Never cut corners.

The Anti-Objectivist says that they hate the rich, and they hate corporate greed. But they want the rich to pay for them to have stuff. So, in terms of analysis, they want to rely upon the rich. They want the rich to be personally responsible for the poor, for society, for the middle class. They want the whole world to be a burden on the shoulders of those who make money. Ayn Rand had something to say about that in "Atlas Shrugged."

Let people try to get away with cutting corners, when there is no one else to pay for it. They won't get away with it. If you rely on yourself, you cannot cut corners, because there would be nobody else to pay for you, so you would not get away with it. So the people who cut corners, want everyone to rely on everyone else, and want everyone to rely on society, and to rely upon reliance upon society. That way, there is always someone else to pay for them to cut corners. There is always someone else for them to rely upon. So, naturally, in politics, they want socialism. Or fascism. Or any system that gives power to society and forces the individual to rely upon society for survival.

Someone can be an Objectivist and not know it, or be one and believe they aren't one. Many people are Objectivists their whole lives, but they don't realize it until they read Ayn Rand for the first time. "An Objectivist" is defined as "a person who has intellectual honesty, and who regards intellectual honesty as a virtue, and who practices that virtue as a habit in their everyday life." So that covers a lot of people. Everyone who truly has intellectual honesty, and has moral integrity to that value, is an Objectivist. Leonardo Da Vinci, who saw what things were, in biology and the human body and mechanics, and made inventions and works of art pursuant to what he saw, was an Objectivist. Even though he didn't know it, and he lived hundreds of years before Ayn Rand was born. Anyone who embraces the spirit of intellectual honesty to know that a thing is what it is, that a thing is itself, is an Objectivist, whether they know it or not, whether they read Ayn Rand or not. Aristotle, who invented the logical statement "A is A," the Law of Identity, which embodies the spirit of intellectual honesty, he was one. Despite living two thousand years before Ayn Rand.

Steve Jobs, the co-founder of Apple Computers, had the intellectual honestly to see what computers and technology are, and to see what they could be because of what they are, to see the possibility of the iPod in 2003 and the iPhone from 2007 and the iPad in 2011 and the original Mac, the first desktop computer, from 1984, and he saw all the stupid things in computers and technology for what they were that could easily be gotten rid of, like ugly boring exterior appearances and complicated user interface and on/off switches, and he was the only one who saw, no one else paid attention and looked, and he then made inventions and designs pursuant to what he saw, and made a trillion dollars by doing so, so, in practice, he was an Objectivist. Even though, in his theory, in his own beliefs, Steve Jobs was an avowed Leftist liberal Democrat socialist, and he once said he had picked up "Atlas Shrugged" at the recommendation of a friend and he had to soon put it down because he hated it so much.

Compare and contrast William Shakespeare, who was a genius and a great writer and a great genius playwright, but he was not an Objectivist: his plays are all about human existence as irony and accepting existential contradiction and the necessity of cynicism and hypocrisy, if you read them carefully enough to care about his message. Shakespeare's message is the Anti-Objectivist message of cynicism and hypocrisy as intellectual maturity, and never the Objectivist message of innocent, honest, sincere, earnest intellectual honesty as virtue.

FROM FACTS TO VALUES

From what something is, to what you should do.

From facts to values.

You are driving a car, on a street, carved into the side of a mountain, above a sheer cliff that drops to an ocean far below.

If the road *is* curved, you *should* hug the corners, and you *should not* cut corners.

If the road *is* straight, you *should* drive straight ahead, and you *should not* drive in a winding curved line.

If you do wrong, your car may fall off the cliff. If you do right, you will drive safely to your destination.

That assumes your goal is to not fall off a cliff. If you don't care whether you do, if you don't care whether you live or die, then there is no right or wrong.

That's morality only if you want to live. The choice to live, the desire to live, your life as the goal of your life, is the Objectivist Ethical Axiom.

The existence of inanimate matter has no conditions.

The existence of Life is conditional.

Ethics is the study of the answer to this question: Human Life stays alive: How, and under what conditions?

X is.

You act in pursuance to the fact that X is.

You treat X like an X, and you don't treat X like a Not-X.

Posit that X is an action with a result that can have an effect upon your chances of long-term survival.

Then action pursuant to X being X, in other words, knowing that X is X (intellectual honesty), and treating X like the X that it is (morality), enables you to live. Or to live a long and happy life.

You are *good* at doing something. Because you are good at it, you succeed.

You do something the *right* way. Because you did it correctly, you succeed.

You are morally, ethically *good* at doing something.

You do something the moral, ethical *right* way.

You are *good*.

You do *right*.

You are morally, ethically *good*.

You do moral, ethical *right*.

You can do the act of being human well (good) or badly (evil). You can live life the right way, or the wrong way. But, ultimately, to do something well, is to do it for a goal of success, and so it is a means, which assumes an end. The ultimately end goal of every action, that translates being good at doing something, to be ethical, moral good, is that being good, causes success, which helps you stay alive, and *life is good*. You can be good at being human, which is ethical virtue, or be bad at being human, which is what defines ethical vice and sin, but, because you are human, that is what you are, being good at being human will cause you to stay alive and to live a richer, fuller, happier, longer life, a better life, a good life. You should have the intellectual honesty to know that humans are humans, and that you are you.

Being good at something causes you to succeed. Success at what you do makes it more likely that you continue to be alive.

Doing the right thing, and not the wrong thing, and making the right choice, and not making the wrong choice, keeps you alive. It makes your life last longer, and be fuller and happier.

Given the Objectivist Ethical Axiom, that life is a value and is the standard of value, doing something well (good) or not well (bad) translates into a good and evil that is based on objective fact, not subjective assignment of meaning. Ultimately, you are (intentionally, by intentionally doing the right things) good at being human, and you are good at being alive and you are good at living your life, which is good. Or you are bad at being human and you are bad at being alive, you (intentionally, from laziness or stupidity or the choice not to think) do badly at being human, you are not good at being what you are, which is evil. But, for this system of morality to be logical, you need the Objectivist Ethical Axiom, that the purpose of all of this is to live, so that doing good and being right has a purpose, which is your life. It is *your* life, hence, selfish.

This is why Ayn Rand described the process of being a moral agent as a constant series of facing choices and making a choice: Right or wrong? Good or bad? Good or evil? Doing an action right or doing it badly, wrongly? Such that, choosing right, and good, and doing actions properly, will have a practical result, to improve and enhance your life. And choosing wrong, evil, vice, sin, will only hurt your life, either short-term or long-term, and make your life sad, unhappy, unpleasant, and, eventually, shorten it, or result in death. Much as, the typical stupid objection is, if rational selfishness is ethical, why not choose to be an alcoholic drug addict, because that is a fun, happy life, despite being a life of sin and vice? But that is not the right way to live life, according to Objectivism, because that is not a good way to have a truly long, healthy, happy life, with a healthy body and a healthy mind and a healthy soul, which is the Objectivist idea of the good life.

The "intentional" element adds a moral sense over and above merely lacking the ability to be good at being human intrinsically and without fault, for which there could be no blame. Moral blame, or moral praise, or moral significance, always arise from a choice, which, ultimately, is the choice to think and the choice to live, or the choice not to think and the choice to cut corners (and hope someone else pays for it). If you do so to the full extent of your ability, then, no matter how little your ability was, there could be no moral blame. But you have to care. You have to care about right and wrong, you have to care about good and evil. And you have to care about discovering what they are, on the basis of objective facts in reality. If you don't, then that is a choice not to live. That is a choice to be evil.

But the Anti-Objectivist (1) doesn't know what the right way to do something is, (2) lacks the ability to do it or (3) is too lazy or cowardly or petty or nasty to actually do it. So someone else must do it for them, must pay for them to not do it, must pay for them to not be properly living their life, or else they will die. They can't drive the car. They don't choose to pay attention to the road and look at the road and make the effort to drive. They need someone else to do it for them. Or they need other people to pay someone to do their driving for them.

In this book I have frequently used the metaphor of driving a car down a road, and treating the road with the intellectual honesty to recognize that it is what it is, or not doing so and forcing someone else to pay for that mistake. The road, and the destination at the end of that road, which destination you reach by driving well (by driving in a good, ethical, moral way), is a metaphor. That destination can represent any goal, any place you want to get to, any desire or need, any end state you seek to achieve. The road to get to that destination can represent any purposeful action, task, or series of steps, necessary to achieve the goal. It is a metaphor, but the idea underneath it is to be taken literally.

The classic phrase: "Nature, to be commanded, must be obeyed," is a related idea, and it implies that the road exists objectively, outside of your mind, in reality, which forces your behavior to act pursuantly to what the road is, in order to conquer it and ascend it, instead of simply closing your eyes and subjectively wishing or willing the road to be different from what it is.

How do you know what the road ahead is? In order to treat it like what it is? You see the road ahead. And you consult maps, and you use reason and logic on a set of maps. So you know what the road is. You know where it winds and curves. You know where it is straight. You know where it is wide, and you know where it is narrow.

Then the Anti-Objectivist philosopher says: But how do you know what the road is? You don't know what the road is. Because perception and the sensations of sight can lie and deceive. You don't know what the road is. Because knowledge of the physical world is impossible. You don't know what the road is. Because there is a deeper reality, behind the realm of appearance, in comparison to which the road is an illusion. You don't know what the road is. Because it's only your subjective belief about the road, and that isn't objective truth, and you can't prove that it is true.

You don't know what the road is. So you can't drive it. You can't trust yourself to drive it. You can't rely on yourself to drive it. Instead, rely on us. Rely on each other. Rely on society. We'll do it for you. It's safer for you, that way. Easier. Less labor-intensive. It requires less intelligence from you. We will help you, and, one day, in the future, you will help us. You rely on us. One day, we will rely on you.

And the Objectivist says: The road is what it is. The road is what it is. The road is what it is. The road is what it is. The road is what it is.

SELF-ESTEEM

Self-esteem: Liking who you are.

Liking your self-esteem (self-esteem)^2: Self-Worth, Egoism. To believe that you deserve to like the person who you are. To have a sense of self-worth that who you are is really good and great, so you deserve to like yourself, so you like the fact that you like yourself.

Self-respect: Having respect for yourself as a person. To have respect for someone is to acknowledge that: (1) someone is a person, (2) they see, think, choose, have a mind, and have a soul, (3) they have a right to make their own choices and choose what to think and what to believe, (4) they have a right to be treated with dignity and respect and to have people be considerate towards them and be considerate of their feelings.

To have respect for your self-respect (self-respect)^2: Self-love. To respect the fact that you deserve respect. And, therefore, that you deserve love.

Being self-reliant will cause you to have self-esteem. If you are a person you can rely on (self-reliance), that will make you become a person that you like, you will like yourself (self-esteem), and then you will enjoy being you. Self-reliance forces you to be a good person, because it forces you to do everything the right way, because there is no other person who will bail you out or pay for it if you cut corners or behave irrationally or stupidly. If you rely on yourself, and then you succeed, that is a win for you. And being a winner will give you self-esteem.

You are a value, you are the highest value, your value is above all others: Subjective.

You are a value for you and to you, you are your highest value, your job is to be personally responsible for yourself above all others: Objective, Factual.

Objectivist morality, ethical egoism, rational selfishness is objective, not subjective. It is a factual description of reality and of your life and your place in your life.

GRAB HOLD AND DRAG UP

You are an appellate litigation lawyer (a lawyer who handles the appeals of cases). You are preparing an appeal for a client, that you will present to a judge. You are doing legal research for this case. You read the main legal case text in the case law at issue in your case. It is 100 pages long. On page 73, there is a footnote, which you glance at, and the footnote makes no sense to you. The opinion makes sense overall and the author seems smart, so you don't know why this footnote would be there. But you don't let it stop you. You keep reading, and finish page 100.

The footnote: It is at the periphery of your awareness, it bothers you for a moment. It nags at you, something doesn't feel right, your subconscious mind tells you the footnote is strange, you have a feeling something is there. Do you just ignore it and go about preparing your case? If you let it go, you will forget about it, and never be aware of it ever again. And you will prepare your case, do oral argument before a judge, and win or lose.

No: You choose to pay attention to the footnote. You *grab hold of it and drag it up* to be front and center in your awareness, and you look at it. You *see* what it is, so that you can *act* pursuant to what it is. You reach out to colleagues and ask them what they think of the footnote. From them, you get a sense of what the judge meant by that footnote. You dig. You do research on it. Now you fully understand what it means. This opens the door to a whole new body or area of law applying to the facts and procedures of your case. You research this law. You use it when you draft your next brief. You argue your case, on both the argument from the 100 page text, and the argument from law from the footnote. The judge is receptive to the argument from the footnote, and appreciates your intelligence, and the effort that went into this appeal. You win your case.

There is perception. Perception^2, the perception of perception, is awareness. Awareness^2, the awareness of awareness, is self-awareness. But self-awareness^2, your self-awareness of your own self-awareness, as a mind, is to pay attention to what you are seeing and what you are thinking and where things are in your field of vision and in your field of awareness, and to grab hold of things at the periphery of vision and drag them up to the surface, if your gut tells you to notice a critical detail that might otherwise get lost, and to then act upon it. This is the hallmark of intellectual work. This is what smart people do and what people who make money do. They do the tough intellectual work and back-breaking mental cognitive labor, which, for the realm of mind and awareness and perception, is equal to what a day laborer lifting wheelbarrows full of heavy rocks all day, in blood, sweat and tears, day after day, year after year, does. The true mental work is to pay attention and to evaluate, judge, reason, identify, what they are aware of, what they perceive, and then, once they know what it is, to act in pursuance to what it is.

Discipline is Willing the self to not do what one desires short-term because doing so enables one to achieve another greater desire or longer-term desire.

Being Thwarted by Temptations, if (Will of Temptation > (is greater than) Will of Discipline).

Overcoming Temptation, if (Will of Discipline > (is greater than) Will of Temptation).

Destroying Temptations, for example, (Deliver us from temptation).

Importance is the property of being such that you should be aware of this thing right now. Unimportance is the property of being such that you should not be aware of it or think about it. The Unimportance of Pain and Problems is a key Objectivist principle, but it can lead to the Repression of Emotions (if you have Assigned Importance to Some Pain or Problem and then you choose not think about it).

Ayn Rand said that pain and problems are unimportant. Rand once said "You should be aware of your enemies for as long as is necessary to defeat them, and for not one moment longer." And, in The Fountainhead, there is the classic scene, where the villain asks the hero "What do you think of me?" And the hero replies: "But I don't think of you." Rand believed that goodness, hope, optimism, and happiness, are important, but pain, problems, sadness, enemies, and evil, are unimportant, and they should not worry you or drag you down, because you shouldn't even be thinking about them at all, instead you should focus on the good things and be optimistic. But, if you assign importance to pain and problems (which is a mistake), then you should think through them and cope with them. To fail to do so leads to emotional repression.

There is doing something. There is the fear of doing something. There is the courage to do something, which is choosing not to let fear stop you from choosing to do it. Then there is the courage to have courage, the courage to choose courage instead of fear as your precondition and situation to be situated in for making this choice to do the underlying action or not. That is (courage)^2. Courage-squared. Courage times courage. This is called being courageous. If you try, and you fail, the worst that could happen is you die, which will happen eventually anyway, so you net lose nothing. But if you try, and you succeed, then you gain something. But, if you don't try, then you do not gain anything, which is the functional equivalent of failing. So, if you want to do something, you should always try, and overcome the fear of failure, and the fear of "what if?", and the fear of "what if I fail? What's the worst that could happen?" So it is always rational to be courageous.

However, the smart person will still ask "what's the worst that could happen if I fail?" and try to mitigate or prevent the most unacceptable risks before they can materialize, as a corollary of making the sincere attempt at it to win and succeed. Avoiding unjustified risks is smart, it's foresight, it's thinking ahead. If you face risks using logic and rationality, that is thinking ahead. If you face risks using emotions and cowering in fear, that is fear. Thinking ahead about risks you will face and preparing to be ready to face them is not the same thing as feeling fear over a set of "what if?" scenarios.

To value things: Ethics. What things you should value.

To value your values: Morality. (Values)^2. Which values you should value. The philosophy of Objectivism.

BONUS CONTENT

Always trust your eyes over your thoughts. Light cannot lie. Your thoughts can lie.

The only thing worse than a democracy is a dictatorship.

We need freedom from "freedom from freedom."

The cowards rely upon government to protect them from the power of big business. The courageous rely upon competition to protect them from the power of big business.

"We are imposing these rules and regulations in order to ensure the safety of all citizens." But safety is precisely what cannot be **ensured**. You can never **guarantee** that you will be safe, because there always might be things outside your control or dangers you don't know about. Risk and danger is inherent in human existence on this half-barren third rock from the Sun full of predators and natural hazards and human violence and human mental illness and human stupidity. You can never be **safe**. You can have a pretense or illusion of safety, which may make you **feel** safe. But you never **are** safe. There is no safety. You are mortal. There are always things that can kill you, and, one day, something will. There is no such thing as safety. But there is such a thing as freedom. Reliance upon self-reliance can give you the courage to act, and to live, under the conditions of lacking safety. Even if you are at risk of death, if you do things the right way, you will probably live to fight another day. But the solution is not to seek safety and the elimination of all risks. By means of government. The solution is to accept and face and master and control and overcome and defeat risk. By means of success. Within freedom.

Rationality is not an iron cage. It is a path to freedom. A person does not benefit from having the freedom to dance blindly off the edge of a cliff and into the abyss. It is only their rationality that would tell them not to do so. That is the extent to which it cages them. It imprisons them in a happy life and deprives them of the freedom to commit an insane and meaningless suicide. Rationality gives them the freedom to do everything they will do, after having not plunged headfirst into the darkness.

Capitalism: the belief that, if you pay for something, then you own it, because you did the work that made the money that paid for it to exist, so you earned it.

Democracy: the belief that people need the freedom to choose between right and wrong in order to live life as human beings.

Capitalism and democracy (democratic capitalism): The belief that, if you are given a free choice between right and wrong, and you choose right, and doing so makes money for you, then you own that money.

Objectivism: the belief that making good choices is what makes money.

If you give people the freedom of speech to attack democracy, then they gain followers and then attack, and then democracy ends. If you don't give people the freedom of speech to attack democracy, then there is no freedom of speech, and then democracy ends. It's a lose-lose. If you give people the freedom of speech to attack democracy, but then you win the war of ideas and the war of activism to get democracy the support and the votes of the people, then democracy survives. Democracy can only last for longer than a hundred years in a well-educated and well-armed population. It's the only way.

The socialists who want to separate the issue of the distribution of wealth, from the issue of the production and creation of wealth, want to cut people in half. But as soon as you don't, it becomes clear the wealth-creation should control wealth-distribution. One, as one, at one with itself, vs. two, in contradiction to each other, as negative-one.

The spiritualists who say that human is a body, opposed to a mind, want to cut people in half. But as soon as you don't, it becomes clear that the mind makes the choices that keep the body alive, and the body then gives the mind a place in physical reality within which to exist, a home. One, as one, at one with itself, vs. two, in contradiction to each other, as negative-one.

"No one survives in this valley by faking reality *in any way*." Ayn Rand, Atlas Shrugged. This is the signature Objectivist virtue: intellectual honestly, opening your eyes and really seeing what exists, identifying things as what they are, accepting that a thing is itself and each thing in reality is what it is. Even if you don't like it, or wish it wasn't true, the truth is all there is. To not pretend, or fake it, or wish it away, or close your eyes to it, to what you don't like, but to fight it, instead, and to live your life in an intellectually honest way.

God: The Other, that which is not the Self, the name for all that which is outside of your control. And your name for whatever ultimately controls that which you don't control.

Faith in God: Hope that what is outside of your control will give you the opportunity to succeed, prayer for good luck. What Ayn Rand called the Benevolent Universe Premise, that reality is good, not evil, is benevolent, not malevolent, so you should have hope that, for each thing, which you need, that you cannot control, it will turn out all right or in your favor. Optimism.

Let's explore some fun Bible quotes from Christian theological Scripture. This is an exercise in Objectivist hermeneutics and Objectivist interpretations of the Bible. It will be fun! Let's go!

"In the beginning was the Logic, and the Logic was God." John 1:1

Often translated as "In the beginning was the Word, and the Word was God," the actual Greek used in the Bible is "logos," which is a direct reference to the word "logos" in Ancient Greek philosophy, especially Plato, Aristotle, and their contemporaries in Greece and Athens. John, the author of the Gospel of John, was a well known Platonist, and he was trying to bring the philosophy of Plato into the Christian Bible. Indeed, the Gospel of John is the most extremist of all the Gospels, and very evidently Platonist, with Plato's rejection of the physical world as mere illusion, in favor of a complete commitment the spiritual realm. But, instead of Plato's world of the Ideas, from Plato's Cave Allegory, John has Heaven and God, and a Christ who ascends to Heaven. "Logos," properly translated, means "things in an understanding that is articulated in language and which are understood so well that they can be explained using language," so "the Word" is a poor translation; in modern English, "logic" might be best as a translation. What the statement actually means is that God is a philosophical understanding of the world that can be articulated in language. It is a direct reference to Plato. So, Christians, who pride themselves as pious, simple men of faith, and who believe that the Bible comes from God directly, should be horrified to learn that their entire theology, and the New Testament itself, rests upon a foundation of the philosopher Plato and Ancient Greek philosophy.

"All those who sin are a slave of sin." John 8:34

Jesus says the truth will set you free, and the men say, but, Jesus, we are free men! And Jesus replies, all those who sin, are a slave of sin. The chains that bind you are inside. Your own sin is what causes you to become a slave of that sin. You are your own enslavement mechanism. No government can be everywhere and watch everything. They rely on internalized fear of the state, so that you censor yourself, you stop yourself from acting, you cause yourself to hesitate, out of fear, and then the state has won, because you render yourself powerless to act against it. If you internalize fear into your own head, then your fear owns you, and you are a slave of your own fear. If you give in to what you regard as evil, you become a slave of sin, but you are the very chains that bind you, and you can take off your chains, at will, and be set free, by a mere act of choice, and of will.

"What should it profit a man, if he gaineth the world, but loseth his own soul?" Mark 8:36

Objectivism is often regarded as a materialist philosophy, where physical rewards are the motive of the ideas. But Objectivism is an idealist morality. You are supposed to have ideals. Based on goodness. And virtue. Those who seek to break you, to rule you, will seek to bait you into compromising your moral integrity, because, if you do, then they have won, then they own you. Material rewards, material pleasure, money, status, sex, romance, career, etc., are all things that the evil ones will tempt you with, and offer

THE MEANING OF LIFE

to you, to lure you to the betrayal of your ideals.

Pretend to be someone you are not, and create a fake persona, to get sex or to get a girlfriend or boyfriend. Then, the more sex, or love, you get, the more deeply you are sunk into living a lie, and being dishonest, and the real you will then never be loved.

Your boss asks you to do something unethical at work, and you go along with it, because you are afraid of being fired, even though you have a feeling that this is bad. And then you tell a lie to cover up the crime, and you get roped in, and before you know it, you are a criminal working with your boss.

You have the opportunity to tell a small white lie to a customer to make a sale and get more money. Then, before, you and your customer were on the same side, and doing business was a win-win, but now it's a conflict of interests, where you win if your customer loses, and it becomes a bloody war of all against all, and life becomes nasty, brutish and short.

These things are evil. They are the path to Hell. This is not Christianity I am talking about. I am talking about what Objectivism holds. You should be true to your ideals, to reason, rationality, independence, integrity, honestly, and courage, because there can be no happy life, in the physical world, if you renounce goodness and concede to evil. Christians say your punishment for sin will come in Hell. Objectivism says your punishment for sin will come much sooner, here on Earth, soon, and well before you die. Much as your reward for virtue would have come, in this life, before death, without needing to wait for Heaven.

"Ask and ye shall receive, seek and ye shall find, knock and the door will open." Matthew 7:7

If you will something to be, it will be. If you ask for what you want, and you will it to exist, you will obtain it. This world is a world in which you have the power. If you use it, you will get what you want. The only way you don't, is if you are bullied into not asking for it, not using your power to will it to be, and then you have a lack of what you want, and sit, alone, and cry, and feel depressed and sorry for yourself, and are sad and angry that you don't have what you want. But you were responsible. In this life, more often than not, you are in control. No one knows more about your life, or cares more about what happens to you, than you do. If you do the right things, and you have desires, and you choose, and will, those desires to come true, you will get what you want. You just have to have the faith (really, the rationality) to be confident that it will happen. And then you will make it happen.

If you take responsibility for yourself, then you have the power, then you control what happens in your life. But if you just want to bitch and moan and cry about bad luck and you never had a chance, and there was nothing you could do, and you never ask for what you want and you never will what you want, then you take what power you could have had, and you concede it, and give it away, and lose it. That is the power of Objectivism, that it gives you the power to live a happy life.

Jesus Christ was fully moral. He tolerated no evil. He did not tolerate sin. And he succumbed to no temptation. He was strict, and perfect, in his observance of virtue. As such, he is a paradigm of morality, for any morality. Including Objectivist morality. The whole spiritual vs. physical, mind vs. body issue, or afterlife, or Son of God issue, is merely an infection of Platonic influence, in what could otherwise stand as a role model, for virtue and values and ethics, as such. Jesus Christ can be understood by philosophy, and philosophical analysis, as distinct from the purely religious understanding of Jesus Christ, as merely a savior to obey who demands obedience to the Church in return for the salvation of your soul and entry to Heaven.

WHAT THEY WON'T TELL YOU ABOUT OBJECTIVISM: THOUGHTS ON THE OBJECTIVIST PHILOSOPHY IN THE POST-RANDIAN ERA

CHAPTER ONE: THE TRUTH ABOUT OBJECTIVISM

Both Objectivism's advocates and its critics treat Objectivism as some sort of right-wing extremist conservative philosophy, as if it is merely a defense of capitalism, and nothing more. Objectivism's contributions to the theories of reason, logic, morality, and atheism are entirely missing from the narratives of the philosophy's foes and friends alike. The advocates of Objectivism and its enemies then argue over free market economics. But they are both arguing about a straw man, a scarecrow. They have taken a deep, thoughtful, detailed philosophy, and thinned it down to a shallow paper-thin cartoon. The followers of Objectivism then loudly proclaim that they are in favor of this two-dimension cartoon, while its enemies attack the cartoon as being a cartoon.

One of my central positions is that people come to Objectivism by reading Rand's novels and find her commitment to rationality, reality, and intellectually honest analyses of philosophy and ethics to be like a breath of fresh air in a stagnant, festering, stinking world of fakeness and evasion, but then, as this initial interest draws a reader deeper into the movement, these ideas, Objectivism's appeal, are used as lure, as bait, to line the person up along traditional partisan political lines, exploiting Objectivism's politics like a crass, crooked ward heeler lining up votes for his candidate through lies and scams. There are two philosophies of Objectivism, the one in the ideas, which people see in the novels, and the one in the movement, which is also what the world at large thinks about the philosophy, and why many view it with cynicism, disappointment and bitterness.

Most Objectivists begin their path in the philosophy for one reason and one reason only, because they found something special and unique by reading *The Fountainhead* and *Atlas Shrugged*, which they believe in after reading John Galt's speech, and now want to study it and make use of it, although they can't really define exactly what that "it" is. As we should all know by now, Objectivists tend to reach the end of their time with Rand's philosophy in one of three positions: (1) hating it, for having let them down in its honest commitment to open-minded rationality and having been a mere cult of fakes disguised as rationality; (2) as an obedient Randroid robot, proudly cultist, with no mind of their own, who thoughtlessly obeys the philosophy as a closed-minded dogma and is a conformist of the worst sort; or, (3) far more rarely, the people like me, who defy dogmatism but refuse to abandon the philosophy, instead seeking to revive the ray of light that made it noble, hopeful, and optimistic to begin with.

My approach is, in a sense, "do as Rand did, not as Rand said": she was a visionary philosopher who challenged the dominant traditions of her era, of both the corrupt liberals and the hypocritical conservatives, and I, for my part, seek to do much the same, taking on the hypocritical Randroids while at the same time opposing Objectivism's leftist critics as a bunch of stubborn idiots. I seek to take that breath of fresh air, that nugget of gold, the thing that readers find in Rand's books but cannot name and then proceed to lose, and try to save it, and define it, and promote it. This could be articulated in more detail: "Do as Rand did as a thinker, and do as Rand said in her novels, but don't do as Rand did or said when she ordered her followers to obey her, in her historical movement of the 1960's."

What is the "real" Objectivism? Only an examination of Objectivism at the source can show that. Here I will undertake a serious analysis of Objectivism, by examining what I see as its two key texts, the two most famous novels of Ayn Rand, *The Fountainhead* and *Atlas Shrugged*.

In *The Fountainhead*, Dominique, after spending a period of time living in a poor neighborhood of New York City for investigative journalism for a newspaper, writes "articles on life in the slums," a "merciless, brilliant account. . . .'" She then attends a dinner part of the rich, and says:

"The house you own on East Twelfth Street, Mrs. Palmer," she said , her hand circling lazily from under the cuff of an emerald bracelet too broad and heavy for her thin wrist . . . "has a sewer that gets clogged every other day and runs over, all through the courtyard. It looks blue and purple in the sun, like a rainbow." "The block you control for the Claridge estate, Mr. Brooks, has the most attractive stalactites growing on all the ceilings."

Soon after telling the rich slumlords that their treatment of the poor is horrible, she speaks at " a meeting of social workers," to speak about the residents of the slums, and says "The family on the first floor rear do not bother to pay their rent, and the children cannot go to school for lack of clothes. The father has a charge account at a corner speak-easy. He is in good health and has a good job. . . . The couple on the second floor have just purchased a radio for sixty-nine dollars and ninety-five cents cash. In the fourth floor front, the father of the family has not done a whole day's work in his life, and does not intend to. There are nine children, supported by the local parish. There is a tenth on its way."

Pages 139-140, Signet paperback edition.

In sum, Dominique tells the rich about the plight of the poor and how horrible the rich treat them, while telling the poor that they are a bunch of lazy deadbeats.

The statements against the rich here come, not from the novel's socialist villain, but from one of the novel's heroes. What is Rand doing here? Let me observe two things. First, there is depth here, and complexity, that requires thought, and not merely a paper-thin dogma.

Second, what Rand is doing through Dominique is pointing out the hypocrisy of both the champions of the rich and the champions of the poor, and declaring that she will call all hypocrites out as such. I point this out because it goes to the heart of *The Fountainhead*, where one of Rand's main arguments is that the idealism she articulates as individualism is an idealism that an idealist can really believe, that it has integrity, whereas collectivism, widely regarded as the impractical idealism to believe in, is just a bunch of sell-outs pragmatically copying other people and selling their souls for power, just as Keating sells his soul to Toohey.

This role reversal, the opposition to people who are fake and phony and to sell-outs, like Keating, and the offering up as integrity and idealism and being true to your own artistic vision as selfishness and individualism, is one of the hallmarks of *The Fountainhead*. Rand's innovation was to take the traditional narrative, that people sell-out for money, and keep their ideals for the sake of the poor, hence selling out is pro-capitalist and having ideals is socialist, and reverse them, showing that Keating, who sells his soul for career success, is actually a second-hander conformist who obeys the other and has the soul of the principle of socialism, whereas Roark, the artist with integrity, is selfish in staying true to his vision of his self, and as such has the soul of the principle of capitalism. This is a total and unexpected reversal of the roles as tradition had understood them prior to Rand's writings.

Let us consider the case of Dominique. She loves Roark and hates Keating and Wynand, yet spends much of the novel trying to destroy Roark's career while marrying Keating and, later, Wynand. Let me, again, make two observations.

First, Dominique's behavior is not inexplicable, but it is a deep, realistic, deeply human psychology that motivates her. This is a far cry from the simpleton robots, otherwise known as Randroids, who believe that Rand calls upon us to be robots programmed by logic, and simplistic logic at that, executing the directive of "capitalism good, leftism bad" without too much deep thought. Dominque is a deep, human, realistic character, one who real people can relate to, although they may not consciously understand why she does what she does.

Second, why does Dominique seek to destroy Roark? Simply put, she believes in his greatness, and also believes that greatness cannot succeed and will inevitably be destroyed in a society of "second-handers," the conformists and sell-outs, therefore decides to put Roark out of his misery, almost like a mercy killing, to spare herself the horror of watching him, the man she loves, be destroyed by society and seeing him be crushed or sell out to the architectural conformist mediocrity. Then, when he succeeds and triumphs at the end of the novel, her pessimism about the ability of greatness to succeed is destroyed, and she can marry him without reservation.

Hers is a deep, conflicted, confused, and complicated character, yet she is one of the main heroes of Rand's central novels. In that sense, to obey the tenets of Rand's written work, one must conclude that it is acceptable human behavior to have complicated feelings, and to be wrong at times, and to have depth and shades of gray to one's behavior, as all of these things describe Dominique. A superficial reading of the novel would not notice this, yet many of both Objectivism's friends and foes seem to be reading the books superficially.

The complexity and depth of Dominique's character is not the only instance of a deep, complex humanity in Rand's fiction. For example, in *Atlas Shrugged*, which I discuss below, the heroes Dagny Taggart and Hank Rearden are deeply conflicted throughout most of the novel, to the point where the main hero, John Galt, is fighting a battle against these other heroes, not against the book's villains, during much of the novel. That is a complicated and deep story, not a shallow and superficial tale of "good rich people" against "evil looting moocher poor people", as many Objectivists view *Atlas Shrugged*.

The heroes in *Atlas Shrugged*–at least, Dagny and Rearden–have emotions and face inner conflicts, they are not blind, perfectly built robots who obey dogma that is programmed into them, although, from a psychological point of view, the main hero John Galt is, essentially, completely perfect and, to that extent, is less humanly realistic and more of just a metaphor for the philosophy itself, although a lot of Objectivists get into trouble by taking Galt as a literal human being and seeking to emulate his robotically perfect behavior. Many Objectivists seek to become mere Randroid robots programmed by the philosophy, and thereby repress and deny their human emotions and inner conflicts, and then either succeed and become blind stupid idiots, or fail and leave Objectivism behind as an unnatural and impractical system. They do this because they seek to model themselves on John Galt, and take him as a literal realistic human role model instead of as a metaphor and a presentation of ideas, whereas Dagny and Rearden are the more human heroes that real people can relate to, but are still heroes in the novel, just as much as Galt is.

There are plenty of other deeply human, realistic characters in Rand's novels, who struggle with inner conflicts and lack perfection. Cherryl, the working class girl who is deceived into entering into an abusive marriage to James Taggart and then commits suicide, and Gail Wynand, a man who had the mind and potential to be an Objectivist hero but lacked the conviction to withstand the pressure that society brought to bear against him to conform, and also Steven Mallory, the depressed, tortured artist who tries to assassinate Toohey. It is characters such as these that the reader relates to, who draw the reader into an emotional involvement with the stories in the books.

But then, at the end, while graduating from the novels to the ideas of Objectivism as a philosophy, the reader is subjected to a "bait-and-switch": instead of being offered as role models those characters, that the reader could relate to as human beings, and taking John Galt as the representation of the ideas that one should apply, the reader is instead told to take John Galt literally, as a human being, and become mentally identical to him–when, as I see it, Galt is not a realistic human being, he is robotic and unrealistic in his character, not because "perfection is impossible," but because the details of Galt's behavior and depiction are just not those of a real person, they are (and I think this obvious if one really reads the book) a metaphor for the defining spirit of the philosophy itself, a metaphor for innovation, thought, courage, etc.

If one took John Galt literally as an ideal for humans to use as a role model, not even Rand herself nor Aristotle would be anywhere near being a truly good person on a realistic scale, as even the super-geniuses of philosophy were not genius physicists and inventors who developed earth-shattering new inventions at the same time, like Galt's static electricity motor. If Rand, the Objectivist super-genius, is a failure by comparison to Galt as a real person, just imagine what normal humans would feel like compared to him, and what robots they might become on their quest to emulate him. Objectivists do not give Rand even the basic decency that every reader should give to a novelist, that a college English major would be required to give to James Joyce or William Shakespeare, or even to Victor Hugo or Ibsen–namely, to read a work of fiction looking for symbolism and metaphors of the meanings that the novelist is expressing. As soon as one does this, John Galt as symbolism and metaphor becomes abundantly apparent, and we can look to the other characters, who have inner conflicts and struggles but overcome them, as our literal role models. It would be interesting to undertake a literary analysis of the symbolism of John Galt's motor, in the context of Rand's catchphrase for the novel that John Galt is "the man who said he would stop the motor of the world, and did," but such an exploration would be impossible for those Objectivists who take Galt literally.

An astute Objectivist might object that, yes, Dagny and Hank face great inner conflict and operate in a moral gray area when they fight to oppose John Galt by saving society from his strike, but this conflict comes from their accepting the looters' moral code, and, at the end of the novel, when they accept Galt's morality, they magically become perfect and cease to have inner conflicts or deep emotional feelings. Upon a close, careful reading, this is incorrect. Yes, Hank does suffer because he accepts the morality of death, especially in relation to his marriage to his wife, and he does achieve something of a deliverance once he accepts the morality of life. Yes, too, Dagny finds exaltation when she joins Galt's strike at the end of the novel. But these are the same people that they were throughout the novel. They do not magically become completely different people, people with no problems, for whom the emotional and ethical issues of life are simple and easy and black and white with no shades of gray. Indeed, I do not think that Dagny ever truly accepted the morality of death; what made her oppose Galt was that she did not believe that the looters themselves were committed to the morality of death, instead, she believed that society could be saved, and would be saved if she and Hank could make enough money to keep everyone from starving to death.

This idea that our society can be saved, and that enough good people exist for that to happen, is not an implausible idea. As such, for real people, for real Objectivists, the moral dilemma and inner conflict faced by Dagny is one that can and will exist, and one can find a great role model for overcoming life's deep, complicated ethical challenges in her determination to triumph over adversity.

So, having mentioned that novel, next let me turn to *Atlas Shrugged*, the great Randian novel that sings the praises of businessmen and shows that businessmen are heroes. Or does it? Let's take a closer look at the text.

In the novel, one of the heroes, Hank Rearden, has a widely publicized court battle against the American government, and, by unapologetically standing up for capitalism, wins. Let's listen to some of the quotes:

"God bless you, Mr. Rearden!" said an old woman with a ragged shawl over her head. "Can't you save us, Mr. Rearden? They're eating us alive, and it's no use fooling anybody about how it's the rich they're after--do you know what's happening to us?"

"Listen, Mr. Rearden," said a man who looked like a factory worker. "it's the rich who're selling us down the river. Tell those wealthy bastards, who're so anxious to give everything away, that when they give away their palaces, they're giving away the skin off our backs."

The businessmen he met seemed to wish to evade the subject of his trial. Some made no comment at all, but turned away, their faces showing a peculiar resentment under the effort to appear noncommittal as if they feared that the mere act of looking at him would be interpreted as taking a stand. Others ventured to comment: "In my opinion, Rearden, it was extremely unwise of you. . . . It seems to me that this is hardly the time to make enemies. . . . We can't afford to arouse resentment."

"Whose resentment?"

"I don't think the government will like it."

"You saw the consequences of *that*."

"Well, I don't know . . . The public won't take it, there's bound to be a lot of indignation."

"You saw how the public took it."

"Well, I don't know . . . We've been trying hard not to give any grounds for all those accusations about selfish greed–and you've given ammunition to the enemy."

"Would you rather agree with the enemy that you have no right to your profits and your property?"

"Oh, no, no, certainly not–but why go to extremes? There's always a middle ground."

"A middle ground between you and your murderers?"

"Now why use such words?" . . .

"It's no time to boast about being rich–when the populace is starving. It's just goading them on to seize everything."

"But telling them that you have no right to your wealth, while they have–is what's going to restrain them?" . . .

"I don't like the things you said at your trial," said another man. "In my opinion, I don't agree with you at all. Personally I'm proud to believe that I *am* working for the public good, not just for my own profit. I like to think that I have some higher goal than just earning my three meals a day and my Hammond limousine.". . .

"I am sorry, gentlemen," Rearden said, "that I will be obliged to save your goddamn necks along with mine."

Pages 449-451, Signet paperback edition.

But surely, the right-wing Objectivist will object, this can be interpreted in such a way that it is not a criticism of the businessman as such? Surely Rand is only referring to rich liberal businessmen, whereas a right-wing or conservative businessman would not count? Let's read on.

In the novel, the evil statist government passes Directive 10-289, the villainous, depraved law that abolishes the free market and puts the economy under the total control of the government. This is a scene where several of the villains in the novel are plotting how to get the Directive passed into law:

"It will give security to the people," said Eugene Lawson, his mouth slithering into a smile. "Security–that's what the people want. If they want it, why shouldn't they have it? Just because a handful of the rich will object?"

"It's not the rich who'll object," said Dr. Ferris lazily. "The rich drool for security more than any other sort of animal–haven't you discovered that yet?"

"Well, who'll object?" snapped Lawson.

Dr. Ferris smiled pointedly, and did not answer.

Lawson looked away. "To hell with them! Why should we worry about *them*? We've got to run the world for the sake of the little people."

Page 500.

Who is the "them" to whom Rand refers? By this point it should be clear on the basis of the quotes that there is a specific type of person Rand is seeking to advocate for, a type of person whom these villains hate and seek to destroy, and, in what should be crystal clear from these quotes, businessmen are not this person. But who is? Who is "them"? That passage in the novel continues in this way:

"It's intelligence that's caused all the troubles of humanity. Man's mind is the root of all evil. This is the day of the heart. It's the weak, the meek, the sick and the humble that must be the only objects of our concern." . . .

"Genius is a superstition, . . . " said Dr. Ferris slowly, with an odd kind of emphasis, as if knowing that he was naming the unnamed in all their minds. "There is no such thing as the intellect. A man's brain is a social product. A sum of influences that he's picked up from those around him. Nobody invents anything, he merely reflects what's floating in the social atmosphere. A genius is an intellectual scavenger and a greedy hoarder of ideas which rightfully belong to society, from which he stole them. All thought is theft. If we do away with private fortunes, we'll have a fairer distribution of wealth. If we do away with genius, we'll have a fairer distribution of ideas."

Page 501.

Rand, in *Atlas Shrugged*, makes a point of stating repeatedly that the intellectual cowards never name their premises, and that to give voice to something, to name it openly, is to define it and articulate it and bring it into the realm of reason and rationality and critical reflection, so that, to openly name a massive con or scam, is to expose it and thereby destroy its ability to fool rational people. The novel itself then becomes Rand's effort to name the unnamed, to name the scam whereby the morality of altruism makes the productive accept guilt and thereby enslaves them to looters. (Rand's analysis of morality is, perhaps, an evolution of Nietzsche's account of slave morality vs. master morality, but we need not answer that question decisively to continue.)

So, I will take the lead from Rand, and name the unnamed, which the conservative Right and the Objectivist movement knows at some level, having read her books, but fears and hides from and pretends is not the truth. Namely, that the type of person who is the glorious hero of *Atlas Shrugged* is John Galt, and the John Galts of the world are what Rand referred to as "men of ability" or "geniuses" or "men of the mind", people who really think and use an incredible capacity of vision to see reality as it really and to see through lies and masks and clouds of smoke and all wishful thinking and self-delusion, and make brilliant decisions, and use the powerful capabilities of their mind to think thoughts at an extremely high level of intellect and make amazing leaps of logical inference to draw conclusions from evidence and experience. These "men of the mind" are certainly not the same thing as the businessmen as such, or the rich as such.

Objectivism is a defense of capitalism because it gives the productive genius the freedom to create, not because it gives the businessman the freedom from paying higher taxes, although the latter is a small detail that is necessarily also contained in the former. There are, in reality, certain men who have been productive geniuses of the caliber of John Galt: one thinks of Thomas Edison, the great inventor, or Steve Jobs of Apple, or Bill Gates of Microsoft, or Larry Page of Google, or Jeff Bezos of Amazon, the self-made Silicon Valley billionaires, for example.

But such men are few, and these are not the ones whom the army of Objectivists is up in arms to praise and defend. The Right, the conservatives, the alt right, the Republican Party, whatever you want to call it, has coopted and corrupted Objectivism, devolving it from a philosophy of reason, into a philosophy of the rich and big business, whose only stated purpose is to serve as propaganda for cutting taxes on the rich. Reason, and the mind, are the things which these people have forgotten about the novel. This can be seen, for example, in such people's Christianity. For Rand, rationality demands atheism, as well as no internal contradictions, so a person cannot be a

Christian and an Objectivist, hence the Right and Objectivism are natural enemies just as much as the Left is an enemy.

Rand, in her own words of the above quotes, did not really give a damn about "the rich" or "the businessmen," she cared about the individualist, the innovator, the thinker, the man of ability, the John Galt. John Galt-like people are rare, and the ranks of the rich and the businessmen do not contain many of them. In the above quotes, Rand contrasts the John Galt-type, Hank Rearden-type hero, to the masses of the rich and the masses of the businessmen in the *Atlas Shrugged* world as such, who criticize Rearden and do not oppose the evil law that puts the economy under government control.

The villainous businessmen in the novel have all bought into altruist Judeo-Christian morality, and thereby support the corrupt statist looters, so the Right can say that the evil businessmen in the novel are really liberal leftist businessmen, not real conservative rich people. Guess what? Most of the Right in the USA, and most of the rich in the USA, and most of the businessmen in the USA, are Christian, and so, as a matter of logic, Rand would condemn them for having bought into evil irrational anti-freedom morality, just as she condemned the evil rich businessmen who are portrayed in *Atlas Shrugged*.

Looking back at *The Fountainhead*, another John Galt-like hero, Howard Roark, is brought to years of poverty and career failure when he rebels against the conformity of the architectural industry and is then punished by the industry for his rebellion. It is even plausible that, along a certain trajectory, not only is not every John Galt rich, but society will tend to make the real John Galts poor. Yet, in practice, the Right holds up Rand as a champion and defender of "the rich" and "the businessman", who, in practical reality, tends to be conservative and Republican (and Christian), while the Left attacks Rand as if that the Right's fantasy were true.

Both sides, it seems, did not give her the dignity of actually reading the words she wrote, and instead base their positions off a general feeling or abstract impressive given off by John Galt's speech that "oh, this book defends capitalism, it must be on the Right and be propaganda for the rich and big business." Rand herself, as we have seen *from her own words*, was smarter than that. As an author of those novels and those quotes, she was not the person both the Left and the Right seem to think she was.

The conservative Objectivist will say that I am some sort of leftist liberal socialist because, unlike him, I actually read the words in the novels instead of just believing what everyone else believes about Objectivism, that I don't "get" the "real" Ayn Rand.

That is a plausible position that can be defended, although I disagree with it. There are vast segments of *The Fountainhead* and *Atlas Shrugged*, especially in the big speeches, that do defend the rich, and businessmen, and seem right-wing in their defense of capitalism. The rightist Rand is plausible, I do not deny it.

But are my arguments wrong? No. Do the previous quotes exist? Yes. Can Objectivists pretend that they don't exist, that reality is not what it really is, and still be

Objectivists? No.

I will also concede that Rand, in her later nonfiction, took a far more conservative and right-wing approach, and, at times, she wrote nonfiction where she did in fact defend the rich from higher taxes as such, and praise the businessman as such. Her nonfiction contains essays where she said that men are superior to women, that she disapproved of homosexuality, and such, which is bread and butter to conservatives. However, even in her nonfiction, she also advocated for abortion and atheism, and she was never the right-wing icon that the conservatives dressed her up to be. She also had some famous nonfiction essays where she attacked conservatives as such and even wrote that she hoped conservatism would die.

But people do not come to Objectivism because of Rand's nonfiction. People come to Objectivism because of the ideas in *The Fountainhead* and *Atlas Shrugged*, most Objectivists read the novels and feel that there is something right and noble and true about those ideas and then discover the philosophy after reading the ideas in the novels. What *those* ideas are is what should define Objectivism. My above quotes tell a story about the novels that is true, and as undeniable as reality itself, but nobody else will tell you the truth about Rand's novels. The key ideas in Rand's novels are being smart, having a mind, thinking for yourself, being intellectually honest and open-minded and intellectually independent. These qualities, or what is perhaps really all one attribute, is what the "men of the mind" have, that their enemies lack. Objectivism, as such, is a philosophy of *reason* and *rationality*, not of capitalism, and defends capitalism only as the political precondition of free thought. But this fact, which exists in objective reality, is inconvenient for both the religious right and the robotic cultist Randroids.

Consider this quote, where Hank Rearden is talking to his steel mill foreman, the representative of the rank and file working class workers whom he employs. The foreman is a man named Tom Colby, who says this to Rearden:

"They've been telling us for years that it's you against me, Mr. Rearden. But it isn't. It's Orren Boyle and Fred Kinnan against you and me."

"I know it."

Page 515. (the final sentence is said by Rearden back to Colby.)

Boyle is the corrupt rich steel mill owner who competes against Rearden by bribing politicians for government favors, and Kinnan is the corrupt crooked labor union boss who represents the working class.

If it's not the workers against the rich, with Rand siding with the rich–and, according to this quote, she rejects that alignment–then what is it? What do Hank Rearden and Tom Colby have in common, that Kinnan and Boyle lack, for Rearden and Colby to be opposed to Boyle and Kinnan? There must be some quality, that both productive geniuses and working class employees can have, that would group them together on opposite sides of whatever this conflict between these two types of people is.

In John Galt's speech at the end of the novel, Galt makes clear that productive genius of the caliber to invent a world-changing new type of electrical motor is the pinnacle of reason and rationality, but there can be a man of reason, with an open mind, intellectual honesty, and a commitment to rationality and actually looking at reality and thinking about reality, in varying and lesser levels of inherent talent and sheer productive capability. These people would be the normal people, the working class people, who are Objectivists.

The example given through the novel of such a man, a normal man who is not a "man of ability" as such but is still a good man and who is rational and productive at a job of lesser responsibility, is Eddie Willers, the heroine Dagny Taggart's personal assistant. Willers is a good man, and a hero, and thinks, and sees, and reasons, and plays an important role in the novel as a conduit of information about Dagny Taggart for John Galt, but he lacks the revolutionary genius of John Galt or Hank Rearden or Dagny Taggart herself.

Thus, it seems to me that this is true: there is something, that could be called thinking, or looking at reality, or reason and rationality, or intellectual honesty, or Objectivist ethics, for which, if a person adheres to this behavior and these values, he is the man whom *Atlas Shrugged* praises, regardless of whether he is rich or poor, businessman or employee, and, if a person lacks these virtues, being intellectually dishonest and corrupt and irrational and defocusing one's mind and blanking out reality to hide from the negative consequences of irrational beliefs and behaviors, and choosing to get through life on shortcuts and taking the easy way out which someone else pays for, this person would bear the mark of villainy, and be evil according to Objectivism–whether he was a poor liberal or a rich conservative.

Colby and Rearden are both the former, despite the fact that Rearden is a productive super-genius and Colby is just a normal man, and, ostensibly, a member of the working class in a factory. Boyle, who is incredibly rich and powerful, and Kinnan, who is too but represents the working class masses, are both the latter. This explains the above quote, and is the most plausible explanation of it.

There are many other things that they won't tell you about Rand, that you will have to see for yourself from reading the books. I'll name two. First, in *Atlas Shrugged*, the heroine Dagny Taggart, the productive genius who makes the railroad successful, is a subordinate of her brother, the CEO James, a crooked corrupt looter who feeds off of her productivity and steals the benefits of her work. It is clear in the novel to any astute reader that Dagny's father gave control of the railroad to her brother, not to her, because she was a woman and her brother was male, and that this was a huge insult to Dagny, who does the work of running the railroad without the status and recognition that society reserves only for men. This is feminism, and the Right does not like it, but nobody ever talks about this, as if they can pretend that it was not important to Rand, despite being in her novel.

Second, in the novel, there is a villain, Dr. Stadler, who creates a super-weapon called Project X, an evil machine that the government uses for mass destruction (in this sense, the novel is science fiction, by the way, which is also rarely mentioned). Nobody ever mentions the fact that Rand's real life associates widely regarded Stadler as based on the historical figure Dr. Robert Oppenheimer, one of the leaders of the Manhattan Project where nuclear weapons were invented during World War II, and that "Project Y" was the actual historical code-name for the development of the nuclear bomb by the Allies in World War II. Rand's portrayal of the evil Project X and the villainous Dr. Stadler is Rand's attempt at an antiwar, anti-nuclear proliferation activism–a position which, during the era of Rand's lifetime, was universally regarded as a leftist, hippie, peacenik dove position that the conservative hawks hated and virulently opposed.

That Ayn Rand was deeper than what both her friends and foes say, that her novels contain characters who are complicated and conflicted and deeply human, that she had positions no one ever talks about, and that her novels mean so much more than mere political "capitalism is good, leftism is evil" two-dimensional depthless propaganda for idiots, are some of the things that they won' tell you about Ayn Rand.

Rand's philosophy is not a philosophy for the rich or for big business or for the conservatives. It is, instead, a philosophy for the smart people, a philosophy for people who think, for people who look at the world with open eyes and really see what is happening, and a philosophy for people with the ethical values of intellectual honesty and all the rest of the virtues listed in John Galt's speech. The Objectivists in the Objectivist movement, by and large, are a bunch of hypocrites who don't do what the novels tell them to do: they don't open their eyes and look at the words in the novel, instead they take the easy of way of behaving like programmed robots and obeying, as dogma, a simplified, stupefied, two-dimensional straw man version of the core tenets of the philosophy.

These Randroid robots are obnoxious, and the leftists then gain the upper hand in their battle against Objectivism by pointing at the cult of Randroid robots and warning smart young minds that you'll end up like these stupid robots if you read these novels and think about them and like them.

I will conclude by telling you the truth about Objectivism that neither the Left nor the Right will tell you, because it is inconvenient for both of them: If you read the novels, and think about them, and think for yourself, instead of just blindly obeying what people tell you about them, you will see that Objectivism is a deep, meaningful, and thoughtful philosophy, and that it is a rich philosophy, not in the sense of money, but in the sense of rich food for your brain to eat that has a lot of good-tasting meat on the bone, with an abundance of interesting, fascinating ideas to chew on.

The remainder of the essays in this book will explore various details of the Objectivist philosophy, using the approach of open-minded reasoning instead of dogmatic obedience.

CHAPTER TWO: RAND'S TWENTY FIVE PERCENT

Atlas Shrugged was published decades ago, and it has also been many decades since *The Fountainhead* was published. In spite of this Objectivism remains in relative obscurity for the public at large, to the surprise of many Objectivists. Ayn Rand is mentioned here and there from time to time, and she has carved out a small place in pop culture and also in Republican politics, but many who know her think of her more as a novelist than as a philosopher, and her philosophy is not particularly famous. To an Objectivist the philosophy of Objectivism makes perfect sense, is downright obvious, and seems like something that every human being on the planet should embrace naturally. So why does Objectivism remain so unpopular?

In his piece "Objectivism: Why Isn't It More Popular?" on The Atlas Society's website William Thomas makes an argument that I consider typical of many, the argument that Objectivism isn't more popular because people are brought up on religion and subjectivism and it is hard for them to adjust to Objectivist ideas. It is true that people often believe whatever they are taught as children, and Thomas is seventy-five percent right. But the other twenty-five percent of why Objectivism isn't more popular stems from two strategic mistakes that Rand made in promoting her philosophy. I believe that Rand's first mistake is one relating to leadership, and that her second mistake is one relating to communication. An analysis of these mistakes can help lead to a stronger, healthier Objectivist movement, and will also shed light on what is at stake in the disagreement between the different branches of Objectivism, by which I mean those who view the philosophy as an "open-system," within which I would include Sense of Life (the open-system group with teeth) and the Atlas Society (the kinder and gentler open-system group) and those who view the philosophy as a "closed-system," i.e. the Ayn Rand Institute. In the course of this essay it will become evident that I think the Ayn Rand Institute has perpetuated a number of Rand's mistakes which hinder the flourishing of Objectivism, although, in all fairness, ARI has been better within recent years.

Rand's first mistake was making her movement, the Objectivism movement of the 1960's, a hierarchical movement, with a structure and leaders. Rand and Nathaniel Branden were at the top, others were in the middle, and the rank-and-file Objectivists were at the bottom. Objectivism is nothing like a religion, but an analogy can be made to the Catholic-Protestant divide. Catholics have a hierarchy because they believe that God speaks to people through priests. Protestants do not have an organized hierarchy because they believe that God speaks directly to individuals. If individuals can know reality directly by means of their reasoning minds then what need is there for a hierarchy? By having such a rigid top-down structure, mistakes at the top lead to huge problems, which is why the conflict between Rand and Branden destroyed her movement and created an obstacle to promoting Objectivism that still haunts the movement 40 years later. Being independent is scary, and having an authority to lean on is comforting, but hierarchy is a dangerous path to follow.

Authority and hierarchy lead to a cult-like mentality. There is a difference between believing in reason as an ideal, and actually using reason as a tool in your life to form independent conclusions. This is a difference between reason in theory and reason in practice. Aristotle keenly observed that it is not enough to know an ethical theory, you have to also be able to put it into practice and make a habit of using it in order to achieve an ethical result. You can know all the most wonderful, spectacular theories, but they don't do you any good unless you know how to actually put them into practice. Rand claimed that her ideas were practical, and it is her followers' task to think about how to put that theory into practice. The unfortunate truth is that some Objectivists live in a world of theories devoid of any concern with practicality. This is the problem that afflicts many "closed-system" Objectivists. These Objectivists believe in reason but fear to actually use reason. This is based on their fear that if they think independently, they might come to disagree with Rand or to believe that Rand made a mistake and was wrong about something. Since their whole belief system is based on Rand's ideas, they fear a psychological abyss if their beliefs are challenged or disproved.

It can be argued that Rand left her philosophy incomplete, that such questions as how reason works in terms of the biology of the human brain, how free will is possible in a physical world of scientific causation, and what a free market society will look like are not answered in sufficient detail, and that in some areas, such as the proper relationship between men and women, Rand's ideas are dubious and questionable. But some Objectivists would rather avoid questions than ask questions, and some Objectivists simply believe that Rand was incapable of making mistakes, and everything that she said must be true because she said it. This is a mindset based on fear and faith, and it leads to conformity among Objectivists. This is the opposite of the mindset that Rand advocated in her writings, in which she called for people to think for themselves, not to feel fear, not to have faith in authorities, and not to conform. There is a great deal of tragic irony in this fact. The Randian irony is particularly painful because it plays right into the hands of Objectivism's relativist critics, who claim that if there is an objective truth then everyone will have to blindly obey it as an authoritative dogma. For Objectivism to resist this criticism the movement must combine objectivity with the possibility of debate and dissent. Just because there is an objective truth doesn't mean that everything is obvious and that everyone should think the same thoughts: that is a clear recipe for conformity, not individualism. Individualism should mean that everyone tries to express their own unique, special voice, not that everyone tries to copy Rand. And you don't have to agree with Rand about every little detail in order to be an admirer of Rand's.

This leads me to the observation that both Rand's admirers and her critics often make the same mistake: they equate the founder of Objectivism with the living embodiment of Objectivism. In a religion which worships its founder there is no difference between the idea and the savior, but with a non-religious philosophy this should not be the case. Objectivism's enemies try to attack Objectivism by demonizing Rand, and her supporters attempt to promote Objectivism by deifying Rand. Both approaches are mistaken; one should praise Rand's ideas, not Rand herself. There is no principle which states that the originator of a belief is also going to be a good example of what that belief looks like when it is put into practice. Of course, some Objectivists believe that Objectivism is suitable only for the elite few, the creative geniuses of this world, and they view Rand as a member of their little clique of super-humans, according to which Rand is a living embodiment of her ideas. However I believe that Objectivism is a philosophy useful for all human beings and so I dispute that viewpoint.

Furthermore, turning the debate about Objectivism into a debate about Rand demeans Objectivism's ideas, which hurts the movement because it is Objectivism's ideas that are truly unique and exceptional. Very few people are Objectivists because they met Rand personally and liked her (in fact, historical biographies paint a picture of a person who was at times rude, arrogant, and unlikeable). Rand's followers are more frequently attracted because they read her novels and were enthralled by the ideas presented in the texts. Rand was a talented philosopher and novelist, but it only helps her critics if we allow the debate over Objectivism to shift from the logic of rational self-interest and the ethical virtues of free trade into a debate over Rand's love life.

I believe that it should be possible to love Rand's ideas and hate Rand herself. I think that if Rand had met me she probably would have condemned me for having independent thoughts that disagreed with her own ideas. I almost certainly would have joined her movement and later been "excommunicated." Yet this does not make me like her philosophy any less, because I believe that Objectivism is a set of ideas and is not a cult of personality. What Rand might have condemned me for does not bother me. The Ayn Rand Institute sees no difference between humanizing Rand, which is necessary in order to appreciate her ideas as separate from her, and demonizing Rand, which is what Rand's critics do to attack her ideas. The logic of Rand's ideas is very difficult to argue against, and it is much easier to attack Rand's flaws as a human being than to debate her ideas on their own terms, so the Ayn Rand Institute does the critics of Objectivism a huge favor by allowing the debate over Objectivism to remain a debate about Rand and her life rather than a debate about the truth or falsehood of abstract ideas and principles.

It is worth going off on a small tangent here to discuss who is an Objectivist and who is not. I must admit that I am myself not an Objectivist in the traditional sense of the word because Rand wrote one book, "Introduction to Objectivist Epistemology", which makes arguments that I have never found to be persuasive, e.g. I do not believe in axioms. It is not that I don't believe in "A is A" and "existence exists," my disagreement is that I believe that existence and identity can be proved, assuming that you define "proof" in the right way, whereas Rand said these principles were incapable of proof, which to me means they must be taken on faith, something I find to be a contradiction within Rand's philosophy. I agree with Rand's political, ethical and metaphysical ideas, but I have a different, more Aristotelian point of view on epistemology. I must also admit that John Locke has had significant influence on my political beliefs, and that I am a big fan of Friedrich Nietzsche (whom I believe had a strong influence on the young Ayn Rand, although the adult Rand would only ever admit to being influenced by Aristotle).

I believe that it is useful to rate how much you agree with Rand on a scale of 1 to 10, with 10 being total agreement and no difference between your beliefs and Rand's, 7 being a healthy respect for Rand, 5 being agreement with about half of Rand's ideas, 3 being minor agreement with Rand on some issues and 1 being total disagreement with Rand. (One might call this the world's shortest philosophical quiz.) The Ayn Rand Institute zealots would define only 10's as real Objectivists, and would call everyone at 8 or below mere "admirers" of Rand's, but not Objectivists. I would say that more realistically, if we do not want to be fanatical dogmatists and we are not so insecure with ourselves as to be obsessed with ideological purity, that we can call anyone from around 6 (which means that more than half of your ideas resemble Rand's) up to 10 as Objectivists, and people from 5 to 3 would probably also be people whose support we could draw upon for certain issues. And if you posit a hypothetical scenario according to which people are evenly distributed along the spectrum from 1 to 10, then a more welcoming definition could group a substantially larger number of people within the movement's ranks than a narrow definition, which ties into the question of how to popularize the movement. If Objectivism is defined, not as a way to copy Rand, not as a cult of personality, but as a system of principles and a way of interacting with reality, if the focus is on our relationship to reality rather than our relationship to Rand, then a broader definition of Objectivism is called for. If Objectivism is defined as the philosophy of objective reality then it becomes possible to say that in some instances Rand was wrong about what Objectivism says, whereas if Objectivism is defined as "the philosophy of Ayn Rand" then Rand was infallible and Objectivism is simply a way to copy Rand. I do not mean to say that Objectivism can ever separate itself from Rand's legacy, but it is certainly the case that Objectivists can be defined, not by their relation to Rand, but by their using and developing a relation to reality that was pioneered by Rand. Objectivism as such is a relationship between a person and reality, not a relationship between a follower and Ayn Rand, and this distinguishes it from religions and cults of personality which are mere shadows of their messiahs and founders.

One might think that in presenting this problem as I have, I am advocating the idea that the open system factions of Objectivism, such as Sense of Life and the Atlas Society, should fight the Ayn Rand Institute for leadership in the Objectivist movement. This is not the case. I believe that the analogy between Objectivism and Christianity lends a great deal of insight to understanding the various groups within the movement and what the future has in store for them. In Christianity some Christians want an authority who will give them orders, while other Christians want to speak directly to God, and so both the Catholic Church and their Protestant rivals fill a need inherent in human nature, and each movement has a strong base and is not going away anytime soon. Indeed, some psychologists would say that conformity and obedience to authority are inherent in human nature, in which case those who pander to these traits will always draw a crowd. But Protestants are no less influential in the world because the Catholics outnumber them. Similarly I would argue that it is healthy for there to be many Objectivist groups without central authority, in the spirit of healthy competition, even if some groups have fatal flaws, and that the job of the open-system Objectivists is not to replace the Ayn Rand Institute, but is merely to present an alternative for those who want one. Christianity is not weakened by having many different sects, in fact it is strengthened by internal competition and by having a wide range of alternatives for the people who want them. The Objectivist movement as a whole can appeal to all people and approach the staying power of Christianity only by having a diversity of groups and styles. Those people who want to worship a savior and communicate with reality through intermediaries can choose the closed-system Objectivism, while those who want to communicate with reality directly will choose the open-system Objectivism. Furthermore, just as there are many different Christian sects each founded by a founder who combined a unique personality with a unique theosophy, so I would posit that, in the future, Objectivism will probably split up into more sects, representing the different psychological needs of every kind of person who might seek Objectivism—just as SOLO appeals to people who want an open system but ideological passion. (Obviously, I do not intend to imply that Objectivism is a religion, because religions are by definition based on faith; however it does have various elements in common with religion as a system of belief that people seek to put into practice in their lives, and so the Objectivism-Christianity analogy is an interesting way to predict the future of the movement.)

Rand's second mistake was encouraging her followers to deal with critics, opponents, and everyone who disagreed with her by directing condemnation and outrage at them, and also allowing her followers to develop an unhealthy sense of arrogance. Some Objectivists view all the people who don't agree with them as stupid or evil. I argue that this is a central stumbling block in popularizing Rand's philosophy. One of the attractions of Objectivism is that it offers a theory of good and evil as absolute rather than relative, but as grounded in reason instead of faith. Good and evil are absolute, but we need to think about how we should put this idea into practice. There is a difference between being stupid on the one hand and being ignorant on the other hand, and there is also a difference between being evil or simply being misguided. Ignorant people lack the knowledge needed to know what the good thing to do is, rather than being too stupid to be able to know. For example, a highly intelligent person might make a bad mistake if they trust bad advice, as for example the ethical lessons received from their teachers or parents. Misguided people intend to do good, but they lack any rational knowledge of the good, as opposed to evil people who intentionally want to cause pain. Most of the people in this world are ignorant and misguided, not stupid and evil.

By viewing all non-believers as stupid and evil Objectivists come to a very pessimistic view of humanity, a view of humanity as being beyond help. A society that could build the skyscrapers of the Manhattan skyline is not hopeless, and Rand might have agreed with me on that. You cannot spread a message of hope to someone if you consider them to be hopeless. Spreading the Objectivist message requires an optimistic view of human nature, a belief that other people can become more rational if they are exposed to reason. Condemning everyone who disagrees with you as "evil" encourages those who already believe as you do, but it reduces the possibility of ever persuading someone who disagrees with you to change their mind, and, more importantly, it scares away people who might be undecided and who quite possibly would have listened to you with a sympathetic ear.

I will admit that there may be devoted, committed socialists and other foolish people who cannot be persuaded to change their minds and who rightfully deserve to be condemned. But loudly declaring "YOU ARE EVIL!!!" might be counterproductive, even though it is satisfying. I believe that the vast majority of people in America are undecided on key ethical and political issues, or even if they have an opinion they might be capable of changing their opinion, and fiery condemnation merely scares people away when we should be reaching out to them. Condemning people who are merely ignorant and misguided isn't fair from an ethical point of view, and drives away some people who might otherwise be persuaded. For a philosophy of reason, rational discussion should be a preferable alternative to condemnation in most situations, and if your opponent is willing to talk to you then you are probably obligated to have a rational debate with them. One problem is that rational discussion requires you, not to agree with your opponents, but at least to understand where they are coming from and to recognize the reasoning and justifications, flawed though they may be, behind their arguments, which requires treating them with some respect.

One other related concern should be considered in assessing the popularity of Objectivism, a concern that I think of as Rand's arrogance issue. Rand's philosophy presents itself as something that is suitable for the smartest, most creative, most talented people, the people who through their ability should easily become rich and successful. Indeed, it seems fair to say based on the historical materials that Rand had a high opinion of herself, and she gave her pride to her followers as part of her legacy. Pride is an admirable trait, but when taken to an extreme it can lead to something that might be called elitism, a belief that Objectivism is for the noble few, and that Objectivists should treat the common masses, the human herd, with scorn and disdain. (As a scholarly aside, I believe that Rand inherited this problem from the influence of Nietzsche, and that it is not attractive in either Rand or Nietzsche, although I'm very fond of both of them.) I believe that some Objectivists view the majority of humanity as idiots or a herd of helpless sheep. If this is the case then it is no wonder that Objectivism is not more popular. Popularity is being liked by the majority, which is not going to happen if you hate the majority. There are two factors that may be helpful in correcting the problem of elitism. The first factor is an understanding that this is a profoundly pessimistic view of humanity, and Objectivism needs to present itself as a philosophy of hope and optimism.

The second factor lies in reinterpreting some of Rand's ideas. One can interpret Rand as claiming that a person's intelligence is predestined and genetically determined. If that is so, then some people are smart and some people are stupid, that can never change, and the stupid people, the masses, will never have any use for Objectivism. But if you interpret "volitional consciousness" as free will in the literal sense, you can argue that a person's intelligence is based on the choices that they make, and that if you choose to think more you can make yourself smarter. If that is true then Objectivism can offer a hope to everyone that if they choose to think, they can become more intelligent and become better people in the process. I believe that this also applies to the political and economic sphere, in this way: free-market capitalism was presented by Rand as something useful for the rich, but if Objectivism is to become more popular, the argument must be made that capitalism also benefits the middle-class and, perhaps most importantly, that it benefits the poor. (This argument can be made, although I won't do so here; see for example my nonfiction books on economics, which are available in bookstores.) Christianity is so popular because it has a message that appeals to everyone: believe in Christ and you will go to Heaven. That proposition might not be true, but it is persuasive. Objectivists must counter that with a message that is simple and also has universal appeal: if you think intelligently and behave rationally then you will live a happy, satisfying life.

Aristotle once said: "Plato is dear to me, but the truth is dearer still." One can say something similar about Rand: she was brilliant, but she did make mistakes. If

Objectivism is to become more popular then Objectivists must avoid authoritarian leadership and be more welcoming and less condemnatory. Rand's mistakes have a very real effect, but as time passes and we enter the Post-Randian era of Objectivism that effect might fade away. If we focus on the future of Objectivism, one day Objectivism will be more than merely the words and ideas of one person, it will be the words and ideas of many different people. Some movements never get over the deaths of their founders, in fact one might say that Christianity is still in mourning for the death of Christ, but if we are willing to be brave and bold we can move beyond the shadow of Rand while still paying tribute to the vision of life and happiness that she preached in her books. If Objectivism is merely Rand's cult of personality then it has no future after Rand's death, whereas if it is truly a philosophy, if it is a set of ideas, then it can live and grow and evolve and remain relevant for centuries to come. Until Rand's two mistakes are corrected, until there is a vibrant non-authoritarian Objectivist movement and a willingness to reach out to the masses, Objectivism will suffer from a popularity problem. "Closed-system" Objectivists tend to refuse to acknowledge that Rand was capable of making mistakes. "Open-system" Objectivists are smarter when it comes to this issue. Objectivism has the inherent possibility of becoming very popular, because Objectivist beliefs do not require faith or divine revelation to be known. Objectivist truths can be sensible to anyone with a functioning reasoning mind, and so every human being could potentially become an Objectivist. But until these internal problems with promoting Objectivism are resolved, Objectivism will have a problem gaining in popularity.

CHAPTER THREE: THE CHICKEN HAWK

I recently had a chance to catch some of the movie "The Passion of Ayn Rand" on television. I do not see any need to do a review of the entire movie, but there is one aspect of the movie that needs to be addressed. Here I am not going to do something that other people do, which is to defend Rand's behavior regarding the Rand-Branden split: I think that Rand behaved very foolishly at that time, but it is for each person to form their own independent evaluation on that topic. However, there is a subtle (or not so subtle) implication in the movie about the way in which Rand influences people. Nathaniel Branden, in the way in which he is swayed by Rand, represents the way in which Objectivists are swayed by the philosophy of Objectivism, and it isn't pretty.

The criticism, as I see it, goes like this: Objectivism sways teenaged boys, because teenagers are at that age when they are seeking the ability to understand the world, and Objectivism offers an easy, simple, convenient understanding. Objectivism makes its followers feel like they are geniuses, when they are really not, and it has an element of the macho to it, which appeals to intellectual boys who need a way to assert their masculinity. I don't agree with any of these ideas, but they need to be rebutted, and a larger issue comes into focus from this: why does Objectivism appeal to teenagers more than it does to adults? This tendency leads some to view Rand as a "chicken hawk," someone who preys upon children.

First I will briefly address the concerns raised in the movie. Objectivism, although part of its appeal is the claim to be able to explain everything, and to do so in such a way as to be rational and persuasive, is not a "quick fix" for curiosity. This is because Objectivism, in contrast to some other schools of thought, tells you to think for yourself and figure things out for yourself and come to your own conclusions. Christianity, for example, offers a simple "quick fix" for curiosity, and it also brainwashes children. Objectivism is far different. The problem, of course, is that the orthodox Objectivist movement, the "closed-system" faction, has never put that part of Objectivism into practice: they don't think for themselves, they blindly obey what Ayn Rand said as if it were gospel, and they have developed a deserved reputation as a cult-like atmosphere. But this is a problem with putting Objectivism into practice, not with the theory itself: the theory calls for Objectivists to be curious, to look that things critically, to explore the world, and the failure to do this contradicts the philosophy.

Part of the lure of Objectivism is that it presents itself as a philosophy for those who are smart, and, by implication, for the smart few who are smarter than the stupid masses. Objectivism does not require you to claim to be a genius, but it comes close. But the fact is that the truth is not simple, it is complicated, and you do have to be intelligent to understand it. Thus, Objectivism appeals to people who really are intelligent, not just to people who want to feel smart but are really mediocre and stupid. Of course the problem with this is that some Objectivists have turned the philosophy into an elitist system that looks down on or condemns the majority of humanity, which I view as a very foolish attitude. But that is another problem with practice, not theory.

Third, Objectivism has a unique appeal for boys because it gives intellectuals a way to be macho. This is a strain in Objectivism that I believe comes from the influence of Nietzsche on Rand. But I don't see this as a valid criticism: after all, a philosophy should tell you to be strong rather than weak; if it doesn't it is trying to make you soft and fragile. And Objectivism certainly welcomes women to its ranks. There is what could be interpreted as an anti-feminist perspective in some of Rand's ideas, but none of those ideas are central to the philosophy, and it would be foolish to think that women can't be Objectivists when Rand herself was a woman.

Now we come to my main point, an analysis of the reasons why Objectivism appeals more to teenagers than to adults. The "chicken hawk" criticism is inaccurate, because it assumes that youths fall for Objectivism because they are ignorant, inexperienced, naïve and gullible. I see a different set of reasons, both for why Objectivism appeals to youth and why many adults leave the philosophy in their later years.

I believe that there are three reasons why Objectivism appeals to teenagers, one psychological and one cultural.

The first reason is that they are at an age when the most conceptual mental abilities develop in human beings, leading them to seek an understanding of the world and, in accordance with human nature, the understanding that they seek is naturally a rational one.

The second reason is that they have not yet become disillusioned with life as a result of the stagnant cultural and philosophical establishment that surrounds them, and they have not yet been brainwashed by the predominant anti-Objectivist forces, such as religion or socialism. Teenagers are, in an intellectual sense, innocent and not yet corrupt, because they have not yet been corrupted by the intellectual influences of anti-reason systems of thought. At the precise point when a human being begins to think, that human cannot yet have thoughts that are faulty or misleading. This is why the point when a person begins to think is the exact time when the unobstructed truth is mostly likely to take root in the mind. Objectivism certainly cannot be accused of brainwashing children, the way a cult does. Objectivism is something that people choose, it is not something that is forced upon anyone: if you don't want to read the book, you put it down and stop reading.

The third reason is that Objectivism is a philosophy of ideals and principles and integrity, which calls for a man to live by his code of ethics with no contradictions. As soon as a person sells out and betrays his ideals and gives in to pressure against his values, he will find himself hating that code of values which he used to love back before he "sold his soul", so to speak. A teenager tends to still have his sense of honor and honesty, but the older one becomes, the more one is in a situation where there is some sort of convenience or success to be had from selling out or accepting and condoning a contradiction. As such, a teenager has not yet given in and developed internal contradictions, and so is still in a position whereby he can accept Objectivism as his philosophy.

But why, then, do so many adults who are influenced by Objectivism as a youth abandon the philosophy is their later years, as adults? The answer to this question is crucial, because the problem must be solved if Objectivism is to become more popular. I see four factors at work: integrity, fear of death, conformity to peers, and the incompleteness of Objectivism.

A teenager still has his sense of idealism, of his capacity to live life consistently by a code of ethics that calls for individual integrity and intellectual honesty. This is precisely the "youthful innocence" that attracts people to Rand, which her critics call naive gullible ignorance, and which her advocates correctly identify as merely not having sold one's soul to the Devil yet. But, along a time line, over every given period of time, a person will face a moral challenge, a test of one's moral character (think Wynand at the end of *The Fountainhead*), and, as soon as a person caves in an conforms on one issue, as soon as a person accepts or condones or embraces irrationality on any one issue or behavior or decision or thought, then they can no longer live the philosophy without a contradiction, at which point they can no longer be good Objectivists, and the philosophy serves merely as a reminder of the person they were before they sold out, so they come to hate it. Over every period of time, one will face a moral challenge, therefore, the older into adulthood one gets, the more opportunities one has to sell out. This explains why, the older into adulthood one becomes, the more likely one is to have abandoned Objectivism.

Note that, yes, Rand does call for perfect rationality, 24 hours a day, 7 days a week, and she says as much in the scene where Dr. Stadler confronts John Galt near the end of *Atlas Shrugged*. I think hers is too high a standard, and I do not believe that total perfection is realistic for most, perhaps all, people, so, to say that as soon as one is imperfect one loses the philosophy, would mean that most people can't be good Objectivists. I oppose that position, and favor what I call "Objectivism for everybody". Total perfection is not necessary, but when faces a true moral test, a serious and significant one, and one fails the test, at that point the philosophy is lost. One need not be inhumanly perfect, like a robot that mindlessly obeys its programming, to be a good Objectivist, but neither can one be an Objectivist if one has embraced something that is true evil according to the tenets of the philosophy, such as a fundamental conforming or lying or tolerating irrationality for one's own convenience or some short-sighted benefit or social approval.

The most simple factor is the fear of death. Teenagers tend to be full of life and to not think about getting old or dying. After all, when you are that young, death seems very far away, so far off that it might as well not exist. But once you reach your thirties, forties or fifties, you are not so young anymore, and old age looms on the horizon. The fear of death always has and always will lead in one direction: towards religion. As much as you might understand that death is a fact that your subjective beliefs cannot help you to escape, there is always the temptation to believe in a spiritual afterlife as a way to cope with the fear of death. This leads people away from Objectivism and towards religion. There is no easy way to put a stop to this problem: after all, it takes incredible strength of mind to have courage in the face of death.

The next factor is conformity. Extensive experimentation in the science of psychology has offered scientific proof of something that was already obvious to anyone with eyes: that human beings have a tendency to conform to the behavior of those around them. It is all well and good to believe in some incredible book when you are a teenager, but to be an adult and to be scorned and disrespected for having some weird, strange system of beliefs is very disheartening. The vast majority of human beings don't believe in Objectivism and reject its key ideas: how could all of those people possibly be wrong? Here, of course, there is something that we can do to help fix this problem, by making Objectivism more popular and by creating opportunities for Objectivists to meet with each other, interact, and gain support and not feel completely isolated and alone.

Another reason, the one that some Objectivists may disagree with, is my belief that the system of thought known as Objectivism is not perfect, is not complete, and still has some holes. I believe that there are some areas where Rand did not fully explain everything, there are some areas where she is very questionable (such as her views on sexuality) and I also believe (and here I will startle some of the Objectivists reading this) that Rand made several serious philosophical mistakes, especially in the details of her epistemology as she worked them out in *Introduction to Objectivist Epistemology*. (I won't go into the details here, since that isn't what this is about.) Even if you dispute that, it is easy to see that many, perhaps most Objectivists, know a whole lot about theory and remarkably little about putting it into practice. It is all well and good to believe in "reason," but if you don't use reason to make choices in your everyday life then "reason" remains merely an empty word, an abstract concept ungrounded in reality. Similarly, if you let the leaders of the Objectivist movement do your thinking for you, then you aren't putting the theory of individualism into practice. Many Objectivists find it difficult to live an Objectivist life, to practice Objectivism, and so step by step they drift away from the philosophy, until one day they abandon it completely.

This problem is worst for those who consider Objectivism to be a "closed system." They believe that the theory is perfect, flawless, and unchanging, like the word of God, and so when they come upon a reality that contradicts the theory, they abandon the theory as completely wrong, instead of integrating the new material into the theory to modify and improve it. Yet this contradicts something that Rand might have said herself, such as, for example, that when you encounter a new context it may be necessary to revise your knowledge.

Putting a system of thought as complicated as Objectivism into practice is tricky, even though some people assume that it is simple. On the subject of free market capitalism, it sounds simple in theory, but it gets complicated in practice: for example, how do you prevent stock market fraud without the Securities and Exchange Commission? There are problems with the theory, but the solution is to think more about the theory, not to abandon the theory. Or regarding your own life: if you can choose a career where you will make lots of money but you will hate your job, or one where you can be passionate about what you do but where you will be poor, which should you choose? Arguments can be made for either side; the only argument I disagree with is the one that claims that the answer is easy and simple and requires no deep thought (as if, for example, the choice that Roark made is one that automatically applies for everyone).

Here also something can be done to fix this problem. We need thinkers who are brave enough to do new things with Objectivism, to tackle problems, to expand it, and to offer ideas that can help Objectivists to lead a distinctly "Objectivist" way of life. This can never be done so long as the "closed system" attitude rules Objectivism, but as time passes I believe that open system Objectivism will gain in prominence.

In conclusion, while I don't think that there is any truth to the "chicken hawk" accusation that some make against Rand, I do believe that Objectivists can gain something interesting by thinking about this issue. I also believe that more can be done so that the people who take to Objectivism when they are young can stick with it as they grow older.

CHAPTER FOUR: WHO IS AN OBJECTIVIST?

My beliefs are not identical with Ayn Rand's beliefs. Not only are my beliefs not identical, but there are a few significant differences, most especially in the area of epistemology. So am I allowed to call myself an "Objectivist"? Rather than making a specific defense of my claim that I am an Objectivist, I feel that it is necessary to examine what we mean by "Objectivist," and who is an Objectivist and who is not. This is a question of what the "distinguishing characteristic" is on the basis of which we can say "yes, he is an Objectivist, but no, she is not." To do this we must arrive at a definition of "Objectivism."

There are two sets of distinctions that are important regarding the definition of Objectivism. The first distinction is whether Objectivism is defined as "the philosophy of Ayn Rand," in other words whether the term "Objectivist" reduces to the term "Randian," or whether Objectivism is defined as that philosophy whose fundamental position is that reality exists objectively. If the first is true, then one is defined as an Objectivist by one's relationship to Ayn Rand. If the second is true, then one is an Objectivist on the basis of the content of one's philosophical beliefs, in other words, if you believe the Objectivist positions then you are an Objectivist. This defines Objectivism on the basis of your relationship to reality.

The second distinction is whether we want to define Objectivism by the content of our thought, or by the method of our thinking. We can define Objectivism based on a certain philosophical content. Or we can define Objectivism as whatever content is arrived at by means of a certain mental process, a process that consists of logic and reasoning based on sensory experience. Which of these paths we go down determines our ideas about who is an Objectivist and who is not.

Let's examine the first distinction. It should be clear that the first definition of Objectivism, defined as the philosophy of Ayn Rand, leads to the "closed-system" approach to Objectivism embodied by the Ayn Rand Institute, and that the second definition, by content, leads naturally to an "open-system" approach, espoused by various groups. If Objectivism is defined as the philosophy of Ayn Rand, then the standard of whether or not you are an Objectivist is your relationship to Rand. The closer you are to Rand, and the closer your ideas are to Rand's ideas, the more you are an Objectivist. This idea leads logically to an approach to Objectivism that is based on your copying Rand in as great detail as possible. This approach creates a separation from reality: instead of thinking your own thoughts and approaching philosophy from the point of view of creating a relationship between your thoughts and reality, in other words with the focus of knowing reality, you approach philosophy as a follower, as a believer in a prophet, and your focus is on your relationship with your prophet, not with reality. If this definition is true then there can only ever be one real, true Objectivist, Rand herself, since only she has total knowledge of the philosophy defined as the beliefs of Rand, and the rest of us can only ever be mere "students of Objectivism." This brand of "Objectivism" is no different from "Randianism," and could be called Randian Objectivism. Sadly, if this is true then the philosophy of Objectivism died when Rand died.

A critic might say: well, after all, isn't it true that Objectivism is the philosophy created by Rand? To which we can reply yes, it is, but that isn't it's defining characteristic. The second approach, the "open-system" approach, defines Objectivism not as the philosophy of Rand, but as that philosophy characterized by specific philosophical positions. These positions are: belief in an objective physical reality, the power of reason based on sensory experience, an ethics of rational self-interest, and the value of capitalism. Which view among these is the most fundamental? I would say that all of the positions are important, but the most fundamental is the belief in objective reality, which is precisely why it is called "Objectivism."

In a general sense, it would seem clear to say that people who share those views, who have those beliefs in common, have something significant in common, something that enables us to say "those people are Objectivists." This enables us to say that not every Objectivist must be exactly the same and believe exactly the same thing (which is a recipe for conformity), but that if they have that same general belief, the specific details of their beliefs might vary considerably. The logical result of this "open-system" approach is that instead of being obsessed with who can be more like Rand or who can be a more loyal follower of Rand's, we become concerned, not with Rand, but with reality and our knowledge of it. We can get knowledge of reality directly, and not by means of Rand as an intermediary.

This creates a distinction between closed-system, Randian Objectivism and open-system post-Randian Objectivism. Only by accomplishing this new definition can we make the defense of Objectivism be about defending a specific set of ideas, rather than defending the life and actions of a single person, Ayn Rand. If Objectivism is defined as an intellectual content, then the philosophy stands or falls by the truths of its ideas, not by the glory or sexual deviancies of the philosopher who created those ideas. The benefit of the open system approach is that it makes Objectivism a living philosophy, something that can grow and evolve, which is the way that living systems of thought function.

A critic might reply: yes, but if we are Objectivists, don't we believe that all, or most, of what Rand said is true? So isn't it natural for all Objectivists to have the same beliefs, which happen to also be the beliefs that Rand had? In response to this I want to introduce an idea that I refer to as "Randian irony." Rand advocated individualism, and yet her followers create conformity in their attempts to follow her. Rand told everyone to think for themselves, and yet her followers act this out by relying upon Rand to do their thinking for them. If someone gives you an order that consists of "Don't obey orders!" there is a certain irony to it, the irony of obeying disobedience. A failure to cope with this irony lies at the heart of problems that plague many Objectivists and also the Objectivist movement as a whole.

But I think that the second distinction I introduced is useful in overcoming the problem of Randian irony. So long as Objectivism is defined as a content, there will always be the question of who decides what content is or isn't in, and how much content you need to qualify. The solution is to look at method as well as content. I argue that Objectivism is a specific content, to some degree, but also that it is a specific method. The method, in simple epistemic terms, is to apply reason to the physical world and learn the truth about objective reality by using logical thought to analyze your sensory experience. But more generally, in ethical terms, the method is intellectual individualism: you don't base your thoughts on those of others, you don't let other people do your thinking for you, instead you do your own thinking and draw your own conclusions, and you aren't afraid if that puts you on the opposite side from the majority. As such, Objectivism is different from every other system of thought, and it cannot be defined in such a way as to have organized leadership and a structural hierarchy, since every individual has the same relationship to reality, and every human being's reason has equal validity. As Objectivists we can have political leaders, but not philosophical leaders, because any philosophical leader would try to do our thinking for us. Objectivist philosophers can try to persuade us by rational discourse, but they cannot have intellectual authority over us.

So even if Rand were completely right about everything, even if Rand was a perfect philosopher, and the truth was precisely what she claimed it to be, (which I don't believe,) we would still need to arrive at the truth by means of the right method. If we reason the truth for ourselves, then we know it, but if we believe the truth only because Rand told it to us, we are what Rand would have criticized as mere "parrots," people who have some idea of the truth but who do not fully understand the truth. Yet this is what the closed-system approach leads to.

One can see this in a quote from Galt's speech: "*Whose* reason? The answer is: *yours.* No matter how vast your knowledge or how modest, it is your own mind that has to acquire it. ... Your mind is your only judge of truth—and if others dissent from your verdict, reality is the court of final appeal." (*Atlas Shrugged*, page 935, Signet paperback edition.) Rand says that you should do your own thinking, not that she should do your thinking for you, and that you have a direct intellectual relationship to reality, not a relationship that goes through her as the prophet. (Of course, in her book *The Passion of Ayn Rand*, Rand's close associate and biographer Barbara Branden recounts that, in person, Rand did not behave that way, often demanding that people obey her edicts without reason, and Rand even took offense when someone cited the above quote from *Atlas Shrugged* back to her in a defense of their right to disagree with her. That having been said, Objectivists must concern themselves with the philosophy as expounded in Rand's books, not from the idiosyncrasies of Rand's personal behavior and private life. It is from Rand's books, not from interacting with Rand in person, that one derives one's desire to learn about Objectivism.)

From this it is clear that intellectual individualism is fundamental to Objectivism. In this respect I believe that Objectivism is unlike every other philosophy or religion ever created. Every prophet and philosopher in the history of humanity has told people what to think, whereas Objectivism tells you to think for yourself. So it is no wonder that some people have been confused by this aspect of Objectivism. But one can hardly believe that anyone could put intellectual individualism into practice and yet fail to see the appeal of the "open-system" approach to Objectivism.

I think that if we define Objectivism partially as a generalized content, a belief in objective reality, reason, rational self-interest, freedom, and capitalism, but that if we also include a methodology of intellectual individualism in our definition, we can achieve a definition of Objectivism that will let us effectively identity who is and isn't an Objectivist, without excluding people unnecessarily or creating a cultish atmosphere. This is the logical solution to the Randian irony, to define Objectivism by including independence as a method. Thus, if my method is sound, even if my conclusions lead me to philosophical content that differs sharply from Rand, so long as I have the right method and the right general beliefs I am still an Objectivist.

In arriving at a definition, we must conclude by examining what our purpose is with the term "Objectivist." If our purpose is to preserve ideological purity and to exclude from the movement anyone who is different from us or who doesn't agree with us, then the "closed-system" approach is preferable. But if our purpose is not to keep others away from us, but is, instead, to connect with other people, to include others in our community and find a way to connect with other Objectivists, then the "open-system" approach is desirable. If we want Objectivism to become more popular and to go from the a strange idea at the radical fringe to something more widespread and mainstream, which should be our goal, then we need a definition that brings us as close to this as possible, and which is as wide and accepting as possible.

Also, aside from a merely pragmatic definition, we must see what our concepts refer to in reality. There are two kinds of Objectivists, the Randian Objectivists and the Post-Randian Objectivists who practice intellectual individualism, the closed-system Objectivists and the open-system Objectivists. The Randians are defined by their relation to Rand, but, ironically, it is the Post-Randian Objectivists who actually put Rand's theories into practice in a consistent, logical manner. If a person believes in all the right Objectivist content but arrives at it from the wrong method, by believing what Rand said without giving the issues any independent critical thought, we don't want to say that such a person is not an Objectivist, but we can say that there is something wrong with this person's approach to Objectivism. Fortunately it is possible for human beings to think for themselves, Rand very clearly told her followers to think for themselves, and so this problem should easily be corrected.

CHAPTER FIVE:
PRACTICAL IDEALISM

In this paper I am going to argue that there is a gap between theory and practice in Objectivism. Objectivists are very clear about what theory to believe, but there is not a great deal of attention paid to how to put that theory into practice. Because of this, Objectivists tend to be impractical idealists. I claim that this is not consistent with the core of Objectivism, which calls for practical idealism, and that Objectivists should put a great deal of thought and energy into developing ways of putting Objectivist theory into practice. I believe that this would result in a new ethical approach, practical idealism. I am going to begin by explaining some reasons why Objectivists lean towards impractical idealism. Then I am going to offer some examples of situations where Objectivist theory is clear but practicality is unclear. I am going to conclude with some thoughts on how to move towards practical idealism.

Here is one reason why Objectivism is impractical idealism, and it is a complex reason with many interrelated parts. During Rand's historical Objectivist movement of the 1960's, she backed Goldwater's presidential campaign and, when he lost, she became disillusioned with political activism, and came to believe that political activism was futile until a culture shift in political philosophy was achieved. This was taught to the Objectivists in the movement in such a way as to evolve into an attitude that theory matters but practice doesn't matter. In a related syndrome, there is an idea in Objectivism that the correct way to win the debate between capitalism is the *moral* argument, not the practical argument. This idea holds that, prior to Rand, people had made the practical argument, that capitalism is more efficient, creates more wealth, makes people happier, etc., but nobody had ever made the moral argument, that capitalism is a holy ethical ideal to strive for according to a rational code of ethics. Rand was the first person to argue that capitalism is a moral ideal, and she even created her own custom code of morality, proven by her reasoned deductions, to justify that conclusion. So, in the minds of some Objectivists, being practical, or caring about results and practicality, is simply a return to that same old mistake, the practical argument for capitalism.

I think this idea is incorrect, because it assumes a concept of ideal vs. practical which is actually opposed to the core tenets of Objectivism. Objectivism holds that the standard of morality is life on Earth, and that rationality is the necessary tool for living a successful life. Therefore, if we define "moral" as "that which is right according to our code of ethics" and "practical" as "what works and achieves good results in life in reality" then the moral must necessarily be practical and, also, the practical, that which is really practical, must necessarily be moral. It's like an if-and-only-if statement: something will work in reality, if and only if it is the result of reason and rationality, therefore the moral causes the practical, and the practical requires the moral, and they go together, side by side, in real life.

Therefore, Objectivists need have no fear of the practicality argument. We must not embrace the bad element of the old pro-capitalism anti-socialism practicality argument, which was the premise of Pragmatism, that an economic system should be chosen on convenience and results without regard to truth, ideas, or ethics, or that good ends can justify bad means. But we can debate the practicality of capitalism without sacrificing our philosophy. If reason and freedom are the precondition of wealth and prosperity, which is a central argument in *Atlas Shrugged*, then the argument about whether capitalism or socialism produces better results is one which Objectivism wins every time.

Indeed, there is an idealism-practicality dichotomy here, which is, I think, as toxic to living the good life as a mind-body dichotomy. There is not a contradiction between what is true and what works, provided that one make decisions based on a rational code of ethics, and not merely on what happens to work without regard to principles and analysis. Debating practicality as such does not implicitly concede a premise of Pragmatism or amoralism, unless one has actually explicitly accepted such a premise and abandoned Objectivism. Applying this to the realm of politics, there should be no dichotomy between political "get out the vote" activism and philosophical "change people's beliefs" activism. We cannot afford to only choose one or the other, because there is a vital, urgent need for them both, right now, in today's world. The fact that, if a sea change in beliefs happened, then getting lots of votes would be much easier, is no excuse for not also doing the tough work of getting as many votes as possible now, since those votes, just like changed beliefs, make the world a better place for every individual to live in.

Consider this quote from *Atlas Shrugged*, that nobody seems to notice: "No matter what dishonorable compromise you've made with your impractical creed, no matter what miserable balance, half-cynicism, half-superstition, you now manage to maintain, you still preserve the root, the lethal tenet: the belief that the moral and the practical are opposites. Since childhood, you have been running from the terror of a choice you have never dared fully to identify: If the *practical*, whatever you must practice to exist, whatever works, succeeds, achieves your purpose, whatever brings you food and joy, whatever profits you, is evil–and if the good, the moral, is the *impractical*, whatever fails, destroys, frustrates, whatever injured you and brings you loss or pain–then your choice is to be moral or to live." (Page 968, Signet Paperback Edition.) Rand was well aware of this, but the Objectivist movement has once again proven that they don't do a detailed and careful reading of her novels, for all that they say they worship them.

Another reason why Objectivism tends towards impractical idealism is because Objectivism is an idealistic school of thought, and historically all idealism has tended to be impractical idealism. I would define idealism as any system of beliefs that believes in good and evil, assigns significance to good and evil, and paints a picture of the good as noble, worthy, heroic, and to some extent perfect and flawless. This picture of goodness is the ideal.

Every idealistic philosophy in history, prior to recent times, has been spiritual. Spiritual idealism presents a view of two worlds, one a noble, perfect spiritual world, the other a dirty, ugly physical world, and defines the good as the rejection of the physical and the achievement of the spiritual. A spiritual ideal is inherently impossible to achieve on Earth, and functions to give to humans an ideal that they cannot achieve. This forces them to fail and to feel guilty for having failed to achieve the ideal, and guilt makes them more easily manipulated. (This analysis comes from Rand's Toohey speech.) Spiritual idealism can never be practical, and contrasts with practicality, which deals with this Earth but cannot make a claim to goodness or ideals. Thus, historically, idealism has been synonymous with impractical idealism.

I am partial to Nietzsche's critique of idealism, but I believe that it applies only to impractical idealism. Objectivism can be something different, and in theory it should be something different. This is because, in contrast to spiritual idealism, Objectivism bases its ideals and its idea of goodness on this Earth, not some spiritual other world, and one of the ways that the good is defined is as that which is useful for life on this Earth. Therefore, in theory at least, it should be possible to have a goodness that is both ideal and practical, both noble and something that makes it possible to handle life in this world. However, many Objectivists, with their focus on the ideals of idealism and not on the practicality of idealism, preach a theory of "this world" without actually bothering to talk about, or be concerned with, the concrete details of how Objectivist idealism is to be put into practice.

Another reason is, ironically, the fact that Objectivists believe that one's theories have direct, significant impact on one's actions. Objectivists believe that beliefs determine behavior. As such, a good theory inspires good actions, and a bad theory, such as Communism, spawns incredible horrors. Unfortunately, the way that this idea has been developed has been, not to carefully examine the interplay between beliefs and results, but to focus all ethical scrutiny upon beliefs, acting on the assumption that all you need is the right set of beliefs and after that everything will just fall into place. Objectivists are deeply concerned with philosophy, and philosophy, as a discipline, tends to be more concerned with theory than with practice, and Objectivism seems to have acquired this unpleasant trait.

This gives rise to the Objectivist tendency to judge people based on what they believe, and only what they believe: if you believe what I believe, with no differences, you are good, but if you believe something different from what I believe, you are evil. This leads to conformity and dogmatism, but it also leads to impractical idealism, because the belief is that the right ideas will necessarily result in good behaviors, without any need to consider how those ideas are to be put into practice. I would argue that the right belief is necessary for goodness to result, but it is not sufficient: for goodness to be real, you need a good idea, and you also need to put effort into applying the good idea to make something in reality, an ethical result in your life.

This point may be illustrated by a thought experiment: assume two people, one of whom supports capitalism and the other supports socialism. But the person who supports capitalism does so because an angel came to him in a vision and told him that capitalism is God's chosen economic system, while the person who supports socialism does so as the result of a process of attempting to use reason to deduce the right economic system from a rational understanding of human nature, a process that was sincere but mistaken. Which one is closer to Objectivism? Many Objectivists would prefer the capitalist, but this is a mistake: in the first place, epistemology is prior to economics, and in the second place, the socialist can change his beliefs when reason shows him that he was mistaken, whereas the capitalist can never check his premises. If a person is judged solely by what they believe, without reference to the other details of their life, this results in a shallow, distorted understanding of right and wrong.

Some Objectivists might object at this point, and say: yes, but according to Objectivism, there is no separation between what works in theory and what works in practice, so there can be no theory-practice gap! To which I would reply, that one way to think about it is that theory is general and abstract, and practice is specific and concrete. Therefore theory, without practice, is a "floating abstraction," to quote Rand. I admit that there is no separation of theory and practice, in that what is true in theory must also be true in practice. However, you can know the theory and still not know how to use it, because you haven't thought about all the details of how to apply the theory to the set of facts and circumstances in your life. Aristotle distinguished between abstract ethical knowledge and practical ethical knowledge in that the latter required developing a "habit" of usage, and that is another useful way to think about it.

A reason for a tendency towards impractical idealism in Objectivist culture is a certain reading of *Atlas Shrugged*. In the novel, the good guys leave the irrational world behind and create a haven for rational individuals, called Galt's Gulch. Some readers long for this idealized place and apply this idea in their lives by shutting out the outside world and seeking to be only with like-minded people. This, I believe, can be done well or badly: it is commendable to seek to form a community of Objectivists, but it is problematic to cut yourself off from the rest of the world and refuse to engage other people, even those who disagree with you and whom you would condemn as irrational. Indeed, the unfortunate tendency is for Galt's Gulch to become a utopia in the Platonic sense of the word, a land of perfection compared to which this world fails miserably. This is not a trap into which one should fall, for it leads to pessimism and negativity, and it also leads the rest of the world to reject Objectivism under the idea that if you condemn me then I'll condemn you. On the topic of the interpretation of Rand's novels, I also claim that most Objectivists are too concerned with *Atlas Shrugged* and do not pay enough attention to *The Fountainhead*, the result of which is that Objectivists view their system as a purely political philosophy, rather than an ethical philosophy capable of informing difficult personal choices. Objectivism's purpose is not just to promote capitalism, it is also to improve the way that people live life in ways that are prior to political ideology.

Now let's look at some situations where theory is necessary but not sufficient to make a decision about one's behavior. Before I present these, I will offer the observation that in many cases Rand's "hierarchy of values" approach will indicate possible solutions, but that theory by itself is not sufficient to solve these problems.

One, the money clip scenario: you find a money clip at work with a hundred dollars in it. You may know who it belongs to, but you're not sure. Should you keep it or try to return it? Would keeping it be stealing? Or would it be greed?

Two, the children scenario: your eight-year-old child misbehaves. Do you try to explain to them that what they did was wrong and convince them to behave by rational argument, or do you punish them in some way? How severely should you punish them?

Three, the dating scenario: you are thinking about asking someone out on a date, and there are two possible choices. You like one person's personality and you think he/she's a nice person, but he/she disagrees with you about politics. You like the other person's political beliefs, even though you don't think he/she's a great person. Whom do you choose?

Four, the politics scenario: You are a politician, and you strongly believe in some positions that are unpopular. Do you remain true to an ideologically pure platform, or do you change your policies and make compromises in order to get elected? Which would be the right choice, considering the fact that you want to make a difference, but if you don't get elected then none of your policies will be enacted into law?

Five, the life scenario: You are in college, and you want to decide what to do with your life. You are in a band and you want to try to make it as a musician, but you are really good at math and you could become an accountant and make loads of money. As a musician you will probably go broke, but you will be doing what you love. Which do you choose?

Six, the hedonism scenario: you are overweight to the point that your health is in danger, but you really love food, especially chocolate and ice cream, and you have a slight metabolism problem that makes losing weight difficult. In order to lose weight you would have to completely give up ice cream and chocolate. Do you give up sweets and try to get healthy, or do you give up on health and just enjoy food? Which would be more in keeping with rational self-interest?

Seven, the phobia scenario: because of a traumatic childhood incident, you are terrified of spiders. You have tried to overcome this phobia but spiders still scare you. A group of your friends asks you to go hiking in the woods with them. You want to go, but your spider phobia makes you think that maybe you ought not to go. Do you go and risk being very afraid, or do you stay home and not take a risk?

My purpose in presenting these examples is not to demonstrate conclusively what the right answer is, but simply to indicate that the experiences of human life require thought and effort in order to apply abstract theories to concrete situations, and nothing that Rand said provides an obvious, blatant answer to these questions. What this establishes is that abstract theory does not automatically show you which choice to make, regardless of the practical concerns of the individuals involved, largely because the choices that stem from those theories are in no way obvious. In many situations, the proper choice will depend upon one's hierarchy of values, as for example in the dating scenario, and so the theory can only be applied in a way that is unique and different for each individual. In some situations, there will be a choice between the seemingly idealistic choice and the seemingly practical choice (as in the politics scenario and the life scenario), and an Objectivist tendency will be to choose the idealistic solution and scorn the practical solution. This, I contend, is not always the best choice, because practical idealism demands not only ideals, but results also.

In some cases, one can say that the good is "obvious," as in the hedonism example where it is obvious that you should not kill yourself for chocolate, but even in this case the situation requires thoughtful evaluation, and it may not seem so obvious to someone who is really in that situation. One might also say that these choices are misleading, because the ideal solution is not given, for example, you should do something you love and make money doing it, or a politician should have ideals and get votes. But this is a perfect example of what someone who believes in impractical idealism would say. The "perfect" solution is possible in theory, but in practice life will not always give you perfect solutions, or else you might need to work very hard in order to find them. This is why the task of applied ethics is so important and so interesting.

As a suggestion on how to move in the direction of practical idealism, I believe that one of the key concepts that needs to be examined is "perfection." Perfection, as the ideal, is that which every idealistic philosophy aims at. Spiritual idealism posits a perfection that is non-physical and can't be achieved on Earth, a perfection that belongs only to God and angels. This corresponds to a vision of human nature as weak and sinful, exemplified by the phrase "to err is human." But for an idealism that is based on life on this Earth, a radically new concept of perfection is called for. Perfection should, I believe, be defined as "the best possible state that humans can achieve." If some accomplishment is impossible then it is not perfect. Thus, if you make mistakes, but you learn from them, you can still achieve the state of perfection as defined by practical idealism, so long as you make a significant effort to be good and to improve. There should also be a certain degree to which making mistakes that is inherent in the state of perfection, because humans do not begin with knowledge from intuition, they learn from their mistakes, and so some mistakes are necessary as part of the learning process for any human endeavor. All of this leads to the idea that perfection should be defined, not as a way to make people feel guilty when they fail, but as a practical tool for living a better life.

Practical idealism, in order to be achieved, needs to shed the conception of ideals inherited from spiritual idealism and adopt a view of ideals that is grounded in life on this Earth and rooted in practical life experiences. The idea of "perfection" needs to be revised in such a way so that it is defined not as the best of all possible worlds, but is instead defined as what results when a rational human being works hard and does the best that he or she can to live a good life. We need shed the idea that the ideal and the practical are incompatible. To do this we do not need to take the real world and bend it to fit our abstract theories, on the contrary, we need to take our ideals and bring them down to the real world and apply them. In conclusion, I believe that there is a great need in the world for practical idealism, and Objectivism has the ability to satisfy this need, but this will only happen if the Objectivist movement moves away from an idealism that defies the world around us and longs for a perfect world of Galt's Gulch, and becomes a practical idealism that embraces the world and finds effective, intelligent means for living as a part of the world and enacting change in the world. Practical idealism calls upon each individual to take Objectivist theories and think about them and find ways to apply them to their the circumstances of their life. This is a task that only you can do. Nobody else, not Rand nor any other philosopher, can do it for you.

CHAPTER SIX: A CRITIQUE OF JUDGMENT

The issue of pronouncing moral judgment upon other people from an Objectivist point of view needs to be carefully examined. Below I will argue that the unintended consequences of unexamined ideas about judgment, uncritically accepted from Rand's work, are causing serious problems for the Objectivist movement. In this essay I will look at the origin of Randian judgment, and then analyze the problems which arise from Rand's concept of judgment, and how to solve these problems.

Objectivists get Rand's concept of judgment from the Galt speech in Atlas Shrugged. The speech says that man's act of living is dependent upon his mind, the primary function of which is to judge. To live, a person must pass judgment upon the world around him, and all the things in that world. The two basic judgments are: right or wrong, good or evil. To quote: "A process of reason is a process of constant choice in answer to the question: True or False?—*Right or Wrong?*" (*Atlas Shrugged*, page 935, Signet paperback edition.) In this way, judgment plays a key role in Rand's ethical theory.

I agree with the general idea that it is the purpose of the human mind to judge, that judgment is one of the key mental acts, and that proper ethical judgment is critical to an ethical life. It seems evident that rational judgment is one of the main building blocks of a reason-based ethics. But I believe that Rand misses something here, something important, an unintended consequence of her theory as it is put into practice by her followers. The problem is that Rand makes no distinction between judging inanimate objects, and judging living beings, to be more specific, she offers no special rules about passing judgment upon other human beings. In fact, she seems to say that passing judgment on everyone and everything is good; for example John Galt has judged the entire society of *Atlas Shrugged*, and everyone in that society, and deemed them unfit to survive.

But by urging Objectivists to judge everyone, and offering only two categories, right and wrong, black and white without any shades of gray, Rand's theory, as applied in the act of judging human beings, causes Objectivists to be very judgmental. There is a difference between someone who judges, and someone who is judgmental: the person who judges looks objectively at the things and people around them, and attempts to evaluate the benefits and liabilities of these things for that person. A person who is judgmental, on the other hand, goes around passing judgment on people, telling people that they are evil, and generally being self-righteous and obnoxious. The judgmental person forgets the purpose of judgment, which is practical, and gets caught up in the act of judgment itself, as if passing judgment were the end rather than the means to an end, which is rational self-interest.

Anyone reading this might identify what I have described as a problem with the Objectivist movement, particularly with its orthodox branch spearheaded by the Ayn Rand Institute. I would point to Rand's concept of judgment as a major source of the problem. The problem manifests itself in two ways: towards outsiders, Objectivists scare them away by condemning them as evil, and towards members of the movement, they scare their own kind into being obsessed with ideological purity and being afraid of being judged evil and excommunicated. This fear motivates Objectivists to become a flock of sheep shepherded by ARI's leaders.

To fix the problem, it is not enough to change our behavior: we must critically reevaluate Rand's theory of judgment. I believe that two points need to be modified: first, that human beings deserve to be in a special category of things that can be judged, and second, that within this category there should be, to some extent, shades of gray, and one should have to be specially and particularly careful before passing judgment as "evil" upon other people. One can judge others as wrong, or ignorant, or misguided, or dangerous and harmful, but "evil" is a strong word and should be reserved for those who truly deserve it. I wouldn't call someone evil unless I believed that they were deliberately and intentionally irrational and intended to cause harm to themselves and others.

There are a variety of things to consider when judging someone as "evil:" did they know any better? What were the results of their actions? Did they intend to do good, or did they intend to behave badly? Also, on a related note, it is just as difficult to judge that someone is "good," a perfect angel, when there may be evidence both for and against a person's sainthood. Being limited to only two categories, good and evil, limits us from having any kind of nuance or sophistication in our moral judgments. Most human beings are somewhere between perfection and atrocity, and they should be judged accordingly.

To give examples of this, I would say that Hitler was evil, that Gandhi was naïve but good-intentioned, and that Kant's actions involving the writing of his books have had malignant social repercussions, and have misled many people, but it is difficult to say that such was his intent. If Kant honestly believed that he was writing the truth in such a way as to help people then it is difficult to say that he was "evil," in spite of the fact that he was ignorant, misguided, and harmful. With Kant we can see that even if we want to judge someone as evil, there are still details within that idea that need to be worked out. As Objectivists we should not do away with "good and evil," we must simply refine and develop them.

There are those Objectivists who will object that there are no shades of gray, that everything is black and white. These are the people who enjoy condemning others, but these people should be willing to rationally analyze their own behavior and see if it stands the test of reason. From the point of view of judging a theory by the results of putting it into practice, we can see that Objectivist judgment needs to be rethought. If the Objectivist theory of judgment were modified in the way that I have suggested, and the new theory were put into practice, some of the more significant problems with the Objectivist movement might be eliminated.

It is perfectly legitimate to take pride in being an Objectivism and, as a part of that pride, to be loud and vocal as an Objectivist, which includes criticizing irrationality where one finds it. But, if this evolves into what I refer to as "bible-thumping," merely a desire to be as loud and visible as possible in one's condemnation of one's opponents, it can be exploited by a dangerous psychological vulnerability in the human mind. Passing judgment on others can go hand in hand with one living a rational life, but it can also be used as a substitute for living a rational life. Passing judgment on others is easier, and feels better, than the hard, difficult, painful task of making tough ethical decisions can doing things the right way, which is almost always the longer, more difficult, less pleasant way, at least in the short term, although over the long term reason and rationality are always better than giving into irrationality and conformity and doing things the easy way. If one is a loud vocal critic, waves Objectivism's sword, and one gets positive feedback on this behavior from one's fellow Objectivists, one might be tempted to forget altogether about the task of actually *being* an Objectivist, namely, looking at reality, analyzing reality by means of reason, identifying rational decisions in one's life, and then applying those rational decisions in one's behavior, against the opposition of whatever forces are assailed against you.

If Objectivists are supposed to be bible-thumping warriors who spend their time condemning and passing judgment upon others, we would expect to see this mirrored in Rand's novels. We find precisely the opposite. Take, for example, the end of *The Fountainhead*, where Roark actively attempts to forgive Wynand, despite Wynand's massive sell-out to conformity that stabs Roark in the back and costs Roark the support of the newspaper for his courtroom trial. How do judgmental Objectivists reconcile that with their beliefs? Or, in *Atlas Shrugged*, Hank Rearden's feelings of forgiveness, and, yes, love, for the Wet Nurse, in the scene where he dies, despite having spent much of the novel as a government regulator tasked with controlling Rearden's steel mill. Then there is Cherryl's suicide, which is unpardonable behavior that Rand casts in a forgiving, sympathetic light. Are Objectivists simply not reading these novels carefully, or do they ignore the bits that are inconvenient for them?

I could continue, but I feel I have proven my point. John Galt has, obviously, passed moral judgment on American society, and found it unworthy, but he is willing to forgive Dagny for making the looters' survival possible, even when she chooses to leave Galt's Gulch and continue to work for the statist establishment. The issue of judgment is a complicated one, which deserves thought and wisdom and an awareness of shades of gray, but which has been tortured into a cartoon ethics that can be applied by idiots. The bible-thumpers are a mere shadow of real Objectivism.

The bible-thumpers will say that they make the world aware of Objectivism by publicizing their repudiation of the philosophy's enemies, that anything less would be the sanction of the victim, and that their moral fervor and extremism will be watered down if they accept shades of gray. In reply, I say only that none of those considerations can come above the primary ethical rule, namely, that A is A, and one should treat reality as that thing which reality really is. If a person truly deserves moral condemnation, in reality, then condemn them. I would support that. But, if human nature, and the consideration of that individual and his scenario, is more complicated, then one's analysis of objective reality must also be more complicated.

One thinks of Rand's quote that "in a compromise between food and poison, only death will win." I do not advocate compromise, at least not on the core beliefs and tenets of the philosophy, in both ethics and in politics. But if a person has made an honest error, and is not a super-villain devil in the flesh, and there are a complicated set of factors in the analysis, then bible-thumping judgment is not what objective reality calls for. You might want to reread this passage from *Atlas Shrugged*: "Learn to distinguish the difference between errors of knowledge and breaches of morality. An error of knowledge is not a moral flaw, provided that you are willing to correct it; only a mystic would judge human beings by the standard of an impossible, automatic omniscience. ... Make every allowance for errors of knowledge; do not forgive or accept any breach of morality." (Signet Paperback Edition, page 974.)

My opponent will cite this as proof that Rand was against forgiveness, while simultaneously blanking out the entire section about errors of knowledge and the fact that one should forgive those. The bible-thumping Objectivists, while waving their copies of *Atlas Shrugged* at those whom they condemn, have not bothered to read it carefully enough to think about what is an error of knowledge, how one would identify it, how one could make every possible allowance for it, and how such behavior could be put into practice. I have called upon them for nothing more than that. For example, when an Objectivist directs his hatred towards someone for disagreeing with him, how does he know whether the person disagrees because of evil and irrationality, or merely because of ignorance and an error of knowledge? In the bible-thumpers' behavior I see no conduct that reflects Rand's theory on errors of knowledge in any way.

CHAPTER SEVEN: THE MYSTICS OF MAGIC AND THE MYSTICS OF SCIENCE

In John Galt's climactic speech in Atlas Shrugged, Ayn Rand describes two foes of capitalism, the "mystics of the spirit" (or, as Rand also put it, "witch doctors"), who promote religion, and the "mystics of muscle" or "Attilas," that is, especially, the communists, who are atheists and promote Marxist materialism as the antidote for religion. What gets lost in a lot of libertarian theory is the fact that, to take Rand's idea and expand on it, people who believe in rationality, science, and technology are not necessarily friends of liberty. Indeed, precisely the opposite is often true. Some of capitalism's most vicious enemies have come from the ranks of scientists and technologists.

Two types of mystics do exist — whom I prefer to call the mystics of magic and the mystics of science. The latter are my main subjects here.

I am an atheist. Not only do I not believe in God, but I am also of the rather abnormal (but increasingly popular) sentiment that the proposition "I know that God does not exist" can be rationally justified, i.e., atheism is knowledge and not mere belief. However, many of the people who share my view go in the opposite direction and elevate science into a new religion. Here I refer not to the cult of Scientology but to the scientific atheism of, for example, famous philosophy professor Daniel Dennett.

Let me offer two examples.

First, in a Facebook group that discusses philosophy I recently saw someone say something like this: "bitterness and sweetness do not exist, what exists is atoms and void, and sweetness is an illusion." This assertion was provided as a scientific approach to philosophy, but it manifests a desire to transform science into a new religion, a mysticism of science. Such a religion would depict the world you and I perceive as an illusion. Instead of saying that access to the hidden truth of reality is revealed by God and the Bible, the mystics of science say that revelation comes from reading science textbooks and scientific journals and knowing the results of experiments and research studies.

Mystics of science love to talk about how neurobiology has figured out all the ways that the human brain is flawed and perceives illusions. Yet, as I explain in my book "The Apple of Knowledge", the truly scientific attitude is that the sweetness of an apple does exist objectively in reality, in that the apple's sweetness, and the apple itself, which physically exists in objective reality, are one and the same thing. The apple's sweetness is what that collection of atoms tastes like when it acts as a whole upon the tongue's taste buds. In other words, qualia exist, but they are not subjective; instead the experience of something that physically exists is identical with that thing in itself, because the brain's means of perception do not alter or create the objects that are perceived. (This is the tip of iceberg, and I needed 400 pages in my book to explain what I mean; the theory is fully developed there.)

The mystics of science would reply that I am ignorant of the fact that taste comes from smell and not from taste buds, so the taste in the mouth must be an illusion. To this I reply that these hate the idea that human beings have direct access to knowledge of objective reality. I say that we can know what an apple tastes like by eating it; the idea that we cannot know, that sweetness is an illusion — this is sheer mysticism. In my opinion, these mystics of science are far worse than the mystics of magic, because at least the religious mystics are open and honest in their commitments.

Second, Daniel Dennett, a popular advocate of the movement called "New Atheism," has expressed a position that I call "biological relativism." This, basically, is the idea that reality looks the way it does because the human body and human sensory organs evolved in such a way that we humans experience this world of our experience. He has actually said that apples look red because the human brain evolved to sort edible objects by color, so that redness comes not from the apple but from the evolution of the human digestive system as expressed in the human brain's hunger regions. This means, ultimately, that the sky is blue because blueberries are blue. (See Dennett, Consciousness Explained [1992].) If that is true, then the world we experience is entirely relative to perception, is completely subjective, and is a creation of the human brain. This, to me, means that access to objective existence is impossible, since we could never get outside our brains to see reality as it exists objectively.

The only thing about Dennett's idea that is scientific is the allusion to evolution and the brain. In every other respect it is mysticism, because it denies the possibility that human beings have direct access to objective reality by means of perceiving the external world. Taking my cue from Rand, I dispute any position which defends that idea, considering it not only false but unscientific. The experience of an apple's redness and the physical reality of the apple are identical, not such that the apple itself is subjective, but such that the experienced apple is objective. Redness exists in physical objects and is not a subjective creation of the eyes, despite all objections from the mystics of science, who would lecture me about the workings of the retina, the optic nerve, and the occipital lobe. Mystics of science might say that the depth and length we perceive are illusions because our brains and eyes process the data subjectively

— despite the fact that measurements of space and time recorded by scientific instruments are accurate and objective, e.g. a building could be 100 feet long but our eyes cannot see this clearly.

Kant once helped to save religion from science by persuading people that the experience of reality is subjective and knowledge comes from intuition. Dennett, in the name of science, simply buys into this Kantian error. To me, if reality is subjective, then wishes and thoughts can control it, which is a religious worldview that tells people to seek to change their lives through the power of prayer. In contrast, if reality is objective, then it exists outside the mind, in which case science and technology are the correct approach to improving human existence, and Francis Bacon's maxim "nature, to be commanded, must be obeyed" is justified because the mind must obey reality in order to succeed. A true philosophical science says that we must learn about reality by observing the external world, instead of trying to use our minds to impose subjective phenomena onto reality.

Now let me explain why atheism has very little to do with libertarianism and, contrary to Rand's assertions, why there is no direct correlation between rationality and freedom. This is obviously true because, historically, the Marxists were (mostly) atheists, and the conservatives who have fought against socialism in America are (mostly) Christians. For one poignant case study, note that the famous science fiction author H.G. Wells was a notorious socialist, as were many men of science of his era. The trend continues to this day, as antisocialists tend to be religious, and socialists and modern liberals tend to be secular.

In The Road to Serfdom, F.A. Hayek tried to explain why men of science tend to be socialists. He argued that scientists seek order and patterns in reality, and this leads them to try using government to impose their ordered plans and schemes onto society; this is a recipe for socialism, especially in the context of the Hayekian belief that freedom is consistent with an order spontaneously emerging from chaos. Just as a scientist might want to design a new plan for a car engine to improve fuel efficiency, a scientist might also want to design a new plan for an economy to improve allocations of wealth. The problem is that a car engine is a mindless tool, whereas an economy is a collection of thinking human beings, each with his or her own plans, standards of "improvement," and rights to life, liberty, and property. Many of the bosses at the American government's regulatory agencies are scientists or technologists with advanced degrees, and many of the nonscientists have degrees in economics and mathematics. The EPA's regulators are often experts in the science of the environment and pollution, and therefore knowledgeable in chemistry, metallurgy, engineering, physics, etc. But their science does not dispose them to become libertarians.

Being a scientist, or being rational, or being an atheist, has very little to do with political support for freedom. If any group has been more responsible than others for saving America from a descent into total communism, it is the conservative movement, which is fueled by a belief, one which I think on its face is irrational and crazy, that God supports capitalism and the Bible demands that the American patriotic tradition of free market economics be defended. As Hayek has noted in his essay "Why I am Not a Conservative," the conservatives love capitalism not chiefly because of any of its virtues but only because it is the old, established, traditional system in America. This attitude is not particularly intelligent or rational, but it achieves a practical result — the defense of liberty by a vast portion of the American voters. To cite only one example, the Tea Party in the House of Representatives, backed by the Tea Party conservatives, has done much to stop Obama's socialist agenda, although there was little it could do to repeal laws that were already passed, such as Obamacare.

Without much exaggeration it can be said that, absent the conservatives, you would not be able just to go to a coffee shop and buy a cup of coffee. Instead, the atheist Marxist central planners, chosen by Obama and his cronies, would assign your beverages to you, just as they want to assign your healthcare to you, and you would drink carrot juice instead of coffee whether you wanted to or not, and see the end of a soldier's gun if you tried to escape from the socialist plan drinking. You owe your freedom to the Bible, at least to some extent, whether you like it or not.

The best defense of liberty, which most libertarians ignore or are ignorant of, is a Biblical idea, the Golden Rule. This principle of ethics asserts that you should do unto others as you would have others do unto you. In "Golden Rule Libertarianism" (Hasan [2014]), I argue that the Golden Rule's implementation in politics is, and can only be, libertarianism: if you desire the freedom to do what you want, you must let me have the freedom to do what I want; but if you force me to obey you, I will be justified in forcing you to obey me, which you cannot possibly want.

In short, the hatred of religion that is felt by some libertarians, especially those who entered the movement through Ayn Rand (but also, to some degree, through Murray Rothbard) is misplaced. If Rand's "mystics of muscle" idea is taken seriously, then there is a basis in her texts for opposing the mystics of science as fiercely and ardently as we oppose the mystics of magic.

CHAPTER EIGHT: THE BATTLE OF THE SOUL OF ATHEISM

Most people think of "atheism" as one school of thought, the school of thought that rejects God, Christianity, etc. Presumably, it then favors science as a replacement for religion. Here I will argue that there is not one, but is in fact two, types of atheism, that they are fundamentally opposed, and that they are locked in a war for the direction that atheism will take in the future. I will argue that, sadly, the wrong, misguided version of atheism is currently dominant, but I will offer hope that the less popular, more accurate type has a path to greater popularity in the future.

First, let me describe the currently dominant form of atheism, which is, I think, incorrect. I call this type of atheism by several names: nihilist atheism, geneticist atheism, amoral atheism, behaviorism, biological relativism, or naturalism.

The leaders of this type of atheism are four writers commonly referred to within the atheist movement as "The Four Horsemen of New Atheism." Their leader is Richard Dawkins, and his philosophy was best articulated in his book "The Selfish Gene." Anyone who has read my own philosophical book "The Apple of Knowledge" knows that I argue against a position that I call geneticism, and in favor of a position that I call post-geneticism. I will not go into detail, hoping that you will see the details when you buy and read my book for yourself, but I will say that "The Selfish Gene" is the most perfect, naked, unapologetic presentation of the position I refer to as geneticism.

This position posits that all human behavior is mindless, determined from physical forces without free will, amoral, and reduces to the selfish, manipulative desires of each human's genes to survive and sexually reproduce. Hence, it is geneticism, and, as atheism, it is geneticist atheism.

Because it posits that there is no code of ethics, values, or honor that governs human behavior--because, first, free will is an illusion, and all of our decisions are made by our conniving, scheming DNA, and second, every morality is simply irrational and anti-science--I also call it amoral atheism, as it posits no values other than biological evolutionary values that are inherent in all human behavior prior to our consciously made choices.

It is biological relativism in that it posits that all of reality is such only in relation to the human brain as it evolved in the context of evolution--there is no absolute truth, only truth for us humans as human DNA and human brains. It is behaviorism, in that it thinks that "the mind" and "thought" and "free will" are illusions, as explanations for human behavior, and it says that all human behavior can be predicted and measured by science, without any need for looking at minds, thought, or free will. It is naturalism, the term commonly used to describe a philosophy of the world without any spiritual element, but this goes farther and rejects ethics and values as a spiritual entity devoid of any basis in physical reality.

Now, is this also nihilism? I say yes, because the nihilists believe in nothing, and the new atheists say that there is nothing there for us to "believe in," in the sense of a morality or virtue or heroic central principle to adhere to.

In the West, for two thousand years, Christianity has laid claim to a monopoly on ethics and values. As such, when the atheists rejected Christianity, they were also tricked into abandoning ethics and values as such, thinking that morality is inherently intertwined with religion. As most religions are moralities, and most morality is religious, this is an easy mistake to make, made even easier because there is no code of ethics that is both famous, atheistic, and well-reasoned, all in one. These atheists cede morality to the realm of religious, and then assert that they reject God and accept an amoral life, where they are content to merely express their DNA and let it control them and make their decisions for them, without the ghosts and goblins of Christian morality to cloud their thinking.

These two alternatives--religious morality or amoral atheism-- were the only two choices available to us, *until* the rise of Objectivism.

In Objectivism, Rand taught us how to take science, reality, reason, and the physical world, and, from these things, to deduce a code of values, which is complete and comprehensive, that we can use, as beings with minds, thought, and free will, to guide our decision-making with ethics and values. Objectivist values are derived from reason, not from religion.

I will not elaborate upon what Objectivist ethics is, or how Rand derived values from rationality--if you need detail, go read her novels "The Fountainhead" and "Atlas Shrugged"--I will instead merely comment upon what consequences Objectivism creates for the future of atheism. Now, we have access to an atheist morality, an atheist code of ethics, and atheist virtues and values--Objectivism has created them in its proprietary code of ethics. In Objectivism, atheists have something to *believe in*.

Now what? Inevitably, there should have been a war within the atheist movement, over the use of ethics and values. But this has not happened, with both sides partially to blame.

Objectivism, in today's world, has styled itself as a politics, not an ethics. It is a right-wing politics, and so has fallen under the control of the Republicans and the right, which, as everyone knows, is ultimately loyal to Christianity, not to reason. So the right has hidden and obfuscated Objectivism as an atheist ethics, instead popularizing Objectivism merely as a free market politics--which it is, but Objectivism, when you study it, is so much more than merely a defense of capitalism.

Then, within atheism, the new atheists have taken control of the movement, and their thinkers and writers attack, reject, and insult Rand, and so urge that atheists not take Objectivism seriously, dismissing it as merely a political theory under right-wing Christian control.

So, as promised in my introduction, I arrive at my conclusion: there is a conflict between amoral atheism and Objectivist atheism, but the former, which is erroneous and misguided, dominates, and the latter is barely putting up a fight, within atheism, instead focusing on right-wing political battles. But the fight for the heart and soul of atheism should happen, and must happen, and Objectivism should win. For, as Rand observed, people follow their values and their ethics, not practicality or pragmatism, and to win the war of ideas, you must put forward a philosophy for people to believe in. An atheism where we are all the slaves of our calculating, manipulative, sometimes villainous DNA, is not something that we can believe in. Instead it is something that all naturally ethical, honorable people will reject, from a gut reaction opposed to a view of themselves as evil puppets, if not from reasoned analysis.

For atheism to overcome religion as a world philosophy, it needs values and ethics, something heroic for people to believe in to motivate them to fight for it. Objectivism offers this type of morality to atheism. It remains to be seen, then, whether the atheists will recognize Objectivism as a type of atheism, and embrace it, and whether Objectivism can evolve into a dominant flavor of atheism and get out from under the shadow of its political right-wing Christian context.

The mind-body conflict comes from philosophy. It is also present in atheism, where the new atheists claim the realm of mindless, thoughtless body, and cede the realm of mind to the religious, with the caveat that they assert that mind, like God, does not exist. On example of this is the pseudo-scientific position called "epiphenomenalism," which claims that all human behavior arises from the different biological regions of the brain, without the mind playing any role whatsoever in controlling human behavior, such that consciousness and free will are mere pointless illusions that happen to be randomly superimposed onto the brain by coincidence. These pseudo-scientists point to the scientific evidence that shows that the physical state of brains influences behavior, and then make the unjustified, wrongful inference that this proves that free will is an illusion. Religion has claimed free will as its own, in seeking its monopoly on ethics and morality, so amoralism is all that was left for the scientists. Objectivism now arises to reclaim free will, and ethics, and morality, from within the scientific physical worldview. Objectivism undertakes a great reconciliation between mind and body, so that we need not choose between life as spiritual disembodied minds plagued by physical urges, or life as mindless flesh-based robots at the mercy of dark, sinister biological drives, where our choices and beliefs are mere powerless illusions, in other words, as mind (or soul) without body or body without mind.

Instead, Objectivism offers us lives as minds *in* bodies, with values based on the physical world, with abstract thoughts and free will-based choices within a world of reason and science and physical human bodies with brains and DNA. To Objectivists, the brain and the mind are identical, so that we can say that, yes, the brain is the thing that defines and controls our behavior, but it is not a predetermined behavior defined by our neurons and brain lobes and hormones and DNA, no, *we* are the ones who control our behavior, our mind makes choices using our free will, but this free will and mind is a process which physically occurs in our brains, minds and free will exist in the physical world as our brains and bodies, minds and free will do not exist in some spiritual, religious, non-physical other dimension that hovers over the physical world like ghosts breathing life into zombies.

As such, Objectivism is the great advocate of atheism, but it is also a champion of morality, and will be, and is, roundly opposed by all those who benefit from the mind-body split, both the religious who claim the world of mind and morality, and the nihilist behaviorist new atheists who claim the realm of body and reject mind and ethics. Although the opposition to Objectivism is widespread, as it must be with what is at stake in the mind-body split, we can also see that the only future atheism has is within Objectivism, with a code of values based on reason instead of God.

If Objectivism does not emerge within the atheist movement, then the fight of atheism vs. religion remains merely a fight between nihilism vs. religious values. The majority of human beings will always choose values, will always want a code of honor to believe--as they should, to be good, ethical, honorable people, and also as they must, as a practical matter, to have an ethics to guide them and to help them make decisions in their decision-making process. This explains why at least 90% of the world's population are religious or superstitious, and less than 10% are atheists (leaving the issue of Marxism as atheism out of these numbers, for the time being), despite the fact that at least 65% of the world's population is reasonably smart and intelligent, and should have become atheists by now. For atheism to expand into a larger portion of the human race, it must put forward atheist values to believe in. Only Objectivism can achieve that.

CHAPTER NINE: THE ONTOLOGICAL ARGUMENT VS. THE PRIMACY OF EXISTENCE

It was once famously said by an atheist that he did not want to believe in the Ontological Argument, but he saw no rational way to escape it. In contrast, I have always felt it is easy to refute.

The Ontological Argument says this:

1. God is the most perfect being possible,
2. It is more perfect to exist than to not exist,
3. Therefore, God exists by definition.

So, let me muster all the best arguments against it:

1. The crucial false premise is "it is more perfect to exist than to not exist." This, I feel, is the right place to attack the argument. For example, consider this statement: "X is a perfect being, and X does not exist." If the Ontological Argument were true, then this would be inconceivable, it would not make any sense. Yet the phrase does make sense, and identifies a thing that you and I can conceptualize. Or, let me say "X is the most perfect being which does not exist." This, too, makes sense, yet it reduces to my prior statement. Now, let me posit this: "X is a home run hit in baseball which scores an infinite number of runs." Of course, to any baseball fan, you know that this would be the most perfect play you could imagine, and yet it is, obviously, completely impossible. (For my non-American readers, this would be like scoring an infinite number of points by making one goal in football, although the metaphor works best in baseball because there really are three-run and four-run home runs.) One could just as easily say that, in baseball, a five-run home run is more perfect than a grand slam, and things which are perfect have a necessary existence, therefore five-run home runs exist in baseball.

We can analogize, from baseball, to God, and say "X is God," God is a perfectly perfect thing which does not exist. This, I assert, is precisely what God really is, the most perfect being possible, which does not exist. If one does not accept the premise that "to exist is more perfect than to not exist," in the sense that a thing's perfection can cause it to exist, and begin with this as an unreasoned assumption, then there is little reason or rationality that would justify that particular premise. And there is no reason to believe this premise, as in the baseball example.

To draw upon a line of thought from Voltaire's Candide, a room full of gold and diamonds and champagne in your house for you to own is more perfect than an empty room, isn't it? But this does not exist. Similarly, if this were true, then we would all live in the most perfect possible world, a world of peace and justice with no evil or crime, yet to believe this is to deny the reality that really exists around us. And, in the end, this is what the Ontological Argument calls upon us to do: to pretend that our denial of what exists, our belief in God, is somehow rationally justified, even though religion is the great enemy of reason and rationality.

2. Secondly, this is sophistry, it is mere trickery with words. What difference does it make how you define "perfection," or what you say, or what arguments you make at all? The question of whether God exists is to be answered by looking at reality and seeing if He exists or not, not by self-introspective analysis of the words and concepts in your own mind. This is something that Rand called the conflict of "the primacy of consciousness" vs. "the primacy of existence." Those who believe in the former, in the primacy of consciousness, think that their minds, their thoughts, what arguments they believe, actually have some impact on the metaphysical nature of reality--it is pure, true subjectivism, in other words. To believe in the Ontological Argument is to believe, in effect, that your analysis of the definition of God will *create* God, will *cause* God to exist, like Athena springing from your own head fully formed. It is to say that your belief that God's existence is necessary will cause God to exist, will require God's existence.

In contrast, if you believe in the primacy of existence, then you believe in a physical reality, and external world, prior to your beliefs and arguments and thoughts. So, even if you believe that God exists, it is still true that God does not exist--because of your belief, from your point of view, you will think that God exists, but, in reality, there is no God, and your belief has no effect whatsoever on this. Thus, no matter how pretty and persuasive and logical the Ontological Argument is, if God does not actually exist, if you have looked out into the real world and failed to see God, then the Ontological Argument, which is just a bunch of definitions and arguments in your own mind, is no reason to believe in God, since your beliefs that God exists will not cause God to exist if He did not already exist in reality. The primacy of existence might just be called the one, core, true, foundational principle of *Objectivism* as such, because, restated, it simply reduces to "existence exists *objectively*," hence the Ontological Argument lacks the power to create God merely by proving that God's existence is necessary.

Let me conclude with the disclaimer that I am not a skeptic, nor am I a pessimist. Knowledge is possible, there are things which we can know, and there are also things in reality which are such as to cause, require, and make necessary certain other things. It is just that this necessity exists in the physical world, as known by science and reason. God, and some overhyped concept of perfection, is not within the realm of reality, the realm of such things as reasoned proved necessity. Moreover, the Ontological Argument exploits the genuine desire that human beings have to believe that goodness, hope, honor, virtue, truth, exist in the world, that this is a *good* world. People want to believe that it is necessary and mandatory for good to triumph over evil in the world, and the Ontological Argument expresses that desire. And I think it is a good world, and goodness does usually defeat evil, although bad things happen in it. But we do not need to believe in God and religion in order for this to be true!

In a way, the Ontological Argument is sort of like one of Zeno's Paradoxes. Zeno, the ancient Greek philosopher, said that a distance, such as an inch, can be broken up into infinitely small units, so, for a thing to move its place one inch from point A to point B, it would have to travel through infinity, which is impossible. This, among all the other Zeno's Paradoxes, was meant to show that the physical world is an illusion. But the solution to this Zeno's Paradox is easy: in fact, in reality, one inch is one inch long, it is not the length equal to an infinite number of infinitely smaller subdivisions, instead, an inch is equal to an inch, A is A. So, for a thing to travel from point A to point B, it only needs to travel a distance of one inch, not a distance of infinity. This refutation, like the refutation of the Ontological Argument, is rooted in the Randian Primacy of Existence, that what exists, exists in reality, not in our heads, so if fancy philosophical sophistry puts weird ideas in our heads, which resolve to things which we know are not true, reality cannot be wrong, reality exists, it is what it is, so, instead, logically, we are the ones who are wrong, and we must check our premises and our logic until we see the error that leads to a conclusion which we know, from reality, is not true.

This is not to say that atheism or reality are known by intuition, and we are then making our reason align with intuition after the fact. The opposite is true: we know from perception that the physical world is reality, therefore God does not exist, and we know from perception that things can move one inch distances from one point to another point. In Objectivist epistemology, reason flows from empirical perception, because we begin with perceiving reality, and then we apply our analysis in logic and reason to reality.

CHAPTER TEN: ATHEISM AND OBJECTIVISM

As Objectivists, we are atheists. I believe that we need to have the proper attitude about atheism, especially when talking to people who believe in religion, which is, after all, the majority of humankind. The attitude that we should have is one in which our atheist beliefs are carefully thought out and grounded in clear logical arguments. Below I will offer counter-arguments against what I see as the four most popular anti-atheist, pro-God arguments, and then I will conclude with thoughts about the basis of religion and how Objectivism might one day replace religion.

The first argument is one that every atheist hears. The difference between an atheist and an agnostic, of course, is that agnostics don't know whether there is a God or not, while atheists believe that there is no God, and claim that this belief constitutes knowledge. But if you say "I know that God does not exist," the immediate response that you will be met with is: "Well, you can *believe* that God does not exist, but you can't *know* that God doesn't exist, no human can know whether or not God exists. You can't prove that God does not exist, so what you have is belief, not knowledge, a belief of no greater value than someone else's faith." This probably throws some atheists for a loop and makes them reconsider their atheistic beliefs.

But I believe that there is a proper atheist reply, which goes something like this: "What do you define as *proof*? I have proof of something if I have evidence that logically demonstrates the conclusion that my reasoning has reached. And the proof that God does not exist is everywhere. Everything about existence that you believe to be the work of God, is explained with much greater logical consistency by science. Every dark place where you saw evidence of God, the light science has shined on it and shown how it really works. Every event, from a bolt of lightning to an earthquake to the creation of humanity, has been explained by science. And when your child got sick and you prayed to God to heal her, some scientist figured out a cure for her disease and actually healed her. Belief in God requires faith, an mental act of defying reason and believing in what you know to be irrational. You believe in God, and you have faith; I believe in science, which, unlike your faith, proves its conclusions based on the evidence found in the physical world, and so I, unlike you, have knowledge." Every atheist should proudly say: "I know that God does not exist."

The greatest source of doubt about God is scientific explanation. Science, by explaining all physical phenomena by reference to natural causes rather than supernatural causes, and doing so in such a way as to be supported by observation, removes any need for God as an explanation. The concept of God, I believe, originated in the myths of ancient civilizations that were trying to explain things like why lightning appeared, why it rained, and why one army won and another lost. God is a simplistic, primitive attempt at explanation. With the explanative power of science, there is no longer a need for the concept of God. Science offers knowledge, in other words conclusive, demonstrable, certain proof, rather than mere refutable opinion, which is all that faith has. God is the unknowable and is defined as the non-human, the non-mortal, the non-physical, the non-perceivable, and so the faithful can never know God, making faith totally irrational, as Rand observed.

The second argument is one that was offered most famously by the philosopher Pascal. This is the gambling argument. Pascal says that since you can't know whether God exists or not, what you believe is a gamble, and you should make your decision based on which choice risks more. If you choose religion and you are wrong and God really doesn't exist, you will lose nothing, but if you choose atheism and God does exist, you will burn in Hell forever. But this argument, while clever on the surface, has no substance. First of all, you can know that God does not exist, so there is no risk. Secondly, if God is loving then He will forgive you for your sins. But if God does not exist, and this life on Earth is your one shot, is all that you will ever get out of the vastness of eternity, it would be a true crime to waste your life with the guilt-induced suffering of religion, when you could have spent your brief time on Earth living a happy, satisfying life according to the tenets of reason. Taking the risk that your life will be wasted, when reason clearly shows you the truth, is a risk not worth taking.

The third argument is the philosopher St. Anselm's "ontological argument." This argument claims that God must exist "by definition," that an analysis of the concept of God proves that God's existence is necessary. The argument is that God is the most perfect thing possible, to exist is more perfect than to not exist, and therefore God must exist. There are a number of different ways to refute the ontological argument. First, one can say that it hinges on something resembling that infamous philosophical villain, the analytic-synthetic split. The ontological argument seeks knowledge from the analysis of concepts without regard to observation of the physical world; this is analytic knowledge. If our observations of the physical world show that God does not exist, then any concept that "proves" that God exists must be wrong, and when belief and perception contradict, it is our beliefs that we must give up on, and not the observable physical world.

One can also refute the ontological argument on its own terms. The argument has two questionable premises: first, that it is more perfect to exist than to not exist, second, that God is the most perfect thing possible. These premises both depend on a concept of "perfection" as spiritual rather than physical. If we are to have a rational definition of "perfection," it must be defined as "the best thing possible." For example, in baseball, hitting a 4-run home run (a grand slam) is a perfect hit, but hitting a 5-run home run is not perfect, because it is impossible to hit a 5-run home run, there is no such thing. So if something is impossible, no matter how great it may be, it is not perfect. God may be a great, omniscient, omnipotent being, but if God is not physically possible, then God is not perfect. The believer may reply: God is physically impossible, but God is conceptually possible. To which we might reply: if your concepts are not based on physical reality, then they have the wrong basis. And there is no reason to believe that something existent is more perfect than something non-existent regardless of the context of the values of individual human beings for whom something existing can be more or less desirable; for example, a plague that exists is less perfect than a health that does not exist. So the ontological argument is a failure.

The fourth argument against atheism concerns what we take as evidence for or against the existence of God. Whenever there is tragedy, or there is incredible evil and human suffering, people question their belief in God and start to doubt God. The existence of evil is taken by some as the greatest challenge to a belief in God, or as proof that God doesn't exist. People are troubled by the idea that an omnipotent God would allow suffering, and so the existence of evil shakes their convictions. Conversely, whenever something incredibly good happens, people take it as a miracle and consider it as proof that there is a God. If this is the way that proof for or against God is defined, with evil as proof of atheism and good as proof of God, then it is no wonder than most people believe in God. As atheists we must make it clear that yes, the existence of evil, and horrible tragic catastrophes that no loving God would allow, does contradict the idea of an omnipotent God. But it is the existence of good, the existence of the noble and pure and sacred, the existence of great things and happiness, that is the best proof that God does not exist. Religion, as seen from every religious text, offers God as great and humans as weak, God as good and humans as sinful, God as powerful and humans as helpless. God controls everything, humans control nothing, and the physical, material life is one that religion condemns as empty and sinful, something that ought to be given up in exchange for the joys of the spiritual afterlife. So for something really good to happen to human beings in the physical world, for human beings to be capable of great things, and indeed for human beings to be happy, God cannot exist. Religion is the last refuge of the miserable who want to think that after their miserable lives are over they will go to Heaven and be happy. Human achievement on Earth, human happiness, and everything good that happens, which some people consider to be "miracles," are actually all evidence that God does not exist.

And on the subject of miracles, as a brief tangent, there is a proper response to those believers who cite miracles spoken of in the Bible as the basis for their beliefs. You never saw those miracles, you have never seen any "miracles" yourself, it is perfectly possible that none of those miracles really happened, and given the ignorance and superstitions of the ancient peoples one can picture them inventing the whole thing and fanatically believing in their own lies. You have no reason to believe that events happened as described in the Bible, so the Biblical narrative is not a valid source of knowledge. To commit the ultimate act of blasphemy, I must say that it is just as likely that grave robbers, or some of his supporters, raided Christ's tomb and removed his body, as it is that he was resurrected by God, or perhaps nobody ever even looked in Christ's tomb and the story that it was empty is something that was created by his followers after his death. This argue applies not only to Christianity, but to all the texts that every religion relies upon as evidence of miracles. Unless you saw it with your own eyes you have no rational basis for believing that it really happened.

The four rebuttals to arguments that I have presented show that religion cannot be given any justification by reason or rational argument. The purpose of using this material is to back believers into a corner by forcing them to admit that their belief, their faith, is not based in reason and is in blatant defiance of reason, that it flies in the face of sensible thought. Rand observed that faith contradicts reason by definition, but many faithful people fail to understand this. If they can be made to see that they must choose between reason and faith, the more intelligent people will choose reason, and that is all that is necessary for social progress to happen.

I would like to conclude by briefly considering religion as morality, and the prospect of replacing religion. As I stated earlier, religion originated in the needs for ancient peoples to explain the natural occurrences that they observed. Lacking knowledge of science, they explained things with spirits or gods. Now, however, we have science, and so there is no need for supernatural explanations. But religion has evolved to fill a new need: not the need for explanations, but the need for morality. Morality is a need based in human nature: most humans, by nature, seek to do good. Some people see religion as the only morality, the only basis for good and evil, the only source of virtues and values. The majority of humans share that opinion, and among those that don't, most see Marxism as the only alternative morality. But with Objectivism we can change that. Objectivism is the first fully rational and complete atheist morality, an atheistic account of good and evil and of how to live an ethical life. Now that we have Objectivism, we can replace morality, the one final role that was filled by religion, and we can show people that there really is no need at all to believe in God. Religion, which most believers consider to be good and noble, promotes irrational behavior, the rejection of science and progress, and guilt-induced human suffering, and the human race will be much better off once religion is replaced with science and Objectivism and we can look back at religion as a relic of the past.

However, to replace religion with Objectivism, which should be our goal, we will need more than just than our beliefs. We need carefully thought-out atheist arguments, but that is not enough. We will need an active Objectivist movement and an Objectivist community. What most people get out of church is not just their belief in God and guidance for how to live life, but also a sense of community and a way to relate to other people. If we are to replace religion, we must have an Objectivist community capable of fulfilling these human needs that people have. Some people believe in God not from any intellectual basis but simply from a need for comfort or a fear of death; the answer to this is to get people to be more self-reliant and self-confident. Religion is not so popular because people hate the physical world, in spite of what some atheists may believe. Religion fills a need that is inherent in human nature, the need for a purpose in life, the need to believe that there is good in the world, the need for a feeling that is euphoric and ecstatic, the need for that "warm, fuzzy" feeling of kindness. Religion is not the best way to meet this need, it fills that need at the cost of denying the physical world, but religion is popularly perceived as the only way to fulfill this need. To promote Objectivism we must explain how Objectivism can fill those needs. The difference between religion and atheism is that religion fills the need for purpose and meaning with God and spirituality, whereas atheism fills the need for purpose and meaning with your own self and your life in the physical world, with the purpose of making yourself happy and the meaning that you derive from the events of your life. Religion condemns individual humans as small and meaningless, but every human being has the power to feel important and meaningful, and Objectivism can tap into that potential. Religion can be overcome, but it will take a smart approach and logical arguments to accomplish this goal.

CHAPTER ELEVEN: PRO-CHOICE FOR OBJECTIVISTS

In this essay I am going to do two things relating to the advocacy of my position regarding abortion, which is the pro-choice position. First I am going to explain why pro-choice should be the Objectivist position and why it flows naturally from an Objectivist account of rights. Ayn Rand was pro-choice, and so this is not terribly controversial. But secondly I am going to make an argument that is much more controversial, which is my claim that Objectivists are intimidated by the pro-life Christian fundamentalist element of the Right Wing, and that this makes Objectivists downplay their support for pro-choice.

First we must see the arguments for pro-choice as the rational position regarding abortion. I am of the view that there are four persuasive arguments in favor of pro-choice as an Objectivist position: potentiality, rights, government, and self. There is the argument that Rand herself put forward, the potentiality argument, which is that restricting a mother's right to abortion for the sake of the fetus amounts to sacrificing something that is actual (the mother) for the sake of something that is merely potential (the unborn child).

The second argument, the rights argument, runs like this: human beings have rights because they have minds that are capable of reasoning, and therefore human beings are capable of living human lives. Only beings with minds have rights, because rights are derived from the social/political foundation that is necessary for human beings to live the rational lives proper to human beings. Rocks do not have rights because they don't have minds, and similarly animals do not have rights because they don't have minds. A fetus, prior to birth, cannot possibly have a mind, because mental activity begins with the mind receiving sense-experience from external reality, and the unborn fetus does not perceive anything outside of the womb. The fetus' brain is only starting to develop in the first part of the pregnancy, and even once the brain has formed, it is still empty of content and therefore devoid of a mind. Since the child does not have a mind until the point of birth, it has no rights up to that time, and if it has no rights then it does not have the right to life. If it has no right to life then there is nothing unethical about terminating the pregnancy. Until the point of birth the fetus is merely biological material within the mother's body that belongs to the mother. The fundamental basis of the right to own property is the right to own one's body, the right to own what belongs to you, and this right is what is at stake in pro-choice.

The government argument, my third argument, arises from our desire as Objectivists to limit the government from interfering in private freedoms to the maximum degree possible. If we approach politics with principles, and with a theory based on the idea of a smaller government, does it make sense to let the government tell women what they can and can't do with their reproductive organs? The pro-life position calls for more government interference, not less. If we seek to be consistent and logical in our application of the smaller government position, then we must leave the decision regarding abortion to the mother, and not force our beliefs onto private individuals. This is the legal justification for *Roe v. Wade*, that the mother has a "right to privacy" that protects her from the government looking into her private life. Even if we would not choose to abort, that does not give us the right to take that choice away from other people. If we do not believe that someone should use the government to forcibly impose their views onto other people, by means of physical aggression, instead of relying on reason to persuade other people, then we must support pro-choice.

The fourth argument, selfishness, makes a great deal of sense from an Objectivist point of view. The selfishness position argues that even if the fetus were alive, and had all the rights of an adult human being, it would still be unethical to force the woman to bear the child, because this would be asking the woman to sacrifice her life for the sake of someone else's life, a clear-cut case of self-sacrifice, altruism and duty. The fact that the child needs the mother to live is not a valid claim upon the mother. As an example, the crumbling society of *Atlas Shrugged* needs Galt and his strikers to return in order to survive, but they choose not to return and to let that society die, because they do not choose to sacrifice themselves for the sake of others. The corrupt society is physically dependent upon the strikers for their life, but that doesn't dissuade the strikers. In what way is there a difference between that and asking the mother to give her life and her most valuable private possession, her body, for the sake of someone else's life? If a rich man could save a beggar's life by giving him some money, is it murder if he doesn't give some money to him?

Because of these four arguments, potentiality, rights, government, and selfishness, it makes no sense for Objectivists to be pro-life, and the only logical position is pro-choice. It is also relevant to note that almost every defense of pro-life is grounded in some way in religion, Christian morality and a belief in the soul of the unborn child, and so long as Objectivism does not accept any of those ideas there is no logical justification for pro-life.

So why don't Objectivists take up the banner of pro-choice and fly it proudly? Why do Objectivists choose to be known for their pro-capitalism position as their main issue, but choose not to make pro-choice a central issue as well? Of course, many of them do individually. But the movement, as a whole, does not. I have a simple, elegant explanation, but many Objectivists won't enjoy hearing it. The root of the problem is that Objectivists, when they address political issues, get caught up in the traditional American political fight, which is the Left (which stands for social equality and economic equality) against the Right (which stands for social inequality and economic inequality). As advocates of capitalism, Objectivists believe in economic inequality, which makes them the ally of the Right. Rand's chief concern was the fight against Communism, and so many perceive her to belong to the Right. Objectivists are focused on the fight against socialism, and socialism is advocated by the Left and opposed by the Right, so Objectivists find their "strange bedfellows" to be the forces of the Right.

But pro-choice is an issue supported by the Left and opposed by the Right. This is because pro-choice is really an issue of female equality. Historically, for thousands of years women have been defined as wives and mothers, forced into marriages without consent and consigned to a life where their primary function is to give birth and to be a housewife. By giving a woman the right to an abortion, you free her from her status as child-bearer and give her the opportunity to live a life of freedom, which had previously been kept only for men. The Left, with their focus on equality, supports pro-choice, and the Right with their emphasis on inequality and tradition opposes pro-choice. I would also argue that many—not all, but not just a few either—of the people who support pro-life do so, either consciously or unconsciously, not because they care about fetuses, but because they hate women: note for example the hypocrisy of murdering a doctor at an abortion clinic because you believe in the sanctity of life. (One can criticize this as a "feminist" interpretation of abortion rights, which I will address later.)

Pro-life Objectivists, and even pro-choice Objectivists who want pro-choice to keep a low profile, are afraid that if we advocate for social equality then we will go down a slippery slope leading to economic equality, but I disagree. To free ourselves from the traditional fight we need a new fight, the Objectivists (who stand for freedom) against politics as usual (which stands for oppression). There is nothing in Objectivism that should lead us to reject female equality, minority equality, or gay rights. After all, we want every human being to have full rights as a citizen, so long as the government does not favor one group over another. Of course, Objectivists approach the issue of gay rights, female rights and minority rights in a different way from the Left: for example, the Left wants affirmative action, whereas we want race blindness. But on these issues, of which pro-choice is one, we are closer to the Left than to the Right, and in order to maintain our integrity we must not sacrifice our conscience to please the conservatives. We can choose to participate in the Right, but we cannot allow ourselves to be cowards who yield to the Christian extremist fringe of the Right. As pro-capitalists we have the right to claim our place in the Right Wing, but we make ourselves weak and useless if we let the evangelical leaders define the Right's agenda for us. We cannot be sissies and let the evangelicals intimidate us, lest we let the Right become nothing more than an instrument of the Church.

To achieve political integrity, and to define ourselves politically as Objectivists, we must disentangle ourselves from the Christian extremists. This will involve a rethinking of the Right. With the Left so firmly in support of socialism, it is the case that we have nowhere else to go but the Right. And there are many conservatives who are not Christian extremists, who have principles, who believe in capitalism and who gladly embrace anyone who hates communism. This being the case, as Objectivists we can find a home in the Republican Party. But the truth is that we do not have to support either the Christian Right or the socialist Left, we can do something new. We can have an approach, not of Left vs. Right, not of equality vs. inequality, but of freedom vs. oppression. We can say that we are not Left-Wing extremists, but we are not Right-Wing extremists either, and I am sure that such a statement would attract attention and support from most American voters, who are somewhere in the Center. With a platform of being conservative on economic issues and liberal on social issues, the politics of Objectivism could become quite popular, and we could provide a real alternative to both the Right and the Left. But that would require us to present ourselves as a politics of the center (which is where most Americans are), rather than as a politics of the extremist fringe, which is what many Objectivists and "radical" Libertarians want. This is the appeal of supporting the Libertarian Party as opposed to the Republican Party. Unfortunately, most Libertarians want to be thought of as pure, idealistic radical extremists rather than practical moderates capable of compromise, and so it remains extremely difficult for any Libertarian to be taken seriously as a candidate by the American public.

The Center does not have to be a compromise between the Right and the Left if we approach it in the right way, if we come to it by way of principles rather than compromises. A conservative economics and a liberal social policy leads naturally to the Center. The only problem with this is that Objectivists, who would be given the gift of popularity if they embraced the Center, might actually have to enter politics and win elections, and then we would not be free to just deal with abstract idealistic theories, we would have the unpleasant responsibility of actually putting our ideas into practice with real flesh-and-blood human beings. I would like to see that day come, but for it to come about we must have a rational attitude towards politics, starting with the abortion problem.

Objectivists should proudly support issues such as pro-choice, stem cell research, gay marriage, and the separation of church and state. This does not mean siding with the Left, it means "transcending" Right and Left to arrive at a politics that is truly ethical. One should try, as an Objectivist, to choose moderate candidates who are economically conservative and socially liberal. Obviously "the enemy of my enemy is my ally," and the conservatives are a valuable ally in the fight against socialism. But if our politics is to remain truly ethical we must recognize that this alliance is a political compromise, and we must hold fast to a distinction between Christian evangelical conservative politics, on the extreme Right, and Objectivist/Libertarian politics, which is on the Right but is closer to the Center. We can work with the Right against our common enemy, socialism, but we must not allow ourselves to be corrupted by the evangelicals. And frankly, I think that Rand herself might have agreed: she called herself a "radical for capitalism" rather than a "conservative" precisely because she didn't get along with the conservatives of her era.

Lastly, I will concede that one can call my interpretation of pro-choice a "feminist" interpretation. But this is misleading: my interpretation is based on verifiable historical fact: it is a fact that historically women have been confined and oppressed. We must distinguish between the different kinds of feminist. Irrational feminism is the kind of nonsense that accuses history and science and capitalism of being "phallo-centric" and claims that we should all be more spiritual and womanly, the kind of post-modernist deconstruction that clearly hates reason and reality. But there is a less philosophical, more practical kind of feminism, which simply says that women should be as free as men. And with Ayn Rand, herself a woman, as the founder of Objectivism, we cannot ignore the merit of this idea. Rand was against feminism, but as anyone can see from her writings, her ideas about male-female relationships are a bit strange and not entirely coherent. The fact that pro-life evangelicals use pregnancy to confine women to the role of childbearing wife and deny them careers in business is, I feel, a factual statement, and so I do not think that I can be dismissed as a "feminist." And since I believe that women should be as free as men, but I am also an avowed supporter of capitalism, I believe that there should be a place in the Right for those of us who are pro-choice, and we, as Objectivists, should be willing to recognize the kind of political realignment that will make such a thing possible.

CHAPTER TWELVE: OBJECTIVISM AND MULTICULTURALISM

The question can be posed: does Objectivism only have use for Americans, or does it have usefulness for the peoples of every nation across the globe? Can it only be appreciated by people in "Western" cultures, or can people from Eastern cultures also appreciate it?

Some Objectivists believe that Objectivism is firmly rooted in "Western" values such as reason and capitalism, and that it can hold no appeal for people in nations whose philosophical traditions do not descend from Greece and Rome. This is a horribly naïve and inaccurate view. In the first place, so-called "Western" culture reads like a horror story of despotism and irrationality. Western culture has historically been dominated, not by reason, but by Christianity, and political democracy and capitalism are relatively recent developments. Europe, the original seat of Western culture, has never fully embraced capitalism, and now more than ever is sliding towards socialism. And America, for all that it gave birth to Objectivism, is not a wholly rational culture, to say the least. One can argue that "Western" values are those rooted in ancient Greek philosophy. The general spirit of the ancient Greeks was better than what had come before them, and Greek philosophy, particularly Aristotle, has informed much of later rational thinking. But the history of Greece does not bear out the idea of Greece as a utopia. Plato is as much a part of Greek philosophy as Aristotle, and Plato can be interpreted as a liberal and someone who scorned reason, so Greece is not a firm foundation for rational culture. Indeed, the Gospel of John in the Bible is a firmly Platonist element of Christian theology. To the extent that Western culture is rooted in Platonist philosophy and also in Christianity and religious irrationality, there is no logical basis to say that Western culture is inherently compatible with Objectivism. This, perhaps, explains why must of the West has not only not embraced, but also actively rejected, Objectivism since the founding of Objectivism in the middle of the Twentieth Century.

Furthermore, this view denies the humanity of people in other cultures, and fails to understand that Objectivism can make a valid claim to be the universal truth, applicable to all human beings as humans. People in Asia are not irrational by nature, and the fact that they have been exposed to Buddhism does not make them antithetical to Objectivism any more so than the fact that most Americans are raised in the Christian tradition. If Objectivism is the universal truth, then it should apply to any being who can call himself a human being. The values of American culture that Rand celebrated, individualism, independence, freedom, and rationality, would be just as useful to someone in China as they are to Americans—in fact, given the repressive Communist Chinese regime, they might be even more urgent for the Chinese than they are for Americans.

In light of this I would argue that Objectivism should carefully reexamine its stance on multiculturalism. Multiculturalism and cultural relativism are liberal nonsense, but the liberals use multiculturalism as a way to prevent rationality from spreading to people from non-American cultures, and so it deserves a serious analysis. Liberals claim that other cultures are not logical like ours and that this anti-logic should be celebrated. If Objectivists reply that other cultures are not logical like ours but our culture is better than the other cultures then we accept the fundamental liberal premise, which is that other cultures are anti-logic and our culture is pro-logic, which is not factually true. Liberals who preach that anti-reason foreign cultures should be worshipped are exploiting other cultures for their own anti-reason ends, they are not doing something that the foreign cultures actually want them to do. Culture, the traditions of artistic expression, food, dance, language, etc., may be twisted by whatever is the dominant religion in that region, but there is nothing inherently pro-reason or anti-reason about most Eastern cultures, and to say that every member of a given culture is irrational is to define people by what group they belong to rather than by their actions as individuals. In fact, "culture" can be a shorthand for a collectivist way of identifying people, as if "Eastern culture" and "Western culture" were a single entity and not a massive number of unique individuals, some of whom are rational and some of whom are irrational.

If Objectivism were to try harder to appeal to foreigners in Asia, Africa and Latin America and the Middle East then it might be possible for the movement to expand to other nations and become a global movement, which, from a purely practical point of view, might really help the Objectivist movement to grow. Unfortunately Objectivism is largely limited to appealing to Americans because we believe that America is the greatest country in the world.

However, there is a solution to this problem. Many people all around the world, in foreign countries, also buy into the Objectivist idealism of America as "the land of the free", this, indeed, is precisely why so many foreigners try to become American immigrants. The notion that America is great can be used in one of two ways. It can be used in a way that borders on racism, by thinking that the American people are generally smarter and better than foreigners. Or it can be used in a way that is rational, by thinking that every human being is a human being and the people in foreign nations do not have a different metaphysical nature than people in America, but the ideas that America was founded upon such as freedom, capitalism and reason are what makes America different from any other nation. If the latter is true then the things that make America great can be copied by other nations, and they could then rise and become just as great as America. The racist wants America to always be on top and for the rest of the world to always look up to us, whereas the rational Objectivist should want to spread America's winning ways to the rest of the world so that everyone around the globe can rise up and we will all one day know the prosperity and happiness that comes from freedom. America should serve as the symbol of reason, freedom, capitalism, science, and everything that Objectivists believe in, but the notion that the American people are inherently superior to the peoples of other nations reeks of racism and will be a huge obstacle to promoting Objectivism around the world. In the era of globalization we should not limit ourselves so foolishly.

Someone who disagrees with me might accuse me of hating America and embracing the irrationality of Eastern culture, but my reply should be evident from what I have already written. I will conclude by mentioning that Ayn Rand herself was a child of Russia, not the United States, and so Objectivists confine their efforts within the borders of America at the risk of ignoring the rational people in other countries.

CHAPTER THIRTEEN: THE SUBJECTIVITY OF PERSONAL TASTE IN OBJECTIVISM

Rand believed that nothing in reality is subjective, and there is no room for any, nor is there any realm of, subjectivity within reality. I tend to agree that in reality, all physical objects exist objectively, and there is no subjective element to the physical existence of any object, any existing thing, in reality.

That having been said, I differ with Rand in that I believe the world of one's artistic, aesthetic judgments is the one area in reality where there is valid subjectivity, and relativity to the extent that what is beautiful or ugly for one person might not be so for another.

Rand disagreed, with disastrous, and absurd, results. For example, Rand, as her historians have noted, had extreme tastes about classical music composers, loving some and hating others, and she sought to impose her musical tastes onto her followers, condemning those who liked the music she hated, and asserting that they, like the musical symphonies, were evil and corrupt. This would be laughable, if not for the fact that it is very real, and very sad, that the end of result of Rand's position is that every Objectivist must impose upon their tastes a carbon copy of Rand's own tastes--which, obviously, helped contribute to the dreadful syndrome among Rand's Objectivist movement, that it became a cult where her followers copied her and worshipped her and were "Randroid" robots devoid of independent thought.

Rand's position leads to both funny, and heartbreaking, results--she hated men with facial hair, and said that beards and mustaches are evil (seriously!), and she also allowed her sexual taste, which found homosexual sex to be ugly and unpleasant, to lead her to denounce homosexuality, which forced her many gay followers to repress and hide their sexuality, within a movement that was supposed to be based on reason and freedom.

In contrast to Rand, let me try to articulate a theory according to which one may have differences of opinion about artistic tastes, while still maintaining that reality exists objectively and, as such, there can be only one truth about what is real, which does not admit of different subjective points of view. Take, for example, a musical song.

The song exists, what notes are in the song, exists, what it sounds like, exists. Hence, for the Objectivist, what the song is, is a matter of objective fact, and is the same for two different people, and for all people everywhere. A scientist could record the sound waves, and have a written diagram of the notes of musical notation, and there is nothing more to the song than this, this exists objectively, and this is what you hear when you listen to the song, which is one and the same for all listeners.

But--and this is true *only* for artistic and aesthetic judgments--whether you like the song or not is not only a function of what the song is, but also of what *you* are, and of who you *choose* to be. Liking a song, for example, may arise because it reminds you of a person you loved a long time ago, which would be true for you, but probably not for another listener sitting next to you. Or, if the song is an angry song that is focused on some political issue you care about, you may like the song because of who you are, and, to extend this example, your liking the song may be, not a reaction to what exists, but your choice about what you do in reality, and, to some extent, your artistic tastes may be how you choose to define yourself as a person, an act of self-expression, not merely an identification of external objects in reality. Indeed, I feel this way about the "prog rock" band Rush, that I like their music more because they frequently put explicitly Objectivist content into their song lyrics.

Thus, the aesthetic judgment of a song does not reduce merely to the physical existence of the song, which is one objective non-subjective fact, it may reduce to the combination of the song, which exists, and its listener, who exists also, but for whom the objective existence of the combination of that song plus that listener is unique to each individual song-listener combination. It may reduce to this, plus to the listener's choice of how he chooses to express himself in his tastes and preferences, which is an exercise of free will and thereby is "subjective" in the sense that it is created, not discovered, and is under the free control of the person who makes the choice.

For a similar example, when a person chooses what career to pursue, this is not merely their discovering what their natural talent and socio-economic circumstances, etc., are, but, in this choice, they define who they are, they choose what person they are going to be, and, in this sense, the choice does not exist objectively until it is created by the chooser, and, once chosen, it is a construct of the person who made that choice. In this sense, then, what job or career a young person should pursue is not entirely a matter of fact that a scientist could discover, it is, at least in part, a choice that the person makes, which is unique and special to that person, as a self-expression of who and what he or she chooses to become.

To conclude, in this essay I have shown that the extremist Objectivist position on artistic tastes as objective reduces to absurdity (and to monstrosity), and I have then explained that a little bit of subjectivity within the realm of art and personal preference actually can be fully reconciled with my core belief that only objective things exist and that reality, as such, exists objectively. In doing so I have made no concessions of any sort to philosophical subjectivism, but I have still proven that, within the physical world, tastes and aesthetic judgments have a quality that can be called "subjective," in that they possess objective qualities which may be unique to, or dynamically created by, the person who makes the judgment.

CHAPTER FOURTEEN: NECESSITY FROM ESSENCE: THE ANTI-KANTIAN REVOLUTION

The rest of this book presents the areas where I disagree with Rand substantively on details of her philosophy, which, as you will see, is mainly in the area of epistemology, in other words, how reason works. This section is designed to give you a taste of my post-Randian philosophy, which I explore in full detail in my other books, which I hope you will please buy. I will try to keep this essay short and easy to understand, despite dealing with the most sophisticated intricacies of philosophical epistemology, a subject where even the name strikes fear into the intellectual capacity of most people, let alone the ideas.

Since the birth of philosophy, philosophers have wondered how to achieve knowledge of the things in the physical world, which is, after all, the world that we see and live in within our own lives every day. Early Greek philosophers took two approaches. There were those, like Heraclitus, who said that, because everything changes and is imperfect in the physical world, knowledge of the physical world is impossible. Then there were those, like Parmenides, who accepted the premise that knowledge of the physical world is impossible, but then said that there is such a thing as knowledge, but it comes from a non-physical world of spirit, and can then shine light on the physical world, revealing physical reality to be an illusion. Plato then came and formalized and popularized the Parmenidean idea, stating that knowledge does not come from the physical world, and physical senses are deceptive and illusory, like watching shadows in a cave, but, through pure non-physical spiritual intellect, the soul can know the Platonic Forms (which should actually be translated as the Platonic Ideas), and, as things in reality get their identity from participating in the Forms, this spiritual knowledge is the only thing we can know about physical reality.

This conception of a conflict between the physical world, of which no knowledge is possible, and the spiritual world, where knowledge is possible but physical reality is nonexistent, persisted, and became the conflict between the Rationalists (the world of spirit, known by reason) and the Empiricists (the physical world known by perception, but without knowledge). Hume, the Empiricist, was also a famous skeptic, and said that knowledge is impossible, we do not know anything that is necessary, and we do not know that the Sun will rise tomorrow, etc.

Then, into the fray entered Kant. Kant's great achievement–if it was an achievement–was to stage his "Kantian Revolution," in which he argued that the world revolves around the mind, instead of the mind revolving around the world, in other words that the world is primary and absolute and the mind is merely a reflection of the truth that presents itself in the objective physical world, which had been a big idea among scientists in the Enlightenment era. Kant called his idea a "revolution" to analogize to the Copernican revolution, where men of science learned that the Earth revolves around the Sun, contrary to the Sun revolving around the Earth, which ancient societies believed.

Specifically, Kant said that the mind, in the act of experiencing a thing in physical reality, imposes certain conditions onto the experience. Because everything that a human being experiences is, after all, experienced, the mind imposes these conditions onto everything that a human being can experience. From this, Kant derived a theory of necessity–that, for example, it is necessary that the Sun will rise tomorrow, because the human mind will impose the Sun rising onto the experience of tomorrow, so it has to happen, it can't not happen, it is necessary. Kant's key idea, the synthetic a priori, means simply that, to translate it into layman's terms, there are thing which arise not from the mind nor from the definitions of ideas and concepts, things that we think of as facts in the physical external world, but these things, too, the mind imposes onto reality. For example, not only "a bachelor is an unmarried male", but also "Frank Jones is a bachelor" are things that the mind imposes onto reality. Thus, knowledge about physical reality could come from analyzing the structure of the mind and its a priori intuition, in other words, these necessary truths that the mind imposes onto experience.

That is the best that academic philosophy could come up with to justify necessary truth in the physical world. I would like articulate a theory which is different and, I think, better.

My theory is something that I call empirical essentialism, or, to name its main idea, pure empirical essential reasoning. My theory enables us to say that the mind revolves around the world, not the reverse, but that necessity comes, not from the mind, but from the things in physical reality, in other words, that necessity is objective, not from subjective experience. How can we say this? Simply by saying that necessity comes from the being of things.

Empirical essentialism holds that things have essences, and these essences are known from perception. Each thing has an essence. For example, the essence of a table is that it is furniture which has a space to hold stuff and stands on legs. (Note that, no, I am not defining the word "table", but rather, I am stating the essence of the thing, and this essence is what the word actually refers to). The essence of a thing is the being that makes it be a certain type of thing.

But let us consider the essence of a table. If you look at a table, you can see it hold stuff on a space, and you can see it standing on legs. Of course, you see *this* table do these things, not an abstract idea. But if you see this table, which is furniture, has legs, holds stuff, is made of wood, is in your office, and you then remove the property of "made of wood" and "located in my office," then you are left with the properties "holds stuff in a space, furniture, stands on legs." You can conceive of this set of properties as the essence of something, and then give this something the name "table." This is how abstraction and reason proceeds.

Here is my key idea: say that this set of properties is the essence of a table. Then, if a thing has this set of properties, it is a table. If it doesn't, then it's not a table. It might be something similar to a table, but it would not be actually a table, as we have identified that essence. So, a shelf might have one property of a table (space to hold stuff) but lack another (stands on legs). So, a shelf is not a table. This is not a matter of semantics, but, rather, a matter of sets of properties: we have identified a set of properties, furniture with legs and a space to hold stuff, as what the word "table" names, whereas a shelf is furniture with a space to hold stuff, and no legs. Here the academic philosopher of language tries to mess with my theory, saying that my theory reduces to the different definitions of words, that is true mere "by definition," etc., or saying that it not clear which properties are the essence of a thing. But, I believe that a thing is a set of properties (being in a specific location and being made of mass being properties), so, for example, the set of properties of "(1) furniture, (2) space to hold stuff, (3) standing on legs" is one thing, which I call a table, while one could define "shelf" as "(1) furniture, (2) space to hold stuff", or as "(1) furniture, (2) space to hold stuff, (3) does not have legs". So, the issue of whether a table is a type of shelf is solved merely by being precise in our identification of essences. Along these lines, pointing to a table that sits atop one giant leg, and saying "is this a table? your theory of essences is rubbish" simply did not begin by identifying the essence of a table with specificity, for, if the essence we identified to reason from is "with multiple legs," then it is not precisely a table, but if it was "with legs," but the property of the number of legs is not present with that set of properties that is the essence of a table, then yes, it is a table. With this *precise* identification of what a thing is by its essence, we can say that a table has the essence of a table. It must, because, if it didn't have the essence of a table, it would not be a table.

Now, why does this matter? Because of two interrelated conjectures: first, if a thing is what it is by having its essence as that type of thing, then every thing of that type must have that essence, or else it would not be that sort of thing. This is not to say in a Platonic that the essence causes the thing to be that thing, rather, the essence is a set of properties of the thing, of each real physical thing, and a thing with that set of properties is what we have identified as that type of thing. So, if x(e) is the essence of X, it follows that every X has the x(e) essence, because to be an X is to have the x(e) property.

Second, that for a thing to have an essence can cause it to have a consequence of that essence, in other words, for a thing to have a set of properties can cause it to also have other properties. This, I think, happens in different ways: one property directly causes another, one property contains or is contained by another, or one property only arises as the result of the other and the other is its means of existing. So, that if we have identified the essence, in a way which is intellectually precise, then, for a thing to be a thing of that type, it necessarily must have that essence, it must have that set of properties in order to be that type of thing, and having that essence also causes it to have the consequential properties, therefore every thing with that essence also have that set of consequential properties. If x(e) is the essence of X, and x(c) is the consequence of the essence of X, and if x(c) is y(e), then we can reason that every X is Y, in a way that is necessary, universal, and true in all places and times, but which exists in physical reality, and which was reasoned only from empirical perception of properties in physical reality and the reasoned analysis of this perceived experience.

For example, suppose that the essence of a table is that it is furniture, with legs, and a space to hold stuff. Suppose further that the essence of furniture is that it is a man-made object to place in a human living space for functionality. From these, we can deduce that there is a property, the property of being man-made, which is (part of) the consequence of the essence of being a table (because the essence contains this consequential property.)

Here, we have the prize at the end of the race: we can now say that every table is man-made, and every table must be man-made, not because the mind imposes this quality onto tables as a condition of being experienced, but because *to be the thing that it is imposes this condition onto the thing as a condition of being that thing which it is.* In other words, necessity comes from being, from ontology, from what things are, from the thing in itself, from what things (sets of properties) are. There is no need to look for necessity in Platonic Forms, or in Kantian subjectivism, or in a world of spirit. The necessity is here, in the things in the physical world, waiting for us to learn them by analyzing what they are and applying reason to perceived things in the world that we experience.

So, if, from a table, which we have perceived and known what it is (its set of properties) just by looking at it, and from this one table we can reason to necessary truths about all tables, and a table must have the essence in order to be a table, and the essence causes the consequence of the essence, then all tables, as a condition of being a table, must have the consequence of the essence. Then, from this one thing, we learn about (a) all tables, everywhere in reality, and (b) tables which we have not perceived nor experienced directly, and might never perceive nor experience. We reason this, from one table, using *induction* and *reasoning* from *perception*.

So, empirical essentialism, by showing how to achieve necessity from things in themselves in the objective physical world, enables a counter-Kantian revolution, where, once again, as in the Enlightenment era among men of science, the mind revolves around the world. We can now achieve *knowledge* from the physical world, not from the world of spirit. And this knowledge is necessary and universal, and can't be wrong, for, if our knowledge of the table was wrong, then the table would not in fact be a table, so we would not be asserting that claim against a table, and the claim to knowledge would not be wrong.

My opponents may raise certain objections, let me briefly address them.

"You are defining the word table in a way so that all tables which are not man-made are excluded, so this is true by definition, not by essence, and your theory reduces to the philosophy of language," they will say.

But a table is a physical object, with legs, and a space to hold stuff, etc. It is not a word. It is seen. It is not spoken. I speak of sets of properties, and the analysis of properties, not of words and their definitions. So, in fact, there are not tables which are not man-made, because a table is furniture, and furniture is man-made.

"But I was walking in a forest and I came upon a tree stump, which I used as a table, and it is not man-made, but it was a table, hence there is an exception, and the physical world is messy and imperfect and ever-changing, unlike the perfect eternal world of reason, spirit, math and geometry, etc., so you have no perfect empirical knowledge from the physical world."

You did not identify the essence with a specific and consistent identification of the set of properties you were reasoning from. What is it to be "man-made"? To be taken from nature and appropriated into human usage. Thus, the tree stump is a table, because you took it and used it as a table, just as a wooden table is also made from a tree.

To which the reply is "then the tree stump being a table comes from human usage? And before I came upon it, this stump, with the same physical properties, was not a table? Then it is a social construct arising from intentionality, and there is nothing objective about it. And, if a tree stump is a table, and a tree stump is not man-made, then a table is not man-made, hence is not furniture, etc."

To which I reply, simply, you came upon it and used it as a table, you physically exist (you are your body and its thinking brain only), your using it is an objective physical fact, and yes, human usage (or, to be precise, being created by humans as something for human usage) is a property of the essence of "man-made". A tree stump is not a table, but it becomes a table when a person turns it into a table, as, for example, if someone dug up the tree stump and put it in their house and kept books on it, anyone would concede that it is a table, just as if someone took a tree, which is not a table, cut the tree up with an axe, and used the lumber to build a table, one could concede that this table was in fact a table, yet before it was a tree and not a table, but cutting up a tree and using a tree stump to put stuff on are both acts of human usage. A tree stump just sitting in a forest is not a table, again as most normal people would concede, but a wooden table would be made from a tree stump. Usage by humans exists objectively in physical reality, hence (a table)(e) (in other words "the essence of a table") is not (a tree stump)(e), but there can be a thing with the property of being a tree stump which also has the property of being a table. The linguist can think of an infinite number of arguments, either claiming that there are border cases where the essence lacks the consequence, or that this reduces to mere semantics and definitions. All such arguments are refuted by being precise and specific in which set of properties we include in the essence.

Similarly, the critic could ask me to define a cat, to which I might reply "a cat is a certain four-legged tailed feline-shaped animal," and the critic then points to a cat that doesn't have a tail, to attempt to prove that my conclusion was not necessary and universal. But here, again (and in most other arguments of this sort), the critic swapped one essence for another while using the same word "cat" to refer to them both. For, if the essence of a cat is in fact that it is a four-legged tailed feline animal, then the cat without a tail is not a cat. It is, of course, a cat, because the swap is replacing the essence "four legs, a tail, feline, an animal", that set of properties, with another essence, "an animal, has feline DNA." In reality, having feline DNA tends to cause the thing which has that property to also have the properties of being a feline animal with four legs and a tail, so the two essences are often coterminous and are spoken of interchangeably. But one set of properties is not the other. So, the cat with no tail is a cat(essence 1) that has feline DNA (and I leave it to the biologists to deduce which genetic properties to include in that essence), but no, it is not a cat(essence 2) meaning a thing that is an animal, feline-shaped, with four legs, and a tail, because it lacks a tail. The two essence might as well have two different words, as the critic is exploiting confusion from using the same word to name two different but related essences.

Here it is worth noting, as I strongly believe, that one must never overestimate one's percentage of certainty, or else one ends up claiming knowledge in something that turns out to be false. 99.9% of the time, having cat DNA (which is probably a good essence to use to define the word "cat) causes the thing to be a cat-shaped four-legged tailed animal, but perhaps 0.1% of the time, physical deformity or mutation might alter this. This does not mean that the consequence of the essence is only true 99.9% of the time. On the contrary, a *necessary* truth must be true 100% of the time, and it is. All cats (feline DNA) have feline DNA 100% of the time, and all cats (cat-shaped four-legged tailed animals) have tails (and the ones with no tails, or three legs, etc., are not "cats" under the second essence), but this does not contradict the assertion that cats (feline DNA) only have four legs and a tail 99.9% of the time. Thus, if the critic says "you can assert claims of cats that are probably true most of the time, but not necessary universal truths," he is wrong. If one is strictly precise about which essence one identifies to reason from, and the actual certainty that one has in one's conclusion, then true knowledge is possible from this type of reasoning.

"Aha! But the set of properties is a choice of the thinker, hence subjective, hence is the mind imposing necessity!" the critics will say.

My reply: Which set of properties you choose to reason from is a choice, but it does not create the set of properties, and the consequential properties are determined by the essential properties, not by your choice. And, whatever set of properties you don't choose to include in your reasoning, also exists and has its own essence and consequence, which exists objectively and outside your mind, like the essence and consequence you reasoned from. So you can choose to define "shelf" as "furniture with a space to store stuff" or "furniture with a space to store stuff with no legs," but you do not create any of these properties, and their consequence comes from their essences, their being, from being the things that they are, ontologically, not from your mind, your definitions, etc. I describe this by saying that which essence you think about is a choice, but what the essence is isn't your choice, or I also say it is objective and relative, and the essence is only relative to the non-essence. A real table is a fully specific thing with properties of location, time, mass, etc., while the essence of a table is arrived at by taking a real table and removing is properties which were specific to just that table, and in the same way, a thinker can manipulate which properties he thinks about, but it all just reduces to that real table, it all reduces to the objective physical world.

My opponent can state: "why do you even seek to prove that a table is man-made on this basis at all? As you say it, a table is man-made by definition, because you have defined furniture as being man-made. This is all analytic and true by definition, so you add nothing new, and there is no purpose in your making this argument."

One can say that a table is man-made by definition. But my theory is a theory of knowing necessity from *empirical* observations. In the first place, I assert that even our concepts of tables, furniture, etc., are empirical, because they are formed in the human brain from empirical observations of our experience while we are infants and children. But, second, reasoning necessity from essence is an empirical essential reasoning, even for all sophisticated knowledge at the adult stage of thought. For an example I am fond of using (I take this example from Ayn Rand and then use it against her), if scientists can establish on the basis of observations that water boils at a certain temperature *because it is water*, on the basis of its molecular behavior, then we can say that this is necessary as a consequence of the essence of being water, hence is universally true– this, despite the claim that "water boils at X degrees" being an empirical claim, it is in no way derived analytically from the definition of "water" as most people would understand it. Indeed, this claim "water boils at X degrees" would be called a synthetic claim if analyzed under Kant's analytic-synthetic distinction.

It is tangential to my argument here, but worth mentioning, that when people say that a thing is true "by definition," as with a table, what they almost always mean is that it is true "by essence", in other words, as a result of the consequence of the essence. When a person asks what the definition of a word is, they often really are asking what are the essential properties of the thing, and when they say that a thing is true by definition, they mean by essence, etc. The philosophers of language have historically been confused by the lack of the theory of essences, and so in place of essence they have clung to the idea of words and their definitions, instead of essences and their consequences. Also, to be fully precise, I must also say that, in this essay, when I refer to "ideas" or "concepts," if I were precise I would really say "the objects of concepts," because concepts exist in the mind, while essences exist in things in reality (ultimately, an essence that exists is a property of a real thing, namely is the set of properties that are its essence as a thing of a certain type. For example, the essence of a table exists in reality, it is the set of table properties that every real table has, it is the four legs of the table in your kitchen, which you can go and look at and touch right now, as well as every other essential property in every real table), and the concept of an essence is merely the mind's means of knowing the essence.

Thus, I have proved the possibility of necessary universal synthetic truth, but in a manner opposite to that of Kant: Kant claimed that the mind imposes it onto reality subjectively by conforming human experience to the laws of "pure reason" which the mind creates, whereas I have shown that it arises as a consequence of the essences of things, the essences of physical things in objective reality, so that the being of what a thing is requires it to be what it is in order to be that thing, being water requires (causes) it to boil at X degrees, being a table requires (consists of) it being man-made, being a cat requires (is the effect of) having feline DNA, etc., and things and their essences and consequences exist in reality, and are discovered by the mind through empirical essential reasoning, and are not imposed nor created by the human mind and its analysis.

We can achieve knowledge from physical reality, through empirical essentialism, and stage a counter-Kantian revolution, and abandon the anti-physical world, pro-world of spirit, intellectual reason vs. physical perception dichotomy that we inherited from Plato and Kant, two outdated thinkers whose time to fade has come. Kant's revolution was actually an anti-Copernican Revolution: whereas the astronomy of Copernicus ushered in an age of science and helped put to rest an age of superstition, Kant undermined science and knowledge of the physical world by ushering in an age of subjectivism and a denial of the physical world in favor of the world of mind, which undermined science and promoted religion. My new revolution is a Counter-Kantian Revolution, and my revolution, like the Copernican revolution, advances science and knowledge by giving them a theoretical foundation, showing that the mind revolves around the world, not that the world revives around the mind in the Kantian model.

This is a scientific philosophical revolution, just as ancient men of faith said that the Sun revolves around the Earth, only to be disproved by observations and rational analysis of men of science who proved that the Earth revolves around the Sun, thereby opening the door to an accurate understanding of the physical Universe.

CHAPTER FIFTEEN: CHECK YOUR PREMISES: HOW THE BRITISH EMPIRICISTS LED TO KANT'S TRANSCENDENTALISM

"Check your premises," Ayn Rand said. Here I will present an example of how dangerous it can be not to follow this advice. Of course, every Objectivist views Kant as a great villain of the history of philosophy. John Locke, in contrast, is a hero, the philosopher whose work in political philosophy inspired the political freedom beliefs of America's founding fathers, like George Washington, Ben Franklin and Thomas Jefferson.

Yet I view the ultimate blame for Kant's philosophy as lying in John Locke's unchecked premises.

Locke, in addition to being a political philosopher, was also an epistemologist (not unlike myself, actually). He believed in physical reality and matter. He was a great empiricist, meaning that he believed that knowledge of reality came from sensory experience. In fact, he was one of the first great members of the group of philosophers known as the British Empiricists. Yet, in his epistemological work, he always assumes that (1) sense perceptions are ideas in the mind, and (2) the things that are perceived are sensations, like yellow or sweet, not things, like a lemon or a candy bar. Locke also articulated another premise, (3),his distinction between "primary" ideas, that were directly known from reality, and "secondary" ideas, which were not.

I think (1), (2) and (3) are assumed, are not reasoned, and, had Locke checked those premises, he would have found them unjustified, on the basis of his observations of empirical experience.

And look at where Locke's premises lead. Berkley, the British Empiricist who came after Locke, said that "to be is to be perceived," which is a logical conclusion from the premise that what is perceived is ideas in the mind, and reality is the empirically perceived world. The question, then, after this is conceded, becomes: if the only thing we have access to from empirical perception is ideas in our minds, *because ideas in our minds are what we are perceiving when we perceive the world*, then how do we gain knowledge of objective reality? Note the italicized portion, which results from Locke's mistaken assumption. This question was never Locke's intention, in fact, quite the opposite, Locke believed in scientific knowledge of the external world. Then, the next question that arises is this: if some of the "ideas" that we "perceive" are real, and some are not, then how do we tell the difference between the ones that are real, and the ones that are not? If they both look the same, since every perceived idea is a sensation, like hot or sweet or salty?

So there are different answers to these questions. Berkeley's answer was that God perceives reality, and we know reality through God. Hume, the later British Empiricist, said that no knowledge of the external world is possible, since everything we perceive is ideas in our minds, and we can't tell the real ideas from the ones that are not real, since they are all just ideas in our minds, which is a reasonable conclusion to draw from Locke's premises. For Hume, the only real indication of which ideas we should believe is whether the ideas feel really clear and strong, or vague and hazy, and whether we can imagine them or not, because, if we can imagine an idea, then our mind is perceiving it, and if our mind perceives it, and to be is to be perceived, then everything in our imagination that is clear and distinct must actually be real (seriously!). This is the origin of the popular idea, still prevalent today, that things which are impossible to imagine are not physically possible–for Hume, to imagine something is for the mind to perceive it, hence it exists, so if it can't be imagined then it can't be perceived and can't exist (again, seriously, and this is truly warped, twisted thinking, if you pay attention to it).

Then came Kant, who, through a detailed, complicated system, said that we can know the external world, despite the fact that what we perceive are ideas in our minds, because we know it through intuition that we have prior to empirical experience, "a priori" (meaning "from before" experience), and our mind imposes laws onto our experience, forcing "a posteriori" (from after) experience to obey our a priori intuitions, and the purpose of philosophy is to help the person "transcend" the world of experience to rise up to intuition of things in themselves, a deeper reality that exists behind physical reality.

For example, Kant said that space and time are categories that the mind imposes onto reality. Of course, every sensory experience is situated in space and time, so Kant's philosophy reduces to sheer subjectivism, with every experience created by the mind. But Kant, through his complicated, muddy arguments, is much more than merely a subjectivist: he justifies knowledge of the external world despite this subjectivism, because, although our senses only have access to the "phenomena" of empirical experience, there is a world of "noumena," of real things, of "things in themselves" as separate from the perceived things, which, although we can never directly know them, our intuition and pure reason can give us a sort of mystical knowledge of them which is prior to empirical experience.

Kant reduces, not only to subjectivism, but also to a loopy, flakey religion, in which the noumena is the spiritual world above our physical world, which our mystical religious intuitions put us in touch with. Kant was the handmaiden of the movement that saved religion from being destroyed by science in the Enlightenment era, at a time when science was increasingly popular, atheist "freethinkers" were on the rise (Hume was one, actually) and the survival of religion was in danger. Kant has dominated academic philosophy ever since, and his impact changed the course of human history by saving religion from science.

And all of this due to three small false premises, easy to correct, totally unjustified, which, to Locke, probably seemed merely a manner of speech, not an intentional assertion at all, coming from a philosopher who believed in the external world of physical matter and who believed that perception could gain some knowledge of that external world.

Check your premises, or you might share Locke's fate, and see your premises lead to a logical conclusion that would be repulsive to you! Sadly, it is a similar error to Locke's that was made by Rand in her "intrinsic-objective-subjective" distinction, where Rand's concept of the objective is something that is really subjective but which she asserts as being objective, without being willing to fully commit to objectivity, and instead then assigns her problems with true objectivity to the intrinsic position. Randian "objective that is not intrinsic or subjective" would inevitably collapse into subjectivism, as it is a contradictory compromise between the subjective and the objective. Fortunately, there is a solution to Rand's problem. It is an evolution in epistemological Objectivism using the empirical essential position, which I have outlined here, and which I explain in fuller detail in some of my other nonfiction essays, such as my books "The Power of Objectivism," "A System of Legal Logic" and "The Apple of Knowledge".

GOLDEN RULE LIBERTARIANISM: A DEFENSE OF FREEDOM IN SOCIAL, ECONOMIC, AND LEGAL POLICY

CHAPTER ONE:
INTRODUCTION TO
NVP AND GOLD

The Golden Rule, which has been called the ethics of reciprocity, states: "do unto others as you would have others do unto you," or, to modernize the language, "treat people the way you want them to treat you in return." The Golden Rule follows as a matter of deductive logic from the existence of right and wrong, good and evil, regardless of what specific details you believe about what is right and good. How could something be evil when others do it to you, but be good when you do it to them, if both you and they are human beings governed by the same ethical rules? It goes to the basic notion of fairness that you cannot treat people badly and then expect people to be nice to you.

In addition to being rigorously rational and logical, the Golden Rule is also stated or implied by virtually every major philosophy and religion. Jesus Christ taught it in the Sermon on the Mount (Matthew 7:12 and Luke 6:31). The Jews derive it from Leviticus 19:18 and Leviticus 19:34 of The Torah. It was recorded as one of the sayings of Confucius. It was a common proverb in ancient Greece during the era of the Greek philosophers. The Golden Rule is mentioned in a line in the Hindu holy book The Mahabharata, and the Muslim Hadith records that Muhammad taught it to his followers. In Western philosophy the Golden Rule formed the foundation of the ethical theory of Immanuel Kant, the most influential philosopher of the Enlightenment.

The Golden Rule's presence in philosophy and religions of both East and West, ancient and modern, speaks to what a deep, universal, clear idea it is. The Golden Rule is a principle that the vast majority of the human race could agree on without altering what they already believe.

Here I will present a new, unique, original idea, the GOLD (Guiding Our Liberty's Defense) justification of the principle of libertarianism. The GOLD theory holds that if you accept the Golden Rule in ethics then it follows as a matter of logical deduction that the best political philosophy is libertarianism.

In order to see liberty's basis in the Golden Rule I must first define what I mean by "libertarianism." Libertarianism is based on a principle that has many different names but one common understanding among libertarians. The principle has been called the Non-Aggression Axiom (NAA), the Non-Violence Principle (NVP), or the Zero Aggression Principle (ZAP). I call it NVP.

NVP is an idealistic non-violence belief stating that no person should ever use violent force in order to coerce another person for any reason, including to redistribute wealth or enforce socially desirable political goals. In contrast to true pacifism, the believer of NVP is willing to use violent physical force for self-defense or to defend private property. Once we define government and laws, enforced by the police and army, as a type of coercive violent force, we reach the libertarian conclusion that the government should leave us alone and let us make our own decisions, both economic and social. This leads us to the belief that one group of people, or voters, lacks the right to use the government to impose their values and visions onto non-consenting groups of other people.

Most libertarians are already familiar with NVP, and we know what policy positions flow logically as conclusions of NVP. However, we are not clear on why NVP is desirable or right, and no consensus exists on the theoretical foundation for NVP. GOLD answers these questions. The GOLD principle is roughly the same as NVP, but it is NVP based on the Golden Rule.

SUBPART 1-A: THE XYAB ANALYSIS, AND A STORY ABOUT ME AND YOU

The GOLD theory argues that libertarian policies are a natural result of applying the Golden Rule to political questions. I will illustrate GOLD using what I call the XYAB analysis, which consists of the example of X, Y, A, and B, an example that I will return to repeatedly throughout this book. X is a person and A is a person. X believes Y, or X does Y, or X's behavior is Y, and A believes B or does B or behaves according to B. X believes that Y is good and that B is evil. Assume that A believes that B is good and that Y is evil. Thus, if X and A know each other, it is probable that X thinks that A should abandon B and do Y, and A wants X to abandon Y and do B.

Because I will be talking about X and Y and A and B a lot in this book, let me note at the outset that these letters represent ideas in political philosophy, not theories in mathematics. My use of X and A has nothing to do with variables and constants, or with rates of change and levels, although X and A are used in math to denote such things. In the political philosophy of GOLD, the use of the letters X, Y, A, and B, indicates that X is a person and shows that Y is something that relates to or belongs to X. Either Y is the religion of X, or Y is the ethics and values of X, or Y is the beliefs of X, or, as will be discussed later, Y might be the goods or services that X produces at his/her business and sells to A, or Y might be X's government that defends X and which X voted for. The name of A and B, in contrast to X and Y, show that A is a person who is different from X, and A has a B which relates to A in much the same way that Y relates to X, in that A's B is A's beliefs or behaviors or political values or economic products. X and X's Y sit on one side on the analysis, while A and A's B sit on the other side. So, in summary, Y relates to X, B relates to A, X is different from A, and Y is different from B. X hates B and believes in Y, and A hates Y and believes in B. The question then becomes, from the point of view of political philosophy, how should X treat A, and how should A treat X?

Assume that X can treat A in one of two ways. X can either let A be free to believe B, or X can try to violently force A to believe Y. Similarly, A can treat X in one of two ways, either forcing X to believe B, or allowing X the freedom to believe Y. If X and A follow the Golden Rule principle, meaning that each one of them will reciprocate towards the other with the type of behavior that he/she receives from the other, then if X forces A to believe Y, then A would force X to believe B in retaliation. This would descend into a war between X and A, with each seeking to use brute force to impose their values onto the other side. On the other hand, if X gives A the freedom to believe B, then A will give X the freedom to believe Y, and the result is the peaceful coexistence of X and A.

Thus, for people who follow the Golden Rule, the only logical path for X to follow, assuming that X believes Y is good and wants A to believe Y instead of B, is for X to respect A and give A the freedom to choose Y or B, and to seek to use reason to persuade A to freely choose Y, because this is precisely how X would want A to treat him if X wants to be able to believe Y and not be forced to believe B. Even if X believes that B is evil, X would still let A believe B or do B, because X wants the freedom to believe or do Y, and for X to be free from A's coercion, A must also be free from X's coercion.

However, force used for self-defense can be universalized under the Golden Rule, because if X forcibly defends himself from A's force, and A also forcibly defends himself from X's force, then neither dominates the other, and each will be forced to let the other do what he wants, so peace and harmony and freedom would result from self-defense for both of them.

GOLD captures the wisdom of liberty, which is based upon the freedom to choose. Political freedom means you are free to do whatever you want so long as you don't violate other people's right to life, liberty, and property. GOLD is the one and only behavior which each person can do to everyone else and which everyone can do back to that person which enables the person to coexist with everyone else in perfect peace, harmony and freedom. As soon as X tries to use force to impose Y onto A, A will try to impose B onto X, and the violation of rights and of liberty dissolves into violent conflict and war, a barbarian savagery where the most violent person wins and the stronger winner imposes his belief onto the weaker loser. X can be anyone and Y can be anything, so GOLD is true freedom for everyone.

You might ask: but if Y is correct and true and good, but A believes B, then A should believe Y, so why can't X force A to believe Y? Under GOLD, X should not force Y onto A even if X is one hundred percent completely, absolutely certain that Y is right and B is wrong, and not even if in actual objective reality Y really is right and B really is wrong, because if X tries to impose Y onto A by force then A's Golden Rule reaction is to try to impose B onto X by force, because A believes B just as much as X believes Y. If GOLD respect for the rights of others is lost from X initiating force against A, then we disintegrate into a world of brute force, and we lose freedom, rights and civilization.

Then you could ask the next question: if Y is true and right, but A believes B, how can X get A to choose Y, the correct, right, true choice? The answer is that if Y really is correct, then X can use reason and persuasion to persuade A to freely choose Y. Even if Y is true and good, nothing can be so good for everyone that it is worth violating someone else's freedom to force the good onto them, because the widespread initiation of violence for noble, good justifications totally destroys freedom and rights.

GOLD is a higher value than Y, even if Y is true and good, because GOLD gives each person the freedom to choose between Y and B, and from the point of view of X and A, who are mortal human beings with fallible human brains and limitations upon their ability to know the truth, for all they know either Y or B could be true, so it is never appropriate for X to force Y onto A and make A's decision for him. Even if Y is true and good, if X seeks to impose Y onto A then A will respond by seeking to impose B onto X, so if people accept that they should use violence to force "goodness" onto others then civilization devolves into a war of all against all. I have named the alternative to GOLD, the principle of X using force against A and A using force against X, by the name EVIL (Everyone Violating Individual Liberty).

Going back to the Golden Rule, that you must treat others the way you want others to treat you, you can deduce that if you assume X, Y, A, and B, and you assume that X can either violently impose Y onto A, or not initiate violence and let A freely make A's own choice between B or Y, then the only two paths are GOLD or EVIL. GOLD means that A lets X be free to choose Y or B, and X in return lets A be free to make that choice, thus, X treats A in a way that respects A's rights and A treats X in a manner which respects X's rights. EVIL means that X seeks to coerce A and impose Y onto A by brute force, which leads to A retaliating against X and violently forcing B onto X. Under EVIL, X uses force against A and has no respect for A's liberty and rights, and A gives precisely this same treatment back to X. X could respect A's rights and A might initiate aggression against X in return, but this is not conceptualized under the Golden Rule as a treatment which could be universalized, with each person treating every other person precisely the same way, and being treated that way by everyone else in return. Under the Golden Rule, the political choice we must make is between GOLD and EVIL.

Now let us explore a story where I am Mr. A and you are Mr. X. This story is an abstract example; you could plug any values into the variables Mr. X, his belief Y, Mr. A, and his belief B, and the logic would remain essentially the same. For a bird's eye view of this story, I am a social liberal and a fiscal conservative, while you are a social conservative and an economic liberal. As can be expected, your X's Y is in sharp conflict with my A's B. This book will explain how GOLD libertarianism rises above the war between liberals and conservatives to find a fair and principled solution that enables everyone to coexist in peace and freedom, including all groups of people who disapprove of or hate other groups of people within the same political community.

A summary of the issues where you and I disagree are: (1) sexual orientation/gay rights, (2) religion, (3) race, (4) freedom of speech/intellectual freedom, (5) occupational licensing, (6) the minimum wage, and (7) welfare for the poor. GOLD says that each of us should be free to do what we want and choose our own beliefs and values, and if I give freedom to you then you should give freedom to me in return.

Having offered the above summary, I shall proceed to flesh out the details. Regarding the areas that are generally regarded as social policy, when it comes to (1) sexual orientation, if you let me be gay then in return I will not use force to impose my beliefs about right and wrong onto your sex life. If I am free to be a gay man then you are free to have a fetish for women's feet or marry a woman who is a member of a different religion, etc. If the government controls marriage then nobody is free, but if every social decision is made privately by each individual then everyone is free. Thus, as you will see when you read the upcoming chapter on gay rights, the GOLD position is that conservatives should not use the law to condemn and criminalize homosexual behavior, but liberals should not use the law to force social conservatives to recognize gay marriage against their will and in violation of their moral conscience. The GOLD solution is to protect gays from homophobic violence while deregulating marriage so that the government no longer gives its approval or disapproval to weddings and instead lets each church and social group freely choose their own views on gay marriage.

With respect to (2) religion, if you leave me free to be a Jewish atheist then in return you get the freedom to practice Christianity in whatever way you see fit. Although this book does not specifically advocate or oppose any particular religion, the issue of GOLD as a defense of intellectual freedom, i.e. the freedom to believe what you want, will be addressed several times, for example in the chapter on capitalism as the economic precondition of freedom, and also in the chapter discussing the civil liberties guaranteed in the United States Constitution. In both chapters I explain why intellectual freedom, social freedom and economic freedom go hand in hand. The alternative to freedom is giving the government the power to regulate religion, which takes the most sacred sphere of life and gives control over it to whoever happens to be the strongest thug or the politician with the most votes.

If I am a Jew and you impose Southern Baptism onto me then in the future someone else will impose Roman Catholicism onto you, and under the Golden Rule that will be perfectly fair because you get the same treatment that you gave to me. Or, for a related example, if you force an atheist to convert to Christianity then you have no right to complain when the Marxists take over and force you to become an atheist. Perhaps the sharpest example of freedom of religion comes in the chapter on sin crimes, where I argue that even if you view drugs, gambling, and prostitution as sins, this does not make it right for you to use the government to criminalize those behaviors, because when you fight to outlaw other people's freedom you pave the road to your own freedom also being destroyed.

In terms of (3) race, the United States has a history that looks a lot like EVIL, which began with whites using violence and the legal system against blacks, first with slavery and later with Jim Crow. The blacks later retaliated against the whites, which is easy to understand given that many blacks are steeped in anger and furious at their history of being oppressed. Blacks sought revenge by deploying affirmative action and reverse discrimination policies to use government force to favor blacks and disfavor whites.

If X is colored and A is white then it violated GOLD for A to use force against X, but it is also wrong and unfair for X to use force against A, even for the noble ideal of helping black people to escape from the past effects of slavery and inequality. This book contains several chapters showing why libertarianism helps the members of racial minorities, and also why capitalism helps the poor and underprivileged, and I take one chapter to spell out in detail the GOLD policy for defending civil rights.

As I discuss later in this book, GOLD gets government out of the business of helping one race at the expense of another race, and GOLD lets everyone be free as individuals to succeed or fail on their own unique merits, which is the policy of true social progress. It cannot be said that "GOLD favors blacks" or "GOLD favors whites" or "GOLD helps the poor" or "GOLD helps the rich" because the truth is best described by the statement "GOLD helps everybody and does not help one group at the expense of another group." This idea may be new to pro-white racist conservatives and pro-black racist liberals, but to someone like me, who is Jewish, gay, and colored, the idea of race-blind political equality, where each individual has the same rights regardless of his or her racial identity, seems like simple common sense.

To conclude the social freedom part of the story about me and you, if (4) you lobby the government to ban my book then you have accepted the principle that the government owns your mind and gets to give you a list of authorized books to read. And if you later want to read a book that the government has banned or you don't like the ideas that are being forced onto you then by that point it is too late because you conceded that the government is allowed to decide right and wrong for the public and that violent force is a proper and appropriate tool to impose values and virtues onto people. One of the unique ideas in this book, explained in the section on economics and also in the section on the law, is that the liberal concern for civil liberties, e.g. my freedom to write atheist books, and the conservative concern for freedom from regulation, e.g. my freedom to buy and sell what I want on my terms, is really two sides of the same libertarian coin, because if the government claims the right to be the boss of your beliefs then it will soon usurp the power to be the boss of your place in the economy and take total control over you, and if the government is the boss of the economy then it will inevitably take over the realm of ideas in order to suppress dissent and stifle criticism of the economic planners.

To deal with economic freedom as it relates to me and you, if (5) you force me to get an occupational license to practice law to protect the public from bad lawyers, then you concede that the state can regulate and control your job too. This same principle taken to its logical conclusion would let the government assign you to a job and force you to work without the choice to quit, since the workplace would be transferred to the public sphere. If you "protect" a poor person by not letting them hire me as a lawyer, then the government will protect the poor from you by making you jump through hoops of regulation and leaving you unemployed and destitute if you don't measure up to the regulator's demands, even if you are good at your job and people don't really need to be protected from you. This point will be examined in detail in the chapter on occupational licensing.

And if (6) you use force to impose the wage that you feel is right onto other people then you open the door to government using violence to impose what the state's experts feel is right onto you even when you disagree with the government. I make the case against minimum wage laws later in this book, in the context of a bold new economic analysis which explains why economic policy can only succeed if it uses capitalism and money prices so that supply and demand can be allowed to function as a tool for people to coordinate production and consumption.

This ties to (7) poverty and helping me as a poor person. In the chapters at the heart of my new theory of economics, I show that GOLD will be better for the poor and the working class than socialism would be, I also prove that my theory, if applied consistently in practice by policymakers, would achieve so much increased efficiently and create enough new wealth that it would help solve the problem of poverty. My theories explained later in this book, including the productivity theory of demand, the choice theory of value, and my refutation of market failure, combine to explain exactly which path we should walk down to move the economy forward. So GOLD is the political philosophy that is truly loving and compassionate towards the vulnerable and helpless, because it will generate the added prosperity that will enable us to afford to help those who are less fortunate.

Both libertarianism and liberalism seek equality, but each does so by means of quite different methods, as I analyze in the chapter on equality and aristocracy and the chapter on how capitalism helps the poor. Liberalism, to the extent that it accepts socialist economic principles, achieves equality not by lifting the poor up to the level of the rich but by tearing the rich down and dragging them into the ranks of the poor. The goal of libertarian economic policy is to make everyone rich by raising the standard of living in order to create upward mobility for the working class so that everyone reaches equality at the top of the ladder. What every able-bodied poor person needs is opportunity, not handouts, so that they can lift themselves up. Economic freedom creates jobs for the working class whereas government intervention destroys jobs, although welfare benefits will go down when freedom leads to tax cuts. In other words, when freedom closes a window it opens a door.

In each of these seven examples, I was just minding my own business and doing no harm to you, but you felt justified by EVIL to use violence against me, by means of the government's police which enforce the laws, to coerce me into doing what you think is right but which I feel is wrong. Having abandoned GOLD and embraced EVIL, there is no principle which stops the next thug or political party from coming along and forcing you to obey them just as I obeyed you. And if you choose EVIL then you are asking for it. By contrast, under GOLD you are justified in using violence to defend yourself against me if I attack you, but you should not use violence against me in a way that you would not want me to use against you if you and I had our situations reversed.

Libertarianism has been likened to "live and let die" by its critics, but we can see that GOLD is really "live and let live." GOLD is not a philosophy of arrogance and elitism. Instead, GOLD is founded upon tolerance and respect for the rights of others, including the most important right, my right to engage in behavior which you morally disapprove of and feel is ethically wrong but which does no harm to you, which is identical to your right to do what you want free from interference by me. GOLD is an interpretation of the Golden Rule according to which I give you the freedom to do what you want, and in return you also give me the freedom to live my life as I see fit, so that we treat each other the same way and the result is freedom for both you and me. The alternative to GOLD is EVIL, where you use force against me to impose your beliefs onto me and I retaliate with violence against you. EVIL leads either to the bloody chaos of open war or, as is happening in the United States of America, it leads to a situation where you vote for politicians who pass laws that constrict my freedom, and I vote for politicians who pass laws that squeeze you and take control of your life, and the end result is a maze of laws where no one is truly free anymore.

SUBPART 1-B: THE ETHICS OF GOLD, AND THE FREEDOM TO MAKE DECISIONS

The reason why EVIL is so seductive, and both social conservatives and economic liberals accept it, and the reason why GOLD libertarianism is so unpopular, is because it seems illogical and counterintuitive to say that if X knows for sure that Y is good and B is evil, and X knows definitely that B will be bad for A, and A stubbornly chooses B and refuses to freely, voluntarily choose Y, then why can't X behave like a responsible parent teaching a child, and use violence to force Y onto A? Why not, if Y would help A and Y being forced onto A is for A's own benefit? The GOLD Principle which says that X forcing Y onto A is wrong, even if we assume that Y is good and B is evil, requires a person to actually think deep, sophisticated thoughts about politics, and to see the logical conclusions which will result from the acceptance of the political principles of either GOLD or EVIL. GOLD demands that you reason the long-term effects of a political system, which might be subtle and hidden and not obvious, and not merely attach your political ideology to the simple and basic feeling that if Y is good then everyone should do Y, so A should do Y, so X should force A to do Y.

If X is only aware of Y, and X is not conceptual enough to know about A and think about B, then X will find it natural and easy to think that Y is the one and only truth. X will seek to impose Y onto A without even being aware of B or thinking the next thought that follows from EVIL, namely, that A believes B, and if X imposes Y onto A, then A will seek to impose B onto X, unless GOLD protects X from A and A from X and leaves X and A the freedom to choose Y or B. GOLD, as an intellectual, intelligent theory, is a political idea for human beings, and not for base animals. Unfortunately, most people, and most voters, do not think the next thought that follows from reasoning where your political principles will lead. Most people get caught on the idea of "B is good, X should do B, we should force X to do B," and they never reach the next thought, a thought that is more complicated but also far deeper, which is "if A forces X to do B, then EVIL, and if EVIL then A and X will go to war, and brute force and savage thugs will decide who rules and who forces their beliefs onto everyone else."

GOLD is consistent with the theory of personal responsibility and individual accountability which holds that X should decide for X between Y and B, and A should not make the decision between Y and B for X, in other words, X should be free to choose and A should not force A's choice onto X. It isn't A's job to make X's decisions. X is the one who bears the consequences of Y. If Y is good then X will prosper, and if Y is bad then X will suffer. Therefore, since X is the one most affected by Y, it is fair and just for X to choose Y, and not have A force the choice of B onto X. If X chooses Y freely then X will bear the consequences of Y, so X's freedom to choose between Y and B makes sense. Having A make the decision for which X will prosper or suffer but which won't have any direct effect on A doesn't make sense. If X does not use violence to violate A's freedom then X's belief in Y cannot possibly harm A or violate A's rights, so A has no right to control X, and A suffers no harm by leaving X alone and letting X believe Y.

Libertarianism has been accused of being the political philosophy of arrogance and hubris, made for those who see themselves as the productive, talented genius elite, but the principle of GOLD is actually based on being humble and having the humility to accept the limits of an individual human being's knowledge. I asked earlier: "what if Y is good and B is evil, why shouldn't X force Y onto A for A's benefit?" But this question accepts a hidden premise, that we, me and you, the reader of this book, are able to look at Y and B and know, like gods or omniscient omnipotent supermen, know for sure that Y is good and B is wrong. But X believes Y and A believes B, and those beliefs are all that we humans will ever have. Nothing inherent in A's mind, other than his arrogance, could let him believe that he is better able to choose between Y and B for X's benefit than X could choose for himself for his own benefit.

In actual practical reality, we don't say that A made X's decision for X and forced B onto X, which obviously assumes that A is an "expert" in a class of superior intelligence compared to X, and X is a lower class citizen in decision-making ability compared to A. We say instead that the government made X's decision for X and imposes B onto X. However, the way this really works is for A to vote for a politician, let us call him C, who will then impose B onto X. Thus, we can see that EVIL assumes a god complex, or a "government as God" complex, which assumes that A and C have a magical, infallible path to knowledge of B, and that the government knows better than the individuals and the government's "experts" like C can make decisions better than the people, better than X can for himself. In true reality, A is a human with a fallible brain and limited, faulty knowledge, so we should let A make his decisions for himself, and let A stand or fall by A's choosing B, but we should not let A drag down X by also forcing B onto X via the politician C's control. B looks correct to A, but since this is the result of A's mind, A might be mistaken, and it isn't fair for X to suffer because of A's mistake. If someone must make the choice which impacts X's life, and a fallible human capable of error must choose for X, and X will suffer or prosper from this choice, then fairness and justice demands that X be allowed to make the choice for X. As such, GOLD is a philosophy for human beings with human brains who can make mistakes, and EVIL assumes a mistaken "government as God" complex.

EVIL appeals to two types of people: First, people who feel so stupid and weak that they want someone else to make their decisions, and they want someone to use violent force to coerce them into behaving properly instead of having their own discipline and willpower to make good choices. Second, people who are so arrogant and elitist that they feel the right to force their personal beliefs onto everyone else, as if they are smarter and know better than everyone else. By contrast, GOLD is for people who know that someone must make a decision to guide a person, so the system which makes sense is for the person who bears the consequences to make the decision, and not let one person ruin another person's life by forcing his decision onto the other person, just because he believed in his own mind that he was right and the other person was wrong.

To illustrate this using an example, first, X is a graduate of Yale College and Harvard Law School. So X is "smart." Second, A dropped out of high school and works as a chef cooking French fries at a fast food restaurant, and A scores low on IQ tests. So some people (not me) would say that A is "stupid." The example works if A is smart and X is stupid, or X is smart and A is stupid, and it also works whether X seeks to force Y onto A, or A seeks to force B onto X, or all of the above. These are abstract variables that represent all people and all values.

Now, if you are smart and I am stupid and you are smarter than me, does that give you the right to make my decisions for me? If you know what's best for me better than I do, would that give you the right to violently coerce my obedience to your decision? If you really went to Yale and Harvard then you would probably say yes. But if the reverse were true and I am smart and you are stupid and I am smarter than you, how would you feel if I forced you to obey my decisions for you and I did not let you make decisions for yourself? To say that A should decide for X if A really is smarter than X, assumes that some authority with God-like knowledge has evaluated that A really is smarter. X, since he favors Y over B, probably does not accept that A is smarter, and who are we to disagree? Who are we to decide for X that A knows what is best for X and to impose our decision by force?

Let us assume that all humans are capable of making mistakes, such that some of our decisions are definitely going to be wrong and mistaken. If something bad happens to you, would you feel better if the problem was the result of your decision or of mine? If you let someone else control you then you can deny all blame for the bad things that happen to you as a result of someone else's decisions. It is comforting to think that "the experts" are protecting you and running your life. But the reverse of this is that someone else gets to control you on the justification that you are not fit to think and someone else is smarter than you.

If you take responsibility for yourself and you make your own decisions then you function as an ethical person who makes good or bad choices and reaps the rewards or punishments of those choices. Whether you are smart or stupid, you are a human being just like me, and I would rather choose for myself than have you (and your government) make my decisions for me. In accordance with the Golden Rule, I am willing to give you the same freedom than I want you to give to me, even if you make bad decisions of which I disapprove. So long as you don't use violence against me, your problems are your issue, not mine. The reciprocal is also true, which means that if I don't use violence against you then how I run my life is really none of your business, at least in the sense of political significance.

X's decision of Y or B is a personal choice, and X's decision is X's path to self-actualization and self-realization as a human being. If X is an end in himself then he has the right to be free to realize his identity through choosing Y. A forcing B onto X, even for a noble, idealistic social purpose, merely turns X into A's means of achieving B, which violates X's dignity and independence as a human being, and effectively makes X into A's slave. This is equally true if A's B comes from a motive of selfish ambition and power, or from a selfless, charitable desire to help X, assuming that A believes that B will be good for X. If A tries to violently force X to believe B, to do B, to think B, to obey B, and X refuses to go along with it or dissents, and X asserts Y, then A's political principle of EVIL will result in A putting X in jail, stealing X's property, and murdering X. Under the principle of EVIL, X has no right to freedom nor to life, liberty, and property, and EVIL does not respect X's right to choose Y. Thus, if X insists on Y, and A commits to violently forcing B onto X, then EVIL must eventually, inevitably result in: "to the gas chamber, go!"

Because everyone is treated the same, GOLD achieves true political equality. GOLD means that you can, and should, use force for self-defense, but you must never initiate violence against another human for any reason, even for a supposedly good, noble, idealistic reason. GOLD doesn't tell you what to do, what to choose, what to think, or what to believe, it only says that you have the freedom to make those decisions for yourself. If we define "liberty" or "freedom" as the condition of you being able to make your own decisions and not having someone else use force to impose their decisions onto you, then GOLD, and only GOLD, can form a foundation for a politics of freedom.

SUBPART 1-C: THE RIGHT TO OWN PRIVATE PROPERTY

When A uses force against X's property, he is using force against X's person, for the following reason. We can infer that property is self-expression if we accept two premises, (1) that the physical world exists objectively in reality, and (2) that a person manifests his/her existence in the physical world by mixing his/her choices, labor and actions into the stuff of material objects. Assuming these, it follows that a person owns his/her own body for the same reason, and to the same extent, that he/she owns his/her private property possessions. The reason that the person owns their body and property is that the physical things express the person's existence in physical reality as the tools of the person making personal choices and decisions about physical existence, and a person's decisions are their means of self-actualization and self-expression. When an artistic clay bowl results from an artist mixing her choices with the material of the raw clay, the bowl expresses her personal identity, and she owns it because she created it.

The day laborer worker does not think of his salary as self-expression, but nonetheless, physical human existence as a person includes the worker making choices to do work to earn wages to buy food, water and shelter. This forms a cycle: the self makes choices which the body acts out to create the property consumed by the body for the furtherance of the self. This cycle of production and consumption by the individual situates the person as a human being in the physical world. By "self" I refer to the person, but you could call it the soul, the mind, the brain, the consciousness, or whatever you believe the self to be. Body and property are extensions of the human self, so violent coercion against body or property is an assault on the freedom of the self. Thus, "life, liberty, and property" actually describes one thing, the freedom to exist as a human being.

Political philosophers have identified three general justifications for private property: (1) utilitarianism, (2) natural rights, and (3) personhood and self-expression. Utilitarianism says that people should own property because owning the products of your labor has the practical pragmatic result of motivating you to be productive and work hard, which benefits society by creating more wealth. For example, the motive of getting a promotion might motivate a worker to work harder. Natural rights says that you have the moral right to own the things that you create because they were created by your hard work, your decisions, and your investments of the money and materials you put in, and it is fair for you to reap the rewards of the things that resulted from your blood and sweat and tears. For example, if a businessman works ten hours a day seven days a week for several months, and goes without sleep or spending time with his family, in order to develop a new product, then he has earned the right to profit from the sales of that product. Personhood says that the things that we make are an expression of who we are as people so we have a right to control those things because they are a part of us. For example, if an artist paints a painting then she owns that image as an extension of her being.

Many libertarians get into fierce, aggressive arguments debating which of these three theories is correct. I sidestep this debate, because I see all three theories as correct. I don't think that one theory being right means that the other two are wrong. All three arguments are true and I agree with all of them, so I have no need to defend one against the others. In the chapters to come which discuss natural rights vs. utilitarianism and the question of whether rich people deserve to own their wealth, I will elaborate on these ideas in far greater detail.

SUBPART 1-D: THE FREEDOM TO BE GOOD, AND X'S Y VS. A'S B

The GOLD principle is politics as meta-ethics, and GOLD is a decision theory. It doesn't tell you what is good or evil, it doesn't tell you Y or B, it only tells you that the person who must make that decision is you, not the government. GOLD as an ethics of freedom comes from the meta-ethical need to choose your own right and wrong, which is the essence of being an ethical human being. In the absence of a person having the freedom to choose what he/she thinks is the good and right choice or evil and wrong behavior, morality and ethics would simply cease to exist or to have any meaning because nobody could express their ethics and values. Where, later in this book, I say what good or evil is, I tell you my belief about Y or B, but I make this merely as a recommendation, as an appeal to your reason to ask you to freely choose, rather than forcing a choice onto you. Any person can nonviolently recommend or request anything, and this does not inherently obey or violate GOLD. The GOLD vs. EVIL question turns on whether I, or you, or someone else, asks you to freely choose what they recommend, or else seeks to use the government to force their vision of morality and good and evil onto you against your will.

The GOLD meta-ethics is a politics that makes ethics possible. Assuming that a person becomes a good person by choosing goodness and choosing to do good, and it doesn't make you ethical or moral to do a "good" behavior because you were violently forced to do it by someone else at the point of the government's guns and not because you chose to do it or wanted to do it, then A forcing X to do B doesn't make X become a good person even if B is a good behavior and is better than Y. Forcing people to "be good" doesn't make people virtuous or moral or build their character, but it commits the sin of violating liberty and denying to individuals the freedom to become good people by freely and voluntarily choosing goodness.

As the simplest example of this, imagine that a person dies and then goes to the gates of Heaven and says to St. Peter who decides to let people in or else send them to Hell: "In life I did not believe in God or Christ, and I wanted to sin, but I was violently forced to do a set of behaviors like not gambling and not buying liquor on Sundays and not having sex with prostitutes. I thought about committing sins constantly and I wanted to sin and I have no feelings of God's love or morality. I obeyed only begrudgingly and with a heart full of hatred and resentment. However, as a result of the government's police forcing me to obey, my actions were fully consistent with the laws of the Bible and I never committed a sinful action, despite the fact that I hate Jesus and I would have behaved differently if I had been free to do so." Do you really think that St. Peter would let this person enter Heaven? Note that in this situation the use of the government to enforce Christian morality has done everything that it can possibly do. If being forced to obey the Bible does not cause salvation for the person in my example then are any souls saved by legislating morality, even if we concede that Christian theology is correct? In contrast, if a person is free to sin but instead chooses to be holy, doesn't that actually increase his moral virtues in the eyes of God? The common folk wisdom that "character is what you do when nobody is watching" comes to mind.

GOLD, and the Golden Rule that you should treat others the way you want them to treat you, is both a pragmatic practical principle and an ethical moral principle. As pragmatism, A should let X believe Y so that X will leave A alone and let A believe B, which is useful for A because A wants to believe B. As idealism, A should respect X's right to Y because A respects X's rights and dignity as a human being, and A believes in freedom and the Golden Rule. A should know that the right thing to do is to let X be free so that GOLD will govern both A and X, and A will be free to do B.

Here let me make a point which is by far the most important argument in favor of GOLD. It makes no sense to say under the Golden Rule that A may force B onto X because A would want X to force B onto A, such that it would be universal for everyone to be forced to do B. It is nonsense because the equivalent of A's B for X is X's Y, not B, so X forcing Y onto A is the equivalent reciprocal of A forcing B onto X. For example, a conservative Christian might say that he treats straights and gays equally because both straight men and gay men have the freedom to marry a woman. But the equivalent of A's B for X is Y, not B. In this example the equivalent of a straight man's right to marry a woman is a gay man's right to marry another man.

The stupid, idiotic A will be perfectly okay with X forcing B onto A because A likes B, and A would be okay with either freely choosing B or being forced to do B. A can't imagine that the EVIL principle means that if X is forced to do B, the reciprocal lets X force Y onto A, so A is actually accepting an EVIL result under which A will be forced to obey Y even though A fanatically believes B and hates Y. Our political structure can be based on either GOLD or EVIL, and if A embraces EVIL to force B onto X then EVIL will destroy freedom of choice for A as well as X. In the gay marriage example, if A says that X has the freedom to marry a woman but not a man then A accepts EVIL, a principle under which gay men might get elected into Congress and then use the law to force X and X's church to recognize and endorse gay marriage against X's will, even to the point of censoring books which discuss Catholic moral theology or putting people in jail if they make statements which offend gay men.

If X uses force to impose Y onto A then it is fair and just for A to retaliate by forcing B onto X, as we can see throughout human history, most recently by American liberals and conservatives fighting over which group can destroy the freedom of the other group as rapidly as possible. Libertarian GOLD, on the other hand, gives A the freedom to belong to a church that condemns homosexuality and gives X the freedom of gay marriage because it gives both X and A the freedom to decide his/her own ethical beliefs for himself/herself, just as it gives each person the freedom to make his/her own economic choices. GOLD is both ethical in terms of everyone receiving the same treatment and practical in terms of each person gaining the freedom to do what he wants by creating a political structure which defends the freedom of X against A's violence while simultaneously defending A from X's violence. If X denies freedom to A by saying that A is free to choose Y but not to choose B then X has destroyed freedom, and in doing so he destroys his own freedom because EVIL fosters a system where society and the government have no respect for anyone's rights.

Small-minded, shortsighted people think that it is okay for them to force their "morality" or their "noble idealism" onto everyone else. They think that what they believe is good for everyone, and therefore everyone should obey it and this is consistent with the Golden Rule since everyone can force everyone else to obey goodness. But their principle is EVIL, not GOLD, because as soon as you use force to coerce others into obeying your vision of right and wrong, you open the door to everyone using force to coerce everyone else to obey their own vision of right and wrong, and this leads to an EVIL world without rights or liberty, because your belief is yours, and others might believe or choose or impose something completely different.

This does not change if you use the government to coerce other people to obey your morality or noble idealism instead of using force yourself individually, and it doesn't change if you say that your belief about morality is what "society" believes. Coercion by the government or society is a majority aggressively coercing a minority of individuals, and the numbers on the side of X or A do not change the principles of GOLD and EVIL. EVIL will always tell X that Y is goodness and virtue and therefore X should force Y onto A, and EVIL will con and scam X into believing that a world based around Y where everyone believes Y will be a happy, peaceful, good place, because everyone will accept and believe X's Y. EVIL is a serpent's tongue which seduces X into abandoning the GOLD principle of freedom and rights and instead choosing a world where force decide everyone's choices for them, a world devoid of the freedom to be good, a world where violence replaces reasoning. The EVIL world is a land of barbarian brute force that no civilized person would tolerate if they understood what was happening and what GOLD and EVIL really mean.

Who are X and A, and what is Y and B? I said that I am A and you are X, but in reality X and A could be any man or woman, any human being, and X's Y and A's B can be any belief, ethics, value, behavior, or choice, be it social, economic, religious, or philosophical. Note that as soon as we plug in a specific choice for Y, the supporters of Y will forget GOLD and want to use force to impose Y onto A. GOLD asks people to remember their understanding and have the discipline to let other people be free, and to advocate Y through persuasion, not violence. For example, Y could be gay pride and B could be the belief that homosexuality is a sin. Or Y could be Christianity and B could be Judaism. Or Y could be Christianity and B could be Islam. Or Y could be a desire to do drugs and B could be a belief that drug abuse is evil. Or Y and B could be two different makes and models of cars that are competing for auto consumers to buy them. Or Y could be the belief that an experimental medical treatment might be effective to treat a sickness, and B could be the belief that it is unsafe and too dangerous to try on humans. Or Y could be the belief that workers should be paid a wage of no less than $15/hour, because workers deserve to be paid well, and B could be someone's belief that it is okay to pay workers $1/hour, if that is what the supply and demand for labor determines as a proper wage.

The principle of GOLD remains the same in each situation, no matter what you plug into Y and B, and that principle is that each person, every X and A, should be free to make their own choice, and be free to do whatever behavior they want to do in their own life, and should not have someone else's choice imposed onto them coercively, nor should they impose their choices onto others. A person should be free to worship in the religious faith of their choosing, without a state religion being imposed on them, but the reverse is that they are not free to legislate their morality and impose their religious values onto others by means of the state. A person should be free to express gay pride, or to disapprove of homosexuality, so long as they seek to spread their opinions by persuasion and get others to voluntarily choose to agree, rather than violently intimidating others or using the law to force their belief onto those who disagree.

GOLD is not an ethics that people must choose, it is a precondition that follows if a person wants to be able to make an ethical choice. GOLD is politically necessary for any ethics or religion or for any choice, and everyone should respect the rights of others and embrace GOLD. If EVIL is accepted then politics disintegrates into a war between X and A to see who is the strongest and most vicious thug, because brute force defines whether X is able to impose Y violently onto A or whether A will triumph over X. The EVIL principle leads inevitably to savagery and the barbarian condition of "might is right" where the strongest muscle forces its beliefs onto everyone else. EVIL is a path leading back to the Dark Ages and the rule of kings, whereas GOLD is the principle which justifies civilized freedom and republican democracy and a society based around "we the people" and each individual's right and freedom to make his or her own choices for himself/herself. GOLD is a world of freedom; EVIL is a world of violence.

The remainder of this book will lift GOLD off the pedestal of abstract theory and show what GOLD means in terms of specific, concrete positions applied to various questions concerning social, economic, and legal policy, and the nature and purpose of government. Part One explains the GOLD analysis of social policy, and introduces the concept of social libertarianism. Part Two presents GOLD economics, and showcases the correspondence theory of money, the choice theory of value, and the story of trade vs. force, as well as the productivity theory of demand. Part Three examines what a legal system would look like if it conformed to GOLD, using the American legal system as an example, and defends the United States Constitution as a libertarian document. Part Four makes the argument, which is quite controversial for some libertarians, that GOLD justifies the existence of a government that actively defends the rights and freedoms of its citizens.

To conclude, I will mention that, although the rest of this book touches upon dozens of different issues, the theme that unites all my arguments is GOLD. You should pay special attention when I discuss X and Y and A and B, because the XYAB analysis is the core of the GOLD theory. The interaction between X and A represents the political relationship between all people as human beings. X and A can be anyone and Y and B can be anything. X can either use force against A or let A be free, and A can reciprocate towards X with force or freedom. XYAB reduces the complicated conceptual analysis of how I treat you and what you do to me in return down to its most basic components in terms of GOLD vs. EVIL.

PART ONE: SOCIAL LIBERTARIANISM

CHAPTER TWO: THE LEGALIZATION OF SIN CRIMES: DRUGS, PROSTITUTION, AND GAMBLING

GOLD libertarians want to legalize gambling, prostitution, and drug usage. Drug legalization includes all drugs, meaning marijuana as well as hard drugs. The basic application of the libertarian GOLD principle is clear, and can be described as follows: X should not force A to do Y, nor should A force X to do B, even though X fervently, passionately, fanatically believed that Y is virtue and B is horrific evil, and also despite the fact that A feels the same way in the sense that A thinks that B is goodness and Y is evil.

To apply the GOLD analysis to the legalization of sin crimes, it might be true that prostitution, drugs, and gambling are morally evil, and GOLD concedes that these behaviors might be extremely evil. Sins might condemn the sinner to an eternity in Hell, and drug abuse might cause brain damage and ruin people's lives. But the decision of whether these things are evil or good, ethical or immoral, belongs to each individual person, because each person has the right to be free to decide for himself/herself. This decision does not belong to "society," which in reality means that one group of people uses the government to impose their moral beliefs and feelings onto everyone else, even if some of those other people want to make a different decision. GOLD is the freedom to do whatever you want as long as you do no violence or aggression to others. Drug use, prostitution and gambling are nonviolent behaviors. Therefore under GOLD each person has the right to do them.

The legalization of sin crimes does not assume that the behavior is good, nor denies that it is evil. Legalization merely embodies the principle that the decision of good or evil should be made freely by individuals and should not be imposed by the government. If the purpose of government was to legalize goodness and criminalize evil, then legalization would imply that sins are good. But this is not the purpose of government. The purpose of government is only to legalize freedom and criminalize violence. So it is possible for a nonviolent evil behavior to exist that should be legal despite the fact that nobody should ever do this behavior as a matter of ethics. Sin crimes are such behaviors.

The criminalization of sin crimes does not make sense from a Christian theological perspective. If sin crimes are evil, then God will punish the sinner with Hell, or evil behavior will punish the person with a miserable life, but the responsibility to decide his or her moral behavior lies with each individual himself/herself, not with the social conservatives. If God punishes the sinner with Hell then what need exists to punish the sinner with jail on Earth? If God's job is to pass judgment on good and evil, then why authorize the courts to pass such judgment? Indeed, is this not "playing God" by mortal men?

If social conservatives know that these behaviors are evil, they are free to persuade other people to agree, and thereby convince others to freely and voluntarily choose to abstain from sin. From a theological point of view, what makes a person be good or evil, destined for Heaven or Hell, is their choices to be good or evil, not merely obeying orders when someone shoves a gun in their face and threatens to throw them in jail. The government imposing certain behaviors onto people actually has no net moral benefit in terms of saving sinners. Legislating morality is merely a pretext for social conservatives to use the state to achieve political power and curtail social freedom.

The social conservative argument that such behaviors are not nonviolent, and are not a "victimless crime," because "society" bears a "social cost," e.g. the costs of healthcare and welfare for drug addicts, is absolute lies and nonsense. The problem of the welfare state would be solved by restoring financial personal responsibility to each individual, and the existence of welfare is not a flaw in the freedom to make individual decisions. None of the sin crime behaviors, including prostitution, gambling, and the use of pot or hard drugs, is actually more dangerous than alcohol abuse or habitual cigarette usage, which are already legal. Legalization of drugs, prostitution and gambling would create jobs and stake out new areas for businesses to develop, by enabling people to get jobs and start businesses in these areas, which would vastly increase economic growth. As a practical matter, criminalization of sin crimes unfairly targets the poor, blacks, and Hispanics, who are more likely to be arrested and go to jail for these crimes than the rich and whites. Criminalization inherently targets the poor, and those racial minorities who are more likely than whites to be poor, for a very simple reason, which every poor person knows but which the rich and middle class voters find difficult to understand. The reason is that being poor makes people sad and miserable, and sin crimes are all ways that humans cope with sadness and misery, so it is intrinsic to the criminalization policies that they will put the poor in jail, but will leave the happy rich and satisfied middle class free and untouched.

And, obviously, if it is okay for the state governments to sell gambling services, in the form of the state lotto, then why should gambling be outlawed when sold by private businesspeople? Similarly, if people are allowed to drink alcohol and smoke cigarettes, then why can't they buy and smoke pot, which is actually far less dangerous that liquor or cigarettes? In reply to the argument that prostitution enables the rich to sexually exploit the poor, I reply that prostitution gives to the poor one of their few opportunities to make a lot of money, and a poor person is free to choose whether or not she (or he) is willing to do sex work. Also, criminalization has not eliminated the existence of prostitution, so some people must want to do it. It is unfair to the poor to criminalize prostitution as a way for the poor to get rich, or to criminalize the drugs which enable the poor to cope with the misery and suffering of poverty. The law as it exists right now has no rigorous logical sense or coherent reasoning to it, other than thinly disguised racism and class warfare. Therefore the need for reform is clear, and reform would be logical and rational.

Bringing the black market of drugs, prostitution and gambling back into the legal marketplace could increase economic growth by a lot, although data on illegal transactions cannot be comprehensively collected due to the absence of tax reporting of sales. If one takes the impressive economic growth that legalized gambling caused in Atlantic City, Las Vegas, and the Native American Indian casinos, and projects it across a larger region, then the projection for added growth is substantial. Not only would sales of these services generate revenue, but they would create new jobs for the poor, which would shrink the number of people who need to be on welfare. Indeed, in answer to liberal critics who say that in reality some 30% to 50% of Americans need welfare, I reply that legalization has a realistic chance of creating enough working class jobs, and revitalizing enough impoverished areas, to cut the number of people in need of welfare in half. Libertarian policies discussed elsewhere in this book, such as abolishing wage regulations and occupational licensing restrictions, would create so many new jobs that the number of people who need welfare could be cut down to zero. Decriminalization will create jobs for the poor who are able to work, leaving only the truly helpless to be rescued by charity.

Some anti-drug crusaders say that legalized drug abuse would add to society's welfare burden, but the opposite is true, the net effect would subtract from social burdens. Consider also the cost to taxpayers of funding the police effort to fight "sin" crimes, and to fight the mafia, and organized crime, and gangs, all of whom are funded largely by drug money and prostitution and gambling. Because sin crime money funds the gangs and organized crime, legalization of drugs and prostitution and gambling would deal a sharp blow to crime, in contrast to the stupidity of "tough on crime" conservatives (and liberals) who think that putting as many people as possible in jail is somehow a good thing for society. Legalization of sin crimes will cut off the funding for organized crime and return the black market economy to the daylight.

The decrease in funding for organized crime might enable federal, state and local police departments to enjoy a huge across-the-board decrease in expenses, which could cut total government spending by a significant amount. So legalization of sin crimes will both vastly increase tax revenues by stimulating economic growth and will also decrease the need for government law enforcement spending, which will enable states and the federal government to enact big tax cuts without increasing deficits. The net economic benefit of legalization might be billions of dollars per year in private business economic growth, a lot of which would benefit the poor, racial minorities, and urban inner cities.

Note that the criminal law has historically followed society's general feelings of morality, and the evolution and trajectory of change in American moral values, as expressed by today's contemporary sentiment, is towards greater freedom and liberty. At times in American history, it was a crime for a black slave to try to escape, or for a white person to help a black slave escape. It has been a crime in the USA to have a drink of alcohol, for people to be openly gay or for consenting adults to have gay sex, and for women to have abortions, or for married couples to use contraceptives in the privacy of their own homes, and for people to read books on the government's list of censored books. In future eras, Americans will probably look back on our times, and view the criminal laws against drug use, gambling, prostitution, and other sin crimes and victimless crimes, as similarly barbaric, primitive and uncivilized.

The final end goal of the evolution of criminal law, if it remains true to the principle of freedom, will be for crime to consist of violence against the life, liberty or property, and nothing else. If that evolution happens, then the purpose of the criminal law will be to authorize the police to use force for the self-defense of the people. The police would be the guardians of our freedom and our liberty to live and make our own decisions, including our personal decisions (life, liberty) and our economic decisions (property). The criminal law's purpose would no longer be to force and impose the moral values and religious opinions of some people, some voters and some politicians, onto other people who do not consent and would not willingly and freely choose to obey those moral values.

The GOLD libertarian attitude is the freedom and personal liberty of "live and let live": I will choose to behave morally and ethically, but it is not my job to force or regulate my neighbor's morality and violently coerce my neighbor's moral or sinful behavior, because that is his/her own private matter, for which the responsibility lies with him or her, not with me. Their punishment or reward will be success or failure in this life or Heaven or Hell to be handed out by God, it will not be jail handed out by me and the government, and I will not use violence against my neighbor to violate their freedom, and I will not let my neighbor use violence against me to violate my freedom.

CHAPTER THREE: THE SOCIAL LIBERTARIAN STANCE ON GAY RIGHTS

Applying GOLD to gay rights is obvious. If X lets A do B then A lets X do Y, and if X wants A to tolerate X then X must tolerate A in return. Y is being gay or believing that being gay is good, and B is being homophobic or believing that homosexuality is a sin. In this section I will first discuss how GOLD can enable X and A to coexist in peace, and then discuss GOLD protecting X from A, and then conclude by talking about GOLD protecting A from X.

Anti-gay conservatives don't need to like gays or approve of gays (and when I say "gay" I mean what is sometimes called "LGBT," i.e. lesbians, gays, bisexuals, and transgendered people), but they do need to see that if they don't want gays and liberals to force them to change their religious beliefs then in return the conservatives must not force gays to be straight through fear and violent intimidation. GOLD does not say whether being gay is morally right or wrong. GOLD says only that everyone has the right to be free to do whatever they want as long as they do no violence to others. A GOLD libertarian could be pro-gay or anti-gay but he or she must have respect for the right of others to disagree and behave differently. GOLD libertarians should be committed to the NVP approach of not using violent force against others unless in self-defense, even to force others to conform to their beliefs about good and evil when they are certain that they are correct. GOLD recognizes your right to be LGBT, straight, or anything else you want, as long as your sexual identity expression does no violence to others and your sexual conduct is consensual with consenting adults. GOLD recognizes the right to morally disagree with LGBT as a lifestyle choice, but only if that disapproval is not expressed through violence, intimidation or government laws.

If "gay rights" is defined as the freedom to be gay, and as legal protection for that freedom, then GOLD supports gay rights, because gay rights means X's freedom to do Y and does not mean that X forces Y onto A. The specific policies which would implement gay rights must begin with the simple requirement that the police protect gays and lesbians from violence, but they also include policies to give gays and lesbians the ability to use self-defense against hateful bigots. This could be accomplished by a "gays with guns" policy of arming gays and lesbians and giving them weapons training so that haters can't intimidate them.

One commentator has said that the civil rights movement can only protect blacks by means of three tools: the ammo box, the ballot box and the jury box. The same thing can be said about gays, and all other nonconforming minorities. Gay rights and Second Amendment gun rights go hand in hand, because a gun is a person's best defense against a gang of haters. If we want a people to be protected from violence, the liberal answer is to make them rely on the government for protection, whereas the libertarian answer is to give them guns and bullets and let them defend themselves and stick up for themselves and not get pushed around. Gun rights as a tool for political equality is equally applicable to protecting blacks and Hispanics from white racists, or protecting women from muggers and sexual predators. The other two tools, the jury box and the ballot box, simply mean that gays and lesbians should run for political office and serve in office, and that juries should be selected from an inclusive cross-section of society so that bigotry will not play a role in criminal convictions.

The First Amendment should be reinterpreted so that hate speech and bigoted political activism which openly calls for and advocates violence against gays and lesbians is not given protection as free speech. The legal theory in support of the criminalization of bigoted pro-violence activism that its only purpose is to incite violence against gays and lesbians, and inciting violence is a criminal act, not a speech act, and violence is a legitimate target of law enforcement as understood by NVP and GOLD. Conservatives would be free to say that homosexuality is a sin, but would not be free to advocate violence against gays. This policy proposal would also reform First Amendment freedom of association so that bigots and hate group members, such as the KKK and Neo-Nazis, could be excluded from joining the police and the military, and possibly any role in government which oversees the use of the government to protect the freedom of the people from violence. This is supported under the theory that guns and weapons training, and political power, given to haters will end up being used as violence against victims. None of this would violate the "right to be a hateful bigot," because this right entails only the right to engage in nonviolent nonaggressive behavior, and does not include a requirement that the government or society give help to violent people or help them to do violence.

Note that GOLD forbids the government to make people's decisions about whether to like or dislike gays for them, but GOLD leaves private groups and private individuals free to persuade people to accept gays and lesbians and to encourage people to voluntarily embrace LGBT rights. This could be accomplished by "voluntary gay pride pledges," contracts or declarations which an individual or business could sign which would declare themselves committed to nondiscrimination and acceptance. Under GOLD, the government could not help or promote this, but the people would be free to voluntarily choose to sign the pledge, and to encourage others to do so, and gay rights supporters could reward people who sign. The people would be free to boycott or speak out against those who oppose the gay pride pledge and what it represents, although, again, the government could not levy legal sanctions against the non-signers. The government does not have the right to force private businesses not to discriminate against gays, but if a business signs a gay pride pledge then it would freely choose not to discriminate, which would be better for gays in the long run because it would protect gay rights in a manner consistent with GOLD and freedom.

If the people are given freedom, then they are free to do the right thing, but society should not force any particular person to do something that someone else, e.g. me or you, considers to be the right thing for them to do. Instead, freedom lets each person decide for himself or herself. If being gay is good then the supporters of gay pride can advocate their position by reason and persuasion, without the government's help. And if homosexuality is a sin, then the opponents of homosexuality have the right to voice their opinion via nonviolent tools, such as the preacher's podium and the conservative think tanks. GOLD recognizes a doctrine from the theory of First Amendment freedom of speech called "the marketplace of ideas," which means that the best ideas will win in the competition of discussion and debate and thinking, and ideas should not be forced onto people by the government.

Having explained how GOLD protects X from A, and defends X's right to Y, let me now discuss protecting A from X, and defending A's right to B. Both conservatives and liberals tend to embrace the principle of EVIL, in the gay rights debate as well as elsewhere. Conservatives seek to use violence to bully gays and intimidate them, while liberals try to use the government to force everyone to be pro-gay and to deny to conservatives the right to disapprove of homosexuality. The issue of the debate over gay marriage is a great example of how the liberal vs. conservative debate should be recast in different terms as a GOLD vs. EVIL debate. When the debate is framed as the liberals supporting gay marriage and the conservatives opposing gay marriage, then the hidden premise of the political dialogue assumes that the government's job is to decide who is allowed to marry. If the liberals win then they force their beliefs onto the conservatives, and if the conservatives win then they force their beliefs onto the liberals. Both sides are EVIL, meaning that Everyone Violates Individual Liberty.

The GOLD alternative to EVIL is to "deregulate" marriage, to abolish marriage licenses and let people create whatever private social relationships they choose, which they can define using legal contracts enforced by contract law in order to create a relationship that both persons are legally obligated to obey. To "legalize" gay marriage is to deny the right of social conservatives to believe that gay marriage is wrong and to oppose gay weddings, but to outlaw gay marriage is to violate the freedom and political equality of gays. Instead of the social conservative answer of denying gay marriage or the social liberal answer of legalizing gay marriage, the social libertarian answer is to remove government from the marriage process, abolish "family law" and marital licensing, and let people engage in whatever voluntary, consensual, nonviolent behavior they choose to do. Thus, each individual, each group, and each religious organization and church, would be free to choose whether to recognize or deny gay marriages.

Because it looks like gay marriage is eventually going to be legalized at both the federal level and in most states, the right of the social conservatives is going to be violated by liberal EVIL. In contrast, GOLD would protect the right of religious conservatives to condemn gay marriage, because GOLD preserves A's right to do B, even if the morality of mainstream society changes so that B is widely viewed as wrong and Y is more commonly accepted as right. As times change and different fads go into or come out of fashion, society will change its mind about whether Y or B is good or evil, so the only system that can offer long-term protection for both X and A is GOLD, by defending the right to do either Y or B. EVIL, even if one side uses it to force its beliefs onto others when that side is the majority, can always end up being corrupted by the other side and being used against the side which at one time was the moral majority but which has become the minority due to changing circumstances.

CHAPTER FOUR: THE SOCIAL LIBERTARIAN STANCE ON ABORTION RIGHTS

The social libertarian stance is that, according to GOLD, a person should be free to do whatever they want, even if other people's ethics or society's morality views their behavior as wrong, so long as they do no violence to others. GOLD also says that a person owns his or her own body, and can do to his or her body what he or she wants, even if society disapproves. The social conservatives make a clever move in their appeal to libertarians on the abortion rights question, to get around NVP. They say that, even if we concede social libertarianism and NVP, the libertarians don't condone murder, and NVP allows the government to use force to prevent murder. Conservatives say that abortion is murder and therefore libertarians should oppose abortion. This argument has persuaded many libertarians, and the libertarian movement is divided between pro-life and pro-choice.

But the social conservative ploy is a sham, and the GOLD stance is pro-choice. Why? Because even if a fetus is a human life with the rights of a person, and we concede the social conservative assumption that abortion is the termination of a human life, a woman would still have the right to choose an abortion. As the libertarian scholar Murray Rothbard argued, even if a fetus is a person with rights, including all the rights of an adult human being, a fetus would not have more rights or different rights than an adult human, and no person has the right to enslave the body of another person. Pro-life would make the mother into the physical slave of the fetus by forcing the woman to host the fetus in her body and give her body to the fetus against her will. Thus, although one could call abortion by the name "murder," it is not the same thing as the traditional concept of murder as the taking of a person's life.

The fact that the fetus needs the mother is no more an entitlement to enslave the mother than is the fact that some poor people rely on government welfare in order to have food to eat, or the historical fact that pre-Civil War Southern white slave-owners needed their black slaves in order to maintain their economic prosperity. Need and dependence are not an entitlement to slavery, so the termination of a slavery-based life support system is not murder, and therefore abortion is not murder even if a fetus has the rights of a person. Conservatives might assert that biological natal dependence is different from political slavery, but no logical principle exists to distinguish the two.

It is also no answer to say that the mother chose to have sex, and the fetus is a helpless victim. One can easily imagine that an alien species exists on a foreign planet, and when human space explorers encounter them, the humans learn that the aliens are capable of attaching themselves to the humans' bodies and feeding off of the human bodies as parasites. Let us assume that the foreign planet's environment is changing and being destroyed so that the aliens' normal food supply is vanishing and they need to feed on humans and they would die without attaching to human hosts. Let us also assume that the aliens have minds and souls, and are persons with all the legal rights of human beings. Even if some humans take pity and choose willingly to let the aliens attach, no reasonable person would say that the aliens have a right to be parasites upon the humans, or that the astronauts would lack the right to forcibly remove the parasitic aliens whenever they choose to do so. The logic of the Rothbardian abortion argument is unassailable, so social conservatives are forced to rely on pictures of cute babies and gross disgusting aborted fetuses to appeal to people, but such emotional ploys are powerless to alter the truth as discovered by thinking.

Judith Jarvis Thomson independently made Rothbard's abortion argument in her paper "A Defense of Abortion," and it is promoted by some liberals, but the argument is a truly libertarian argument and is not a plausible liberal argument. This is true because the argument's premise is that biological need and dependence do not give one person the right to enslave another person in order to survive. The obvious analogy is between the government forcing the mother to be the physical slave of the fetus and the government forcing the productive taxpayers to be the economic slaves of the welfare parasites. The Marxist motto "from each according to his ability to each according to his need" could easily be cast as a pro-life maxim such as "from each mother according to her body's ability to each baby because of its need."

Social libertarianism, of the kind based upon GOLD, views pro-choice abortion rights as the one true libertarian position, in line with our belief that an individual owns her own body and has the right to do with her body whatever she wants, free from the government and social conservatives forcing women to obey their morality. The social conservative argument that abortion is murder, and therefore NVP would authorize the use of force against abortion, is a logical fallacy.

CHAPTER FIVE: THE LIBERTARIAN ANTIWAR FOREIGN POLICY POSITION

Libertarians believe that war is only appropriate in national self-defense, against a clear and present danger which threatens the people. Our general foreign policy favors isolationism and rejects interventionism. NVP says that violence should never be initiated and should be used only for self-defense. Wars of aggression should never be started against foreign countries. Foreign nations should never suffer military occupations. And one nation should never impose a political system upon another nation. Libertarianism opposes the War on Terror, the Iraq War, and the Afghanistan War, just as we opposed the Vietnam War, because none of these involved a specific foreign enemy who initiated aggression against the United States. The job of the USA is not to be the world's policeman.

The only real purpose of a pro-war "hawk" foreign policy is to enable America to intimidate the rest of the world and create an American Empire. Some conservatives quite openly desire a "Pax Americana" similar to the "Pax Romana," which is a Latin phrase meaning "Roman Peace" that was the historical name for the Roman Empire's domination of Europe in ancient times. While giving a lesson on the Latin language as it relates to antiwar policy, let me illustrate the Roman method by reference to the word "decimate," which comes from a Roman practice of gathering the peoples of the conquered village and cities, lining them up, and going down the line and murdering every tenth person in the line. This thuggish intimidation scared the Roman Empire's enemies and kept Rome safe, but this safety came at the price of liberty. We Americans love being kept safe by our soldiers, but we must be ever vigilant in staying true to the freedom that America has stood for since the American Revolution rebelled against the British king.

The libertarian antiwar stance is a logical extension of the principle which also justifies free market competition, this principle being that each person should be free to choose for himself or herself, which by extension means that a voter should be free to choose his/her government, and a people should be free to determine their political identity for themselves instead of having a different foreign nation violently impose a political system upon them. In this sense, libertarianism is the political philosophy which gives power to the people. Instead of wars, libertarians see international trade as the most efficient, effective, peaceful tool of diplomacy. If trade with a capitalist democracy produces prosperity for a poor struggling people who are currently oppressed by socialism, Marxism or dictatorship, then those people will look at their trading partner and see freedom and happiness, and this will motivate the oppressed people to rise up and choose libertarian pro-American policies for their country.

Because trade produces increased wealth, whether it be trade among citizens or trade between nations, voluntary international trade will naturally and inevitably lead to world peace, if trade is kept free and allowed to function over a period of several decades. Prosperity is the path to world peace because most wars have one of two motives, either (1) a people's desire to achieve self-government and break free from foreign control and occupation, or (2) a desire to steal wealth from conquered peoples. Trade-based prosperity and political independence answer both motives peacefully. The sadness of poverty is a significant cause of a people becoming warlike, angry and aggressive, as can be seen historically from Nazi Germany and Communist Russia. The prosperity resulting from free international trade would make a World War II or a Cold War far less likely to reoccur in the future.

The principle of libertarianism is the principle of democracy and free market competition, which means that each person should be free to choose for himself/herself. This principle demands that each group of people should be able to make their own political decisions. The libertarian principle requires that each people be free to choose their own political system and to govern themselves in a democratic, independent self-government, on the condition that they do no violence to their neighbors and do not start wars of conquest. Antiwar foreign policy flows logically from NVP.

However, libertarian theory justifies wars of self-defense against foreign nations who seek to conquer us. Military activity and government military spending are desirable to the extent reasonably necessary to protect the American people. The world is full of the enemies of freedom and democracy, and we have the right to defend ourselves. Libertarianism is not true pacifism. Contrary to some libertarians, I go farther and say that if we know for sure, or to an extremely probable and likely extent, that a foreign nation is a serious danger to us, e.g. a crazy dictator is developing a nuclear weapon and has missiles that can reach us, then a preemptive attack may be justified to eliminate the threat. But this is only justified on the basis of reasonable knowledge grounded in objective evidence which shows that this foreign enemy can and will attack us, and not due to mass hysteria or fear mongering. I participated in antiwar demonstrations in Washington D.C. prior to Bush II launching the Iraq War, and I can tell you from my personal experience that every reasonable American at that time knew that Iraq did not really have dangerous weapons of mass destruction that posed a danger to the USA. It was obvious to us that this was merely a case of the American Empire flexing its military muscle under the leadership of conservative hawks.

By contrast, the writing was on the wall in the 1930s that Nazi Germany posed a danger to every free country in the world and that Hitler's goal was to rule the world. So it would have been proper and ethical for America to attack the Nazis preemptively prior to Pearl Harbor. Also note that our involvement in World War II was morally justified and we protected and saved freedom on planet Earth. World War II is the perfect example of what a war that is right and moral under GOLD looks like. Smart and logical people can easily tell the difference between a real threat like World War II and a pretext scare like the Iraq War. The political mechanism and system to tell the difference between good wars and bad wars consists of the voters and Congress having a debate prior to the nation going to war. If the need for war is not obvious to the voters then the war is probably not justified under GOLD.

To conclude, note that "foreign aid" in the form of the United States government shoveling out billions of dollars in American taxpayer money to prop up supposedly "pro-U.S." foreign nations, including foreign dictatorship, e.g. South America and Egypt, or using NGO "charity" to influence foreign peoples, e.g. Africa, is in total violation of the NVP principle of political independence and self-government for each nation of people. Each nation must produce its own wealth to consume, and not feed off others as a parasite. If a nation stands on its own and achieves independence and economic self-reliance, instead of being reliant on foreign aid, then the nation's government will be forced to answer to its own voting citizens, instead of answering to foreign politicians and diplomats who control the flow of foreign aid money. Instead of taxing hundreds of billions of tax dollars out of the American taxpayers, the better foreign policy would be to cancel all foreign aid, cut taxes by the amount of money that had gone to foreign aid, and implement total free trade policies free from tariffs and regulations. The US could then let the American businessmen use those billions of dollars that they kept from lower taxes and invest that money into business to trade with foreign people. The GOLD position is the diplomacy of money, whereas the EVIL policy is the foreign policy of war.

In practice, the United Nations and the USA have used a combination of military intimidation, through the War on Terror and American military bases in foreign countries, combined with the corrupt bribery of dictators called "foreign aid," justified on the lie that foreign aid will help the poor in foreign nations, to impose an American Empire upon the rest of the globe. Only if the circuit of independence and autonomy is allowed to function in each nation for each group of people, so that each nation's government answers to its own people and is controlled by its own people's votes, can the people of each foreign nation achieve freedom and wealth. Personal responsibility at the national level, and the end of foreign aid on the pretext of charity to prop up pro-U.S. foreign regimes, will naturally motivate the peoples of each foreign region to voluntarily choose free market capitalism and prosperity. The political decisions of a foreign body of people are rightly for them to make, not for us to violently impose onto them. For example, the job of governing Iraq belongs to the Iraqis, not to the Americans. The same is true for Afghanistan, for every nation in Africa, and for every country in the world.

CHAPTER SIX: DISTINGUISHING THREE DISTINCT TERMS: SOCIAL LIBERTARIANISM, LIBERAL-TARIANISM, AND LEFT-LIBERTARIANISM

In order for our libertarian political discourse to be precise in our use of terminology, we must not confuse three similar but separate concepts: social libertarianism, liberal-tarianism, and left-libertarianism.

Social libertarianism means the application of libertarianism to "social" issues and questions, like gay marriage, abortion, and drug use. Just as social liberalism is the liberal stance on social issues, and social conservatism is the conservative stance on social issues, social libertarianism is the libertarian stance on social issues. Social libertarianism bases itself on what most libertarians would agree as the fundamental principles of liberty, the principles of ownership of private property, and the freedom to do whatever you want so long as you do not commit acts of aggressive violence against other people. The libertarian principles say that individuals have the right to make their own decisions, the government should not violently impose morality upon people, and each person is the owner of his/her own body. If a woman owns her body then abortion rights follow. If a person has the right to decide what social relationships to enter into with other consenting adults, but the recognition of personal relationships should not be forced onto those who disapprove, then gay rights and the privatization of marriage follows. And if a person should be free to engage in any nonviolent behavior they choose, then a person has the right to do drugs, use prostitutes or gamble.

Social libertarians believe that decisions about morality should be made by each individual, not by the government, whereas social conservatives want to force everyone to obey the conservative "traditional" Christian morality through government and laws. As such, social libertarianism is sharply in conflict with social conservatism. Within the Tea Party and the American Right, many conservatives believe that no conflict exists between conservative principles and libertarian principles, as if libertarianism is only an economic theory which says nothing about social policy. Such people are confused. Libertarianism is a political philosophy based on idealistic ethical principles. It is not difficult to see that the application of those libertarian principles to social issues demands the freedom to do what you want within the social sphere of life. This freedom contradicts the social conservative vision of imposing Christian traditional values onto dissenting minorities by means of government laws.

But social libertarianism is not social liberalism, because liberals think about social issues in a way that is very different from how libertarians think. For example, compare the social libertarian and social liberal positions on gay rights. Libertarians would say that an individual has the right to be evil so long as their evil behavior is non-violent and commits no aggression against others. Hence, libertarianism would say that every person has the right to be gay or lesbian, while asserting no value judgments on the matter, and letting each person decide for himself or herself, rather than letting the government impose social decisions onto individuals. Libertarians would equally defend the freedom to be gay or the freedom to be homophobic, provided that one never uses violence against others to advance one's position, and one limits oneself to voluntary persuasion in the furtherance of one's social goals. Social libertarians would say that marriage should be privatized and deregulated such that each individual and church would be free to choose whether to recognize gay marriage. We would agree with the social conservatives that it is unfair for liberals to force conservative Christians to approve of gay marriage by giving the authority of state legality to gay weddings.

Unlike social libertarians, social liberals would assert that being gay or lesbian is a good, virtuous lifestyle and would demand that everyone else agree with them and they would use government force to coerce obedience to their value judgments, such as by legalizing gay marriage while maintaining state control over wedding licenses. Social liberals incorporate gay rights and abortion rights into their socialist/Marxist narrative by saying that the Republican rich white male conservative upper class is waging war upon the sexual freedoms of the working class, and that homophobia and restrictions on abortions are a tool of oppression used by the privileged against the underprivileged. Social liberals would happily use the government to force everyone not to discriminate against gays and lesbians, even in a person's private decisions and in the use of their private property, e.g. workplace discrimination laws. Even though both social libertarians and social liberals generally support gay rights and women's rights, the two groups envision the use of government in completely different ways, with social libertarians committed to freedom of choice and with social liberals willing to use government force to coerce everyone into doing what they feel is good.

For another example of the difference between social libertarians and social liberals, social liberals would decriminalize drug use because they see the War on Drugs as a war by the rich white male aristocracy against poor inner city black youths who tend to use illegal drugs. In contrast, social libertarians would decriminalize drug use because we see the War on Drugs as an attack on individual rights and the freedom to own your body and to do with your private property, including your body, whatever you want to do with your property. If you own your body then you should be free to damage your body with drugs if you choose to do so, because you have the right to make the decisions that affect your life even if other people disapprove of those decisions and even if your decisions really are mistaken, dangerous or immoral. Social libertarianism is generally based on self-ownership and individual rights, including ownership of one's own body, whereas social liberalism is based on the Marxist/ socialist narrative of the oppression of the lower class by the upper class. Social libertarianism and social liberalism are two separate, distinct doctrines.

Liberal-tarianism is not a theory or group of ideas. It is merely the name for a strategic political approach, namely, the strategy of seeking to sell libertarian ideas to liberals and members of the American Left and the Democratic Party. Liberal-tarianism might seek to carry out its mission by pointing out positions where social liberals agree with social libertarians. But liberal-tarianism has no substantial theoretical ideas of its own. Historically, liberal-tarianism was a failure as a tactic for promoting libertarianism, because liberals tend to disagree with libertarians, especially on the economy, but also on social issues. Liberals think about freedom and equality differently than libertarians, and most liberals hate the libertarian free market radicalism which the majority of libertarians embrace as our defining ideal. Although this term has a somewhat complicated history, one can also use the term "Neo-Liberal" to mean the same thing as "liberal-tarian."

If liberal-tarianism is the attempt to make libertarian ideas appeal to liberals, one might say that left-libertarianism is the attempt to make liberal ideas appeal to libertarians. Unlike liberal-tarianism, left-libertarianism is an actual body of theories and ideas, specifically, ideas which mix leftist principles of the interests of the working class with libertarian ideas, especially anarcho-capitalism. One flavor of left-libertarianism is anarcho-socialism, which simply takes the concepts of libertarian anarcho-capitalism, and asserts that they would benefit the workers and harm the interests of the rich. Once one has embraced anarchy, the line between anarcho-capitalism and anarcho-socialism can get quite blurry. Another flavor of left-libertarianism argues that the libertarian concept of private property is valid only if people were just and ethical in the original acquisition of their wealth. They assert either that land can never originally enter into the realm of private property, and therefore land should be shared communally even in a capitalist society, or else that wealth may properly be redistributed to the extent that its origin is not perfectly just and ethical.

Some left-libertarians assert that capitalism is the most efficient producer of wealth and economic growth, but we should use libertarian policies to create added growth and then tax the added growth to provide welfare for the poor and helpless. Other left-libertarians take the set of ideas that traditional libertarians agree with, like radical free market capitalism, private property, and deregulation and tax cuts, and present arguments showing that these policies actually help the poor and hurt the rich. Left-libertarianism as a theory has some impressive intellectual pedigree within the libertarian movement: many libertarians forget this, but F.A. Hayek mentioned in "The Road to Serfdom" that he believed a social safety net funded by taxes is the price we must pay to enter the world of free market competition, and Milton Friedman in "Free to Choose" made the case for a negative income tax as a form of welfare consistent with capitalist freedom.

As more and more people enter the world of libertarian political philosophy, the theories of libertarianism will become deeper and more varied. While this happens, we must fight to keep our terminology clear and precise, to avoid the linguistic errors of confusion which can have negative consequences for the evolution of a relatively nascent set of ideas.

CHAPTER SEVEN: PROSTITUTION AND COERCION

Why is prostitution illegal? As a libertarian I think that it should be legal, as an extension of people's absolute right to own their own bodies. But many Americans disagree. If there is a rational, persuasive argument against the legalization of prostitutes (or "sex workers," as they should be called) it is that a need for money would coerce poor women into becoming sex workers and selling their bodies. Poor women who need money to buy food and pay bills would feel economic pressure to become sex workers, this argument goes, so we need to protect them from coercion by denying them the opportunity to sell their bodies.

Some version of the coercion argument underscores a great deal of anti-libertarian sentiment: poor people will be coerced into selling their organs and body parts, which justifies denying them the right to do so. Poor people are coerced into accepting dangerous, low-paying jobs such as coal mining, or are coerced into working long hours for wages that are lower than what they want. They are coerced into buying cheap high-fat fast food, or are coerced into buying cheap meat, packed at rat-infested plants, and so on. The coercion argument is a thorn in the side of laissez-faire politics, because socialists argue that poor people aren't really free in a capitalist system where they face economic coercion.

An example of the grave seriousness of the coercion myth is legal scholar Robert Lee Hale's famous law review article "Coercion and Distribution in a Supposedly Non-Coercive State" (1923). Hale brainwashed generations of law students with his argument that capitalist employers exert coercion upon workers, and socialism would not produce more coercion or less freedom than capitalism. The coercion argument goes far beyond the issue of prostitution; it is crucial for the integrity of libertarian theory that we have a definitive refutation to offer the public. This essay presents two strategies for refuting the coercion argument. I will focus on sex work to develop my ideas, but my arguments extend by analogy to every application of the coercion myth.

Assume that a poor woman (or man) cannot pay her utility bills and grocery bills and healthcare bills, and she does not want to sell her body, but if she becomes a sex worker she will earn enough money to pay the bills. Is this coercion? Two different approaches exist for arguing that this is not coercion. The first approach is to argue, as a matter of deductive logic, that economic pressure can never amount to coercion, and therefore this scenario does not satisfy the definition of "coercion." The second approach is to argue that economic pressure can be coercion, but that capitalism is better than socialism at preventing the situation in which a poor woman has to do work she hates in order to have enough money. This requires showing why libertarian economic policy will create an abundance of economic opportunity for American working-class women.

In the remainder of this essay I offer my thoughts on how to use each approach, focusing on the analytical approach first and the empirical approach second. I argue that economic pressure is not and can never be coercion, because economic pressure does not fit the definition of "coercion." What is coercion? My "Oxford Dictionary of Current English" identifies it as the noun form of the verb "coerce," which it defines as "persuade or restrain by force." Dictionary.com defines "coercion" as "the act of coercing; use of force or intimidation to obtain compliance." A serious question is whether coercion requires, by definition, physical force or the threat of it. I don't feel it's necessary to answer that question. I think a good common-sense definition of coercion is "threats of physical force or psychological intimidation that pressure someone into doing something he or she doesn't want to do."

To make my point, permit me to present what academic philosophers call a "thought experiment." Imagine an English sailor in the late 1700s who is marooned on a desert island after his ship was blasted apart by cannon fire from a pirate attack. This person washes ashore, explores the island, and finds that he is the only human there. Some animals and plants and trees exist on the island, and he sees some land that he thinks could be farmed. This sailor faces a choice. Either he hunts for animals or farms vegetables and perhaps gets enough food to support his life, or he starves and dies. He could choose to seek food, which would require doing a lot of sweaty labor, or he could choose to be lazy and sit around and wait and eventually die. Work or death is the choice that he faces.

Few people would say he was coerced into working the job of hunter or farmer. Why? Because the thing that forces him to work is the nature of reality and the circumstances of the desert island. Coercion is typically regarded as an action, as something that one person does to another person to force the latter to conform to the former's wishes. Where there is only one person there can be no coercion. Reality can be such that you must do something or face an unpleasant punishment, but reality has no mind capable of intentions and therefore has no intent to pressure you to obey some sort of scheme or plan.

It seems counterintuitive to say that reality coerces you, or that the aspect of reality called a desert island coerced you. It is the nature of reality, of humanity in the state of nature, that you work or die. If the sailor resents being forced to work by the human need for food, in a situation where it is obviously reality itself that poses this requirement, then he is rebelling against reality and the nature of human life. The demands of reality are not coercion; they are merely human existence.

This sheds light on the phenomenon that I call "worker's rage," a rage that most people feel sometimes and some people feel most of the time. Worker's rage is a fear-fueled hatred of the fact that material success requires hard work and entails the risk of failure. Many socialists are motivated at a deep psychological level by the feeling that a strong socialist government could somehow create a magical utopia where there is no risk of failure or any need to do work in order to enjoy material comforts. Money and capitalism have come to symbolize the need to do work in order to survive. But as the desert island thought experiment suggests, the "work or die" condition of human existence is the result of humanity in the state of nature. It cannot be the result of capitalism if it exists someplace where there is no economic system. Thus "work or die" is perfectly natural; it is the condition of humans in the state of nature. The actual cause of worker's rage is reality and not capitalism.

But now let us change the scenario slightly. Suppose that two sailors are shipwrecked on the desert island. One sailor, let's call him John, finds a plot of land and sows some fast-growing fruit seeds and produces an orchard (or, for simplicity's sake, let's say a crop) of edible fruit. This sailor also builds a fence around his land, topped with sharp spikes. This fence cannot be scaled without serious risk of death. The second sailor, James, just sits on the beach, doing nothing but watching the waves.

Now James faces the same situation that the sailor in the first thought experiment faced: either he works or he dies of starvation. The new wrinkle is that if John were to give some of his fruit to James, then James would have a third option, to eat John's fruit, not work, and not starve to death. Let us assume that James asks John to give him some fruit, and John says "no" and refuses to open the gate to his fence to let James in. Has John coerced James?

Here, for reasons similar to those of the first hypothetical, it's difficult to say that John has done anything to James that constitutes "coercion." In the first place, there isn't anything that John wants James to do. Therefore there is no intent or plan of John for James to conform to. We can hardly say that John coerced James into doing something when nothing exists that John wanted James to do.

In the second place, if James dies from starvation, it will not have been John who killed him. Everything bad that could happen to James (such as starvation), will have been caused by the island, by the circumstances of not having an abundance of free food waiting to be taken, and by James' own decision not to work. John has not directed any threat at James, and any harm that befalls James will not have been caused by John. James' death by starvation will have been caused by his own decision, combined with the nature of reality and of human beings, and the laws of physics and biology. Of course, John can prevent James' death by giving him free fruit, but if he doesn't, he has still not taken any direct action toward him, so it can't truly be said that John caused anything that happened to James.

"Ah, but John built that fence, and in so doing he murdered James!" the hardened socialist will say. If you don't believe that anyone would seriously claim that the protection of private property constitutes coercion against the poor, let me inform you that the Robert Hale essay used precisely that argument.

My reply is that, in the first place, coercion requires the use of force or threats, at the very least to reduce freedom of choice. James' freedom of choice has not been reduced. He is free to hunt, farm, sit on the beach, or do anything else he wants to do. John has done nothing to interfere with James' freedom. Coercion is what would happen if John aimed a gun at James' head and said, "Sing and dance or I will shoot you in the head." That is what the government does when it gives orders to be enforced by the police and the army. John's staying behind his fence, farming and minding his own business, while James does whatever he wants on the other side of the fence looks nothing like coercion. John is not doing anything at all to James, and therefore is not "coercing" him.

The only thing that John prevents James from doing is invading his land and stealing his fruit, actions that are not properly within James' scope of freedom. It strains credulity to think that protecting property that you have the right to own is coercion against people who try to steal it from you. If James were to steal John's fruit, then James would be feeding off John as a parasite, and John would become James' slave. James would be using force to steal from John. John's attempt to prevent him from doing so, by building a fence, is not the aggressive initiation of force; it is merely self-defense. Self-defense protects the defender's own freedom of action; it in no way pressures or controls the attacker. As can be seen from this example, James' freedom of action and his ability to survive are in no way impeded. The only thing the fence does is prevent James from stealing from John. Even if John had fruit to spare, which he could give to James without missing it, the fact remains that John has done nothing to control or pressure James. If James cuts a hole in the fence and steals fruit from John, then one might say that James used violent force to coerce John into growing fruit for James to eat, and that James is trying to force John to stand between James and reality so that James can escape from the fact of having to work or starve. But it is reality and the desert island that punish James for his lazy choices.

John faced a risky situation. If he had chosen to reap his crop too late in the summer, a tropical storm might have wiped it out and condemned him to death. James wants to avoid the risks of having to make such choices. He wants to steal the bounty of John's good choices, acting on the ground that John does not need all the fruit, but he himself does. This is robbery. For John to build a wall to prevent James from robbing him does not force James to make any of the choices available to him. The fence merely prevents James from exploiting John's choices. Thus, John's fence cannot reasonably be

THE MEANING OF LIFE

interpreted as a form of coercion.

Now consider a third thought experiment. Assume that John and James are both stranded on the island, and that John has grown crops and built a fence, while James lies on the beach and enjoys the cool breeze in his hair. James asks John to give him some fruit, and John says "no." But now, with this third and final fact pattern, let us assume that John tells James that he would be willing to give him some of his fruit if in exchange for it James would be willing to do something for him. Here at last we have some elements that suggest the possibility of coercion: John has some purpose or intent that he wants James to fulfill, and James can avoid death by starvation, at least for a few days, if John gives him that fruit. The socialist would say that John has the power to coerce James with the threat of not giving him the fruit, and therefore John can pressure James into doing what James does not want to do. This is the heart of the coercion argument.

But let us look more closely. John does not want James to obey him blindly. John is proposing a trade whereby James does something for John (some sort of sex work, let us assume), and in exchange John gives something of value to James. This would be a free trade of value for value. John does not really want James to "obey." He wants James to make a rational economic decision in which he gives John something of value to John, in exchange for something of value to James. When a baker gives twenty pizzas to a mechanic and receives a bicycle repair in return, both sides receive something that they wanted or needed more than the things that they traded away, so both sides end up happy. In a free trade both sides are always better off, at least in the sense that they always get what they want or what they choose, because if you don't think you will be better off from making a trade you simply walk away from it.

But the socialist says that James cannot simply walk away. He says that James has no other choice than to make this deal, because John is the only farmer on the island and so owns all the fruit, and James might die if he refused John's terms. But if we look at the scenario carefully, we see that nothing has fundamentally changed from the first and second scenarios. What will kill James is the desert island and starvation, not John; no aggressive physical force was used by John against James. James is free to go off to another part of the island and build his own farm, and John is not restricting any of James' abilities, with the single exception of his ability to steal. John owes nothing of his fruit to James. He would therefore be fully justified in not giving any of it to him.

Having established that James has no right to John's fruit, we can see that it is good for James that John offers to trade some fruit in exchange for some work. Unless John chooses to give some of his fruit to James, no reason exists as to why James should be entitled to any of John's fruit. It is perfectly right and ethical for James to have to come up with some value he can give to John in order to persuade John freely and voluntarily to give some of his fruit to James. It simply isn't true that John is threatening James or trying to intimidate James, because James' danger of starvation is caused by the island

and not by John. John is not doing anything to prevent James from going off and doing anything he wants, including starting his own farm.

Whether or not John has "unequal bargaining power," as socialist lawyers like to say, is irrelevant. The fact remains that John has every right to make a proposal that James is free to accept or reject. John is free to accept or reject James' request, and James is free to accept John's offer or reject it and face the consequences of the dangers of life on planet Earth.

James' freedom to choose is real and substantial. The socialists say in a capitalist system a poor person's freedom is illusory. Actually, however, capitalist freedom is the only kind of freedom that lets you make your own decisions rather than having someone else run your life. This freedom benefits everyone, rich and poor alike. When the socialists say that James' alternative to accepting John's offer is death, what they mean is that they don't want James to have to do the work and take the risk of starting his own farm. They want to use their guns to tear down John's fence and let James steal from John so that James won't have to face risk and make choices, as is proper for a human being trying to cope with the harsh problems of life on Earth.

My inquiry thus far has been about whether John is coercing James, not whether John should give James charity voluntarily and out of compassion. Obviously he should; in most cases it is a sin to let other people die, especially if you can help them without putting yourself in danger and they have not committed any morally repugnant crimes. It would be cruel for John not to give some fruit to James, but cruelty is a concept that is separate and distinct from coercion or injustice. And a real market economy always features competition, so no businessman can ever have the kind of monopoly on trade that John does. But I stand by the arguments presented above, which show that John's offer of money for sex is not coercion. Leftists equate the mugger's "your money or your life" with the employer's "work for me on my terms or I won't pay you, in which case you might starve." The difference is that the former is a threat of murder, whereas the latter is merely the expression of "work or die," a reiteration of the natural condition of human life. To say that in practical terms the cases are identical is to ignore the reasoning in this thought experiment. Where there is no threat there can be no "coercion."

I will now shift gears and present the second approach to refuting the coercion myth, which is the empirical factual approach. This approach allows that economic pressure might be coercion, but GOLD libertarianism would actually produce less economic pressure than EVIL criminalization and would therefore be preferable.

The first step is to frame the question properly, in this way: assuming that economic pressure is coercion, which is the economic system that produces the least economic coercion and the most economic freedom? Is it the capitalist libertarian GOLD system, which would legalize prostitution, or is it the socialist, protectionist, EVIL system, which criminalizes prostitution and uses either central planning or a welfare state? Also, assuming that neither capitalism nor socialism has the ability to erase all poverty (poverty being, after all, a relative term), the question is not which system will eliminate coercion; the question is which system will minimize coercion, because that is the achievable goal.

The logic of this argument must begin with a key observation. Even if prostitution is illegal, poverty will still put pressure on poor women to become sex workers. Criminalization makes prostitution more dangerous and therefore a less attractive choice, but it does not completely prevent poverty from coercing women into becoming sex workers. The widespread existence of sex workers in America proves just how ineffective the ban is. Therefore, whether or not prostitution is illegal doesn't factor heavily into this analysis; the crucially important question is whether capitalism or socialism is more efficient at creating jobs for poor women.

So long as poverty exists and sex work is a way to make money, there will be economic pressure for women to become sex workers, so one might think that legalization of prostitution would necessarily increase coercion. But libertarianism is not the reason why sex work is repulsive to some women, or why it frequently pays well. That has its roots in human nature and the nature of sexuality. Assuming that the availability of other jobs is the best way to decrease economic pressure, it is perfectly reasonable to examine GOLD libertarianism and EVIL protectionism to try to determine which one would be better at providing more choices for women. We can say that a system in which most poor women are not forced to become sex workers is one that is not generally coercive.

More wealth in an economy and a higher average standard of living will create more opportunities and career choices for everyone, including poor women. Capitalism is simply more efficient at producing wealth than state-socialism, because it is better at providing the incentives that motivate people to be productive. The explanation for why, under laissez-faire capitalism, there will be more opportunities for the poor than under socialism is that in a capitalist system the entrepreneurs and business owners depend on the skill, talent, intelligence, and hard work of their employees in order to compete. The manager can't do everything, so if the employees do a bad job, the business fails. Thus, management must always be searching for people who will do a good job, and seeking them wherever they may be found. An employee who is smart and works very hard is valuable. Employers will hunt for and abundantly reward productive employees.

If a poor woman chooses to work hard and be a good employee, under capitalism she is likely to find a non-sex-work employer who will hire her. The public education system traps the poor in poverty by giving bad educations to children who can't afford private schools; but privatization of education, using a voucher system, can solve this problem, and we can assume this as a feature of the libertarian system we are considering. We can also assume that wealthy people would support banks willing to give student loans to well-qualified poor people in order to develop the workforce necessary to compete with rivals. Because free-market capitalism will create more career choices for poor women than state-socialism or protectionist liberalism, women will actually feel less economic pressure in a libertarian society than they would under socialism or liberalism. Banning prostitution, on the other hand, simply eliminates a way to make money. A ban does nothing to solve the problem of poverty or to reduce the pressure to take unpleasant jobs.

One variation of the coercion argument is that a woman might choose to become a sex worker, but she would not want to if she had a choice (or, to be more precise, if she had money), and therefore the government should make her choice for her. This argument claims that protectionism actually increases freedom by giving people the situations that they would have chosen if they had been free to choose. But no one's choices can be predicted; the human mind is too complex for that. The only way to know what choice someone would make is to give her the freedom to choose and then see what choice she ends up making.

If a woman (or, again, a man) is horrified by the idea of becoming a sex worker, in a libertarian society she would be free to seek another job and persuade some employer that she would be a good worker and should be hired. F.A. Hayek's famous argument in "The Road to Serfdom" is that when people face a difficult choice (such as whether to become a sex worker or else have money trouble), they often want the state to eliminate this choice. But if the state destroys their freedom to choose, it has not eliminated the problem of a difficult choice. It has merely made that choice for the people instead of letting each person choose for herself. The poor woman who does not want to become a sex worker but who faces money problems must sometimes make a difficult choice, but outlawing prostitution does not magically solve the problem of poverty or help poor women pay their bills. It merely deprives women of the possibility of becoming sex workers if they wish.

There would probably be a sharp increase in sex work if prostitution were legalized. But we have no reason to assume that such an increase would be caused by coercion, since the increase might be caused by the freedom accorded to women who would view sex work as comparatively easy money. Some human beings view sex as a physical act devoid of emotional or spiritual significance and would view sex work and washing dishes as comparable. The idea that no woman could possibly want to become a sex worker is rooted in a very conservative, old-fashioned religious ideology. The government has no right to take the religious views of some people and force them upon others.

Looking beyond prostitution to broader issues of coercion, it is also worth remembering Hayek's classic argument that when government makes people's choices for them, there is but one authority that everyone must depend on, whereas in free-market competition there are hundreds of thousands of employers and millions of sales and deals happening constantly. The government has the power to coerce you by using its guns to force you to obey, but no capitalist can own every business or control every job. A worker under capitalism always has options and choices. If a woman faces poverty and hates the prospect of becoming a sex worker she is free to seek another job, and if one employer refuses to hire her then she can apply for positions with fifty others. The number of employers it is feasible for any one person to seek employment from, and the costs and sacrifices that any person must make in order to find a job, are real, empirical questions that vary for each individual. Some people may need to move to find a job, or to make other adjustments in their lives, just as they often do when seeking a spouse, getting an education, and so forth. Generally, however, in competitive capitalism there will be many more choices than in a socialist system.

To conclude: economic pressure is not coercion, but even if it were, GOLD libertarianism would produce less coercion than EVIL government control. Opposing arguments are common in American culture, especially among leftist or Marxist intellectuals and people influenced by them. The coercion argument is the foundation of many socialist illusions. It is the justification for laws that attempt to protect people from the tough choices that they would feel pressured to make in a free market. The truth is, however, that when the government tries to protect us by eliminating our freedom, that government action is coercion. Libertarian capitalism, in which people can make whatever choice they want, is freedom, and freedom is a good thing. I hope that this essay's framework of a double-barreled shotgun approach to refuting the coercion myth, with one barrel comprised of analytical deduction and another barrel coming from empirical fact, is a step in the right direction on the path toward replacing the state's coercion with the people's freedom.

CHAPTER EIGHT: THE ANTI-DRUG ARGUMENT FOR LEGALIZATION

In an episode of the libertarian TV show "Stossel," John Stossel debated Ann Coulter about ending the War on Drugs. At one point Coulter exclaimed in a tone of shocked outrage that Stossel could not possibly be serious in saying that legalization would lead to a decrease in drug abuse. Here I want to argue precisely that point.

It is possible for someone to believe that nobody should ever do drugs but also to support the libertarian proposal for ending the Drug War and legalizing all recreational drugs. The two positions are fully consistent, because both legalization and the end to widespread drug addiction will flow naturally from a psychological and philosophical shift toward a culture of more personal responsibility and away from a culture of irresponsibility. The cause of most drug addiction can be traced to irresponsibility, and irresponsibility is the psychological precondition of the welfare state. This explains why the drug subculture is dominated by the Left. We libertarians can silence some of our most vocal opponents if we undermine the alliance between the anti-drugs movement and the EVIL War on Drugs. This essay is one step toward achieving that goal.

I hate "recreational" drugs, and I do not think that anyone should use them. But I firmly believe that recreational drugs of every type should be legalized. I could argue that drug use is a victimless crime, or that human beings own their own bodies and have the right to do to themselves whatever they wish. I could argue that the War on Drugs is racist because it targets substances commonly used by members of racial minorities. But such arguments have been made many times before. Libertarian think tanks such as the Cato Institute have already produced ample empirical evidence showing that legalization does not correlate with drug abuse. I have no need to repeat this evidence. My argument is different. I am going to argue that legalization, if accompanied by a psychological and philosophical shift towards a culture of personal responsibility, would lead to a long-term widespread decrease in drug abuse.

Legalization might cause a temporary spike in drug use, as curious Americans would be tempted to experiment. Then again, there might not be a major spike, because despite the War on Drugs, most Americans have already experimented. But even if there were a spike it would not last long. The rational, intelligent American public would soon learn, or reaffirm its current conviction, that drug use is self-destructive and stupid. Indeed, if the foes of drug use are so sure that drug use is bad, then why are they so afraid of their inability to persuade consenting adults to abstain from drugs? The truth, of course, is that the arguments against drug abuse are so obvious that rational people can be persuaded to freely choose not to do drugs. Human goodness and happiness depend upon reasoning and reason's ability to perceive reality accurately; mind-altering drugs impede this process.

I have seen firsthand how drugs can ruin lives and how difficult it can be to quit once someone becomes addicted. While in college I had a serious substance problem, but since then I have been able to quit drinking alcohol and smoking cigarettes, and as of the publication of these words I have been perfectly sober since 2010. Without providing any detailed horror-story anecdotes, I think that it is widely known that alcohol makes people stupid and aggressive, that cigarettes are a deadly, lung-destroying poison, that marijuana makes people lazy and apathetic, that drugs cause people to lose their grip on reality, and that hard drugs are physically self-destructive and can ruin lives in any number of ways. There can be some debate about whether or not moderate, infrequent recreational drug use is a bad thing. I think that it is, because it accepts the principle that drug use is appropriate and sets the person up for a slippery slope descending into severe drug problems. Regardless of whether or not you approve of recreational use in moderation, there is no question that habitual serious drug abuse, in other words drug addiction, is both physically and psychologically poisonous. Drugs are a mess, and every sane person knows it.

The question, for me and other drug-haters, is: how to get people to stop using drugs? One possible approach is to outlaw them. This policy has undeniably failed, as drug use of every kind is rampant, despite the government's best efforts to eliminate it. But if you can't force people not to do drugs, then what can you do?

A more sophisticated and refined approach would look at the reasons why people choose to do drugs, and would fight the choice to use drugs at its source. People become drug addicts because they make a choice to be weak-willed, lazy, and irresponsible. A drug, after all, is a substance that functions by going between you and reality, so that your experience of reality becomes more pleasant than it would have been sober. The drug does not change reality; it merely changes the chemicals in your brain. It is undeniable that sober reality is the reality that objectively exists in the physical world, and drug-experienced reality is a fictional reality which does not actually exist. Therefore, in a sense, drugs are the ultimate subjectivism and solipsism, in which you choose to cope with the problems in your life not by facing reality soberly and seeking to improve it, but by choosing to change your brain so that you will not feel the pain of your problems anymore, so that you won't have to be aware of what is really going on. The tremendous appeal of drugs is their usefulness for escapism.

Addiction is usually more psychological than physical, because every human being has the power to quit doing drugs at any time if he makes a genuine choice to do so. Although many drugs exist that have withdrawal symptoms of sickness and agony, rare indeed is the drug that will actually kill you if you stop abusing it. Sobriety is beneficial to one's health. Addiction usually comes from the mind, not from the body. What, then, is the nature of an addiction?

The cause of most drug addiction is pain and suffering. A drug addiction is merely a manifestation of the sadness inherent in the condition of being human. Pleasure, wealth, friendship, love, romance, and happiness are not given to humans; we have to work for them. When we make mistakes we lose what we want. The fight to be happy is difficult and messy and full of misery and horror. A person can, however, cope with the human condition responsibly by choosing to face and try to improve reality. This means that he assumes responsibility for both success and failure; he accepts the rewards for good choices and the punishments for bad ones. Alternatively a person can choose the irresponsible choice of abandoning reality, not trying to make things better, and trying to hide from or escape from sorrow.

The essence of irresponsibility is seeking to break the causal connection between the choices you make and what happens in your life. Drugs are addictive because they are uniquely useful for living life irresponsibly. They kill your awareness of your life and blind you to the punishments for your choices. Drugs are as popular as they are because everyone experiences the pain of the problems in life. But this pain evolved as nature's way of motivating people to solve their problems.

The problem with addiction is not merely that you use the drug constantly and it damages your physical health. It is that a human being becomes ethical by thinking and making choices, and drugs make the drug user's choices for him or her. The essence of personal responsibility is taking responsibility for your choices and not using easy shortcuts around doing the work that is necessary in order to be happy. Drug addiction is fundamentally irresponsible, not merely because it is a lazy way to cope with problems, and not merely because it impairs the ability to choose, but because it is easy and tempting for drug users to blame their actions on the drug, shifting causation away from themselves. That is the core of irresponsibility.

The issue of whether a person chooses to live responsibly or irresponsibly is at the heart not only of the issue of drug addiction, but also the issue of which form of government to choose. Drug use is a personal manifestation of irresponsibility, but a political manifestation of irresponsibility is socialism or liberalism. An irresponsible government will hide from society's problems and use any quick-fix snake oil it can imagine to make people think that it is doing the right thing, without ever actually addressing the causes of society's problems and trying to fix them. The irresponsible person blames his problems on something else and looks to external saviors to solve his problems instead of taking responsibility and solving his problems himself. The liberal voter looks to government to make his choices for him and give him wealth instead of creating wealth for himself. Government, in short, acts upon the body politic like a drug, blinding the people to reality. The more we rely upon government to live our lives for us, the more we lose control and the farther we fall from the condition of being able to solve our own problems.

Because drug abuse and big government are two manifestations of the same irresponsible attitude towards life, it is no coincidence that the drug culture is permeated by the liberal and socialist Left. On the other hand, a culture of personal responsibility, such as is embodied by the libertarian political philosophy, would militate against the problem of drug addiction.

Personal responsibility is inconsistent with using government to force people to behave ethically regarding activity that does no violence to others. We libertarians must make a stand for legalization, but we should fight this battle not for the sake of drug addicts, but for freedom as a matter of principle, supported by rational arguments for individual responsibility.

Many drug foes seem incapable of grasping the notion that you can persuade a reasoning mind to choose sobriety freely. Perhaps this is because the anti-drug interest groups have shown not one iota of understanding of how to talk to people about drugs. Instead of running anti-drug ad campaigns that treat people like rational adults, the anti-drug groups (usually in conjunction with government agencies) run ads designed to scare or guilt-trip people into quitting drugs. People who have chosen to use drugs as a way to cope with reality are already more afraid of facing reality than they are of death, and they have chosen to be irresponsible. So appealing to the fear of death and the guilt of letting down your loved ones is a silly strategy. A manipulative emotional trick never has the same impact as persuasive reasoning. The proper anti-drugs approach is to convince people rationally.

It is notable that when a special interest group wants people to behave in a certain way, but lacks any well-reasoned arguments, it petitions government to pass a law to coerce obedience. Some fools actually may believe that people know better than to do drugs but are too weak to resist temptation and therefore need the government to force them to choose sobriety. Only weaklings and cowards would buy this argument. The government has no special knowledge of the dangers of drugs, no knowledge that the American people lack, nor does it possess a magic wand to make drugs any less appealing. The most effective anti-drug strategy is rational persuasion in a free, legalized society.

When the government forces you to do something that you aren't persuaded you should do, it is treating you like a child, and the condition of being a child is precisely the condition of not assuming responsibility for yourself, the very condition that leads to drug addiction in the first place. Legalization would send a message that we as a people need to take responsibility for our own choices. It is the best thing the government could do to combat drugs. Rampant drug abuse and the War on Drugs would both be killed by a cultural shift towards personal responsibility.

If the socialists and the anti-drug warriors actually wanted to solve the drug problem, marijuana would be legal today. Marijuana is far less dangerous than alcohol. It is the opposite of a gateway drug; it is merely a convenient means of experimentation for curious people making the transition from child to adult. Over the long term, legalized pot would decrease hard drug use. Unfortunately, we cannot depend on the state to do the rational thing and legalize marijuana.

At this juncture, the libertarian movement should try to have it both ways: we have already gained significant popularity by appealing to drug users who want drugs to be legalized, but we could also gain a loyal following among drug haters. We should preach that our path of social and political self-responsibility is the way best suited to sober, clear-headed, rational adults. We can thereby attract to our ranks many of the people whose lives have been ruined by drugs and who are looking desperately for an escape from the drug-induced carnage. But because responsible adults are more likely to support free market capitalism than people who are irresponsible and immature, I think that libertarianism can only triumph with the support of sober voters. GOLD does not say whether drug usage is right or wrong, it only says that the decision of whether drugs are good or evil should be made by each individual person, not by the government. Thus, GOLD can appeal to both the stoners and the straight-edge.

One might wonder why the many voters who abuse illegal drugs do not swarm the polls and vote libertarian politicians into elected office. My explanation is simple: voters with drug-addled brains are too lazy and irresponsible to become political activists, even though they stand to gain the most from legalization. It is the sober voters (albeit ones who may smoke cigarettes and have an occasional glass of wine) who largely control America's politics, so they are the ones to whom we must sell the libertarian message of legalization.

Right now the anti-drug, anti-legalization lobby is a powerful foe of libertarianism. The anti-drug activists are passionate and fanatical because they understand the horror of drugs and take inspiration from the virtue of sobriety. But so do I, and my hatred of drug abuse does not make me think that the sins of the Drug War are in any way justified. If we could chip away at the link between the anti-drug movement and the anti-legalization movement, libertarianism would lose some of its most zealous opponents (perhaps including Ann Coulter and conservatives like her). We should try to persuade some of the anti-drug advocates to abandon the prohibitionists and back legalization as the clever solution to America's drug addiction problem.

PART TWO: ECONOMIC LIBERTARIANISM

CHAPTER NINE: THE FREE MARKET ECONOMY VS. THE PLANNED SOCIALIST ECONOMY

In ancient times the same group of people in one village would all farm, hunt, build houses, make tools, and do all labor. The invention which produced the birth of civilization was the development of farming. Once agriculture was invented, the existence of economics arose from the division of labor. The division of labor, which began in ancient times but which increased as civilization progressed, meant that one person specialized in hunting, another in farming, a third in building houses, a fourth focused on making tools, etc. Specialization in separate areas enabled each person to master a craft, which was far more efficient than one hunter/farmer doing everything for himself. The division of labor created the problem of economics: how do we properly coordinate all the different productive activities of different people? Two fundamental alternatives answer this question. The first answer is coordination by trade. The second answer is coordination through someone being the boss and giving everyone else orders about what to do.

Trade assumes that each person knows what is best for himself or herself. You produce goods or services and trade them to others, and, because the trades are voluntary, you only do a trade if it gets you something you want, or, at least, if what you receive is something you wanted more than what you traded away. Trade-based coordination enables you to trade what you produced but someone else wants to consume in exchange for what you want to consume which the other person produced.

Command economics, another term for the Marxist/socialist planned economy, is the alternative to a trade-based economy. Central planning by a boss assumes that an expert or specialist exists who knows what is best for everyone and can make decisions for each person better than that person could for himself or herself. The free market capitalism vs. planned economy policy debate is a matter of where to place the decision-making powers: with the people, or with the government? If people are allowed to trade then each individual decides three economic decisions for himself or herself: (1) he/she chooses what to produce, (2) he/she chooses what trades to make, and (3) in conjunction with the first two choices, he/she chooses what to consume. If the government imposes an economic plan then the bureaucrats make these economic decisions, and they impose those decisions onto the people.

Capitalism is preferable to the planned economy for two reasons. First, the free market is pragmatic and efficient. As will be discussed below, a money-based trading economy is more effective and practical at allocating productive resources to maximize satisfaction than a planned economy. As Marxist nations have learned, a planned economy is notoriously inefficient. Marxism is always inefficient because money and prices are the most effective means of measuring supply and demand.

Second, the free market encourages political freedom, whereas planned economics favors, and forms a slippery slope leading to, dictatorship. Marxism, in theory, has always believed in dictators. Marxist dictators are asserted to be noble and have the best interests of the poor at heart, but they are dictators nonetheless.

A good reason exists which explains why socialism leads naturally to a loss of the freedom to engage in political dissent, which is vital to any true democracy. If a boss coordinates economic activity by giving orders, then he will inevitably be forced to rely upon a system of violent force, swords in the olden eras, guns and police nowadays, to force people to obey him. The economic planner must use force because if some people were to disobey the master plan then the economic czar's plan wouldn't be able to work as intended.

If the economic planners of a planned economy want you to be a farmer, and you want to be an astronaut, then the secret police of a Marxist/socialist state will force you to be a farmer. Or, if you are a doctor treating a patient who suffers from a rare life-threatening illness about which little is known, then you might want to treat your patent with Treatment Y. But if the government's medical oversight board has only approved Treatment B, and has disapproved Treatment Y, then the police will throw you in jail if you try to use your best medical judgment to treat your patient using Treatment Y. Or if you try to publish criticism of the economic plan or the bureaucratic regulations or medical controls then the government will censor you. And if you become a political activist working for reform then the secret police will search your house and arrest you. Political dissent, if it becomes widespread, is fatal to any centralized government plan for the economy. Thus, despite the Left's preaching about civil liberties, socialism naturally leads to dictatorship.

All economics reduces to this simple alternative: trade vs. force. Libertarian economics is based on trade. Trade enables voluntary behavior and free economic decisions. As such, trade is the political principle of freedom. Marxism and socialism, and liberalism to the extent than it accepts socialist economic principles, is based on force. Force is the political principle of dictatorship.

The narrative offered here can be understood a different way, as seen through the lens of GOLD vs. EVIL. GOLD applied to the realm of economics lets each individual make his or her own economic decisions. Each person takes responsibility for his or her own choices and lets others be free to make their own different choices. EVIL applied to economics is one person, namely one bureaucrat or one leader of a group of voters, using violent force and the government to coerce everyone else into obeying his beliefs about what is good or bad for the economy. If a person believes in freedom as an ideal, then they must accept GOLD and reject EVIL. GOLD is a necessary, practical precondition for an economic system compatible with political freedom.

Note that this theory does not dispute the possibility of conservative right-wing dictatorships. But historically such nations merely pay lip service to free markets, while in reality they use government power to favor the nation's aristocracy and the ruling party, rather than leaving people free to compete according to productivity and freely chosen trades. Such "crony capitalism" is not what true libertarian capitalism looks like. For a similar reason, namely, the significant difference between the ideal of capitalism and the flawed implementations of that ideal, the United States of America is not viewed by libertarians as a utopia or a perfect capitalist system. America is a combination of capitalist freedom and socialist government controls, with the socialist elements dating back to FDR's New Deal and the policies of JFK and LBJ. Therefore the sins and errors of the American economy, such as the continued existence of poverty, do not disprove the merits and virtues of capitalism. America's mistakes and failures can be attributed to the EVIL elements of the American economy.

CHAPTER TEN: THE NATURE OF MONEY AND SUPPLY AND DEMAND

Having presented the basic narrative of trade vs. force as solutions to the problem of coordination using the division of labor, we must complete this picture by explaining money as an evolution upon barter of goods for goods, and showing how money calibrates supply and demand. Money is a common medium of exchange. Money does not alter the basic nature of an economy, it merely facilitates trade by enabling each person to trade with more people. You can trade your goods and services to someone in return for their money, and then trade that money to other people in exchange for their goods or services, instead of only being able to trade goods for goods with the limited group of people who want what you make and also make what you want. Thus, when the division of labor existed in a small village, the farmer would trade directly with the blacksmith, but money enabled them to have a common, standardized measure of value, something everyone would want (and usually a valuable metal or commodity in ancient times). Money, as a common medium of exchange, enabled a series of trades among many different people in one town, and also enabled people from different towns and villages to trade with each other.

In a very real sense money is an illusion, because it hides the fact that a capitalist economy is really a network of trades, and all money is merely a common medium of exchange for the trades of everyone trading with everyone else. Such trades include employees selling their labor to employers in return for money and then trading this money to other producers in return for consumable goods and services made by other employees. If one looks at the illusion of money, one might see Mr. X, who works for Employer A, and A owns a company that makes widgets. X gets paid $10 as a salary for an hour of work, and it takes X one hour to make one widget. X gets paid on payday and X then spends $10 to buy a cake from Baker B. This looks like X gets paid in money for making widgets, and the cake was a purchase and sale for money. But removing the money from the analysis, and looking past the money illusion, yields a deeper, more accurate account of what actually happened.

In this example, X is an employee of A, and A's factory makes widgets. X produced a widget while at A's factory using A's tools. Baker B produced the cake by baking it.

Unknown to X when he bought the cake, B has a home which needs a widget, and later that week he bought a widget made at A's factory from A's widget store and installed the widget at B's home. What has really happened is that X produced W, X traded W to A in exchange for $10, B traded C to X in exchange for $10, and behind the scenes, invisible to the naked money analysis but visible to us, is that B traded X's $10 to A in exchange for W, which gave A the $10 to give to X. Thus, the only economic activity that happened was production, consumption and trade. X produced W and consumed C. B produced C and consumed W. And A made a profit from facilitating the production and trade of W.

In general, all employees are willing to sell their labor for dollars instead of consumable goods because money is a common medium of exchange and as such can be traded for anything else, including whatever consumable goods the workers could possibly want to buy when they spend their dollars. And sellers accept money in exchange for sold goods and services for the same reason, because they know that the dollars they get can be traded for other goods and services in the future. So what happens in a money-based economy is production, consumption and trade, and the money simply blinds us to what is going on.

As a common medium of exchange, money enables the comparison of the value of a good or service relative to other goods and services in an objective quantifiable manner from the goods and services being cheaper or more expensive than others as shown by the marketplace of trades. When consumers spend more or less money to buy a good or service, these money-based trades send price signals of demand to producers to produce more of what people buy and less of what isn't selling, or to produce more of what sells for more money and less of what sells for less money. This causes an increased supply of desirable goods as producers shift resources to making what sells, and to making what sells more expensively, by shifting resources away from producing goods and services which are commercial failures, in other words, what consumers choose not to buy. Increased supply makes the desirable goods cheaper until supply reaches the point at which demand is satisfied and consumers won't buy more or for a higher price. In economics this condition where supply and demand meet is known as the "equilibrium point."

Similarly, when something doesn't sell well or for a high price, it is then sold for a cheaper price until it reaches an equilibrium point where it clears the market, and this lower price motivates producers to shift resources away from making it, and to only assign the efficient amount of resources equivalent to the price at which consumers will buy it. If demand remains constant, then supply will increase or decrease to meet that demand at the equilibrium point, which is the precise point where the level of consumer demand justifies producers' investment of Earth's scarce resources in creating that supply. And those producers who were able to satisfy the consumer demand by producing what people wanted will have made a healthy profit as a result of making sales, which both motivates producers to focus on what consumers want and rewards the capitalists who do the greatest service to the people in meeting our needs and making us happy.

This use of price to send signals to coordinate the economic activity of millions of different producers and consumers is the profit motive's method of enabling a socially efficient allocation of resources to produce the most desirable goods and services. Every individual economic decision to buy or sell, both by manufacturers, suppliers, distributors, retail sellers, and buyers, sends signals to the market, and the market price sums up and aggregates the collective economic desires of the economic actors to show how the market values any given good, service or resource. This principle can also be thought of as Adam Smith's "invisible hand," which, among other things, uses the motive of personal profit to motivate people to give to buyers what the buyers want in order to make sales, such that a person's selfish greed is an incentive to give to other people what those other people want. This motivates people to increase the wealth of society as much as possible, when society's wealth is measured as an aggregate of each individual's wealth. It also uses money to achieve maximum efficiency under the theory that optimal efficiency is attained at the price located at the equilibrium point where supply and demand curves meet, because nobody could be made better off by doing anything more.

Note that none of this happens unless all trades are entirely voluntary, because the motives and results of involuntary transfers of goods and services would be entirely different, since the people would not be making trades based on their own choices, and therefore the price signals would not show consumer demand aggregated from millions of different individual producers and consumers. Price can be set by a central planner, but it would not show the choices of the people, it would instead show merely one bureaucratic central planner's individual opinion.

The problem of a politician or bureaucrat knowing what the public wants is an example of what I call the "grain of sand" problem, which is that the central planner might think that he knows and understands one million grains of sand because he has the abstract concept of "one million grains of sand," but he has not conceptualized each grain of sand to know each one individually. There is a difference between "10 numbers" and "1+4+6+2+9+6+8+1+1+5," which is a set of 10 numbers. The content of the former is 10 and the content of the latter is a sum of 43. The difference between 10 and 43 in this example is the difference between abstract theory and real-world knowledge. A central planner might know the broad trends of consumer needs in the abstract, like knowing "ten thousand mothers need diapers for their babies," but he cannot know the details of each one of those ten thousand mothers, such as the shape of diaper they want, the material they want it made from, how many they need, and how much each diaper is worth to the mother in terms of the work she does to pay for it.

A free market economy is a massive mathematical calculator that aggregates every individual's economic decisions to give people what they want relative to their willingness to pay for it, with price being the mechanism that coordinates different people's choices. The decision of each one of those ten thousand mothers factors into the price of each type of diapers. A government central planner, even with a staff of thousands of economists, cannot know the choices and desires of three hundred million Americans. There are simply too many of us for the bureaucrats to talk to each of us and learn what we want and need. But a free market economy can know 300,000,000 individuals with enough precision to calculate price signals based on each and every individual within that group of three hundred million because price is affected by everyone's decisions to buy and sell. Even if a planner was very familiar with the details of one woman, he would need to read her mind to know what decision she would actually make if she was given a choice between the alternative diapers that exist. When faced with the reality of the situation, she might make her decision based on color or design or price or any combination of factors, which nobody else can predict. The only way to know what each mother would choose is to really give her the choice and then let her pick what she wants.

Wealth consists not of money but of goods and services which are traded using money as a common medium of exchange, and an analysis of any economy must look at its production, trades, and consumption, with the money serving merely as a distraction (although money can be used as a means to store wealth and has some limited intrinsic value, e.g. gold during the gold standard era). When a person creates more wealth, he/she then has more value which they can trade to others. Having made more trades with others, such people then have more wealth to consume. This is a simplistic, but adequate, explanation of income inequality between rich and poor in a free market economy.

Let me offer an example to illustrate the nature of money and supply and demand. Assume that you work as a software computer programmer at a company that writes software. Assume that each day you buy a cup of coffee and an egg and cheese sandwich from a coffee shop and you eat this for breakfast. You think of yourself as an employee who gets paid a salary and who then spends money to buy coffee and the egg and cheese sandwich. But the money is an illusion which hides the fact that you are not merely an employee who spends money, you are really a trader who produces and consumes. You create value, the software that you produce at work. You then trade this software to your employer in return for money which the employer pays you. Your employer, the firm, then trades your software to buyers, and these buyers use your software and then pay your employer the money out of which comes the salary that you are paid. Basically, you do a trade where you give software to users and users give money to you.

Similarly, when you buy your coffee and sandwich, you do a trade where the coffee shop gives the coffee and sandwich to you and in exchange you give some money to the coffee shop. Ultimately and indirectly, you are trading your money to the people who made the coffee and food, so that they get your money and you get your breakfast. The coffee beans were grown by coffee growers in South America, the eggs were collected at a farm by a poultry farmer in the Northeast, the bread was made from wheat grown by grain farmers in the Midwest. You are trading with the coffee growers and the poultry farmer and the grain farmer, because you trade your money to the coffee shop for the coffee and food, and the coffee shop uses your money to trade with the coffee grower and the farmers.

So what has really happened is two trades: you give software to users and get money back, and you give money to the coffee shop and get breakfast back. Why is the coffee shop willing to give you breakfast, which has obvious nutritional value, in exchange for mere pieces of paper with green ink printed on them? For the same reason that you give something useful and good, your work and your software code, in exchange for these same dollar bills. And the reason why you, and the coffee shop, and everyone else, is willing to trade value for money, is because money symbolizes and represents consumable value, so that anyone can take money and go into the marketplace and buy anything and everything which is for sale by means of that money. This is what I mean when I say that money is a common medium of exchange which enables the division of labor, e.g. you can specialize in technology while someone else can specialize in agriculture because you can trade with them by means of money.

The money is an illusion which makes what really happens in a free market economy, which is a massive network of trades of goods and services for goods and services, look like employees get paid salaries and buyers buy and sellers sell. As I will explain in the next section, all economic activity is based on trade, not on mere buying and selling. For example, you traded your software to a user for the user's money, and a coffee shop traded breakfast to you for your money, but somewhere out there, invisible to you but enabling this circuit of trade to be completed, a person exists who bought for and used your software but who also built a table and chairs which the coffee shop bought from him and installed at the coffee shop. In this way trade is a triangle, where you trade your value (your work) for other people's money (your salary) and you spend money (you buy) to get other people's value (they sell), but in the background millions of other trades happen which complete the cycle of a trade of value for value by means of money, which matches your value that you produce and someone else consumes to the value that someone else produced and which you consume.

Also note that, since a free market economy is simply a massive network of millions of trades, for example your trade of software for money and your trade of money for breakfast, the only way to coordinate all this trading is the mechanism of the price system. When people want something then they buy it, and when someone buys something this makes the price go up, which tells producers to invest more in satisfying that demand because when the price goes up it means that people can make more profit by selling an increased supply. When people don't want something they buy less of something which makes the price go down, which tells people this is less valuable and to invest less in producing it because there is less profit to be made in selling it. Price gives information so that the efficient amount of resources goes into increasing supply when price goes up or decreasing supply when price goes down, and then when the supply of something desirable goes up the price then comes down, or when supply of something undesirable goes down the price goes up, so that demand and supply meet at the perfect price which embodies the equilibrium point, which is the ideal efficient price.

For example, if you and all your friends buy the egg and cheese sandwich at the coffee shop instead of buying the blueberry muffins, this tells the coffee shop that the sandwich is desirable and the muffins are less desirable. This information enables the coffee shop to make intelligent decisions about what to sell, which raw materials to buy, and how to run its business. In other words, price is the mechanism by means of which the coffee shop knows what you want and gives it to you at the price you are willing to pay for it. If everyone loves the sandwiches then the coffee shop might raise the price of the sandwich, at which point if its price is greater than your desire for it then you will switch to buying a donut for breakfast, after which the coffee shop will lower the price back to a range where lots of people buy the sandwich. So price tells the coffee shop exactly how much people want the sandwich, and the coffee shop will price it at the precise price which reflects exactly what it is worth to you.

Price also enables people to compare apples to oranges using a common measurement of value, and because of this it enables every business to measure all goods and services in the economy relative to one another. For example, if you want to measure how much the sandwich is worth to you relative to the amount of effort you put into coding software, money prices are the only way to measure this. If you earn $6 after-tax dollars for one hour of labor, and the egg and cheese sandwich costs $6, then you can judge that one hour of work buys one sandwich. If the coffee shop sells the sandwich for $6 and sells one donut for $3, then you can evaluate that two donuts cost the same as one sandwich, and you can use that information in making your economic decisions to compare donuts to sandwiches to decide what to buy.

For another example which sums up all these principles nicely, consider the minimum wage, which is intended to help the poor by giving them higher wages, but which actually hurts the poor by eliminating jobs and encouraging American manufacturers to outsource jobs to foreign countries where labor is cheaper. In a supply and demand free market economy, the wage will be the equilibrium point where employers find it profitable to pay wage X and workers find it better to work for X than to choose any alternatives. If Employer Y believes that it can sell 100 widgets

THE MEANING OF LIFE

and it will need 10 workers to manufacture 100 widgets and it will make a profit on selling these widgets by paying wage X, then Y can afford to hire 10 workers for wage X. But if the minimum wage is X+$10, and demand for widgets does not increase, then Y will not be able to profitably employ 10 workers, and will only be able to hire fewer workers, such as, for example, sales of 100 widgets could pay a salary of X+$10 to 5 workers. So the minimum wage gives 5 people a wage of X+$10, and destroys five jobs, which will probably be sent to Mexico or China. And, if jobs exist for X but the minimum wage is X+$10, then many workers will seek jobs illegally and an entire labor force will be criminalized because the people will want to disobey the central planners' scheme for economic order out of their desire to get a job. This is an apt description for the illegal immigrant labor force in the USA, who compete against U.S. citizens by working for far less than the minimum wage.

Liberal voters are under the mistaken belief that Y wants to pay X because they are greedy capitalists who want to exploit the working class and rip people off, but, under the hypothetical scenario as posited, employer Y wants to charge the wage X because that is the price the market calls for as a result of supply and demand for labor and widgets. X is the market wage because consumers want to buy only 100 widgets, no more and no less, so Y's personal feelings of greed or selfless love could not influence the result even if Y wanted them to. The liberal believes that a minimum wage of X+$10 will give 10 workers a wage of X+$10, whereas in reality it kills five jobs, and the five people who get fired will probably be the less educated, less talented, unlucky workers who would have benefited from those jobs, thus the liberal policy of government intervention in the economy on minimum wage produces a result opposite from the noble liberal intentions. The only solutions to the wage problem are no minimum wage, or else banning outsourcing of American jobs to foreign countries. But, obviously, the foreign countries would retaliate with devastating trade embargoes, so the best thing for workers is to abolish the minimum wage.

Marxist and socialists generally want people to think that the world is a nice place where we could all retire to a life of luxury and take vacations three days each week if we merely take their yachts and mansions away from the rich and give the rich's wealth to the people, of which the minimum wage is merely one step on their long-term path towards the socialist utopia. The cruel, awful truth is that planet Earth is meaner and nastier than the socialist idealists' dreams, and we must first create a life of wealth and plenty in order for us to experience and enjoy such a world. The government cannot create wealth merely by executive order or by means of taxation, nor can the government create safety and eliminate risks and dangers via regulation unless the people already possess the economic means to afford such safety, assuming that safety is expensive (which is usually true). A leftist might reply that the people would have the money if the government gave it to them, to which my reply is, in free market economics a voluntarily chosen trade is usually a win-win situation where both sides are better off, because each side would not have chosen the trade if he/she did not want it, but when the government taxes and spends that is a zero sum game, because the state giving $1 to one person requires first taking that $1 away from another person via taxes, such that no net benefit to society accrues from taxing and spending as such. In fact, society suffers a net loss from tax and spend liberal policies, e.g. if the government collects $1 from taxes, loses $0.30 to bureaucratic inefficiency and red tape, and ends up spending $0.70 on welfare, then $0.30 was destroyed.

CHAPTER ELEVEN: THE CHOICE THEORY OF VALUE, THE CORRESPONDENCE THEORY OF MONEY, A THEORY OF PROFIT, AND REFUTING "AUSTRIAN" ECONOMICS AND "KEYNESIAN" ECONOMICS USING A NEO-CLASSICAL MODEL

The task of libertarian economics is to put forward theories in order to explain and justify three principles. The first principle is "you cannot consume what you have not produced, unless someone else gives it to you for free or you steal it from someone else." The second principle is "in a free market, traders trade value for value, so each side to a trade benefits and neither side gets screwed over." The third principle is "money, prices, and supply and demand are necessary for an economy to function, and they cannot be done away with or replaced by any alternative system." This section will offer a new, comprehensive mini-treatise of economic theory as a foundation for those three principles. In developing my own theory I will argue against some of the ideas of "Austrian" economics, and I will also refute the basic premise of "Keynesian" economics. I present three libertarian Neo-Classical ideas: the choice theory of value, the correspondence theory of money, and the theory that profit corresponds to the value added to raw materials by the worker's labor, such value being quantifiably measured by the choices of the purchaser in relation to competing goods and services.

My original ideas are a new, unique interpretation of the "Neo-Classical" economics approach. Neo-Classical economics, attributed to a revitalized modernization of Adam Smith, is economics based around the idea of supply and demand as the basic framework for understanding economics. Keynesian economics posits that economic growth is caused by government spending, and inflation enables the government to spend, and growth creates jobs, so policymakers face the continual choice of inflation and growth or spending cuts and unemployment. Austrian economics is a complicated set of ideas which I will discuss in detail during the remainder of this section.

SUBPART 11-A: THE METHODOLOGY OF PHILOSOPHICAL ECONOMICS

In the libertarian movement during the 20th Century, a debate raged among two competing schools of libertarian economists. The debate, which was known by the name "the controversy on method," was fought between the libertarian Austrians, led by Ludwig Mises and F.A. Hayek, against the libertarian Chicagoans, led by Milton Friedman. The war can be characterized as a conflict between the Chicagoan economist approach and the Austrian approach. Chicagoan economics is based around using empirical data to predict future trends by means of complex statistical mathematics and computer models. The Austrian approach uses analytical logic and abstract reasoning to deduce conclusions from fundamental concepts and first principles. The Austrian method begins with a first principle, called an axiom, and then seeks to deduce all economic truths as a matter of logic from the axiom. In other words, the Chicago approach is scientific economics, based around research into empirical fact which then draws inferences from data, vs. the Austrian method, which I call "philosophical economics," a method that uses abstract deductive logic and reasoning to deduce necessary truths from basic self-evident ideas and principles. Scientific economics is based on empirical data, and philosophical economics is based on ideas and reasoning.

My approach, which is embodied in GOLD economics, embraces philosophical economics and rejects scientific statistical mathematical economics. So, at the start of my deep detailed presentation of my economics, let me make it crystal clear, and I cannot stress this enough, that my method is not based on empirical data, and unlike conventional economists I am not seeking to justify my theories on the basis of trends in statistics and sets of numbers. Instead, I present self-evident ideas, which you can see are obviously true by looking at the ideas themselves, and I then show that if these ideas are true then the need for free market capitalism follows as a logical necessity from the nature of economics as such.

I reject scientific economics for two reasons. First, most people are not university professor-caliber mathematicians or economists, but everyone needs to understand economics, so economic truth and wisdom must be captured conceptually in order to be useful for most humans. Second, it is implied by the scientific method that data and facts are neutral and unbiased, but in practice the supposedly empirical data-based, "neutral" economics actually is exploited by partisan economists to fit their politically biased desires. Any hidden desire or bias can be justified by a skillful manipulation of the data that is available, and most good economists are capable of manipulating the facts to justify their desired outcome. Someone who knows math and statistics can easily manipulate any set of economic data to reach a desired conclusion. This is why liberal economists take the data and argue that it proves liberal theory, and conservative economists say that the data supports conservative economics, and libertarians take the data and prove that it shows libertarian truth. Who are you going to believe? And why?

The only way to sort through all the different competing interpretations of economic data presented in the research papers of economists is to look at the premises and ideas at the foundation of their analysis and try to use reasoning and common sense to see what makes sense. A serious debate about economics will always reduce to a debate over ideas and theory and principles, so scientific economics is really useless, and philosophical economics is quite useful. Mathematical duels over data and statistics and scientific calculations are irrelevant and won't be found outside esoteric, redundant university journals.

Note that economics is not even a hard science, like chemistry or physics, and can never achieve the true scientific method, despite the economics professors who say that they are scientists. Economics does not perform controlled experiments like the hard sciences, and instead takes data collected from economic research and interprets it. The collection of data from observations of the economy can always be biased by the person who collects the data, and a lot of the data used by economists is collected by government agencies, and it should not be trusted in a neutral unbiased evaluation of the role of government in the economy. In controlled experiments, variables are rigorously controlled for in order to isolate cause and effect, like applying an experimental chemical to a group of lab rats to evaluate the biological effects of the chemical acting as a cause upon the lab rats. In contrast, the data in economics is collected from measurements of the economy, which are messy and imperfect compared to measuring the effect of a chemical upon a set of lab rats. Economics can never use the scientific method in the sense of hard science like physics, chemistry, and biology, because we cannot run tests on humans in the same way that we run tests on lab rats. A soft science like economics will never achieve the neutral, unbiased, objective conclusions of true empirical science. A demonstrated logical proof is more likely to be trustworthy than a complicated statistical research study.

Of course, if you want fact-based scientific empirical research, the libertarian Chicagoan economists have undertaken a mountain of research presented in papers and books, proving that the data shows that free markets produce prosperity and leftist socialist economics destroys wealth. The books and studies authored by Milton Friedman and his followers are ample evidence of this. But if you are looking for empirical research, I suggest that you go read those books, not this one. Then, when you grow weary of numbers and math, and you want to actually understand what it all means and why it is true, please come back and read this book.

Having embraced philosophical economics as my solution to the controversy on method, let me say that my axiom of economics, my self-evident truth from which my ideas flow as a matter of deductive logic, is quite different from the axiom of the Austrian economists. The Austrian axiom is "human action", whereas my axiom is "the division of labor", which I call the Neo-Classical axiom. I will analyze the division of labor axiom, which is the idea that X produced Y and A produced B and X wants to consume B and A wants to consume Y, later in this chapter. For now, let me turn a critical eye upon the Austrian axiom.

The Austrian method of deducing economics analytically from first principles is correct, but the Austrian axiom is the wrong first principle to deduce the truth from. The axiom of human action, first developed in Mises's "Human Action" and later expanded in Rothbard's "Man, Economy, and State," states that "humans act (for a purpose)." From the axiom of human action the Austrians deduce that humans create a scale of value preferences and act according to their scale of preferences in order to maximize their perceived utilities, which means that humans prioritize scarce resources for the purpose of achieving their goals. The Austrians conclude that only a capitalist economy (and anarchy) properly enables humans to allocate scarce resources based on their preferences. The axiom of human action also states that resources are converted into consumable goods by means of "recipes," i.e. ideas or techniques for how to use raw materials, and because recipes are supposedly not scarce they should not be owned and are not subject to the laws of economics, according to Rothbard.

The problem with the Austrian axiom is that "human action" is too vague and broad to justify capitalism. My argument here is that humans acted for purposes, in the sense of wanting food to eat and wanting to satisfy their various desires and prioritizing their resources in order to achieve their goals, in the economies of Communist Russia and Nazi Germany. But those were not libertarian economies. If human action existed in socialist economies, and according to obvious factual analysis it did, then the axiom of human action does not require a capitalist economy. Indeed, a human stranded on a desert island could act for a purpose and prioritize his scarce resources, but in that situation no economy would exist at all, which points out the weakness of human action as an explanation of economics. The axiom of libertarian economics should be a principle that makes capitalism necessary and gets at the fundamental difference between capitalism and socialism. Human action does not require capitalism so it is not the proper libertarian axiom.

The correct axiom of libertarian philosophical economics is the division of labor, not human action. The GOLD XYAB Neo-Classical axiom states that X produced Y and A produced B, and that X wants to consume B and A wants to consume Y, and X and A can either trade freely using money or be commanded to obey someone else's economic plan. From this axiom we can logically deduce supply and demand, money prices, and the need for trade-based economics to coordinate the economy. All of this flows logically as a necessary requirement from the axiom, as I explain below. The axiom of the division of labor requires money, trades, and supply and demand, so it requires capitalism as an economic necessity. The biggest problem with the axiom of human action is that it does not adequately explain trades, money, or supply and demand. And as a matter of logic the axiom of human action is compatible with either capitalism or socialism.

Let me conclude this section by noting three things. First, I am not saying that Austrian economics as a whole endorses socialism. The Austrian economists have taken their axiom of human action and coated it in thick layers of interpretation which justify capitalism and reject socialism. The entire body of Austrian thought does make some valuable contributions to libertarian theory. But if you strip away the outside and look only at the axiom of human action as such, the idea that humans act for a purpose and prioritize scarce resources does not really tell you very much about economics. A socialist could agree that resources are scarce but claim that socialism makes use of scarce resources better than capitalism.

Second, baked into the Austrian axiom is the absurd, stupid idea that intellectual property is so abundant and plentiful that it appears by magic and grows on trees and should therefore be free for everyone to take it away from the people who create it without paying for it. By contrast, GOLD Neo-Classical economics recognizes that inventions, works of art, and creative expressions cost labor and money to produce and therefore inventors and artists and writers deserve to own the things that they created by their hard work. Intellectual property should be treated as private property which can be traded and owned by its producers and creators. The mistake of intellectual property is additional proof that the axiom of human action is not very logical or rigorously reasoned.

Third, let me conclude by saying that my Neo-Classical economics could probably be reconciled and made compatible with Austrian economic theory, and my XYAB analysis could be incorporated into Austrian ideas. But examining what a Neo-Classical plus Austrian harmony would look like is outside the scope and purpose of this book. I will not speculate on whether the right path forward is to improve Austrian economics or else to replace Austrian economics in its entirety.

The remainder of this chapter shows the details of why Neo-Classical economics is better than Austrian economics as a libertarian economic theory.

SUBPART 11-B: SUPPLY AND DEMAND

I posit that the central idea of Neo-Classical economics is supply and demand. But we must be precise in what we mean by "supply" and "demand," terms which become confused when politicians talk about them in policy debates. I argue that supply and demand can be used to analyze a market consisting of a good or service and trades involving that good or service, but not for people or groups of people. Here I offer the key idea of GOLD economics, which is the XYAB trade analysis as an explanation for the supply of and demand for Y relative to B.

To present this idea I will return to the XYAB analysis that I offered when I presented GOLD, but I will change it slightly in order to use it to illustrate the division of labor in the economy. The division of labor states that different people do different jobs, and the task of economics is to figure out how to coordinate production and consumption among people who produce and consume different goods and services. I take XYAB and redefine X and A as two different workers who work two different jobs and produce two different products, and who also consume values other than the values that they produced. Let us say that X is a worker or employee or producer or businessman who produced or created or made Y, and Y is a good or service, either a consumable good or service or a tool that can be used by someone else to produce or manufacture or create something else. Similarly, A is a worker/businessman/etc. who produced B, which is a good or service. Now let us add that X wants to consume B, and A wants to consume Y. So, in summary, X produced Y, and A produced B, and X wants B, and A wants Y.

If X produces Y and sells Y to A, and A buys Y from X, we are tempted to say that X is a producer and X is the "supply" of Y, and A is the consumer and A is the "demand" for Y. This is misleading, because the hidden part of the picture is out of view. The hidden side is that A produced B, and A trades B to X in exchange for Y. Thus, A and X are both consumers and producers. If this is true, then it makes sense in policy debates to speak of free trade vs. control, and not to speak of supply side vs. demand side.

The truth is confused and obscured by the role of money in the trade. For example, in a more realistic model, a triangle of trade will exist. Say that X produces Y, and X trades Y to A in exchange for A's money. Let us say that Y costs $1 and call A's money by the name "$1", so A buys Y from X for $1. It looks like A is only a consumer and X is just a producer of Y, because X sells Y for $1 to A and A buys Y for $1 and consumes Y. A gets Y, and X gets $1. The hidden side of the triangle of trade in this example is that A also produced B while consuming Y, and it is B that enables A to buy Y from X, but for a complicated reason. In this triangle of trade, assume the existence of a third person named C, who produced a good or service called D. While A bought Y from X for $1, A also produced B, and A traded B to C in return for C's money of $1, and C produced D, and C traded D to X in exchange for X's $1. This is somewhat confusing, so let me try to simplify it. X gives value to A, A gives value to C, and C gives value to X. It is really as simple as that. The money in the analysis merely hides what is really happening, which is why money is an illusion which disguises the trade-based nature of a capitalist free market economy. X gives value to A and A gives money to X, and A's money is a placeholder for the value that C gives to X. A's money symbolizes and represents value because it can be redeemed for value.

As I argued in the earlier chapter on supply and demand, money is the tool which functions as a medium of exchange to enable trades of value for value among large numbers of people with specialized jobs in a division of labor economy, but money hides what is really happening, which is trades between traders. So in the example of the triangle of trade, X produced Y, A produced B, and C produced D, and Y, B and D get traded in a three-way triangle of trade. X consumed D, C consumed B, and A consumed Y. The $1 that went in the other direction than the value, when each buyer received a value and gave $1 to the seller in return for that value, was merely a tool for a three-way trade to take place. In reality, nobody is just a buyer or just a seller. Instead, X, A, and C are all traders.

To visualize this, simply draw a triangle, label one corner X, label one corner A, and label one corner C. Along line XA, Y went from X to A, and $1 went from A to X. Along line AC, B went from A to C, and $1 went from C to A. And along line XC, D went from C to X, and $1 went from X to C. I really do encourage you to draw the diagram to make this easier to understand.

To make the terminology precise, we can say that X and A are the primary traders in the trade where X sold Y to A for $1, and the trades involving C, i.e. the trades between X and C and between A and C, were the secondary trades, which happened behind the scenes from the point of view of A and X doing their trade with each other, and C was the secondary trader. In actual reality, when X and A do a trade, perhaps millions of secondary trades may happen behind the scenes. For example, when X builds a car in Los Angeles, and A bakes gourmet bread in New York, and X orders a loaf online from A's website and pays for the bread by credit card, then eventually a trade of money will connect the two, such that the circuit of trade is completed. Perhaps C, a doctor in Cleveland, buys a car from X and pays X with cash, and C also invents a medicine to treat A's daughter for which A pays C with cash. GOLD economics says that for every primary trade that happens a secondary trade must also exist to complete the circuit of trade, because A's $1 has usefulness for X only because X can use A's $1 to buy D from C, and C will give D to X for $1 only because C receives B from A.

From the XYAB trade analysis I deduce a concept which is key to GOLD economics, namely the idea which I call "the productivity theory of demand". The Keynesian model, as some economists envision it, holds that demand creates supply, and the goal of economic policy is to stimulate demand. But A's "demand," meaning A's ability to buy Y, actually consists of A's ability to produce B. A's demand for Y does not consist of A's need of Y or want for Y. If by "demand" we mean purchasing power and whatever causes and enables A to buy Y, then A's demand for Y consists of A's production of B. A's ability to buy Y is A's ability to create B so that A can trade with X and C and trade B for Y. I call this analysis "the productivity theory of demand."

Thus, Keynes was wrong. Demand does not "create" supply, but demand motivates supply and holds supply accountable. GOLD could be called "supply side economics" because GOLD says that the best way to enable A to buy Y is to help A produce B, or to get government taxes and regulations out of A's way so that A is free to create B, instead of the demand side economics notion that A's need for Y or A's desire to consume Y has any economic significance in giving A the ability to buy Y. GOLD rejects the notion that demand, which really means those people who make demands to be given goods to consume without having to pay for them, should enslave supply, i.e. productive people who create and trade value. However, to speak of supply and demand one must be talking about Y (relative to B or D), not about X and A and C, all of whom are people who both produce and consume and trade, all at the same time.

In economic policy, the question is not whether we should stimulate demand or encourage supply. The question is whether we should allow freedom to trade or restrict trade and impose a planned economy. Freedom to trade lets X, A and C be free to produce and consume and trade as they choose. Under a centrally planned economy the government steps in and controls what X, A and C do, in both production and consumption. GOLD holds that freedom to trade is preferable to planned economics. Trade is the engine which drives the economy and causes economic growth, because a division of labor economy is a network of trades, and the economy requires trading between individuals as the facilitator for organizing production and consumption across a group of millions or billions of people each with a specialized job capacity. More trading aligns more production and consumption so that the people produce and consume more wealth. To return to the XYAB example, trade motivates X to produce Y and enables X to consume B or D, so more trading leads to more production and consumption for X. Hence the engine of economic growth is increased trading. Therefore the policy of the freedom to trade is always preferable to government control.

The cynical socialist or liberal politician will attack this story by asking "what about the helpless and disabled people who cannot produce but who need to consume?" For example, what if A needs Y but A is unable to produce B? The answer is that if A consumes Y but does not produce B, then X must have produced Y and given it to A for free, or else someone must have forcibly stolen Y from X and given Y to A. One man's misfortunate and misery does not justify doing injustice to another person who has done nothing wrong. If free trade creates an abundance of wealth, as it would, then someone will probably give Y to A as charity, because it is in the nature of human empathy for most people to want to help other people if it is within our power to do so. However, absent voluntary charity, it is wrong for the government to steal Y from X and give Y to A just because A needs it, even if A would die without it, since X created Y and was Y's legitimate owner, and injustice and tragedy is not an excuse to commit further injustice and do evil deeds. Ironically, if economic slavery destroys X's ability to produce Y, as it eventually will, then socialist distribution is bad not only for X but also for A, because Y is not created by X for A to consume it, so A dies anyway, and A probably would have received Y as charity from someone else if liberty had been allowed to vastly increase the pool of wealth in the economy.

The idea that government will "help people" because its purpose is "not for profit" and the state will be more charitable than private individuals who are "selfish and greedy" is absurd, and assumes the "government as God" complex. The government consists merely of individuals. Individuals within the government and outside the government share the same fundamental human nature. So private human beings are as kind, nice and charitable as government officials, and politicians can be as arrogant and cruel as private individuals. Nor can the government magically create wealth to distribute by taxing the rich, since taxation merely takes what someone else created, taxing does not itself create wealth. "We must rely on the charity of the rich" is no worse than "we must rely on the charity of the government," indeed it is better since the government officials are obsessed with power, as they must be to have the ambition and ruthlessness to reach high office, and they will tend to use the government's noble, idealistic, altruistic mission as an excuse to seize power over the economy and dominate us and destroy our freedom. The government will con good people into thinking that this is the only way to help the poor and the disabled, helpless, elderly, etc. The truth is that "we must rely on the charity of our fellow human beings." So the GOLD "live and let live" is not "live and let die," it does not "let the poor die." Instead it is the best policy for everyone.

The XYAB supply and demand model also shows how government has conned the public into thinking that the government has the power to give things away for free when in reality it is the people who pay for what the government distributes. The government gives Y to the public, saying that Y is free, and the public only sees Y and fails to see the deep complicated economic analysis showing that A's B is what enables A to consume X's Y. If more Y is consumed but no extra B is produced to pay for Y then, under the laws of supply and demand, the per unit quality of Y must go down, because the same B purchasing power is buying a larger number of units of Y. When the government forces trades to happen, e.g. forcing people to buy healthcare, it is forcing trades between doctors and patients that the people would not voluntarily choose. This distorts supply and demand, leading to inefficiencies and problems, which is why Obamacare will lower the quality of healthcare in the United States. And when the government pays for something by raising taxes, then it has not created something for free, because the "free" service is actually paid for by the taxpayers. The tax dollars appropriated by the government could have been spent more efficiently by investment in the private sector, which helps small business, which creates jobs, which benefits the poor far more than welfare.

SUBPART 11-C:
MARGINAL UTILITY

Early economists pointed out a problem that they sought to understand, namely the fact that diamonds are expensive despite having no practical usefulness while water is cheap despite being vitally necessary for human survival. Austrians argue that water is cheaper than diamonds even though water is vital and diamonds are useless because of the "marginal utility" theory that a commodity is always priced at the value of its least important use. The diminishing marginal utility theory is a complicated theory and I argue that it is not quite correct. Instead of the principle of marginal utility, I argue that the principle of supply and demand explains the water vs. diamonds mystery. Assuming a constant demand, then the bigger the supply the less is the value of each individual unit. Water is less valuable than diamonds because a huge supply of water exists relative to the demand for water and a small supply of diamonds exists relative to the demand for diamonds.

If each marginal unit had a different value then a rational businessman would not price each unit at the cost of the least desirable use. Instead he would divide up the units and value each unit according to its usefulness. In reality the first unit to be sold has the lowest cost because a rational businessman would sell the unit which fulfilled the least necessary use first, but this does not mean that every unit has the same price as the marginal unit. In other words, if one takes the Austrian theory of marginal utility seriously, and the businessman who sells water collects his water in a vast pool, then the water at the edge of the pool is cheaper than the water in the middle of the pool. By contrast, in reality we do not find that one portion of a commodity is valued differently from the price of another chunk or group of it. If it is summer and a lot of water gets used up to fill swimming pools and then there is a drought and the demand for drinking water goes way up relative to the remaining supply of water the price of water will go way up, but this will be because supply decreased and demand increased, not because the use of the unit at the margin changed. It is unclear what the principle of marginal utility adds to economics that is not already fully explained by supply and demand.

SUBPART 11-D: THE CHOICE THEORY OF VALUE VS. THE SUBJECTIVE THEORY OF VALUE AND THE LABOR THEORY OF VALUE

Austrians counter the Marxist "labor theory of value" which holds that a good or service is worth the labor that created it with the Austrian "subjective theory of value" which says that a good or service is worth the personal satisfaction that it gives to people who use or experience it. Based on the subjective theory of value, it is Austrian dogma that if one product or service is more expensive than another competing good or service this does not indicate that it is objectively more valuable than the other, since value exists only subjectively in people's minds. This leads Austrian economics to the counterintuitive claim that $5 is not more valuable than $4. The idea that value is completely subjective and cannot be objectively measured is bizarre, irrational, and totally unnecessary for a defense of capitalism. This theory originated because the Austrians wanted to oppose the Marxist labor theory of value, which holds that a good's value is the effort that went into producing it. Instead of using price signals and free markets to assign values, the Marxist thinks you can calculate an object's intrinsic value by reference to the effort that created it, and sell it at a price based on its labor value. The Austrians tried to counter the Marxist argument by saying that value is subjective and not intrinsic to the object. This hints at and grasps towards the truth but does not quite reach the truth.

The truth is that goods only have values when they are used by and for human beings, and an object's intrinsic physical qualities only have value when a human desires them or finds them useful. But the solution to Marx's labor theory of value is not the subjective theory of value. The solution is, as I describe it, "the choice theory of value." The choice theory of value holds that the value of a good or service is the amount of money that a person will freely choose, or has freely chosen, to spend to buy it. Thus, only the free market in which people actually freely buy things can figure out what is the value of a good or service. A central planner cannot objectively measure values because the bureaucrat does not know the consumer's desires and thoughts and choices, consumers have free will and can make any conceivable choice, so only the free market where trades really happen can properly determine a product's value. In summary, an object's objective value is what someone freely chose to pay to buy it, so only the free market can measure objective values because free economic decisions only happen in a free market. The choice theory of value refutes the Marxist labor theory of value but enables us to say that an item that is purchased and sold in a free market has an objective value measured in dollars. $5 is obviously more valuable than $4, and my theory enables us to understand why this is true. It is also incorrect to speak of the goods as removing urgently felt uneasiness, as some Austrians do, since the accurate thing is to simply say that the consumer chooses what he chooses, and this is usually what he wants or thinks that he needs.

Value is created by the consumers' preferences and is subjective in that sense, but the money that a person actually pays for a good is a perfectly valid objective measure of the value of that good, and money prices are numerical mathematical quantities that can be objectively measured relative to other prices. The Austrians run around in circles trying to hide from the fact that the price at which an object is sold is an objective measure of the buyer's and seller's choice, thus it is an objective measure for the choice theory of value. This makes sense, because when supply of a product goes up the price goes down and this tells people to produce less of the product, why? Because the price has told businessmen that the value of the product has decreased. If money was not an objective quantitative measure then it would be impossible to compare the values of different goods. The Austrians say that $5 vs. $4 means only that the five dollar item is preferred to the four dollar item and only ordinal rankings and not cardinal rankings are possible, but this flies in the face of reality because dollar amounts are quantitative, and all other things being equal, $2 is always worth more than $1, and $3 is worth more than $2, and $4 is worth more than $3, and so on, and $10 is worth less than $20, etc. The Austrians struggle to say that economic actors want "satisfaction" but do not act to maximize their monetary wealth, which is absurd.

The Austrians would also disagree that one can say that objectively a television that is priced at $500 is objectively more valuable than a television that sells for $450, which is an absurd, ridiculous thing to disagree. I say this not only from common sense, but also from rigorously logical theory. The Austrian might say: "But one TV is worth more than the other to whom? The televisions have no objective value. They only have subjective value for the consumers who experience satisfaction from them."

It is true that the TVs only have value from their use by human beings, and any given person might actually prefer the $450 TV to the $500 TV. The televisions only have value for individual human beings, that is quite true and I agree. But because money is a medium of exchange and can be traded for any good or service that is available for trade on the market, the seller who sells one TV for $500 and the other for $450 thinks that the more expensive one is worth more of any other good or service than the less expensive one, and the seller's price is set by the impact of supply and demand upon competition, so the price is essentially an average of the valuations of every trader in the market about what that good is worth in terms of every other good on the market. And when a consumer actually buys the $500 TV, and at the same time (or nearly the same time, in the same time frame) another consumer actually buys the $450 TV, or, as might actually happen in reality, that brand and model of TV is priced at a uniform price in many stores and large groups of consumers buy those TVs for the producer's prices, and the transaction is paid for in dollars that could have been used to buy any other good or service, then the traders' choices have been made and one can say with certainty that the TVs were objectively worth the prices at which they were labeled.

Marxism fails because only free consumer choice can reveal what consumers actually want, not because value is subjective rather than objective. When I pay $6 for a chocolate ice cream sundae and I say "this sundae was worth the $6 that I paid for it," I mean that the value was comparable to other goods and services on the market that generally sell for a price of $6, although I might also mean that the reward of the sundae justified the work that I did to earn that $6.

SUBPART 11-E: INTEREST

Austrians explain interest on loans purely from the time value of money, namely the difference between the value of money in the present and the value of that money in the future. I argue that interest is the payment for the use of capital/means of production, not merely an arbitrage between present goods and future goods. In the first place, actual futures contracts, e.g. those traded on a Chicago exchange, do not resemble any interest rate. Secondly, if I loan a person money, my understanding is that the interest is a payment in exchange for his use of my money and is not based on my understanding of future prices. Third, if a person borrows money to produce a present good, and no time elapses, he would still owe some interest, although no time-based interest would have compounded (depending upon the terms of the loan).

For example, if X has a machine that turns $100 into $500 instantaneously, and A gives $100 to X, and X feeds the $100 into his magic machine, and in that same instant X gives A's $100 back to A, then A would reasonably expect his fair share of the $500 created by the machine from his $100, even though no time value exists in this thought experiment. What A expects, the interest, is the price X pays to use A's money. Merely saving assets does not create additional wealth beyond what was saved. If I borrow $10 from you at 10% interest and I do nothing with it then tomorrow when the loan comes due I will have to return the $10 to you and I will no additional money with which to pay the $1 of interest owed to you. I would still owe interest, but it would be payment for the opportunity that came from having $10 to invest, and not merely from the time value of one day of time. I would have failed to use that $10 productively as the loan envisioned. One must do something productive with the asset to produce added wealth, and some new wealth must be created in order to pay the interest. Banks evolved as loan-giving organizations so that people's savings could earn interest by being put to use through bank loans to businesses.

SUBPART 11-F: PROFIT

Profit is not merely a reward for correctly predicting uncertainty, as the Austrians assert. Not only are the Austrians wrong here, but their theory in no way justifies a belief that businesspeople earn and deserve to own their profits. In the first place, the Austrians view economic decisions about the future as possessing total uncertainty, so predicting the future is luck and guesses and not actually doing work, so if profit is a reward for predicting the future then it is like being paid for luck, and luck does not justify earning money or ownership of the rewards of effort, whereas work does. Second, the Austrians believe that the entrepreneur simply predicts the future and then assigns "resources" to the future demand, and is rewarded for it. On such a theory the resource does all the real work and the businessman does nothing. This Austrian view is strangely similar to Marxism.

The better pro-capitalist theory is that profit represents the value in the goods and services that was created by the businessman, and he recovers the money value of what he created as his profit when he sells the item. For example, if a businessman invests $10 worth of raw materials into a product and sells it for $15 then his profit of $5 represents the value that he contributed by turning the raw materials into a consumable finished product. The difference here between the choice theory of value and the labor theory of value is that the choice theory of value holds that his profit, i.e. what he earns and deserves to own, is defined and determined by the choice of the consumer to buy the object for $15 and cannot be evaluated independently of the purchasing decision.

SUBPART 11-G: INFLATION AND THE CORRESPONDENCE THEORY OF MONEY

The Austrian theory of inflation is flawed. They claim that increased credit causes interest rates to rise, but there is no reason why this should be so. Also, any rational businessman who knew Austrian economics (as they all would if it was a rational theory) would simply ignore the inflationary business rate and choose to expand at a rate slower than the interest rate would suggest when the data on credit expansion came out. A simpler, and more truthful, explanation of inflation is that the total amount of money in circulation symbolizes and corresponds to the total amount of wealth, as it must because there is a finite amount of wealth and a finite amount of money and the money can be redeemed for the wealth, because of the government's gun declaring that paper fiat money is legal tender. So when the government prints more money, the total amount of money increases but the amount of wealth remains constant. Then there are more units of money per each unit of wealth, so it then requires more units of money to purchase the same unit of wealth. This adequately describes why prices go up.

Under this analysis, inflation is theft. Inflation is the government stealing money from the people because, when the government prints money, this money immediately corresponds to and symbolizes the wealth that is proportionate to the ratio of that printed money to the total money supply. The government can spend that newly minted money to acquire that wealth which the money represents. The government is buying this wealth and not giving anything in exchange for it except the printed money backed by nothing, so when the government prints money it takes wealth away from all of the people who own dollars.

Let me offer an example to explain my theory of inflation. If the economy contains 100 apples, and the money supply contains 100 dollars, then one apple would usually cost $1 (100/100). If the government prints an additional $100, then there are 100 apples and 200 dollars. So now one apple costs two dollars (200/100). The government has stolen 50 apples from the private sector, because the government can buy 50 apples of wealth through spending its newly minted $100. The private dollar-owning citizens must now spend $2 to buy an apple which used to cost $1. And the original $100 that was in the hands of the people now has a purchasing power of 50 apples, whereas it previously could have bought 100 apples before the government's newly minted $100 of money was printed.

This narrative explains the price increases that are the most visible symptom of inflation. The value of money is a direct function of the money supply plus the total wealth in the economy, because money represents wealth, so inflation, and deflation, are entirely the result of the money supply expanding or contracting relative to the value of wealth. It might be true that when the state prints paper money certain prices of certain goods might experience temporary short-term decreases, attributable to their relation to whatever the state is spending its newly minted dollars on, but what we generally mean by "inflation" is a long-term trending rise in prices, and this is precisely the inflation which is explained by my theory.

The Keynesian theory that inflation enables government spending which fights unemployment, such that inflation and unemployment are locked in a constant duel, is incorrect. If the government steals money via inflation, and then spends that money inefficiently and in a manner which does not hold the decision makers accountable from competition and the profit motive, as it usually does, then inflation will increase unemployment by ruining the economy. Government spending in the short term might artificially inject growth into the economy, since it might take dollars that would have gone into savings and instead spend them on present-day spending, which could create new jobs in the short term, but over the long term it will stall growth and cause a net loss of jobs.

So the choice which policymakers face is precisely the opposite of the Keynesian premise: if the government chooses inflation then the long-term result will be unemployment, although voters, especially liberals and socialists, might shortsightedly prefer short-term artificial growth. And if the government chooses to hold the money supply constant, or, as they really should do, abolish the Federal Reserve and privatize the management of the national currency so that the free market will decide whether and when to print money, then government will no longer be able to use inflation to steal wealth, and government spending will shrink. This will cause short-term pain unpopular with many voters, but this would achieve a long-term result of greater financial stability, and more economic growth which creates more jobs.

More generally, Austrian economics refuses to acknowledge that all market activity consists of trade, and when a seller sells X good to buyer and buyer pays Y dollars, buyer "bought" those dollars by doing work and trading his work to his employer in exchange for the dollars, so the dollars symbolize and correspond to the work that buyer has done, and buyer is trading buyer's work to seller in exchange for seller's work embodied in the product X that seller made. Even in an advanced specialized division of labor economy where money is the medium of exchange, all trades are actually a trade of value for value, i.e. of work for work. If you fix my shoes and then I bake a pizza for you, this is the same as my paying you money to repair my shoes, and you then buying a pizza from me for money. The money is merely the medium by which all goods and services are translated into a common frame of reference so that it is easier to compare the values of different goods.

This analysis is completed by the understanding that when a worker works for a salary, he trades his labor to his employer in exchange for money, so the worker is "buying" dollars of wage salary with his labor. Austrians claim that money replaces "in kind" valuation, when in fact money's only value is to ultimately buy consumer goods and services, so all valuation reduces to the in kind valuation of what you consume measured relative to what you produce and what others produced. All money reduces to work done in the economy, i.e. all money reduces to wealth, each specific dollar can be traced back to some work that someone did to get that dollar, and when you spend that dollar you are trading that work in exchange for the product that you buy. The money is just a symbol, the money in itself adds nothing and the free market itself is a trade of economic value for economic value. This is the correspondence theory of money, in concise summary.

SUBPART 11-H:
RETROSPECTIVE HINDSIGHT
VS. PROSPECTIVE FORESIGHT

The Austrians are wrong to claim that economic activity is entirely prospective and never retrospective. The best example of what the Austrians mean is that if you buy shares of a stock for $100 and the price drops to $50 you should make your decision about when to sell looking only at where the price might be in the future, and you should totally ignore the $50 loss you will take if you sell now relative to the price in the past when you bought the shares of stock. The Austrian idea is wrong because profit equals revenues minus costs, so the goal of making a profit requires that costs be considered in making financial decisions.

It might be true that as a matter of logic a trader should sell his assets in the most profitable way that the present or future can permit regardless of what it cost him to buy those assets in the past. But in practical reality, a person does not feel good by selling for the best deal available, he feels good for making a profit and he feels bad for taking a loss, so the cost of acquiring the assets will usually figure into any human being's calculations when he or she makes economic decisions. Throughout the history of the Wall Street stock market there have been millions of people who should have sold their stock for a loss to avoid a bigger loss, but did not because they wanted a gain instead of a loss and decided to hold while the stock market was declining. Any economic theory should take account of the practical reality of the free market trader's psychology, especially when the psychological phenomenon is so widespread as to have a significant impact.

I concede that the Austrian approach is a good general rule for stock investors and is helpful for people who should take a smaller loss to avoid a bigger loss in the future. But in general it is unrealistic to expect people to ignore their net profits and losses. Even if one ignores human psychology and focuses entirely on economic logic, the goal of a trade is generally to make a profit, and profit is the excess of revenues above costs, so past costs should always factor into present economic decisions about profit. Austrians are incorrect to say that economic traders should ignore the past and choose the best path based entirely on the present and the future.

SUBPART 11-I: TRADING VALUE FOR VALUE AND OBJECTIVE RELATIVE VALUATION

In order for you to consume what you have not produced, someone else must not consume what they have produced, because it has to come from somewhere. Thus two types of production-consumption circuits exist. The produce-and-consume circuit is the healthy circuit where you consume what you have produced. The parasite circuit is the unhealthy circuit where you consume what other people have produced, but you yourself produce nothing. Healthy people consume what they produce, whereas the lazy feed upon others as parasites. When the sick, elderly, and disabled take charity given voluntarily by productive people, then their circuit is a hybrid of the other two, in which the unproductive consume value but as part of the healthy cycle of human life. The trade economy and trading for money instead of bartering some goods for other goods obscured this, but if you create Y, and you trade Y to A in exchange for B, and you then consume B, then you are really consuming the value (i.e. substance) that you created in Y, but in a form that A created, which is B. Trade magnified the value of Y by the trade for B, but the value that X consumes is the value that X produced. X consumes the substance of Y in the form of B, so when X consumes B he is actually consuming the productive labor that went into producing Y because Y paid for B.

Trade theory holds that traders in a free market "trade value for value," but if X trades Y to A in exchange for B, how can you say that Y and B are of equal value at the time of the trade if X values B more than Y and A wants Y more than B? They are both better off from trading, but why are Y and B equal? X might want B more than Y, but Y is what X is willing to give up in order to get B, so for purposes of the trade X values B at the price of Y, X converts Y into B, so Y was worth B. But what does "for purposes of the trade" add when if X will give up Y to get B then X wants B more than Y, so for X the value of Y and B are not equal? If X buys B for $1.50 does that mean that B is worth more than $1.50 to X because X traded $1.50 for B? If B were worth precisely $1.50 to X then why would X do the trade? Also you can make a bad trade and trade Y for a B of lesser value by choice, and you can consume what you have not produced if someone gives it to you as a gift. "Trade value for value" means that you give A something that A wants and in exchange A gives you something that you want, and "you cannot consume what you have not produced" means that if A gives you B then A had to produce it, and to get A to give you what you want you must give A some reason to give it to you, i.e. give A some value in exchange, either financial from profit or emotional for charity. "Trade value for value" means that in order to give Y to someone as a gift for free, someone else had to produce Y and pay for it. The theory confirms that the best way to get value is to create value to trade away in order to receive value back.

Also, what if I sell Y for $5 because someone was willing to pay $5 but I would have been willing to sell Y for $3? Is Y worth $5 or $3? If you assume economic profit-maximizing rational actors then the seller will seek to sell for as high a price as possible and the buyer will seek to buy at as low a price as possible, so the trade will happen at the equilibrium point where supply curve meets demand curve, and that is the point at which both buyer and seller want the trade to happen.

The market is an averaging of evaluations, so money price enables comparative valuations of different goods/services, but the money price is the objective value only relative to everything else in the market, e.g. "an apple is worth $2" only has objective meaning relative to "an orange is worth $1" because money only has value for what it buys, it is only a measure of the value that it corresponds to. If an apple costs $2 and an orange costs $1 then an apple is worth two oranges, and money is an objective measure of value in the objective relative sense only. The price mechanism of money reduces to the relative value of one good in terms of other goods, in the context of the fact that money merely represents bartering one good for another good. Assuming rational actors everything is priced as close as possible to the money value which is the average of how much people value it i.e. how much people choose it. If Y buys an apple for $2 at a farmer's market in New York, and A buys an orange for $1 at a grocery store in Los Angeles, then the price system coordinates the supply and demand of fruit and links the trades of X and A, and the trades' prices tells farmers and the agricultural industry to invest more resources in producing apples than oranges and matches supply to demand, under the supply and demand money system described in a previous section.

This theory of objective relative valuation follows from the choice theory of value and the correspondence theory of money. I call it "objective relative" valuation because it is both objective and relative. $2 is objectively worth more than $1, in the sense that the laws of math and logic are objective and 2 is objectively greater than 1. But price valuation is relative, because it measures apples in terms of oranges, or measures one good in terms of the average of values decided by all trades for all other goods in the marketplace using a shared money supply. For the best example of objective relative valuation, consider one economy where one hour of manual labor typically commands a salary of $6, and a chicken sandwich in a deli also typically costs $6.

Now consider another economy where one hour of labor normally earns $200, and a chicken sandwich costs $200. I argue that the price of a chicken sandwich is the same in both nations, because the price of the chicken sandwich exists only relative to the objective amount of work that earns it, despite the fact that $200 is $194 more than $6 in absolute terms. Note that this theory does not ignore inflation, because, for example, inflation is the process of the price of a chicken sandwich going up from $6 to $200, which is harmful to the economy for reasons discussed in my explanation of inflation, and which is not the same thing as an objective relative price remaining constant.

Profit is also usefully explained by the correspondence theory of money and objective relative valuation. If I buy raw materials for $10 and build a mousetrap and sell it for $20, the work that I put into it is represented by my $10 profit and my labor's contribution corresponds to $10 of the $20 I received, because if there are enough trades in the market to average out, i.e. if there are millions of sales of goods/services for dollars, then the value of one dollar averages to the relative value of one good/ service relative to all others traded for dollars, so $20 represents a specific objective amount of value as does $10, e.g. $1 is worth one orange and $2 is worth one apple so $10 of raw material is worth 10 oranges or 5 apples, etc. The market values the mousetrap at $20 and the raw materials at $10, so my labor must be worth $10. Thus, profit is value that is earned by doing work and producing value, and profit can only be valued and measured by choices in the marketplace. Profit is not merely an unnecessary addition added by capitalists to prices in order to exploit laborers, as Marxism claims.

Let me describe how a correspondence monetary analysis works. The correspondence theory of money begins at the macro level. For example, if there are 500 dollars in an economy and 50 pineapples then each pineapple must be worth $10. It looks at the total value in the economy as represented by the total money supply and then deduces the micro level value from the total economy of wealth divided by the money supply. But absent a market large enough to produce averages, e.g. if on a desert island I trade a mousetrap for a pizza, there is no way to know that the objective value of the mousetrap was worth the objective value of the pizza, since nothing else exists relative to which to value the pizza, e.g. you can't say that ten pizzas were worth a bicycle so one mousetrap is worth one bicycle if no bicycles exist in the desert island.

If you assume rational actors who know what goods they were trading, then does the choice theory of value say that a mousetrap is what I would choose to trade for 1 pizza? If I trade mousetrap for pizza then I value the pizza more than the mousetrap, but if I could trade 1 mousetrap or 2, and I trade 1 because the pizza is worth 1 but not 2 mousetraps to me, then the objective value of the pizza is in between 1 and 2 mousetraps: you can only measure value relative to another value. 1 mousetrap traded for 1 pizza by itself merely says I value pizza more than mousetrap, but if I sell 1 mousetrap for $5 in a market then I value $5 more than the mousetrap i.e. it is worth less than $5 and the buyer values it at more than $5. In a widespread marketplace the averaging means that if seller sells Y to buyer for $5, it is worth $5, because seller is willing to sell for $5 or more and buyer is willing to buy for $5 or less, and so Y is worth the amount of other goods/services that $5 will buy elsewhere, Y is worth the average of the value that you can buy for $5 in the market elsewhere.

If you assume profit-maximizing rational actors who know the goods/services they are trading then you can eliminate scenarios of trading a good mousetrap for a bad pizza or buying for more than the lowest price that you were willing to pay. Since you can say that people should be rational and the law of contracts should prevent deception, lies and misrepresentations in trades, you can deduce that if there is a market economy and seller sells a mousetrap to buyer for $5 then under the choice theory of value and the correspondence theory of money the objective relative value of the mousetrap is $5. Y is worth what a person would choose to trade for Y, and the choice theory of value says that value exists only for individual humans, it is relative but objective. Y's value for a person is what that person would choose to trade for Y. If a person would trade B for Y, then Y is worth B. But generally a rational actor will value Y for the pleasure or satisfaction or usefulness that Y will give to him, so the demand will inform and motivate the valuation of Y.

The value of a dollar will always be total value of the economy divided by total number of dollars, and the total value of the economy must be prior to its dollar value, because the economy is the objective physical matter of all goods/services and how much pleasure/satisfaction they can create, the economy is the wealth represented by money. It is impossible to say that one person could choose the entire economy, so it can only be valued by one part relative to its other parts or by its objective attributes of being able to produce satisfaction, pleasure and happiness.

The choice theory of value reflects that only the individual himself/herself can know what he/she would choose in a given situation, and a bureaucrat central planner cannot possibly figure out what each of the millions of individuals in the economy really want. No government official can predict what each consumer and producer and trader would choose if he or she is given the freedom to choose, and no politician can guess what will produce satisfaction or pleasure or happiness for a person better than the person knows for himself/herself. The only way to know what choice a person will make is to give them the freedom to choose and see which choice they make in reality. Therefore, under the choice theory of value, free choices in the marketplace of trades must actually happen in order for us to know what are the prices that the goods and services are objectively worth. The government cannot accurately set prices so the free market is necessary in order for an economy to function because only money prices can use supply and demand to coordinate the production and trading of millions or billions of different people.

CHAPTER TWELVE: REFUTING MARKET FAILURE

A theory exists known as "market corrections of market failures." This theory asserts that the natural, unregulated operation of the free market will inevitably produce "systemic market failures," which are "structural defects" that interfere with the public's ability to make free voluntary informed choices. The market failure theory asserts that it is the government's job to step in and regulate in order to give the people what they would have chosen if they had been able to freely choose. Thus, market failure is a theory which seeks to justify government intervention, but it does so using the language and ideas of free market competition and capitalism, asserting that the government helps and assists the free market, rather than promoting regulation using a framework of socialist/Marxist or liberal theory. The market failure theory has hypnotized many people who believe in free market capitalism, including economists and professors, as well as scholars and lawyers who follow the "Law and Economics" school of thought. I will take this opportunity to offer a principled refutation of market failure theory, in order to strengthen the theoretical defense of capitalism and prevent pro-free market theory from being used to justify the destruction of the free market.

The remainder of this section is broken down by parts. The first part discusses the general principle of market failure and points out the flaws in the principle. Each subsequent part begins by offering a detailed presentation of a market failure that is recognized by economists and then breaks the idea down and refutes it using reasoned analysis. My list of asserted market failures includes antitrust, transaction costs theory, information costs theory, negative externalities and positive externalities, game theory/the collective action problem, and the Hold Up Problem. This list includes all of the most famous asserted market failures.

SUBPART 12-A: THE THEORY OF CORRECTING MARKET FAILURES

This theory asserts that the free market develops structural defects and systemic problems which prevent consumers and traders from making free, voluntary, informed choices. Therefore, in order for the market to produce the benefits of competition and capitalism, government must act to give the people what they would have chosen if they could have made choices.

The problems which are asserted to be "systemic market failures" are not failures in how the free market works. Rather, they are merely facts about the free market that people dislike. They can't be changed without destroying capitalism, and the attempt to use government corrections to correct market failures abandons GOLD and embraces EVIL, even while spouting the language of voluntary informed choices and free market competition. Generally, market failure theory says that the government should give to people what they would have chosen if they could have made choices. The basic flaw in this logic is that the one and only way to know what someone would have chosen if they had been free to choose is to really give them the actual choice and let them choose and then see which choice they made. The market failure, market corrections theory shares the same fundamental problem as liberal/leftist/socialist economics, the belief that the government can assign wealth and manage the economy and give people what they want.

The government cannot succeed at giving to the people what the people really want because the only person who knows what an individual wants is that individual, so the only way to give the person what he/she wants is to let the person choose for himself/herself. The thought that the government can predict and estimate what choices people would have made is a leftist/socialist/liberal assumption, and it is an anti-market premise disguised under a supposedly pro-market justification. A is imposing B onto X because A believes that X would choose B, not Y, if X were "truly free to voluntarily and intelligently choose between Y and B." This is EVIL, the opposite of free market competition GOLD. Also, several details of market failure theory assume that people are idiots too stupid to make the choices which are truly in their best interest. Under GOLD, a person is assumed to be a human being with the right to choose their own right and wrong, and the government's job is not to make that decision for them.

Note that the real purpose of the market failure theory is to target people who believe in free market competition but who feel sympathy for the poor and helpless, and to persuade them that government regulation can be used to "help" the free market instead of "hurting" it. This seduction tempts free market advocates with the poisoned apple of the supposedly good and noble things that government can accomplish if the government seeks to assist the free market. If a person accepts market failure theory, then they have accepted the EVIL premise, even if they don't understand it yet, and EVIL will lead them down a slippery slope so that they will think it okay for more and more regulation to happen, and for less and less unregulated voluntary trading in the marketplace to be allowed, until these people, who once believed in capitalism, end up on the side of the liberal socialist Left, led there by the market failure premise that government control can somehow assist with or be compatible with true market liberty. Only two basic political and economic principles exist. These two alternatives are GOLD or EVIL. If you accept a theory which holds one as its premise, then you will inevitably end up at the logical conclusion of your belief and its principle, and be led to reject the other.

SUBPART 12-B: ANTITRUST

The theory of antitrust asserts that when a monopolist achieves a monopoly, he is no longer restrained in his ability to raise prices by his competitors, so government must break up the monopoly so that the public can make choices among competitors and purchase goods at efficient prices. Also, when two or more businesses make an agreement to collude and not compete against one another, it creates an oligopoly, which must be broken up for the same reason, namely, to give people choices and restore the functionality of competition-based capitalism.

The basic idea of antitrust is that a monopoly or conspiracy not to compete will raise prices and gouge consumers, because it is price competition which generally forces every business to sell goods and services at a competitive, reasonable price. However, the hidden crucial assumption of antitrust is the existence of "barriers to entry." My reply to the threat of a monopoly or conspiracy not to compete is that if a monopoly or oligopoly actually exists or businessmen conspire not to compete and they raise prices to a "monopoly price," then this creates an opportunity for someone else to go into business to compete with them and steal their customers by charging a lower, competitive price. Thus, temporary antitrust violations are feasible, but if antitrust problems arise then the free market will solve the antitrust problems.

The theory of "barriers to entry" posits that a monopolist or oligopoly that corners the market enjoys a "structural, systemic" advantage that prevents other businesses from entering the market to compete with them. Examples are economy of scale, i.e. the advantage from being very big, or owning a large supply of a raw material necessary to make a specific good. My reply is that barriers to entry are imaginary and do not ever really exist. If the price charged is higher than what demand dictates, then a profit opportunity will motivate someone else to enter the market, and someone will find some way or some technology to enable them to compete.

Note that a person does not need to actually enter the market and compete against the monopoly or oligopoly to protect consumers so long as the potential for new entrants exists, because the possibility of new competitors entering the market will make it unprofitable for a monopoly or oligopoly to charge a monopoly price, since doing so would set up the opportunity for someone else to enter the market and steal all their consumers and destroy their business. If no barriers to entry exist, and I argue that they do not, then the long-term prospects of competition, combined with the never-ending possibility of technological development of alternatives and substitutes, renders the fear of antitrust irrational.

It is true that in the late 1800s some trusts existed which posed antitrust problems, such as the oil trust, the steel trust and the railroad trust, among many others. These antitrust problems led to the trust-busting antitrust laws that were passed circa 1900 and which form the core of antitrust law today. But if the free market had been allowed to solve these antitrust violations then new technology, such as biofuel/vegetable oil-based energy (which technology existed in 1900), plastic-based buildings, and cars-based transportation (which developed soon after 1900), would have created alternatives which would have led to competition with the trusts. Absent government force, a monopolist cannot force others not to compete with him in a free market, so it is impossible for a monopolist to suppress competition in profit opportunities.

The general premise of antitrust is the same as the liberal leftist socialist idea behind redistribution of wealth. This premise holds that wealth is stable and permanent and motionless and it just sits there in a bank vault or a factory waiting to be distributed or exploited. In reality, wealth is fluid and active and mobile and it must continuously be created. If a business does not continually fight and compete to retain market share and improve profits then the marketplace will leave it behind and the business will collapse and fade into dust, no matter how big and rich it used to be. AOL (America On-Line) and Bethlehem Steel are two examples of huge corporations which at one time dominated their markets (the former for internet access, the latter for steel) but which later disintegrated into nothingness.

The application of GOLD to antitrust is that the defense of private property, and a person making a decision about how to make use of his/her property and exercising control over his/her property, is inherently nonviolent under NVP. Therefore NVP affirms the absolute right of a person to own his property and to dispose of his property as he chooses, including by charging any price he chooses or choosing not to compete. Yet in practical reality any choice on how to run one's business which disobeys the market, such as choosing not to set a competitive price, will be punished by a devastating loss of sales and customers.

My cynical realist critics may assert that I am being a naïve idealist and that I am blind to how things work in reality. But I am being a realist in this assessment. I do not deny the existence of monopolists in the late 1800s, or the fact that monopolistic price gouging is bad for consumers, or the tendency in human nature for lazy people to want to find a way to succeed without competing. I do not dispute that sometimes antitrust laws have helped solve such problems. Antitrust problems are possible, and in the short term they can cause serious problems, but over the long term the functioning of the free market would correct all antitrust problems without any need for government intervention. It is simply contrary to how the free market works for a business to succeed over the long term by any means other than by giving the people what they want at the price they want to pay for it. If barriers to entry do not exist and technological progress is possible then no monopoly or conspiracy will last for very long.

SUBPART 12-C:
TRANSACTION COSTS

This theory says that for some things, the theory of free market capitalism would posit that every citizen would come together and make an agreement about what to do, but the practical pragmatic costs of a large-scale contractual negotiation are prohibitively expensive, and the costs of making an agreement among millions of people prevents the agreement from happening. Since the people would have made an agreement if they had been able to, the government must step in and create the agreement that the people would have made had they been able to make one. Environmental regulation is often asserted as a good example, e.g. the 300 million American citizens can't all agree on what level of pollution they are willing to put up with to achieve the benefits of technology and industry, so the Environmental Protection Agency must figure this out and give to the public what the people would have chosen if they could have chosen.

Two reasons exist explaining why Transaction Cost theory is flawed. First, if the transaction really is desirable and beneficial then the supposed costs are not so big as to prevent a large group of people from coming together and doing a deal and signing a contract, since the only obstacle is expense, and nobody is holding a gun to people's heads and forcing them not to transact. Second, litigation would solve all of the specific problems asserted by Transaction Cost doctrine. The people should be left free to come together and create a broad social contract or not, without the government forcing a contract onto them under the justification that they would have chosen it if they could have.

At the point at which someone violates someone else's life, liberty or property, let them sue in court and use litigation to protect themselves. For example, instead of a social contract administered by the EPA whereby everyone agrees on the cost-benefit levels for permissible pollution, the GOLD system would instead control pollution by letting any affected person sue a polluter for damages. Any person affected or poisoned by pollution could sue, and would recover damages by persuading a jury by a preponderance of the evidence using scientific data that they were harmed. The science for this proof already exists. And if a large number of people are affected, as often happens with pollution from a major polluter or factory, and as Transaction Cost theory posits, then the size and number of lawsuits would make the environmental litigation cost-effective, and would justify the expense of legal fees for the victims to decide to litigate. Instead of viewing pollution as a problem owned by "society," solved by a social contract under the theory that society can't privately handle a competent transaction, GOLD would view pollution as an individual problem, and empower each individual to decide his or her own cost-benefit level and protect the individual from pollution.

Under a litigation-based system, pollution would be very expensive for polluters, because they would be forced to pay the people injured by their pollution to make those people whole and undo the harm they caused. The litigation system might actually lead to less pollution and a cleaner environment than EPA regulations currently impose. But the system would be based on the defense of individual rights rather than government control, and it would transfer the decision-making power to the people and away from the bureaucrats and politicians and the EPA's elitist "experts."

Such a system could also handle the global warming/climate change problem asserted by liberal scientists and politicians. If the climate change problem is real and is supported by hard science and empirical data, then an individual could sue to recover the damages that he and his heirs and his property will suffer in the future, e.g. by rising oceans destroying beachfront property, upon a showing of proof persuading a judge or a jury. The defendants in the lawsuit would be the polluters whom the evidence showed as being to blame. Thus, if climate change does damage to life, liberty and property, then a lawsuit would solve the problem, but this decision should be made by the people and not by the EPA's anointed experts and bureaucrats. If climate change is a true threat to human survival then the GOLD system would produce litigation costs than would make it profitable for businesses to develop cleaner technology and solve the problem. A private solution to pollution exists, and a government solution is unnecessary.

If a person has the ability to sue to recover upon violent injury to their life, liberty and property, then no need exists for everyone to come together and do a transaction, and the expenses of such a transaction cease to be a valid justification for government regulation. Note, however, that if a group of people wanted to do a large-scale transaction, they could do so, as nobody would be forcing them not to. If they really want to do it, and the benefits were significant, then they will choose to pay the expenses of doing the large-scale deal. The actual legal costs of large-scale contractual negotiations would shrink under GOLD because, as discussed in a later section, the deregulation and de-licensing of lawyers would enable the public to purchase cheap legal services, and also do-it-yourself legal websites already exist, and more are on the way, that can make it cost-effective for large groups of people to enter into agreements without being dissuaded by transactional expenses. Indeed, if a demand existed for a system whereby millions of people could negotiate a large-scale multi-party contract, then some entrepreneur could probably design a website whereby millions of users could sign in to the website and negotiate one massive contract with other people using the internet to coordinate the negotiations. The fact that nobody really tries to do massive social contracts or shows a real interest in wanting to do them proves that the basic premise of Transaction Cost theory is flawed.

SUBPART 12-D: INFORMATION COSTS, A.K.A. INFORMATIONAL ASYMMETRY

This theory asserts that the benefits of free economic choice are lost if the traders cannot make informed choices. Various obstacles prevent people from obtaining the information necessary for their choices to be informed, so government must step in and either give people information or, as more commonly actually happens in policies so justified, the government collects the information and then imposes a choice which is asserted to result from the information. An example is the information costs of knowing that a given restaurant or food supplier sells clean food which is not dirty or contaminated. Because the restaurant or food vendor owns the kitchen or facility which prepares or processes the food, the public is not free to enter the premises and inspect for cleanliness, nor would it be feasible for each individual to do so if the kitchen was open to the public. Therefore, the information costs theory asserts that the government should send in health inspectors to forcibly enter the facilities and inspect the food for quality and cleanliness. Since no person would make an informed decision to eat unclean, dirty food, the government can then shut down food vendors or restaurants which its inspectors deem unsanitary, under the justification of giving to the people what the people would have freely chosen if they could have made informed decisions.

We must respect property rights, and understand the wisdom that under GOLD and free markets, if the consumers have demand for something then profit will motivate the supply to rise to satisfy that demand. Specifically, if government were to get out of the way, Information Cost problems would be solved by consumer-driven voluntary disclosure programs combined with forced information collection as part of the discovery phase of litigation. Government food health inspectors can be replaced by private voluntary inspectors and consumer info groups whose reports and ratings can be accessed via smart phone or mobile device instantly by anyone who wants it. Restaurants that don't let inspectors in won't get customers, if we make the reasonable assumption that people want to eat clean food.

For example, if a restaurant in a GOLD free market economy has led the public to doubt its health and cleanliness, it will lose customers unless it invites in a consumer watchdog group to inspect its kitchens and publish an unbiased report, and the people will have access to all the information which the government could collect, although the decision to eat will be made by each individual and not by the government. And if a person eats at a restaurant and gets sick from food poisoning, this is equivalent to violence done against the person's life, and the person could sue the restaurant and force the restaurant to disclose all information about its kitchen relevant to the lawsuit as part of the "discovery" phase of litigation. Discovery is the phase of litigation which enables each side to coerce the other to disclose all information necessary for the lawsuit to discover the truth and enact justice. Thus, the free market could solve this problem, and lack of information is a shadow, a lie and misunderstanding, designed to serve as a justification for the government taking over an area of private consumer choice, in the area of food and also in the various other areas regulated under this pretext. The general GOLD idea is that the free market will protect consumers from all health and safety dangers.

SUBPART 12-E: NEGATIVE EXTERNALITIES AND POSITIVE EXTERNALITIES

This theory asserts that certain types of behavior do harm to other people while not having any negative consequences or punishments for the person who actually did it and made the choice to do it. The theory says that if an act does harm to third parties, then the government must step in and "internalize the negative externality," meaning that the government should shift that harm from the third parties to the first party who made the choice to do it. The reasons for the policy are both so that a person can make an informed decision about whether the benefits of a choice justify the costs of that choice, and also fairness that a person should not be made to suffer for someone else's choices.

A typical policy is to tax the behavior and then spend the tax revenue on social programs for the behavior's victims. An example would be to tax pollution to fund clean energy research on the theory that pollution kills innocent people with no connection to the polluters, or to tax cigarettes to fund anti-smoking ad campaigns on the theory that secondhand smoke kills innocent people, as well as the argument that smoking cigarettes creates health problems and "society" pays for the healthcare for smokers so society should recover its costs by taxing cigarettes. The reverse of this theory is "positive externalities," the theory that some behaviors have benefits for third parties which do not benefit the person who does the behavior. Theorists assert that it is in "society's" best interest for the government to encourage and fund positive externalities, since the people themselves won't be motivated to do the things that are good for society. One example is education. The proponents of this theory say that a good education for a student is good for society in ways that go beyond the education's selfish benefits to the educated person, so the government should internalize the positive externality by funding public education or giving state-backed educational loans to students.

Regarding negative externalities, we must ask a simple question: is one person's behavior doing violence to another person's life, liberty and property? If the answer is "no" then the government has no right to do anything with respect to the behavior, no matter how "society" feels about it. If the behavior violates individual rights, then the government's proper job is to provide courts for the person who suffers harm to sue the person who harmed him, and to provide police to enforce the court's judgment. The government's appropriate response would not be to regulate the economy. We should let the affected persons litigate negative externalities if they do violence to life, liberty and property, and leave them alone if they do not violate individual rights.

Regarding positive externalities, we should persuade people to voluntarily choose the positive externalities, and not use the government's coercive taxing power to forcibly redistribute property for a supposedly idealistic goal. If an education for a student really has such great benefits for society then someone somewhere will choose to fund it voluntarily. Despite the whining and complaining of the Left, it is a fact that billionaires and millionaires already donate a lot of money to charity, and if education is good for society then people will donate to groups that fund educations for low-income students (leaving aside the fact that if an education benefits a student's future career prospects then for-profit lenders such as banks would make a profit by handing out student loans). The choice of whether the positive externality is good or not should be made by the people, not the government. Similarly, for taxing a negative externality like smoking, if smoking truly is bad then we should persuade people not to do it, and we should not force them to obey us, treating them like a young child or an animal. If cigarettes produce healthcare costs then force each smoker to pay for his own healthcare instead of using social payment to justify government control over people's lives. If secondhand smoke causes illness, and the victim can prove it, then let the victim sue the smoker and recover in court.

SUBPART 12-F: THE COLLECTIVE ACTION PROBLEM AND GAME THEORY, E.G. OBAMACARE

This theory is derived from work done in the academic field called "game theory." Game Theory's paradigmatic thought experiment is the "prisoner's dilemma." Assume that two criminals have been caught by the police and each is being interrogated separately from the other. If both deny wrongdoing then both will go free. If one confesses and turns state's witness and the other denies wrongdoing then the state's witness gets immunity and the liar will go to jail. If both confess then both go to jail. The Game Theory asserts that it is in the best interests of the two criminals to both deny wrongdoing, since both would go free, but their selfish interests will lead each to seek to become state's witness to get immunity, so the selfish interests of people in a condition of freedom will lead them to make choices which are harmful to them, because they choose as individuals and not as a group.

The Game Theory postulate has been modified into the Collective Action Problem, which asserts that the government should impose decisions onto people in cases where, if the people had chosen collectively, they would have made a choice that is good for them, but if they choose individually then they will make choices which are bad for them. The best example, which most people will understand, is insurance. Collective Action proponents say that the best thing is if everyone chooses to buy insurance, because this will result in insurance performing its proper role of shifting risk from the people who have claims to the pool of insured people, and everyone will benefit from lower risk and added safety, as well as affordable premiums. More people buying insurance leads to cheaper premiums because the pool of money to pay claims goes up. But if people choose as individuals, and not as a collective group, then the low-risk people will selfishly choose not to buy insurance, and the pool of insured people will end up containing only high-risk people, who won't have the premium payments for the actuarial risk-spreading to decrease their risk. Thus, in a free market insurance will be expensive, but insurance would be cheaper if everyone was forced to buy insurance.

The government solution asserted by the Collective Action Problem is for the government to force everyone into the pool of insured risks so that risk is spread and decreased, which is what the people would have chosen if the defect in the structure of the market had enabled them to make a wise choice that truly benefits them. The most clever, cunning advocates of this theory say that they are merely giving to each individual what he or she would have freely chosen as an individual in the free market if he/she could have made a choice as part of a collective decision and forced everyone else to share the same choice. The best real-world example is the "individual mandate" in Obamacare, which forces everyone to buy health insurance.

If the desired behavior is good then the solution to the problem is to get everyone to choose it freely, rather than forcing everyone to do it. Each human being is an individual, and a group or "society" is only a group of human beings, so a group is a group of individuals. Only individuals exist, although individuals can be added up to form a number of people in a group. So when the "group" or "society" makes a "collective decision," what this really means is that one group of individuals used the government to forcibly impose their decision onto everyone else within the group, on the pretext that the dissenters did not exist and what really existed was one big blob, "society," which made the decision "as a group."

The specific refutation of Game Theory and the "prisoner's dilemma" is that the solution is not for the group to impose a group-beneficial choice onto each individual, it is for each individual to freely choose the right choice that benefits the group. If the benefits of the supposedly right, good-for-the-group decision are really so great, then each individual can be persuaded to freely choose the right, optimal, efficient choice. Each person has the right to choose for himself, and benefit to the group is not an excuse to violate individual liberty and impose a supposedly better choice onto each person. Let us return to the prisoner's dilemma. If both prisoners choose to deny wrongdoing, then they both go free, but if this really is a good choice then both prisoners will be smart enough to choose it voluntarily. Each prisoner should have the right to freely make his decision for himself, since the choice to confess or deny is ultimately a personal choice for which the prisoner is responsible. Each prisoner's choice belongs to him and not to the other prisoner.

Indeed, the Game Theory and Collective Action Problem ideas are, in reality, merely excuses for one person to force others to do something that the person thinks they should have chosen but which the others would not have otherwise chosen. This is straightforward EVIL, with A forcing X to choose B instead of Y, with the EVIL justification that B is better for X than Y would have been. Game Theory is a pretext for forcing other people to do what the EVIL expert thinks that the group should do. The concept of "collective decisions" is a smokescreen for X to impose Y onto A on the pretext that if X and A were to decide "as a group" then A would choose Y, not B. This is absurd, because X and A are individuals, and X has chosen Y, but A has chosen B, or would choose B, not Y. If Y is so much better than B, let X persuade A to freely choose Y, rather than forcing Y onto A via the government's force.

Regarding Collective Action and health insurance, if everyone buying insurance really is a reduction of risk and is not naked redistribution of wealth from rich to poor, then the low-risk people won't "opt out" and ruin it because they will recognize the benefit to them of the existence of a system for risk reduction which functions effectively. Indeed, I personally believe that health insurance is a good thing for everyone to have, and I think that in a free market the vast majority of people would freely choose to buy health insurance if they understood their risks and the potentially devastating impact of unexpected medical bills, such that no need for government force exists to make health insurance function properly. But if people do not choose to buy health insurance then "society," whatever that is, does not have the right to force a choice onto them. If everyone buying health insurance is such a good, great, brilliant idea, then we should persuade everyone to choose it voluntarily, and if not enough people choose it then it was not so good or wasn't what everyone really wanted.

The implicit, hidden, unstated premise of the advocates of Obamacare, the socialist healthcare law, is that the people are idiotic helpless sheep, and you can't reason with people to make them do the right thing, so you have to force them to do what's good for them but which they are too stupid to understand, e.g. force everyone to buy health insurance so that premiums are cheaper. My reader should understand what I mean when I say that this is EVIL, not GOLD, and the theory offered in support of Obamacare is irrational, illogical nonsense.

SUBPART 12-G: THE HOLD-UP PROBLEM

This asserted market failure is the socialist/leftist argument which "explains" why the free market values the labor of workers at wages which are cheap and below what they are really worth. The Hold-Up Problem has two parts, first, the "threat of death," the asserted market defect that if a poor worker doesn't get hired, or gets fired, then he or she might not have the money to buy food, and might starve to death. This, they assert, forces workers to make choices about employment which are not what they would freely choose if they were free to choose. Second, the "proportions problem," which asserts that the ratio of many poor workers to a few rich businessmen makes it easier for a businessman than a worker to negotiate in labor and wage negotiations, because the equivalent of one businessman's bargaining power is, for example, ten workers combined, and the one businessman has one interest whereas ten workers are ten different people with ten competing interests.

The government correction of the market failure would, first, tax and spend to create a social safety net, taxing the rich so that poor unemployed people are given welfare benefits so that they won't die, which eliminates the threat of death. To the extent that this policy has a theoretical justification, it couches itself in the language of voluntary choice by workers to enable workers to freely choose their jobs, but it also claims that the unregulated, untaxed free market is "live and let die," and for a rich person to not pay taxes to feed a poor person constitutes the rich person "letting the poor person die," which, it claims, is morally equivalent to the rich person murdering the poor person,. Therefore the government has the right to forcibly redistribute the rich person's wealth to the poor person.

Second, the government correction of the market failure would pass laws to help labor unions and force all workers to become union members, so that the workers would negotiate as one body through the mouth of the labor union, which changes the proportion of workers to businessmen. This is called the "Hold-Up Problem" because the theory's advocates believe that when an employer says to the employee "work for me on my terms or I won't hire you," it is the same as "work for me or die," which is like a robber saying "your money or your life."

I am a libertarian, but I am a nice, kind, loving person, and I would not be okay with a political system which does the horrible things that the liberals and socialists say about capitalism. Will freedom "let the poor die"? Is cutting taxes on the rich and ending a poor person's welfare benefits that they live on the practical equivalent of "to the gas chamber, go"? No, it is not, because freedom will unlock the economy's potential for growth and prosperity. For every one welfare benefit that gets eliminated, ten new working class jobs will be created, so nobody will suffer or die in the absence of a social safety net. The working poor will be given opportunity, self-sufficiency and pride, instead of dependence, helplessness and parasitism. In other words, when freedom closes a window it opens a door. GOLD is a policy of "live and let live," not "live and let die."

Five specific GOLD policy platform planks would accomplish this: (1) abolish the minimum wage, (2) abolish occupational licensing, (3) legalize drugs, prostitution and gambling, (4) cut taxes, and (5) deregulate small businesses, especially in their fundraising, e.g. the JOBS Act. If small businesses can raise money then more small businesses will open, and that creates working class jobs. Right now in order to start a new small business an entrepreneur must pay tens of thousands of dollars in legal fees to cope with a vast spider's web of regulations, which stifles small business. If we deregulate then we open the door to thousands of new businesses and jobs across America. Cutting taxes gives the investors more money to invest in small businesses. Legalization would create legitimate legal jobs for drug sellers, sex workers and gambling workers. Ending occupational licensing would eliminate a legal barrier that prevents people from entering into the high-paying occupations, like doctors and lawyers. And abolishing the minimum wage would create jobs that can only exist cost-effectively if the employer pays the employee the price dictated by wage supply and demand.

These five policies would create a tenfold increase in jobs for the working poor, which would replace the poor's need for welfare or a social safety net. As ambitious as this is to say, total GOLD economic policy could create so many working class jobs and produce so much wealth that we would eliminate poverty, and all the poor would rise to the middle class standard of living, and freedom would eventually make everyone rich. When someone gets a job and makes more money, then they have more money to spend, which creates jobs for other people making things for them to buy, which in turn creates more jobs, and so on, such that productivity is an upward spiral. It is possible for libertarian policy to cause enough economic growth to reach escape velocity and to solve the problem of poverty once and for all.

Now let me give a specific answer to the Hold Up Problem. The constraints on human choice from the risk of danger and death caused by a person's economic failure is due to the human condition, the situation of life on Earth, and is not due to the functioning of free market capitalism. See my desert island argument in the "Prostitution and Coercion" section for my analysis of why "work or die" is not coercion and does not impair voluntary choice, even if a poor worker might really die. Poor workers would face the threat of death from economic failure under socialism, the only difference being that if socialism destroys capitalism's efficiency then more poor workers actually will die, because fewer jobs will exist and less wealth will be enjoyed by everyone, poor and rich alike.

Redistribution from rich to poor, or a social safety net, cannot alter these facts: (1) you die if you don't eat food and drink water, (2) you need to produce wealth and trade with others in order to consume wealth, (3) if you have bad luck or do bad work then you might lose your job. These facts come from the human condition, not from capitalism, and the problem of poverty would continue to exist under socialism. If we sacrifice GOLD freedom for EVIL's so-called "safety" of a social safety net, then we get neither freedom nor safety, because the principle of a tax and spend welfare state social safety net is socialism, which destroys wealth while eliminating economic freedom. A government intrusion to protect employees from employers, even if justified under the pretext of protecting the workers' freedom and voluntary choice from "work or die" coercion, accepts the principle that the free market doesn't work and government control is necessary. This principle is EVIL. This can only end in Marxist socialist dictatorship as the logical end result of government interfering with the market to protect the poor from the rich. The politicians do well under Marxism, but the poor do not. The failed experiment of Stalin's Communist Russia was ample empirical proof of this.

Regarding labor unions exploiting government force to coerce workers into becoming union members to counteract the proportions problem, GOLD would permit voluntary labor unions, and GOLD upholds the right of the workers to strike, and rejects the employers using government or violence to break strikes and force workers to work. Every person should be free to decide their own behavior so long as they do so non-violently. This is basic NVP, and a worker strike is simply a non-violent refusal to work, and joining a labor union to organize can also be done non-violently. However, labor unions under GOLD must be completely voluntary, and government may not help the unions or force workers to unionize, because this is an EVIL violent force coercing workers into doing something they did not freely choose to do, namely joining the union. In practice, the labor union bosses force their decision onto workers who would voluntarily make a different decision when they use labor laws to force involuntary labor organization. If a labor union actually benefits the workers and assists in their contract negotiations, rather than being merely a ploy for union bosses and Democratic politicians to seize power and organize votes, then enough workers will freely choose to unionize so that no need will exist for the unions to use force to get members. And if not, then violent coercion of union membership is EVIL.

CHAPTER THIRTEEN: UTILITARIANISM IN ECONOMICS: REJECTING THE "LAW AND ECONOMICS" SCHOOL OF THOUGHT

In legal scholarship, a school of thought exists called "Law and Economics." This theory, which is partially a legal theory and partially a theory of economics, is known for several ideas, including the theory of Transaction Costs and Information Costs as market failures. Law and Economics seeks to apply economic principles to questions regarding the proper role of government. It is known as a generally pro-free market theory. The Law and Economics school has many followers who are thought of as libertarians, such as law professor Richard Epstein and Judge Richard Posner. However, the Law and Economics movement, as a whole, must be rejected by GOLD libertarianism, for the following reason.

The stated goal of the law according to Law and Economics is "efficiency." Efficiency, as the Law and Economics school envisions it, means that you should make the choice with the most benefits and the fewest costs, no matter how evil and unethical that choice might be. Their doctrine of "efficient breach," which says that businessmen should intentionally choose not to perform their contractual obligations to others when the benefits of doing so outweigh the costs, is one good example. This view naturally leads towards Marxism or socialism, because it is a fundamentally Utilitarian belief. To answer the question "Whose costs? Whose benefits?" when undertaking a cost-benefit analysis forces the Law and Economics adherents to try to standardize every individual's desires into a mass calculation of equalization. The comparison of one individual's costs and benefits to the costs and benefits of other people inevitably leads to measuring costs and benefits in terms of society, not individuals.

Individuals are unique, and only a person can know that person's own desires. For example, in order to get a woman a dress that she wants, she must go to the clothing store and try on dresses and choose it for herself. No person other than that woman herself can possibly know which dress at which price fits her precise profile of cost-benefit analysis for paying money to get a dress. The woman has direct access to her thoughts, feelings, and desires regarding clothes, and the government lacks the same sort of access to the woman's mind. The only way to know the efficient dress for the woman is to let her shop and look at the price tags and make her own decision.

Since each individual's desires are unique, one person's cost-benefit analysis cannot be merged with or measured against another's. The free market is necessary because it lets each individual make his own cost-benefit analysis, by letting each person make his own individual buying and selling decisions. It is the system of money prices that coordinates one person's economic decisions with the decisions of all other people by means of the impact of supply and demand upon price. But the mechanism which does this coordination consists of each individual's choices acting upon prices. The money system cannot be replaced by the government or economists performing a cost-benefit analysis for society as a whole. The only way to know what someone would have chosen is to give them the options and let them choose. A person's choice preferences can only be learned after the fact empirically from seeing what they actually chose when they were given the choice. Their cost-benefit profile cannot be predicted before the fact analytically in order for an economic planner to make decisions for us which accurately predict our desires. Social cost-benefit analysis contradicts the premise of capitalism and can end only in socialism and Marxism.

Utilitarianism is an inherently socialist/Marxist doctrine, dating back to its chief founder John Stuart Mill, for one simple reason. Utilitarian economists seek "the greatest good for the greatest number," and prefer political policies which achieve the maximum amount of happiness using the "hedonic calculus." The vast majority of people in America, and around the world, are poor, and they are certainly not rich. Giving $1 to a poor person who thinks of $100 as a lot of money does far more good for that poor person than giving $1 to a rich person who thinks of $100,000 as a small sum of money. Therefore the theory of Utilitarianism can only end in the redistribution of wealth, specifically a progressive income tax which will take $1 as taxes away from the rich people and give that marginal $1 to the poor people. Utilitarianism, taken to its logical conclusion, must take $1 away from each rich person, and keep taking $1 over and over again until he or she is taxed into poverty and everyone is equally poor.

More generally, let me state that economics as a discipline can study economies and measure the efficiency of resource allocations on supply and demand curves, but economics as a set of ideas is not deep enough to explain all human behavior, nor can it explain every law and legal doctrine. That, however, is what the Law and Economics school's leading scholars claim. The alternative to economic efficiency as the goal of law is the protection of individual rights as the law's ultimate goal. Through the free market's "invisible hand," the protection of individual rights and freedoms lets each individual make his/her own choices. But this economic individualist freedom achieves economic efficiency better than would be possible if the government were to think up a plan for efficient resource allocation and impose the plan upon the people. This is Adam Smith's invisible hand applied to the law: the law will achieve maximal economic efficiency when the law ceases to concern itself with efficiency and social cost-benefit analysis, and instead focuses on the defense of each individual's rights and life, liberty and property against violent aggression.

Whenever someone tells you "economics says this," reply: "Whose economics? Which economic theory?" Economics is a field with various competing theories, and each of them sharply disagrees with the others. Theories include the Keynesian, the Marxist, the Austrian, the Chicagoan, the Neo-Classical standard, and the Neo-Classical GOLD. If economists do not themselves have a settled, established idea of how the world works then we must wonder whether they can help the rest of us understand the world.

CHAPTER FOURTEEN: NATURAL RIGHTS VS. UTILITARIANISM

The battle between libertarians who believe in natural rights and philosophical idealism on the one hand, with those who believe in pragmatism and practicality on the other hand, the conflict between those who believe that capitalism is virtuous vs. those who believe that capitalism works, is legendary within the libertarian movement. For decades the followers of Ayn Rand and Murray Rothbard, the natural rights idealists, have dueled with the followers of Milton Friedman and F.A. Hayek, the Utilitarian pragmatists. R.W. Bradford's famous essay "The Two Libertarianisms" (Liberty Magazine, reprinted March 2008) captured the gist of this war.

I have one thought which sums up my feelings regarding this matter. Isn't capitalism ethical and noble for precisely the same reason that it is functional and practical? Capitalism gives financial rewards to people who work hard and make good choices. That makes capitalism the most efficient way to motivate people to work hard. Profit is the most effective incentive for productivity, so capitalism maximizes the creation of wealth. Thus we have the pragmatic side.

But this very same act of rewarding productivity also gives rewards to the people who work hard, which gives to a person the wealth that the person has earned, and puts the results of good choices in the hands of the person who made the good choices. Getting what you deserve is the very essence of justice and fairness. Capitalism is ethical because it creates the freedom within which people who make virtuous choices can get what they deserve. From this we reach the ethical side.

Pragmatism and idealism are not in conflict, and capitalism is necessarily both ethical and practical. Freedom is both ethical and practical because it rewards people for doing good work. Therefore the libertarian Utilitarian vs. natural rights war makes no sense.

CHAPTER FIFTEEN: ABOLISH OCCUPATIONAL LICENSING

Generally, occupational licenses should not be used to restrict the supply of labor in the supply-demand curve in order to artificially raise wage levels and gouge consumers, which is all that professional licensing regimes actually accomplish. Licensing system propaganda focuses on professions where the professional requires technical expertise which can only be properly evaluated by other experts who also hold this expertise, and the expertise is necessary to do the job correctly. The best examples are doctors and lawyers. GOLD holds that no licenses should exist in areas where consumers are competent to make informed decisions about the qualifications of service providers, e.g. hairdressers/barbers or food truck vendors.

Lawyers should also be deregulated, and the requirement of a license to practice law abolished. As a licensed lawyer and law school graduate, I can tell you that law school is a great experience which teaches valuable knowledge, and the bar exam weeds out the less talented lawyers, but legal reasoning is a skill that any intelligent literate person can do. In a republican democracy governed by the rule of law, it should be clear that every citizen has the right to know what the law is and to participate in the legal life of the community. The people should be free to choose whom they hire, and should be free to pay less and hire a cheaper legal service of lower quality. The government should not boss people around and say that you can't hire someone who hasn't spent the $100,000 in tuition to obtain a law degree and the $3000 for a bar review study class to pass a bar exam. The real beneficiaries of law licenses are the lawyers. The real losers are the many poor people who need legal help but cannot afford to pay the legal fees of a highly qualified lawyer.

The law license is a classic example of licensing used to restrict a supply of labor in order to artificially raise wage levels and protect a class of workers (educated lawyers who passed the bar exam) from wage rate competition from hungry rivals (smart but ordinary people who could read and interpret laws and make legal arguments). It goes to the basics of supply and demand that when demand remains constant and supply goes down (from the people who do not have a law license being removed from the supply of lawyers) then price goes up. With the example of the law, we can also see how the poor, who can't afford to hire expensive licensed lawyers and aren't allowed to higher cheaper unlicensed ones, are the true victims, forced to rely on "pro bono" legal services charity to meet their legal needs, when deregulation would give them the power to pay for themselves by lowering the overall price when supply increases.

Although medicine is a technical scientific body of knowledge, it would also be possible for the reliability and qualifications of doctors to be vetted privately by consumer watchdog groups and websites, and the government's medical license boards are not necessary. For doctors and lawyers, and any "learned profession" where the profession requires legitimate technical expertise (e.g. architects, engineers, dentists), the license should be made purely informational and voluntary, such that you can still get a license which demonstrates expertise, but the licenses will be granted by private consumer advocacy organizations, not by the state.

Consumers should be allowed to choose to hire whomever they want, licensed or not, with the license as merely an informational factor in each individual's purchasing decision. Because a real need exists to know who are the service providers with adequate expertise, the free market will do the same function that the state license had performed, but in a manner consistent with freedom and economics. This GOLD policy will benefit the poor in two ways. First, by lowering the cost of professional services due to an increase in supply. Second, by lowering the costs of entering the learned professions, which will give poor ambitious intelligent workers easier access to higher-paying jobs.

CHAPTER SIXTEEN: WE MUST PRIVATIZE

The libertarian position is always looking to enhance competition as a means of driving efficiency. One of the great sins of government is that it is a monopoly, so there is no competition in areas where government provides services. Absent competition and the profit motive, there is no psychological mechanism to cause innovation and progress or to achieve accountability and personal responsibility. A libertarian policy is privatization to the maximum extent possible, so that the delivery of government services is transitioned to a competition-based scheme in which people are allowed to choose among competing service providers. Two examples of the need for privatization follow.

SUBPART 16-A: PRIVATIZING EDUCATION

The k-12 public education system in America is a mess. American children routinely score badly relative to foreign children, especially in math and science. A lot of "failing schools" exist, especially serving ethnic minority communities in urban areas. The source of the problem is the fact that teachers in public schools are not accountable to parents. Schools do not compete for students, so parents lack the power to choose their child's school from among competing alternatives. The teacher's unions hate merit-based pay schemes and insist upon a seniority-based pay system which runs completely contrary to the wisdom of personal responsibility, which knows that rewarding success and punishing failure is the best method for encouraging good results. Children who are too poor to afford private schools usually have no choice about where to attend school. Schools are generally funded by property taxes, so children who live in poor areas go to poor schools with bad quality, and then grow up to become adults without a good education or job skills. Uneducated children become low wage-earning adults, so a badly-performing public school can become a long-term black hole that swallows an entire neighborhood into poverty.

The rich can afford private schools, so public schools hurt only the poor and middle class. Education is opportunity, so the failure of the public school system traps the poor in a void where they are doomed to poverty. Indeed, for all that liberals complain obsessively about the supposed oppressive class system in America, the public education system, championed by those same liberals, is a chief culprit for the solidification of upper and lower classes into a caste system. The poor caste goes to public school and the rich caste goes to private school.

The solution to the public school disaster is obvious. Abolish the property tax-based system of publicly funding schools, privatize primary education, and eliminate mandatory schooling. Then parents will have the freedom to choose where to send their children to school. If the parents pay the school fees then they will have the power to hold schools accountable and to control what the schools are doing to their children. Otherwise, under the nationalized public school system, parents are powerless, and the system encourages irresponsibility and failure. When parents choose where to send their child, badly performing schools will improve or else go out of business, and the good schools will make money and grow. Control of primary education will be taken away from the bureaucrats and given back to the people.

The great argument against privatizing schools is that it will hurt the poor because the poor won't be able to afford school and it will increase the privilege of the rich. This is faulty logic, for several reasons. If the education of children is profitable, then the free market and the profit motive will pay for it. To the extent that the education readies children for the workforce and makes them better, higher skilled employees as adults, and to the extent that an education makes a student into a better person with socially desirable qualities, businesses and private charity will give loans or scholarships, and schools will create endowments. The college system is partially private, and many college students pay their educations with student loans that eventually get paid back when the college education enables the borrower to get a better job. The university system works far better than the public school system, so the criticism is wrong. The argument against privatization ignores the basic principle of economics that if the education will actually benefit the child, then it will be profitable, and if it is profitable then it will be paid for.

When the government gives the people something that the free market would not have paid for, it gives the people something that the people themselves would not have voluntarily chosen to buy or pay for via free economic consumer choices, so people are given something that they don't want. That is inefficiency at its worst. Only the useless, ineffective public school educations will be eliminated, while the good educations which improve productivity will pay for themselves. Since the public schools are paid by property taxes, which are usually assessed locally, the poor are still ultimately paying for their children's schooling, only with the added heavy burden of government bureaucracy and inefficiency instead of free market competitive effectiveness. Paying for school with taxes tricks the poor parents into thinking that the schooling is free. In fact, the families in the taxpaying school districts are the ones who must pay the school's bills, but the taxpayers get none of the benefits of control and accountability that would come from directly controlling the flow of payments. This is why the liberal solution to failing public schools, namely raising taxes and increasing spending, will never solve the underlying problem at the root of why the public education system is broken. Competition is efficient, in education as well as in every other area.

The state-owned, state-controlled, mandatory public schools are a system of indoctrination and propaganda, while also teaching legitimate subjects like English, history, math and science at the same time. Indeed, in the early 1900s, the advocates of the nationalization of education argued explicitly that control of the ideology presented to young impressionable children's minds for political purposes was a benefit of their proposed system, and the government officials who nationalized primary education agreed. The teacher's unions' arguments for public education are largely a sham. Break up the public schools and we will set the minds of children free from partisan political motivations in terms of what they are taught.

Also, competition leads to experimentation and innovation, because each school is free to try different things, instead of every school answering to the state and federal standards. If a child excels at a certain subject, he or she will be free to enroll at a school to learn it, and if one school would be best for a child then a parent will be free to choose it, instead of relying on the magnet public school system which gives freedom to the lucky few children while leaving the majority of children trapped in the ordinary failing school systems.

In reply to the argument that poor children will be encouraged by their parents to take jobs instead of going to school, if the schooling has all the great benefits which the advocates of education say then the educators will persuade the parents to choose to send their kids to school. If the parents feel differently then they deserve the freedom to make their own choices, which is the GOLD Principle in action. Note that the legal principles of GOLD would emancipate a child who has reached the level of maturity such that he or she is able to knowingly make informed decisions and understand personal responsibility and the consequences of his/her actions such that he or she may legally be held accountable for his/her decisions. Thus the decision of whether the student wants to go to school would eventually be made by the student himself/herself, at around the legal age of adulthood, which would probably be 16 or 17 years old. The student could choose school for himself/herself in time for any teen who wants an education to make up for lost time and obtain one.

The benefits of privatization are extremely obvious, and the only reason for the educational establishment to oppose the market-based system is a hatred of merit-based competition, and partisan loyalty to the political influence of the teacher's unions. The teacher's unions have amply demonstrated that they care more about achieving job security for teachers than about educating the students.

SUBPART 16-B: PRIVATIZING INFRASTRUCTURE, RETIREMENT, AND BANKING

Privatization accomplishes the benefits of free market competition and could be easily applied to many other areas. For one example, management of the roads, and other public transit like buses and trains, could be privatized. Privatization would motivate success and create accountability through the profit motive and competition among competing alternatives, and it could be done without any risk that private owners will abuse their power by excluding members of the public from obtaining vitally necessary services. Drivers who must use a road in order to reach their home or place of business could be given a right not to be prevented from using a necessary road, by a modification of a legal doctrine which already exists, called the law of easements. The roads might be privately owned, or they could be publicly owned and leased to private management firms, to make sure that the people have continued access, or else roads could be sold with sales contract terms that would place policy-based limits upon the private owners' ability to exclude drivers from use of the roads.

Another example is garbage collection, or water and sewage services. If one water system exists then the administrator can sit back and relax, whereas if two water services compete for customers then each service must be constantly inventing new ways to attract and retain buyers, such as by making water cheaper or else by making the water cleaner and healthier by innovation in water treatment plants or sewer lines.

One pro-government argument for public ownership of, for example, roads, power lines, subways, sewer lines, and television licenses, is that for these things only one or a small number of avenues of delivering services to consumers exists, which makes them a "natural monopoly." Because they will naturally be the monopoly of whichever business owns them, it is appropriate for the government to regulate them, so that a private monopolist does not improperly gain power over the public. I discuss antitrust elsewhere, but let me say here, to refute the natural monopoly theory, that technology will always find alternative delivery methods to enable competition, so government control is never truly justified. For example, cable TV replaced broadcast television, breaking up the limited number of TV stations on bandwidth frequencies (and ending the justification for the existence of the Federal Communications Commission, whose job was to regulate the bandwidth natural monopoly).

If the roads were deregulated and privatized, and the Environmental Protection Agency also cut back on regulations to mandate and standardize transportation emissions, then technology combined with the profit motive and free market competition would give us "flying cars" or some sort of air-based individual transportation in a matter of decades, and the natural monopoly problem for transit would be solved. This will always happen in a situation of natural monopoly, because the profit motive will motivate scientists to develop technology to get a piece of the action in that marketplace. If this seems like science fiction, let me remind you that cars, and televisions, and electricity seemed like science fiction to every human being alive from the origin of the human species until the rise of electric-based technology, e.g. everyone during the Middle Ages and the Roman Empire, which was a lot of people. Freedom, free market capitalism, and the profit motive inspire technology and scientific innovation, whereas government control and orthodoxy stifle and suppress progress. That explains why Nineteenth and Early Twentieth Century America, and Renaissance Europe, the two eras of relatively well-developed reason and freedom, were the main engines of recent growth in the human species' standard of living.

The total privatization of healthcare and health insurance would eliminate the bureaucratic inefficiencies of Obamacare, Medicare and Medicaid. The privatization of retirement would produce payroll tax cuts enabling people to buy private retirement investments to replace Social Security. Social Security should be replaced with a private retirement investment system, whereby a worker is given a tax cut in the amount of the payroll tax which currently funds Social Security, which he/she can then use to can buy an investment in any public company stock, annuity, bond, or investment of his/ her choice, on the private Wall Street market. The worker can decide what he or she needs for retirement, and buy an investment which will guarantee that amount at the desired retirement age.

The basic idea behind the origin of Social Security was that the government would help the working class invest for retirement, but Social Security evolved into a Ponzi scheme. The government pays current Social Security benefits out of current taxes and not out of the proceeds from investing prior years' Social Security payments. In fact, the government does not ever actually invest Social Security payments, it instead spends them during the year in which they were received. For the elderly working class to retire on their savings and investments, saving and investment has to actually take place, so that some money is saved or created by investment to pay for the retirement benefits. Investment functions by the investor giving money to the recipient, who then uses the money to do something which creates a profit, and the recipient then gives some money back out of the profits to the investor to compensate him for the investment of capital. Similarly, the concept of saving money is that you give money to someone, and they save it for a period of time and then give it back to you.

Conservatives and libertarians seem to understand this, whereas liberals have blinded themselves to how the economics of retirement works.

The privatization of Social Security and its replacement with a private retirement system would have double political benefits from a leftist point of view, by achieving long-term viability for the retirement prospects of the American elderly, and also by shifting equity ownership of American business away from the Wall Street rich and to the Main Street working class as the owners of their invested stock shares. It is already the case that most Wall Street investment is ultimately owned by the 99%, not by the 1%, by means of the ownership of stock by mutual funds and pensions which invest for the benefit of the working class. The liberals are the fiercest critics of "privatizing" Social Security, but they are obviously only concerned with increasing the state's political power, because increasing the working class investment stake in the public companies would actually give more economic power to the people than does Social Security. In reality Social Security merely increases the tax burden on workers due to the payroll tax, and uses the Social Security payroll tax to fund government spending without any direct benefit to taxpayers or seniors.

I advocate that the mechanics of Social Security privatization be structured so that a worker gets a tax cut equal to the amount which right now is taxed as payroll taxes that go to the government to fund Social Security, so that, as a matter of logic and mathematics, the working class will not possibly experience any net loss of money due to privatization. The money would go directly from employer to worker to retirement investment, and we could remove government from the picture, instead of money going from employer to government, with government then giving money to the retiring worker years later. Since the Social Security system is broken and it will go bankrupt in the future (2050 is a safe estimate, if not a few decades earlier or later), privatization is the one hope for our generation and our children's generation to have a sane, rational option to retire.

Privatization would have an added benefit: it will take issues which public services have inappropriately converted into political issues, and convert them back to private issues. For example, the problem of schoolyard bullying, although it is a true menace to our children, is something that each school should find a way to solve, with teachers helping bullied children and punishing bullies, and it should not be a matter of getting laws passed and public political outrage to make politicians "do something." Similarly, the fact that traffic fines are criminal makes no sense, because minor traffic violations are not an evil or moral wrong, and the common sense understanding of a crime is that it is a wrong which society seeks to punish or prevent. The privatization of transportation would properly make traffic violations a private civil matter between the driver and the business entity which owns, maintains or manages the roads.

I will conclude by arguing for the privatization of banking and the end of the Federal Reserve, the central bank which sets the interest rate and controls the money supply. Let free market supply and demand and the price system set the interest rates, instead of a government bureaucrat Fed Chairman. The privatization of banking would cause the economy to experience vastly increased efficiency in loans and borrowing and lending, for the reasons stated in the discussion of the principles of supply and demand in Neo-Classical economics. The premise which justifies the Fed, which is that it must control inflation as a tool to strike the correct balance between inflation and employment in order to fight unemployment without severe inflationary recessions, is based on faulty, flawed, disproved Keynesian economics. The Keynesian worldview has no place in our modern, rational economic world.

Regarding money, the privatization of money would mean that each bank (or business, or person) would be allowed to print its own money, and economic forces of supply and demand would set the money supply, although I expect that currencies would tend to be tied to the banks that issued them, to encourage traders to use and accept the credit. Thus, ironically, GOLD does not equate to a uniform gold standard-based American currency, because every bank will have the freedom to choose to issue gold-backed currency, currency backed by other hard assets, or paper money backed by promises to pay in the future, depending on what each bank's consumers want and choose. Banks will tend to choose to back their currency with gold or assets to foster trust, but this would not be legally mandated.

If a danger exists that the failure of a few big banks will trigger a run on the banks and could cause economic disaster, then the understanding of this threat will motivate banks to voluntarily form and pay into an insurance pool against a run on the banks and an economic crisis, such as is currently done by the FDIC. Because most people in banking and finance are very knowledgeable about economics, they will generally understand the dangers which the economy faces, and will act to avoid those dangers out of economic self-interest. If the free market makes a big mistake then the economy will suffer or unravel, but that is also true if the Federal Reserve makes a big mistake. The only difference between private mistakes and government mistakes is that the free market gives thousands of people the ability to reason and think and act and solve problems, while the Fed gives one person, the Fed Chairman, who is one faulty, fallible, lone human being, the ability to single-handedly crush the American economy by making a big mistake. The Fed Chairman, and the Fed's Board which assists the Chairman, can easily make mistakes because they do not receive accurate price signals about where the market forces of supply and demand want the interest rate to be set, because they set the interest rate by command instead of letting the market set the interest rate.

Under GOLD, X, not A, is the person who gets to make the decisions that control X. GOLD is a decision theory which states that we should let X decide for X and let A decide for A, and not let A violently impose his decision onto X. If A is the Fed Chairman and X is you or me, then the consequences of freedom vs. control are obvious. The government's experts, such as the economists of the Federal Reserve, are fallible, flawed, oftentimes foolish humans, just like the rest of us. They do not possess any special powers or access to knowledge that the public lacks. So it makes sense to let each individual choose for himself/herself, and not let the government's experts violently impose their plan of what they think is best for us onto everyone. This is true of letting each banker decide where to set the interest rates for loans he gives out, and generally for every economic decision that can be made by each individual.

CHAPTER SEVENTEEN: THE ECONOMICS OF IMMIGRATION

Immigration is an economic question, not a social question, because the right at issue is not ownership of the body, as in social libertarianism, it is ownership of tangible personal property (jobs and land), as in economic libertarianism. Also, the immigration policy debate is being driven by an economic concern, the impact of immigrants upon supply and demand for blue collar jobs held by American workers, e.g. "they'll steal our jobs!"

The libertarian immigration policy is open immigration. To state the argument as simply as possible, illegal immigration is a victimless crime. Immigration is peaceful and nonviolent. Immigrants come to America in peace, seeking jobs and freedom in the land of opportunity. Therefore NVP and GOLD sees no justification for using force to ban or regulate immigration. Let everyone who wants enter the USA and be given a free and easy path to citizenship, and give citizenship and amnesty to all illegal immigrants in the USA who are willing to take an oath to defend the U.S. Constitution.

Immigration has been compared to the front door of a house, in that it maintains order and safety in the entry and exit of persons. The difference is that you own your house, but the federal government does not own the USA. Therefore you may exclude or invite whom you want, but the government does not possess a similar authority to dictate to American landowners whether to allow immigrants onto their privately owned land. According to GOLD the government has the right to guard the border, but only against invading foreign armies, not against non-violent foreign immigrants seeking jobs in the USA. The crucial distinction for the NVP (Non-Violence Principle) analysis is that foreign armies are violent but immigrants do no violence to the life, liberty and property of others. Because under NVP the government may only use violence to defend the people's life, liberty and property, the government lacks the moral right to use force to regulate immigration or any other non-violent behavior.

Opposition to immigration is rooted in two factors. The first factor is racism designed to maintain the white European-descended majority in America and to protect American white culture from the influence of cultural and ethnic diversity. The concept of racism is not limited to whites hating blacks. I think that racism is the correct term for white hatred of Hispanics, for English hatred of the Irish and Italians, and generally for any ethnic group's animosity towards another ethnic group. I will not bother to explain here why racism is evil. Assuming that the evil of racism is obvious to the reader, we can see that open immigration is ethical to the extent that it opposes a policy founded on racism.

Some libertarians have made the argument that immigration should be restricted because, for example, immigrants from Mexico will be criminals, immigrants from Muslim countries will be terrorists, immigrants from South America will be liberal Democrats and be anti-libertarian and change American culture, etc. Although I know that many intelligent libertarians are sincere in their belief that closed immigration is consistent with freedom, I see these arguments at rooted in the racist idea that we must protect white American culture from foreign colored cultures. It is a racist argument that if some members of a race have a problem then all members of the race share that problem, which stems from the racist premise that problems are caused by DNA and not by the choices made by individuals. Just because some Mexicans are criminals does not mean that all, or most, Mexicans are criminals. The fact that some Muslims are terrorists does not mean that all Muslims are terrorists. I explain this later in this book in the section on racial minorities.

The danger of immigrant criminals is real, but the police and the legal system are adequate to defend us. If immigrants come to America and commit crimes then we have every right to jail or deport them, but if they come in peace and live here in peace then they have done no violence to us and it would be wrong of us to use force against them. It is true that many foreigners are Marxists, but so are many native-born Americans. It poses a danger to intellectual freedom for the government to favor or disfavor people based on cultural trends in people's ideas. The history of America shows that a culture of freedom can evolve out of a melting pot of foreign cultures. Note that every native-born American is the descendent of immigrants, because only the Native Americans were here prior to the immigration of the colonial Americans from Europe, and even the Native Americans are believed to have come to America from eastern Asia in prehistoric ancient times.

The second factor fueling the opponents of immigration is the fear that immigrants will "steal" American jobs. American citizenship is being transformed into a de facto national license to work and hold a job. This is a license which is being given to white American citizens but is denied to poor immigrant Hispanics and Asians and other foreigners. We must oppose closed immigration because it is a racist policy, but a free market libertarian must also oppose it because the policy of protecting lower class white Americans from wage competition from poor immigrants who want to work those jobs at a lower salary is an obvious violation of the free market idea that supply and demand in the labor market must be allowed to set the level of wages in an efficient economy.

The idea that immigrants will steal American jobs is simply not true, because increased economic efficiency is a net job creator, not a job eliminator. Let us assume that an American named Mr. A works as an orange picker at an orange grove in Florida. A Mexican Mr. M is willing to do American Mr. A's job for $2 an hour, when A was doing it for $9/hour. Let us also assume that M is given citizenship, and A is fired and M gets A's job. What A doesn't see, but rational economists do see, is that M should do the job for $2/hour, because M and M's fellow Mexicans working as orange pickers results in more oranges being picked, since the orange grove can hire four orange pickers instead of one with the same $9, because each picker gets $2/hour instead of $9/hour. More picked oranges, specifically four times more oranges, creates a new job as an orange delivery truck driver to deliver the fourfold increased amount of oranges, and this truck driver job pays $12/hour, and A will get the truck driver job.

And if M eventually gets the job as truck driver by working for a cheaper wage than A, then the increased delivery of oranges will create a job as an assistant accountant and bookkeeper at the orange corporate office, with this job paying $15/hour, and A would get this job before M does. If we assume that A is a high school graduate and M is illiterate, then A letting M "steal" his job will create a new job where A will make more money than A did before. Open immigration will achieve efficiencies and create added wealth which will open up new job opportunities, such as a different job requiring more advanced job skills where Americans will make more money because of the immigrant labor force. Libertarian economics has been called the art of seeing economic relationships and policy consequences which are difficult to see and not obvious, but the GOLD argument against "foreigners steal jobs" is actually very simple and easy to follow.

One can make a coherent argument that giving amnesty to illegal immigrants is unfair to all the immigrants who came to the USA legally, and it rewards people for breaking the laws governing immigration. The counter to this argument is simply that two wrongs don't make a right. The first wrong was forcing prior generations of immigrants to obey immigration law. The second wrong is forcing the present generation of immigrants to navigate immigration law. We don't need to worry about punishing immigrants for breaking immigration laws that were stupid or crazy to begin with.

A similar anti-immigration argument warns that if open immigration is allowed then the United States will be flooded with poor immigrants who will strain the welfare system and place an added heavy burden on taxpayers. This might be true, but two wrongs don't make a right. One wrong is taxing the productive to help the lazy, while another wrong is forcibly restricting immigration. The solution to the welfare danger from open immigration is to eliminate the welfare state. Maintaining closed immigration is not necessary to solve the welfare problem.

The motive of most illegal immigrants is coming to the land of opportunity and creating a better life for themselves and their children. Their motive is not crime and wanting to break the law. America is a place of peace and prosperity, and most Americans are so sheltered that we do not understand the dismal hopeless horror of the poverty in many foreign countries, which immigrants are fully justified in seeking to escape. While it is generally a good thing to obey the law and a bad thing to break the law, the policy of preserving the sanctity of legal immigration is far outweighed by the irrationality and injustice of using the government's violence to outlaw a nonviolent behavior. Because immigration is nonviolent, NVP and GOLD can find no justification for criminalizing illegal immigration.

CHAPTER EIGHTEEN: DEREGULATION AS A PRECONDITION OF CONTINUED TECHNOLOGICAL PROGRESS

In the early 20th Century, some 70 or 80 years ago, people believed that in "the future" we would have flying cars, a cure for all diseases, and other technological marvels like robot butlers and maids. So why don't we? Not surprisingly, the libertarian answer to this question is: government regulation.

Regulation kills innovation because the businesses must invest so much in regulatory compliance for what they already have that they can't afford to innovate and then spend the money which would be required for the newly developed innovation to comply with all the regulations. Regulatory compliance in today's world costs millions of dollars. This is why the carmakers don't try to create flying cars, because of EPA car emissions regulations, which currently fills thousands of pages with hundreds of detailed laws and mandates. Can you imagine what a regulatory nightmare it would be for a car manufacturer to invent a flying car and then try to clear the EPA's emissions review, to say nothing of the liability nightmare of tort lawsuits they could face for any minor defect, or the host of other safety regulations from myriad other bureaucratic regulatory agencies who could put an end to the flying car design if they feel it is unsafe? No carmaker will spend a billion dollars to design a flying car that really could work, only to have regulators kill it off in the name of safety and then take a total loss on their research and development investment.

The same thing is true of innovative new medications, perhaps even more so. The Food and Drug Administration (FDA) requires a complicated multi-stage clinical trial to prove both safety and effectiveness before any new medicine can be put on the market. The clinical trial required by the FDA is both time consuming and extremely expensive. This makes regulatory approval of new drugs so expensive that the drug makers can only afford medical research for drugs which are certain to clear the clinical trials and be big sellers so that they can be sure to recover their high up front cost of regulatory compliance. They don't find it economical to experiment freely with possible new medicines such as might lead to a cure for the common cold. A cure for the common cold might sell well, but a bold new idea might fail the clinical trials, and the culture of free experimentation in medical research has been gutted by the fact that significant sums of money can only be invested in research that is sure to clear the FDA's clinical trial requirements. If a devastating sickness exists but it only afflicts three hundred people then the amount of profit could never justify drug makers assigning their research scientists to find a cure because of the expense of FDA regulatory compliance, so the FDA's mandate of safety actually condemns those three hundred people to death.

The FDA will force the drug makers to take a total loss on the research which fails the FDA's clinical trials, so drug makers cannot fund innovative creative experiments which think outside the box for fear of not passing the FDA's clinical trials. In the name of safety the FDA has destroyed the sort of scientific innovation and experimentation which might actually achieve progress in medical science and cure a lot of sicknesses, including the common cold. Interestingly, the FDA's authority to regulate medicine began in the early 1900s to fight a wave of "snake oil" medicines, absurd poisons which were sold to foolish people on wild promises that the snake oil would cure all their diseases. In the modern era, where medicine is the result of science and biological research, the justification for the FDA no longer exists.

Regulation destroys innovation and kills the ability to be experimental and creative. The regulators say they are protecting us and creating safety. They probably have the best of intentions. But as a result of the structure and nature of government regulation, the EPA and FDA only do harm. And it is the people of the USA, who would enjoy the use of flying cars and an end to the common cold, who suffer because of the government's lack of political wisdom.

CHAPTER NINETEEN: EQUALITY AND ARISTOCRACY: UNRAVELING THE LEFTIST NARRATIVE

Leftists tell a story about America. The story goes something like this: the American Revolution was about the Founding Fathers fighting for the cause of equality against the British aristocracy. Dating back to the Declaration of Independence and the Constitution, the central principle of America has always been equality. Inequality continued to exist after the Founders won the war, and it grew and festered as Southern slavery. But the Civil War was a new victory for the cause of equality when Lincoln freed the slaves. Now, in modern times, rich white men are the new American aristocracy. The Left is fighting the battle for the cause of equality by socializing all wealth and eliminating ownership so that the poor, blacks, Hispanics, women, etc., will become equal to rich white men.

Millions of liberals in the USA would eat this story up like a chocolate sundae. But according to libertarians, of which I am one, this narrative is total nonsense. The libertarian version of American history is quite different, although we also tell a story about equality and aristocracy. Our story goes like this: the British King and his aristocracy of nobles wanted to rule the Americans as a big strong powerful central government from across the ocean sending soldiers over here to us to tax us and control us. We rebelled in the name of freedom from the King's government, using the slogan "no taxation without representation!" The American Revolution was a victory against aristocracy and for political equality, but that aristocracy was tied to the British government. Later, the Southern whites used the Southern state governments to enforce the Slave Code, the set of laws which enslaved the black slaves. The Civil War was a victory for the cause of political equality, because it resulted in whites and blacks becoming politically equal before the law, so that white people and black people would each be free to stand or fall by their own individual efforts, and not because of what race they were born into. In both the American Revolution and the Civil War, big oppressive government was the tool of the aristocracy, and freedom from government control was the device used to achieve political equality.

The issue of rich vs. poor in the contemporary USA is completely different. We are not ruled by a new American aristocracy of rich white men from "old money" families, as the leftists claim. Yes, there are still some "old money" families, but in America many rich people are self-made millionaires or self-made billionaires. The rich in America contain many "new money" families, people with wealth which they themselves created. America is not a caste system where the poor are trapped in poverty and you must be born rich in order to become rich. Yes, the Ivy League legacy admissions system slants in favor of upper-class Old Money people. Yes, being rich is easier if you are born rich. That much is obvious. But throughout American history thousands of self-made people have pulled themselves up by their bootstraps, including blacks and women.

The rich are not an aristocracy. The cause of "economic equality" championed by the Left is completely different from the political equality which the principle of America has always stood for. Political equality is the right to be a full citizen with the rights of every other citizen. So-called "economic equality" is merely an excuse for socialist Big Government to boss us around. A Communist dictator is no different from a British King, as the Russians learned to their horror under Stalin. A socialist dictator's only purpose is to seize power, and socialism is the agent of the new aristocracy, the aristocracy of the government bureaucrats who want to rule us like a new kingdom. Equality, on the other hand, demands that each person be given the right to work and live in freedom, just like everyone else. Freedom is the true meaning of political equality.

Does capitalism give freedom to the rich that is more meaningful than the freedom which it gives to the poor, such that rich and poor lack political equality? Not if precise terms are used. To develop F.A. Hayek's argument, don't ask: "does a poor person have the freedom to buy an expensive car?" Instead, ask: "if a poor person had the power to buy an expensive car, and he/she decided to do so, would anybody use force to prevent him/her from doing it?" If the answer is "no," then a poor person does in fact possess the freedom to buy an expensive car, but he/she lacks the means of doing so. What the poor lack is purchasing power, not freedom. Capitalism gives freedom equally to all people, rich and poor alike.

Once the leftist story is unraveled, and its rhetorical manipulations are exposed, we can see that the Left seeks to corrupt the American ideal of equality and to disguise the tyranny of Big Government so it appear compatible with that freedom which we Americans have loved since 1776.

To complete this analysis we must look at the leftist story which equates white Southern racism with capitalism. During the pre-Civil War era, and continuing on until the civil rights movement and even into today, whites in America tended to be richer than blacks, and men tended to make more money than women. In any society which features oppression, the oppressors will usually be richer than the victims of oppression. But the fact that oppression causes the oppressors to be rich does not prove that the rich are always oppressors. We can imagine a libertarian utopia where no oppression exists but the rich will still be richer than the poor. The difference between the libertarian utopia and oppression-based wealth is that in the libertarian utopia income inequality is the result of the rich making good economic decisions and the poor making bad choices. Such inequality does not come from a class/caste status-based system.

This is not to say that modern-day America is a libertarian utopia. Contemporary white-black and male-female income inequality reflect oppressive racism and sexism that continue to exist. But to equate capitalism with oppression is simply untrue. Capitalism, as the economic system required by freedom, is the natural enemy of oppression, and the natural ally of political equality.

CHAPTER TWENTY: THE WALL STREET SYSTEM OF INVESTMENT DECISIONS

Socialists and Marxists like to define the American political debate as Main Street vs. Wall Street. In fact, the name "Wall Street" is merely the term for a system in which investment of capital in growing businesses is done privately by private investors, instead of publicly by the government as in a Marxist system. Let me explain why the Wall St. system works, and could not be replaced without losing part of the benefits of capitalism, namely the benefits of competition in the investment decision-making process.

The rich need to make their wealth keep pace with inflation, which forces them to invest most of their money, either in their business or in other people's businesses. Who do we want to make business decisions about investing in small businesses and entrepreneurs, to decide who receives society's investment capital: people who know finance and economics and take personal responsibility for their decisions, or government officials lost in a mess of bureaucracy and red tape, who experience no personal accountability from gains, losses, and the profit motive?

Capitalism is merely a system in which capital is invested by private people, as opposed to the state. "Wall Street," that much-maligned entity, is the process followed by rich people, and the financial managers who invest money for them, as they make decisions that fund the talented and hard-working middle class. Small businesses are carefully chosen by Wall Street's investors because they have the capacity to succeed and expand, thus creating more jobs for the poor. Wall Street investors become rich or poor by making good or bad investments, so they are highly motivated to be financial experts, to understand economics and the economy, to determine what goods and services the consumers want or will want in the future, and to put the talent and intelligence of society to work in making investment decisions.

The recent tech start-up IPOs, circa 2000 to the present, show that Wall Street works in funding science and technology to improve the people's standard of living. Every start-up entrepreneur who has a good idea or product but isn't rich needs investment, often from an angel investor or venture capitalist who gives both capital and expertise. Later, in order to grow, the business secures more capital from investors. The investors and finance people teach and impart wisdom to the start-up businessmen, and put financial reason and logic and experience-based knowledge into the small businesses of America. Ultimately, if the business is looking to grow from a regional to a national scale, the company might do an IPO and go public. An IPO, contrary to being a windfall of wealth for the rich, enables the people to own corporate America, not the other way around. Corporate America does not own the people, instead the investing public owns the stocks of corporate America.

Wall Street is Main Street's best friend, even though most people don't see the complicated economic relationships that form the substructure of a trip to buy a loaf of bread at the local grocery store. Someone made a decision about which grocery stores to invest in, and which bakers to invest in, and the success of those decisions helps determine whether you pay $2 for bread, as we can today, or $20, as we might in the socialist nightmare of tomorrow. The socialist leftist liberal dogma that the rich are a few crusty old white men locked away in the towers of distant mansions, counting gold coins like Scrooge, and that the corporations have enslaved us and the only practical thing is for "working people" to rebel, is totally contrary to the way the world works.

Note that once a company is "public," it is owned by the shareholders, which means that it is owned by the people, specifically every member of the public who invested in it and owns shares of stock. Public ownership is real and means what it says, as the shareholders possess the legal power to vote in the board of directors, which has the power to fire and hire executives, who manage the company. The power of the people is enforced by shareholder plaintiff's class action litigation, which is very real and a viable tool for forcing corporate America to obey its populist bosses, the share-owning public. Also note that in Wall Street, the investing ability of the rich is roughly on par with that of the pensions and mutual funds, which generally are beholden to the working class and middle class, not the upper class. Wall Street is really the American workers' tool for saving for retirement, because Social Security is a fraudulent Ponzi scheme, as explained elsewhere in this book.

CHAPTER TWENTY ONE: HOW LIBERTY HELPS THE POOR

As a libertarian I want the policies I prefer to actually become the law. But libertarian policies will never be enacted in a democratic society if poor and lower-middle-class voters stand against libertarian ideals. A significant number of Americans can be classified as the working poor. It is inherently difficult for laws to come into being that oppose their perceived interests. The solution to this problem is not to rail against the poor. The solution is to convince the working poor that free market capitalism does not oppose working-class interests and that the free market favors the working class just as much as it favors the rich. Libertarians must be able to make a persuasive argument that free-market capitalism benefits the poor, and that it is better for them than socialism or socialistic programs. Here are four kinds of arguments that may be useful.

1. The Efficiency Argument

Socialists like to appeal to poor people by proposing a redistribution of wealth. The idea is that when a pie has been cut into pieces so that some people get big chunks and other people get crumbs, the fair thing is to re-slice the pie into equal portions. But that is only one way to increase what people get. If you make the whole pie bigger, everyone's portion gets bigger, and you don't have to mess up the pie by re-slicing it. Everyone can understand this metaphor. What it means is that the economy is not a zero-sum game. When new wealth is created, everyone can win, without the inefficiency of social disruption.

Under capitalism the poor can buy products that are both good and cheap, because competition forces market efficiency. The standard of living for poor people in wealthy economies, economies operating by means of the profit motive, is visibly higher than that of poor people in poor economies. Capitalism is the most efficient producer of wealth. A poor person in America benefits from the productivity of the entire free market system, which creates jobs paying wages that comparable workers in third-world countries can only dream of. If poor people in America compare themselves to rich people in America, it seems that they have little, but the comparison that is relevant to the point at issue, namely capitalism vs. socialism, is with similar people in non-capitalist societies. Only that comparison reveals what capitalism offers to the working class, which is a larger and larger economic "pie."

A classic libertarian observation says that because consumers are the ones making choices in a free market, the market supplies what people want at the prices they are willing to pay. By contrast, in a socialist economy the choices are made by bureaucrats who, even if they are saints, will still lack the detailed information about each consumer's wants and needs that can enable goods and services to be distributed efficiently. Some rich people splurge on yachts and some poor people splurge on chicken sandwiches, but capitalism will get you your chicken sandwich more efficiently than socialism.

Socialists like to argue that their policies help the poor people whom the efficient market ignores, for example, by providing a minimum wage to make sure that everyone has enough money. But regulations that interfere with the market also interfere with people's ability to get what they choose at the price they can pay for it. For example, if an employer is not free to offer a lower salary, then he will simply not be able to hire people, or will hire fewer people, whereas with an unregulated salary he would have been able to offer more jobs. This would be true even of a government-owned business. And when the minimum wage for the people who work in the grocery store goes up, the price of food goes up too, because the salary is a cost of the grocery which is factored into the food prices so that the grocery can continue to exist, and the poor have to pay that higher price for food.

2. The Ambition Argument

Under socialism, the rich (if any) and the middle class are taxed according to how productive they are, whereas the poor are given goods and services in proportion to how much they need them. This tends to solidify the classes. The more successful a worker is and the more productive he becomes, the more he will be taxed and the harder it will be for him to rise from one class to the other.

An inability to profit from one's individual efforts destroys all ties between the work one does and the reward one gets, rendering meaningless the concepts of personal responsibility and deserved rewards. When the fact that socialism diminishes your responsibility for your own life and severs rewards from achievements becomes clear to people, they often become uneasy about it, in spite of all the free lunches that socialism promises.

It is, of course, unrealistic to think that every poor person can become a millionaire. But a diligent worker can realistically aspire to the middle class, and someone in the lower middle class can realistically aspire to the upper middle class. Capitalism does not have a rigid caste system, despite the assertions of the sociologists, because capitalism does not have laws which force a person to remain in his or her class. The American dream is rags to riches, and capitalism offers that hope to everyone.

3. The Freedom Argument

Socialists like to scare poor people into voting for them by tapping into the fear and misery that poor people feel. They make the argument that if we have less freedom we can have more safety. Poor people are naturally fearful that they will not have enough money to buy things, especially if they lose their jobs. They fear becoming destitute and starving to death or being homeless. Socialism promises to give them money taken from the rich, and to give them financial security in the form of jobs they cannot lose.

The libertarian reply is simple: if you give up freedom for the sake of safety, you get neither freedom nor safety. This argument can be made by merely pointing out the practical realities of socialist societies: in theory the poor may own the wealth, but they don't have a way to voice their will except through the government officials who purport to represent them. There is no other way for the system to work besides the government's taking control, and when it takes control, it takes control of the working poor as well as everyone else. Socialism is not the people's system. It is the dictator's system.

Under capitalism your boss can fire you, but if you do your job well you probably won't be fired, your hard work will be rewarded with a decent salary or a promotion, and you continue to enjoy political freedom and rights as a citizen. Under socialism, instead of a job provided by a boss competing with other bosses, you have a job under the control of a government official. If the socialist government official decides to terminate your employment, then no other employers can exist who might hire you. This is not freedom, and it is not safety either. A system of economic redistribution takes wealth from the rich and gives it, in the first and sometimes the final instance, to government officials. The poor will be as poor under socialism as they are under capitalism, or poorer, but they will have lost their freedom in exchange for promises of safety. The failed "experiment" of Russia during the USSR era proves this. You don't have to be rich to like freedom; and libertarianism, which is basically the love of freedom, is as relevant to the poor as it is to the rich.

4. The Workers' Rights Argument

Socialists argue that you need to be rich in order to enjoy individual rights or economic freedoms, such as the right to choose where you work or what you spend your money on. They also argue that workers can't make meaningful economic choices because of their unequal bargaining power.

The libertarian reply is twofold. First, social freedoms such as free speech and freedom of religion are inseparable from economic freedom. A government with unrestricted power over the economy will waste no time in accumulating as many other powers as possible. There is no rational principle that distinguishes one kind of freedom from another.

Second, a worker's choices are in reality not limited to one employer's take-it-or-leave-it offer. Turning down one employer's offer of a certain wage doesn't mean starving to death. There are thousands of employers, and a worker in a capitalist society has the unconstrained ability to choose whichever employer he prefers out of all who may be willing to hire him. If no employer will give him the terms he wants, he is free to seek a loan from one of the hundreds of banks in existence and start his own business, or to learn a trade that makes him more valuable to employers. Everyone has the option of getting an education and learning some trade to put him in a better bargaining position.

To say that some people lack the intelligence necessary to do so is both patronizing and untrue. The qualities necessary to accomplish such a feat are discipline and the willingness to make tough choices. Neither of these qualities is a magical ability that some people are born with and some are not. In no industry is there a monopoly such that a worker must choose to accept one specific set of terms or starve. Even if there were, the worker would be free to start a company to compete with the monopoly, on at least one of its product lines, assuming, of course, that there was a free market. Hungry, ambitious start-up companies often compete very efficiently with fat, bloated would-be monopolists.

It is misleading to say that working-class people cannot appreciate the right to choose a job or the right to use money. A worker who earns his money has earned the right to spend it on something he wants, and to enjoy any product or service that the other hardworking citizens of a capitalist country will sell to him. The worker's enjoyment from spending money is not an illusion, even if he has comparatively less money than an upper-class person. The fact that rich people own yachts does not make a chicken sandwich taste any less delicious.

Any libertarian candidate who runs for office on a platform of helping the rich and ignoring the poor will lose. But after all, libertarians are not in the business of using government to help any class of people. Their concern is with preventing government from hurting everyone's legitimate interests. It may seem counterintuitive to think that low-income people can be persuaded that economic freedom is in their best interest, but it only seems counterintuitive because of the pervasive influence of socialist propaganda. Fortunately, this propaganda has the weight of American history against it. Generations of low-income people arrived at Ellis Island and looked up at the Statue of Liberty, and they did not come here because they wanted to be exploited. They came because they wanted the American dream, the dream that hard work can earn you a decent wage and a good life. That dream, in the vast majority of cases, became reality. America has been called the land of opportunity, and the USA is a capitalist society in which economic opportunities appear to people who make simple, honest, persevering efforts.

In spite of all the obstacles that may stand in the way of working-class people trying to support themselves and their families, it remains possible to say that the American dream is still alive and that economic freedom still has a place in the American way of life. Socialists tell workers that capitalists exploit the workers and steal their wealth. The libertarian reply is that capitalists create wealth, make the economy function, and thereby benefit workers, who are always free to make use of capitalism for their own dreams and ambitions. Libertarians should be proselytizing to the poor as well as the rich. We cannot promise to provide free lunches to the poor, because, indeed, "there is no such thing as a free lunch," but we can promise to give everyone an unfettered opportunity to earn lunch money. Almost everyone on the political scene maintains that a political philosophy designed for America as a whole should be beneficial for all Americans, not just one class or special interest group. And free market capitalism is the one economic system that truly benefits everyone. If a libertarian platform were able to draw support from high-income, middle-income, and low-income voters, if we were able to say persuasively that freedom benefits all Americans, then there would be virtually no limit to the realization of libertarian political goals.

CHAPTER TWENTY TWO:
HURTING THE POOR,
HELPING THE RICH

Coming from Randian roots, I have a deep appreciation for the virtues of business, and of wealth that has been earned. I do not consider myself to be a liberal-tarian. I usually agree with the Right and disagree with the Left. But the more I look around, the more I see that socialism is really a tool by means of which millionaire elites keep the poor masses from rising up. Libertarianism, on the other hand, can accurately be described as the friend of the poor and the enemy of the rich. I have written in the previous section this book about how GOLD helps the poor. What I want to focus on in this section is how EVIL helps the rich, especially the old money aristocracy, the metaphorical "Atlas Shrugged" James Taggarts of the United States.

The evidence is overwhelming. Look at education. Rich people send their own children to expensive private schools, which put them on track for Ivy League universities and white collar jobs; meanwhile the political establishment makes sure that the only choice available to poor children is a horrible public school system that teaches nothing and trains students only for low-income jobs. The public schools are controlled by teachers' unions that oppose merit-based pay and favor a seniority system, which is a terrible model for achieving high educational excellence. The liberal reply is to say that the system is broken but could be fixed by raising taxes to give more funding to public schools. The real solution is to use school vouchers so that poor children can attend the rich children's schools, a prospect that few wealthy parents care to consider.

Or look at business. Big Government EVIL helps wealthy corporations in many ways, not by giving them tax breaks as the liberals complain, but by giving them handouts such as farm subsidies and defense contracts or municipal contracts like a monopoly on garbage collection. Ending all subsidies and all pork barrel spending would be a huge loss for rich people with political connections, yet the liberals have bamboozled the poor into thinking that the government actually helps the poor and hurts the rich. On Wall Street, the Securities and Exchange Commission's maze of rules and regulations makes legal compliance so difficult that it is virtually impossible for newcomers to compete with the old established investment banks. The engine that maintains the power and privilege of Goldman Sachs is the SEC, a government agency, not the free market-based Wall Street stock markets.

Established businessmen use taxes and regulations to stifle competition from start-up entrepreneurs and up-and-coming small businessmen who can't afford to hire compliance lawyers and tax consultants, as their "old money" rivals can. Yet small business is precisely the engine of opportunity for hard-working ambitious people from poor backgrounds.

Now look at the professions. Affluent professionals in the medical and legal fields enjoy salaries that are artificially increased because the American Medical Association (AMA) and the American Bar Association (ABA) maintain systems of doctor licensing and lawyer licensing that restrict the supply of new doctors and lawyers. I predict that if Obamacare does lead to a socialist single-payer national healthcare system, that system will be run by AMA-approved bureaucrats whose inefficiency and nepotism will drive up the price of healthcare, allowing doctors favored by the government to make more money than they would have in a free market. In the Obamacare nightmare, the rich will probably be able to afford to obtain treatment from high-quality doctors, but the poor will be faced with no alternative to the low-quality healthcare that the system is certain to produce. Obamacare will be a disaster for the working poor.

In every situation mentioned, liberal policies help the rich and hurt the poor, creating a caste system in which vast fortunes can be inherited but cannot be built up from scratch. The instances described above have all been justified on the ground that they benefit society as a whole or protect the whole public from the dangers of free markets, which in itself is a distinctly socialist justification. But a logical person would expect socialism to favor the wealthy, because it vests tremendous economic power in the class of bureaucrats and government officials, and one would expect the upper class to have the means to exploit that power. The rich are the ones most likely to be able to afford to run for office and to purchase influence among politicians by means of campaign contributions and special interest lobbying.

What I am offering is not an empirical claim but a deductive argument: the wealthy are inherently better positioned than the poor to exploit the government's power through lobbying, therefore the more powerful the government becomes, the more advantages the rich have over the poor in terms of the opportunity to make money. Ayn Rand hinted at this idea when she contrasted "the aristocracy of money," that of people who earn wealth, with "the aristocracy of pull," that of people who exploit the government to obtain wealth. But in the end I think Rand loved the rich so much that she failed to see how socialism may actually be a plot by the rich against the poor.

My criticism is directed mainly at wealthy members of the socialist or extreme-leftist wing of the Democratic Party. It is no coincidence that many of the most famous Democratic politicians who preach that they are the champions of the poor graduated from Ivy League universities that most poor people could never get into because they could not afford to attend the most prestigious private high schools. Many of these liberal millionaires could not possibly imagine what it is like not to have enough money to pay your bills or to have to work two shifts to make ends meet.

Consider Democratic presidential candidates, past and present. President Obama comes from Harvard Law. John Kerry has the Heinz fortune. Bill and Hillary Clinton were products of Yale Law. And the members of Joe Kennedy's clan have vast amounts of wealth and several Ivy League degrees behind them. Looking farther back, Franklin D. Roosevelt, the champion of the socialist New Deal, was a man of wealth and privilege; the Rockefeller family inherited an enormous fortune, yet produced many left-leaning politicians, one of them a presidential candidate. People like the ones just mentioned have no right to say that they speak for the poor and underprivileged. Such people are merely exploiting leftism to maximize their already substantial influence.

It is true that the higher taxes championed by liberals would hurt the rich. But the bottom line is that in the American capitalism-socialism hybrid, the leftist rich retain the ability to own their vast fortunes while also exploiting the advantages of socialism to prevent ambitious poor people from competing with them. While socialist interference in the economy drives up prices and eliminates jobs, the rich retain their connections, their ability to land good jobs, and their ability to pay for what they want to buy. By contrast, the poor have no choice other than to accept whatever goods and services the government-ruined markets have to offer, and they must desperately seek jobs in a market crippled by taxes and regulations.

The socialist wing of the Democratic Party thinks that decades of the welfare state have made the American poor so lazy and dependent upon government charity that they can be controlled like dogs and trained to bark at capitalism whenever the liberals blow the dog whistle. This twisted scheme has worked to some extent: common sense and conventional wisdom now hold that lower-class economic interests are aligned with the welfare state.

Libertarians would be well served to focus our ideological energy on fighting this myth. The working poor in the United States have enough trouble to worry about as it is, and it's not fair to them to tolerate a political system that hurts the poor and favors the rich.

CHAPTER TWENTY THREE: BROADENING THE APPEAL OF LIBERTY TO RACIAL MINORITIES

Liberals tend to view the ideology of free market capitalism as a tool of white males, especially white Anglo-Saxon Protestant men, whom they condemn as conservative oppressors. It would come as a surprise to them to learn that I, Russell Hasan, am the son of a brown-skinned Bangladeshi Muslim father and a white Jewish mother of Russian Jewish lineage. As a person of mixed race living in the northeastern United States I feel a constant pull from liberals, trying to draw me in with their claim that theirs are the only policies beneficial to racial minority groups. I believe that libertarians, with our commitment to free markets, individualism, and race-blindness, are actually far better for minorities than liberals. We should try to attract more members of racial and ethnic minorities to the libertarian movement, but in order to do so we need a coherent set of arguments proving that capitalism isn't racist.

Liberals who view capitalism as inherently "white," and who believe it is impossible for the members of racial minorities to prosper except with government aid, fail to understand the principled approach to fighting racism. They assume that either you are for the government helping minority groups or else you must hate minority groups and want the government to help only the white race. As in many other areas, liberals embrace EVIL, the principle of Everyone Violating Individual Liberty, under their belief that either conservative whites will use government-backed violence against racial minorities (e.g. "separate but equal" and the Black Code Jim Crow laws of the South) or else liberal racial minorities must use government-backed violence against whites (e.g. reverse discrimination and Affirmative Action to force blacks into favorable positions).

Most liberals (and many conservatives) view EVIL as the only option, thinking that our only choices are X coercing A or A coercing X. EVIL means that liberals must dominate conservatives or else conservatives must dominate liberals, and it means that the white race and the black race are competing for which group can use the government against the other group. The liberal way of thinking about race cannot comprehend the concept of libertarian GOLD, which respects the rights of both X to do Y and A to do B, and which defends freedom for both whites and racial minorities, as an alternative to EVIL.

The liberals think that pro-minority favoritism, enforced by the government, is good for the minority races. Actually, however, libertarians hold that a race-blind government is more helpful to minorities than a meddling liberal government. Race-blindness is based on the ethical premise of individualism, the idea that a person should be held responsible for his or her own actions and not for the actions, good or bad, of people who happen to share the same ethnic identity. The principled ethical solution to the problem of racism is race-blindness, and capitalism is race-blind.

Here I will make the Clarence Thomas argument, which is that the achievements of United States Supreme Court Justice Clarence Thomas, who is one of the most brilliant and talented legal minds of our generation, have been obscured and reduced because most lawyers think he owes his position on the Court to the fact that he is black as a racially motivated Supreme Court pick, and that he did not earn his place due to his individual accomplishments. Liberal reverse discrimination is unfair to Justice Thomas and to all blacks and ethnic minority members who have the talent to succeed as individuals. Only race-blindness can give to blacks the respect and dignity that is currently possessed by whites.

In a free market economy individual talent and hard work tend to be rewarded. Businesses depend on the talent of their employees in order to compete with their rivals. If a racist businessman refuses to hire a talented person, it is in the interest of some other businessman, who is not a racist, to hire him and by doing so be able to compete successfully against the racist. The invisible hand of the market punishes the racist and dispenses rewards to talented workers, regardless of their ethnic identity.

It is sometimes argued that racism forces members of minority groups to overpay for the retail goods they buy. Yet any racist who based his business model around overcharging in this way could be put out of business by the first nonracist who was willing to undercut his prices. If you want lower prices, unfettered competition is the most efficient way to get them. It is plausible to think that some unscrupulous people have victimized low-income racial minority groups in places where the market is not large, but as a large scale business model such a strategy doesn't make any sense.

Nothing in the nature of capitalism gives a competitive edge to any particular race. In fact, it is demeaning to think that the members of racial minorities would not be competent enough to prosper under economic freedom. If the government meddles in the economy to help people in racial minorities (or majorities!) who do not have the talent and determination to succeed in a free market, it will reward them for their race but not for the work they do. Anyone should be able to see that this isn't fair.

That is a simple argument. Yet a "sophisticated" critique of capitalism insinuates that capitalism is de facto racist because it is "only" individuals, not racial groups, who succeed or fail in the market system. True, wealth, in this system, is not held by races; it is held by individuals, and it is individuals by whom it is enjoyed. What difference would it make to you if your race were doing better than another race, according to some set of economic statistics, if you yourself were not allowed to prosper? In nations dominated by racial economics, few people do prosper. It should also be pointed out that economic statistics that are focused on racial groups tend to obscure the significance of individual effort for individual success.

Liberals often argue that racial minorities need government help because minority races do not have the same opportunities in America as white people. But why is this? Free-market capitalism creates jobs, and jobs are opportunities, created by capitalist enterprise for people of all groups. It cannot be said that members of racial minorities lack opportunities to get high-paying jobs because racism prevents us from getting degrees from good colleges. University admissions officers who reject deserving applicants because of their race will decrease the quality of their student body and lower their school's academic reputation, whereas schools that accept hard-working people from minority groups will benefit their academic rankings. If the public schools that serve minority communities do not properly encourage children to aspire to college, then we should blame the public schools, which are run by the government and the teachers' unions, for the failure to provide opportunities.

The general truth for both white people and ethnic minorities is that life is not easy but perseverance and hard work usually pays off. Some whites do not face the same obstacles as some members of minorities, but happiness is not automatic for anyone. Whites do not live in a fantasy paradise, the doors to which are locked against others. President Obama might not be good for much, politically, but he does prove that members of racial minorities can now achieve any station in life that we desire if we exert ourselves with hard work and determination. No one is owed a life that is easy; all we are owed is the chance to succeed, which is precisely what the free enterprise system gives us.

As to the claim that government should help to end residual racism by acting "affirmatively" in aid of ethnic minorities: if it is obviously unethical for the government to help the white race at the expense of the minority races, why wouldn't it be unethical to help minority races at the expense of whites? People who argue otherwise sometimes claim that African Americans, in particular, are owed various kinds of restitution for past abuses. Slavery is indeed an ugly scar on the face of American history. Yet America fought the Civil War in order to eliminate slavery, and our goal as a nation should be to reach a time when we will be able to move beyond the past and embrace the future. The people who participated in slavery are all dead; no further restitution can fairly be exacted for the crime of slavery, a crime that, incidentally, was licensed and maintained by law and government, not by the individualism of the free market.

Similarly, the white Southerners who perpetrated the "separate but equal" era in the South are all either dead or elderly and dying, so the American people cannot properly be held guilty for the crimes of those individual white racist Southerners. And the sins of the members of the KKK and Neo-Nazis, although gruesome and horrific, also are not faults for which the American public as a whole should be punished. The concept of racial guilt, as used against white Americans, shares the same principle as the concept of the inferiority of blacks. Only individualism is a true alternative to racism as a principle.

The free market gives to the members of minority races the freedom that matters, the freedom to choose whom we deal with and on what terms. In this day and age, with no remaining state-enforced racism, the sins of slavery are the liberals' excuse to turn the government into a perpetual restitution machine that will "equalize" the white race and the minority races by artificial means. Such a program can only damage the people it is meant to help. People who earn their own wealth in the free market earn the right to be proud. They enjoy their prosperity and independence. But when the leaders of minority special interest groups buy their followers' loyalty with government favors, they create a perpetually poor, weak, needy, helpless, hopeless, welfare-addicted subculture.

Racism was at one time widespread and state-enforced. It is a good thing that civil rights movements arose to combat it. But now, though it is still a problem, enough progress has been made for us to shift gears and promote race-blindness as the only feasible long-term program of achieving racial equality. Leftists sometimes try to scare members of racial minorities by saying that libertarianism "protects the right to be a racist." Yes, and it also protects our right to be free from racism having the power of law. Libertarianism calls for an end to the use of force except in self-defense. That is NVP, the Non-Violence Principle, pure and simple.

Racial discrimination should by all means be eliminated, even when it operates without the power of law or violence, but non-violent racism, as in speech or employment, is properly combated by means of persuasion, by educating people on the virtues of race-blindness, and not by trying to outlaw thoughts. If you can't persuade a person that racism is evil (and any person worth dealing with will be persuaded), and the other person is not threatening you with violence, what gives you the right to force that person to obey you? Political correctness easily snowballs into censorship. It is used as a means of getting what its purveyors want, as when people who oppose the liberal agenda are automatically labeled racists. I am optimistic that future generations will leave racism behind without sacrificing the freedoms to which American citizens are entitled.

Are traditional American ideas of freedom really just "white" ideas, as professors of ethnic studies often assume? Of course, the writers of the Declaration of Independence and the Constitution were white; they relied on the ideas of such philosophers as John Locke, who were white; and the early theorists of the free market, such as Adam Smith, who were white. Yet the ideas they propounded have universal applications. They account for the experience of people of all races, throughout the world. They speak for the rights of every man and woman. If an idea corresponds to reality and human nature, it is equally true for everyone, with no advantage given to "white" culture.

Capitalism flourished in that vaguely defined set of territories, "the West," in most of which the population was predominately white. For that reason it developed an early association with Western culture. So what? Economic freedom can exist everywhere, and exists today in nations throughout the world. It matters not because you are white, but because you are a human being. People in China, Venezuela, North Korea and Iran need freedom just as much as Americans do. Their cause is not well served by cultural relativists, who constantly desire to protect other cultures from the dreadful influence of "hegemonic" Western culture. These liberal scholars merely patronize nonwhite people with the belief that we are too primitive to understand useful ideas such as capitalism and individualism.

Racism is a monstrosity that should be destroyed. But a government that is truly race-blind, which treats every citizen with the same evenhanded justice, would act as a role model for ending racism, and should be more effective at fighting it than a government that promotes a utopia of reverse discrimination, insidiously based on the idea that your race determines your value. Only race-blindness is a true alternative to racism. Racists in America are not so powerful that they have the means to cripple the resiliency of American minorities, and the members of racial minorities are not so weak that we need a welfare state to take care of us. Only if we get the government and its poisonous interference out of the race game can we create attitudes and motivations that can solve the problem of race in America.

Libertarians are in the vanguard of the fight against racism. Whether they call themselves libertarians, free-market conservatives, objectivists, or "radicals for capitalism," thinkers who have adopted libertarian ideas have taken landmark positions against racism. Many examples come to mind, though I am thinking particularly about Ayn Rand's famous essay "Racism" (1963) and Thomas Sowell's several works in the field, especially "Race and Economics" (1979). I want to see this tradition continue. Some prominent members of racial minorities, such as the black conservative United States Supreme Court Justice Clarence Thomas, are living examples of the ability of individuals to succeed and flourish in the American system, but many members of minorities remain fooled by liberal propaganda. We need to spread the message of race-blindness in order to add more people to the libertarian movement.

The issue of racism in America is particularly important to me because, as I mentioned in the opening of this section, I am myself a member of two racial minority groups: I am part Bangladeshi Muslim and part Russian Jewish. I consider myself to be living proof that racial diversity can be achieved without state-controlled social engineering. Drawing upon Thomas Sowell's analysis, I would observe that in spite of their history of persecution, many Jewish immigrants have achieved considerable prosperity by pursuing higher education and seeking high-paying jobs, not by relying upon state charity. On the other hand, many Bangladeshi immigrants, coming from a nation permeated by various strains of liberal and socialist thinking and emerging out of a culture that was ransacked by the British Empire, face substantial poverty and have not yet accomplished what they have the potential to achieve. The only real difference between Jewish immigrants and Bangladeshi immigrants is that the Jewish culture teaches Jews to pull themselves up by their bootstraps and pursue intellectual excellence (partly stemming from the duty to study the Torah and Talmud), whereas Bangladeshi culture lacks the same strong emphasis on individual achievement and scholarly knowledge (although I must note Bangladesh once had a rich intellectual culture that the British deliberately destroyed).

The world has seen what horrors are spawned by a government obsession with helping some races and ethnicities at the expense of others. Racism was the principle behind Nazi Germany's Holocaust, the Russian Pogroms, and the persecution of European Jews during the Middle Ages, as well as the enslavement of black Africans by white colonial Americans and Europeans. Racism has caused countless ethnic wars and ethnic cleansings, dating as far back as Egypt's enslavement of the Jewish race during Biblical times. For the United States government to treat some races differently, even for a supposedly noble purpose, elicits an intense distrust from me, both as a student of human history and also because I believe that the Equal Protection Clause of the United States Constitution was intended to safeguard legal equality, not to legalize new kinds of inequality. How long will it be before America realizes that members of racial minority groups can achieve prosperity and pride without becoming helpless victims, needing to be rescued by liberal politicians?

CHAPTER TWENTY FOUR:
CIVIL RIGHTS AND GOLD

GOLD is keenly aware of the policy need to protect blacks from racism. The GOLD set of civil rights policies is summarized here. First, we must protect blacks from white racists. Instead of relying on a protectionist liberal government to accomplish this, we should enable black men and women to protect themselves, by means of Second Amendment gun rights. The GOLD policy is "blacks with guns," meaning that we should arm blacks and enable them to defend themselves from violent white bigots and racists. The various scandals where white men shoot black youths and then claim self-defense, e.g. Getz, Trayvon, does not alter the logic of "blacks with guns" as a civil rights policy. The truth is not "more guns make us safer," the truth is actually that "more guns in the hands of good people to counter the guns in the hands of bad people" make the good people safer.

Second, the police and the armed forces should also have a quota, for example 10% of the police force must be black, in order to have black policemen who will defend the black citizens. (Similarly, at least 20% should be women and 5% should be gays and lesbians). A quota is a deviation from the principle of race-blindness, and as such it is not ideal. The race-blind ideal would be for all policemen to be race-blind, in which case no need for quotas would exist. However, this sort of perfect intellectual purity is not something that can be feasibly achieved in today's world. And as a realist I believe that blacks will receive better protection if some of the cops are black.

This result is not inconsistent with the Equal Protection Clause of the United States Constitution. In fact, a textualist reading of the plain meaning of the Equal Protection Clause may mandate a police racial quota. The clause requires the government not to "deny to any person within its jurisdiction the equal protection of the laws." If "protection of the laws" means the police protecting you, and "equal" means what it plainly says, then if whites in upper class communities receive adequate police protection of their life, liberty and property, by policemen who share their race, then blacks in lower class communities are legally entitled to also receive adequate police protection under the Equal Protection Clause. Also, as I see it, a 10% racial minority quota for the police and the army would not constitute affirmative action at all, because it consists not of the government reaching into the private sphere to force employers or schools or businesses to consider race and hire minorities, so it does not violate any particular person's freedom, and it concerns only the government internally achieving an optimal delivery of services which legitimately belong to the government, i.e. protecting the citizens from violence. If having black cops helps the police to protect black citizens then it is justified despite my principled adherence to race-blindness.

Third, we should not force people to use their property contrary to their free choices and desires, even for a noble idealistic reason. This means that all laws outlawing nonviolent discrimination should be repealed. This would not result in a net harm to blacks, because the white racists would be free to discriminate against blacks, but the blacks and liberal whites would also be free to discriminate for blacks and against whites. It is not society's job to achieve racial equality. Instead it is the role of each individual to work and trade with consenting others in a manner which is race-blind and thereby do his or her part for social change. However, one exception exists to the principle that a person should be allowed to discriminate. At the point where widespread organized discriminatory use of property transforms a group of people into second class citizens, such as blacks in the Jim Crow South who were subjected to "separate but equal," then economic discrimination transforms into political discrimination, which is not allowed under GOLD. At that stage a legal remedy is proper to achieve political equality, e.g. I think Brown v. Board was rightly decided. This is a narrowly limited exception because in general the use of property is not coercive.

Non-violent racism is evil, but it is properly treated by persuasion, education and activism, not by law and government force. In principle the government passing laws that are pro-white laws or pro-black laws will only result in a tug of war between whites and blacks over who gets to use government force against the other. That is an adequate explanation of the Civil War. Race-blindness is probably the only solution which will prevent a new North vs. South, liberal vs. conservative war in the future. The better approach to policy debates is GOLD vs. EVIL, not white vs. black. A white person and a black person are both individuals, and as human beings we are all in this together, so white racist groups and black partisan political groups both betray the anti-racist principle of race-blindness and GOLD individual rights.

CHAPTER TWENTY FIVE: THE DEMOCRACY OF MONEY

Who is the servant and who is the master? The popular understanding of politics is that in capitalism everyone is bossed around by the rich owners/employers, whereas in socialism the politicians, bureaucrats, and government officials serve the public, and therefore socialism is the "People's System." But which system really serves the people?

If I walk into a store and the store clerks aren't polite to me or I don't like the products offered for sale then I can (and will) choose not to shop there. Money forces the store to please me and satisfy me and do what I want. This is as true in stores that sell to the poor and middle class as it is for luxury stores targeting the rich. By contrast, in a socialist dictatorship the government officials answer to no one, and nobody pressures them to do what the people want. Nobody has the power to punish the government bureaucrats if they disobey the will of the people, not in the way the market punishes the capitalists if they don't produce goods and services which are pleasing to the consumers. In fact, the socialist dictator's power has no real limits, and no political or economic mechanism forces him to do what the people desire.

So, the pop culture idea is really quite backwards. Capitalism is the system that gives power to the people, by fostering competition and leaving consumers free to exploit the power of their spending dollars, whereas socialism is the elitist movement that gives unbridled power to the political rulers.

Some time ago I debated someone on social media about economics, and I argued that capitalism is the people's system and socialism is an elitist system, because under capitalism the people decide what their money gets spent on, whereas under socialism the government bureaucrats and elitist "experts" plan the economy and decide how to spend the people's money. In politics, democracy is the people's system, because it gives power and freedom to the people, whereas dictatorship and aristocracy are the elitist system. Similarly, capitalism is the people's system because it vests economic decision-making power in the people, with each person choosing what to buy for himself/herself, whereas the Marxist/socialist planned economy is an elitist system, because the class of government officials and bureaucrats make our choices for us, and steal decision-making authority from the people, under the "we know what's best for you" ideology.

To which the person I debated gave various replies, such as that the socialist bureaucrats are the people's system because they make decisions with the goal of helping the people, helping the poor and vulnerable, and other good intentions. Even if we assume that socialist and liberal politicians are good, noble persons who have the best interests of society at heart, such an assumed premise simply cannot alter the fact that either we, the people, make our own decisions, or someone else decides for us. If someone else imposes their economic decisions upon us by force, this meets the definition of aristocratic elitism.

Another counterargument to capitalism is that the people will make bad decisions if given the freedom to do so, because the experts really do know better than the unwashed masses. This might conceivably justify socialism, but it certainly does not dispute the aristocratic and elitist nature of liberal policy. Freedom assumes that the people deserve the responsibility to be treated like adults, to be given personal responsibility, and make choices for themselves.

For example, drugs are evil and self-destructive, but the libertarian proposal is to legalize them, because people should be free to make those bad choices which only harm the person who made the choice, and do not harm other people. Libertarianism legalizes only "victimless crimes" which do no violence to anyone besides the person who makes his or her own choices. The person who makes bad choices will only hurt himself/herself, and will not hurt other people or "society." It is consistent with justice and fairness for a person to be punished for making bad choices (or to be rewarded for making good choices). Indeed, ethics and justice demand such a system in which choices are meaningful. Also, the flip side of not having the freedom to make bad choices is not having the freedom to make good choices. Decisional control by the government results in the people being helplessly at the mercy of bad choices made by the experts, who make our choices for us because think they know what's best for us, despite the fact that the experts are only fallible ignorant humans like the rest of us.

My opponent in the social media debate made one truly clever argument, that socialism is the people's system because in democratic socialism the people vote the politicians into power, and the politicians control the economy, so the people control the economy. Let me put this myth to rest. American voters make a choice once every two or four years between two alternatives, Republicans and Democrats, each of which differs little from the other. We are forced to choose a package of policies and can't pick precisely what we want. And the voters have no ability to hold the politicians accountable for their broken promises until the next election four years later, by which time many voters will have forgotten what they were promised to begin with. The so-called choice here described is no real choice at all. Elections are not even a pale shadow of the real, deep, meaningful choices that consumers have in a free marketplace. Making a choice every day, and choosing between five or ten or twenty different competitors, each of whom differs from the others in meaningful ways, is much closer to real choice, and to true competition.

Thus, because elections happen so infrequently in the United States and only two major political parties exist in the USA, elections leave little room for true choice. The political world is run first by the elitist political establishment, and second by local grassroots political activists, who are a small but vocal minority. The American democracy is not run by the masses. It is run by the activists and politicians who tap into the sentiment of the masses. In capitalism, everyone, including all members of "the people" or "the masses," gets to make economic decisions to control their own lives in the free market. Each individual person makes the choices which have the greatest impact on that person himself/herself. Everyone get to make choices constantly, and competition exists, and choosers have options.

If freedom to choose in a socialist economic democracy were to be given true effect, then each voter would require the right to choose among five or ten local politicians and their different plans for how to bake and sell a loaf of bread, and we would need the right to vote daily and to cast a new vote every time we buy a loaf of bread, in order to hold the politicians accountable for their economic plans for baking bread for us. If the choice to buy a loaf of bread is conceived of as a vote for the local economic production plan of the baker, and each producer is re-conceptualized as a politician and each consumer as a voter, then free market capitalism would be conceptually indistinguishable from a socialist democracy in which the people are given real meaningful freedom to choose. Thus, the liberals who say that they believe in liberalism only to the extent that it is democratic, and who would not endorse a dictatorship, have already accepted a principle which in practice calls for economic libertarianism.

Here it is worth also mentioning the Robert Nozick postulate. Nozick argued that if socialism were to achieve true income equality for all people, but if everyone were then given individual control over their own assets and allowed to do whatever they wanted with their money, then income inequality would naturally reappear. This would happen because, as production and consumption happened, the smarter and more talented people, and the people who experienced good luck, would inevitably attract more money than the lazy, stupid, and unlucky people. So the existence of income inequality is to some extent natural and inevitable, and income inequality cannot be charged against capitalism as an accusation of elitism, as the Marxists and socialists assert.

Free market capitalism is desirable precisely because it will help the poor. If we get government out of the way then business will create more wealth and everyone will benefit. Let me return to the metaphor of the pie, and refine the metaphor further. I agree with liberals that income inequality is a bad thing, and the existence of poverty is intolerable. But two approaches exist to solving the problem of income inequality, which can be visualized as a pie with uneven slices. You can re-slice the pie to make every slice equal. But an unintended consequence of re-slicing is that the cutting of the knife as you slice might destroy some of the pie. Or you can let the pie slices be unequal, but bake more pie so that the pie gets bigger. If the pie gets bigger then even though some slices are smaller relative to others each slice will be bigger from an absolute measured point of view. And if every slice gets bigger, then the smallest slices also get larger, and the people with the smallest slices then have more pie to eat. The evenly sliced pie is the redistribution of wealth, but the pie which grows larger is capitalism, creating new wealth which raises the standard of living for the poor. The poor will be better off from a much bigger pie with uneven slices, as libertarianism promises, instead of the socialist and liberal Left's evenly sliced but much smaller pie for everyone to share.

The premise of the free market system is that economic decisions should be made by consumers, not by politicians. Politicians are driven by the lobbying efforts of special interest groups, whereas consumers are driven by their own individual needs and desires. The consumers are the people who are most affected by the economic decisions of what they produce and what they consume, and each consumer has the best set of knowledge to decide for himself/herself what to buy. For example, the question to ask is not "should transit by car be replaced with transit by rail?" The question to ask is: "who should decide whether trains should replace cars? The consumers in the marketplace, or the politicians and bureaucrats?" If all negative externalities, e.g. pollution harm to third parties, have been properly negated by a litigated liability system enabling every individual to defend his life, liberty and property from external accidental or intentional violence, then why not give the consumers the freedom to make this decision by means of their choices to buy cars or else buy commuter rail passes and train tickets? If the consumer desire for trains exists, then the private market will invest in rail, because consumer demand will make it profitable. And if the consumer demand isn't there, then government investment in rail is an inefficient waste of our scarce resources, because the people don't want trains and wouldn't freely choose to buy train tickets.

CHAPTER TWENTY SIX: POLITICAL SCIENCE AND THE SOCIAL SCIENCES, AND USA VS. USSR IN THE 20TH CENTURY

Economics, political science, and the law are generally considered to be "social sciences." The problem with social science is that it is impossible to run controlled experiments which collect precise empirical data and control for variables, so the social sciences cannot actually use the scientific method. A true science such as physics or chemistry runs a controlled experiment in which a variable is controlled for, and empirical data is analyzed using statistical math to demonstrate what influence the variable has upon the physical phenomena. For example, one subjects one piece of iron to acid and another piece of iron to nothing, and if the iron dissolves under acid but remains stable in the absence of acid, and one runs the same experiment enough times to be statistically significant and reliably accurate, then it offers support for a hypothesis that acid causes iron the melt. The social sciences simply cannot do something like such an experiment, because it would be both extremely unethical and pragmatically impossible to use human beings to experimentally control for variables like economic deregulation or tax increases.

How can the social sciences employ the principles of the scientific method when we cannot run experiments to test social science hypotheses? The best attempt at doing something modeled upon the scientific method is to look at history and historical data, which was reliably collected and is broad enough to be statistically significant, and then use "a posteriori" after-the-fact analysis using statistical math, combined with analytical deductive reasoning, to attempt to explain what are the causes which produced the trends and structures which can be seen in the historical data. Such is already the basic methodology employed by many economists and professors of political science. The unfortunate and serious mistake made by economists and data-driven political scientists is to think that economics and politics can actually use the scientific method in its pure form.

For the reason just explained, the social sciences will never be true sciences, and the social scientific method should be a combination of data and analysis, a marriage of statistical math as well as logical deduction from first principles. Because in the social sciences controlled experiments are impossible, data sets in the social sciences will always admit of competing interpretations, and different competing interpretations will often find support in the same set of data. Therefore only analytical deductive reasoning will be able to go into the areas where interpretations compete and the data is ambivalent in order to answer the question of what is the true answer to a hotly debated social sciences question.

The closest thing to a controlled experiment testing capitalism vs. Marxism/socialism is the United States of America vs. the USSR, i.e. Communist Russia, during the Twentieth Century, circa 1900 to 2000. Called "the noble experiment" by Marxists at its founding, the USSR under Stalin became a brutal dictatorship, in which secret police terrorized the people and the leaders used mass imprisonment of political dissenters to solidify their power. By many historical accounts, most of the Russian people hated the USSR, and the USSR ultimately collapsed due to economic inefficiency and poverty combined with the people's hatred of their government. By contrast, America survived. The United States also achieved some level of freedom and political satisfaction, combined with a vast increase in prosperity and growth in the standard of living, when the USA in year 1900 is compared with the USA in year 2000. Periods of recession existed in America, such as the 1930's Great Depression and the 1970's Stagflation, but by and large America was more successful than the USSR.

It is impossible to scientifically determine which precise features of the American political/economic structure were the causes of American success, because America used a mixture of free market capitalism and welfare liberalism, to say nothing of actual socialism during the New Deal, during the 1900-2000 era in question. The Twentieth Century included liberal Democrats like FDR, JFK, and LBJ, as well as conservative Republicans like Eisenhower and Nixon, and the conservative/libertarian Ronald Reagan.

Liberals say that the 1929 stock market crash was the result of an unregulated stock market, and the stock market crash caused the Great Depression. They also say that FDR's New Deal ended the Great Depression. Libertarians say that the Great Depression was triggered by a run on the banks caused by the Federal Reserve's tightening of the money supply, that the Great Depression was made worse by the New Deal, and that the economic impact of World War II and Eisenhower's post-war rebuilding programs was the root cause of the long-term recovery.

Let me note the liberal vs. libertarian explanation of the post-2008 Great Recession also. The liberals say that unregulated Wall Street trading of mortgage-backed credit default swaps caused the Great Recession, and Obama's liberal policy, such as the

Dodd-Frank Wall Street Reform Act and Obamacare, will end it. Libertarians say that government guarantees for subprime loans through the federal agencies Fannie Mae and Freddie Mac caused the widespread phenomenon of home loans being issued which were beyond the borrower's ability to repay, which caused the subprime mortgage crisis, leading to the bursting of the real estate bubble which caused the Great Recession. We think Obama's Dodd-Frank Wall Street Reform Act has made the Great Recession worse. Only libertarianism can end the Great Recession and achieve a long-term sustained recovery, which might result from the influence of the Tea Party-controlled House of Representatives and their "Sequester" austerity measures.

You can take any given decade of the Twentieth Century and make a liberal argument or a libertarian argument about what the facts are and what the facts show, but the overall trend of the 100 year period from 1900 to 2000 favors the libertarian historical economic interpretation. The social sciences cannot control for variables in experiments, so a general experience-based analysis using enough factual data to approximate statistical significance, such as "The USA vs. the USSR in the Twentieth Century," is the best we can achieve at approximating the scientific method in the social sciences. And this "experimental economic history" showed that capitalism, in general, is superior to a planned economy, in general. But let me be the first to concede that America was not, and has never been, pure capitalism, so the experiment is not pure and perfect, and it can only suggest mere inferences, without offering hard scientific proof. But we must concede that is all that the social sciences can ever do, if we are honest about the limitations of our methods.

CHAPTER TWENTY
SEVEN: THE PSYCHOLOGY
OF SOCIALISM

Everyone knows the explicit, logical, reasoned arguments in favor of socialism. Here I offer a "realist" analysis which explores the deep psychological factors that drive people to embrace socialism.

The appeal of socialism stems from a desire for what socialism promises, but also from a hatred of capitalism and everything that the profit motive represents. To the working class and the poor, capitalism and money have come to represent the condition of poverty. If we are to be honest, we must recognize that being poor is horrific, that for some people to not have enough money to buy food to eat or the goods and services necessary to enjoy life is a totally unacceptable tragedy, and also that it is sheer torture to have to work a job that you hate in order to survive. The great con game of the socialists is to trick the working class into believing that the condition of poverty comes from capitalism, rather than from scarce resources on planet Earth or from bad government policy that mismanages the economy and destroys wealth.

The socialists appeal to the pain and sadness of the working class and manipulate them into seeking to alter the metaphysical nature of reality through transforming the economy from capitalism to socialism. The socialists preach the belief that eliminating money will eliminate hunger and poverty and want and need, which will change the world so that nobody will need to do hard work in order to survive, and so that the risk of failure will cease to exist. The poor see that they have little and the rich have plenty, so they reach a simple-minded, naïve conclusion that their poverty could be eliminated by taking wealth from the rich and giving it to the poor. Libertarian economics has adequately demonstrated that socialism will destroy all wealth and crush the standard of living for everyone, but reason and logic have a difficult time fighting the emotional appeal based on the agony of the working class. To the extent that the human brain makes decisions based on emotions and not reason, libertarianism must paint a compelling, beautiful picture of what life will be like for everyone, including the poor, once freedom from government interference is achieved.

Other elements to the psychological appeal of socialism also exist. The hatred of money is frequently hatred of the physical world and of the fact that human beings are fallible human brains in mortal vulnerable human bodies. Money represents physical wealth and material success, and many people are angry that they live in a physical world and not a perfect spiritual world, so they blame money for their sadness and anger. Unfortunately for these people, destroying money and capitalism does not destroy the physical world, it merely destroys a lot of wealth while leaving the root cause of their frustrations intact.

As argued elsewhere, money is an illusion, it hides the fact that what is happening in a capitalist economy is production, trade and consumption. Only altering human nature so that people don't need to have food and shelter, or moving to a planet where resources aren't scarce, or changing reality so that wishes are granted by magic and money grows on trees, could give these miserable people what they really want. The free market, on the other hand, is capable of producing more wealth and a higher standard of living for the poor and lower middle class, which would cheer most people up if the "invisible hand" were allowed to function properly.

Envy is another key psychological factor for leftism. The poor wish that they were rich and successful, so they direct their envy, jealousy and resentment towards people who are richer and more successful and have more money than they do. The poor know that socialism would take away wealth from the rich, and the working poor are manipulated by socialist hate into wanting to tear down the happy rich by destroying capitalism, instead of seeking to become happy themselves. Capitalism offers economic opportunity to the poor by giving them the freedom to work hard and rise to the middle class, so the poor could direct their energy towards achieving success instead of pouring fuel onto the fires of hatred. It should be obvious to any emotionally mature person that if you direct spite and hate towards other people you can tear down other people but you will never make yourself happy by doing so. Instead you will merely achieve a result where both you and everyone else are sad. The alternative to envy is to let other people be successful but to also strive for success in your own life so that both you and others are happy and content.

The basic economic principle that "you cannot consume what you have not produced," or, more accurately stated, "you cannot consume what has not been produced, therefore either you consume what you have produced, or else you consume what someone else produced, whether given to you as a gift or stolen from others by force, or else you don't consume," comes from the nature of physical existence. Socialists appeal to the psychological weaknesses of those people who hate the nature of reality and wish it were different. I call the hatred of the metaphysical nature of reality and of human nature, disguised as a hate directed towards money and capitalism, by the name "worker's rage." No external cure for worker's rage exists, since we can't change reality, and biology has not yet achieved a technology of genetics which can evolve our brain's DNA to eliminate the neurology of suffering and sadness. Worker's rage can only be alleviated by creating more wealth to increase our material happiness, or by a philosophical and psychological acceptance of the harsh conditions of life in our Universe.

Socialists argue that the poor do not have true economic freedom because they are not free to choose to buy expensive luxury items, so only the rich have true freedom to choose. This is perhaps an honest description, but in its underlying premises it is untrue, and it mischaracterizes the nature of economics and the policy choices available to us. Expensive items are expensive not because they are a privilege belonging to the rich, but simply because it is in their nature to be highly desirable, which causes supply and demand to set them at a price where one must trade away a lot in order to receive them. If greater value were not more expensive than lesser value (e.g. higher vs. lower quality), then the price system would not function properly to send signals of supply and demand. Something being expensive expresses the fact that it is highly desirable, i.e. it has a high demand relative to supply, and desire comes from the nature of economic reality, and is not imposed artificially by capitalism.

For example, a trip on a plane is scarcer and more valuable than a trip to the corner store in a car, so a plane ticket is more expensive than a tank of gas. Thus, expensiveness and cheapness is itself the price we must pay for the free market to function. Yachts and mansions are expensive merely because they are in short supply and produce a high degree of satisfaction. If entrepreneurs were to develop means of making many more of them, and producing them more cheaply, then supply would increase and price would fall, as happened for televisions and washing machines and cars, all of which were once expensive luxury items owned only by the super-rich. The culprit for expensiveness is not capitalism, it is reality, in which resources are scarce.

Similarly, socialists view the principle of "buy low, sell high" as an imperative to screw people over, since people are encouraged to sell things for more than what they are really worth in order to maximize profits. On the contrary, it merely encourages people to do the most with the least, which describes economic efficiency and the maximally efficient use of limited resources, which is necessary for human survival on planet Earth.

Lastly on this point, socialists hate the fact that many workers must work tough, sweaty, difficult jobs for long hours for relatively low pay, including jobs where people risk death. But this work must get done, it is the work that enables the human race to survive and produces the goods and services which make life bearable, and the human race needs a lot of people to do this type of work, and scarce resources mean that there isn't enough money in the world for everyone to be paid a high wage. This situation is unavoidable in the context of life on Earth during our relatively un-evolved, low technological progress, uncivilized phase of the evolution and development of the human species. If money and capitalism did not exist then we would still need janitors and store cashiers and factory assembly workers and truck drivers and coal miners. Under socialism, resources would remain too scarce to pay them all high income salaries. But under socialism their salaries (and all other economic transactions) would not be paid as efficiently as happens under a free market system.

The capitalist ruthless relentless ambition to make money and the drive to "sell, sell, sell" is not mere greed. It is the desire to produce as much as possible and trade as much as possible in order to consume as much as possible. It is natural to want to be happy, and material comfort is the type of happiness which the human brain most easily recognizes. Therefore the profit motive is not "greed," in the bad sense of that word. The profit motive is merely the natural human desire for happiness.

CHAPTER TWENTY EIGHT: DO RICH PEOPLE DESERVE TO BE RICH?

In order to justify a system of ownership of private property in which people are allowed to be rich, do we need to say that rich people deserve to be rich? Does the justification for private property depend upon the concept of earning wealth and deserving to own the results produced by your work? And, if so, can we actually look at the facts and the evidence and say that most rich people deserve to be rich, and do not owe their wealth to mere good luck? Obviously ownership of property cannot be justified entirely on the basis of possession, because if it was then a thief who stole a car would own the car because he possesses it. So some sort of understanding of ownership as the result of productivity and doing work to create value is necessary. But on the other hand, the fact that a person was born is the result of good luck, and the fact that a person exists on Earth is a matter of chance for which no individual can be responsible, and all ownership exists in the context of a person having been born into life on Earth. Therefore a person cannot be denied ownership entirely on the basis that he did not create the value of what he owns and that his property is due to good luck and not to his effort.

The theory of ownership of private property which addresses these concerns is the theory which I presented in the Introduction to this book, namely, that a person earns ownership of the value which they create when they mix their labor with the raw materials in nature. A person's labor, including his effort, his work, and his choices, is something for which he is personally responsible, and as such he causes his labor to exist and he earns and deserves the results of what he produces. But the materials into which his labor is mixed in order to produce value are the result of good luck, not personal achievement. If an artist comes across a lump of clay in the woods, and she molds it into a bowl, then she owns the bowl as private property because she created it through mixing her labor into the clay. She owns it, even though having the lump of clay to begin with was sheer good luck. And in a real economy, the materials into which we mix our labor should be thought of not as lumps of natural clay out in an untamed forest, but as the entirety of whatever the economy gives us as the tools, means and resources with which we can be productive.

A person mixes his effort with what exists out in the world, including knowledge, teachings, the goods and services of others which can be employed in new productive ventures, as well as the various raw materials that can be transformed into manufactured goods. Private property is produced when a person mixes his labor into preexisting materials in order to produce a new value, a new good or service. The person is individually responsible for his labor, but good luck is the cause of the raw materials into which his labor is mixed. Thus, good luck does not negate a person earning and deserving to own what he created, so long as he mixed his labor into the materials that were given to him by good luck.

If a rich person does productive work to make money, then he has the right to own his wealth, even if good luck gave him advantages which helped him to get rich, provided that he actually mixed his productive labor into the physical material of reality in order to create the value which he claims ownership of. For example, if an artist finds a lump of clay that is naturally red then it will be easier for her to sculpt a model red sports car using that clay than if the clay had been naturally gray. But this good luck would not mean that the artist does not own her sculpture of a red car or that she does not deserve to own it. She owns it because she created it, even though she created it out of red clay which she found in nature as a result of her good luck.

Ownership must be reconciled with a mixture of individual responsibility combined with good luck in order for ownership to be justified, because, as a practical matter, it is impossible to examine each item of property owned by every person and evaluate whether or not they created it by good work or were given it by good luck, or, if they possess it due to a combination of good work and good luck, then what is the portion attributable to their labor and what to good luck. Any economic theory which might seek to tax income to the extent attributable to good luck and leave as owned that portion which is actually earned would collapse into socialism, because no precise calculation of that kind can be made.

Having established that ownership is justified and that the rich should own their wealth, we must next ask: as a practical matter and a question of empirical fact, do rich people actually deserve to be rich? The answer to that question is quite complicated. The existence of many poor and working class people throughout American history who rose to success and became self-made rich proves that America is not a caste class system. But the existence of the self-made rich does not prove that economic status is the result only of good work and not good luck, because for every self-made rich person, we can also find a rich person who inherited their wealth and privilege. But also, just as many poor people are born into poverty, many poor people exist who experienced good luck at some point but made bad choices that contributed to their economic failure, such as alcohol abuse and drug addiction, or simply not having the ambition to do well in high school and go to college in order to get a better job.

Some poor people are born into poor inner city areas and are sent to failing public schools which don't give them the job skills for high-paying jobs, and their families can't afford to send them to college. One can say that bad luck condemned these people to poverty and they are not to blame for being poor. But other poor people really are lazy and stupid. For example, many poor people let themselves get caught in alcohol and drug abuse, which lowers IQ and destroys ambition and motivation. Drugs are addictive and useful for coping with the sadness of poverty, but drug use is something that any given person has the power to avoid if he/she makes disciplined decisions, because drugs are not usually forced onto people and people use drugs because they choose to do so. If it is possible for a poor person to do well in school and seek better job skills through higher education, if it is possible to avoid doing drugs and to stay clean and sober, and if it is possible for a person who does good work in a working class job to impress his/her employer and get promoted, e.g. from cashier to shift supervisor, then poor people have the ability to rise to the lower middle class by means of hard work and good decisions. If that is true then, although it seems cruel to say this, in the sense of being personally responsible for their condition the poor deserve to be poor.

On the other hand, relatively few rich people exist in the world as compared to the poor. But of the people who are wealthy, a lot of them inherited some or all of their wealth, and many were born into rich families with rich parents who sent them to good schools and used legacy admissions to get them into top universities. Good luck set many wealthy people on the path to success, so one could say that they did not earn their wealth and they do not really deserve to be rich. But many rich people also exist who are self-made, who were born into poverty but rose to wealth through their own efforts, and the self-made rich have historically always existed in America. In the 1800s there were notable poor people who became very wealthy, like Andrew Carnegie, and in the contemporary USA there continue to be people who succeed by means of their intelligence and determination, like the billionaire founders of Google and Facebook and Twitter. If a person rises from the lower or middle class to the upper class, as many entrepreneurs in capitalist economies have done, then they made their money and they deserve to be rich. And if such a person leaves his wealth to his heirs, be they his wife, children, or grandchildren, then it seems reasonable to say that because the fortune was earned and the person who made money chose to give his fortune to his heirs that they also deserve to be rich.

The issue of good work vs. good luck is further complicated by the fact that government's interference in the economy is involuntary against the people it affects, and therefore government help or harm is not earned or deserved, and is unfair. Many rich people get rich through corporate welfare, meaning that their businesses do deals with the government or benefit from various laws, such as the bailout of the auto industry and AIG, or farm subsidies to rich corn farmers, or billions of military spending to defense contractors. The rich have the money to hire lobbyists and give campaign contributions, and therefore the rich, be they Democrats or Republicans, have an inherent advantage over the poor and middle class in every area where government officials make decisions. Some rich people deliberately milk the American taxpayer through pork barrel spending, while other rich people benefit unfairly through no fault of their own.

For example, the fact that rich children can attend good private schools while many poor children are trapped in the government-enforced failing public school systems gives rich children an unfair advantage over poor children, although in this case the blame rests with government policy, not with the rich themselves. Rich children attending private schools is an "unfair" advantage, not in the sense that it is unfair for a rich child to be able to buy better things than a poor child could buy, but in the sense that the government has used violent force to take over the public school system and destroy all merit-based competition in the delivery of education from teachers to poor children, and the poor were helpless to prevent this. Similarly, the government can unfairly hurt the poor, as for example if the United States' irrational, cruel drug policy puts a poor person in jail on a drug charge, which could plunge the family of the jailed person into poverty if he/she had supported his/her family, and being in jail for years turns people into hardened criminals, introduces them to gangs, etc. Government public schools and zoning laws can turn neighborhoods into poverty traps, and minimum wage laws eliminate potential low-income jobs, and the poor who are victims of government activity cannot justly be said to be at fault for their plight.

Even this description is not as detailed and complex as reality. In fact, a rich person could have been born into wealth but made use of his/her good luck in attending a top-ranked private school to work very hard to get good grades and get a good university education which then gives him/her job skills for a profession that generally pays a high salary such as law or medicine or science, and to make breakthroughs in his/her chosen field through determination and intelligence and talent. In that case his/her success is partly due to good luck and partly due to good work. And a poor person might be born into poverty, but then use his/her bad luck as an excuse to give up and be lazy and not struggle and fight to try to rise to the middle class, and perhaps also have the bad luck of being around drug addicts among parents, friends or family, and then make the individual choice to give in to peer pressure and do drugs or drink liquor and then spiral into drug addiction or alcoholism. In this case the poor person's economic failure is partly due to bad personal decisions and partly due to bad luck and circumstances. This is the reality that is true for most people, both rich and poor, and human achievement is a spectrum with work at one end and luck at the other end, with most people falling somewhere along the middle between these two extremes.

Do the rich deserve to be rich? Are the poor helpless victims? The real answer is that some rich people deserve to be rich and earned wealth through good work, but some rich got rich through good luck or corporate welfare, and some rich owe their wealth to a mixture of factors including good work, good luck, and unfair advantage due to government. Some poor are to blame for their poverty and could have done better by working harder, and some poor were helpless victims, and some poor were screwed over by government policy, and some poor owe their situation to a mixture of various factors including all those described. Empirical data cannot accurately map what caused what for who, and who falls into which category, because the hard data to prove this cannot be measured, other than possibly by intensive academic scrutiny making case studies of a handful of study subjects. The conservative answer that the rich are hardworking geniuses who deserve to succeed and the poor are lazy idiots who are to blame for their poverty, or the liberal answer that the rich all had incredible good luck and the poor are helpless victims, are both far too simplistic to accurately describe reality.

Let me conclude this section with an answer to another question: what do we mean by "doing work"? Doing work, as I understand it, consists of five basic components: (1) physical labor, (2) mental labor, which consists of paying attention to what you are doing and concentrating and not getting distracted, as well as, more generally, employing one's brain and cognitive resources productivity, (3) math and science work, (4) social interaction, persuasion, human relations/people skills, and talking and listening, and (5) thinking and planning, which includes thinking about what you are doing under a long-range big picture view, and anticipating risks in order to avoid problems before they happen.

Assuming a worker/employee vs. entrepreneur/small businessman vs. upper management/owner/investor distinction, it seems clear that (usually) the employees do 1 (physical labor), 2 (mental labor), 3 (math/science), and 4 (human interaction), the entrepreneur or small business owner or floor manager might do all five, and the investor, owner or upper management does only 5 (thinking and planning), and perhaps 4 (social interaction). Contrary to the liberal belief, it is clear that upper management, businessmen, owners, and learned professions like lawyers and doctors, do a lot of very difficult, important, challenging intellectual work, although their work is not mainly physical labor. But, although a rich successful businessman works his ass off, so too does a janitor or a store cashier. The three qualities which enable a person to do work are: (1) experience and knowledge, (2) talent/intelligence, and (3) discipline/work ethic. An examination of work shows that rich people and poor workers do different types of work, but they both do productive work, and most owners and workers earn the money that they make.

CHAPTER TWENTY NINE: FINANCIAL RESPONSIBILITY

The recent recession, which some call the Great Recession, has been around for years, yet it simply refuses to go away. I believe that American business is strong enough that not even Obama's socialist agenda can permanently destroy our prosperity. But even if a Republican President is elected and this recession ends, what is to prevent another one?

The question of what causes recessions is perhaps the single most important and most highly political question that the science of economics seeks to answer. The Keynesians and socialists have one answer, the Austrians have quite another. Perhaps the Federal Reserve's manipulation of interest rates has caused or exacerbated the recession. However, I think that from an empirical, factual standpoint the linchpin of the Great Recession was the American public's financial irresponsibility, as manifested in the collapse of the real estate bubble.

Many thousands of Americans irrationally believed that home prices could only go up, and they incurred real estate mortgage indebtedness far in excess of what a financially responsible person would incur. When real estate prices collapsed, very many mortgages went into default, which led to foreclosure sales, which further reduced home values, which triggered a downward spiral. It is probably true that government efforts to encourage low-income home ownership and government home mortgage guarantees contributed to inflating the real estate bubble. But the disaster would not have been so widespread if more home buyers had been committed to living within their means or had been more risk-averse.

This is the most dangerous error, and also the easiest to correct. If the American public, especially the lower middle class, learned to understand the concept of "financial responsibility" then this syndrome would never happen again.

What precisely is financial responsibility? I think that the main point that people should understand is that money does not grow on trees, and there is no such thing as a free lunch or easy money, and that money is not magical and cannot be created by waving a magic wand. The great Randian contribution to economic theory is the idea that in a free market people trade value for value, and to "make money" is to create value. (Yes, Ayn Rand did not invent this idea, but she perfected it.) In order to make money you have to do work to produce the value; in other words, you need to make the money that you trade with others when you buy things from them. If you don't produce value, then you have nothing to trade.

This not only means that people earn and deserve their salary by working at their job; it also means that people do not deserve to consume more value than what the other traders in the free market are willing to purchase in exchange for money. "From each as he chooses, to each as he is chosen," to quote a Robert Nozick saying that captures this concept.

Financial responsibility is the understanding that you cannot spend more money than the amount you earned because of the work you did, unless someone gives you charity or you steal wealth from others, and that you cannot consume a value that has not been produced by someone. To use Rand's phrasing, you can't have your cake and eat it too, or as I would prefer to say, you can't eat your cake before you bake it. Understand this, and you will probably not spend money that you don't have or use borrowed money to buy stuff when you can't repay your loans. If you want to buy something, then you will be more likely to do the work necessary to earn the money before trying to get what you want.

This understanding that money is finite and must be created before it can be spent is the essence of financial responsibility. Implicit in the concept, however, is the notion that charity and theft are exceptions, and the general rule is that you, and only you, must do what is necessary to make your own money and control your individual financial destiny.

But if you understand this principle then you will be very careful about economic risk, because you will understand that you will be required to assume responsibility if you make a mistake. You will be on the hook for your losses and no government will bail you out. Financial responsibility means being held responsible, which means that you are held accountable and you will accept the rewards and punishments that result from your economic choices. Thus, you will not assume risks in excess of the amount of sweat or skill you are willing to put in to compensate for your mistakes. A person who is financially responsible would not assume a gigantic mortgage on real estate if he had an annual income in the lower-middle class range, because he would understand that the debt would actually need to be repaid.

It seems to me that the solution to the problem is for high schools or colleges to incorporate personal finance management training into their liberal arts educations. Simply teaching people how to write up a personal budget that matches income and expenditures, and keeping a running record of expenses, would go far toward creating the practical skills of financial responsibility. Some high schools have such classes, but they are treated like trivial afterthoughts compared to the more important subjects. Also, merely teaching students how to spend money is not enough; the financial responsibility class would somehow have to simulate earning income in proportion to productivity, possibly by tying fake money to GPA or class performance, to give students a feel for the fact that you cannot spend what you have not earned. The ideal personal finance class would teach career ambition, how to budget to spend within your means, and the crucial importance of saving money and not borrowing beyond your ability to repay.

One would expect the poor to appreciate the crucial importance of saving money. But it is precisely the low-income families that are most vulnerable to financial irresponsibility. The poor face a dark temptation to borrow beyond their ability to repay and not worry about repayment until it is too late, so that for a short time they can live a more affluent lifestyle before their debts catch up with them. The temptation to take shortcuts to one's desires is deeply seductive even to rational, honest people. But people with no money to spare can least afford to make mistakes. Good finance classes in high school would help poor families budget properly, save for retirement, and avoid predatory lenders. This would help the poor much more than all the liberal nonsense of entitlement spending, welfare, food stamps, consumer lending regulators, etc.

Middle- and upper-income people could also benefit. A 2009 study cited on Yahoo claims that the average New Yorker is $200,000 in debt and the average Californian is $300,000 in debt. The American economic system encourages credit card debt, home mortgage debt, and student loan debt. I personally have struggled with handling my finances, which were made worse in 2011 by roughly $90,000 in law school student loans that I needed to incur; and I wish that there had been a serious class in this subject that I could have taken, particularly in college where young people are supposed to learn how to live like adults. When I say that ignorance regarding financial responsibility causes suffering and crisis for borrowers, I speak from personal experience, as well as a macroeconomic analysis of the recession.

If such personal finance classes were commonly available, the average American would actually be exposed to the concept of financial responsibility, and the odds of another recession happening would be greatly reduced. If it were customary for every American student to take a class in financial responsibility, it would be more likely for voters to vote for financially responsible fiscal policy. And if American politicians had taken such classes, they might have better training in the art of living within a budget and be more appreciative of a balanced budget and the dangers of excessive debt and irresponsible spending.

Of course, if the public were financially responsible, it would not put up with a government that steals money from others or borrows excessively and spends money that it does not have. So the leftist college professors who control most colleges and the teachers' unions who control the high schools would fight to keep people from understanding the truth about financial responsibility and how to prevent another recession. But while government is the primary source of economic problems, even in a libertarian anarchy recessions would still exist if the majority of individuals were financially irresponsible.

CHAPTER THIRTY: VOLUNTARY LIBERALS AND VOLUNTARY CONSERVATIVES

GOLD does not tell you what specifically to do or to believe, it only tells you that you should have the freedom to do what you want and to believe what you want, and to respect that freedom for others as well. Thus, in theory, it would be possible to be a "voluntary" liberal or conservative, someone who was a liberal or conservative but who followed GOLD. For example, a voluntary conservative could oppose abortion but would recognize that women own their bodies and can't be forced to bear an unwanted pregnancy even if abortion would terminate a human life. He or she would seek to prevent abortions by persuading women to freely choose to bear their pregnancies rather than by passing laws outlawing abortion clinics. The same would be true regarding prostitution; the conservative would oppose it through persuasion and not through legislation.

Similarly, a voluntary liberal might feel that the working class poor are exploited by the rich and that charity should be given to the poor, but he/she would donate to the poor using his/her own money and would not steal other people's money to help the poor through tax-funded government welfare. Or if the voluntary liberal believes in "fair trade" which gives favorable terms to sellers in poor foreign countries then he or she could choose to only buy fair trade goods and to only shop at businesses which respect his/her ideals, but he or she would not use the law to force other people to do so. This analysis fleshes out a picture of the scope and limits of GOLD as a political philosophy.

PART THREE: LEGAL LIBERTARIANISM

CHAPTER THIRTY ONE: THE LIBERTARIAN INTERPRETATION OF THE UNITED STATES CONSTITUTION

The libertarian interpretation of the United States Constitution deduces conclusions about the Constitution using deductive inferences from the First Amendment, the Fourth, Fifth and Sixth Amendments, the Takings Clause, the Commerce Clause (Article I, Section 8, Clause 3), the Taxing Clause (Article I, Section 8, Clause 1), and the Sixteenth Amendment. The First Amendment protects freedom of speech and freedom of the press. The Fourth, Fifth and Sixth Amendments are the Bill of Rights criminal procedure sections, which protects our civil liberties. In other words, those Amendments place limits on what the police can do to the people, place limits on when and how the police may search people or houses or property, gives rights to criminal defendants, etc. The Commerce Clause gives the federal government the right to regulate "interstate commerce." The Takings Clause says that the government may not take private property for public use without giving just compensation to the owner. And the Taxing Clause gives the federal government the power to tax, augmented by the Sixteenth Amendment which explicitly authorizes the federal income tax.

The libertarian constitutional argument infers a conclusion as a matter of deductive logic from two premises, which I discuss separately. The first premise is that the U.S. Constitution creates freedom and is incompatible with dictatorship. The second premise is that socialism leads to dictatorship and freedom requires capitalism.

First Premise: Freedom vs. Dictatorship. Freedom of speech and of the press represents the right of the citizens to dissent and criticize the government. Assuming that free speech and free press are the tools that the people use to muster support when they seek to force the government to do what they want and abandon bad policies, the First Amendment is essential to a society where the people have the power of self-government, and the First Amendment is incompatible with a dictatorship where the government is not controlled by the desires of the people. Limits on the police and limits upon the ability of the police to search the citizens represent the freedom to do what you want without the government snooping around and seeing what you are doing in order to manage your behaviors. Freedom from a secret police is not a judicially invented "penumbra right to privacy" never mentioned in the Constitution, instead is it a plain, clear, obvious direct inference from the text of the Fourth Amendment.

The plain meaning of the text of the Constitution, as a document that defines a republican democracy where the lawmakers are elected by vote, shows that the American system is one designed to give freedom to the American people. I define political "freedom" to mean that power belongs to the people, and that the people have the right to govern themselves, and not to be governed by an elitist class of experts and rulers, or a king, or a dictator using a secret police and censors, who search us and control us and stifle our dissent. A dictator must violate the free speech and free press guaranteed by the First Amendment, and a dictator must also use secret police who will breach the civil liberties promised in the Fourth, Fifth and Sixth Amendments, because those are the most natural tools for a dictator to use to prevent rebellion and rule his subjects. Therefore, under the Bill of Rights, and also under the system of republican democracy whereby power is vested in elected representatives, the U.S. Constitution is incompatible with dictatorship.

Second Premise: Capitalism as Freedom. As famous libertarian economist and Nobel Prize winner F.A. Hayek argued in "The Road to Serfdom," and as economist Milton Friedman, who also won the Nobel, showed in "Capitalism and Freedom," liberalism will inevitably evolve over the course of decades or centuries into democratic socialism, which within a few generations will slide down a slippery slope to dictatorial Marxism. This is unavoidable because liberalism is watered down socialism in moderation, and socialism concedes Marxist principles and the Marxist ideology that the government's job is to protect the people from the businessmen. Socialism and Marxism naturally create a dictatorship with secret police and no freedom of the press nor freedom of speech, because if the economy is managed by a boss with a plan for the economy, then the boss will need the power to force people to obey him in order to make his plan work, and dissent and disobedience are incompatible with the boss's need for control to implement his plan.

Logical Conclusion: the libertarian argument. Capitalism is the alternative to a planned economy. A planned economy will lead to a dictatorship. The U.S. Constitution is incompatible with dictatorship. Therefore the Constitution is incompatible with socialist or liberal economics, which means that the Constitution implicitly specifies a distinctly capitalist economy. Such an interpretation of the intent of the Founding Fathers who drafted the Constitution is confirmed by the Takings Clause, because it would be impossible to achieve a socialist/Marxist nationalization of all private property, which is the end goal of the liberal Left, without violating the Takings Clause. The Takings Clause codifies the concept of private property, which forms the basis of capitalism.

To put this argument in terms of GOLD, the U.S. Constitution is a GOLD document because it protects the freedom necessary for and intrinsic to GOLD, such as free speech (the First Amendment), freedom from searches by a secret police (the Fourth Amendment), and freedom not have the government take private property at will (the Takings Clause). The Constitution is incompatible with EVIL because EVIL in moderation will inevitably collapse into total EVIL. The spirit of the American Revolution and of the United States is GOLD, the spirit of freedom in which each person is free to do what he or she wants without other people or the government forcing you to do something else that you don't want to do.

The most important basis for the Constitution as GOLD comes not from the text of any clause but from the structure of the document itself, because the Constitution limits the government to a set of explicitly defined powers and implies that the government has only those powers and it lacks the power to do anything else or to do whatever it wants to the people without the people's consent. The many laws passed by Congress which embrace the principle of EVIL, and which twist and torture the text of the Constitution in order to claim un-enumerated powers, are in contradiction to the fundamental vision of the American Founding Fathers who drafted the Constitution as a tool to protect the rights of the people to life, liberty and property. The purpose of the Constitution is to protect the people from the government by means of the law, which is an inherently libertarian idea.

However, the U.S. Constitution does authorize taxing and spending, and it also allows regulation of the economy: the Commerce Clause, the Taxing Clause, and the Sixteenth Amendment quite openly state the government's right to regulate, tax, and spend, so the Constitution authorizes a minarchy, i.e. it justifies the existence of a small government with limited powers but does not require anarchy and the total end of government. This was made quite explicit in the Federalist Papers, as the argument between the federalists who favored the ratification of the Constitution, and the anti-federalists who opposed it, was really a debate between the libertarian minarchists (those who want a small government) and libertarian anarchists (those who want no government at all) of that era, and the minarchists won.

The only real question is whether "interstate" commerce includes purely local activity. In the 1700's, when the U.S. Constitution was drafted, most economic activity was local activity within towns and villages which were distantly connected by horses and ships. In today's economy all economic activity is interconnected at the national level by the internet, highways, planes and rail, so a reading of the Commerce Clause which authorizes federal government regulation of the entire American economy is plausible under the theory that every local economy is connected to the national economy.

However, the better argument looks at the text to infer the true meaning. The language of the Commerce Clause grants two powers, (1) the power to regulate commerce among the several states and (2) the power to regulate commerce with foreign nations, using precisely the same words to grant both powers. So the federal government's power to go within the economy of an individual state is the same as its power to go into the economy of a foreign country, meaning that the Constitution did not grant the power to regulate any commerce within a state, and the Commerce Clause was intended to mean only that the feds may regulate goods and services which cross state lines, and only while they are crossing state lines. Such an interpretation can successfully eliminate all the vagueness and confusion regarding the meaning of the Commerce Clause, and this would limit the government to the economic regulatory power that the Framers accepted as constitutional during their own era.

A corollary libertarian interpretation exists, which is worth mentioning here. Conservatives argue that the United States Supreme Court's use of a "penumbra right to privacy," which is never explicitly granted in the Constitution's text, in order to judicially create the right to use sexual contraception, the right to have an abortion, the right to gay sexuality, and, perhaps, the right to gay marriage, finds no textual basis in the words of the Constitution. But the conservative reading simply ignores, and refuses to look at, the Ninth and Tenth Amendments. The Ninth and Tenth Amendments state that every right which is not given to the federal government remains with the states or with the people. Therefore, like all other individual rights, the right to have an abortion remains with the American people because the government did not receive an explicit grant in the Constitution to regulate it or ban it. The conservatives argue that if the Constitution did not mention abortion then the states are free to regulate it, but the Ninth and Tenth Amendments create the opposite presumption, that the government may not violate any individual rights unless the grant to do so is given in explicit constitutional text.

Nowhere in the U.S. Constitution does the text say that the government has the right to ban abortions, or to regulate marriage, or to criminalize recreational drug usage, or to regulate prescription medications. Under the constitutional presumption of the Ninth and Tenth Amendments, if the text doesn't specifically say that the government may do it then the government cannot do it. The United States Supreme Court has held the Ninth and Tenth Amendments to be a "truism" or a "nullity" and to have no legal impact, and the Court protects individual rights using the Due Process Clauses. However, the Supreme Court was never given the authority to amend the Constitution, so it lacks the authority to choose not to enforce Amendments IX and X, and those Amendments offer a textual basis for social liberty, which is as clear as many other legal interpretations that are widely accepted as settled law.

The debate between conservatives who embrace an "originalist" interpretation of the Constitution that the original meaning of the text controls and we should look back to the colonial era to interpret the text, and liberals who embrace the "Living Constitution" interpretation that the document continuously evolves and we should look at today's world to interpret the text, is highly irrelevant and misplaced. It is moot because the fact is that the meanings of the words in the Constitution, in the English language, have not changed or transformed enough between the Eighteenth and Twenty-First Centuries for the meanings of the text back then to be different from the meaning of the words today. The fight is not really over old meaning vs. new meaning, it is really a fight between leftist desires and right-wing desires for how to make use of the document's meaning, because colonial-era legislators leaned more towards the conservative side and today's modern judges generally lean more towards the liberal side. The interpretational battle is merely a pretext, a duel between conservatives who want to use the Constitution for conservative legal goals, and liberals who seek to squeeze the Constitution into liberal purposes.

The actual meaning of the Constitution gets lost in the partisan arguing, and can only be found by each American citizen actually sitting down with the document and reading the words for himself or herself and thinking about it to individually understand what the document says. The U.S. Constitution is a very short, simple, easy to read document, and so lends itself to direct reading rather than secondhand interpretation from legal "experts." In an ideal world, the U.S. Constitution would be read and referred to in everyday life as frequently as the Bible.

I will proceed to discuss a few more detailed areas of the law which are governed by constitutional clauses.

The First Amendment should be given a stricter and more rigorous application, including both freedom of speech and freedom of religion. The text of the First Amendment uses clearly absolutist language which neither defines, nor implies permission, for exceptions of any kind. The proper test for First Amendment violations is a simple one: "is it censorship?" For example, FCC censorship of curse words on television is censorship, which should be held to violate the First Amendment freedom of speech. The censorship of vulgarity and sexual imagery is censorship, and therefore violates the First Amendment.

And freedom of religion, the separation of church and state, should mean not only that the state cannot officially endorse a state religion, it should also require that no religion may impose its religious moral values upon other people by means of government laws, because so doing would allow the state to make the citizens' decisions for them about which religious values to embrace. State religion makes the church into an agent of the state, but religious laws which legislate morality make the state into an agent of the church, which also violates the separation of church and state. Thus, the social conservative movement, whose goal is to pass laws that legislate conservative traditional Christian morality, actually violates the First Amendment. Religious freedom is obviously what the First Amendment religion clause was intended to protect. This is the most natural, logical reading of the plain meaning of the text of the First Amendment.

In various places in this book I have said that the best tools for protecting oppressed minorities from the violence of majorities, such as protecting gays from gay bashers or blacks from racist whites, is "the ammo box, the jury box, and the ballot box." All three of these tools originate from the Constitution. In a democracy, the people elect their representatives, and the right to elect minority politicians is a right rooted in the structure of the American government. That is the power of the ballot box. Now let me discuss the other two tools.

The plain meaning of the text of the Second Amendment defines the right to bear arms and does not admit of exceptions permitting the government to regulate the right to bear arms by law-abiding citizens. The Second Amendment's text says that the right to bear arms is protected so that citizens may serve in militias to assist in national defense. So it is plausible to say that if convicted criminals or the mentally ill would not be welcome in the armed forces then the government may deny the right to own weapons to criminals convicted of serious crimes of violence and the insane. But the text of the Constitution makes clear that every law-abiding citizen has the constitutionally guaranteed right to own and use a gun.

Obviously the Second Amendment is supported by policy arguments. Gun control strips the law-abiding citizens of their ability to defend themselves, while leaving guns in the hands of the criminals who won't obey gun control laws or any criminal laws. And it robs the people of our independence and empowerment to make us more dependent on the government. But, policy debates aside, the Constitution has already answered this question, and gun control is unconstitutional in the absence of a new amendment.

Note that gun rights are justified under NVP and GOLD because the use of a gun for self-defense, to defend an individual's life liberty and property (which I abbreviate as "LLP"), is legitimate under NVP (the Non-Violence Principle). As long as the gun is not used aggressively against others to violate the LLP of other people, ownership of a gun is considered non-violent under NVP, therefore the government has no right to regulate it. Also, under the Golden Rule, if the government were allowed to disarm the people then the people would be equally justified in disarming the government, which would leave everyone without a means of self-defense. If we abandon the "government as God" complex then we have no reason to believe that individuals within the government would use guns more responsibly than individuals outside the government. So gun control reduces to an absurdity.

A legal procedure which is not widely known by the contemporary general public, but which is dear to the hearts of libertarians, is "jury nullification." Although lawyers generally believe that in a criminal trial the jury decides "the facts" and the judge decides "the law" which is applied to those facts, jury nullification is an exception to that structure. Jury nullification is the right of the jury to disagree with the content of the criminal law applied in the trial and find a not guilty verdict because they believe the facts showed guilt beyond a reasonable doubt but the law is too cruel and unjust to convict and send someone to prison. An example is drug use charges. For example, if owning a dime bag of pot can get someone a mandatory minimum sentence of ten years in jail, and if the jury feels that this law is evil, then jury nullification permits them to find not guilty.

Judges hate jury nullification because it undermines their authority, and the establishment legal profession doesn't believe in it, but a very persuasive constitutional law argument supports it. The argument is that the Bill of Rights explicitly granted the right to a jury trial to criminal defendants, and at the time of the ratification of the Bill of Rights to right to jury nullification was widely understood to be a part of criminal trials by jury, see for example the trial of William Penn. So the drafters would have understood that in enacting the Bill of Rights they codified the right to jury nullification as a right of criminal defendants, and the people of that era would have also understood jury nullification as part of the meaning of the right to jury trial in the text of the Bill of Rights. Therefore jury nullification is constitutionally protected. This theory is further supported because one of the best reasons to have trial by jury instead of trial by judge is so that the people, not the government, are the ones who get to pass judgment. This suggests that the values and feelings of the public are intended to be a part of the jury trial process. Because the criminal law is one of the chief methods by which majorities persecute minorities, e.g. a disproportionate number of people sent to prison are black and poor, jury nullification is a tool for protecting the public from a criminal justice system gone mad. Some judges say that it is undemocratic to have unelected jurors rewrite the criminal laws, but we should not object to a limited exception to legislation whereby a jury can change a finding of guilty to a finding of not guilty, when decades trapped in a jail cell for real people who are truly innocent is at stake.

CHAPTER THIRTY TWO: LEGITIMATE LAWS, PARTICULARLY WITHIN THE COMMON LAW

GOLD sees the purpose of legitimate laws as self-defense, specifically, the defense of the three expressions and requirements of the self: life, liberty, and property. The law defends these three areas as follows:

Life: defended by criminal law and tort law.

Liberty: defended by constitutional law and criminal law

Property: defended by criminal law, tort law, constitutional law, property law and contract law.

The role of constitutional law is to defend the individual from the government, and, as such, it is the primary tool for the defense of liberty in a justice-based legal system. Constitutional law interprets the clauses of the Constitution, which is the legal document that cages the government in a cage made of laws to protect the people from tyranny. I discussed the libertarian interpretation of the Constitution in the previous section. The remainder of this section will discuss the bodies of law commonly known in the American legal system as "the common law," namely criminal law, tort law, property law, and contract law.

The legitimate job of criminal law is defending life, liberty and property from intentional violent force, and the legitimate job of tort law is defending life, liberty and property from accidental violent force. Criminal law protects life from intentional force, e.g. murder, assault, attempted murder, attempted assault. It protects liberty from intentional force, e.g. kidnapping, rape. And it protects property from intentional force, e.g. theft, robbery, burglary.

By contrast, under tort liability, if force damages your life or property as the result of an accident, and you are not at fault, but someone else's choice to be negligent resulted in the risk that caused the accident, so that other person who engaged in risky behavior is to blame, then fairness and justice permit you to recover restitution from the person who is to blame for the accidental harm to your life and property.

Accidental force is a violation of the individual's right to be free from force, and an accident which does violence to the plaintiff and results in harm to the plaintiff entitles the plaintiff to recover. The defendant made a choice to be negligent, which means that he chose to take a risk which caused the accident. The defendant's negligence entitles recovery from that defendant in order to hold him responsible for his actions and his choices. The negligent choice entails blame and the right to recover damages, despite the fact that the violence was accidental and the defendant did not make a choice to intentionally cause the harm.

Property law generally functions to adjudicate and litigate a decision about who owns what piece of property. Ownership is important for the other laws to be able to protect a person's property from theft or accidental damage. For example, prior to a tort lawsuit for damage to a house, the parties would need to litigate a case involving conflicting deeds of title to determine which of two claimants actually owns the parcel of land containing the house. The law can only protect a person's property after property law has resolved the issue of who owns what and whether a person does or does not own the property which he asserts his right to defend.

Contract law makes possible trading in a free market economy. Specifically, a contract is one person giving his promise or something of value (called "performance" by contract lawyers) to someone else in exchange for the other person's promise or performance. When you and your trading partner agree and consent to a trade, each party has the right to enforce the contract against the other, because once the parties agree to and consent to the contract, each party becomes the owner of the property that the contract gave to him, and each party cedes and gives ownership of what he had previously owned to the other party. This is true of physical property, performance, or a pair of promises which are traded one for the other. Thus, when X owns Y, and A owns B, once X and A sign a contract to trade Y for B, then the contract transfers the property and enacts the trade. At the precise moment when the contract takes effect and the trade happens, Y ceases to be X's property and Y becomes A's property, and B ceases to belong to A and now belongs to X. The legal event that happened is a trade, meaning that Y going from X to A is the legal justification for B going from A to X. X executing his end of the trade gives X the right to force A to carry through with A's end of the bargain, and vice versa. This is the rationale of the contract law doctrine called "consideration," which basically says that X may only force A to hand over B if the contract gave Y to A, i.e. if there was a "bargained-for exchange." Consideration makes clear that the trade is the legal basis of a contract.

Once the contract is signed and the trade happened, then X owns B, and X's ownership of B gives X the right to legally defend his ownership of B as the legitimate defense of his private property, including X defending B against A or against anyone else trying to take it, steal it or assert ownership over it. Once the contract is signed, X can force A to hand over B because the true owner of B at that point is X, not A. This is true even if B consists of A's promise to do something for X or A's doing something for X in the future. The fact that X owns B after the contract is signed explains why contract law permits X to force A to perform on A's promise. It also explains why if A does not hand over B then X may force A to pay X the value of B, because X owned B and if A does not hand over B then A has stolen B from X and A must pay restitution to give B's value to X.

Assume that Y is a car and B is a motorcycle. X and A sign a contract whereby X trades Y to A and in return A trades B to X. Contract law enables X to get his property, which is now the motorcycle, and enables A to receive and defend his property, the car which X traded to A. The same holds true of contract law if X owns a car and A owns $8000, and X sells the car to A for $8000, which trades the car for the money. This is also what contract law does if X owns a car and A is a car mechanic and X pays A $500 to repair the car. Once the contract is signed, A has promised to repair the car, and A has sold his promise to X in exchange for X's $500. Once the contract terms are met or A receives the $500 payment, X is the owner of A's promise. Contract law enables X to defend and protect his property interest in what he owns, namely A's promise, by forcing A to fix the car (to "perform") or forcing A to pay back the value of the promise, which A would owe X if A breaks his promise and breaches the contract.

Contract law is necessary for a trade-based capitalist economy to be able to function, because it enables people to enforce their trades and to trade promises. Trading promises enables economic calculations based upon what other people will do in the future. The ethical, moral basis of contract law is that a person freely chooses to consent to and enter into a contract, and a responsible autonomous consenting adult should have the freedom to bind himself to his promise by means of his choice, expressed through the language of the contract and his signature on the document. A person has the right to do whatever he wants with his property, including trade his property away in return for other property, and contract law is the legal basis for the right to trade.

Note that under contract law, no contract exists unless the freely given, voluntary consent of both parties exists ("offer and acceptance," in the terminology of contract law). As I will discuss in a later section, a contract should not be enforced unless both parties fully understood and gave their informed consent to each and every term in the document after a process of discussion and negotiation and bargaining, which would nullify the "take it or leave it" boilerplate contracts that people sign without bothering to read or understand what they have signed. Also, no contract exists unless a trade actually happened, such that each party traded property or a promise to the other party, meaning that both parties had to give something up in order to get something back (called "consideration" by contract lawyers, as mentioned above). If you have problems with the concept of owning a promise, contract law can also be conceptualized as owning property that exists in the future, not the present, which is embodied in the present as the other party's promise.

Generally, the only areas of law which have a valid role to play in a legal system whose purpose is to protect life, liberty and property are those discussed above. All the various dozens of other legal regimes invented by the American legal system could be abolished without any serious loss to the quality of life of the USA's citizens. The libertarian must seek to reform the law to refine it down to its proper tasks.

Note one major point, however, that the discussion above assumes that the law known as "criminal procedure," is included under "constitutional law," because criminal procedure in America is largely derived from the Bill of Rights in the U.S. Constitution. Criminal procedure is the law that defines what the police may or may not do to the people, e.g. where the police may not search without a search warrant. Obviously, if it needs a separate mention to make sure, I would also add criminal procedure to the list of legitimate laws.

The one body of law that might or might not be added to this list, where libertarians suffer from major internal disagreement over its inclusion, is intellectual property law. Intellectual property law sounds like it would be included in the list of legitimate laws as a type of defense of property. But Mises and Rothbard, two of the founders of the libertarian movement, advocated for the abolishment of intellectual property, and their many followers carry on their opposition to intellectual property (IP).

Intellectual property law, which is authorized by the Intellectual Property Clause of the U.S. Constitution, protects property consisting of inventions (by patent law), works of art, literary expression, and creativity (by copyright law), and brand names and logos which contain the goodwill and reputation built by a business (by trademark law). I argue that IP is legitimate, for precisely the same reasons that tangible physical property is legitimate. If intellectual property is created by an individual mixing his labor (his thinking and effort) together with the raw clay or stuff of existence (language, science, ideas and principles, etc.), if it results from doing work and making choices, then the creator of intellectual property has earned the right to own it, like an artist owns a clay bowl which she sculpted.

The various distinctions between physical property and intellectual property are "distinctions without a difference," as lawyers say. The argument that patent and copyright laws enable rich corporations to exploit the working class and that communal sharing would be preferable to private ownership is a socialist or Marxist argument. The IP exploitation argument is EVIL and opposes GOLD, despite the many libertarians who claim to believe precisely that argument with respect to intellectual property. Intellectual property and physical property are indistinguishable from a legal justification point of view, so patent law, copyright law and trademark law are valid under GOLD.

The pseudo-libertarian argument that intellectual property ideas are not physical and therefore can't be used up, and are not subject to the laws of economics because they are not "scarce resources" and should be free like air to breathe, is flawed for two reasons. First, an idea can't be destroyed by being used up, but an idea's financial value is finite and can be used up. For example, a limit exists to the number of people who will buy a book, see a movie, or buy an invention. Thus, an invention might be worth $200,000 because only 20,000 people will buy it and it sells for $10, even though the abstract idea of the invention can't be used up by the buyers. The inventor of that invention has earned ownership of that $200,000 of money from the invented device's sales, because he did the intellectual work of creating the invention.

If intellectual property was truly not scarce then supply would be so abundant that nobody would ever bother to try to sell it, as is the case with the supply of air to breathe on planet Earth. For example, if the supply of inventions is not scarce, then where is the invention that enables humans to breathe air in the natural environment on the Moon or Mars, so that we could colonize other planets? Obviously it does not exist until someone invents it, and this invention, like most intellectual property, is quite scarce and precious.

Second, a good theory justifying private property should not depend on the specific details of one theory of economics, since reasonable people differ in their opinions about the details of economic theory, but we want all reasonable people to believe in life, liberty and property. In the first section of this book I offered a theory of property based on GOLD and the Golden Rule, which everyone can agree with. Property is justified by creating value and mixing one's labor with the stuff of reality, like a sculptor turning a lump of clay into a bowl. Property is not created merely by prioritizing scarce resources.

The enemies of IP argue that IP robs people of their physical property, for example if I own a painting then my control over the physical object that I own is interfered with by the artist owning a copyright in the painted image. My reply is that in most cases the value of the object comes from the intellectual property, not from the physical matter, e.g. people buy a book to read the book not to own ink and paper, or people buy a car to drive a car not to own lumps of metal and plastic. If the value of a physical object comes from the IP, for example from the literary creativity or the design of the car engine, then the creator of the IP has earned the right of ownership and the right to reap the profits of his or her productivity.

The idea of John Galt's motor comes to mind in the context of intellectual property: profit was his motive and his just reward, and it would be stupid to steal John Galt's motor away from him without paying him his due, because this would be pavement for the road to socialism and the enslavement of the inventors, just as it would be blatant theft to take the literary creation of "Atlas Shrugged" and sell copies of it without giving regard to the work of Ayn Rand who created it by paying her a literary royalty. It goes to the basic notion of fairness and justice that a person should get what he or she deserves, and a creator has earned the reward of his/her work. In conclusion, the thieves and pirates who steal intellectual property are free riders who unfairly rob the creators of IP of the profits they have earned and rightly deserve, not vice versa as some libertarians assert.

CHAPTER THIRTY THREE: CIVIL LIBERTIES

The law of civil liberties, also known as criminal procedure, is the law which defines what treatment the police are allowed to give to the people, and which behaviors police are not legally allowed to do to people. Civil liberties law represents our right to be free from a police state, and to not have a secret police search us to look for political dissent and throw dissenters into jail. Historically, every dictatorship, be it a socialist dictatorship or a fascist dictatorship, requires a secret police in order to suppress dissent and hold onto power. Civil liberties law, if it functions properly, is the mechanism to prevent the FBI and CIA and NSA from mutating into a KGB or a Nazi Gestapo. Democracy demands that the police are limited to their proper role, and that the people have a legal device to protect themselves from abuse at the hands of the police.

The analysis of civil liberties in the context of the contemporary USA must distinguish between the criminal law "as it is" and the criminal law "as it should be." What it is right now is X's tool to put A in jail when A does B and refuses to do Y. What it should be is the police defending the life, liberty and property of the people, in other words, police assistance for individual self-defense. First I will discuss what civil liberties would look like if the criminal law was what it should be, and then I will discuss which civil liberties policies we must pursue because of what the criminal justice system actually is in today's America.

In an ideal legal landscape, no general need would exist for the police to conduct searches. If a person needed help for self-defense, they could call or text the police, given the widespread usage of smart phones and mobile devices. The only general need for searches would be to fight the mafia and terrorists. Legalization of drugs, prostitution and gambling, and an end to the War on Drugs, would dry up the mob's funding and money supply. Antiwar foreign policy based around trade and an end to foreign occupations and foreign military bases would start the United States down the path to world peace and end the motives of most anti-U.S. terrorist groups, so that we could phase out the War on Terror. Organized crime and terrorism could be reduced down to a size small enough so that the police could effectively fight it without infringing our civil liberties.

Now I will discuss civil liberties in light of what the criminal law really is, and not what it should be. The mafia and terrorists are used as an excuse to erode criminal procedural limitations and move us down a path towards the legal acceptance of a secret police who can search, inspect and arrest anyone they wish with impunity. And the criminal law has become, in part, a war against the poor and against blacks and Hispanics, specifically in the form of the War on Drugs. Other libertarian think tanks have offered ample research proving that too many Americans are in jail, and I will not repeat those studies here, but let me briefly state the facts showing that the criminal law in America is a monster out of control.

The three countries in the world with the largest incarceration rates are the United States, Russia and China. But in the latter two countries many inmates are political prisoners, so we are jailing people at rates comparable to dictatorships. In the USA we use the criminal law to criminalize poverty, because drug use and petty theft are ways that the poor cope with their grief and misery, and these crimes face stiff jail sentences. Empirical fact proves that a disproportionate number of America's inmates are poor, black, or Hispanic, as compared to whites and the rich, both because the War on Drugs fills prisons with such people, and also because jail sentences are overly strict for minor theft and minor drug offenses as well as other victimless crimes like gun possession or prostitution. Roughly 2.5 million American adults are in jail right now. Another 7 million have been processed by the criminal justice system in some way, e.g. a charge or parole or acquittal or post-release. This means that almost 10 million people have been touched by the criminal justice system, which is almost one person out of every 33 people. Even if you have been the victim of a crime at some point in your life and you support "tough on crime" policy, it is still undeniable that we send too many people to jail.

Because criminal law is what it is, not what it should be, we must use criminal procedure as a practical pragmatic way to keep people out of jail, as the only tool we possess to protect people from unjust laws, rather than as a theoretical idealistic scheme to organize the limits of what police can do to citizens. The War on Drugs turns the police, who are naturally good and noble individuals, into thugs who arrest poor and truly innocent people when they commit victimless crimes. What follows is a list of eight specific civil liberties policies we must pursue.

(1) Protect and enforce the civil liberties spelled out in the Bill of Rights in the U.S. Constitution, specifically the Fourth, Fifth and Sixth Amendments. The most important provision is the Fourth Amendment, which requires no warrantless searches of a person's body, home or personal property absent a true emergency or a search warrant supported by probable cause shown to a judge. Like most of the libertarian-leaning sections of the U.S. Constitution, the Fourth Amendment has been given an interpretation by the United States Supreme Court which fundamentally destroys and rewrites its true meaning as a safeguard of civil liberties. Here I explain the Supreme Court's distortion and offer a path forward to reform the law.

The text of the Fourth Amendment states that "the right of the people to be secure in their persons, houses, papers, and effects, against unreasonable searches and seizures, shall not be violated." Early case law was obsessed with the words "persons, houses, papers, and effects," and held that the Fourth Amendment only protected the inside of a home from searches, and left everything else open to intrusion. But the rise of new technology, specifically the telephone, led judges to update the law. Modern case law replaced the old interpretation with a new interpretation called the "reasonable expectation of privacy," which holds that one is protected from warrantless searches only where one may reasonably expect to have privacy and where what is searched is not open to the public. The practical, pragmatic embodiment of the reasonable expectation of privacy doctrine is that electronic data on the internet is not protected from government searches because the data is transmitted over public data lines and is held by third parties such as email hosts or remote servers. This means that you have no reasonable expectation of privacy in your emails, electronic documents, logs of what you do on the internet, etc. The NSA's massive electronic spying program is constitutional under this doctrine.

I argue that the Supreme Court made its original and most serious error by looking at the words "persons, houses, papers, and effects" when the truly important and legally significant word was "searches." A textualist interpretation of the plain meaning of the Fourth Amendment is that it forbids "searches" done without a warrant or in the absence of a true emergency (i.e. a warrantless search in an emergency is not "unreasonable.") The clause "persons, houses, papers, and effects" simply describes everything that could have been searched when the Bill of Rights was ratified, and it is a list which embodies a general category of all searchable things and was not written in order to denote some categories as outside the scope of protection from searches. The plain meaning of "search" is "to purposefully look at, look through, or inspect and examine, something, in order to learn about it or discover information or to find something from the search." Electronic data can be searched, and when the NSA collects data they are looking at something, so under the textualist analysis of the Fourth Amendment the NSA's spying is a warrantless search and is unconstitutional.

An example to illustrate the Fourth Amendment jurisprudence debate is something I call "the roommate argument." Say that you and your roommate share a studio apartment. Under the reasonable expectation of privacy doctrine, you do not expect to have privacy from a roommate in a one room apartment, so you would have no reasonable expectation of privacy from your roommate. Now say that you leave the apartment, and you have a pile of your clothes on your bed, and while you are away your roommate looks through your pile of clothes in search of a dime bag of pot. Under the reasonable expectation of privacy doctrine, no search has taken place. But under any grasp of common sense, logic, and the obvious and plain meaning of the word "search," the most natural description of what just happened is that your roommate searched your pile of clothes. It cannot be said that whatever lay beneath the pile of clothes was open to the public, because he had to search for it in order to find it, and you did not hand a dime bag of pot to your roommate, instead he searched for it without you having given it to him or given him permission to take it or look for it. I advocate a wholesale reinterpretation of the Fourth Amendment to retire the reasonable expectation of privacy case law and to instead say that whenever a "search" happens there must be a warrant or a reasonable excuse or else the Constitution is violated.

(2) Fight for the law to give teeth to the exclusionary rule. The exclusionary rule is the legal doctrine which says that evidence collected by the police in violation of the law of criminal procedure is inadmissible at trial and cannot be used to convict. The "tough on crime" politicians who crave a police state hate the exclusionary rule, they say that it lets criminals go free, and they assert that it is merely a matter of convenience and is not a right that belongs to the accused. The exclusionary rule is the one and only way that the drafters of the Fourth, Fifth and Sixth Amendments could have imagined that the Bill of Rights would be enforced. Just as judicial review enforces the Constitution, the exclusionary rule enforces criminal procedure. Given that the Bill of Rights exists, and is the law on the books, it follows that a criminal defendant has the right not to be convicted unless the conviction is supported beyond a reasonable doubt by admissible evidence not excluded by the exclusionary rule.

(3) The burden of proof in a criminal trial is that guilt must be proved "beyond a reasonable doubt," in contrast to the civil trial burden which is "by a preponderance of the evidence." The burden of proof must be given sharper teeth. Specifically, if the only evidence is what someone says or a few people say, and someone else disputes it, and no corroborating forensic evidence such as DNA evidence or crime scene analysis or a neutral corroborating witness's testimony is presented, as a matter of law one cannot achieve proof beyond a reasonable doubt. We as political activists must propose and fight for a legislative law which will say that contradicted verbal narrative testimony in a criminal trial fails to meet the burden of proof unless supported by forensic evidence, the testimony of a neutral unbiased witness, or the testimony of three or more witnesses who tell the same story.

The enemies of freedom will say that a person who gets victimized while alone and who by bad luck has no forensic evidence to support his/her story will be stripped of his/her legal protection. But the ability to invent and fabricate stories, combined with the scientific biological research which shows that the human brain's memory is a delicate, fragile, fallible structure, demands that we not put people in jail purely on he said/she said testimony. When you say that I mugged you and I say that I did not, and there are no other witnesses or facts and this is the only evidence, then the judge and jury can have no objective basis to know what really happened, which in my opinion rules out certainty beyond a reasonable doubt.

(4) The motive of most criminal prosecutors and district attorneys is maximum punishment, not truth and justice. This is so for two reasons. First, because they want to look "tough on crime" to appeal to voter fear of crime in order to be reelected. Second, because they view their role as being the person who advocates for the toughest, harshest sentence possible, as if it is the job of the criminal defense lawyer to get the defendant an acquittal or a light sentence if the defendant is truly not guilty, so that the prosecution's job has nothing to do with actually achieving a just sentence which reflects whether the defendant is really guilty or not. The best way to break up the prosecutorial "tough on crime" culture is to privatize criminal prosecution. Fairness demands that decisions about the prosecution, such as whether to prosecute and which sentence to seek, be made by the victim, not the prosecutor. Rights belong to the individual, not to the government, and the right to sue and the decision to sue is not the type of thing that the social contract delegates to the government, even if the lawsuit is for a crime, i.e. intentional violence against life, liberty or property. The privatization of criminal prosecution would take decision-making power away from the politicians and give it to the people.

(5) The criminal justice system as it currently exists is a factory designed to churn out as many convictions and as long jail sentences as possible. The engine of the factory is the plea bargain. Criminal defendants are warned that it is difficult to get a fair trial. The system is designed so that the jury decides guilt or innocence but the judge decides what sentence to impose, and many judges are fair, honest people who will not impose harsh sentences for minor crimes. But the prosecutors use "mandatory minimum" sentencing laws to scare the accused with the threat that if he is convicted then he will get a harsh, severe mandatory minimum, and the judge will have no power to impose a fair sentence, which pressures the defendant into a plea bargain. For example if the mandatory minimum is forty years in jail for possession of a small amount of cocaine then a plea bargained sentence of four years in jail looks attractive and reasonable, even though the defendant might have a strong case if the case went to trial. We must abolish all mandatory minimum laws to restore fairness to sentencing and break the motor which pressures those who are innocent, and know that they are innocent, to accept plea bargains which treat them like the guilty.

(6) We should also fight to pass a new law saying that a judge cannot approve a plea bargain unless he is persuaded that the admissible evidence could prove guilt beyond a reasonable doubt and also that the judge honestly believes based on his impression and knowledge of the facts offered by the prosecutor that the defendant is probably guilty. This would not require a bench trial for every case, and could be done with a quick, fast-paced judge's review of the case and hearing from counsel for five minutes, and it could easily be added onto a normal hearing to enter a guilty plea. This would not burden or inconvenience the criminal justice system, but it would help prevent the innocent from entering guilty pleas. This might force more defendants to go to

trial, but the purpose of the criminal justice system is to punish the guilty and free the innocent, not to let people game the system via the plea bargaining process.

(7) Another piece of a "civil liberties reform" package would reform the grand jury indictment process. Grand juries in the federal system and some states decide what cases can be prosecuted. The system as it currently exists enables the prosecutor to run the show, and the common wisdom among criminal lawyers is that "a grand jury would indict a ham sandwich." We should pass a law to restore sharp teeth to the grand jury, by requiring that a grand jury be told and made to understand that they really should not indict someone unless evidence of guilt exists and is persuasive to them that the person might be guilty. We should also reform the indictment process so that it is run by a neutral third party, not by the prosecutor. Civil liberties reform would prevent unjust prosecutions and limit the abuse of prosecutorial discretion.

(8) We must seek to get legislatures to pass laws spelling out the right to "jury nullification." Jury nullification, discussed in the section on the U.S. Constitution, is the right of the jury to find a criminal defendant not guilty, not because they think he didn't commit the crime but because they feel that the criminal law used to convict is unjust and unfair. Most judges do not recognize the right to jury nullification, so we must seek to get state legislatures to pass laws explicitly granting this right, to say that all jury instructions must include a paragraph spelling out the right to engage in jury nullification and explain it to the jury. Jury instructions should also specify that jury nullification can cause innocence but cannot be used to find guilt.

CHAPTER THIRTY FOUR: JAIL

The unstated premise of a system which uses jail as a punishment for non-violent crimes is that humans are animals who can be thrown into a cage whenever we do what "society" disapproves of. The libertarian position advocates that fines and corrective programs replace jail as the main form of criminal punishment: non-jail penalties must always be used for non-violent crimes, which includes all drug abuse offenses which do not endanger others (e.g. smoking pot, but not Driving While Intoxicated because that involves a risk of violence to others). None-jail penalties could sometimes also be used for violent crimes at the judge's discretion, if the judge believes that a correctional program could rehabilitate the convict. Jail should only be mandatory is situations where the actual danger to others of violence by the convicted criminal exists as shown by the violent crime of which he/she was convicted and also violent criminal history, such that the convict must be imprisoned to protect the public.

The libertarian system has four premises. First, that humans have free will and should be given the opportunity to change and improve wherever possible instead of being swept into the cracks out of sight. Second, only a violent crime deserves a violent punishment, and forced incarceration is a type of violent retribution. Third, that jail for drug offenses unfairly imprisons racial minorities like blacks and Hispanics, who tend to smoke pot or crack, while leaving free whites, who tend to smoke cigarettes or drink alcohol. Fourth, jail increases gang violence and organized crime by placing youthful drug offenders into jails full of hardened criminals.

We must rethink the concept of jail as a punishment for crime. It makes sense to incarcerate violent criminals who are a danger to society. But for criminals convicted of non-violent crimes it makes more sense to develop a program like parole combined with community service and a rehabilitation and civic education program to help the person become a productive law-abiding citizen. Reason suggests that long jail terms be reserved for the worst crimes of violence like rape and murder. The premise of jail is that the criminals are too dangerous to roam free, whereas the premise of rehabilitation is that people can be helped.

Once we remove all victimless crimes from the law, then we can feel better about harsh punishments, such as jail, for real crimes. GOLD is not "soft on crime," if crime is defined properly. Jail as a punishment for crimes of violence can be justified under GOLD because if the criminal treats the victim with violence then it is fair and just for the victim to reciprocate to the criminal with violence as punishment, in other words "if you do that to me then I will do this to you" is consistent with the Golden Rule. "An eye for an eye, a tooth for a tooth" is the basic idea, but jail is more humane and civilized then actually killing or injuring people to punish them, so in a civilized democracy jail must be our tool of punishment for legitimate crimes of violence.

But jail should not be draconian even for serious crimes. Reasonable sentencing guidelines might be 20 years in jail for each murder, 10 years for each rape, 6 months for each assault, and 1 year for each assault with a deadly weapon. A kidnapper's jail sentence should correspond to the length of time that the victim was held for, e.g. if someone is captive for three months then the kidnapper is jailed for nine months. A reasonable sentence for theft might be one day in jail for each $10 of property stolen, e.g. $300 = 30 days, $3000 = 300 days. The amount of time that a thief spends in jail should be comparable to the time that the victim spent making the money which was stolen, and $10 an hour is a good estimate of average wages, but sitting in a jail cell is a lot easier than doing productive work so one day of jail for one hour of labor is fair retribution. The purpose of a judge's sentencing discretion is to avoid unfair sentences, so the judge should be allowed to impose a less harsh sentence but not a harsher sentence than what the sentencing guidelines recommend. Also, teenagers should be processed with children in the juvenile justice system, which should only use rehabilitation programs and should never send kids or teens to jail.

Note that tax evasion, as a non-violent crime, could not be punished by jail. It would be punishable either by the forcible taking and removal of wealth equal to the back taxes owed, or by economic sanctions such as courts declining to enforce the person's contracts. In its most extreme form, dissenters who refuse to pay taxes could lose police protection, or be asked to leave the country and go somewhere else where they will not receive benefits from the government system which they refuse to support.

On a related topic, the GOLD position soundly rejects the death penalty. Even if murderers and rapists actually deserved a death sentence, we would still oppose it, because no jury ever has perfect knowledge, and the inherent ignorance and uncertainty of the criminal trial system means that we should not risk killing the innocent in order to punish the guilty. Although in justice one might think that death is a fair retribution for the crime of murder, or rape, death is so extreme and final that it is inconsistent with the practical observation that the courts and legal system are fallible, flawed, and imperfect. Many cases have happened where a criminal defendant was convicted and spent years in jail, only to be freed later when DNA evidence or new witness testimony proved his innocence. The death sentence as an irreversible punishment eliminates our ability to appeal wrongful convictions.

If even a 0.01% chance exists that a person might have been wrongfully convicted, and I believe that criminal trials never achieve a degree of knowledge higher than that level, then the price we would pay for the death sentence is too severe to justify the benefit of death as retribution. If a piece of evidence were misinterpreted by the jury, or a witness convincingly and persuasively lied, or a jury was somehow misled, or the judge made a mistake in an evidentiary ruling, or ten witnesses all told the same story that they saw the murder take place which looks like credible evidence but all ten of them were wrong, all of this means that no guilty verdict is ever perfectly reliable. Also, we do not want the government to claim the power of life and death over us, because this would make the government too powerful. No need for the death penalty exists given that a long prison sentence as punishment for murder is in reality a suitably chastising, life-ruining, agony-causing punishment.

CHAPTER THIRTY FIVE: CONTRACT LAW REFORMS

From a minarchist point of view, the legal system of the courts litigating business disputes and applying contract law is a valid role for the government to play. It is proper for us to turn a critical eye of scrutiny upon contract law, and see areas where it can be improved.

In a free market capitalist economy, sometimes in a sale of goods or services two people trade value for value, and both trade what they produced or wanted less for what they desire to consume or wanted more. For example, I want a sandwich and the deli sandwich shop wants my $5. If both traders knowingly and voluntarily choose the deal then both traders usually end up happy. But sometimes the seller seeks to screw over the buyer (or vice versa) and trick him/her into buying something that wasn't worth the money he/she paid for it. When I say that someone got ripped off, I do not mean that they bought a cheap product at a low price. So long as some goods and services are better and more desirable than others, a cheaper price will always correspond to lower quality. No method exists to eliminate this problem for the poor, other than by helping them to make more money with which to buy more expensive desirable goods. A price/money system is necessary to send price signals and coordinate economic activity, and producers/sellers should receive economic reward for producing more desirable goods and services, which they receive from charging a higher price.

But sometimes buyers get ripped off and screwed over, like paying $6 for a pastrami sandwich with Dijon mustard, only to learn later that it is a bologna sandwich with plain mustard, which in the marketplace commonly costs $3. Or, as may happen more realistically, I bought a used car for $5,000, only to later learn that it is a piece of junk really worth $1,000, but I can't return it because I signed a contract, and the fine print does not legally give me the right to return it merely because it wasn't worth what I paid. We must permit price-based trades while at the same time preventing the poor (and middle class, and, to the extent necessary, the upper class also) from being victimized.

Various policies can solve the rip off problem. It could be solved by a strong private legal cause of action for consumer protection false advertising, with damages including attorney's fees. It could be solved by reforming contract law. Under contract law as it currently exists, if both parties to a deal are mistaken about the facts of what is being traded, then the contract is generally voidable, but if one party is mistaken and another knows the truth, a contract will legally be enforced in most situations, unless the party who knows the truth lied to or misled the mistaken party. Contract law should be reformed so that no contract exists unless both parties have knowingly chosen to do the deal which actually exists in the facts, such that any material mistake on the part of a party about the facts of the trade should be grounds to void the contract. This would force the party with knowledge to disclose the truth to the ignorant party.

A critic might reply that this will seriously interfere with economic transactional activity, because everyone will be worried that their contracts will be voided. This contracts reform proposal envisions voiding only where the mistake was important and causes the deal to be something other than what the person understood as the deal he/she was choosing to do. This importance/misunderstanding materiality requirement would be a legal requirement limiting the law.

For example, if Farmer X sells a cow to Farmer A, and X believed at the time of the sale that the cow was sterile, and the cow later gives birth, then this mistake would not void the contract, because the contract as understood by X was to sell a cow, not to sell a fertile cow, and X could not have understood any part of the purpose of the sale as the cow giving birth in the future since X believed the cow was sterile. Courts would be asked to interpret the legal requirements of this proposal of voiding from unilateral mistake strictly, so that it would not put regular ordinary day-to-day deal-making in the marketplaces of the USA in danger of added legal liability and litigation costs.

But the best solution to the rip off problem might be a "default returns policy." Let me begin by explaining the concept of a default rule, which is widely recognized in contract law and commercial law. In a contract, the parties negotiate and discuss the terms of their deal. But if they sign a contract that leaves out a key term which they never discussed, and the term becomes important, then the law must step in and provide the terms necessary in order for the contract to function. For example, if a buyer and seller sign a contract to sell a car, and they could have defined in the contract whether delivery of the car was to take place before or after the money changed hands, but the contract did not actually define that and the parties did not discuss it, then the law must provide an answer if the time of delivery becomes a litigated issue. The law has evolved default rules for contracts which provide the default for unspecified contract terms, such as the Uniform Commercial Code and various bodies of case law. The default rules are "default" because the contract begins with them, but they can be replaced if the parties actually define those terms in their contracts.

The default returns policy I am proposing would mandate a money-back satisfaction guarantee for all sales of all goods and services, lasting 24 hours from the time of the sale for perishable goods and 7 business days for durable goods. That way a consumer who got screwed over can get a return for a refund and be protected. Practicality would require keeping the receipt or proof of sale and precautions against fraud on sellers, but it could be done. It might be best if the 24 hour/7 day period was for returns for any reason, plus a 30 day return period if the product later proves to be "obviously" defective or substandard or the seller lied about it (the "obviously" to prevent unnecessary litigation.)

This reform could be accomplished through contract law as a default provision of all contracts, meaning that if the buyer and seller do not mention or discuss it then it applies, but the buyer could voluntarily waive his/her right to use the default returns policy if he/she expressly chooses to do so as part of negotiations to get a better deal or some other benefit. Opting out should not be done as easily as the seller including an opt out clause in fine print in the form contract which the buyer is told to sign without reading the fine print, or else sellers collectively would render the default returns policy ineffective. Rather, the policy proposal would require a verbal discussion in which the buyer is informed of his/her rights, and that the buyer read and sign a special form detailing the opt out in large print and easy to understand language. It cannot be said that government would be imposing its opinions upon the marketplace, since everyone could opt out of the default returns policy if they chose to do so. And one can't say that it would eliminate competition by equalizing all returns policies, because every trustworthy seller already does this, and the ones who wouldn't want to are precisely the ones who like to screw people over.

The Uniform Commercial Code would need to be modified to reflect this, but the default returns policy should apply to all consumer transactions, not only UCC sales of goods, and something like a reverse default returns policy should apply to sales by individuals to pawn shops and consignment shops, etc., that a person who sells something can ask for it back within the time window. The default returns policy would need details for goods and services which cannot easily be returned. One possible detail would be that the consumer gets a return of 50% of the purchase price, e.g. if a person buys a $5 sandwich and eats the sandwich and hates it and wants a refund, he gets $2.50 back to reflect his dissatisfaction, but the deli keeps $2.50 to reflect the price of the ingredients and nutritional value which the buyer retains. An alternative to the 50% rule would be that the seller would be entitled to keep the cost of the raw materials but would refund his profit margin. A similar rule could be enacted for services, like legal representation or accountant's services, which cannot be given back.

For goods like car gasoline, which cannot be returned and either you benefit from it or you don't, a return should require proof that the gas was defective, or else the buyer must siphon it out of his tank and give it back, because making the gas station lose the gas and the payment price would be unfair and give a windfall to the buyer, who would get the gas for free. A return assumes that the buyer did not enjoy or want the good or service and would not have bought it if he had known what he was getting, and regulations and details to implement the default returns policy would reflect this basic premise.

The default returns policy would not interfere with the free market, instead it would augment the free market, by helping to make sure that every trade in the market is one which both sides really wanted, which requires that the buyer has fully knowingly and voluntarily chosen to do the deal and got what he had chosen to buy. If a business's business model depends upon no refunds, or a no refunds policy can lead to lower costs and a competitive advantage, then that business will be free to persuade buyers to waive the default refund policy for those sales.

In the modern economy, consumers have seen a proliferation of "adhesion contracts," standardized contracts which contain pages upon pages full of fine print, which buyers typically sign without reading just for the sake of convenience to get the contract out of the way so they can buy what they want to buy. An adhesion contract is a form contract with fine print boilerplate which the seller expects the buyer to sign without any bargaining or negotiations and usually without even actually reading it. An example is a website's "terms of service" agreement; the custom is for people to simply click the "I accept" button as a trivial technicality without ever reading the contract or thinking about whether to consent to the terms and be legally bound.

Since nobody ever bothers to read these contracts, courts have created the "doctrine of reasonable expectations for adhesion contracts," under which the fine print in an adhesion contract has no legal power, even if the person actually signed it, and the person who signs an adhesion contract is bound not by the fine print but by what he "reasonably" would have "expected" the fine print to say if he had read it. The problem with the reasonable expectations doctrine is that it undermines the premise of contract law, that consenting adults have the right, and the power, to bind themselves to their promise by means of a freely chosen contract, and the signature on a contract represents a knowingly and freely made choice.

My proposal for an alternative solution to this problem is to not allow people to sign a contract without first reading it and knowing what it says. Specifically, I propose a "mandatory contract summary of key terms," which the seller must get the buyer to read and either (a) record or videotape the seller giving a verbal explanation of the key terms and the buyer's verbal expression of understanding, or (b) give a quiz testing the buyer's understanding of the key terms (e.g. a multiple choice quiz on a website), and the buyer must demonstrate his understanding by answering enough questions to get a passing score. The summary obviously need not present every detail, but the seller must put the buyer on notice of any term which the seller will seek to enforce through later litigation against the buyer, and absence of a record of notice by the seller would be an affirmative defense that a buyer could assert in later litigation. The premise of this policy is that a party to a contract must first know what it says in order to consent to it, and nobody reads or understands pages of fine print and boilerplate, until the seller's lawyer looks at it and tries to start a lawsuit using it. The fine print can still be there for legal protection, but contract law would be more practical and up to date if the seller was not allowed to sue under any contract term which the buyer did not give his informed consent to.

CHAPTER THIRTY SIX: CENSORING SOUTH PARK AND THE HORROR OF DEFAMATION

Some time ago I read an interview with Matt Stone and Trey Parker, the creative duo behind the hit animated comedy South Park, in conjunction with the opening of their Broadway play The Book of Mormon. What struck me was one of them saying that in the episode of South Park in which they lambasted the cult of Scientology, they had wanted to say that Tom Cruise is in the closet. Their lawyer advised them that Cruise could sue them for defamation, so instead they put the cartoon version of Tom Cruise in a literal closet that he refused to come out of. The result was laugh-out-loud comedic gold, but it highlights one of my major peeves about legal causes of action, which is the law of defamation.

Defamation is a cause of action under which a plaintiff can sue a defendant for damage to his reputation. In "For a New Liberty," Murray Rothbard wrote that he believed defamation law should be abolished, because a person's reputation exists in the brains of other people, and the plaintiff has no property right in other people's minds. My concern is broader; I believe that defamation law scares people away from making statements that might offend those among us with the money to hire lawyers. This fear of being sued for defamation chills people's ability to say what they want. It scares them away from criticizing others, even when the criticism might be justified and deserved.

This danger is often poignant in the case of such artistic representations as South Park, which makes deep, meaningful social commentary by making jokes, often offensive ones, directed at people who could easily take offense and who generally have money. The strange thing is that the First Amendment has a clause that guarantees freedom of speech. Why isn't the First Amendment regarded as making charges of defamation unconstitutional?

There is a larger and a smaller answer. The larger answer is that the members of the Supreme Court, even the supposedly "textualist" and "originalist" conservatives, do not take the words of the Constitution literally. They make interpretations that twist and mangle it into something that looks like what they want, something that deforms the meaning of the words on paper, written by the Founders. The smaller, more specific answer is that the Supreme Court has grappled with the conflict between free speech and defamation, and has chosen a middle ground that tries reconciles the two.

In the landmark case of New York Times v. Sullivan (1964), an overseer of Southern police officers sued the Times and members of the civil rights movement under a defamation theory, accusing them of damaging the policemen's reputation by publishing an ad indicating that the police had committed crimes against demonstrators. Instead of holding defamation unconstitutional, the Supreme Court found for the defendants, holding that when public officials assert defamation they must prove "actual malice," meaning that the defendant knew his statement was false or acted with reckless disregard for truth. This is a much higher standard than the "negligence" requirement that applies to defamation against private individuals on matters of public concern or the mere "publication" requirement that applies to defamation by private citizens on a matter of private concern. However, after Sullivan the Supreme Court expanded the actual malice rule to cover "public figures" as well as public officials, so most celebrities, such as Tom Cruise, must prove actual malice.

Actual malice was designed to prevent censorship. I am sure that the Court believed it was being quite generous by creating such a high barrier to recovery. But because defamation continued to exist, the fear of being sued and the expense of litigation remain a serious impediment to American free speech and to our ability to criticize people of political and social importance. Speaking freely about the flaws (real or alleged) of our political and cultural leadership is a basic requirement for democracy to function.

A more recent important case is Hustler Magazine & Larry Flynt v. Jerry Falwell, a 1988 United States Supreme Court case in which evangelist Jerry Falwell sued a pornographic magazine for printing a joke that accused him of having sex with his mother. The accusation was obviously a joke that no one could take seriously. It was also clearly an example of the use of charges of defamation to censor criticism and take revenge against people who offend you. The jury found against Falwell on his libel claim, but found against Hustler on the "intentional infliction of emotional distress" claim, which is a somewhat similar cause of action that is also used to censor criticism and punish offensive behavior. The jury awarded substantial monetary damages. The Supreme Court, however, found in favor of the magazine on the "IIED" (as lawyers call it) claim, citing the need to protect the American tradition of political satire cartoons, and held that the New York Times v. Sullivan "actual malice" standard for defamation against public figures should also be used in cases involved intentional infliction of emotional distress claims against public figures, in order to protect free speech and create breathing room for vigorous debate. Regarding the right to be offensive towards other people, the court said that offensive speech is protected by the First Amendment.

But again, the Court refused to see the truth sitting right under its nose, which is that the only real purpose of claims of defamation (or intentional infliction of emotion distress claims alleged against plaintiffs because of what they say or write) is to censor speech; and this violates the First Amendment.

More recently, some legal scholars have argued that defamation does not violate the First Amendment because it allows publication to take place and only penalizes via economic penalties after the fact, under an injunction vs. recovery distinction, meaning that people are free to speak (i.e. the government will not get an injunction), but they must pay for what they say (the plaintiff can recover money damages). That argument is absurd, because being penalized for saying offensive things creates a fear that accomplishes the same result as the police forcibly muzzling the speaker or shutting down the printing press. The law of defamation has no place in a society that believes in intellectual freedom for all citizens. We libertarians are basically the only group of people in America who say that the emperor has no clothes and who criticize governmental mistakes that liberals and conservatives ignore or condone. Defamation is an obvious abuse of the law and of the government's coercive power to repress independent thinking, and we should all get angry about it.

CHAPTER THIRTY SEVEN: TORT REFORM VS. LOSER PAYS

The concept of reforming the American legal system to adopt the "loser pays" system used in most foreign countries, by which the loser pays the winner's attorney's fees, is popular among libertarians. "Loser pays" is proposed as a means of deterring frivolous litigation and solving the problem of excessive lawsuits. When Texas recently adopted the system, it was championed as a victory for small business. I have seen John Stossel advocate it, and in Liberty Magazine I have seen Gary Jason endorse it in a comment on one of my essays. "Loser pays" is a policy that might seem reasonable to a non-lawyer layperson. To a lawyer like me, unfortunately, it looks like a policy with unintended and unfavorable consequences, and also like a policy that has little chance of accomplishing its purpose.

The idea that it will deter frivolous litigation hinges on the idea that the frivolous litigant will lose. Yet if frivolous litigants actually stand a good chance of winning, then "loser pays" deters nothing except poor people, who would find it riskier to access the justice system. In torts lawsuits, the laws are such that bad plaintiffs with bad suits often have a good chance of winning. For instance, Liebeck v. McDonald's was a lawsuit in which a woman sued McDonald's because she spilled hot coffee and burned herself, for which McDonald's was held liable at trial for millions of dollars (mostly punitive damages) and ultimately settled the appeal. We can argue about whether the coffee actually was unreasonably hot, but this case can be viewed as the quintessential bad lawsuit, and it was held up as a poster child for tort reform. Yet the plaintiff won at trial, on the argument that the coffee was excessively hot and the cup's warning label was too small.

This lawsuit could have been stopped by reforming the law, that is, by creating a bar to punitive damages whenever there is a warning label. Because the case settled, it would have been unaffected by "loser pays." Under "loser pays" the risk of having to pay McDonald's' legal defense fees if the plaintiff lost might have factored into her calculation of whether or not to sue. But she won the case at trial, and if cases like this happen, then who really expects plaintiffs with bad cases to be excessively afraid of losing? As I will explain below, you don't win a lawsuit because of the rationality of your claim but because of the emotions of the jury. So if a tort plaintiff can reach a jury, the jury trial system will be favorable to stupid lawsuits. The best solution is to reform the tort laws so that plaintiffs with ridiculous cases have no legal way to reach a jury.

Meanwhile, "loser pays" is likely to scare poor people with valid claims away from court, by inspiring the fear not only of losing but also of paying the huge legal fees of a wealthier opponent's high-powered law firm. The landmark civil rights litigation that helped to end Southern segregation might never have been filed in a "loser pays" system.

As for frivolous suits, legal ethics rules and civil procedural rules already forbid and punish lawyers for bringing "frivolous," "vexatious," "abusive" suits, and various provisions enable judges to quickly dismiss baseless or groundless claims. "Loser pays" will add little to the tools that already deal with the frivolous. In fact, the only way to prevent bad litigation is to eliminate the bad laws that form the legal basis of bad lawsuits.

Let me be clear: I am an advocate of tort reform, just not of "loser pays" in particular. There are many tort reform policies to choose from that would reduce unnecessary or harmful litigation without toxic side effects. We could, for instance:

1. Reduce the percentage of the tort plaintiff's contingent fees that are considered "reasonable." Legal ethics rules ban lawyers from charging "unreasonable" fees, but a whopping 30% is considered reasonable, and 30% is the typical rate. This means that if a plaintiff wins a million dollar verdict their law firm gets $300,000 and the plaintiff takes home merely $700,000. I think a cap of 5% (plus the firm's expenses of litigating the lawsuit) as "reasonable" would cut the amount of frivolous litigation in half. In this way, torts plaintiff lawyers would enter their practice with some other goal than becoming multimillionaires by exploiting the tragedies of their poor clients.

2. Eliminate class actions. The whole concept of class actions has always bothered me. To say that someone else has the right to litigate my claim without my consent or involvement, just because our claims are identical, is absurd, even if there are requirements of judicial consent and competent representation and the ability to opt out. Judicial efficiency, which is the valid motive of class actions, is not an excuse to let someone else litigate my case. Because class actions have millions of plaintiffs but only one law firm, the lawyers often make millions while the plaintiffs each get a few cents.

There is already a rule in legal ethics codes that bans lawyers from representing multiple clients who have conflicts of interest with one another, something I believe most class action clients have, because each client's claim is slightly different and might benefit from the case's being tried differently, e.g. a settlement could benefit one client and harm another. The conflict of interest rules are considered to be among the most important for lawyers to obey, yet class actions have a loophole. So instead of enacting a statutory ban, I propose simply to close the loophole and force class action lawyers to vet every member of the class for conflicts of interest. Any conflict would remove that class member. This would sharply reduce the volume of class action litigation.

3. Change the products liability tort standard from strict liability to negligence. Products liability cases are typically tried under a theory of "strict liability," which means that fault (i.e. blame) need not be proven. Strict liability is an affront to logic, an abomination. While some see the purpose of tort law as deterrence, I see it as compensatory justice, which means that damages are supposed to restore a victim to the condition he or she would be in, had the defendant not made a bad decision leading to the accident. I view tort law and contract law as twin aspects of free will and personal responsibility, as recognized by law: contract law means that your choices will bind and control you, whereas tort law means that someone else's choices will not be allowed to ruin you. If the defendants have not made bad choices then no reason exists to justify making them pay.

Although a layperson might think of negligence as something that happened to cause an unintended accident, the better understanding is that it consists of the choice to be careless and risk-prone. The strict liability standard has been justified on the grounds that product defects are technologically complicated and it would be too difficult to prove negligence, but this is no excuse for bad law. We should force plaintiffs to prove negligence. Then everyone will benefit from cheaper prices, because manufacturers' litigation costs will decrease.

4. Reform the standard of negligence for medical malpractice, so as to create a safe harbor. Medical fees skyrocket when doctors are forced to pay huge medical malpractice insurance premiums, and the practice of medicine is compromised when doctors based their decisions on fear of being sued, not the health needs of their patients. My safe harbor proposal is that if a medical practice or hospital had a written policy of procedures designed to prevent the type of malpractice that is at issue in a case, and the policy was implemented and regularly enforced and internally audited for compliance, then negligence cannot be proven. Similarly, if a surgeon or delivery obstetrician had a checklist of risks to prevent, a list that multiple doctors double-checked at the time of the surgery or childbirth, and the negligence at issue was on the list, then the doctor would have entered a safe harbor.

This is simply common sense: if the doctors were taking every possible systematic action to limit risk, then they were not negligent, even if something bad actually happened. Such precautionary policies would protect patients from accidents far more effectively than the tort lawsuits that drive up medical costs. Such a negligence test would cut frivolous lawsuits. State legislatures can codify my safe harbor rule, but clever judges could tacitly incorporate it into preexisting common law medical malpractice negligence standards.

5. Put a statutory dollar limit cap on damages. My understanding is that a civil trial is really just a popularity contest in which the jury votes for the lawyer it liked

the most. Instead of faithfully interpreting the judge's instructions to the jury (which are often so technical that only a lawyer could properly apply them), the jury awards lots of money to the party it likes and punishes whichever parties it disliked, based on their emotions and feelings, by making them pay huge damages. Usually poor old helpless plaintiff Mr. P, the janitor with a wife and five children who is suing because he broke his leg, is more sympathetic than the rich big business defendant Corporation D, especially when Mr. P's lawyer slyly insinuates that D cut corners on safety in order to make a profit. This is the open secret, the 800-pound gorilla in the room, when people talk about tort lawsuits and tort reform. This is also one reason why "loser pays" is ridiculous: from a practical, pragmatic, no-nonsense point of view there is no reason to believe that the loser is the one who deserved to lose.

The right to a jury trial in cases that are "at law" (i.e. where the plaintiff seeks money) is constitutionally inviolate, and I leave for another essay the question of whether jury trials should be comprehensively reformed. However, at a bare minimum justice demands that we solve the problem of headstrong juries by removing jurors' discretion to award damages in excess of what the intent of the law indicates, simply because they happen to feel sympathy for one side or another. Activist judges who do not faithfully apply the law are a problem, but so too are activist juries. A legislative statutory solution to place reasonable, honest dollar value caps on each of the different types of damages, or to lower the caps that already exist, is one feasible fix. Amendment VII of the U.S. Constitution does not forbid this, because the text never explicitly says that dollar limits cannot be codified into the law as an element of the cause of action, although it makes clear that judges cannot second-guess the facts found by a jury.

In conclusion: "loser pays" is far inferior to the American Rule, in which each party pays his own attorney's fees regardless of who wins or loses the trial. But I have described tort reform solutions that are available if voters elect legislators and judges who will use them.

CHAPTER THIRTY EIGHT: TEXTUALISM

Lawyers find it difficult to explain to non-lawyers what precisely it is that law school teachers us. Law school is the sort of thing that you need to experience firsthand in order to know what it is like, sort of like colors or scents. One thing that can be explained is that the law school classroom is dominated by the "Socratic Method," in which the law professor questions the students in order to encourage critical thinking. The vast majority of law school professors, most of whom are liberals, use the Socratic Method to teach law students that the answer to every question is another question, that everything can be debated, that a good lawyer can make any argument in support of any position, and that legal questions do not have objective right and wrong answers because it is always possible to argue both sides of any issue.

The result of the law school establishment mindset is that lawyers and judges believe that no such thing exists as an objectively correct, right, definite answer to a legal question. This approach is probably good for the lawyers' clients because a lawyer can see a bad case and still be confident that he or she can think up some sort of argument to turn it into a winning case. But the problem with legal subjectivism is that if no objectively correct legal answers exist then the lawyers and judges can transform the law into anything they want merely by means of a new interpretation. The legal theories known as "Legal Realism" and "critical legal studies" take this no-right-answers mindset and then reach the conclusion that, since the law can be anything we wish it to be and the judge has no way of knowing what the correct answer to a legal question is, the law should always be interpreted to favor the interests of the poor and underprivileged, which in practice means that the judge should always favor the liberals and Democrats in their court cases. This is the philosophical justification for the "activist judges" that conservatives complain about.

Conservatives and libertarians have created an alternative to the school of thought promoted by the law school establishment. This alternative is the legal interpretational theory called "textualism." Textualism holds that the law lives in the words on the pages of the statutes and court opinions, not in the minds of the judges or the intentions of the congressmen. The law is what the legal text (cases, statutes, and constitutions) says it is, as interpreted by the basic rules of the English language, for example, dictionary definitions and grammatical sentence analysis, as well as the commonly accepted legal canons of construction, for example, in a correct legal interpretation every word and every item of punctuation in the text should mean something, definitions in one part of a law usually apply in every other part, or a long list of specific items can be inferred to cover the general category of everything which shares the defining attribute of the items in the list. Everyone is legally entitled to rely on the text as a complete and accurate description of the law, and textualist interpretation is a set of rules which can be predictably applied to demonstrate a correct result. Textualism has several benefits which I will discuss below.

(1) Textualism benefits the public, because it enables the people to know what the law is. The purpose of laws is to control how people behave and to force them to conform their behavior to the non-optional mandates imposed by the decisions of the government acting as the representatives of the body politic and the American people. The law's purpose can only be fulfilled if law-abiding citizens know what is and is not illegal so that they can obey the law. Therefore the law must be objective, not subjective, and the law must create predictive clear rules, and not vague feelings or judicial discretion. If a person cannot predict the legal consequences of his or her actions with some degree of accuracy then he/she has no way to make important decisions about what to do.

(2) Textualism benefits lawyers and judges because it enables them to perform legal reasoning for them to know what the law is. Lawyers and judges have nothing certain to rely on other than the text, so if they want to know that they are correct in their conclusions they must turn to the text. Textualism gives legal reasoning the tools to work with in order to deduce what is the correct result of applying a legal text to a set of facts to determine the correct outcome. It lifts legal reasoning out of the murky, muddy waters of subjective feelings and into the realm of demonstrated proof and rationality. If the law is mere argument and interpretation without right and wrong answers then the law becomes merely a system for talented lawyers and constitution-violating politicians to change the law into whatever they want by reinterpreting it. Textualism gives judges a tool to use to decide cases, and it gives lawyers a tool with which to craft arguments grounded in legal reasoning.

(3) Textualism benefits the legislators and politicians because it enables the law to be applied in the way that they intended it to be applied and prevents judges from rewriting their laws from the bench via judicial misinterpretation. The legislators can draft a law in such a way as to know that their intentions will become the law applied by the courts only if a commonly known body of canons of construction, English definitions and grammar rules exist, and also only if the judge applies the legal text as written and does not "legislate from the bench" and impose that judge's personal feelings onto the law in the judge's interpretation of the text. Because textualism offers a set of rules showing whether a legal interpretation is true to the legal text, the politicians can be fairly sure that the law is what they intended it to be (if they drafted

the law while keeping the rules of textual analysis in mind, and presumably they were smart enough to make their intent clear from the text), and the judges will be obligated to flesh out the details and create interpretations that obey the text.

(4) Even if "the law" actually consists of the decisions and/or intentions of the legislators and judges, the people have no means of knowing it other than the text published by the legislature or the court, so textualism is necessary as a matter of legal epistemology. We can't read minds, but we can read texts. We can never know the subjective intentions and desires of the lawmaker other than by taking the legal text written by that lawmaker as an authoritative statement of the lawmaker's law which transforms their subjective decisions, desires and intentions into an objective formulation for us to read and analyze and understand and talk about. In other words, if the law can be known at all then textualism must be the proper interpretational tool, because only the legal text interpreted by clear understandable rules enables something that can truly be called "knowledge" of the law. If you want right and wrong answers instead of mushy subjective feelings, then textualism is a practical necessity and should be chosen simply for its usefulness.

The benefits listed above all come from textualism as a method and are not altered by the fact that some interpretation is needed to interpret a text. Two textualist judges or lawyers might apply the same textualist method to the same text and reach two different results. This does not mean that one objectively correct result did not exist. It only means that the law was so complicated, as it usually is, that the right answer was not perfectly obvious, and one of those two textualists simply made a mistake and/or was politically biased in some way. It is possible to demonstrate that the answer to a legal question is correct, but a demonstration will not necessarily persuade everyone that you are correct, and a lack of consensus does not negate knowledge of objective truth.

For example, "2+2=4" cannot be debated, but the theories of advanced theoretical physics can be debated, and the debate does not transform objective truth into a subjective matter of opinion. Similarly, we can debate complicated legal questions, but we cannot debate the textualist interpretation of "It is a crime to kill another human being unless as an act of self-defense where no reasonable retreat was possible; 'Self-defense' means that the defendant saw someone initiate a violent attack against him or heard someone threaten to attack him; Taking someone off life support or assisting a suicide or terminating a pregnancy shall not be construed as an act of killing because it merely withdraws life support and is not an active act of killing someone." The facts could be debated in applying the law to a real case, but the text of this law has one clear plain meaning.

The two alternatives to textualism that are frequently discussed are purposivism, which holds that a law should be interpreted to carry out the purpose of the law or the intent of the lawmaker, e.g. the judge should look at the legislative history and floor debates and seek to decipher the feelings and intentions of the congressmen instead of limiting himself to the words of the legal text, and consequentialism, which holds that a law should be interpreted to accomplish a result that achieves justice, typically defined as liberal "social justice," e.g. cases should be decided for blacks and women and against rich white men regardless of what the law says. The doctrines promise to give the judge discretion and flexibility to carry out the law's purpose or to avoid unfair, unjust outcomes. But the proper method of avoiding injustice is to amend or repeal bad laws or pressure the legislature to rewrite badly written laws; the proper method is not judicial activism to undermine the unbiased neutral fair application of the law.

Textualism reflects America's "separation of powers" structure: the congress makes the law, and the judge interprets and applies the law. This system enables political activism to participate in the making of laws while still enabling the application of the law to real people to be politically neutral and unbiased. A system that is more fair and just than the separation of powers legal system could not be imagined.

CHAPTER THIRTY NINE:
THE COMMERCE CLAUSE

The next three sections present my journalistic coverage of the Obamacare Case litigation, which I wrote for Liberty Magazine while it was happening. The articles, although covering current events in 2011 and 2012, discuss issues of American constitutional law from a libertarian perspective which are timeless, and they matter now more than ever. The three articles follow.

Federal Judge Roger Vinson of the Northern District of Florida has declared Obamacare unconstitutional in a lawsuit joined by numerous states seeking to escape from the onerous burdens that the law places upon them. But when I read that his rationale is that the mandate requiring people to buy health insurance exceeds the power of Congress under the Commerce Clause, I became a little bit sad; sad not because Judge Vinson is just dangling the dream of a new attempt to use commerce clause jurisprudence to limit the government's meddling in the economy, but because there is only about a one in 100 chance that the United States Supreme Court will agree with his reasoning.

There was a time when Congress could only pass laws authorized by the specific enumerated powers of the Constitution. (This is ostensibly still true, but most congressmen don't take it seriously.) One of those powers, indicated by the Commerce Clause, is the major one that Congress uses to destroy, I mean, to regulate, the economy. The Commerce Clause states: "Congress shall have power… to regulate commerce with foreign nations, and among the several states, and with the Indian tribes." In my constitutional law class final exam, I argued that the Commerce Clause clearly gives Congress precisely the same power to regulate economic activity within a state that it has to regulate economic activity within foreign nations, and since we obviously cannot march into France and order them to have a minimum wage or a health insurance mandate, and we can really only regulate goods from France that come across the Atlantic Ocean, the Commerce Clause means that Congress can only regulate goods that physically cross state lines. I got an A in the class, despite the fact that my law professor was a liberal.

However, most lawyers don't think that way. Even back in the 1800s the Commerce Clause case law said that Congress could regulate anything that did not take place entirely within one state. There was a time before the New Deal when the Supreme

Court still took the Commerce Clause seriously and tried its hardest to allow Congress only to regulate interstate commerce. But this interfered with the New Deal. So, after FDR threatened the Court with his infamous court-packing scheme, the Court made a "switch in time that saved nine," in the landmark case of NLRB v. Jones & Laughlin Steel Corp. (1937); it began to undermine the Commerce Clause by permitting the commerce power to extend wherever commerce within one state had effects across state lines.

Later, US v. Darby (1941) made it clear that the Commerce Clause was now a joke and Congress could do anything it wanted. To throw a little paint on the feces, the Court decided Wickard v. Filburn (1942), which said that a private individual's private behavior within one state could be "interstate commerce" under an aggregation theory that proposed the questions: "What if everybody did this? Would the aggregate cumulative effects have an impact on interstate commerce?" This meant that a person growing tomatoes in his own farm for his personal consumption could be engaged in interstate commerce, even though the tomatoes never left his farm, because he was somehow magically connected to all the other tomato farmers out there, a conclusion that is ridiculous only if one does not understand that it is the road to socialism. FDR's supporters argued that economics had somehow fundamentally changed since America's founding, and the law needed to change with it.

Commerce Clause jurisprudence remained buried for decades, but in a shallow grave. In the 1990s, Chief Justice Rehnquist, with help from Justice Thomas and the Court's other conservatives, tried to revive the distinction between economic and noneconomic, and national and local, in cases such as US v. Lopez (1995), which struck down a gun ban under the commerce power, and US v. Morrison (2000), which struck down an anti-gender violence law as having nothing to do with interstate commerce. Then Justice Scalia murdered Rehnquist's Commerce Clause revival in Raich v. Gonzales (2005), saying that the commerce power authorized the criminalization of medical marijuana because of the Necessary and Proper Clause: "Congress shall have power . . . to make all laws which shall be necessary and proper for carrying into execution the foregoing powers." For some reason, Scalia failed to understand that the Necessary and Proper Clause is irrelevant if Congress cannot pass a law under the Commerce Clause in the first place, because the necessary and proper power only assists laws that are already valid under other substantive clauses.

The fate of America's healthcare system now turns on how the Supreme Court will interpret the Commerce Clause, whether the Justices will hold that the aggregate effects of choosing not to buy health insurance constitute interstate commerce. I predict that the vote will go along political ideological lines, as the choice of whether to take the Commerce Clause seriously as a limit on Congress's power is as much a political as a legal decision. But there is no way to tell how Justice Kennedy will vote, and it is still too early to tell how Obama's appointees will vote. Still, I estimate that there is only a 1% chance that Obamacare will be struck down. It has been many decades since the Commerce Clause limitation had teeth; and the Court will be afraid of accusations that it is frustrating the will of the American voters if it strikes Obamacare down, even though it is the role of the judiciary to check the tyranny of the majority, and most Americans don't like Obamacare, anyway.

Nonetheless, if libertarians are to make ourselves known in the legal world, then the Commerce Clause is one of the main weapons that we will need to be in our arsenal. We can hope that one day our constitutional jurisprudence will return America to the Founding Fathers' vision of a federal government that cannot do whatever it wants. As my constitutional law professor was fond of saying, constitutional doctrines fade away but they never die, they can always come back, and there are libertarian legal doctrines from American history that we can revive if and when we develop the power to make our voices heard within the legal system.

CHAPTER FORTY:
JUDICIAL REVIEW VS.
JUDICIAL ACTIVISM

Last week the Supreme Court of the United States heard oral argument on whether to overturn Obamacare. I had previously suspected Obamacare would stand, and estimated a mere 1% chance of the vile, disgusting step towards socialized medicine being struck down.

But amazingly, Obama's Solicitor General, who argued the case, was, by most accounts, totally incompetent. He got so tongue-tied that he had to be verbally bailed out by Justice Ginsberg, several times. He could not articulate a limiting principle for where the powers of government would stop if Obamacare stands. This frightened some of the justices (although, in fairness, no such limit can be articulated, because Obamacare is a slippery slope towards socialism).

Most importantly, Justice Kennedy said things suggesting that he would probably vote to strike Obamacare down. Kennedy is the moderate Justice who holds the crucial swing vote between four liberals (all of whom are thought to support Obama's health care bill) and four conservatives (who are believed to oppose it). So the legal community now suspects that Obamacare is doomed. The so-called "individual mandate" is most likely going to die, and the entire convoluted, ungodly abomination might get dragged down with it, thus ending America's nightmarish experiment with socialized medicine.

This is great news for libertarians and bad news for President Obama.

How did Obama respond? This is how: by holding a press conference in which he bullied the Justices, threatening them with the charge that overturning his law would be "judicial activism" and noting that the Supreme Court is not elected whereas Obama's Congress, which narrowly passed his healthcare plan, was elected. His statement contains two glaring flaws.

1. Yes, Congress is elected and the Supreme Court isn't. That is the beauty of the Founding Fathers' scheme, that the rights of individuals are safeguarded by courts which do not answer to the whims and emotions of the hysterical and easily manipulated masses. Yet voters had sent a clear message that they did not want Obamacare passed, when they elected Senator Brown of Massachusetts. The Brown

election was widely viewed as a referendum on Obamacare. It was an election in which a Tea Party candidate won in a strongly left-leaning state. The bill only passed because of procedural maneuvering by the then-Democratic House. The 2010 election of the Tea Party House was a resounding rejection of Obamacare by the American people. Once again, Obama has the facts wrong.

2. The practice of "judicial review," the name for courts overturning unconstitutional laws, dates back to the famous case of Marbury v. Madison (1803). Since that case was decided, it has been well established that the courts have the power to overturn laws that violate the Constitution.

It is true, of course, that conservatives often bemoan "judicial activism," and now Obama is bemoaning it. So what is the difference between judicial activism and judicial review? Is it merely that if you like it you call it judicial review and if you dislike it you call it judicial activism? I do not believe that the difference between judicial review and judicial activism is subjective personal bias. The law is written words with defined meanings, and the text of the Constitution has a meaning that we can see if we read the words. A legal interpretation that obeys the text is correct, and an interpretation that twists or manipulates the text is incorrect.

I offer a deeper libertarian analysis to show that it is objectively true that Obamacare is unconstitutional. The Constitution of the United States was designed to limit the powers of government and protect citizens from the state, as a reaction by the Founding Fathers to the tyranny of the British Empire that they had defeated in the American Revolution. Democrats love to say that the Constitution is a "living document," which means that the Constitution changes to reflect the desires of the public (which, they believe, have become ever more leftist since the American Revolution). But the meaning of the Constitution is clear, and it does not change. The argument to overturn Obamacare comes from the fact that Congress has only the enumerated powers given it by the Constitution. Obamacare sought to use the Commerce Clause, which gives Congress the power to regulate "interstate commerce," in order to effect a partial nationalization of the healthcare industry. But as I argued before, and as Justice Kennedy implied at oral argument, this is far beyond what the Commerce Clause and the cases interpreting it explicitly permit.

So it will not be judicial activism but judicial review, which consists of faithfully conforming the law to what the Constitution allows, if the Supreme Court overturns Obama's health care plan. It is judicial activism when liberal judges follow the philosophy embodied in the legal theories called "Legal Realism" and "critical theory" or "critical legal studies." These theories hold that there is no such thing as an objectively correct or incorrect interpretation of the law, and therefore a judge is free to rule as his or her subjective feelings on morality and justice dictate (and note that somehow these feelings are almost always Marxist or liberal feelings).

Critical legal studies, which explicitly attacks the legitimacy of "legal reasoning," is hugely popular on many law school campuses. Many of the lawyers and judges of the future may buy into it. But when the Supreme Court rules on Obamacare in June of 2012, I hope it will be clear to the Marxists that they don't run America quite yet.

CHAPTER FORTY ONE: THE HISTORICAL SIGNIFICANCE OF THE OBAMACARE CASE

In my last article on the legal challenge to Obamacare I expressed optimism that Obamacare would be struck down. However, in an earlier Liberty article I had said it had only a 1% chance of being overturned. As it turns out, Obamacare was upheld, in a 5–4 decision that is a devastating loss for libertarians and the death of hope for saving the US healthcare industry from a slow decline into socialized medicine.

What happened? In my last essay I said that Justice Kennedy was the swing vote, and he was expected to vote against Obamacare. And that's what he did. With his vote we should have won. But he was not, in fact, the swing vote. Chief Justice John Roberts, whom George W. Bush appointed to be a conservative bulwark, turned traitor and voted with the court's liberals. Why?

When I was in law school the Chief Justice was still newly appointed, but he had already gained notoriety as a person deeply concerned with how the public viewed "the Roberts Court" (Supreme Court eras are often named after the chief justice who presides over them, e.g. the Rehnquist Court, the Warren Court). Roberts has proven himself a conservative in other opinions. He is reported to be a brilliant man, and surely knew what was at stake in the Obamacare case. But it appears he was so deeply worried that the public, influenced by both the Citizens United and the Obamacare decisions, would perceive the Roberts Court as an extremist ultra-Right court that he cared more about what other people thought of him than he did about his own ethical convictions. Judges do not face reelection, but the famous ones often care deeply about how history will view them. To simplify things, he was too embarrassed to be a principled conservative.

In that sense I liken him to Peter Keating, the "second hander" in Ayn Rand's novel "The Fountainhead." Peter Keating has no conviction or integrity, but "selflessly" lets other people create and define the goals and aspirations that he then pursues with ruthless ambition. Chief Justice Roberts has no internal principles, but simply goes with the public sentiment, or what he perceives to be other people's perceptions of his court. The Supreme Court was designed by America's founders to be a check on the actions of Congress in order to protect the American people from unconstitutional laws. The Court has failed, and the Commerce Clause has now lost all meaning. But the origin of this crisis lies with human psychology, not legal doctrines.

History will look back upon the Obamacare decision by the United States Supreme Court, and point to it as one of, and perhaps the most important, turning points in the process whereby the United States Republic collapsed into the American Empire, just as the Roman Republic became the Roman Empire during the Julius Caesar/Augustus era. The Obamacare Case is historically important because the Founding Fathers designed the US Constitution deliberately and intentionally under a "separation of powers" "checks and balances" system, so that the liberty of the people would be protected from the tyranny of the state by each branch (legislative, executive, judiciary) selfishly seeking power at the expense of the other branches, so that no branch could grow in power and assume dictatorship. The courts were designed to prevent Congress and President from collapsing democracy into dictatorship. The principle of Obamacare is socialism and the replacement of individual freedom with government control, more so than any law passed since FDR's New Deal.

The principle of the Obamacare decision is that nonpartisan, unbiased legal reasoning no longer has any place in American courts, which will now by dominated by partisan political bias, starting with the U.S. Supreme Court and trickling down to every lower court as well. Chief Justice Roberts' opinion was the very model of bad legal reasoning and political bias. If Obamacare was constitutional at all, it would have been under an interpretation of the Commerce Clause based on Wickard and the other New Deal cases, which had already gutted and mutilated the Commerce Clause. Chief Justice Roberts's rationale that the Obamacare "individual mandate" forcing every individual to buy health insurance is a tax, valid under the Taxing Power but not the Commerce Power, is so absurd and silly that no intelligent person can take it seriously. It is obvious what it was, and the truth cannot be hidden. It was a made-up justification and rationalization for a politically motivated decision for the United States Supreme Court to rubber stamp Obamacare and not get in the way of America's slow but steady collapse into Big Government socialism.

The destruction of the Commerce Clause as a limit to the government's ability to regulate the economy is the death of the United States Constitution as a limitation upon government power. Thus, Chief Justice Roberts has killed and buried the vision of the American Revolutionaries and Founding Fathers, who envisioned the Constitution as the political mechanism to protect our freedom from governmental tyranny. Unless the Tea Party or the libertarian movement can win at the ballot box and vote into office politicians who will repeal Obamacare and restore our individual rights, it looks inevitable for the USA to decline and fall into an American Empire. And with the entrenched establishment of Democrat liberals and Republican conservatives in power, the prospects for liberty don't look good. The only useful wisdom for such a situation is what Ayn Rand said, that "those who fight for the future, live in it today," because the harsh reality of the present isn't nice to experience, and the hope for freedom looks dim and dark, both for today and for tomorrow.

PART FOUR: MINARCHIST LIBERTARIANISM

CHAPTER FORTY TWO: WHAT IS MINARCHIST LIBERTARIANISM?

If we unpack the term "libertarian" we see that two basic types of libertarians exist, (1) the minarchists, who believe in limited government, and (2) the anarcho-capitalists, who want no government at all and believe in total anarchy combined with individually enforced private property rights. The anarcho-capitalists are the bigger subgroup, with a more extremist, loud, vocal membership, and the anarcho-capitalists dominate the libertarian movement, such that many people equate libertarianism with anarcho-capitalism. Anarcho-capitalism claims to be the one true libertarianism, possibly because Murray Rothbard, who coined the term "libertarian," was himself an anarcho-capitalist. The anarchists verbally beat up on the minarchists regularly, asserting that minarchists are unprincipled sellouts and that minarchists are really "statists," the libertarian insult which means a slave of the evil Big Government "state."

The minarchists thus far have not really had a good theoretical principle to justify themselves. Minarchists believe that the government should provide police, army, and courts, and should defend life, liberty and property, but they have not presented an idealistic and principled theory according to which an active government is vitally necessary for a good society to function. One of the purposes of this book is to offer GOLD as the principle which justifies and defends minarchist libertarianism, by showing that government is a truly necessary precondition of freedom. Government, when it is limited to its legitimate role, helps free markets to operate correctly by providing courts to resolve contract disputes and enforcing litigated court judgments through the police, as well as defending the free market from foreign conquest of invaders through the military. Freedom cannot exist in the absence of a group of armed defenders to defend it, and government is the easiest and most efficient system for defending our freedom.

Minarchist libertarians challenge the other group of libertarians, the anarcho-capitalists, by showing that anarchy won't work in practice, because it will lead inevitably to wars between competing governments or wars between competing police departments. Anarchy, if attempted in reality, would eventually collapse into a bloody mess from which the most brutal group of thugs would emerge as the new government, and it would look no different from the EVIL society where might makes right. The libertarian utopian society will achieve better results if it vests the power of violence in one body and uses the law, and democratic republican elections of politicians, to restrain and control that one body.

Anarchy doesn't make sense, because in one sense the government requires the consent of the governed, and in another sense it does not. It does in the sense that you as a citizen have the right to be politically active and participate in the political process which governs you. But it does not for the same reason that a murderer doesn't have the right to deny his consent to his victim for the victim to use force to defend herself. In other words, you do not have the right to be free from other people's systems of self-defense which they use to protect themselves from your ability to use violent force. To the extent that the government is the body to which the people have delegated their right to use violence for self-defense, and to the extent to which the government governs people only be protecting individuals from other aggressors' violations of their life, liberty and property, you do not have the right to be free from being governed, since this equates to the right to harm others.

As a practical matter, providing police, army, and courts is very simple, and can only be done properly one way, so no need exists for experimentation and innovation from free market competition. The voters have an adequate ability by means of political activism to control and restrain a democratic republican government, and the constitutional law, properly applied, would enable the U.S. Constitution to protect individuals and minorities from the tyranny of the majority. Government can be held accountable without us needing to have competition among rival governments to hold the state accountable to us.

The anarcho-capitalists are naïve idealistic fools who are not cynical enough in recognizing the flaws in their plan, and the way in which anarchy won't work unless everyone is already nice and civilized and decent to everyone else. To quote James Madison in The Federalist No. 51: "What is government itself, but the greatest of all reflections on human nature? If men were angels, no government would be necessary. If angels were to govern men, neither external nor internal controls on government would be necessary. In framing a government which is to be administered by men over men, the great difficulty lies in this: you must first enable the government to control the governed; and in the next place oblige it to control itself. A dependence on the people is, no doubt, the primary control on the government."

The anarcho-capitalists argue that in their anarchist utopia the legitimate functions of government will be performed by multiple governments who will be paid by users and compete for customers, and each government will protect only its customers. This would look no different from mafia protection rackets. If the competing governments in an anarcho-capitalist utopia are kind and gentle and virtuous enough to respect the rights of the consumer-citizens and the rights of the subscribers of rival protection agencies, and not to abuse their organized power of violence to intimidate the people and fight against their competing rivals, then they would be angels, not humans, to resist the temptation to use their guns for personal gain. So it can truly be said that anarcho-capitalism can only work if men are angels, not humans.

A practical, pragmatic evaluation can see that competing governments is a recipe for wars between governments. The Marxists and socialists committed a grave error in thinking that politicians and bureaucrats are all-powerful, all-knowing, loving, kind, generous, great, good people, in other words, the "government as God" complex. The anarcho-capitalists make the same mistake, in thinking that their competing governments or competing police departments will be saintly and noble, instead of using their guns and organized violence to fight against rival governments for a greater share of consumers. Not only does the possibility exist, but it would be natural for bloody battles to result, because the defeat of a rival government will lead to more profits for the victor in the war, so constant war is a logical result of the situation of anarcho-capitalism.

The problem with privatizing the police, army, and courts, is: "who will protect us from our protectors?" James Madison, in the Federalist Paper just mentioned, offered a different view for how to safeguard freedom, based on checks and balances and separation of powers and federalism, so that one branch of government, or one group of people, or one alignment of special interests, prevents the others from growing in power to reach the point of oppression and tyranny. The Federalist vision, in which we have one unitary government chained in a cage of laws and structures to protect us from it, is the more realistic, practical, pragmatic, workable vision, based on better wisdom. The Federalist minarchist plan enables a police and army who can legitimately use violent force to defend life, liberty, and property, but it designs a political structure to prevent the use of force from evolving into despotism, tyranny, and dictatorship. One can argue that America owes her greatness, and her freedom, and her status as the world's oldest current democracy, to that vision.

The anarcho-capitalists say that modern America has evolved in a socialist welfare state, which proves that minarchy, as embodied by the U.S. Constitution as a system for protecting the people and limiting the government's ability to grow and seize power, didn't work and doesn't work. To which I reply that in a republican democracy, the voters will always get what they want, and the political system gives to the American people what the people want, and what the voters have chosen. The anarcho-capitalists have not invented a design, other than in their fantasies and imagination, which would prevent anarcho-capitalism from evolving into socialism or Marxism, if the people wanted and demanded a Marxist socialist government.

If competing governments exist, and the people want socialism, then a government will offer to sell socialism, and everyone will buy it because the people will want it. Anarcho-capitalism could dissolve into socialism, to the same extent and for the same reason that minarchy could. The ability of consumers to hold sellers accountable is roughly comparable to the ability of voters to hold politicians accountable, although a superior democracy would hold elections more frequently, and allow a greater diversity of political parties and candidates on the ballot, than the USA does currently. The only thing which could prevent the anarchy to socialism scenario would be if the public had a healthy respect for individual rights, and were mostly libertarians. But such a society would need no government because men would be angels, and such is not the situation with which we must deal.

Wishing anarchy as the solution for the evils of big government, and believing that anarchy will solve the problem of government, is unrealistic and misguided. Anarchy would not solve the problem of crime, nor the need to defend the people from foreign enemies, nor the need for judges who have the power to enforce their judicial resolutions of conflicts between people, so that the hundreds of conflicts that happen between people every day can be resolved peacefully in a court and not by bloody armed violence in duels or wars. If men were angels who respected each other's rights, then competing courts, competing police, and competing armies might work, but we must deal with human nature as it really exists, and not how we wish it would be in a utopia.

The principle of libertarian freedom is not ultimately minarchy or anarcho-capitalism. Liberty is, at its root, democracy and republicanism, a government of, by and for the people, where the people have control, such that the political decisions which affect the people are made by the people themselves, and not by a privileged class of elite nobles or experts or bureaucrats or politicians. This is the political manifestation of freedom and the right to make self-determining choices, which underlies both economic libertarianism and social libertarianism as expressions of GOLD. The problem of designing a government in the context of the right of the voters to make the political decisions is how to prevent the people, and the voters, from letting the majority violate the rights of the individual or the minority. This question was specifically answered by the U.S. Constitution, and the system presented in James Madison's Federalist Papers makes more sense than anarcho-capitalism.

The extent to which freedom still exists in America, and the fact that we the people retain the power to reclaim our freedom if the voters can be persuaded to want it, and our right to advocate libertarian policies without fear of being thrown in jail by the statist establishment thanks to freedom of speech, is owed entirely to the minarchist libertarian vision of the Founding Fathers and American Revolutionaries in drafting the United States Constitution. The U.S. Constitution is and always has been a libertarian document, the document which locked the government in a cage of laws to protect the people from the government while allowing the government to protect the people.

The problem with anarchy is that it won't work. The government has an important role to play, such as in national defense, funding and organizing the police to prevent crime, and enforcing contracts so that the free market economic system of purchases and sales is able to function. Also, the government through the police generally prevents one person from committing violence against another person, so anarchy would lead to a net increase in aggression and violent coercion, but at the same time we would have lost the system of democracy-based government introducing some degree of civility and thoughtful deliberation into the widespread systematic use of force by the government. The minarchist position would drastically cut government spending compared to what liberals want for social programs or welfare and what conservatives want for military spending, because the American government has grown too big, and spending has become wasteful and excessive. But a minimalist state, a "minarchy" as we libertarians call it, is necessary for society to function properly.

CHAPTER FORTY THREE: THE GOLD MINARCHIST ARGUMENT

Assume that government is a true "natural monopoly," in that it is in the nature of the services it provides that competition between governments won't work and cannot function properly. If one assumes that premise, it follows that, since one government must govern all, all should equally be given a voice in how the government runs. From this it follows that public participation and political decision-making would best be accomplished by voting for policies and candidates in a republic democracy.

The only type of competition which is viable and feasible is to vote on political candidates who compete against one another and who embrace different competing platforms and policies. Assuming that elections happen once every two to four years, the electoral system gives power to the people, and lets the people choose their government and hold the politicians accountable. Also, if a person dissents, then they are free to withdraw into the wilderness, or move to another country. It would also follow that, since one service provider must provide the service to all, and everyone benefits from the service, that because each person receives a benefit it is just and fair to require that each person pay for the benefit of the services they received. Therefore taxation is just to the extent that it funds services which everyone needs and which the free market cannot provide. Taxation for a minarchist state is not theft, it is forcing someone to pay for the benefit which they already received, which is fair and just.

Now, to return to the first assumption, let me explain why government is a natural monopoly. Assume X, Y, A and B. Assume that Y is X's government that X votes for or pays for and which protects and defends X. Assume that B is A's government that A elects or hires and which employs force to defend A's life liberty and property. The basic argument is that if government's main role is to protect someone from violence by others and to resolve disputes and conflicts, and competing governments exist, and X hires government Y and A hires government B, and X has a conflict or dispute with A, then it will be impossible for Y and B to reach a resolution peacefully, because, as governments, both Y and B are organizations dedicated to the organized use of force, so it will be natural and inevitable for Y and B to go to war against one another in order to resolve the dispute between X and A. Competing governments would collapse into constant wars between governments, and the result would be a brutal, bloody, horrific perpetual anarchy, where the winners of the wars would be the most vicious, toughest thugs. This is precisely what an EVIL world looks like. Anarcho-capitalism is actually the practical path to a violent dictatorship, or a land governed by mafia protection rackets.

Conflicts between X and A can be peacefully resolved only if X and A are both governed by one single unitary minarchist government which claims jurisdiction over them both, let us call it the YB State. X and A are not slaves of YB, because they are free to vote for the politicians who lead YB, and to engage in vigorous political activism to influence the path of YB. If YB is a true minarchist state, then the YB Constitution will lock it in a cage of laws to force it to respect X's freedom and A's freedom and GOLD, such that YB will be limited to providing police, military and courts for the defense of life, liberty and property. GOLD does not demand that X and A get to choose whether or not they are subject to YB in this sense: GOLD does not give you the right to choose how someone else protects themselves from you and from your ability to force your beliefs onto them. X does not have the right to prevent YB from protecting A from X. Nor can A forbid X from protecting himself using YB. Therefore as against X for A and A for X, neither is justified in refusing to grant legitimacy to YB, because it is in the nature of force and violence for others defending themselves from you not to be voluntary or freely chosen by you. YB is the organized use of force for force's legitimate purpose of defending life liberty and property, i.e. YB is a government. YB protects X from A and A from X, so both X and A should not complain about YB.

CHAPTER FORTY FOUR: THE CITY MOUSE LIBERTARIAN AND THE COUNTRY MOUSE LIBERTARIAN

While reading an article by Bruce Bartlett on Forbes.com, I encountered an interesting idea about libertarians, which I will elaborate upon here in the context of the minarchist vs. anarcho-capitalist debate. The idea is that two types of libertarians exist: the "survivalist" and the "metrosexual," whom I would instead call the country libertarian and the city libertarian.

The country libertarian believes in libertarianism for very practical reasons. He lives in a rural wilderness, possibly in a mountainous area, is probably a member of a militia, and he has three basic desires: to own gold and canned food, to own a stockpile of guns and ammo, and for government to leave him alone. If civilization collapses or the USA becomes a Communist dictatorship, he is ready to go into hiding and fight for freedom. He might be slightly eccentric or crazy, and he may also believe in conspiracy theories. The city libertarian, on the other hand, lives in a city or suburbs, and believes in libertarian ideas because of reason and logic and abstract theory. He is worldly, and he sees the long-term rational self-interest of society embracing freedom. He probably doesn't own a gun, and he buys his food from grocery stores, works a regular job in an office, and doesn't own a stockpile of gold or ammo, but he has a bookshelf in his apartment full of libertarian-themed books, as well as an e-reader loaded with e-book copies of every libertarian classic.

I relate this to minarchy vs. anarchy because I think that the country libertarian's life experiences and intellectual context deny him the empirical information to refute anarchy, whereas the worldly, experienced, intellectually sophisticated city libertarian is more likely to see the need for a minimal state. The three arguments which persuaded me to declare myself as a minarchist are: (1) Competing governments will lead inevitably to bloody wars between governments, because a unified government will not exist to prevent one competing police department from going to war against its rivals, and the motive of profit and expansion combined with each government's organized military power will lead each police department's leaders to the natural human temptation to engage in wars of conquest; (2) No mechanism can be devised to prevent competing police departments from intimidating citizens into buying their services and evolving into protection racket gangs of thugs, since no government will exist to protect the buyer from the seller of police protection services; and (3) If one unified system of courts does not exist, and the courts lacks the authority to enforce their judgments universally, then the hundreds of various fights and arguments that happen every day between people, which are now resolved by litigation, will instead become violent duels, and civilization will deteriorate into savagery.

The empirical data which proves that competing governments will not coexist in peace, and will definitely go to war, is that, if one thinks of planet Earth as one place, then every government is competing with all the others for the human race's support, which the people can give or deny to any given government by leaving one nation and immigrating to another nation. Every nation's government "competes" with all the other nations nearby for Earth's scarce economic resources. Global competition between nations is no different from what Rothbardian competing governments would look like within a limited geographic scope. Rather than Rothbardian peace and harmony between governments, human history is full of hundreds of wars between national governments, so many wars that I could fill page after page naming them, and making two governments compete for the same group of dues-paying customers won't make them get along any better.

The country libertarian has no reason to see logic in these minarchist arguments, because the arguments contradict his life experiences. When he has a fight with his fellow militia member, they are both nice guys, and they work it out, or else they let one of their friends act as judge and decide who wins the argument. Everything is nice and chummy and peaceful, and police or courts are unnecessary. And the country libertarian has no worldly experience to see, for example, that if two major multinational businesses have a contract dispute, and millions of dollars are at stake, the CEOs of both corporations might hire mercenary soldiers and attack each other unless society provides a legal system to nonviolently resolve the dispute and the court forces both CEOs of both corporations to abide by the court's legal judgment.

Yes, the police use force to enforce court orders, but the legal system is "nonviolent" compared to the system of anarchy which would resolve such a conflict through a war that might see hundreds of mercenary soldiers shot and killed, whereas police enforcement of a litigated contract dispute in the United States is usually bloodless. The country libertarian is always armed and knows how to use his gun, so he can't imagine that a lot of people rely on the police for protection, and that competing police departments could easily intimidate and victimize such people, who would be unable to defend themselves from such intimidation.

In the country libertarian's sheltered little world, everyone is nice and friendly and good, so problems requiring government don't exist. To once again paraphrase James Madison in The Federalist, "if men were angels then we would have no need for government." In the country libertarian's brotherhood of friends, family and militia, everyone really is an angel, so anarcho-capitalist theory has fooled this type of person into thinking that anarchy can be made to work in practice. Maybe anarchy would work in rural, sparsely populated areas, but it would destroy civilization and shatter peace if implemented nationally in America. Many city libertarians are also anarchists, and some rural libertarians are minarchists. Nonetheless, anarchy's biggest flaw is simply a lack of experience-based knowledge which would make the country libertarians see the problems in their theory, which problems are obvious to the more sophisticated city libertarians.

CHAPTER FORTY FIVE: THE ROTHBARDIAN ERROR

Murray Rothbard, one of the most famous founders of libertarianism, asserted that government has a problem, namely, that it is a monopoly. He asserted that this problem is solved by anarcho-capitalism, which would create competing governments to break up the monopoly. The problem with Rothbard's analysis is that government has two distinct problems, not one unitary problem. The Rothbardian solution solves one problem while making the other problem worse.

The first problem is that government appropriates a monopoly in offering the services which it provides. The second problem is that the government uses violent force, and claims the right to legitimately use large-scale organized force. Competing governments would eliminate those flaws and defects of the state which are attributable to it being a monopoly. But if each of the competing governments continues to use force, then the second problem, the ability to use force, goes untreated, and that problem in fact becomes worse since governments could evolve into gangs of thugs running mafia-style protection rackets, and "competition" would most naturally take the form of wars between governments. The best solution to the second problem is to chain all large-scale organized legitimate force into one political entity, and to then give the people power over that entity via the vote and lock it in a cage of laws via constitutional law.

CHAPTER FORTY SIX:
GRADUALIST MINARCHY

If we can ask "who will protect us from our protectors? Who will protect us from our government?" then why not ask "who will protect us from our anarcho-capitalist competing police departments and our competing courts?" The anarchist's only coherent answer is that, as if by magic, economic competition will restrain the thuggish brutality sure to emerge among competing police departments or, as they should properly be called, competing governments. But it is unclear how economic competition will create any greater accountability than the democratic system of government, in which political candidates compete and if the people do not approve of a government's leadership they simply vote it out of office.

Wars between competing governments would be bad for business only if your side does not win the war. If the people are willing to be ruled then anarcho-capitalism will not prevent them from being ruled, and if the people want to be free then minarchy will not prevent them from voting libertarians into elected office. If consumers can bankrupt a corrupt privatized police system then voters can vote out a corrupt state. If the other competing police departments can band together to defeat a warmongering police system then the people can revolt against a warmongering state.

If people are threatened by widespread violent crimes and armed, aggressive foreign governments, then some kind of mechanism is necessary to protect people. A minarchy could do the job, but a unitary government which is the sole judge of its own limits could expand beyond its legitimate scope and seize tyrannical powers. On the other hand, competing police and competing courts, i.e. competing governments, will lead inevitably to wars between governments, not only because the taste of power is addictive but also because the governments will compete and it is natural for a competitor to seek to defeat its rivals, by any means at its disposal, and violent force will be an easy tool for each competing government to use. If we had true anarchy then there would be no force to prevent a group of organized armed thugs from banding together and declaring themselves kings. And if, in fact, a group of bandits did declare dictatorship and the people took up arms and went to war for freedom and organized itself to fight the self-proclaimed bandit kings then this group of protectors would either disband once the threat was over, in which case a new threat could emerge, or it would stabilize itself, in which case it would naturally evolve into a government. As a practical matter any organization organized for self-defense will inevitably evolve into a government (see, for an elaboration of this argument, Robert Nozick's "Anarchy, State and Utopia").

Anarchy can only work, i.e. can only be feasible and viable in pragmatic practical reality, in a populace of honorable people committed to the NVP principle of not initiating aggression. Otherwise there will need to be a mechanism for the just use of force to prevent the unjust initiation of violence, and this mechanism will develop into a government. So long as violence exists the people will need a system to use force for self-defense. Such system will only be as effective and as limited and restrained as the ethics and honor of the people who run it, of the public who votes for it (if a minarchy) or of the consumers who pay for it and the leaders who run it (if competing governments). An unchecked minarchy can evolve into a dictatorship, and an unrestrained anarchy can evolve into a civil war. As such, minarchy and anarchy both have incurable fatal flaws.

But this problem only arises if you assume that individuals must be protected from violence. The only solution to the question of minarchy vs. anarchy is to change people, not government, because if we had a society of great wealth in which no one was poor, and a psychologically healthy populace in which people were not jealous and hateful and resentful towards the rich and successful, then crime might possibly be reduced to the point at which no government would be needed for self-defense. If we lived in a utopia of vast wealth and happiness and extreme psychological health, and nobody was motivated to commit crimes, then it might be feasible to do without government, because crime would be so rare that it could be prevented on a case-by-case basis by armed citizens, and most people in disagreements would debate and reach an agreement on the strength of reason and logic. But anarchy cannot be feasible until our standard of living rises so high that no one lives in poverty and everyone has enough wealth to be happy, and a vast philosophical/psychological shift away from envy and laziness and towards rationality and personal responsibility would also be necessary to eliminate the pervasive threat of theft and warfare. Only a capitalist minarchy lasting one thousand years could possibly create material and social progress like that. And if free trade made all the nations of the world rich and satisfied then it would also be unlikely that foreign nations would want to invade us.

Of course, the same kind of people who would not need government are the ones who would not want it, and the closer we get to free market capitalism, the more wealth we create and the happier and less resentful people will become. In the Twenty First Century the idea of an entire nation or world of rich, happy people is a horribly unrealistic, impractical dream utopia, but on a purely theoretical level I think that it can eventually be achieved, and the closer we get towards freedom the more we set up a foundation that could create a perfect world in flesh-and-blood reality. In such a world, which I would call a libertarian utopia, there would be no need for government, because men would be angels.

Our task, then, is not to create anarchy by fiat overnight, it is to gradually increase economic freedom and libertarian thinking step by step so that we begin in reality and end in libertarian utopia 1000 years later. The natural next step towards libertarian utopia for America is minarchy, while criminals and foreign nations still exist for which an armed protection system is necessary. Indeed, I think that both libertarian minarchists and libertarian anarchists have their hearts in the right place and want the same result, a world free from coercion and the initiation of violence, but the anarchists want to create radical change overnight in a way that the American public will never accept, and they cling to their impractical ideological purity as their highest value. The minarchists, on the other hand, want to work from within the preexisting political structure of government to create free market capitalism in a world which right now is full of crime, war, and violence, such that we might achieve libertarian change gradually. Thus, although from a purely theoretical point of view I actually think that anarchists are more realistic than minarchists about the human ability to create a perfectly just and self-regulated government, I think the minarchists are more realistic about actually making libertarian change happen in reality rather than in our fantasy daydreams, and so I proudly consider myself to be a libertarian minarchist and not an anarcho-capitalist.

The fact of the matter is that it is absolutely impractical, naïve, and hopeless to think that we have any possibility of creating anarchy or competing governments in the United States. The government would have to be so blatantly corrupt and evil that the American people would rise up in rebellion, and as a tactical matter it would be far easier simply to vote libertarian candidates into Congress and the White House than to overthrow the entire American state. No viable politician in the United States is proposing anarchy, and if they did the public would react with fear and anger, but there are a few viable politicians proposing minarchy or, at the very least, a much more fiscally responsible government. Therefore one either renounces reality or one accepts the government and seeks to shrink it down as small as possible by using libertarian minarchism. And it seems to me that we do have some actual possibility of making government smaller if we fight our battles using logic, common sense, and a commitment to pragmatism and practical reality.

It may be bemoaned that if we do not start off by advocating total immediate anarcho-capitalism today then such will never be achieved, and a 1000 year minarchy plan is a weak-willed watered-down compromise to the statists. One thinks of Rothbard's claim, to paraphrase, that a plan which seeks freedom in 50 years through gradual changes endorses slavery for the next 50 years, or that advocating a 5% tax reduction from a 45% tax rate down to 40% endorses the 40% progressive income tax. This attitude is unrealistic and impractical, but it is also highly unethical and irresponsible. If instantaneous freedom is a viable possibility then the ethical choice is to choose it. That much is obvious. But if freedom today is simply not possible and our only choice is between freedom in 50 years or freedom never, then freedom in 50 years is the ideal (I define "ideal" as "the best possible") and choosing it is not an endorsement of slavery for the next 50 years. In fact, because the only real choices in that scenario are freedom in 50 years or no freedom ever, the "choice" of choosing freedom today reduces to the choice of never achieving freedom, which is absolutely wrong and immoral.

Short-term compromises, e.g. calling for a 5% tax reduction or voting for a conservative Republican or liberal Democrat political candidate who embraces some libertarian policies to achieve incremental increases in freedom, will not result in us forgetting our ultimate goals. We libertarians do not forget so easily. Those radicals who denounce gradualism, refuse to work within the American electoral system, and who dream of a blood-soaked anarcho-capitalist revolution have abandoned the fight for freedom in practical reality and can do nothing more than sit back helplessly, daydream about a utopia and criticize everyone else. Therefore the Rothbardian position, which prides itself on the purity of its noble idealism, is actually far less ethical than the gradualist minarchist position.

Lest it be said that minarchy is a betrayal of the true libertarian ideals, let me proceed to offer my best defense of minarchy. First there is the question of taxation. The anarchists claim that taxation is obviously theft because it is the taking of property against the owner's will. But a host of insurmountable problems emerge if government is funded by voluntary payment for services rendered (e.g. bias/bribery of the courts, wars between governments, and, where courts compete, the finality of judgments). However, I think that the question of tax is a straw man, because if the government was limited to defending the citizens from violence and all of the nonsense of the welfare state was eliminated then the government's budget would be small enough so that taxes would be too small to be noticed.

For example, why bother complaining about a 10% flat tax on income? If you earn a $3,000 monthly salary, who would really care about paying $300 per month in taxes? Would you actually notice it if you kept $2,700 per month? And don't tell me that the issue of taxation is one of principle, not degree: a real difference exists between a 10% flat tax and a progressive income tax at the combined local, state and federal levels with an effective average rate of 45% or more. A person who earns $3000 monthly could live a very happy life on $2,700 after-tax dollars per month (a 10% flat tax), but would probably be miserable on a $1,650 monthly after-tax income (a 45% tax). The anarchist asks what gives government the "right" to collect taxes, but the minarchist's reply is: the government provides you with a service, protection from violence, so it is entitled to collect some form of payment. You need to be protected, and the government protects you, so it would be unfair for you not to pay the government for the service it provides to you. If protection from violence is a necessary service, and it is not feasible for the service to be provided by the free market, then it cannot be said that the government "forced" the taxpayer to buy its services.

There is also the issue of consent. The anarchists claim that they have not consented to be governed by the United States government. I concede that the right to vote is not the equivalence of consent, although actually casting a vote is a form of consent. However, you are not required to give your consent in order to be born, or in order to require food to eat or air to breathe. Similarly no reason exists for you to need to consent in order to be subject to the political life of the community and the human species, assuming that such is a necessary precondition for your survival. As a practical matter you can consent to be governed and accept the government and seek to improve it by casting your vote and engaging in political activism, or you can sit back and complain about your lack of consent and choose to do nothing pragmatic to stop tyranny and watch as the nation slides into dictatorship. More to the point, if you refuse to consent to be an American, then you are (or should be) free to leave and move away from the USA.

From a more theoretical point of view there is the minarchist argument that government is based on the retaliatory use of force against aggressors and therefore the aggressor need not consent in order to be governed. If a criminal attacks me I don't need my attacker's consent to defend myself from him. One can apply this more broadly to say that the individual does not have the right to be free from other people's self-defense against that individual. Every other person's systems for self-defense aggregate to form society's system of self-defense, which is what the government consists of. Therefore the individual does not have the right to live in a non-governmental anarchy. Consent to being governed by a minarchy is unnecessary because minarchist activity consists entirely of self-defense. Note that the enforcement of tort law, where lawbreakers negligently injure victims in ways the victims did not consent to, and contract law, where people defend their property which they own as a result of trades embodied in freely chosen contracts, are forms of self-defense. The anarchist reply is that this theory treats everyone like convicted criminals. But if the role of minarchist government is really and truly limited to protecting citizens from violence, and defending life, liberty and property, then in reality it is only the criminals and foreign invaders who will be affected.

Let me now present the state of nature social contract analysis of minarchy. In a state of nature, if you believed that someone was a criminal who had stolen money from you and you sought restitution from him and to punish him, you would owe him some sort of procedural right, some kind of trial, before you enacted vengeance upon him. The other person who harmed you is not entitled to justice as a criminal, but as a human being he is entitled to fair treatment from you. If you attempted to enact vengeance without an adequate trial then you would run a serious risk of punishing the innocent because you, the injured party, would be making the judgment of guilt and innocence, such that your decision would inevitably be biased. A trial could never be fair and impartial if you were the judge of your own case, so an impartial judge would be necessary. The basic justification of government, at least as far as the government providing courts, and the police to enforce court judgments, is that it is inherently necessary from the condition of the state of nature for the people to enter into a social contract that delegates the decision-making power for adjudicating cases and conflicts to a neutral judge. The judge is given life tenure and a secure salary, so that he or she cannot be influenced, and the police are given the power to enforce court orders, so that the judge's decision is binding and conflicts are resolved with finality by the courts and do not transform into violent wars, duels or feuds.

It is inaccurate to say that every person can see the objective truth with his own eyes without being biased, and therefore no need exists to delegate litigation decisions. In many conflicts both parties to the conflict will believe that the other party is at fault and will stand to gain significantly if the other loses, resulting in bias. For example, did you steal from me, or did I not own that object? Did you breach our contract, or did I? Did you murder my brother and should you be put in jail, or are you really innocent? The ability to know the truth does not eliminate the potential for bias inherent in human nature if a strong self-interest or emotional stake motivates the decision-maker. Any belief to the contrary is woefully naïve about how the human brain and human perception works. The people need an impartial, neutral party to adjudicate conflicts in order to see that justice is done. A system of courts and police departments carries out the function of the enactment of justice which was delegated to the government by people in the state of nature. Thus, under what I have described here, which I call the decision theory of government, the need for some sort of a minarchist government is inherent in human nature, no matter how perfect or flawed or good or bad the people are.

The anarchists argue that competing courts and police departments could solve the decision problem. Robert Heinlein painted a picture of an example of this in his libertarian novel "The Moon is a Harsh Mistress," where two people who have a dispute hire a friend to act as judge and then agree to abide by his decision like gracious gentlemen. But this is mere fiction, not fact. An anarcho-capitalist competing police department or a competing judge that is paid per use and which competes for consumers in a free market will be hopelessly biased in favor of its or his customers, since it or he will not want to lose customers. Essentially, in a competing courts system the judges and the police will continually be taking bribes in the form of payments from their customers. Given the widely understood fact that bribes create bias, it would be no wonder for such a system to slant justice.

It will be argued that in competing governments the governments would compete over who could be more fair and neutral, but this is silly when one considers that a human being will not value some abstract ideal of fairness over the concrete benefit of a judge who is essentially bribed by the plaintiff to rule against the defendant. Nor can it be said that biased judges will suffer bad reputations and no one will adhere to their rulings, because the economics of the system itself will tend to make every judge biased, so people will have no choice but to accept it. Thus, even assuming that coercive taxation is unjust, it would still be better for the enactment of justice if one unitary government operated one set of police and one set of courts which all citizens paid into. One might argue that the government will pay the minarchist judge's salary so that judge will also be biased. But bias will be minimized if the judge's salary is paid by a neutral third party (the state) and not by one of the two parties to the litigated dispute. This judicial neutrality is achieved if a judge is appointed to life tenure paid for by the community, rather than hired by a competing government which will take profit or loss based on the judge's decisions. America's Founders recognized as much when they described their proposed judiciary in the Federalist Papers.

Reality will always contain only one set of facts which are objectively true. Therefore one ruling in a litigated case will be correct, and all others will be incorrect. Only one justice exists, and one truth exists, and one right and wrong exist. Truth and justice define only one general guideline to the type of laws and procedures by means of which the legal system can be just and ethical. From this it follows that we only need one government, a government that discovers the truth at trial, enacts libertarian laws, and executes justice in protecting the public from criminals and aggressors. Even the Rothbardian anarcho-capitalist who wants competing governments would concede that one general set of libertarian legal principles exists that every government should follow. Then what precisely is there about the law for competition between governments to discover?

In an economy with 300 million consumers there are 300 million different unique sets of preferences and desires for businesses to sell to, and each individual knows his own desires better than anyone else, so a central planner bureaucrat cannot satisfy the public's desires as efficiently as capitalism, because each consumer can make choices for himself or herself better than the bureaucrats. An infinite number of potential products and services can be developed and offered, so free market competition enables experimentation which produces consumer satisfaction through trial and error in matching supply and demand. But in a state with 300 million citizens, only one truth exists for a court to discover, and only one just law exists for legislators to enact, and only one uniform product exists for the police to sell, namely defending citizens from violence. So it makes less sense for governments employing differing legal approaches to compete, and it makes more sense to have one central government with every citizen-voter striving to make that one government conform to the demands of truth and justice.

The American courts of law with their monopoly on legal authority and the use of force necessary to produce binding authoritative resolutions of disputes prevent thousands of disagreements and conflicts between human beings from erupting into violence. Litigation is made possible by government, and as much as libertarians might hate the law and lawyers, the anarchist alternative is for conflicts to escalate into violent battles. No voluntary or competing system of courts will possess an equivalent power to ensure that the litigated resolution is binding upon the parties so that they don't turn to bloodshed if they dislike the result. It is all well and good to abstractly theorize that no inherent conflict of interests among human beings exists. But practical reality paints a different picture.

For example, if a patient loses a leg through the negligence of a doctor and she can no longer work, and she wants one hundred thousand dollars of compensation from the doctor, and the doctor thinks he acted reasonably and doesn't want to pay, then a conflict exists. Or if a businessman loses millions of dollars because his supplier breaches their contract and the businessman wants compensation, and the supplier disagrees, then a conflict exists. These types of conflicts will not generally be resolved peacefully by reasoned dialogue and debate. Either some neutral third party will be empowered to pass final judgment in resolving such disputes, with a police force to enforce the judicial decision, or else such conflicts will become bloody violent wars. Rothbard claims that the finality of judgments problem could be solved by a rule that if three different courts rule on a case then any two courts' judgments will be final. But who will enforce such a rule? And what if the consumers who lose their court cases refuse to agree to it? No meta-government would exist to force the various competing governments to abide by good rules.

It is no answer to say that the free market would solve such problems because the doctor's or supplier's reputations would suffer, because this will not provide sufficient enforcement of tort law or contract law for our society to be able to function, nor would it accomplish justice. Government must have a monopoly on force so that judicial conflict resolutions have finality. And how can anyone say that competing governments would not go to war because war would be bad for business, when the competitors will each have tons of angry customers screaming at them and threatening to withdraw their business if the police do not find a way to obtain favorable judgments against the people with whom the consumers have disputes and hate? If the people are peaceful and non-aggressive then they will have no need for government. But if the people are war-like then anarcho-capitalist competing governments is a recipe for inter-governmental wars.

Competing governments have been tried before, and most anarchists didn't like the result. America's Founders intended the three branches of the United States government: legislative, executive and judicial, to compete and restrain each other. That is the idea of separation of powers and checks and balances. They also intended the states and the federal government to compete. That is federalism. The Founders' plan failed when the voters demanded a bigger, more powerful government, as they did with FDR's New Deal after the fear and panic of the Great Depression. All that would be needed in a nation of competing police departments would be one major scary crime wave with a few dozen grisly murders to get people frightened, and all the consumers would be driven to whichever government promised to take the most drastic, cruel, draconian measures to fight crime, and that government would become huge and corrupt and harsh, and the competing government system would produce a powerful unitary government, a dictatorship police state which no libertarian could possibly want.

If a unitary government can grow itself and claim powers that it has no right to, what is to prevent one government from among a group of competing governments to do the same? Given the hypothetical competing government, what force will ensure that it does not decide its own scope of powers and grant itself a tyranny like any unitary government? In Rothbard-topia, what if consumers wanted, and would pay for, socialist non-libertarian law? Who would stop them? Either the competing governments will be unregulated, in which case each government, which the anarchists admit will have the capacity to use organized force, will simply seek to expand as much as possible, or the governments in the competition will regulate each other, in which case wars will erupt frequently whenever two or more governments disagree, or else some kind of meta-governmental body will arise to regulate the competing governments, and this body will evolve into a unitary government.

In a sense the planet Earth as a whole is a set of competing governments. Almost two hundred different national governments exist, and it is frequently possible to move from one to another, immigration laws notwithstanding. Yet this competition accomplishes nothing beneficial, for two reasons. First, because governments compete over who can provide the most services and not over who can provide the most freedom. Nations compete over who can accomplish the most, not who can govern the least. This is fully to be expected. For example, imagine the advertisement: "Buy my service and I will do absolutely nothing for you!" Second, because the nations limit who can join or leave each government, i.e. immigration restrictions. In an anarchist's competing government scheme there will be no authority regulating the competing governments to force them to allow easy entry and exit from a protection service for their consumers if they don't want to.

Then we see the most glaring area in which governments compete, which the anarcho-capitalists blatantly ignore: politicians compete over votes in elections, and the government is controlled by the winner, so each political party and each ticket of candidates is essentially a competing government. The Democratic Party competes with the Republican Party, and they both compete against the Libertarian Party. Politicians compete with one another in elections, yet this political competition does not produce the freedom that competing government advocates would hope for. Yet elections provide a lot of the accountability and competition that would be accomplished if there were rival competing police and courts. It is no answer to say that elections happen only once every two or four years because competing governments could easily lock consumers into long-term contracts.

Of course, in a sense competing governments do show some promise, since the checks and balances system and republican democracy designed by America's Founding Fathers has prevented the United States from devolving into total dictatorship for over 200 years. However, competition within one government is preferable to competing separate governments, because absent a monopoly on the use of force the competitors will resolve their differences through warfare rather than through courts of law.

Why let a minarchy have a monopoly on the use of force? Well, why not let it have a monopoly? If it doesn't, then whoever else claims the right to use force will effectively set up their own government and compete against the minarchy, and then the competing governments will be at war with each other. If total anarchy happens, and no governments exist, then there will be no mechanism stopping people from robbing and murdering each other. But if the government has a monopoly on force, who is to stop it from abusing its powers and enlarging itself through violent means, even if it is bound by a constitution and laws that supposedly limit it to enumerated powers?

The answer to that question is simple: you, my reader, you are the one who is supposed to stop it, you and your friends who vote and participate in political activism. In a republican democracy such as the United States the voters and the political activists ultimately control what the government does. If the libertarians win at the polls and win the battle of ideas then the minarchy will be limited to self-defense. And if we don't have the power to control the minarchy, then how do we have the power to create some utopian anarchy instead? If people want a big government, how is a state of anarchy going to stop the people from forming a big government? The anarchists are upset because a minarchy government could grow itself and seize dictatorial power and no mechanism prevents this from happening other than the honor of politicians. But what they are really upset about is that no mechanism prevents this from happening automatically. The libertarians and libertarian-allied conservatives, which together make up over fifty percent of the voting populace, are fully capable of keeping a minarchy small and limited to the ethical use of force only for self-defense. But it will take a lot of never-ending work on our part in order to make that happen, and anarchy seems like a much easier, less troublesome, more automatic way to prevent government abuse.

What really matters is not the political system, either anarcho-capitalism or minarchy. What matters is whether we the people, meaning me and you and all of us, do the work necessary to create a just government of GOLD principles, or whether we let the stupidity and arrogance of others condemn us to a political establishment status quo dominated by EVIL. In a democracy, the laws and politics comes from the people, so only the people can change things. You might feel that your political activism is hopeless and your actions have no effect on American politics. Libertarians are a small minority, and we often feel hopeless and give up. Such is, perhaps, a reasonable reaction to trying our hardest and getting nowhere. Nonetheless, "if at first you don't succeed, try and try again." It is up to you, my reader, to get involved in political activism and try to achieve a political landscape consistent with truth and justice.

CHAPTER FORTY SEVEN:
TOTAL OPEN GOVERNMENT

If we cannot control the government by choosing alternative governments in a paying marketplace of government services, then how can the people control the government? First, by locking the government in a cage of minarchist laws, via a renewed commitment to the United States Constitution as a libertarian document. Second, by the ballot box, by political activism to organize the voters so that the EVIL politicians will be voted out and the GOLD libertarians will be voted in. Ultimately the voters will exercise control over the government and hold the government accountable by means of the vote. But for the voters to hold the government accountable, they must know what the government is doing, and be fully informed. For this reason, an important libertarian minarchist proposal is "completely open government," a policy to pass laws mandating openness in government using a "no secrets, online disclosure" system.

A "No Secrets" system would video-record every government office, except military and law enforcement offices, and have live streaming video online showing what is happening in every government office, as well as every floor debate in every legislature, and every proceeding in every courtroom. Each government official, in every agency and department, would also have an email inbox, and would be legally obligated to answer each and every question emailed to him/her by a citizen, truthfully and completely, unless national security or state secrets might be compromised. And each legislator and legislative house would be required to have a blog and to post an entry summarizing what they did on a daily or weekly basis.

The "total open government" policy is the best answer to this question: if the free markets won't hold them accountable, then how can we hold politicians accountable, and prevent them from making mistakes? The best answer is that the voters must pay attention to what the politicians are doing and hold them accountable by political activism. But this only works if the people know what the government is doing.

The present system is based around the idea that regulators are "experts" who know what's best for us better than we know for ourselves, and the people are too stupid to understand economic, scientific or medical regulations. This is EVIL elitism in which the experts force the laypeople to obey them on the flimsy pretext that the experts are smarter than the public. This EVIL blatantly contradicts the GOLD libertarian idea that we the people are smart enough to make our own decisions and we have the right to choose for ourselves even if we make mistakes. Under GOLD, the government is merely our tool to implement our decisions, and they, the regulators, work for us, the voters.

Eventually our goal is total deregulation, but a No Secrets Law would be a good step in that direction, especially applied to regulatory agencies, because it would let the public see all the stupidity and evil of the regulators. Regulatory agencies like the EPA, FDA, the FTC, the Justice Department antitrust division, and the Federal Reserve, should have no secrets, and every detail of every action they take and each decision they make should be available in an online database of open government information. Right now the agencies generally must publish accounts of their rulemaking promulgations in the Federal Register, but they are not forced to answer citizens' questions, and they are free to delay for months if not years, with no consequences. Agencies are not mandated to disclose everything that they do, to disclose each detail completely, and to disclose it in a timely manner with enforceable deadlines, so the current system pales in comparison to total open government.

The "Audit the Fed" idea has great merit, and should be brought to its logical conclusion as a total open government No Secrets Law controlling every bureaucrat not directly involved in national security or state secrets. Also, every citizen's application for any kind of government benefit or program should be made public on a website, so that the people can see every detail of what the government is doing, and whether the bureaucrats are being stingy or reasonable in their processing of applications, and what actually goes into a government decision which determines the fate of human beings, which I think would amaze the people with how arbitrary and sadistic the government's decision makers are. Open applications would enable watchdog groups and legal aid groups to intervene if the system is being abused by the government officials' discretion. With this detail added, it may be possible to muster bipartisan support among small government conservatives and honest sincere liberals to get a No Secrets Law passed.

Even the Pentagon, FBI, and CIA should be forced to disclose every detail of their decisions unless some specific reason exists to maintain a secret. Upon the request of any person, classified material should be reviewed "in camera" by a judge, and be published for the public unless the government can prove to a judge or administrative law judge that the secret is vital and crucial and the lives of soldiers or police or civilians might be jeopardized if the secret is revealed.

CHAPTER FORTY EIGHT: A NEW AMERICAN REVOLUTION

If one unitary minarchist government exists, and no competing governments are allowed, then the ultimate tool which will protect the people's freedom is the people's ability to rise up and revolt against an unjust, corrupt government. This section discusses the prospects of American revolutions.

There have already been comprehensive accounts of the "Arab Spring" revolutions in Tunisia, Egypt, Libya, and Syria, circa 2010-2013. I think that it is possible to look at those revolutions and apply what can be learned to the United States. My specific inquiry focuses on questions that many libertarians and Tea Party patriots might soon be asking: if the Republican Party fails to deliver fiscal responsibility, either from inability or complicity in the status quo, then will the Tea Party stage a revolt? And would a Tea Party revolution be a good thing? The overarching lesson of Tunisia, Egypt, Libya and Syria is that when a people is no longer willing to tolerate a ruling government, they possess the power to rebel against it, and the ability to rebel is as alive today as it was in historical eras.

The lesson of the possibility of revolution is not new. There were revolutions and slave revolts in ancient Greece and Rome. Famous Enlightenment-era revolutions include the American Revolution, the French Revolution, and the 1848 European revolutions. There have been modern-era revolutions such as the Russian Revolution, Gandhi's resistance movement against the British in India, the revolution in Iran, the failed revolt of Tiananmen Square, and the recent Mideast revolutions, to name a few. What all of this makes clear is that generally it is possible for a populace ruled against their will to rise up and throw off their chains. Is there something special about America that makes us different? And, given that most countries have horrible governments, why doesn't every oppressed people revolt?

Many factors exist that prevent revolutions, but here I will focus on two: the structure of the government and the show of force that the military is capable of. One might be tempted to think that a dictatorship with a powerful army can prevent rebellion, but if the entire people rise up and refuse to be intimidated and engage in guerilla warfare then they can create a quagmire-type unwinnable situation for any government that tries to control a geographical region, such as the United States learned in Vietnam and more recently in Iraq. Even if an army can crush any rebellion, it remains true that a general strike by the workers can usually shut a nation down. Of course, sheer superior brute military power can force a populace into submission against its will, and a revolution is a war that can be won or lost. Nonetheless, it is very difficult to govern a region for a prolonged period of time without the consent of the governed.

So why doesn't every oppressed people around the world revolt? What matters is not the power of an army as much as its show of force to scare the citizens into thinking that resistance is futile so that they will not organize. A strong military and secret police can simply scare a people into submission, even though the people have the power to rebel. The police and army cannot be everywhere, but fear of the police and army can be everywhere, and fear does the dictator's work of keeping the people from rebelling.

This reflects an idea I first encountered in a Liberty Magazine article written by Liberty's editor Stephen Cox entitled "The Threshold Effect" (Liberty Magazine, April 2010), in which Mr. Cox postulated that libertarian candidates outside of political orthodoxy can only win once they reach a threshold in which the public considers them to be viable and capable of success. If you think that your candidate can succeed then you actively support him, whereas hopelessness leads to lethargy and apathy. Similarly, one can posit that for any given government a certain threshold point exists at which the masses will consider a revolution to have a practical chance at succeeding, and to be more preferable than not rebelling. At that point revolution becomes viable. The threshold point is raised not by military power, but by the fear inspired by the army and secret police. Indeed, Egypt's people were docile sheep until the example set by Tunisia showed them that a revolutionary protest can actually succeed, which lowered Egypt's threshold.

Why does this matter for the United States, and especially for libertarians living here? First of all, America is not inherently immune from revolution. Two American revolutions, the original American Revolution and the Civil War, have both been fought on our soil, so Americans who have a sedate, content, lackadaisical, couch-potato attitude that "it can't happen here" are living in a fantasy world. The question is, will it happen again, and should we want it to happen again? I would answer: it probably won't happen again, and we definitely should not want it to happen.

Many libertarians, particularly of the Rothbardian anarcho-capitalist school, are radical revolutionaries. After reading Rothbard's "For a New Liberty: The Libertarian Manifesto" I became absolutely convinced that between the lines he was advocating a violent overthrow of the state and its replacement with anarcho-capitalism by revolutionary methods. However, despite the robust vitality of the revolutionary tradition in the libertarian movement, I believe that revolutionary radical libertarians are hopelessly impractical, because the structure of the American government was designed so that the threshold can never be reached. In order for the threshold to be met so that the American people will revolt, not only must the public think that revolution is possible, which is unlikely, but there has to be a popular sentiment that it will be easier to accomplish change through revolt rather than by engaging in reform from within the preexisting political order. In a dictatorship this is a minor concern because the people possess no viable way to change from within. But the brilliance of America's Founding Fathers is that they established a republican democracy, which enables real policy change via voting in regular elections.

For revolution to happen it would need to be easier to revolt than to vote into office candidates who will enact your preferred policies. Given the might of the American army and the ease with which popular grassroots movements can win elections (for example, the Tea Party won Congress in 2010 and 2012), the threshold in the United States is virtually impossible to reach. There will never be another American revolution because it is so much easier to enact change by means of voting than it would be to revolt. This is why American socialists and communists have abandoned the truly Marxist call to uprising and now seek to enact their agenda by means of the socialist wing of the Democratic Party. And this applies to the Tea Party radicals for capitalism just as much as it applies to socialist revolutionaries.

Politicians in a true democracy must pander to voters and actually try to help voters in order to be elected and re-elected. Every politician constantly does favors for voters to seek support. Even liberal Democrats sincerely try to help their constituents. The true fault lies not in the politicians but in the liberal voting public, and the Democrats give liberal voters precisely what those voters demand. In America a network of regional and local political bodies exist which are devoted to serving the local and regional voters, and every interest group with a voice loud enough to be heard also has a political niche and politicians who seek its support in exchange for favors. So it is implausible for any group of people within the system to feel like it is hopeless for them to get what they want via the electoral system. Libertarians are rare in feeling such hopelessness, but until recently libertarians have been a small, geographically dispersed minority with issues that had been championed by other larger interest groups, such as conservatives on economic freedom and liberals on social freedom. Now that libertarianism is becoming more popular we are electing people like Rand Paul and Paul Ryan and Marco Rubio, so we should also not feel hopeless.

If the majority of the American voting public actually wants to end the welfare state and balance the budget then nothing prevents them from voting out any incumbents who refuse and voting into Congress politicians who will take the task of saving America seriously. If the Tea Party movement fails to enact real change then it will be because the American people were not serious about insisting upon change. America is ruled by the voters, not the politicians, and although it would be naïve not to see that the political establishment has a system of control that keeps the voters spellbound in a hypnosis of apathy, nobody is holding a gun to the voters' heads and we are free to vote for politicians who are not idiots, but only if we actually want to.

By definition the majority always gets what it wants in America, so from a practical point of view why would the people of the United States want to rebel? The entitlement tax and spend welfare state is a horror, but if Americans truly hate it then we are free to vote in a new President and Congress who will abolish it. Fighting for electoral change is, from a practical standpoint, infinitely easier than advocating revolution. The libertarians who advocate radical revolution want to impose the desires of the minority upon the majority. Not only are they hopelessly impractical, but if they succeeded then it would be a short time until the disenfranchised majority turned socialist and staged a counter-revolution.

Some libertarians are totally pessimistic about electoral change. They imply that the Washington establishment will never end the welfare state and the prospects of political change are futile and hopeless. But here is a riddle for those libertarians who are pessimistic about our ability to enact change via the vote and who see revolution as the alternative: how can you drum up enough support for a libertarian revolution if you don't even have enough popular support to vote libertarian candidates into office?

To return to my original question, if it turns out that the political establishment refuses to change then the Tea Party movement may feel like elections are worthless and the revolution threshold will go down. I still believe in the efficacy of our elections, and I think that the structure of our government is such that politicians will cave to the will of the people long before it comes to rebellion. It would be one thing for the U.S. government to disobey the will of the voters, in which case the revolution threshold would plummet, but so long as the voters control the politicians we must make our case to the voters and not take up arms. I often fear that the war between liberals and conservatives could evolve into a new North vs. South Civil War in the United States, and right-wing militias and left-wing radical groups exist who would take up arms if a new Civil War erupted. But I think that peaceful democratic advocacy in the United States is the superior method of change, and we libertarians will only win our "revolution" when we persuade the American people to vote for us.

A revolution would be war, which is always a bloody nightmare, and even if avowed rabid socialists were elected into the White House and took every seat in Congress I would still prefer electoral activism to revolt. Egypt and Libya are nice to look at, but this is the United States, after all, not Egypt or Libya, and we are still a free country, protected by our Constitution and the virtue and values of the American people, the welfare state to the contrary notwithstanding. I believe that America is the world's greatest experiment in capitalism and freedom, and restoring free market liberty by means of elections is not hopeless. American citizens owe a patriotic duty of loyalty to support the U.S. Constitution and to promote the United States rather than turning against this great nation.

CHAPTER FORTY NINE: A REASONABLE POLICY PROPOSAL FOR TAXES AND GOVERNMENT BUDGETS

The policy recommendations in this section are based on data and analysis from the United States during the Great Recession era, but the suggestions can be adopted to fit any time period or nation. The source for the following data is Wikipedia. In 2013, the United States federal government collected $2.77 trillion in tax revenue. In 2012 the US federal government collected tax revenue of $2.45 trillion, and in 2011 it collected $2.3 trillion. Deficits have generally run about $1 trillion annually under President Obama. The federal government's total annual spending in 2013 was about $3.45 trillion. In 2012 total federal spending was approximately $3.54 trillion. Entitlement spending, including Social Security, Medicare, and Medicaid, totaled about $1.563 trillion in 2013 and was about $1.482 trillion in 2012. Total military spending was $608 billion in 2013, it was $655 billion in 2012, and it was $665 billion in 2011. An inexact estimate of intelligence spending by the Department of Homeland Security and other departments including the FBI and CIA is $108 billion in 2013. An imprecise estimate is that the federal courts have a budget of about $6.7 billion annually, with $4.8 billion of this going to judicial salaries and expenses, and the rest going to public defenders for criminals' right to counsel.

Based on research into the Tax Code, the various income tax brackets average out to an effective federal tax rate of about 30% to 35%. Because the long-term capital gains and stock dividends tax rate is much lower than the income tax on salary, someone (such as a rich investor or a retiree who lives on his/her pension) who gets most of his/her money from those sources might pay as low as a 15% to 20% effective rate. With local property taxes and state sales tax and income tax added together, the total effective tax rate for Americans with normal income sources, including middle class employees and working class people, could be as high as 40% to 50%, if not higher in states with a high state income tax.

Let us assume that it is not America's job to be the world's policeman and enforce the Pax Americana and establish an American Empire. Let us instead posit GOLD, which holds that the government's job is the police, the army for national self-defense only, and the courts, and those are the only legitimate jobs for the government to perform. The federal government's proper role is the military for national defense and the federal courts. What I offer here is a federal budget based around the idea that the purpose of the government is police, army, and courts, for the defense of life, liberty, and property.

A reasonable military spending budget, with a focus on protecting America and not on policing the world, might be $300 billion per year. The budget for the courts, where most of the work is done by low-paid judicial clerks, could be estimated at $5 billion per year. This would go mainly to fund a sufficient number of judges to end the backlog of cases that get stalled and wait years for resolution, because the need for public defenders would decrease since the deregulation of lawyer licensing would make lawyers far more affordable for poor criminal defendants. The federal law enforcement, for anti-mafia and anti-terrorist work, should need no more than $25 billion, because the legalization of drugs, gambling, and prostitution will dry up the mafia's funding, and antiwar foreign policy will numb the motivations of Islamic terrorists. $20 billion per year should be included in the federal budget for various miscellaneous expenses, such as legislative staff and the staff for downsized federal agencies before they are fully phased out. Thus the federal budget should be $350 billion per year. This is a 90% cut down from $3.5 trillion. So federal taxes should be cut by 90%.

Based on an anticipated 90% tax cut, combined with a 90% reduction in federal government spending, I propose a federal 5% flat tax on income, and the total elimination of all other federal taxes, to replace the progressive income tax. As part of this reform, all the loopholes and politically motivated deductions and complicated various tax brackets, such as different rates for long-term capital gains and dividends, or deductions for home ownership or investments in medical equipment, must be repealed. Obviously, since a GOLD government has never been tried in recent American history, we would need some trial and error to find the right budget and tax rate, but the 5% federal flat tax would be a step in the right direction.

The primary role of the states would be to provide local police and state courts. It is a fact that the state criminal justice systems play an important role in protecting the people from crime and most lawsuits are resolved in state courts, so the states are no less important than the federal government. The states would be able to do a good job of fighting crime in the cities and towns and providing the state courts to resolve litigated disputes from funding through an additional state 5% flat tax on income. All state sales taxes and local property taxes should be abolished.

The total American government's effective tax rate, combining the federal, state and local tax rates, would be a 10% flat tax on income, with 5% for the federal government and 5% for the states and towns. My 10% flat tax would be a 90% tax cut relative to the current effective combined federal and state tax rate of approximately 50%, which corresponds to my proposed 90% reduction in government spending. My policy would treat everyone equally and would be fair and just for all citizens. Because the amount of taxable income would skyrocket from economic growth and job creation once we get government out of the way of business, a 10% flat tax would be ample to fund all of the legitimate roles of the federal, state, and local governments. Taxes would go down but taxable income would go way up due to economic growth, so the actual tax revenues might be significantly higher than these estimates.

It will take time for economic prosperity to flow from libertarian fiscal policy, so entitlement welfare should not be cut completely all at once. Instead it should be phased out gradually. A nine year plan can be advocated that would cut Social Security, Medicare, Medicaid, and all other forms of welfare, government spending, and state programs, by 10% every year for nine consecutive years, resulting in a total net 90% cut in taxes and spending, so that the working class can transition from welfare dependence to gainful employment gradually as new jobs are created. Or an equally ethical proposal would be an 18 year plan that would cut spending by 5% each year for 18 consecutive years. GOLD economics is based on policies that are smart and logical without being cruel or heartless. Any promises of benefits to the poor, elderly and disabled that have already been made must be honored, but welfare programs can be phased out slowly by ceasing to make new promises to future generations.

Note the warning of libertarian economist Milton Friedman, who theorized that when welfare gets cut, things will get worse before they get better. The short-term loss of welfare will hurt the poor prior to the long-term effects of tax cuts causing economic growth and creating new jobs. Therefore any abrupt, rapid transformation will hurt too many people and could cause a short-term panic before the long-term growth kicks in. Libertarian theory is pointless if the practical reality causes voters to turn against freedom. Our goal must be a long-term smooth transition to GOLD free market capitalism, fueled by a public that wants long-term growth and understands fundamental economic principles. Trying to enact libertarianism all at once, or during one term when we might happen to control Congress or the White House, would be a short-sighted plan, blind to the real long-term consequences of rapid economic restructuring.

PART FIVE: CONCLUSION

CHAPTER FIFTY: SUMMARY OF GOLD AND NVP

GOLD stands for:

(1) Antiwar, and the use of trade as our primary tool of foreign relations,

(2) Legalization, of all drug use and victimless crimes,

(3) Civil Liberties, and strict constitutional limits on police powers.

It should no longer be a crime to be a poor person.

It also stands for:

(4) Free Markets, and capitalist economic efficiency,

(5) Deregulation and Cutting Taxes, to get the government out of the way of productive progress,

(6) Laws defending freedom, so that the freedom to choose is protected from coercion and violence.

It should not be a crime to be a rich person either.

GOLD believes that the use of violence, and the government as the organized system of force, should be limited to the defense of life, liberty and property (LLP). GOLD has the wisdom to know that the LLP of women, blacks, gays, and other oppressed minorities, can only be protected through a triad of tools: the ammo box, the ballot box, and the jury box.

The GOLD libertarian motto is "live and let live." This sharply contrasts with the conservative motto, "live and let die," and with the liberal motto, "we know what's best for you."

GOLD assumes X, Y, A and B, and assumes that X can be either peaceful and respectful or forceful and violent towards A and A can be respectful or violent towards X. GOLD shows how libertarianism follows as a logical conclusion from XYAB. GOLD means that X lets A choose between Y and B, and A lets X choose between Y and B. If X respects the rights of A and shows tolerance towards A, then A does the same to X, and peace and harmony result. X may use force for self-defense only if A violates X's right to life, liberty or property. Absent damage to X's LLP, X does not have the right to initiate force against A, and X is free to non-violently persuade A to choose Y, but if A refuses to be persuaded, but A does not injure X's LLP, then A's behavior is not X's problem. Thus we see that GOLD (Guiding Our Liberty's Defense) is the best justification of NVP (the Non-Violence Principle).

The alternative to GOLD is EVIL (Everyone Violating Individual Liberty), in which X tries to force Y onto A, and A seeks to violently impose B onto X. EVIL leads to a war between X and A, and EVIL is primitive barbarian savagery and no respect for rights or freedom. For X to think that A should force A's decisions onto X, for X to want someone else to make all his decisions for him and force him to obey them, X must think of himself as an incompetent idiot, totally incapable of living and thinking as a human being and choosing for himself between Y and B. Yet at the same time, for X to think that he as a voter has the right to use the government to force Y onto A means that X is a supremely arrogant maniac who thinks that he knows what's best for everyone else and he has the right to beat people and throw people into jail to force them to obey him. EVIL also assumes the "government as God" complex which believes that people in the government are somehow magically superior and infallible, such that individuals within the government, e.g. politicians and experts, are capable of things that individuals outside the government cannot do, like making good decisions or possessing factual knowledge.

The Golden Rule is bigger than Kant, but GOLD can be thought of as Kantian libertarianism, in the sense that GOLD is a categorical imperative as the behavior that everyone must do everywhere universally under the rational, logical rules of ethics applied to politics. For those unfamiliar with Kant, let me explain the concept of the categorical imperative. Kant's ethical theory of the categorical imperative states that if some behavior exists such that it is true that everyone should behave this way everywhere and at all times, with no exceptions, as a universal truth, then humans have a duty to behave that way. Such behavior is called the "categorical imperative." My GOLD argument states that X and A should treat each other according to the rules of GOLD and NVP. A and X represent anyone and everyone in every place and time. Hence I argue that GOLD satisfies the test to qualify as a Kantian categorical imperative.

Kant himself might have disagreed with GOLD, because, as I interpret Kant, he thought that people everywhere should help others and should be forced to help others. His argument is that if X needs A's help then X should force A to help X, and the reverse would be true if A needs X's help. In order to analyze the Kantian argument, I find it useful to distinguish between different scenarios where people need help. I believe that if I were in an emergency or crisis situation and I needed to use force against you in order to save my life, and this did not involve any serious long-term injury to you, e.g. me stealing a loaf of bread from you to keep me from starving to death, then I would use force against you to save my life. This is only natural given human nature and our genetic desire to survive. I would expect you to do the same to me if our situations were reversed, and I would suffer no great injury from it, so I could not complain if it came to pass that you stole bread from me. This reciprocity of treatment is all I must establish in order for my belief to comply with the Golden Rule. Later in this section I will explain why this limited crisis/emergency rule conforms to

GOLD and NVP and is not actually an exception to NVP.

But we can imagine a situation where I need your help and I have to kill or injure you or harm you to get your help, like stealing bread from a poor needy family so that I could survive, or killing and eating a fellow traveler if our plane crashed and we were stranded together in the mountains with no food to eat. In that situation I think that I should not force you to help me, and I hope that if I really had the opportunity to do something like that I would not, even if I died as a result. If your situation and mine were reversed it would be wrong for you to do that to me, just as it would be wrong for me to do that to you, and I would rightly use force to defend myself despite your desperate need for help. So GOLD is not refuted by this situation.

Then, at the extreme end of the spectrum of needing help is the idea that the poor need help by taking wealth from the rich, and the government should take from the rich to help the poor. The Kantian justification for this is that the poor need help so they should force the rich to help them because if the places of rich man and poor man were reversed then the rich would steal from the poor. Something similar is at work in John Rawls's notion of the "veil of ignorance," which says that the rich should be forced to help the poor because any individual can be born into wealth or poverty so if the rich had been born poor they would want the same help from the rich. This society-wide "social" help can be twisted into a shape that looks like it follows the Golden Rule.

This idea opposes capitalism and justifies socialism, and I reject it as meeting the requirements of the Golden Rule. This idea is wrong for two reasons. First, as a factual matter, the government stealing wealth from the rich to give to the poor does not help lift the poor up, instead it merely tears the rich down and causes poverty for everyone. The only political system that can achieve prosperity for everyone is a system where property rights are universally recognized. Second, under the Golden Rule, if I force my decisions about how to help, and whom to help, onto other people, then I also justify destroying my own freedom of choice. It is true that if I want other people to help me and give me charity and support me in my moments of helplessness or disability, then I should also help others whenever it is possible for me to do so. So helping others is ethical under the Golden Rule.

But an ethical duty is not the same thing as a political obligation. Politics deals with the question of when it is right to use violent force, not with the question of what is right or wrong as such. Contrary to Kant, the fact that I should help others does not mean that I should force everyone else to help me through the government. Help should be given freely and voluntarily, aside from the limited exception of the crisis/ emergency that I mentioned earlier. Help for me from others and from me to others can all be done voluntarily. Nothing is inherently better about the decisions of who receives the rich's charity money being made by the government instead of private donors making those decisions, because individuals within the government are not actually smarter or more generous than individuals outside the government.

It is irrelevant under the Golden Rule that not every person will actually treat you right if you treat everyone else right, as long as you treat everyone the same way that you want them to treat you. It is a misinterpretation of the Golden Rule to force others to help you or to force people to be good as payment for your being good to them.

To conclude the discussion of the philosophy of GOLD, here I will answer the challenge of those who say that exceptions to NVP and GOLD exist such that GOLD is not universally true. First I will refute an argument that GOLD is self-contradictory, and then I will show that NVP has literally no exceptions.

The first argument that I want to refute states that GOLD is self-contradictory because GOLD says that two people, called X and A, should be free to choose between any set of competing choices, named Y and B, but GOLD does not give people the ability to choose between GOLD and EVIL and demands that all people choose GOLD and reject EVIL, so GOLD collapses if GOLD is Y and EVIL is B. This idea demonstrates a total lack of conceptual understanding of GOLD. GOLD simply means that each individual is free to make choices for himself/herself. EVIL (Everyone Violating Individual Liberty) means that one person uses violence to coercively impose his/her choices onto other people. GOLD is the freedom of both X and A to choose between Y and B, but for X to "choose EVIL" means that X violently imposes Y onto A, and X choosing to violate A's freedom is not within the scope of X's freedom to make choices. It is not "freedom" for X to impose Y onto A. Thus, the "freedom" to "choose" EVIL does not exist because EVIL necessarily entails the destruction of freedom. EVIL is not an individual choice, it is the violation of the freedom of choice for individuals. The "freedom to choose EVIL" does not exist because GOLD is the freedom to make choices and EVIL is the denial of free choice for individuals. Stated another way, I would not force GOLD onto other people but I would also not let other people force EVIL onto me, and if I am to be free from EVIL then the set of policies detailed in this book are necessary.

A good comprehensive set of possible exceptions to NVP (the Non-Violence Principle) was listed in Mr. Stephen Cox's article "Rand, Paterson, and the Problem of Anarchism" (The Journal of Ayn Rand Studies, July 2013). I will list Mr. Cox's objections in terms of XYAB, although some additions and reinterpretations factor into my presentation of the Cox cases.

(1) Nation A attacks Nation X. If X counterattacks then X will injure C, the innocent civilians living in the capitol of Nation A. Mr. Cox argues that if X attacks then this will violate NVP by initiating violence against C.

(2) A attacks X. X would be best able to defend himself if he assembles a machine gun on the top of a hill. C owns the hill, and C is a pacifist who does not want X to use the hill to defend himself, and has a locked gate around the hill. Mr. Cox says that if X breaks the lock X will violate NVP against C.

(3) A lives next door to X. A builds a tall unstable shaky tower that looms over X's house, but it has not collapsed yet. Mr. Cox says that if X uses force to remove the tower

it will violate NVP against A, in part because A has not yet done harm to X.

(4) A lives next door to X. A builds a bird house that attracts violent wild predatory birds which attack X's family and poop on X's house. Mr. Cox says that if X uses force to remove the bird house then he will violate NVP against A, in part because the agent causing the harm to X is not A.

(5) A lives in the same town as X. Some sort of deadly infectious disease is spreading. A vaccine has been developed but the disease can only be eliminated if everyone gets vaccinated. A has chosen not to take the vaccine. May X force A to get vaccinated? Mr. Cox says that the use of force here would violate NVP.

(6) A lives next door to X. A owns a puppy of a breed of canine which becomes aggressive and dangerous as an adult dog. A refuses to build a fence around his property. Mr. Cox says that if X forces A to build a fence then X has violated NVP against A.

(7) Here I add one hypothetical which Mr. Cox did not offer: X is walking past a mob of people. A is a demagogic orator giving a speech. A inflames the mob of people and starts using hate speech directed at X. X has a gun and X knows that if he shoots A he will stop the anger of the mob. If X does not shoot A then A's hate speech will inflame the mob and they will come after X and murder him. However, A is too physically weak to use force so A will not personally use violence against X. Would it violate NVP for X to use force against A when all A has done is use words and no violence has happened yet?

(8) C has a heart attack at a restaurant where X and A are eating. A is a doctor who knows how to save C's life, but A decides that he does not want to help C. May X use force to coerce A into helping C? Mr. Cox posits that here the noble idealistic commitment to NVP comes into sharp conflict with the ethical duty to save C's life, such that C's life would be "sacrificed on the altar of A's freedom."

(9) C attacks X. X is near the door to A's house, and he could escape from C, who is trying to murder him, by fleeing into A's house. Mr. Cox says that breaking the lock on the door and entering would violate NVP against A. To make this point clearer, Mr. Cox hypothesizes that A is at the door and A refuses to let X in and tries to keep X out. May X use force against A to escape into A's house and avoid death at the hands of C? Is this a case where idealism is impractical and realistic pragmatism betrays the principle of NVP?

Mr. Cox, a brilliant libertarian scholar, sees these nine cases as scenarios which force us to rethink the Non-Violence Principle (NVP) as a universal categorical imperative. I disagree with Mr. Cox. NVP states that we may not use force other than in self-defense against someone who initiated violence against us and that we may not initiate violence against other people. My answer to the Cox cases is that the real-world application of NVP depends on how we define "the initiation of violence," and it also depends on how we define "self-defense," with the definition of self-defense being informed by the definition of initiating violence. I define "self-defense" and "the initiation of violence" broadly, not narrowly as Mr. Cox seems to have done. The initiation of violence is a choice or action that threatens or causes danger of death or injury to self or property. Self-defense is the choice to use or the act of using violent force to protect the life and property of self or others from death or injury or the danger of them.

From my two definitions I can deduce three principles of NVP which solve the Cox problems without making any exceptions to NVP. First, if self-defense has an unintended side effect or accidental byproduct of causing harm to others this does not alter its ethical justification as self-defense. For example, if A attacks X and to defend himself X shoots a gun at A but the bullet misses A and hits C by accident and kills C then this is not murder, it is imperfect self-defense. X could be liable for C's death under tort law for the accidental killing, but this would not be murder as categorized under the criminal laws, and X would be within his rights to have done what he did. I call this the side effects rule.

Second, a choice or behavior that creates a probability of danger or an unreasonable risk of injury constitutes the initiation of violence. For example, if A shoots a gun into the air to have fun and X lives close by then this creates an unreasonable risk of bullets raining down on X, so X could use force to remove the gun from A. I call this the risk rule.

Third, force used for the purpose of saving lives counts as self-defense. For example, if A attacks X and X steals a gun from C to use to defend X from A then X's act towards C was self-defense, not the initiation of violence against C, i.e. it was self-defense and not theft that could be prosecuted under the criminal laws. The same is true if X is shipwrecked and finds a box of A's food floating in the ocean and X breaks the lock and steals the food in order to survive. I call this the saving lives rule.

For all three rules, keep in mind that a behavior is either self-defense or the initiation of violence and it cannot be both at the same time with respect to different people. A choice is either right or wrong, and cannot be both right and wrong at once. So an action is either self-defense or the initiation of violence, not both at once in relation to two different people. If the use of force is ethical then it counts as self-defense, and if the use of force is immoral then it counts as the initiation of violence.

These three rules can be applied to the Cox cases to prove that NVP has no exceptions. I will show this for each Cox case, one by one.

The side effects rule solves the first two Cox cases.

(1) The injury to C would be a side effect of X's self-defense of attacking Nation A, so it is not the initiation of violence.

(2) X's act towards C's property is a side effect of X's self-defense, so it is not the initiation of violence when X uses C's hill to defend X.

The risk rule solves the next five of the Cox cases.

(3) A has caused an unreasonable risk of injury towards X, so A initiated violence against X and X may rightly use self-defense to remove the threat of the tower without waiting for it to fall on him.

(4) A's actions created an unreasonable danger to X, so A initiated violence against X, and X's use of force to remove the bird house is self-defense.

(5) A's choice not to be vaccinated creates an unreasonable risk that A will catch the illness and then spread it to X, so it does not violate NVP for X to defend himself from A's risk by forcing A to be vaccinated.

(6) A's dog is a danger to X, so A initiated violence against X and it is self-defense for X to force A to build a fence to eliminate the danger to X.

(7) When A told the mob to murder X what really happened is that A initiated violence against X, so X's shooting A constitutes self-defense.

The saving lives rule solves the final two Cox cases.

(8) X's use of force to make A save C's life counts as self-defense because it saves C's life. The fact that A did not initiate violence against C does not change this analysis because the self-defense is not directed to protect C from A but rather is intended to save C's life as such. However, this would only be self-defense if X's force against A did not rise to the level of doing serious injury to A, and if X seriously injures A then X initiated violence against A. Note that this analysis justifies tax collection for a GOLD minarchist government because the tax rate is low enough that it doesn't affect the taxpayers and the government saves lives by protecting people from crime and foreign armies.

(9) X's use of force against A counts as X's self-defense against C and does not count as the initiation of violence against A.

My theory of NVP as elaborated here is somewhat counterintuitive and unorthodox, but if the definitions and ideas are analyzed according to reason and logic then my arguments make sense. Having refuted all nine Cox cases, I can say that NVP does not have any exceptions. GOLD is a universal truth which describes the correct political relationship of one person to every other person, e.g. GOLD says how X should treat A and how A should treat X in return. GOLD can be made universal as a categorical imperative because each person can do it to everyone else and the system of politics works successfully if each and every person applies GOLD as a political principle.

CHAPTER FIFTY ONE: A CALL FOR ACTIVISM

If GOLD is true and EVIL is wrong, then you, dear reader, must fight with all of your strength to get involved in political activism and struggle for political and legal reform. Strangely, many libertarian groups and movements exist which reject activism from within the preexisting political system as a matter of principle, e.g. the Agorists and Voluntaryists. Because most libertarians care passionately about politics, if we were to become activists then we could achieve an influence disproportionate to our presently small size. The widespread libertarian rejection of activism neutralizes our potential advantage. Here I address the various reasons why many libertarians aren't activists. I then offer a list of practical tips and suggestions for the budding GOLD activist.

SUBPART 51-A: THE FEELING OF HOPELESSNESS

Apathy, hopelessness and pessimism have made many libertarians feel frustrated, as if being outnumbered by liberals and conservatives leaves us helpless, so we get sad and depressed and give up. We see a two-party system where the liberal Democrats and conservative Republicans control the election process, and the Libertarian Party is horribly inept and incompetent. The irony is that, generally, libertarians, as a group of people defined by our politics, care more about politics than mainstream people, so our voices could travel farther than our competitors not because of more throats but because we could shout louder. If each libertarian did one act of political activism every week, four times each month, and was active regularly, then the result could change the world.

The Libertarian Party recently received 1% of the total presidential vote in 2012. About 50% of "voting age" Americans vote and roughly 200 million American are voting age so about 100 million Americans vote. 1% of 100 million is about one million people who voted for the Libertarian Party in 2012. Let us assume that an equal number of libertarians did not vote for the LP, since they do not believe in activism or else voted for the Republican candidate. Thus, let us assume that two million libertarians exist in America. Now let us assume that a libertarian activist does four acts of activism every month, which means once a week. Four times twelve is 48 act of political work per year, which can be rounded to 50. Fifty times two million would be one hundred million (100,000,000). If our feeling is that activism is hopeless, I believe that one hundred million acts of activism in one year, consisting of donating money or going to an event or giving voice to an opinion or voting in an election, would transform America and change the world.

Why am I so optimistic? Assume that undecided and independent voters, as well as honest open-minded liberals and conservatives, could be converted to libertarianism if the libertarian arguments were persuasively presented to them. Assume that someone could still think of himself or herself as a liberal or conservative but could embrace a libertarian position on one or a few important political issues. Now also assume that many people don't vote because they are sick and tired of the liberal-conservative establishment, but they don't know about libertarianism or have a general uninformed impression that libertarians are crazy. Such people might vote libertarian if they knew what libertarianism was, but they do not. The brainwashed nonsense sold to the voters in public schools and on political TV news shows depicts a world where only liberals and conservatives exist, and libertarianism is not a reasonable political alternative. Assume that principles and integrity are sexy and appealing. Assume that many people simply adopt the beliefs of their friends and family, so conversion will always tend to grow by an exponent. If we reach one person, then we also reach all of the people whom they reach, and if each person reaches two others then the libertarian movement doubles.

A certain critical mass can be reached where a political movement will grow exponentially. The argument that "I am only one person, I don't make any difference, I am helpless unless other people also help" is idiotic and stupid. Like a virus, one person can become 2, which becomes 4, which becomes 8, then 16, then 32, then 64, and in a matter of time it is hundreds, then thousands, and then millions. This is the "viral" internet marketing concept, which has been proven to work with viral videos. It also works in politics, such as with libertarian "money bomb" fundraising. Voters are often motivated by their "common sense" or "political imagination" or "paradigm," the body of political ideas which they take for granted as generally accepted and which they think are known by knowledgeable people and experts. If we shift common sense in the direction of our ideas, then we can join the liberals and conservatives in the political mainstream.

Another set of assumptions shows that if we could achieve exponential growth, and go from one million voters up to roughly four million voters, we could have an immediate Election Day impact. Assume that libertarian politicians would get liberal votes on social issues and conservative votes on economic issues. If 48% of the legislature is liberal, 48% is conservative, and 4% are libertarian, then we would form a 52% coalition in our favor on every issue. Then, assume that libertarian politicians could beat conservatives in a few Republican Party primaries, which has been proven as a viable strategy by the Tea Party, and assume that left-libertarian politicians could sometimes beat liberals in Democratic primaries by being left-of-center on immigration, drug legalization, civil liberties, and antiwar foreign policy. Thus, libertarians have three shots at winning political races, via the Republican Party and Democratic Party primaries, and also by fielding a Libertarian Party candidate. All of this adds up to the fact that if libertarians get really active, we can win, and sooner rather than later.

By doing something, you actually contribute to the cause, and if everyone did so then it would make a huge difference, so your contribution matters and you count as part of the movement. Your action is a necessary part of reaching a critical mass of numbers, and without you the rest of us are diminished. A political movement, like an economy, is a group made up of individuals, so no group exists in the absence of each individual member of the group. Under the Golden Rule and GOLD, each individual seeks to behave in a way that would be proper and good if everyone universally behaved that way, so we must act in the way that would make a difference if everyone did it. Since it would be good for everyone to get politically active, and it would be bad if everyone were politically passive and apathetic and lazy, GOLD calls for political activism. Even if you feel that you don't make a difference, how can you possibly know whether or not your activism will have an effect, until and unless you actually do it? And until you do it regularly for several years to assess a good sample size from which to judge its impact?

Let me conclude this section by noting that, although it is true that the Democratic Party and Republican Party dominate the two-party system, and the Libertarian Party is inept and clumsy, this fact is deceptive and misleading. This is so because it is only the national Libertarian Party, and the Libertarian National Committee, which has demonstrated incompetence and stupidity. Each state has its own state LP, and some of these 50 groups are smart and competent and capable. It is a good strategy to win at the state level before moving to the national level because competition in federal races is fiercer and local politics is more favorable to a small but active movement. And, in addition to the 50 state LPs, countless other local LP groups exist. So instead of focusing on the race for President, which we cannot win right now, we should instead look at the 100 other local and state elections where we can win, and enact change gradually.

SUBPART 51-B: PERSONALITY

The libertarian typical personality type does not favor political activism, for two reasons. First, because many libertarians are too intellectual and we would rather read and write than vote and donate. Second, because we have been pushed out of the political mainstream and into the crazy fringe, which causes the movement to encounter and accept people who are literally insane, such as conspiracy theorists who believe that the Illuminati rule the world. If we have no awareness of reality then we lose our motivation to change reality. The fight for freedom is sane and rational and it matters for every human being, so libertarianism is sane and it is the liberals and conservatives who are crazy. Note that "The Illuminatus Trilogy," where a lot of insane libertarians discover their paranoid delusions, was written as a sarcastic parody to mock conspiracy theory, but many people are too stupid to get the humor and instead take it literally. The political establishment of liberals and conservatives are responsible for libertarians being marginalized to the crazy fringe, and it is up to us to reclaim the reasonable mainstream.

SUBPART 51-C: EXTREMISM

Libertarian anarcho-capitalists do not accept the legitimacy of the American government, so they refuse to participate in American political life, and they see committing crimes like black market trading, which they call "counter-economics," and defying the law, which they view as moral protest, as their form of activism. Civil disobedience has its place, but the best path to progress is to get good candidates elected to office, because America is a democracy where the politicians express the will of the people. Political activism via the U.S. political process is legal, whereas plotting revolution or subversive "counter-economics" is illegal. Instead of spending $5 to act and $5 to hide from the police, we should instead spend $10 to act openly, and double our effectiveness. Political activism is the gift that the Founding Fathers gave to us through the First Amendment's guarantee of free speech, to give us the power to fight for freedom.

The Rothbardian who has accepted Rothbard's "all or nothing" extremism would rather do nothing than promote gradual, continuous change, and he won't lift a finger to do anything unless he can get everything he wants all at once. This "all or nothing" attitude serves to neutralize and disarm the libertarian movement's potential for activism. Like the crazy fringe which contaminates the libertarian movement with their insanity, the theoretical, doctrinal mistakes which lead to apathy and inaction can only help the agents of EVIL and can only serve to prevent the GOLD libertarian movement from "winning" and making a real difference in reforming politics in the United States.

Whether they manipulate us intentionally or not, the EVIL political establishment benefits from every error in the libertarian movement which leads libertarians away from activism and political involvement and towards lazy inaction and passivity. I would say that the biggest reason why libertarianism has not yet dominated in elections is not because we are too small a movement, nor because of a lack of passion on our part. The leading culprit is that we are a principled, intellectual, theoretical sort of people, and our ideas and theories up to this point have not made the case for sustained, loud, assertive political activism on the part of each individual. Here I have made that case, as a matter of principle.

SUBPART 51-D: WHAT YOU CAN (AND SHOULD) DO TO HELP

Many libertarians don't know what to do to get politically active. Let me offer some suggestions:

Item 1. Vote in every election for which you are eligible, and keep track of which politicians lean towards your positions on your issues, such as by looking at the voting records kept by the libertarian political think tanks.

Item 2. Donate money to good groups and causes, not too much but a reasonable sum. For example, evaluate how much money you make in one hour of work. Then choose an issue advocacy group that you like. Once every month, take the sum you earn in one hour, and donate that amount of money to one of your favorite issue advocacy groups.

Item 3. Join good groups, locally and nationally, both online and in person.

Item 4. Sign petitions, which are frequently circulated on the internet.

Item 5. Talk and write: discuss politics with people you know, or get on the internet and social media and participate in a discussion, or share a link to something libertarian online with your social media friends and followers.

Item 6. Write to or call your local, state and federal elected representatives and congressmen. They obey what they perceive as the will of the people, because they want your vote in order to get reelected. It is best to call or write about a specific issue or law that is being debated, and to have some sort of argument ready to explain why they should agree with you.

SUBPART 51-E: APPROACH, LOCAL VS. STATE VS. NATIONAL

It is important to note the difference between federal government, state government, and local government, in the focus of your efforts. The closer you are to the process the easier it is to influence the politicians, but the bigger it is the more people it affects. This is why the major well-funded special interest groups dominate national and state-wide elections, but in local elections it is possible for a charismatic and likable libertarian-leaning politician or group to gain traction. This explains why the Tea Party has fared well in the House but not in the Senate or the White House. It also explains why the EVIL socialists always try to take power for the federal government and away from the state and local governments, because this puts the power where only the special interests can reach it and where the people cannot touch it.

If libertarians continue to be a small but extremely passionate and motivated minority then the dynamics of small local elections will always favor us and large statewide big-money elections will always favor the EVIL special interest groups. EVIL special interest groups have money to spend because they are the sell-outs of politics and economics and they exploit government crony funding, e.g. public campaign financing for incumbent Democrats and Republicans. GOLD libertarians are the noble idealists and we care passionately about freedom, but we are a small minority, so we do best in small venues where we can make our voices heard.

Under the legal principles of federalism and separation of powers, it is plausible to think of each part of the local, state and federal government as its own independent government. Your local town or city's government is one government, the state government is a government, and within the federal government the White House is one government, the Supreme Court is one government, and the House of Representative is a government, and the Senate is a government. Each government has its own powers and laws which affect people, and each government is worth targeting with activism.

For example, most criminal laws are enforced by the police departments of the states and cities, so decriminalizing marijuana in one state makes a big difference despite failing to alter federal criminal law. Even making a difference for the cause of freedom in a town's zoning board or board of education can have a big impact on real people. Instead of thinking in terms of changing "the government," which is so big and full of such entrenched establishment powers as to be impossible in the near future, we should think in terms of altering the political realm one government at a time, e.g. one city at a time and one state at a time. It is especially important for libertarians to focus on local elections, such as elections for your city's council and mayor, your regional representative to the state legislature, and your district's race for Congressman in the House of Representatives.

As a general tactic, you should focus on the issues and seek to build alliances. Instead of advocating GOLD as such, a superior approach is to choose your favorite political issue, find an issue advocacy group which supports your position on that issue, and then do activism for your issue through those groups that are committed to that issue. Most issues already come with either a liberal or conservative support group attached to it, e.g. conservative gun rights or liberal antiwar pacifism, so issue-based advocacy can reach beyond the narrow group of GOLD libertarians to achieve a broader appeal. While engaging in activism, you can try to nudge and shift the groups advocating that issue towards GOLD. Libertarians are a minority, so we must form alliances with conservatives and/or liberals on each individual issue in order to succeed.

SUBPART 51-F: A LIST
OF GOLD ISSUES

A short, incomplete list of issues to choose from follows:

1. Economic libertarianism: cut taxes, deregulate, privatize banking, privatize retirement

2. Abolish occupational licensing

3. End the minimum wage

4. School choice/privatize primary education

5. 2nd Amendment gun rights

6. Legalization of sin crimes (drugs, prostitution, gambling)

7. Antiwar foreign policy

8. Civil liberties

9. Open immigration

10. Gay rights from a libertarian point of view (gays with guns)

11. Abortion rights/pro-choice from a libertarian point of view (girls with guns)

12. Civil rights from a libertarian point of view (blacks with guns)

13. Jury nullification/jury rights

14. Support for the Libertarian Party and ballot access

15. Support for the fiscal conservative/Tea Party candidates in the Republican Party

16. Support for the pro-legalization, pro-civil liberties, antiwar candidates in the Democratic Party

Remember, you doing something once a week, four times each month, makes a difference. Pick one day, perhaps Friday afternoon right after you get out of work, or Saturday afternoon, or Sunday night, and get into a habit of doing one act of political activism each week on your activism day.

For a final conclusion to this book, let me return to the idea that I presented on page one, the Golden Rule, which is the ethics of reciprocity. As Jesus said, "do unto others as you would have others do unto you," and as Kant theorized, it is a categorical imperative for ethical behavior to consist of actions that can be done by everyone to everyone else everywhere and at all times. I should treat you in the same way that I want you to treat me. The absence of a double standard between me and you is the essence of fairness and justice. For both you and me to receive the same treatment that we give out is the right way for each of us to interact with the other person. GOLD simply says that freedom is the political embodiment of the Golden Rule, because if I let you be free then you should also let me be free. According to GOLD, to be ethical, right, noble, idealistic political activists we must believe in libertarian freedom and take action to translate our ideals into practical reality.

LIBERTARIAN ECONOMICS: A MANIFESTO AND AN EXPLANATION

LIBERTARIAN ECONOMICS:
A MANIFESTO

This paper will use the following abbreviated notations:

L&E: law and economics.

C/C: the approach based on Coase and Calabresi.

Max EE: the goal, or condition, of maximizing economic efficiency. Specifically, a maximum amount of money made (AMM) net sum of all economic actors in a scenario.

L&E1: the view of L&E that the goal of L&E is to internalize negative and/or positive externalities by simulating zero transaction costs. Law and Economics version 1.0.

L&E2: the view of L&E that the goal of L&E is Max EE. Also known as Law and Economics version 2.0.

P: a Polluter.

R: a Resident.

R1: a first radio station.

R2: a second radio station.

C: Cost.

AMM: Amount of Money Made.

PAMM: Potential Amount of Money Made (AMM plus opportunity cost).

The OPIE Principle: Output = Process of Input Plus Error. In economic terms, the input is the Cost, and the output is the Benefit. If Benefit exceeds Cost, the difference is the Profit. If Cost exceeds Benefit, the difference is the Loss. Cost and Benefit are precisely mathematically defined by a given Process.

The $1 Principle: If economic rational self-interest is conceded, then, to the same extent that a $10,000 profit is better than a $250 profit, it is equally true that a $10,001 profit is better than a $10,000 profit. If you can get an extra dollar of Benefit for an equal or lesser Cost then there is no rational reason not to do so.

The Opportunity Cost Principle: If X makes $500 and Y makes $100 and you can do X or Y but not both, then not doing Y is the Opportunity Cost of doing X, which means that, to sum all Benefits and Costs for X, you must also include a $100 loss from not having done Y. The Opportunity Cost is real, not merely theoretical, because, had you done Y instead of X, then the $100 would have been real, not mere abstract theory.

Let us begin with Coase Theorem.[1] Assume that P (Polluter) has $1 million AMM (Amount of Money he Makes) if he pollutes, and further assume that his pollution is toxic pollution which will seep into the property of R (Resident) and this will make R too sick to work. Assume R's AMM is $30,000 from his day job as a laborer. Assume that if R sues and blocks P from polluting then the $1 million AMM is lost. Assume that if R gets sick from toxic pollution his $30,000 AMM is destroyed. Posit a goal of Max EE defined such that the sum of AMM of all economic actors is maximized.

So we can summarize the scenario as:

R: $30,000.

P: $1,000,000.

R Minus P = -$970,000 (R = +$30,000 and P = $-1,000,000).

P Minus R = $970,000 (P = +$1,000,000 and R = $-30,000).

If R sues and blocks the polluting conduct of P then $1 million is lost but $30,000 is gained, a net loss of $970,000. Therefore let P pollute is the Max EE result. But then R dies (although, in most of the cases of this example in the literature, it is noise pollution, so R just loses $30,000 worth of the quiet enjoyment of his estate.) How do we solve this problem so R lives while P is free and Max EE is achieved?

Coase Theorem became famous as an innovative solution: Let P pay R an amount in excess of R's loss so that R will consent to P's pollution, freely and without coercion.

If P pays R $60,000 to let P pollute, P's after the fact AMM is $940,000, R gets sick and loses $30,000 but gains $60,000 so his net AMM is $30,000, and the sum of AMM of R and P is $970,000, which represents a swing of $970,000 compared to R blocking P.

Let's Summarize this as:

P: $1,000,000.

R: $30,000.

P minus R = $970,000.

P Gives $60,000 to R.

Now P = $940,000 ($1,000,000 - $60,000) and R = $30,000 (-$30,000 + $60,000). So the net sum of all parties is still $970,000, but P has freedom and both P and R have made a profit.

Here we reach some conclusions of Coase Theorem: let P pay R to pollute, and unless blocking P nets over the $1 million cost of blocking P and have some profit on top of it then don't block P. So let P pay R in this hypo, but if, to change the fact pattern, R is an entrepreneur who makes $1,200,000, then R should block P, because $1 million is lost but $1.2 million is saved so there is a net profit of $200,000 as the net sum of AMM of all economic actors. All entirely by reference only to Max EE.

Guido Calabresi is widely viewed as having achieved the one great innovative improvement upon Coase's original work. His theory became known as "Rule 4."

We can arrive at Calabresi and the "Rule 4" theory that he famously articulated in this way.[2] Rule 4 posits that, instead of P paying R to bear pollution, if R can force P not to pollute (in an environmentalist utopia) then P should be able to force R to pay to P the cost of not polluting. P should be allowed to pollute unless R can pay P his cost not to pollute, then if we let P force R to pay him not to pollute, either R can and does (if the benefit to R exceeds $1 million then this results in Max EE) or if he does not and cannot (and on the previous numbers he can't afford to because his benefit is $30,000) then P should pollute and Max EE is achieved, and the benefit to R is destroyed, and AMM equals $1 million minus R's lost AMM. R's benefit must exceed $1 million for him to pay P because P could only be paid the cost of not polluting if the payment equals or exceeds P's lost AMM, which is $1 million.

Diagram this as:

P = $1,000,000.

If $R > $P, R pays R – P to P and keeps the difference.

If $P > $R, P makes $1,000,000 and either P keeps 100% and R suffers a loss of $R or else P keeps $P – $R and P gives $R to R.

Assume R and P in a Rule 4 world, where P could pollute a little bit less and lose $30,000 and R would then not get sick. In this scenario the Cost of $30,000 of P's AMM is $30,000 of Cost to R, meaning R loses $30,000 for P to make a marginal additional $30,000, therefore the net sum of AMM remains the same whether P pollutes or R forces P not to pollute and R keeps his wages or R forces P not to pollute but P forces R to pay P what it is worth to not pollute. A $30,000 gain to P is a $30,000 loss to R, and vice versa, so the net sum of all parties is constant.

If R keeps his wages, R makes $30,000 and P makes $970,000 and the sum of AMM of all parties is $1 million. If P forces R to pay him $30,000 to pollute less, R pays $30,000 but gains $30,000, and P makes $970,000 and gets paid $30,000, hence nets $1 million, or at P's discretion he chooses full pollution and makes $1 million. Rule 4 is proven because in terms of AMM the results are identical if P has freedom to pollute or force R to pay P his cost of not polluting if R forces P not to pollute.

We can diagram this as:

R forces P to pollute less and R doesn't get sick:

P $1,000,000 – P $30,000 (the cost of polluting less) + R $30,000 (now R doesn't get sick, hence R's income) = $1,000,000.

Or:

P forces R to pay P the value, to R, of P polluting less:

P $1,000,000 – P $30,000 = P $970,000 + R $30,000 (R's income) – R $30,000 (R loses what he pays to P) + $30,000 for P (what R pays to P) = $1,000,000.

In contrast, if P fully pollutes, P = $1,000,000 + P $30,000 (what P avoids losing) – R $30,000 (what R now loses) = $1,000,000.

So the Calabresi Rule 4 Conclusion is that, in this scenario, it doesn't make any difference, to P or to us, whether P fully pollutes, or is forced by R not to pollute, because, as weird as this sounds, if R can force P not to pollute and achieve a Max EE result then P could force R to force P not to pollute and achieve the same Max EE result, that is, if R forces P to pay R the cost of the negative externality of P's pollution, this achieves a result identical to P forcing R to pay P the negative impact, upon P, that R has on P by forcing upon P the internalizing of the negative externality that P forced onto R. Basically, it all sums net to the same result, because the Benefits and Costs are the same.

The only question is how those Benefits and Costs are distributed, whether R gets them or P gets them, which is a political question, not an economic question, as will be discussed below. For the economy, the only thing that the economy wants is Max EE, because Max EE is maximum profit, maximum Benefit over Cost net sum of all parties, and that maximizes the wealth that humanity has to spend for the survival of the human species.

However, let us now turn to the question of distribution. You might assume that distribution is defined by the initial distribution of rights: If R has the right to block P's pollution, then P will be forced to pay R. But if P has the initial right to pollute, then P won't give R any money. But Coase Theorem says no, that is not really true, we end up with the same result regardless of initial distribution. Why?

This paper goes "back to formula" by examining the Radio Station Scenario, which was the first hypothetical Coase analyzed before he turned his attention to the more popular Pollution Nuisance Scenario.

Let us next consider two radio stations where the federal regulators must choose one and only one to assign a license for a radio spectrum (essentially a license to operate) to.[3] Assume radio stations named R1 and R2. R1 has a bigger market and a better product than R2. R1 has a PAMM (Potential Amount of Money it will Make if licensed) of $90,000. R2 has a PAMM of $30,000 if licensed.

If R1 gets the license, R2 goes out of business, net AMM is $60,000 ($90,000 of R1 minus lost R2 $30,000). If R2 gets the license and the license is alienable, R1 can buy the license from R2 for $30,001. R2 still goes out of business and loses $30,000 PAMM but gets paid $30,001 so is $1 better off and R1 nets $59,999 AMM ($90,000 in AMM minus the $30,001 payment). So $60,000 in AMM results either way, because this is equal to R1's AMM ($59,999) plus R2's AMM ($30,001) minus R2's loss of PAMM ($30,000), proving the Coase Theorem that it doesn't matter who gets the license in a free economy because the Max EE result will happen either way.

We can diagram this as:
R1: PAMM $90,000.
R2: PAMM $30,000.
R1 – R2 = $60,000.
R2 – R1 = $-60,000. (R2 – R1 = $30,000 – $90,000).
Or:
If R2 gets the license and then R1 buys the license from R2:
R1: +$90,000 -$30,001. Net plus $59,999.

R2: -\$30,000 +\$30,001. Net plus \$1.

R1: \$59,999 (final).

R2: \$30,001 (final).

AMM net sum of all parties: \$60,000 (\$59,999 + \$1) (Max EE).

The central thesis of L&E2 is that, if zero transaction costs exist, the initial distribution of rights and decision-making authority does not matter. R1 or R2 may have the license. P or R may decide who is forced to pay. It does not matter. The maximum economically efficient outcome will naturally arise from any scenario, because it will either exist initially or it will pay for itself to arise and come into being if it did not exist initially. By having the most AMM, the Max EE outcome can outbid any alternative and is therefore a logically necessary outcome as a result of free market capitalism. It is inevitable.

The key takeaway from this is that the initial distribution of rights does not matter, because, if the economy is perfectly free (with zero transaction costs), then the Max EE result will naturally be the end-result, no matter what. Whether Radio Station One or Radio Station Two is given the license initially, the one that makes the most profit will emerge as the owner and victor, although the other one still ends up being better off than in any alternative possibility. Max EE is the "pareto-optimal" condition, to use an academic phrasing, which means that no one could be made better off by any changes.

To paraphrase F.A. Hayek, this means that order will naturally emerge from chaos, automatically, because the economics will cause it to happen, regardless of which chaotic scenario is the starting point. By analogy, this applies to the Liberty Movement: given any starting distribution of power, whether power is given to kings and emperors and dictators, or feudal lords, or to corrupt Liberal or Conservative politicians, or to the public democratically, the Liberty Movement will win, eventually, and Libertarianism will be the end result, one the wars and conflicts of politics sort themselves out and resolve, into a historically predetermined and inevitable conclusion, because Liberty is the Max EE political and economic system.

We are at a moment in history when the Liberty Movement has just begun, when there are still people alive today who met Ayn Rand and Murray Rothbard in person, but, given enough passage of time, and future generations, we can foretell how history will unfold.

Law and Economics dovetails with Public Choice Theory, the school of thought which examines the motivations of politicians in the most cynical lens possible and assumes that each politician just acts to maximize their own self-interest, and never purely for the good of society, in this way: if government and politicians try to block the Max EE outcome, the Max EE outcome will simply bribe them or pay to create a structure where their self-interest aligns with itself, because the maximum profit will result if and to the extent that the money made from doing so exceeds the costs, so the money spent will pay for itself. Government can only prevail when its control is so oppressive that the costs of circumventing it exceed the profits in the condition of economic freedom.

For example, assume R and P, P has AMM of $1 million, R has AMM of $30,000. Assume an environmentalist lobbying group and a politician who favors them. Assume P can buy the politician with a $200,000 campaign contribution, can sway the lobby by donating $100,000 to fund clean energy research, and faces at worst a $500,000 fine if accused of bribery and corruption. The AMM is $1 million and the Cost is $830,000, so the pollution will happen, regardless of whether P or the politician holds the initial decision-making power.

So we can diagram this as:

P: $1,000,000.

R: $30,000.

Bribe the political system (Liberals, L): $800,000.

Because P > R + L, P is the Max EE Result, so P will happen, and P will keep $P – $L as a profit, and $R is just a negative externality loss that R suffers.

You might think that the Libertarian would just let the pollution happen, and let P keep the full amount of $P, while the Liberal would want P to pay the corruption and bribery fee to the political system to let the pollution happen. However, if R has an individual right, such as ownership of body (health) or property (land) which P's pollution would violate, then P would have to pay R, because R could block the pollution as of legal right, because moral natural rights are prior to economic efficiency according to Libertarian political values. Thus, the key Coase Theorem insight that you would pay people an amount equal to their cost of your benefit holds true.

From the economy's point of view, it makes no difference to society whether the profit is distributed to P or to the Liberal politicians, because Max EE is achieved regardless, so long as the pollution happens. P will make $P, and R will be paid according to R's role in the profit-making, to the extent that P must internalize negative externalities.

Only the Marxist socialist would completely block the pollution. Here we reach a point in our analysis where we Libertarians can gleefully prove that the Marxist socialist will never overcome the resistance of moderate Liberals among the Left: If the cost of funding a political system for the Liberals to usurp and control the Marxist socialists, thereby allowing business to make a profit, is less than the value of capitalism to the rich businesspeople, then big business will simply pay for a corrupt Liberal political system that will not allow the Marxist socialists to ever completely block business or to block the pollution of a P on behalf of an R.

In any society with the rule of law and which lacks a Marxist socialist dictatorship, if a rich business party to a lawsuit can afford far better lawyers than a poor individual party, and the profit to be made from winning the litigation exceeds the cost of the lawyers for the business, then the maximally efficient result is for the business to do the objectionable conduct, hire the lawyers and win and pay the legal fees, which are the cost of winning. And of course the lawyers and the judge both went to Harvard Law School where they were friends and frat brothers and went to the same parties and were at each others' weddings and all it takes is a wink and a nudge from the law firm, and P wins the case, and poor R with his local small law firm attorney never had a prayer. This is the corruption of Liberal economics, which only Libertarian economics can overcome.

If a business can make $1 million from pollution, and win an environmentalist lawsuit by paying $750,000 of legal fees, then it has to pollute. Economic rational self-interest dictates this. Much as we might feel this is repulsive, or unethical, basic economics and math defines this as the necessary and logical result.

Business breaking law (Benefit): $1,000,000.

Legal fees of breaking the law (Cost): $750,000.

Profit: $250,000.

Going back to the $1 Principle, even if Liberals impose a high Cost of doing business in a regulated Liberal economy, the rich businesspeople will pay it, because they benefit more by paying it and making the money than by not doing business at all (being blocked). The Liberals don't want to stop Capitalism, they just want to redistribute its results, to the poor (so they say) or, for the corrupt Liberal politicians, into their own pockets on behalf of their poor voters. It is only the Marxist socialists who truly want to destroy Capitalism, in the interests of their pure ideals, but the purity of their ideals collapse to the extent that economics is rational and a necessary and ethical component of human existence for life on earth.

And, much as their ideals seem pure but are really not, so, too, all Marxist socialism will inevitably disintegrate into Liberal corruption, that, as a Liberal politician just wants a bribe or a fine to be paid, the Marxist socialist dictator who enslaves an economy will end up using corruption to line his own pockets at the expense of his people. It is inevitable, and is what the science of economics would predict and expect.

Assume the following scenarios:

P is a public company, R is a shareholder, C is the cost of paying a fine to the SEC for breaking an SEC rule. If the value to P of breaking the law exceeds C, then P will break the law and pay the fine to the SEC. If the benefit to the SEC of collecting the fine exceeds the benefit to the SEC of enforcing the law, then the SEC would rather have P break the law and pay the fine than have P obey the law. In this way, the existence of the rules and regulations creates a system whereby people find it in their economic self-interest to be corrupt and to promote corruption. Regulations lead inevitably to institutionalized bribery.

A Liberal political system, where the Liberals say that greed is evil, and pass laws and regulations to prevent big business from doing business and making money, but which laws the businesspeople must break to make the money that pays for humanity to survive, and then must pay fines to the Liberal government as the cost of doing business, constitutes little more than a "protection racket," much as the mafia or organized crime frequently runs. The Liberals "protect" business and "protect" the free market, and "protect" the public from the free market, and let business be free, in return for taking a bribe, collecting fines and legal fees and lobbying donations, skimming something off the top, taking a haircut.

The Liberals say they hate business and greed, but their only desire is to take as much money from the rich for themselves as possible, which is both hypocrisy and corruption. The true Liberal secretly loves Capitalism because Capitalism maximizes the amount of wealth available for them to steal. I will concede that, if Capitalism exists, the PAMM is roughly constant between Liberty and Liberalism, the only difference between Liberty and Liberalism is that they both allow Capitalism but the Liberals distribute the proceeds and profits into corrupt politics, while Liberty lets everyone be free to own the rewards of their own hard work, so you keep your own profit. Liberalism holds business hostage, and demands as ransom that business pays taxes and pays the fines and penalties of disobeying regulations. The Liberty Movement will set business free.

As such, Liberty is better than Liberalism because it is more ethical, and so is favorable to all humans in our capacity as moral agents. From the point of view of economic efficiency, Liberty says that pure free market economics actually makes more money than Liberalism, because getting the bad laws and rules out of the way makes more business and more profit possible, but the Liberal counter is that, from a Max EE point of view, Liberty and Liberalism are identical, because the Liberal never expects Capitalism to actually obey the rules, they expect the rich and big business to break the rules and then pay the fines, which fines the Liberal politicians and activists happily collect and pocket for themselves.

Only by means of Libertarianism, where there are no laws or fines, would it be in everyone's self-interest to be ethical and honorable. And, in a Liberty Utopia, R does not need the Liberals to protect R from P, because R can protect themselves from P by means of private lawsuits, and thereby force P to internalize any negative externalities for R. If R enforces R's moral natural rights by private lawsuit, not by regulation and taxation and redistribution, then P is forced to pay R the cost of P's conduct, assuming that R can prove damages and culpability of P to a jury and judge. It is textbook Libertarian law that every human has the right to own body (health) and property (land, possessions), so the rich could not trample these rights at will, and must pay to buy consent in a Liberty Utopia.

For example, if a public company stock commits a fraud upon an investor, in Liberalism, R relies on the SEC and its regulations to protect R, but P can just pay a fine to the SEC and walk away. In a Liberty Utopia, R would sue P directly, asserting fraud as a violation of moral natural rights to property embodied by contract law, and thereby R has control, and R can force P to compensate R and pay the cost of P's evil conduct. This is why both the rich Conservatives and the rich Liberals hate Libertarians and the Liberty Movement, because we would actually enable poor R to hold rich P accountable, in a way that does not currently happen in the corrupt Liberal-Conservative status quo.

It might be objected that P will just hire better lawyers than R, and so get away with murder, much as I described above. If the profit to be made from bribing judges and bribing the legal system exceeds the cost, then P will try to do so. But, I answer that, in a Liberty Utopia, we have gotten rid of all the hypocrisy and corruption, so that the judges and the legal system will have moral integrity and consistency and coherence. With just, simple, basic laws, laws written and intended for people to be able to obey while living happy lives, and not laws "made to be broken," it should be pretty obvious whether R deserves to win or lose according to the letter of the law, and we can assume judges who will act with integrity, honor, and justice, which it would be impossible to bribe by hiring rich fancy lawyers or handing bribe money under-the-table.

No system is perfect, but Libertarian laws, and Libertarian justice, would be upheld in a Liberty Utopia, and it should be illegal for P to violate R's right to life, liberty and property, absent R's consent, in such a system, even if P is rich and R is poor and it is Max EE for P to do so. In that narrow scenario, P will just pay R a sum to buy R's consent, and R will make a profit on selling whatever permissions P wants, which, if R is poor and P is rich, could let R make far more money than R otherwise would.

Here is where a Liberty Utopia diverges from the Conservative L&E fantasy, because the Conservatives would like the rich to be able to do whatever they want, including violate the rights of the poor and the middle class, at will, just because it might be the Max EE result for those with more money to always win. In contrast, in a Liberty Utopia, there are Libertarian laws, and both rich, poor, and middle class, are equally held to obey those laws, without any corruption or hypocrisy.

In a Liberty Utopia, if rich P wants to steal from poor R, and it is actual theft of R's life, liberty or property, that R legitimately owns, then P cannot. And, in a Liberty Utopia, there is no fine nor bribe that P can pay to be able to do so, unlike in the Liberal-Conservative nightmare, because either P pays R a sum that R consents to for the release of R's right, or else P is blocked, by a judge and police when R sues P and wins.

But, in a Liberty Utopia, with zero transaction costs, P has the freedom to negotiate and bargain with R and pay R for R's consent to what P wants, making both R and P better off than they otherwise would be, whereas the Marxist socialist just blocks P from doing anything, as of right, without recourse, and thereby leaves no free path along which business can operate.

Assume the point of view that a capitalist economy PAMM will make $20 trillion GDP (this is roughly the amount of US GDP in 2020, source: Google and Wikipedia), but that, if it is unregulated "cowboy" free market capitalism, then the working class will rise up in Marxist socialist revolution and destroy it. Assume further that the PAMM of the same nation in a Marxist socialist economic system is $2 trillion, because they block lots of things that businesspeople need to do in order to make money, with regulations and red tape and just flat out not letting businesses operate because they hate greed and they hate money.

Assume that the rich capitalist businesspeople believe that, if they pay 20% of capital gains tax and corporate income tax to the government, that would be $4 trillion in taxes, which could fund a government Liberal welfare state, and that, if a Liberal welfare state exists, there won't be enough angry poor people to start a revolution. Then the welfare state becomes a cost of capitalism and of making a profit, which, if the rich feel the benefit exceeds the cost, then they make a profit, and will happily pay the tax, indeed their economic self-interest dictates they must, and must want to, pay taxes, because they maximize profit more in capitalism than in Marxist socialism.

In this way, the capitalist economy will motivate a Liberal movement where the Left will be trying to distribute as much for the working class as they can get, by means of enabling and conceding to a corrupt system. The only alternatives to this, are two systems, which have ethical integrity and honor, and those would be Marxist socialism, which can't exist because the rich will pay the political fees to prevent it from happening, or Libertarian Anarcho-Capitalism, where everyone will be perfectly free so there will be no occasion to pay bribery and corruption costs to the political system.

So we can diagram this hypothetical fact-pattern as:

Capitalism: $20 trillion.

Marxist socialism: $2 trillion.

Capitalism – Marxist Socialism = $20 trillion – $2 trillion = $18 trillion.

Then Capitalism could spend up to $18 trillion minus $1 in order to defeat Marxist socialism and still make a profit on the transaction.

The only question then becomes, from Capitalism's view, how to spend that $18 trillion? The Liberal answer is: pay it to the government for the welfare state, which means, bribe the politicians with money, and bribe the working class with entitlements, to get the Liberals to allow Capitalism to exist. Such as, for example, a $4 trillion welfare state. $4 trillion means nothing to rich people who would own $16 trillion, it is crumbs to them.

The Libertarian answer, in contrast, is: spend that money on business, and reinvest it into capitalist free enterprise, which really means, let each person keep, and own, the money they make, instead of stealing some or all of that money as taxes for Liberal politicians to distribute to their voters. This is more honest and therefore less corrupt.

The Liberals and Conservatives both seem to concede that some of that money should be taxed and spent to bribe the working class into allowing Capitalism to exist, they just fight over exactly how much, with the Liberals wanting a little more for the poor, and the Conservatives wanting a little more for the rich. But they fight over distribution, not over the principle of corruption. Only the Liberty movement has an alternative to corruption as the cost of Capitalism. That alternative's name is: freedom.

Capitalism is going to exist. So why not let it exist? Why not let it be free? We do not need the welfare state to bribe the Left and the working class into allowing freedom to exist. You can never achieve victory for freedom by conceding to the State that the State has the right to destroy freedom. The Liberty movement is all about principles, not making compromises with corruption, not forcing life to bribe death for the right to be alive. The more money you pay to death, the shorter your life will become. Freedom, to be truly free, must be legalized, with no taxes and no regulations, and, if a Marxist socialist revolution rises up, you could spend up to $18 trillion to put it down. But, with a democracy, we decide things by votes, not by revolutions, so the Liberty movement can win, even without any bloodshed.

If AMM of Capitalism = $20 trillion, then, from society's point of view, it doesn't make any difference what portion of that is kept by the rich business world or is distributed to the poor welfare state, provided that, assuming that AMM of Capitalism = $20 trillion and AMM of Marxist Socialism = $2 trillion, the system will do anything possible to keep capitalism and avoid socialism to thereby prevent society and the human species from suffering a $28 trillion loss. So Left vs. Right, Liberals vs. Conservatives, is just a fight over whether the AMM of their corrupt political system of corruption is distributed to the rich or distributed to the poor, they have no self-interested motivation in reform or honor or ethical integrity.

Ayn Rand made a clever and insightful argument: the Liberals and Conservatives concede Capitalism as the means of production, but then they fight over distribution. But this is like saying that we must have theft and stealing from a business so that we will let the businessperson work without us putting our foot on their neck and kicking them in the face. This is like saying that business is a necessary evil, which we will tolerate so long as they pay money to the welfare state, so the poor and the working class don't revolt. But that concedes the morality of Marxist socialism, which says that business doesn't have the moral right to be free, that Capitalism is immoral.

Concede this premise long enough, and Liberal corruption will collapse into Marxist socialism, which nobody really wants, other than a fringe group of far-Left radicals who are too naïve and foolish to realize that Marxist socialism was just supposed to be a phantom carrot and stick to funnel Capitalist money into Liberal distribution for the benefit of rich Liberals.

I repeat: Nobody wants Marxist socialism, because then Max EE is not achieved, the money output declines, for example, from a $20 trillion economy to a $2 trillion economy, and then the nice standard of living for the middle class goes away, and there isn't even any money to give as charity to the poor because all the money goes up in smoke, and everyone is sad, angry and miserable. Like the poor nations behind the Iron Curtain in the Communist Russian USSR, which history shows was a horror story of poverty and corruption, with all political dissidents jailed or shot and killed.

Living on a communal farm and growing your own food and knitting your own clothes and smoking cannabis all day and never using money or trade (and never bathing or showering, and never having to take a bath or shower), is a nice way for a bunch of college kids to spend a summer, but it is no way to run a major economy with hundreds of millions of people. It won't pay for the elderly to retire, it won't pay for the young to be educated, and it won't pay for food on the table. Capitalism makes stuff, and gives people jobs, and enables people to buy stuff, and creates opportunity (by making the money that pays for new opportunity), and, yes, we humans are physical, material beings, and having stuff, owning things, making money, having money, spending money, makes us happy, so Capitalism is ethical, Capitalism is good. Because life is good. Being alive is good. So we must set Capitalism free.

And to those Marxist socialists who say that Capitalism leaves us feeling empty, that we are alienated from our own souls, that money can't buy happiness: no, money does not directly buy happiness, it's not like there's a happiness store where you pay $100 and are given the meaning of life in return, but it buys you the time and the means to live your life, thereby giving you the opportunity to find something that means something to you and which can make you happy. Like money paying for a nice wedding dress: the wedding is what matters, not the dress, but the dress is a nice picture frame for the picture of the wedding, metaphorally speaking. The Grinch can't steal Christmas, but you should still use giving Christmas presents in order to show your Christmas love and affection, because opening the presents gives joy to people. Money is a means, not an end, but, absent having means, having power, people would be helpless and powerless, and have nothing.

Voters like integrity, and activists like ideals and honor. Corruption attracts Reformers, and Crusades for Reform are inevitable. The corruption of Liberalism will collapse under the weight of its own contradictions. And, if Marxist socialism is the only option, it would be that which would win. So Ayn Rand (and Murray Rothbard) created the Liberty Movement, where we have ideals and ethics and heroes to believe in, for Capitalism, and for free market economics. Not as a necessary evil, but as a noble ideal.

The historical inevitability of Liberty can be proven in this way: Liberty will have a higher PAMM than Marxist socialism, and so a Libertarian future will pay for itself to come into being over and against a Marxist socialist alternative. However, while a Liberal economy might have the same PAMM as Liberty, it achieves this only by paying bribes and political corruption as the cost of letting free market capitalism have a sphere of freedom within which business can operate.

Corruption is anathema to the human soul, and the hearts and minds of human voters will not tolerate a permanently corrupt political solution, so that, because Liberty is consistent and has integrity in its freedom-based laws, while Liberalism suffers a contradiction between the economic need for freedom and its commitment to controlling and manipulative and freedom-restricting laws and regulations, the ethics and honor of the voters and political activists will prefer Liberty to Liberalism, and so Liberty would win long-term against both Marxist socialism and Liberalism, as a matter of historical necessity.

The Coase Theorem scenarios can be explained by L&E1. For example P internalizes R's positive and negative externalities. P is forced to pay R so that P will suffer the negative externalities of his pollution or of taking his radio broadcast license. P did something bad to a third party, which is the quintessential negative externality, so P must be punished by bearing R's cost.

It is also possible to explain all scenarios entirely by reference to L&E2 alone, to achieve the Max EE outcome, without any reference in the explanation to internalizing negative or positive externalities or transaction costs. Of course the Max EE is not achieved unless the two sides can trade and buy and sell benefits and costs. The transaction costs must be zero for this condition to be met. But L&E1 is often intended merely to let regulators impose the result they subjectively believe would have happened if there had been zero transaction costs and all externalities were internalized.

The key insight from L&E2 is that whether P should be blocked or allowed to proceed depends upon which option produces Max EE, and that Max EE is achieved if in the first instance the license is given to the radio station with the highest PAMM or if P is allowed to pollute even without cost redistribution to R. By a similar extension of analysis, a voter should, and eventually all voters will, choose Liberty over Liberalism. Because it is Max EE. Liberty will never make less money or be less Capitalistic than Liberalism, but it has more ethics and honor and integrity, which is worth at least $1 more, so Liberty is always superior to Liberalism.

We conclude this section with nice examples that contrast L&E1 with L&E2, with our first example using cigarettes. L&E1 might tell regulators to tax cigarettes to pay for smoker healthcare costs to internalize the negative externalities of smoking, where the negative externality is that society pays for the healthcare system that treats the health consequences of the smoker's self-destructive behavior, because hospitals will not turn smokers away for inability to pay (given the unrealistic assumption that government will give smokers' tax dollars to hospitals in ratio to healthcare services rendered).

L&E2 might say Max EE is achieved if we either let each smoker pay for his own individual healthcare costs or else let him die and spend no marginal additional cost of healthcare. Taxing cigarettes raises prices, which runs contrary to economic efficiency, whereas the L&E2 solution caps cost as equal to the PAMM lost from each smoker's death.

Another example, which is not so nice, is public education. Suppose that a politician is thinking about things, and she thinks, when a child is educated that benefits society, therefore education has positive externalities, so she thinks in her subjective opinion that if zero transaction costs existed then everyone would willingly pay for every child's tuition, and she uses that unproven subjective feeling as her basis to raise taxes and make every college and university tuition-free. That is an example of how L&E1 works, in practice.

L&E2 might say, completely deregulate and privatize all education, and then whatever is the order that emerges naturally from the chaos will be the maximum economically efficient outcome, because that is how economics works.

L&E1 says that zero transaction costs are impossible, but the economy should have what would happen if they existed, so government must guess what that outcome would be and impose it onto everyone by force.

L&E2 says no, that is a misinterpretation of C/C. Let people be as free as possible, and the Max EE outcome will arise naturally. It will arise precisely because it has more PAMM to spend to bring itself into being than any alternative scenario. We might not have perfect zero transaction costs, but no reason exists why P cannot pay R, no legal or practical barrier constrains P, in a multitude of situations, so the theory of L&E2 can and will work.

One can do some interesting things with L&E2, such as, for example, solving the Israel-Palestine problem. If the value of the Palestinian land is more valuable to Israel then to Palestine, then the Jews would pay the Palestinians the cost of having that land, namely, by paying the cost for the Palestinians to pack up and move and buy some nice land somewhere else and go somewhere else, and then the Jews could claim all that land for Israel, and the Palestinians would (be paid to) fully consent and agree, and the Jews could spend an amount of money equal to the difference between the benefit of that land to the Jews, compared to the benefit of that land to the Palestinians, in order to do so. But, if the cost exceeded the benefit, and the Jews could not do so, then the Max EE Result would be to get the Israelis out of the Palestinian-held lands, and let the Palestinians form their own state. Economics, and relative costs and benefits, would dictate the proper solution.

Similar thinking can be applied across a broad range of problems, for example, let the Pro-Lifers pay pregnant women to bear their babies, and, if they don't choose to pay the cost of the pregnancy that they demand to let happen, by paying the costs of having the baby and raising the child, plus a bonus bounty to pay the woman in order to compensate her for choosing childbirth. Then also give the woman the freedom to have an abortion, if the Pro-Lifers won't pay the Cost of pregnancy, because the Pro-Choice result is what would happen absent the Pro-Life objection. And so on.

In this way, Coase Theorem can solve many thorny policy debates using a precisely logical, mathematical, economic approach, which is purely objective and deductive, and not subjective or emotional. It is textbook Libertarian economics that TANSTAAFL, "there ain't no such thing as a free lunch," so, if you want a benefit for yourself from something that you will force onto someone else, you should pay for it, to internalize the negative externality.

The Liberal Conservative status quo has naturally arisen from the class warfare between capitalism and Marxist socialism according to the economic principles outlined above. Emerging fro the Industrial Revolution, it maximized profit and PAMM and AMM for capitalism to exist, but the corrupt states and nations and governments, which had evolved from the kingdoms and feudal estates of the past, demanded payment as a cost of allowing freedom to exist.

This naturally evolved into the Liberal government corruption we see today, where the rich get freedom in return for paying million dollar fines to regulators for breaking the law and bribing politicians through lobbying and corruption and the rich then do whatever they want while the middle class gets screwed over and the middle class is at the same time then confined by the laws and regulations which no longer apply to the rich.

The rich and the politicians become the ruling class, while the middle class and the poor are second-class citizens, and the more this Liberal system works, the more corrupt it becomes. But it is institutionalized corruption, and so cannot survive, because it will kindle in the hearts of humans a fervent desire to abolish it, because humans are good and ethical naturally, and good will always triumph over evil in the end. So the corrupt Liberal state is doomed.

But Marxist socialism does not maximize PAMM and so it too will never survive. The survival of the human species still depends on making as much money as possible, so humans will never choose socialism, and, even if they did, it would go bankrupt and collapse, much as the USSR did against the Capitalism of Reagan and Thatcher.

The only system which maximizes PAMM and AMM, thereby paying for itself to come into existence by affording to pay the cost to defeat any lesser-PAMM system and still take a profit on its existence for society, while at the same time having moral integrity and ethics and honor and internal consistency and coherence, by being capable of honest law-abiding behavior by all system participants, is Libertarianism and Anarcho-Capitalism.

For example:

Capitalism: $20 trillion.

Marxist socialism: $2 trillion.

The Liberty movement, taking a loan today from future generations, could afford to spend up to almost $18 trillion in order to win, while the Marxist socialists could only spend up to $2 trillion. So Liberty must win.

Against Liberalism, even assuming a net $20 trillion AMM compared to Liberty either way, Liberty has one benefit, ethics and honor and integrity, because people need to be free and it lets people be free, as compared to the corruption of Liberalism, where people need to be free but it says people should be taxed and regulated so people use corruption to steal the freedom that they require in order to survive and so, PAMM being even, other than the people who benefit from the way Liberals distribute wealth, namely, the very corrupt politicians and the very poor incompetents who rely on the welfare state for their survival, no one likes Liberalism, and nobody wants Liberal corruption.

The great innovation of the Liberty movement, which did not exist before today, is that it achieves Max EE plus moral integrity. This is a combination that voters will tend to choose, in comparison to political corruption, over a long enough time line, because ethics is inherently more desirable than corruption, for human beings. So Liberty will win.

In Liberty, everyone is free to achieve Max EE, so there is no need for corruption as a cost of Max EE, and everyone is free to pursue their natural economic self-interest. At the same time, if rights are assigned in the first instance to the individual, not to society, then the poor and the working class does not get screwed over, as, for example, going back to Coase Theorem, P must pay R the cost to R for P's conduct, such that both P and R are better off, because the Liberty legal system begins with the assumption that R owns R's body and R's health, and therefore P would lack the right to violate R's property absent paying R for R's consent to do so.

Because both P and R are better off for having made the deal, we assume that P and R will freely choose the deal because they are motivated to maximize profit by their economic self-interest, and so freedom in Liberty becomes a perfect system that everyone can abide by and which everyone becomes the better off for. Ultimately, Libertarian deregulation and economic freedom is the practical application of the condition of zero transaction costs, because everyone is free to shift money to pay for costs of benefits.

As such, the Liberty Movement's historical rise and eventual triumph is inevitable. You, the Liberals and Conservatives and Marxist socialists, give up. Resistance is futile. You will be assimilated. Liberty will win. We will win.

WHAT IS THE LIBERTARIAN AXIOM?

Most libertarians would point to the principle that one should never initiate violence, and use force only for self defense, as the core axiom for liberty—the axiom that I call NVP, the Non-Violence Principle. Here I write to propose a second axiom, based on some recent conversation with my fellow Libertarian Party members.

I know one LP member who opposes big government except for public education to give poor kids a leg up. I know another who opposes big government except for Social Security for retirees, on the belief it isn't fair to deny someone benefits they paid into for decades. I know a third who opposes big government except for welfare and food stamps for the very poor. This person is convinced that a Marxist revolution will happen if all welfare is cut. I have also heard a Libertarian talk about the "real" pain and suffering of the poor that is alleviated by welfare, as if the pain caused by big government is not equally real.

These people, and I now suspect most Americans, understand libertarian economics, but they think that theft (in the form of taxation) is justified if it is for a good, worthy cause. Each person has his own pet cause that he wants government to fund, even while wanting taxes cut to pay for anything else. There are Social Conservatives who crusade for freedom and want freedom for everyone, except for the freedom for pregnant mothers to abort or for LGBTs to exist, because they think gay sex and abortion are sins, and the ends justify a limitation or compromise of (other people's) freedom. Everyone wants freedom, they just don't want absolute freedom.

But we Libertarians really do want absolute freedom.

I propose a new axiom: that the ends never justify the means. Good ends do not justify evil means. I term this the Anti-Marxist Axiom.

If you believe this, then theft (taxation) is never justified, even for the noblest purpose, and even if the rich have more money than they need. My justification for this axiom is moral, not pragmatic, and, in a weird way, Kantian. Kant's signature contribution to ethics is the theory of the Categorical Imperative, which I interpret to mean that, for something to be good, it must be right at all times and places universally. If there is an exception to an ethical (or political) principle then it was not rational or true, it was merely an expediency of the moment.

To be a coherent theory, libertarianism needs the Anti-Marxist Axiom, otherwise it is just a rule of thumb to be compromised or abandoned when someone feels justified in doing so. If you use evil means to achieve good ends, logically the result will not be ethical, because you conceded to evil in order to achieve your goal.

If you want to fund a good cause with taxes then you conceded the validity of statism. If you accept that people make and earn money, and thereby morally deserve to own wealth, and then say that you can take someone's money away from them to spend as you see fit, even for a good cause, you have conceded and condoned widespread systemic theft. It should not then surprise you that a bunch of crooks, literally thieves, actual criminals, will run for office to acquire this opportunity and then will raise taxes on you to pay for evil things while spouting all sorts of virtuous good causes to justify it.

There is a saying "power corrupts, and power attracts the corruptible." (Attributed to Frank Herbert.) I can say something similar: theft attracts criminals. This is a necessary and sufficient explanation for why big government is evil and will always become evil even if it begins as good.

Absent this axiom, you will find good cause after good cause, requiring tax raise after tax raise, and more and more theft to pay for your virtuous plans, until, from a libertarian starting point, you inevitably collapse into socialism. Either you have a universal, absolute axiom, or you face a very realistic slippery slope—even if sliding down it takes a nation 200 years.

Libertarians should consider abandoning their pet causes and commit to the Anti-Marx Axiom, to protect the purity of our principles. Libertarianism as a political theory needs an axiom, a self-evident principle to justify itself. If it does not have a principle then it is not a theory, it would be a mere pragmatic movement, or merely a feeling that government is bad. NVP is a good axiom, but many libertarians feel justified in making exceptions. The axiom that the ends never justify the means says there are no exceptions. If people want compromise, let them vote for the establishment. If they want principled politics, then they should vote for us. But how can we be a party of principles if we don't know what our core principle is?

THE MATHEMATICAL ARGUMENT FOR WHY LIBERTARIANISM WILL END POVERTY

Being a big fan of Friedrich Nietzsche, I have a fondness for clever, memorable aphorisms, on the model of his "All that which does not kill me makes me stronger," which is one of my personal mottos. One such aphorism is: "Socialists believe that no one should own anything. Libertarians believe that everyone should own something." What this aphorism gets at, among other things, is that both socialists and libertarians have an answer to the problem of poverty, but our answer differs sharply from theirs. In terms of the political appeal of libertarianism, this is an important point to hammer home to voters.

The leftists and socialists say that they want to help the poor and that the libertarians and conservatives are the enemies of the working class and we don't care about the poor. This naturally drives working class voters to vote Democrat when they should be voting Libertarian. I can't speak for conservatives, and I can't speak for other libertarians either. But, speaking for myself, I can say that I do care about the poor, and my brand of libertarianism, which comes from a liberal-tarian or neo-liberal strain, is very intently focused upon ending poverty. Poverty eradication is one of my goals. It is not the only goal. But it is a valid goal, and it is an achievable goal.

I would tell voters that libertarianism will end world poverty. That is a bold claim, and I expect most voters would reply: "Why? And how?" One answer can be found in my unique reinterpretation and application of the business management philosophy called Six Sigma.

Six Sigma is a technique developed in the manufacturing industry, and it is widely credited with the high quality of electronics devices that are manufactured today. Six Sigma is a mathematical approach to business management and products manufacturing, which states that hard math and statistics should be used to manage a business and to control the work product of a factory. The key mathematical equation used by Six Sigma practitioners, which I would like you to understand, is: $Y = f(X) +$

e, where X represents input, f(X) represents the process that is applied to the input, Y represents the output, and e represents the errors and imperfections inherent in human existence.

The core teaching of Six Sigma is that most business processes are inefficient and generate waste, and vast amounts of money can be saved by redesigning the process to eliminate waste. The Six Sigma process analyzes the X and the f(X) in order to find the most efficient method of achieving the desired Y. The Six Sigma process uses math and science to find the best process to achieve efficiency, quality and success. Six Sigma believes that with the exact same input X, e.g. with the same amount of work, labor, effort, and raw materials, the output Y can be very different if the process, the f(X), is different. What matters is the f(X), not the X, because you need a good process to get the most output out of your input.

Six Sigma is not mere abstract theory. It has been used in practical reality, for example by Motorola, Bank of America, and major car manufacturers in Detroit. The data suggests that when a Fortune 500 company implements Six Sigma, and when they do it correctly, and especially when they use it on their manufacturing processes and factories, on average their net profits increase by as much as one billion dollars per year.

Now, let me get to the main argument in this essay. We can consider a national economy to be akin to a business or a factory. The work that people do, and the natural resources and raw materials that go into their work, are the input. The money that is made and the consumable goods and services that they produce are the output. And the political system, be it libertarian capitalism or socialist left-liberalism, is the process which takes inputs and creates outputs. My argument is that the process of heavy government intervention in the economy, pioneered by the New Deal and implemented by Obama and the Democrats today, is very wasteful. If Motorola could save a billion dollars by more efficient processes, then the United States of America could probably save trillions of dollars by a more efficient politico-economic process.

And the trillions of dollars of added wealth would end up in the hands of the people, of the working class. I fully believe that if all the economic waste was eliminated, in the USA and also if the rest of the world implemented free market economics, then the added wealth would be enough to end poverty, so that the vast majority of humans would achieve a middle class or upper class standard of living.

Why would capitalism be a more efficient economic system than Democratic left-liberalism? The answer to that question is so big that it is beyond the scope of this article. In my nonfiction book "Golden Rule Libertarianism," I take 100 pages to explain why a system of money and prices and free choices among competing businesses is the best way to coordinate the diverse economic activity of billions of different producers and consumers in a division of labor economy. The arguments in my book can be called the Hasanian answer. There is also the Randian answer, the Rothbardian answer, the

Milton Friedman answer, etc. Between you and I, let's both of us take it for granted, for the sake of my argument, and leave the details for a different discussion.

Why would libertarianism put money in the hands of the poor and middle class, as opposed to the rich? As a factual matter, the government spends trillions of dollars taken from the taxpayers, so if you end the tax and spend leftist policies, then that money remains in the taxpayers' hands, to be spent by the people. Of course, leftists claim that the rich are the ones who pay taxes, and that tax and spend helps the poor.

However, in fact, the lower class and middle class bear a tax burden that is far worse than the taxes actually paid by the rich. This is because of the low tax rates for long-term capital gains and dividends, where the rich get their money, and the ability of the rich to hold their money in offshore tax shelters, which enable the rich to avoid paying taxes, as well as the tax burdens that target the poor, such as the property tax and the sales tax, social security withholding as a tax, and also the high tax brackets for middle class salaries. $1000 is a ton of money for a working class person or a middle class person, whereas one million dollars is meaningless to a billionaire, so taxes hit the lower class with a proportionate impact far higher than they hit the upper class. The working class and middle class actually are the ones hit hardest by taxation, while the rich find ways to avoid paying taxes, or can afford to pay the taxes they pay. Given that this is true, tax cuts actually help the working class and middle class and have minimal direct benefits for the rich.

A libertarian Six Sigma approach would eliminate the waste in government spending, creating huge savings for the American people. In terms of hard data, the United States government, including the combined federal, state, and local governments, are the biggest spenders of the taxpayers' money, and the examples of bureaucratic failure, waste, and incompetence in government spending are too many to list. There are bridges to nowhere, statues built for no reason, railroad lines constructed that nobody wants to use, all costing the taxpayers billion upon billion.

The government is necessarily inefficient, because the government does not need to compete against someone else to satisfy people, and people are forced to accept what the government does, so competition does not exist to hold bureaucrats accountable and force them to do what the people want. Simply be eliminating all government waste, at both the federal, state, and local levels, we could probably save four trillion dollars of Americans' hard-earned money. Then, if you let people be free to be productive, and you unlock the money-making potential of every worker, especially the highly intelligent and creative people, and if you give people broad freedom to trade with other people without regulatory controls, I believe that another $4 trillion would be added to GDP. $4 trillion plus $4 trillion is $8 trillion.

The US GDP is roughly $20 trillion in circa 2020 (Source: Google and Wikipedia), and it is plausible to think that if we replace a bad, flawed f(X) with a good, efficient, waste-free f(X) then Y could vastly increase, which is in line with what Six Sigma improvements have achieved for businesses that replace bad processes with good processes. So Liberty pays for itself. In terms of Six Sigma using math and science to discover the correct process for a business, which is a core tenet of Six Sigma, I think that the work done by Milton Friedman, who completed an exhaustive, thorough scientific research using hard data and statistical math to show that capitalist-leaning economies generate more wealth than socialist-leaning economies, is true to the Six Sigma approach of statistical analysis. So my application of Six Sigma would take it as a given, proven by the libertarian economists, that the libertarian process is the right one to use to redesign the economy.

Let us consider the number I mentioned: eight trillion dollars recovered due to libertarian policies. America has about 300 million citizens. Let's assume that the poorest 90 percent comprise 270 million people. If we eliminated economic waste and save or create eight trillion dollars, and divide that amongst 270 million people, and just give them the money as a "negative income tax," to use a phrase from Libertarian economist Milton Friedman, then each poor and middle class person would get an additional $29,600 a year. That would give a reasonable amount of money, enough to live a decent, happy life, to each and every working class person in the USA.

Note that, if we eliminate most regulations on the economy, then, because regulations focused on safety tend to make things more expensive, deregulation will make everything cheaper to buy, so when I assert $29,600 more for each poor person I think that when adjusted for real purchasing power every poor person will achieve middle class buying power.

We would lift the poor out of poverty, using a mathematical Six Sigma methodology focused on redesigning the process to eliminate waste and improve efficiency, which experience has already proven to be highly effective in the business world. We could end poverty by using reason and logic, instead of the mushy illogical stupidity of the Left. I conclude by repeating the same point I opened with: Libertarians are not the enemies of the poor and the working class, we are their best friends with their best interests at heart. The leftist Democrat poor don't understand this, but we would be well advised to teach this to the working class voters. Remember the aphorism: Socialists believe that no one should own anything. Libertarians believe that everyone should own something. And our policies will create the new wealth for the poor to claim as their own private property.

TO WORLD PEACE: THE PRINCIPLE OF ETHNIC SOVEREIGNTY

(Author's note: This was written in 2015, so some of the references are dated, but the principles are still relevant and remain the same, and will still apply 10,000 years from today!)

What do the recent Black people vs. white police race riots in St. Louis, the recent Israeli vs. Palestinian conflict, and the Russian annexation of East Ukraine, and the US military operations against ISIS in Iraq and Syria, all have in common? My answer is that these crises were all caused by the same problem, and they could all be solved by one solution. This solution, which I call the principle of ethnic sovereignty, is something that I propose as a giant step in the direction of achieving world peace, and an end to all wars. Libertarians are generally antiwar pacifists, and my theory will be of particular interest to libertarian doves.

What is the principle of ethnic sovereignty? To explain it, I must begin with a personal anecdote. I was born and raised in New York, but my father is an immigrant from Bangladesh, which is a small, poor nation in southeast Asia, and I have been taught Bangladeshi ethnic identity my entire life. Bangladesh was a part of the British colony of India. When the Indian resistance movement, led by Gandhi, was finally able to drive the British Empire out, the lands of the colony of India were divided up into new nations. The modern country of India was created, and all Hindu people were forced to move to India. In the west, Pakistan was created, and in the east, East Pakistan was created, to be governed by West Pakistan. The Muslims were forced to move to West Pakistan or East Pakistan. The political leaders who partitioned India and Pakistan believed that if the people of a nation shared one religion then they would get along and be unified. India would be Hindu, and Pakistan would by Islamic.

But in the case of Pakistan and East Pakistan, this religious unity failed to come true. The people in West Pakistan spoke the language of Urdu, and were ethnic Pakistanis. The people in East Pakistan spoke a different language, called Bangla, and we were ethnic Bangladeshis. Bangladesh has a strong cultural identity, dating back to a rich tradition of literature and music, and the Pakistani culture was completely different from the Bangladeshi ethnic culture.

The Pakistanis grew angry at Bangladeshi culture, which was different from the Pakistani culture embraced by Pakistan's leaders, and the Pakistan government used aggressive force to suppress Bangla culture and to seek to impose Pakistani culture onto the ethnic Bangladeshis in East Pakistan. We, of course, did not like this, and the cultural animosity evolved into a political movement aimed at liberating East Pakistan from Pakistani control. East Pakistan called itself Bangladesh, and Bangladesh eventually began a War of Independence against Pakistan. Many Bangladeshis, including members of my family, died in the conflict. In the end, with help from allies in India and the West, Bangladesh won the War of Independence, and was set free as its own country. In the 1960's, The Beatles played a concert to raise money to support the Bangladeshi War of Independence, so even The Beatles cared.

What lessons can we learn from the story of Bangladesh and Pakistan? I draw a broad conclusion, which is that when an ethnic group occupies a geographic region, those people are going to want to be free, and to rule themselves in democratic self-government, and if you let people from a different ethnic group, in a different region, rule over a people from afar, then you are asking for war. It is natural and inevitable for an ethnic group to fight for freedom if they are being rule by a different ethnic group.

Generally, if every ethnic group on planet Earth was given sovereign rule over the territory that it occupies, if all national borders were redrawn so that each ethnic group had self-government, then I believe that we would be one giant step closer to world peace. In terms of right and wrong, I think that each people has the right to be governed by themselves, because when you let a different group govern them, this is tantamount to tyranny and oppression, whereas self-government is a vital component of freedom, as America's founding fathers knew when they rebelled against the British Empire.

How would the principle of ethnic sovereignty solve the world crises I listed above? The application of the solution to the problems, listed in order, is: the police who impose order are a part of the government that governs an area. If the ethnic group in a community is African American, then they should have African American police to govern them, to give them political sovereignty. The data shows that the St. Louis suburb where the race riots are happening is 85% African American yet almost the entire police force is white (and the local politicians are all white too).

White racist conservatives may say that the Equal Protection Clause forbids letting police recruiters in black areas favor blacks, and that race blindness is the proper solution to the problem. I reject this argument, despite the fact that I like race blindness as an antidote to racism, because the actual text of the Constitution says only that everyone should have equal protection under the laws, so that if whites are protected by white policemen, the equal protection of the law for blacks would actually be for blacks to be protected by Black policemen. Draw police recruits and political appointees from the community that they will be protecting or serving, and you end a lot of the impetus for race riots and civil rights struggles.

Note that I am not advocating redrawing the city and state lines within the USA for each ethnic group to rule its own areas, but that, within the context of the unity in the United States, our goal should be for each area within the US be under the control of its own people, be they blacks, Hispanic immigrants, Irish Catholics, etc.

In the East Ukraine crisis, instead of making Ukraine into an issue in the conflict between the USA and Russia, simply let each region be governed by its own people. This would let the ethnic Russians in East Ukraine join Russia if they wish. But, by the same principle, you then draw a line around the non-Russian Ukrainians in Ukraine, and you use the NATO military to prevent Russia from conquering non-Russian ethnic territory. Under the principle of ethnic sovereignty, the borders of nations drawn on a map are not a game for the rulers of the world to play, using people and soldiers as pawns in a global game of chess. Instead, the lines of the maps become an exercise in designing freedom for each group of people on the planet.

Regarding ISIS, it is widely understood that ISIS rose to power by appealing to the Sunni Muslims in Iraq and Syria, who were oppressed by the Shiite Muslims in Syria and ignored by the Shiite Muslim government in Iraq. The United States, like the world rulers dating back to the British Empire, consider the lines of national borders to be inviolate, even if two rival ethnic groups are trapped within the same national boundaries. I say, redraw the lines, and break Iraq into a Shiite South, a Sunni North, and a Kurdish Northeast. But, in each region, create strong ties of trade with the USA, and seek to give the new nations a government modeled on the freedom and individual rights of American-style government.

And, in Syria, recognize the Syrian rebels as a government, and let the Sunni Muslims govern the Sunni Muslims, while opposing the Shiite dictatorship of Assad. It is too late to do this in time to stop ISIS, but, if the United States does the right thing and leads a military operation to defeat ISIS, then this redrawing of the lines on the map for freedom and democracy is necessary to stabilize the Iraqi region. (Note that it is perfectly appropriate for the USA to use military force to defeat ISIS, because ISIS has made it clear that they intend a terrorist attack against us, so this is the legitimate use of force for national self-defense.)

I conclude with the most politically sensitive issue, Israel and Palestine. On my mother's side of the family I am ethnically Jewish, and I believe that the state of Israel has every right to exist. If you look back 5000 years earlier in human history, Israel belonged to the Jews, it was taken from us by force over and over again, by the Egyptians, the Babylonians, the Romans, and the Medieval forces which controlled it during the Middle Ages. Despite this, however, the Palestinians are a different ethnic group, and they occupy a distinct geographical scope, in the West Bank and the Gaza Strip.

The state of Israel has no right to prevent the Palestinians from forming their own Palestinian state, nor does the state of Israel have the right to regulate or control the Palestinians within their own borders, nor to blockade the Palestinian border, and it is none of Israel's business whom the Palestinians choose to act as the government of Palestine. Israel may defend itself from Palestine if Palestinian terrorists attack, but this right begins and ends at the border between Israel and Palestine. So long as the Israelis behave as though they own Palestine and have the right to control it, so long as the Israelis refuse to recognize the state of Palestine, and while Israel denies to the Palestinian people the right of ethnic sovereignty, the Palestinians will know that they are being treated like slaves or dogs by the Israelis. In this condition, the Palestinians will rebel, and fight for freedom, as is their right.

Instead of one state, if we had two states, an Israel that minds its own business, and a free Palestine, then the Israel-Palestine conflict can, and will, be extinguished, because nobody will have any motive to fight any longer, and everyone will get what they want. The right-wing bigots of the Israeli Right will say that this would constitute the Jews surrendering to the Palestinian terrorists. The terrorists have sinned, I will concede that. But two wrongs don't make a right, and an ethnic group of people still deserves its freedom even if some of them fight for freedom using evil methods. Also note that, while all the Palestinian land could rightfully be claimed as part of Israel, I think the generous and charitable move by Israel would be to gift that small slice of land to Palestine, and not begrudge it or seek to retake it. The Torah states "Love thy neighbor as thyself," and the Palestinians are, quite literally, Israel's neighbors.

During the 1800s and early 1900s, the European colonial powers, including Britain, France, and Belgium, especially in dealing with their colonies in Africa and the Middle East, developed an explicit policy of sowing strife and discord by taking different ethnic groups that disliked each other and trapping them within one nation within the borders they drew on the map. This is why, in Africa, many nations contain warring African tribes, and why in the Middle East countries there are opposing Sunni and Shiite sects of Muslims who hate each other within one nation. The colonial powers knew that the ethnic groups would fight each other, seeking their freedom, which would weaken them and make them easier to rule by the Western empires.

Indeed, I would define the idea that one ethnic group should rule another ethnic group as a fundamentally colonial idea, which should have been discredited by now in our post-colonial age of democracy. I can say, as a Bangladeshi, that each ethnic group which lives in a geographic region will naturally chafe at foreign control, and will seek the freedom of democratic self-government. It is natural for freedom fighters to fight, and to die, and to kill, for their ideal of freedom. We must abandon the colonial attitude that the national boundaries of borders drawn on the maps are sacrosanct. Instead, let's redraw the lines on the map so that each ethnic group owns its own nation. Give the peoples of the world their freedom, and you pave the path to world peace. And what ideal to fight for is there that is any better than world peace?

So I would define the principle of ethnic sovereignty as the statement that each geographical ethnic group dominant in one region should have the right to political autonomy and democratic self-government. But what, then, if an ethnic group becomes a tyranny or dictatorship, and seeks to repress the rights of the individual or of ethnic minorities or racial minorities in that area? Then the oppressed person should simply get up and leave, and move to somewhere else, where they can be free and live life as they want. The Pilgrims and Puritans leaving England for religious freedom in Colonial America is a good example.

This is why the principle of ethnic sovereignty only works if paired with a principle of free, open, and unrestrained immigration borders. Let any individual leave or enter any nation freely, and have a cheap and fast path to citizenship.

No quotas, no visas, no ten-year wait. Just come, apply, pass an two-hour-long multiple choice exam to prove you understand the English language and know how the American political system works, swear to uphold the US Constitution, and become a US citizen. Or move to any other country you want, until you find one you like, where you can be free.

The Conservative will scream in reply: Then they'll all come to America! I say: Let them come. They do no harm to me, nor to you, so we have no right to keep them out.

The Conservative counter: but immigrants from poor countries, who are uneducated and unskilled, drain the United States welfare system, raising taxes on the middle class. I say: Then end the welfare system. That is the only correct solution. Closed borders and choking immigration is not the correct solution. Either let them in and end the welfare state, or let them in and eat the higher taxes. But don't keep them out. Otherwise they are trapped in the foreign dictatorship, which is an insult to freedom and liberty everywhere, including here, and an insult to the dignity of all human beings, including you.

For ethnic sovereignty to work, the ethnic majority must not have the ability to trample and violate the rights of individuals in that society. For which the individual must be able to leave at will, and cross borders, for which there must be open borders. Freedom demands ethnic sovereignty, and the open immigration rights to protect the rights of individuals within that ethnic sovereign nation.

MAKING IT WORK: LIBERTARIAN SOLUTIONS IN HEALTHCARE AND PRIVATIZATION

Libertarian policy proposals are often ridiculed for being too impractical and naively idealistic. This article will put forward practical solutions for implementing libertarian policies in ways that can, and will, work in the real world. Privatization and healthcare, two areas in which libertarian policy is hotly contested, are the focus.

I'll start with a summary of two objections to freedom and follow with a solution for overcoming that objection. I will then add details.

First Objection: Infrastructure—such as roads and train lines—and utilities cannot be privatized because they are natural monopolies: two operators cannot compete along the same line at the same time.

First Solution: If the right to operate the space, be it the road, or train line, or power line, were auctioned off for very short periods, such as 6 to twelve months, at open competitive bidding, it stands to reason that the efficient privatization company would make enough money to place the highest bid at the next round, and would have operated in the best way possible to maximize profits and consumers (if consumers cared to listen to reason). In other words, private operators would compete along the vector of time, not space, with the most efficient one winning the highest profit and likely making the highest bid for the next slot of time.

Second Objection: Under the current system, that evolved under capitalism, health insurers pay for the healthcare of the people who pay healthcare premiums, the premiums bearing no direct relation to the healthcare actually received. The health insurer is the "payer," who pays the doctor, while the person receiving healthcare is the "patient," and there is no direct relationship between payer and patient at the point of sale. The system would have to work this way, because the whole idea of insurance is that you pay for the risk that you may one day need insurance, not for the actual healthcare you receive thereafter. This system causes a disconnect between the healthcare buyers and the healthcare sellers, enabling the sellers to jack up their prices.

The patient is like someone walking into a candy store with the ability to charge anything he wants to someone else's credit card (the payer), and never see the person who owns the credit card. We would expect the candy store to charge exorbitant prices, and the purchaser to get fat on candy, and then sweep the prices under the rug and expect the person who pays for the credit card to clean up the mess and find a way to pay for the candy somehow.

This is a broken system, and the socialists say the solution is "single payer," which would mean that the government would make healthcare public and have socialized medicine, and healthcare will be "free," which really means that the taxpayer, not the patient, will pay for healthcare, and the disconnect between payer and patient will be complete. Only big government and a bunch of crusty, arrogant, elitist bureaucrats have the power to step in and force prices down to affordable levels by setting or capping prices by laws and regulations, because the greedy private health insurers want higher prices to make more money.

Second Solution: To the extent that health insurance as such poses a structural tendency to sever payment from delivery of service, the problem can be solved not by leaning toward big government but by moving toward greater freedom in free market competition. Require doctors to publish schedules of what services they offer and at what costs, as would be reasonable in any capitalist system in which sellers must be honest about what they are selling. Then drastically deregulate health insurers so that any entrepreneur can start a health insurance company and compete in any state, across state lines. In this ideal world, health insurers would compete in a marketplace —not a fake Obamacare Exchange but a real capitalist free market.

What will naturally evolve from this is a situation in which, to pass along as much cost saving to customers as possible, in order to get as much business as possible, some health insurers will develop a system for the insureds to pre-pay for the price services they want, from specific doctors at specific prices. Then, if they get sick and need those services, they will get what they shopped for and paid for. The actual payment mechanism would still be the insurer pooling all payments and then paying after the fact for the people who got sick, but price competition would force doctors to lower their prices to competitive levels to get buyers, and this same pricing pressure would force health insurers to pass along the best deal to the buyer. Premiums would be applied after the fact, pro rata, to the healthcare that people chose to buy before the fact. A buyer will compare prices and choose a seller, and buyers and sellers will naturally converge at the equilibrium price point between supply and demand-- which as (smart, sane, rational, libertarian) economists know, is the right antidote for monopolistic price gouging.

Details:

Examples of so-called natural monopolies include transit routes, bandwidth, electric utilities and power lines, cable service, garbage collection, and air space for planes or drones.

"Natural monopoly" public infrastructure can be privatized. And they should be privatized. Most people are aware that public monopolies are often mismanaged by operators who have no accountability to the public.

But it is assumed that there can be no competing alternatives, since the land or space simply isn't there. So let there be a monopoly, but have the government regulate it so it will be forced it to sell at price points below the monopoly price. What this natural monopoly thought process ignores is that there are many ways for companies to compete, if you think outside the box.

Competition in running natural monopoly infrastructure can take place along the dimension of time, not of space, such that, when the natural monopolies are privatized, what is sold is a lease, essentially, to last six to 12 months, but no longer. The buyer would have every right to do whatever he likes with the land or infrastructure and monetize and run it as he pleases, but only for the term of the lease, at which point the right to buy the next period of time would be up for open bidding and awarded to the highest bidder.

Economic efficiency and capitalist theory dictate that the company that can make the most money from such an enterprise will tend to be both the highest bidder and the company that can continue to run it the best. If a transit route is run badly, sales will flag, profits will drop, and the opportunity will arise for someone better to place a higher bid in the next round. Thus, even with only one owner, there will be competition in the economic sense.

Additions to the scheme may need to be made, such as requiring a pro rata portion of an operator's profits to be paid back to previous owners who invested in long-term durable equipment or improvements from which the current owner benefits. But such additions are not difficult to design. As a bonus, if any contractor commits massive fraud against the consumer, this will be easy to see, because if a competing operator wins the next lease bid, when he looks at the infrastructure he will see what the previous operator did to it, and consumers will be protected better than we would be under heavy regulator scrutiny.

Today's economy already proves that this will work. There are hundreds of huge corporations that buy some downstream service from only one seller, for the term of a lease; and there is ample price competition, even though only one seller can get the deal to be a supplier at one time. The companies that sell "back end" human resources (HR) services (outsourced services such as paychecks and benefits management) to Fortune 500 corporations are an example: a buyer can sensibly go with only one seller at a time, but there is a ton of competition. Another example: Places exist where various owners own the rights to different heights above the ground of a single plot of land, so that two companies can compete by owning different floors of the same building, competing along the dimension of height, not of length.

The person who made the original objection to privatization will object again, saying that the rich will bid big to get ownership of the monopoly, charge high prices while offering crappy service, and run away after their lease ends--taking profits derived from forcing people to pay a lot for a service with no alternatives. The operators' costs would have been low, since they didn't give a damn about infrastructure investments. But this objection reduces merely to the general argument against free market capitalism. The Marxists and socialists think that rich people get rich by fleecing their victims. If you believe instead, as smart people do, that money is made in a free society by creating high quality at an affordable price where supply meets demand, then the objection collapses. Specifically it is wrong because an operator who does a good job will always make more, net, long term, than a con artist;, hence the good operator will have more money and more motivation to outbid the crooks.

This is not to say that the system can never be abused. No system is perfect. Privatization is certainly not less perfect that a regulated natural monopoly, and it would ultimately be far better. Just ask anyone who rides the subway in New York City: in addition to being a vital means of transportation for millions of New Yorkers, it is also the location that the wonderfully brainless liberal politicians of New York have chosen as the de facto living space for the mentally ill homeless people, just to get them off the streets. The bigger picture is that the economic demand for the subway would justify a rise in fares that is politically unpopular and therefore impossible.

So New York City as subway operator does not, and cannot, spend the money it should to maintain the subway service as it deserves and needs. The New York Times even ran a crusade to get more spending for the subways, noting how horrible they are and how many people use them, which crusade did not succeed, and could not succeed. The free market would do better.

I have suggested six to 12 months as the basic contract period for the operation of natural monopolies; it could be two or three years, but it needs to be short enough to enable consumers to hold bad operators accountable so that better ones can step in. Employees may not want six or 12 month contracts, and somewhat more may need to be paid them on this account. Nevertheless, we need to get away from the labor union mentality, according to which the labor pool only works if employees are chained to their jobs and employers are chained to long-term labor contracts.

The United States is becoming "the gig economy," as they say; led by the Uber and Lyft drivers. A lot of industries are moving toward hiring employees for a temporary, shorter duration and away from hiring them for permanent, full-time jobs. Employees with strong professional skills are so valuable that no one who purchased a short-term lease on a natural monopoly would want to get rid of them.

As far as planning goes, there are examples in today's economy of businesses drawing up plans for long-term operations, because that is how they can best succeed, but if their basic contracts are not renewed, they just tear up the plans. In business you need long-term plans, but you also need to face the risk that these plans may fail dramatically, at any time.

If you don't get investors in your second year of operation, you just eat the third, fourth and fifth years of your business plan, no matter how great those years might have been.

Now to some details about healthcare. Free market economics doesn't work if there is a disconnect between the person who pays the money for a benefit and the person who receives the benefit. The disconnect causes prices and costs to skyrocket, because the buyer cannot force the seller down. Many libertarians already know this: one of our objections to government spending is that the government will overspend because there is a disconnect between the taxpayer and the beneficiary. Healthcare, where the health insurer pays but the patient receives the treatment, and does not directly pay the doctor, and the doctors don't compete for each individual patient on price, is a great example of a buy-sell disconnect.

The problem with health insurance is that, originally, it was in fact insurance that a person bought to mitigate the risk of getting sick, but it has become a behemoth that pays for all medical expenses and then collects exorbitant and arbitrary amounts from the public, with no connection between payments and collections in an individual patient's case. The problem arises because, by the time people become sick, their medical costs are typically too great for them to pay, so they must have already had insurance to get treatment, and the insurance will then end up paying all costs.

To reform healthcare, first, require doctors, as a condition of receiving their license to practice medicine, or merely by means of laws mandating truth in advertising, to create a schedule of fees and prices for each of their services, and publish it, and let individual patients receive that care if they pay that fee from the schedule of rates. Second, break up the regulations of health insurance companies so that anyone can start one and can compete in every state with a minimum of red tape. Third, require that each health insurer publish the actuarial tables that each insurer is using, showing what portion of your payment will pay for what medical treatment in the future from what doctor's schedule of fees. Fourth, allow the consumer to "buy" his future medical treatment by choosing what portion of his premium he chooses to allocate to the doctors' services that he could potentially get, from the competing doctors' fee schedules, "through" his health insurance company.

The health insurer would pool the buyers' payment to make the actual payment to the doctors for the insureds who become sick, but each buyer could take the income that he has allotted for health insurance and "spend" it by choosing the slate of healthcare services he would pay for at that price, selecting his doctor from among the competitors. Doctors would compete on the price to be chosen by each buyer when he decides how to allot his healthcare premium spend.

This would combine two novel approaches: "shopping" for treatment from the doctor, not the insurer, and expanding competition among health insurers by allowing small startup health insurers, akin to what was done for poor businesses in Asia by the "micro-credit" revolution that enabled any poor woman or man to open a business on a small loan. Thousands of small businesses will pop up to become micro-health insurers and facilitate the trade, between doctor and patient, of treatment for money.

This would connect the buyer to the seller and enable massive price competition among doctors, so costs would plummet, because many doctors would seek patients by offering cheaper prices at affordable levels of quality. Obviously this would not lower the quality of healthcare, because the doctors who succeeded would be those who proved they could deliver successful, effective treatments, but at cheaper prices. In today's world, where everyone finds ratings and reviews online, the doctors with the best value propositions, defined as higher quality at cheaper price, would be readily apparent.

The micro-health insurer could also prepay, locking the buyer and seller in at that price while taking profit up front and not when the healthcare is delivered. This would keep healthcare costs locked down at the competitive price the buyer chose to pay, and complete the sale for the buyer at the time of purchase, not after the fact when the patient-buyer becomes sick and his very life depends on paying for healthcare. Right now there are maybe a handful of insurers and 20 health insurance plans that compete in any given state Obamacare Exchange, but the initiative I have outlined would open the door to thousands of health insurers, and potentially hundreds of thousands of healthcare "menus" and "menu items" available to buyers pre-paying doctors a pro rata share of the healthcare premium cost of treatments received.

The analogy of healthcare options to a menu at a restaurant is a propos. People need food. If you don't have it, you die, just as a sick person who needs medical treatment gets it or dies. This does not enable the farms to jack up the price of food until it is out of sight, as doctors, hospitals, and pharmaceutical makers are doing. Instead, thousands of restaurants and grocery stores compete, buying food from farms and selling it as a selection of options on a menu.

People buy what they want, within the limits of their budget. Consumers win, and have tasty meals and full bellies. Yes, poor people may have to eat at cheap fast food stores, but they don't starve to death (and the food at Dunkin Donuts is not that bad!).

If you are willing to make do with less, such as by purchasing vegetables and cooking your food at home, you can eat quite nicely. So, too, could a free market system work for the benefit of all Americans by introducing price competition into the healthcare industry, which would create affordable options across a range of price points.

The conclusion to infer from this article is that, while the statists object that libertarian policy cannot be implemented in a practical manner, this is simply not true. Thinking outside the box, and being creative and innovative about policy solutions, will meet the challenge of making liberty work for America.

END.

---

[1] R.H. Coase, *The Problem of Social Cost*, 3 J.L. & Econ. 1-44 (1960).

[2] Guido Calabresi & A. Douglas Melamed, *Property Rules, Liability Rules, and Inalienability: One View of the Cathedral*, 85 Harv. L. Rev. 1089 (1972).

[3] R.H. Coase, *The Federal Communications Commission*, 2 J.L. & Econ 1-40 (1959).

ABOUT THE AUTHOR

Russell Hasan

Russell Hasan (pronouns: He, him, his) is a graduate of Vassar College, where his major was philosophy, and he graduated with Honors from the University of Connecticut School of Law, where he was an Editor of the Insurance Law Journal. He is a proud member of the LGBTQ community and an equally proud member of the Libertarian Party. Mr. Hasan has served as a member of the LGBTQ Rights Committee of the New York City Bar Association. He has been a volunteer program leader at the Triangle Community Center, which is the largest LGBTQ community center in southwestern Connecticut. He has also served as Vice Chair and Secretary of the Libertarian Party Affiliate of Fairfield County, Connecticut. He loves coffee and chewing gum, and he enjoys watching sports (Yankees baseball, Giants football, UConn Women's Basketball), comedies, and science fiction/fantasy tv shows and movies. His favorite novels are Atlas Shrugged, The Fountainhead, and Catch-22; his favorite tv show is Friends; and his favorite movies are Star Wars: The Empire Strikes Back and The Matrix.

Mr. Hasan accepts fan mail and questions from readers at this email address:

author.russell.hasan@outlook.com

Bibliography:

Russell Hasan is the author of these books:

NONFICTION ESSAYS:

A System of Legal Logic: Using Aristotle, Ayn Rand, and Analytical Philosophy to Understand the Law, Interpret Cases, and Win in Litigation (A Scholarly Monograph)

Everything is Something: A Philosophical Dialogue About Logic, Language, Words, Meanings, Truth, and The Theory of Things

If P Then Q: Why Philosophy Can Teach You How to Think and Help You Live a Happy Life By the Methods of Applying Logic to Solve the Problems in Your Life and Achieve Success (A Scholarly Monograph)

Moral Logic and Economic Logic: On Knowledge, Choice, Will, Desire, The Moral Ideal, Economics, and Economic Value, with a System of Symbolic Logical Notation

On Moral Psychology and Moral Philosophy: Towards a New Theory of Emotions, Motivations, and Ethics, Using the Insight that Emotions Pay Moral Debts and Moral Credits Owed to Self and Loved Ones (also published under the alternate first edition title: On Forgiveness)

The Power of Objectivism: Ayn Rand and John Galt and Atlas Shrugged and The Morality of Life, Intelligence, Greed, Selfishness, Rationality, Individuality, Integrity, Capitalism, Desire, and Freedom

What They Won't Tell You About Objectivism: Thoughts on the Objectivist Philosophy in the Post-Randian Era

Rand's Axiom Problem: On Objectivity, Ontology, Essence, Epistemology, Deduction, Induction, and the Foundations of Knowledge

An Essay on Reason and Perception

Golden Rule Libertarianism: A Defense of Freedom in Social, Economic, and Legal Policy

Libertarian Economics: A Manifesto and an Explanation

Economics: A Theory of Capital (also published under the alternate first edition title: XYAB Economics: A GOLD Libertarian Analysis of Money, Trade, and Freedom)

The Ethics and Morality of Human Sexuality

SELF-HELP:

To Be Loved, Love; To Be Liked, Be Nice to People; To Be an Adult, Forgive People: Emotions and Social Interactions, Explained

On Self-Reliance, Self-Esteem, and Intellectual Honesty